ECONOMICS 73/74 ENCYCLOPEDIA

CONTRIBUTORS

Khamis Abdul-Magid, Chairman, Department of Economics, Guilford College, Greensboro, N.C.

Peter Asch, Department of Economics, Rutgers College, Rutgers University, New Brunswick, N.J.

Frank J. Bonello, Department of Economics, University of Notre Dame, Notre Dame, Ind.

George E. Brandow, Department of Agricultural Economics and Rural Sociology, Pennsylvania State University, University Park, Pa.

Robert L. Brite, Department of Economics and Finance, Louisiana State University in New Orleans, New Orleans, La.

Thomas O. Depperschmidt, Department of Economics, Memphis State University, Memphis, Tenn.

Martin T. Farris, Department of Economics, Arizona State University, Tempe, Ariz.

T. Aldrich Finegan, Department of Economics, Vanderbilt University, Nashville, Tenn.

John P. Formby, School of Business and Economics, University of North Carolina, Greensboro, N.C.

Irving Goffman, Chairman, Department of Economics, College of Business Administration, University of Florida, Gainesville, Fla.

Josef Hadar, Director of Graduate Studies, Department of Economics, Southern Methodist University; formerly, Department of Economics, Case Western Reserve University

Walter W. Haines, Chairman, Department of Economics, University College of Arts & Science, New York University

Clyde A. Haulman, Director, Marshall-Wythe Institute for Research in the Social Sciences, College of William and Mary, Williamsburg, Va.

Joseph M. Jadlow, College of Business Administration, Oklahoma State University, Stillwater, Okla.

Algin B. King, Department of Management, School of Business Administration, College of William and Mary, Williamsburg, Va.

Allan B. Mandelstamm, Department of Economics, Michigan State University, Lansing, Mich.

John R. Matthews, Jr., Department of Economics, College of William and Mary, Williamsburg, Va.

Anne Mayhew, Department of Economics, College of Business Administration, University of Tennessee, Knoxville, Tenn.

Charles W. Meyer, Department of Economics, Iowa State University, Ames, Iowa

Carlisle E. Moody, Jr., Department of Economics, College of William and Mary, Williamsburg, Va.

Clarence C. Morrison, Department of Economics, Indiana University, Bloomington, Ind.

Walter C. Neale, Department of Economics, College of Business Administration, University of Tennessee, Knoxville, Tenn.

Lawrence H. Officer, Department of Economics, Michigan State University, East Lansing, Mich.

Francis W. Rushing, Department of Economics, College of William and Mary; formerly, Graduate School, University of Georgia, Athens, Ga.

Leonard G. Schifrin, Chairman, Department of Economics, College of William and Mary, Williamsburg, Va.

Charles Staelin, Center for Research and Economic Development, University of Michigan, Ann Arbor, Mich.

William D. Wagoner, Department of Economics and Finance, Louisiana State University in New Orleans, New Orleans, La.

All of the contributors listed here were involved both as consultants and authors of articles in the encyclopedia. The publisher wishes to acknowledge, especially, the efforts of Dr. Leonard G. Schifrin of the College of William and Mary, who not only served as senior adviser but also created much of the basic structure of the volume.

ECONOMICS 73/74 ENCYCLOPEDIA

The Dushkin Publishing Group, Inc.
Guilford, Connecticut

Library of Congress Catalog Card Number: 72-90094

Manufactured in the United States of America
Second Printing

PUBLISHER'S PREFACE

An understanding of the tools of a science is essential to understanding the science—its development, accomplishments, and problems. Modern economics is a science in all senses of the term. Economics has developed an extensive methodology for generating theories and hypotheses to explain man's role and behavior in the economic system and the relationships that exist among the numerous components of the system. Economics has also developed a language that is frequently as technical as that of any of the physical or natural sciences, and nonprofessional readers are often surprised—and sometimes annoyed—to discover that discourse in economics—lectures, books, even popular press articles—not only relies on technical terms but also uses ordinary language in special ways. In the language of economics, even familiar words—"accelerator," "capital," "demand," "efficiency," "marginal"—have specific and, for the layman, unfamiliar meanings.

In this encyclopedia we have attempted to provide a comprehensive treatment of the language of economics and of the full range of its theories, practices, and institutions. Our goal has been to answer specific questions as clearly and as concisely as possible. For maximum utility—because the editors insisted that you should be able to find the information you want in the first place you look it up—we adopted the short-entry, alphabetical form. More than 1,000 relatively short articles—arranged alphabetically and tied together by a system of direct cross references and item guides—form the book's web of easily accessed information. Because of this interweaving structure, almost any article in the encyclopedia can serve as the point of entry for a systematic study of the entire field.

Organization of the Encyclopedia

The encyclopedia is fully comprehensive. It was constructed topically first and then arranged alphabetically for ease of access. Because of this organization, we have been able to build a number of guidance functions into it as integrated parts of its information system.

Cross references are of two kinds. *See* references, which appear as individual entries in the alphabetical sequence, take the place of a separate index and send you directly to the location of the information you want. *See also* references at the end of an article direct you to carefully selected supplementary articles.

Subject maps show in a single display the interrelationships among the book's 1,000 articles for each of twenty-one major areas of economic study. These subject maps allow you to see at once the encyclopedia's full coverage of the area you're exploring. The maps appear in the book under the following headings:

Antitrust Policy
Banking System
Business Cycles
Capital
Circular Flow of Income
Demand
Economic Systems
Factor Markets
Federal Budget
History of Economic Ideas
International Trade Theory
Labor Market
Labor Movement
Market System
Money and Monetary Policy
National Income
Price Level
Regulation
Supply
Theory of the Firm
Wages

Item guides point out specific relationships between individual articles in the book and lead in a meaningful sequence from one article to another. They accompany fifty key articles in this edition.

Consult references at the end of an article are numerically keyed to a classified bibliography at the back of the volume. All of the bibliography titles have been selected by the authors of the encyclopedia articles as suggestions for further reading. Except for classic works, the bibliography includes mainly recent publications especially useful to nonprofessional readers in the field.

Illustrations are used functionally in the encyclopedia. The computer-composed format permits the inclusion of tables, graphs, charts, photographs, and other illustrations wherever the editors considered them valuable.

Authority

All of the articles in the encyclopedia were prepared by authorities working in their own specialities. Articles of 200 or more words in length bear the signature and affiliation of the contributor. The shorter, unsigned pieces were prepared by the same authorities who wrote the longer pieces. The decision not to sign these shorter articles was made for space reasons only.

Making an encyclopedia of this length is as much a problem of deciding what to leave out as of what to include. The advisers and authors were involved in a process of assembling an enormous body of information and, at the same time, of paring it down to essentials. We have sought to be of most value to nonprofessional readers, and this purpose guided our decisions about how best to present the information. Thus, all of the authorities listed on the contributor's page were chosen for their long experience in helping people with no training in economics to understand the field. An examination of the bibliography at the end of this volume will show that many of our authors have made important professional contributions in their own areas of specialization, but for this book each was asked, first, to approach our articles from the viewpoint of the nonprofessional's information needs. Next, each writer was asked to give careful consideration to those points that his experience has shown to be problem areas for nonprofessionals. Finally, each contributor was asked to ensure that every article would be as complete as possible within the limitations of the space available. Thus, we sought to provide the best presentation of information possible within the limits of our chosen length.

Availability and Limitations of Economic Information

Economists use a number of analytical techniques in their attempts to determine empirically the relationships that their theories suggest. Clearly, the key element in their analyses, beyond theory itself, is the nature and availability of information.

The information available to economists comes from a number of sources. Often the data have been collected with the needs of economists in mind. A large number of statistical series providing measures of social and economic variables have been devised by governments, international organizations, and other institutions. The information is collected through systems developed for complete reporting of all relevant data or of statistically significant samples. It generally appears in the form of time-series data, recorded daily or over periods up to a decade or more in length. Most nations have extensive data collection systems and obtain information on all aspects of their economy. International organizations such as the United Nations, the International Monetary Fund, and the World Bank also gather and publish data from their own collection systems as well as from national governments. All of these sources were extensively explored by the researchers and writers of this encyclopedia.

The information obtained by governments and other institutions, however, is not without problems. Incomplete reporting or inadequate collection procedures can significantly affect the validity of data. Every effort is made to correct known faults in data series and to improve the quality of the information available to decision makers, but that task is difficult in complex modern economies. Even where major problems in the collection process have been eliminated, aggregation procedures can introduce new errors.

But perhaps the most difficult information problem is with the many nonmeasurable phenomena that influence an economy. Because economists cannot use controlled experiments, they can only observe actual outcomes of economic processes and attempt to account for all the simultaneous events surrounding a given aspect of the economy. Some events cannot be measured by statistical series. How do you measure the economic effect of a war? Or the effect of a change in the legal framework that governs business? How do you measure the psychological values people within an economy place on its products and its activities? Several techniques are available to avoid some of the problems of nonmeasurable phenomena, but, clearly, these phenomena create difficulties and often effectively block the application of economic analysis.

Stanley Schindler
Publisher

A & P CASE. *See* United States v. New York Great A & P Company.

ABILITY TO PAY, a wage criterion which is an important consideration in union-labor negotiations: namely, that justified cost-of-living wages can only be granted if management is in a position to be able to pay the higher wage rate. However, determination of whether management is able to pay is often a very controversial issue. It often involves undesirable exposure of company operations to unions and often leaves unions in unfair bargaining positions.

See also Wage Criteria.

ABILITY-TO-PAY PRINCIPLE, The theory that taxes should be levied on individuals according to their ability to pay, with relatively larger taxes being paid by wealthier persons, irrespective of the direct benefits received from the state.

See also Benefit Principle.

ABRAMOVITZ, MOSES (1912-), American economist and educator, noted for his contribution to the study of business cycles and economic growth and development. He graduated from Harvard in 1932 and received his Ph.D. in economics from Columbia in 1939. His publications include *Price Theory for a Changing Economy* (1939); *Inventories and Business Cycles* (1950, with Vera Eliasberg); and *Allocation of Economic Resources* (1959). Professor of economics at Stanford since 1948, he was economic advisor to the Secretary-General of the Organization for Economic Cooperation and Development (1962-63) and has been a member of the research staff of the National Bureau of Economic Research since 1938.

ABSOLUTE ADVANTAGE. Adam Smith said trade between nations would increase real wealth via the division of labor. He assumed an absolute advantage necessary in that an exporting industry must be able to produce, with given inputs, a larger output than any rival. Assume that two countries use the same composite input mix of land, labor, and capital with the result that country A produces twice as much of two commodities as country B. Country A has an absolute advantage with respect to both commodities; therefore, B cannot produce for export trade. Smith's analysis could not deal with the situation of B; this awaited the formulation by David Ricardo in terms of comparative advantage.

See also Comparative Advantage; International Trade Theory.

ABSOLUTE COST ADVANTAGE, the ability of a firm in an industry to produce an item at a lower cost than another firm in that same industry. When a firm has an absolute cost advantage, it can sell its product at a lower price than other firms in the industry, thus gathering a greater share of the market and possibly forcing out other firms. As a second alternative, it can sell its product at the same price as other firms but receive a larger profit, because its costs are lower.

ABUSE THEORY OF MERGERS, thesis, first developed in the United States Steel decision (1920), that one firm's domination of an industry, however obtained, did not violate the antimonopoly provisions of the Sherman Act unless specific abuses of power were proven. Allowing "intent" to be disregarded and ignoring the market influence which can result from mere possession of power, this interpretation severely limited antitrust enforcement until contermanded by the 1945 Alcoa case findings.

See also Antitrust Policy; Sherman Antitrust Act; United States v. Aluminum Company of America; United States v. United States Steel Corporation.

"SHOO, FLY, DON'T BOTHER ME!"—From the *Evening News* (Detroit).

"Abuse Theory" developed in 1920 U.S. Steel case gave antitrust enforcement a severe setback.

ACCELERATOR, the humped pattern of induced investment that causes larger variations in investment demand than the causal variations in demand. A firm or industry operating at or slightly below capacity will have a fairly constant investment demand for replacing worn out capital goods and sold out inventories. If demand rises above capacity or previous level of sales, there will be an induced demand for capital (or inventory) goods in order to increase capacity. But once this new capacity is installed investment demand will fall to replacement level again.

When the capital goods have a longish life (several years), the fall will first be to the original replacement level of demand, followed later by a rise to a higher level of replacement demand as the new equipment wears out. When the increased investment is in inventory to service a higher level of wholesale or retail trade, the first hump of inventory investment will be followed immediately by the new, higher replacement demand. The importance of the accelerator is that it introduces into the level of investment an instability, which magnifies the changes in the demand for the products from which the investment demand derives.

—Walter C. Neale, *University of Tennessee*

ACCELERATOR PRINCIPLE. *See* Accelerator Theory of Business Cycles.

ACCELERATOR THEORY OF BUSINESS CYCLES (Accelerator Principle) was first introduced in 1917 by John M. Clark to explain the larger variations in investment than in product output that occur during a business cycle. In 1936, the accelerator principle, which states that small changes in demand induce disproportionately large changes in the amount of investment needed to meet that demand, was combined with Keynes' consumption function to generate a model of a business cycle.

The accelerator principle is used to assay future growth when the economy is close to full employment, but it erroneously assumes that gross investment can fall below zero and that industry is already operating at full capacity.

See also Business Cycles, Theories; Consumption Function.

ACCOUNTING PROFITS are the profits that occur when the income from sales or other sources of a business concern exceeds the expenses of the firm over a designated period of time, usually one year. All expenses, including non-cash items such as depreciation, are recorded. Accounting profits of a business are calculated on the income statement.

Gardner Ackley

ACKLEY, (HUGH) GARDNER (1915–), American educator and government official noted for his work in macroeconomics and economic growth and development. He received a B.A. (1936) and L.L.D. (1964) from Western Michigan University, and his A.M. (1937) and Ph.D. (1940) in economics from the University of Michigan. His publications include: *Macroeconomic Theory* (1961). He was a member of the Council of Economic Advisors from 1962–68, and was chairman from 1964–68. In 1968 he became U.S. ambassador to Italy.

ACREAGE LIMITATIONS. *See* Crop Restrictions.

ACREAGE RESERVE. *See* Soil Bank.

ACT FOR INTERNATIONAL DEVELOPMENT OF 1950. *See* Point Four Program.

ACT TO REGULATE COMMERCE. *See* Interstate Commerce Act (1887).

ACTUAL COST. *See* Original Cost.

ACTUAL INVESTMENT, OR REALIZED INVESTMENT, the amount of spending on currently produced capital goods that occurs during a year, equal to planned investment only when planned investment equals planned savings. When planned savings exceeds planned investment, actual investment is likely to be greater than planned investment because inventories will accumulate when households do not buy as much as expected; but actual investment could be less than planned investment, if induced investment falls more rapidly than inventories accumulate. When planned investment exceeds planned savings, actual investment is likely to fall short of planned investment, because households will buy more than expected and reduce inventories, but actual investment could be more than planned investment, if the higher incomes induce more investment than originally planned. The unexpected accumulation or reduction of inventories is called *unintended,* or involuntary, investment, or disinvestment.

See also Disinvestment; Investment Schedule; Marginal Efficiency of Capital.

ACTUAL RESERVES. *See* Multiple Expansion of the Money Supply.

ADELMAN, MORRIS ALBERT (1917–), American educator and economist who has won recognition for his contributions to the understanding of market behavior, particularly under imperfect competition. He graduated from the City College of New York in 1938 and received his Ph.D. in economics from Harvard in 1948. He is author of *A & P: A Study in Price-Cost Behavior and Public Policy* (1959) and *Alaskan Oil: Costs and Supply* (1971). He was an economist for the War Production Board from 1941–42 and was a member of the Federal Reserve Board in 1946. He has been on the faculty at M.I.T. since 1948.

ADMINISTERED PRICES are the result of a type of pricing policy that is found mainly in oligopolistic industries. An administered price is a predetermined price that is derived after accounting for all costs of the industry and deciding upon a desired amount of profit. Administered prices must also take into consideration approximately how many items will be sold at the predetermined price. When an administered price has been selected, all firms in the industry must adopt this price in order for it to be effective. It is for this reason that administered prices cannot be effective in purely competitive or monopolistically competitive markets.

Oligopolistic market structures, because there are only a few firms in these industries, are able to carry out administered pricing policies effectively by the use of collusions or tacit agreements.

ADMINISTERED PRICING, hypothesis which states that a large part of the United States economy is characterized by firms with enough market power that managers have a large range of discretion in determining product prices. Thus, when demand drops in recession, these firms may hold prices relatively constant and adjust their output, employment, and inventories. When this pattern is combined with a willingness to raise prices in expansionary periods, the result is a ratchet effect, with prices rising during expansion but failing to decline in contractions. The result could be a creeping inflation that persists in recessions.

See also Inflation.

AD VALOREM TARIFF. *See* Tariffs.

AD VALOREM TAX. *See* Taxation: *Glossary.*

ADVERTISING, DECEPTIVE. *See* Deceptive Advertising.

ADVERTISING COMPETITION. *See* Promotional Competition.

AFBF. *See* Farm Bureau Federation, American.

AFDC. *See* Aid to Families with Dependent Children.

AFFLUENT SOCIETY, THE (1958) attacked what author John Kenneth Galbraith called the "conventional wisdoms" of production. Galbraith suggests that economics traditionally has been concerned with productivity, insecurity, and inequality. However, in American society (the affluent society) the emphasis has switched to productivity because insecurity could be cured if production were large enough and inequality can be eliminated only when the rich have satisfied their demands and have enough left over for the poor.

Galbraith feels that the key to America's economic problems is the emphasis upon private production which results from our society's belief that only the private sector produces wealth. This view combined with a distaste for taxation leads to a rejection of governmental expenditures. Galbraith, feeling that public sector expenditures are many times the only means of correcting the problems of society, advocates increasing governmental participation in the economy.

See also Galbraith, John Kenneth.

—Clyde A. Haulman, *College of William and Mary*

AFL. *See* American Federation of Labor.

AFL-CIO. *See* American Federation of Labor and Congress of Industrial Organizations.

AGENCY SHOP exists when workers in a bargaining unit are not required to join the union that represents them but must make a payment to the union equal to the dues. This protects the workers' freedom to join the union or not but does not permit "free riders" to benefit from union representation without helping support it. Agency shops are particularly important to the unions in states with "right-to-work" laws, which outlaw compulsory union memberships.

AGGREGATE CONSUMPTION. *See* Consumption.

AGGREGATE DEMAND. *See* National Income Determination.

AGGREGATE OF INCOME. *See* National Income.

AGGREGATE MEASURES OF ECONOMIC ACTIVITY. *See* National Income Measurement.

AGGREGATE SUPPLY-AGGREGATE DEMAND EQUALITY. *See* National Income Determination.

AGGREGATE SUPPLY CURVE. *See* 45° Line.

AGRARIAN ECONOMY. *See* Traditional Economy.

AGRICULTURAL ACTS OF 1965, 1970. *See* Price-Support Programs.

AGRICULTURAL COLLECTIVIZATION. *See* Collectivization.

AGRICULTURAL MARKETING ORDERS. *See* Marketing Orders, Agricultural.

AID, FOREIGN. *See* Foreign Aid.

AID TO FAMILIES WITH DEPENDENT CHILDREN (AFDC). The largest of the federally subsidized categorical public assistance programs, it provides income maintenance and social services for needy families with dependent children. Originally intended for women with dependent children, about half the states now provide assistance to families with an adult male member if he is unemployed and cannot find a job.

See also Public Assistance.

AID TO THE NEEDY BLIND, the smallest of the federally subsidized categorical public assistance programs, is administered by state or local welfare agencies. It provides income support and services for needy blind persons and their dependents. Like other public assistance programs, aid is granted only to those whose financial resources fall short of a state-prescribed minimum.

ALCOA CASE. *See* United States v. Aluminum Company of America.

ALLOCATION, decisions as to what is to be produced in the economy and who is to receive what is produced. Because of the scarcity of resources used in production, these resources and the products they create have to be allocated efficiently and profitably.

ALLOCATION

A definition of allocation in its economic usage is found in the adjacent article. For a consideration of the pervasive nature of the allocation question, see ECONOMIC SYSTEMS. The allocation process in our economy is explained in detail in MARKET SYSTEM. For a somewhat more specific analysis of how a market economy answers the three component questions—the production, technological, and distributional questions—of the larger allocation question, see the articles on FACTOR MARKETS and PRODUCTION. For the methods and criteria of evaluation of how well the allocation process is accomplished, see EFFICIENT RESOURCE ALLOCATION.

The student will also find it useful to consult the Subject Map accompanying the article MARKET SYSTEM for clarification of other relationships of the allocation process to the economy.

Allocation of natural resources in a capitalistic economy is usually done through the price system. Those products in the greatest demand and with the highest prices have priority in the allocation of resources. Allocation of the four factors of production is done in very much the same way as allocation of natural resources. Land, labor, capital, and management are usually channeled into the most profitable production areas. The price of labor is wages, for example, and wages are usually higher in high-demand areas.

In the allocation of resources, price is the determining factor. Allocation is determined by who is willing to pay for the products and how much each person is willing to pay. Therefore, in a capitalistic economy, it can be said that the price system acts as the main allocator of both the inputs and the outputs of production.

Consult (11) Mansfield, 1970.

—Robert L. Brite, *Louisiana State University*

ALTERNATIVE COST. *See* Opportunity Cost.

ALTERNATIVE HYPOTHESIS. *See* Hypothesis.

AMERICAN AGRICULTURAL MARKETING ASSOCIATION. *See* Farm Bureau Federation, American.

AMERICAN CAPITALISM: THE CONCEPT OF COUNTERVAILING POWER (1956) by John Kenneth Galbraith develops his theory of countervailing power that: (1) the force which compels oligopolistic industries to meet consumer wants and maintain prices close to cost is not the traditional inter-firm competition that economic theory indicates, but powerful buyers exercising countervailing power and (2) this power on the buyers' side emerges systematically in response to power on the sellers' side.

Economists reacted strongly to this concept. The historical record was examined, and the picture of strong unions and retail chains rising sooner in industries with powerful firms was not supported. Also, even if strong buyers can obtain price reductions, there is no guarantee that these will be passed along to consumers.

See also Countervailing Power.

AMERICAN DILEMMA (1944). *See* Myrdal, Gunnar.

AMERICAN FARM BUREAU FEDERATION. *See* Farm Bureau Federation, American.

AMERICAN FEDERATION OF LABOR (AFL), conceived and organized in December, 1886, was skilled labor's major claim to unionism. Headed by Samuel Gompers, the AFL represented the skilled trades which did not want to be associated with the Knights of Labor and its activities.

The organization, though threatened by the advocates of socialism and other political groups, was deep rooted in the principles of American capitalism. It basically opposed government intervention in industrial relations and labor organization.

In its infant state the AFL was not an immediate success, due mainly to struggles with the Knights of Labor and failure to win any major strikes. However, as the strength of the Knights began to decline and several victories were won by AFL unions, membership began to grow. The most important single event, as far as membership growth is concerned, resulted from a victory by the United Mine Workers in 1902. This victory increased membership to 1,675,000 in 1904. After this date, however, the organization suffered some major setbacks, including the failures of the Amalgamated Meat Cutters in New York, The International Brotherhood of Teamsters in Chicago, and the Amalgamated Association of Iron, Steel, and Tin Workers. Because of the bitter battles involved in these strikes, public opinion turned against labor.

The AFL at that time was also feeling the pressures of the unskilled who, feeling neglected by labor unions, often tended to undermine strikes. Membership in the organization began to drop steadily. In addition to strike failures, the unrest of the unskilled, and the opposition by public opinion, improvements in technology and the development of mass production techniques made craft unionization all the more futile.

In 1924, after the death of Samuel Gompers, William Green became the organization's president. In 1932, just when it seemed the AFL was nearing its end, Congress passed the Norris-La Guardia Act outlawing injunctions and yellow dog contracts, thus giving labor its first legislative victory.

Under the pro-union legislation of the thirties the AFL again began to thrive. Having been given the legal right to organize, labor began to gain a bargaining position. However, there was still the problem of the unskilled workers. Under the leadership of John L. Lewis the Congress of Industrial Organizations rose as the representative of the unskilled unions, and in 1955 the two organizations merged, forming the AFL-CIO.

See also Labor Movement.

—William D. Wagoner, *Louisiana State University*

AMERICAN FEDERATION OF LABOR AND CONGRESS OF INDUSTRIAL ORGANIZATIONS (AFL-CIO), formed in 1955 by merger of the AFL and CIO. The AFL was founded in 1886 under the leadership of Samuel Gompers to represent the skilled trade unions who did not want to be affiliated with the Knights of Labor. It experienced mild success in its formative years but did not become a powerful group until the 1930s, with passage of the Norris-LaGuardia Act in 1932 and the National Labor Relations Act in 1935.

It was also during the 1930s that the unskilled groups began to find fault with the AFL. Its refusal to grant charters to several industrial unions such as steel, automobile, and rubber workers led John L. Lewis, then vice president of the AFL, to help these workers organize. He was so successful that the AFL ordered these groups to disband. They refused and left the AFL to form the permanent Congress of Industrial Organizations in 1938.

Both the AFL and the CIO experienced individual success in the late thirties and early forties. However, in 1947, with the passage of the Taft-Hartley Act, union power was curtailed. So, after much deliberation, the two organizations decided to merge in 1955 thus forming the AFL-CIO. The organization now comprises over 125 national and international unions with a total membership of about thirteen million. In addition, there are about 350 local unions affiliated directly with the organization. Only two major unions do not belong to the organization: the Teamsters, who were ousted in the late fifties, and the United Auto Workers, who left voluntarily in the late sixties.

See also Labor Movement.

—William D. Wagoner, *Louisiana State University*

AMERICAN TOBACCO CASE. *See* United States v. American Tobacco Co.

ANALYSIS OF VARIANCE is a technique used to separate the variation of a variable into two components: systematic variation (caused by other variables) and random or chance variation. It is often used to test for significant differences among several sample means.

See also Dispersion; Significance.

ANALYTICAL SOCIALISM. *See* Pre-Marxian Socialism.

ANARCHISTIC COMMUNISM presumes that men are born good, reach fulfillment in voluntary and spontaneous cooperation with others, and thus instinctively seek communal life. Proponents feel that the state and the economic institutions it supports, especially private property, are artificial agencies of exploitation that restrict the individual. Therefore, the state should be abolished; free cooperation in ideal communities would eliminate oppression and make government superfluous. Leading figures in the movement have included W. Godwin, P. J. Proudhon, P. A. Kropotkin, and M. Bakunin.

See also Associationism; Cooperativism.

ANCILLARY AGREEMENT, one secondary or subsidiary to the main purpose of a business agreement, the ancillary agreement being a minimum condition necessary to effect the main legal purpose.

In common law, the sale of a business might be conditioned on the seller agreeing not to compete with the buyer for a certain time or within a certain geographic area, the latter agreement being ancillary to the sale agreement. Common-law courts judged such agreements according to the limitation on competition they imposed. Agreements limiting competition in a whole market for an indefinite time were considered general or nonancillary restraints of trade, *per se* illegal; those with less comprehensive limitations were considered partial or ancillary restraints and judged on the "reasonableness" of the limitations.

Interpreting the Sherman Act prohibition on restraints of trade, the Supreme Court adopted a similar distinction until 1911 (*United States v. Standard Oil Company of New Jersey).* In this case, the test of reasonableness ostensibly was applied to nonancillary (price fixing, market sharing) as well as ancillary restraints. Since then, however, federal courts rather consistently have condemned nonancillary restraints as *per se* illegal.

See also Antitrust Policy; Per Se Illegality; Restraint of Trade; Rule of Reason.

—Thomas O. Depperschmidt, *Memphis State University.*

ANGELL, JAMES WATERHOUSE (1898–), American economist and educator who has worked extensively in the fields of monetary and fiscal theory and international trade theory. He received his Ph.D. (1924) in economics from Harvard. His publications include *The Theory of International Prices* (1926); *Investment and Business Cycles* (1941); and *Measures for International Economic Stability* (1951, co-author). He has held positions as assistant administrator to the Foreign Economic Administration (1945), as minister to the Allied Command on Reparations in Germany (1945–46), and as a member of the National Security Resources Board (1948–50).

AN INQUIRY INTO THE NATURE AND CAUSES OF THE WEALTH OF NATIONS. *See* Wealth of Nations.

ANNUITY BOND. *See* Bonds.

ANTI-CHAIN-STORE LAW. *See* Price Discrimination.

ANTIMERGER ACT. *See* Celler-Kefauver Act.

ANTITRUST DIVISION, DEPARTMENT OF JUSTICE, formed in 1903, is one of two federal

Samuel Gompers helped found the American Federation of Labor to represent workers in skilled trades. He served as its president for 37 years.

An AFL vice president in the 1920's, John L. Lewis also headed the United Mine Workers, which he later led in a breakaway to the new CIO.

government agencies (along with the Federal Trade Commission) charged with enforcing the Sherman and Clayton Antitrust Acts and some forty related laws designed to maintain a competitive economy. Enforcement includes advising and counseling services to businesses and prosecution of violators.

The division staff, including about 300 attorneys and 30 economists, receives over 1000 complaints alleging antitrust law violations annually, of which about 250-300 are pursued to the filing of suits, mostly settled by consent decrees.

See also Antitrust Policy; Consent Decree; Federal Trade Commission.

ANTITRUST POLICY

Antitrust policy encompasses three main sub-areas. The first of these is the expression of this policy in the antitrust laws, among which the most significant are the SHERMAN ANTITRUST ACT, CLAYTON ACT, ROBINSON-PATMAN ACT, and the CELLER-KEFAUVER ACT. The second sub-area deals with the interpretations of these laws by the courts. Important cases expressing these interpretations include UNITED STATES v. U.S. STEEL CORP., UNITED STATES v. ALUMINUM CO. OF AMERICA, UNITED STATES v. AMERICAN TOBACCO CO., and BROWN SHOE CO. v. UNITED STATES. And the third sub-area deals with the enforcement of the law by the ANTITRUST DIVISION OF THE DEPARTMENT OF JUSTICE and the FEDERAL TRADE COMMISSION. For the major prohibitions of the antitrust laws, see the articles on RESTRAINT OF TRADE, MONOPOLIZING, COLLUSION, PRICE FIXING, MERGER, and SUBSTANTIAL LESSENING OF COMPETITION.

The student will also find it useful to consult the Subject Map accompanying this article for further coverage of Antitrust Policy in the Encyclopedia.

ANTITRUST POLICY, the central ingredient of antitrust policy as it has emerged through court interpretation of the three major antitrust laws (Sherman Antitrust Act of 1890, Clayton Act of 1914, and Federal Trade Commission Act of 1914) and amendments thereto, is the promotion of competition among business units and the prohibition of anticompetitive practices. Only secondarily and indirectly are consumer interests protected. That is, the consumer is thought to benefit through the lower prices, more efficient allocation of resources, and better quality products the more competitive economy yields.

Method. The promotion of competition in major legislation is through blanket prohibitions on restraint of trade and monopolization (Sherman Act. Sections 1 and 2) and unfair trade practices (Section 5 of FTC Act). In addition, price discrimination, tying contracts and exclusive dealings, mergers, and interlocking directorates are prohibited where such practices may affect competition adversely (Clayton Act, Sections 2, 3, 7 and 9).

The vigor with which these practices have been checked in the 80-plus years of antitrust enforcement gives a truer picture of what antitrust policy is today than does legislative intent.

History. In the area of restraints of trade, courts have condemned flagrant price fixing, market sharing, and exclusion of competitors, but hard evidence of such overt practice is rarely available. Use of the doctrine of conscious parallelism as a substitute for such evidence increased the effectiveness of Section 1 through the mid-1950s (when a judicial reversal set in) but has yielded only occasional results consistent with the policy of competition. The reluctance of courts until 1945 to find untoward behavior in the dominant size of a firm severely limited enforcement of the prohibition on monopolization. Except for the ban on deceptive advertising, Section 5 of the Federal Trade Commission Act has been virtually useless, prohibition of "unfair trade practices" being vaguely worded and overlapped by the Sherman Act. The law on price discrimination has been clouded by judicial protection of competitors, not competition. Interpretation of the prohibition on tying contracts and exclusive dealings has bogged down over the definitions of what is a "substantial" lessening of competition.

The law on mergers has been effective when enforced, especially since the passage of the Celler-Kefauver Act in 1950, but the magnitude of the task, when mergers run in the thousands per year, has meant less than effective overall enforcement. The prohibition on interlocking directorates—limited to those in the same plane of commerce, where firms are direct competitors—is a dead issue.

Significance. Central to the problems of antitrust policy resolution and enforcement is the nature of competition. Economists tend to emphasize market structure as an indicator of illegality, while lawyers stress performance of firms. In addition, antitrust policy at any time is influenced by the will of an administration to enforce the laws, by the general economic climate (typically, less vigorous enforcement in recession), and by the preoccupation of the nation with other pressing problems. The nation's antitrust policy reflects the fact that antitrust enforcement has not, historically, been a top priority concern of government.

See also Conscious Parallelism; Exclusive Dealing; Federal Trade Commission; Market Sharing; Monopolizing; Price Discrimination; Price Fixing; Restraint of Trade; Tying Contracts; Unfair and Deceptive Practices.

Consult (16) Heflebower and Stocking, 1958; Kaysen and Turner, 1959; Letwin, 1965.

—Thomas O. Depperschmidt, *Memphis State University.*

APC. *See* Average Propensity to Consume.

APPRECIATION, CURRENCY. If the rate of exchange on the French franc were to rise in the United States from $.25 to $.33f1, the number of francs required to buy dollars in Paris would drop from four to three. The franc has appreciated relative to the dollar, and Frenchmen have more purchasing power in the dollar market. There can be no appreciation of a currency unless there is depreciation elsewhere.

See also Depreciation, Currency; Devaluation; Exchange Rates.

Consult (23) Wexler, 1972.

APPRENTICESHIP, a training period in which a trainee works with master workmen on the job in order to learn the necessary skills of a trade. Although apprenticeship programs have been in existence throughout history, in 1937 the United States established its apprenticeship policy with the National Apprenticeship Act (Fitzgerald Act). This act is administered by the Bureau of Apprenticeship and Training in the

ANTITRUST POLICY

ANTITRUST POLICY
enforcement of competition

ANTITRUST DIVISION, DEPARTMENT OF JUSTICE
FEDERAL TRADE COMMISSION (FTC)

ANTITRUST LAWS

COMMON LAW
FAIR TRADE LAWS
BANK MERGER ACTS
u.s. v. philadelphia national bank
u.s. v. first city national bank
u.s. v. provident national bank
SHERMAN ANTITRUST ACT (1890)
CLAYTON ANTITRUST ACT (1914)
WEBB-POMERENE ACT (1918)
NATIONAL INDUSTRIAL RECOVERY ACT (1933)
schecter bros. v. united states
section 7
ROBINSON-PATMAN ACT (1936)
MILLER-TYDINGS ACT (1937)
non-signers clause
WHEELER-LEA ACT (1938)
CELLER-KEFAUVER ACT (1950)
anti-merger act
MCGUIRE-KEOGH ACT (1952)
schwegmann v. calvert corp

The Subject Maps in the Encyclopedia illustrate the coverage of particular aspects of economics, showing the interrelationships among the articles in twenty-one critical areas of study. Entries in capital letters are subjects for which there are separate articles in the Encyclopedia. Entries in small letters are references to the article immediately above and provide some idea of content.

The Subject Maps are arranged alphabetically in the Encyclopedia under the following titles:

Antitrust Policy
Banking System
Business Cycles
Capital
Circular Flow of Income
Demand Theory
Economic Systems
Factor Markets
Federal Budget
History of Economic Ideas
International Trade Theory
Labor Market
Labor Movement
Market System
Money and Monetary Policy
National Income
Price Level
Regulation
Supply
Theory of the Firm
Wages

ANTITRUST CASES

BROWN SHOE CO. v. UNITED STATES
FEDERAL TRADE COMMISSION v. CEMENT INSTITUTE
cement case
UNITED STATES v. ALUMINUM CO. OF AMERICA
alcoa case
UNITED STATES v. AMERICAN TOBACCO CO.
american tobacco case
UNITED STATES v. E. I. DUPONT AND CO.
dupont case
UNITED STATES v. N.Y. GREAT A&P CO.
a&p case
UNITED STATES v. STANDARD OIL CO. OF N.J.
standard oil case
UNITED STATES v. U.S. STEEL CORP

PROHIBITED ACTIONS

MONOPOLIZING
RESTRAINT OF TRADE
conspiracies in restraint of trade
combinations in restraint of trade

TYING CONTRACT
tying agreements
FULL-LINE FORCING
EXCLUSIVE DEALERSHIP
INTERLOCKING DIRECTORATE

UNFAIR METHODS OF COMPETITION
UNFAIR AND DECEPTIVE PRACTICES
DECEPTIVE ADVERTISING

COLLUSION
tacit collusion
overt collusion

PRICE FIXING
MARKET SHARING
PRICE DISCRIMINATION
anti-chain-store law
RESALE PRICE MAINTENANCE
retail price maintenance
price maintenance

CARTEL
PREDATORY PRACTICES

ANALYTICAL CONCEPTS

MERGER
tight-knit combinations
CONGLOMERATE
reciprocal dealing
HORIZONTAL MERGER
VERTICAL MERGER
DIVERSIFICATION
MULTI-PLANT FIRM
MULTI-NATIONAL COMPANY

TRADE ASSOCIATION
loose-knit association

PATENT

CONSPIRACY DOCTRINE

PER-SE ILLEGALITY
ABUSE THEORY OF MERGERS

QUANTITATIVE SUBSTANTIALITY
proportional substantiality
SUBSTANTIAL LESSENING OF COMPETITION

ANCILLARY AGREEMENT

BASING-POINT SYSTEM
PHANTOM FREIGHT
CROSS HAULING
cross-shipping

CONSCIOUS PARALLELISM
COUNTERVAILING POWER

CONSENT DECREE

DISSOLUTION, DIVESTITURE, DIVORCEMENT
TRIPLE DAMAGES

RULE OF REASON

MONOPOLY THRUST UPON A FIRM
passive beneficiary of monopoly

ECONOMIES OF SIZE
diseconomies of size

Kenneth J. Arrow shared the 1972 Nobel prize in economics with Oxford's Sir John R. Hicks for "pioneering contributions to general economic equilibrium theory and welfare theory."

U.S. Department of Labor. Its main function has been to promote apprenticeship programs.

Although apprenticeship training programs vary greatly, there are some general characteristics common to most. Usually special requirements must be met before an applicant is accepted, often a written or oral exam must be passed, and the wage scale normally increases with the length of training as the apprentice approaches journeyman level. Apprenticeship programs usually last from one to five years.

APPROPRIATIONS. *See* Federal Budget.

APS. *See* Average Propensity to Save.

ARBITRAGE, the simultaneous buying and selling of two or more currencies in different markets for purposes of gain. The most prevalent forms are exchange and interest rate. *Exchange arbitrage* eliminates discrepancies in cross rates; *interest rate arbitrage* eliminates interest rate differentials. *Gold arbitrage* exists where there are free markets in the metal.

See also Capital Movement; Exchange Rates; Gold Movement.

ARBITRATION, a process by which labor-management disputes may be resolved, utilizing a third party to render a decision. Arbitration may deal with controversies arising in the determination of a new contract (contract arbitration) or with disagreements over the interpretation of an existing contract's provisions (grievance arbitration).

Arbitration Characteristics. Grievance arbitration is common in labor-management relations and is an extremely useful method of resolving disputes that otherwise might lead to work stoppage. For this reason, it is almost always "compulsory" in that the process is automatic and the decision binding. Contract arbitration, much less common, is usually strictly voluntary, that is, not automatic and perhaps not even binding. The best known cases of compulsory contract arbitration are those disputes in the railroad industry in which Congress has intervened to resolve bargaining disputes and impose its decisions on the industry and the workers.

Arbitrators. In grievance arbitration, the arbitrator may be permanent or temporary, full or part time. Contract arbitrators are not permanent because of the irregular nature of their duties. Arbitrators usually are paid, thus "employed," by both the company and union. Among the several good sources of arbitrators are those suggested by the American Arbitration Association or provided by the Federal Mediation and Conciliation Service of the Department of Labor.

—Leonard G. Schifrin, *College of William and Mary*

ARC ELASTICITY. When the coefficient of elasticity of demand is to be computed between two widely separated prices, the concept of arc elasticity should be used. Because elasticity measures the percentage change in quantity demanded caused by a percentage change in price, the problem encountered in large price changes involves choosing the appropriate base upon which the percentages should be calculated. This problem is handled in the arc-elasticity format by using the arithmetic mean of the two quantities demanded as the base for percentage change in quantity and the arithmetic mean of the two prices as the base for percentage change in price.

ARITHMETIC MEAN. *See* Central Tendency.

ARROW, KENNETH JOSEPH (1921–), American economist and educator noted for his work in growth economics. He graduated from City College of New York (1940) and he received his M.A. (1941) and Ph.D. (1951) in economics from Columbia University. His publications include *Social Choice and Individual Values* (1951); *Studies in Linear and Nonlinear Programming* (1958, co-author); and *Capital-Labor Substitution and Economic Efficiency* (1961, co-author). Arrow was an economist on the Council of Economic Advisors in 1962 and he has been on the faculty at the University of Chicago and Stanford. In 1968 he became professor of economics at Harvard.

ASSESSABLE STOCK. *See* Stock.

ASSETS OF THE BANKING SYSTEM. *See* Balance Sheet, Bank.

ASSOCIATIONISM, the utopian socialist concept that the solution to social problems would be provided by voluntary association on the basis of some preconceived plan, predicated on natural harmony, with the identity of the individual preserved. Such association was deemed the only means of both suppressing competition leading to monopoly and preserving individual liberty and freedom of producers. The best known representatives of associationism were Robert Owen and F.M.C. Fourier.

See also Cooperativism; Fourier, Francois Marie Charles; Owen, Robert.

Consult (26) Spiegal, 1971.

ASSUMED BOND. *See* Bonds.

ATOMIC ENERGY COMMISSION (AEC), independent federal agency that regulates the development and control of fissionable materials as a source of power. It was created by the Atomic Energy Act of 1946 and is composed of five members appointed by the president for five-year overlapping terms. The commission is advised by a liaison committee representing the armed forces and a committee of civilian scientists. The work of the commission is subject to the surveillance of a joint committee that consists of several members of Congress. The AEC is specifically prohibited from entering commercial power production.

ATOMIC POWER INDUSTRY. *See* Regulated Industries.

ATTRACTION TO RISK. *See* Expected Utility.

AUTHORITARIAN SOCIALISM. *See* Command Economy; Socialism.

AUTONOMOUS INVESTMENT, investment—demand for new capital goods—that occurs independently of changes in aggregate demand—consumption, government, and foreign demand for goods and services. Autonomous investment occurs because there are opportunities to increase profits by investing even if aggregate demand does not rise. Examples would be new technologies that replace old ones and save on costs (cash registers with built in calculators allow supermarkets to hire fewer checkout clerks more cheaply), or that produce new goods to replace older goods (the bus and the airline replacing the passenger train). In most elementary treatments of national income determination the investment considered is autonomous investment because limiting the examples to autonomous investment simplifies the arithmetic.

See also Induced Investment; Investment; Investment Schedule; Marginal Efficiency of Capital.

AVERAGE. *See* Central Tendency.

AVERAGE COST is obtained by dividing total cost by the number of units of output associated with that total cost. Average total cost is the sum of average variable and average fixed costs.

See also Marginal Cost; Total Cost.

AVERAGE FIXED COST OF PRODUCTION (AFC), the cost of all the fixed inputs (overhead) per unit of output. If TFC is total fixed cost, and X is output, then AFC = TFC/X.

See also Cost Function.

AVERAGE PRODUCT, total quantity of output produced divided by the total amount of one of the inputs used. If X denotes output, and Z is one of the inputs, then X/Z is the average product of input Z.

See also Production Function.

AVERAGE PROFITS. *See* Normal Profits.

AVERAGE PROPENSITY TO CONSUME (APC), the ratio of consumption at a specific level of disposable income to that income. APC has no role in national income analysis.

AVERAGE PROPENSITY TO SAVE (APS), the ratio of saving at a specific level of disposable income to that income. Although having no role in national income analysis, in development economics the APS is useful in estimating a country's capacity to invest and, hence, to develop.

AVERAGE REVENUE is computed by dividing total revenue by the number of units produced and sold. Where all units are sold at the same price (in the absence of price discrimination), average revenue is simply the sales price of a unit of output, and the demand curve and average revenue curve are identical.

See also Marginal Revenue; Total Revenue.

AVERAGE TOTAL COST OF PRODUCTION (ATC), the cost of all the inputs used per unit of output. If TC is total cost, and X is output, then ATC=TC/X.

See also Cost Function.

AVERAGE VARIABLE COST OF PRODUCTION (AVC), the cost of all the variable inputs used per unit of output. If TVC is total variable cost, and X is output, then AVC=TVC/X.

See also Cost Function.

AVIATION INDUSTRY. *See* Regulated Industries.

AVIATION REGULATION. *See* Civil Aeronautics Board; Federal Aviation Administration.

BACH, GEORGE LELAND (1915-), American economist whose major contributions have been in macroeconomics. A graduate of Grinnell College (1936), he received his Ph.D. in economics from the University of Chicago (1940). His publications include *Federal Reserve Policy Making* (1950); *Economics: An Introduction to Analysis and Policy* (1954); and *Making Monetary and Fiscal Policy* (1971). Bach has served as senior economist on the Board of Governors of the Federal Reserve System (1941-44), as principal economist of the Department of Commerce (1946), and as a member of the executive committee of the American Economic Association (1959-62). He became professor of economics and public policy at Stanford University in 1966.

BACKWARD BENDING SUPPLY CURVE depicts the situation in which, after a certain wage level is reached, workers begin to leave the labor force. The supply of labor, under normal conditions, has been found to be a function of the wage level. As wages increase, the decision to enter the labor force becomes more attractive and the supply of labor increases. This is due to the fact that, as wages increase, the economic cost of leisure hours rises. Thus, there is a positive relationship between wage rates and the supply of labor. However, it has been found that, after a certain wage level has been attained workers again begin to leave the labor force. One explanation of this occurrence is that there is often no longer a need for the income of secondary workers in the household because of the higher income of the principal wage earner. Another is that a worker may feel he can work less hours at a higher wage rate and still maintain the standard of living he desires.

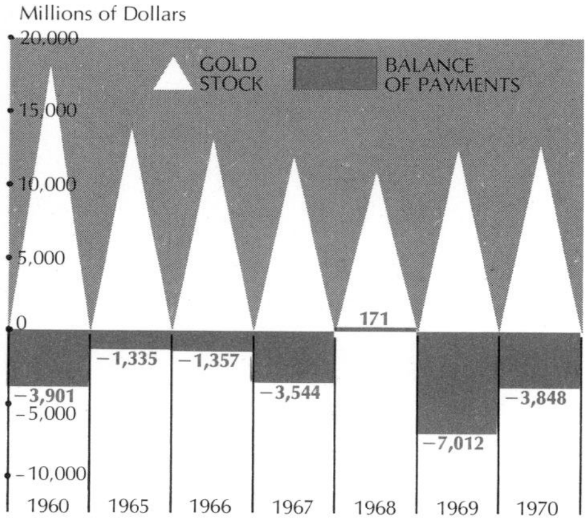

BALANCED BUDGET, budget policy calling for annual government expenditures to equal annual government revenues. Therefore, no deficit and no debt will arise. The case for this type of budget is based on the following arguments: (1) selling government debt to the private sector causes fewer funds to be available for private capital goods, which hinders the economic development of the private sector; (2) deficit spending causes the public sector to expand in relation to the private sector; (3) inflation stems from deficit spending. The Keynesian era in the 1930s brought opposition to the balanced budget principle.

BALANCED GROWTH, system by which a country creates and expands its industries in the same proportion and at the same pace as domestic demand, supplying almost all its needs from its own production and reducing the traditional reliance on imports and exports. The severe depression of the world market for the primary product exports of most less developed countries (LDCs) before and after World War II led many development economists to look unfavorably at the traditional pattern of growth through exports. Instead, many LDCs embraced the balanced growth doctrine of P.N. Rosenstein-Rodan and Prebisch.

There were two supposed major advantages to this strategy. Investment in an integrated set of industries—each demanding the products and supplying the needs of its neighbors and benefiting from each other's external economies—would be more profitable than investment in isolated industries. Secondly, the autarchic (self-sufficient) commerical policies which shut off imports and allowed the establishment of the domestic industries required to "balance" the economy, would lessen the reliance on exports and allow the economy to grow faster than would the then stagnant demand in exports markets.

Unbalanced Growth. The opposition approach was typified by the unbalanced growth doctrine of A.P. Hirschman. He argued that no LDC has the requisite entrepreneurial and managerial ability, skilled labor, and capital to set up and operate any balanced industrial system in a short time. Unbalanced growth, on the other hand, concentrates the available talent and capital on certain key sectors, creating demands that "pull" subsidiary industries and infrastructure into existence by creating obvious shortages to which private investors can react. Furthermore, the autarchic commercial policies associated with balanced growth fly in the face of comparative advantage, giving rise to grossly inefficient domestic (import substitution) industries producing goods that could be imported far more cheaply.

Consult (24) Hirschman, 1958; Rosenstein-Rodan, 1961; Streeten, 1963.

—Charles Staelin, *University of Michigan*

BALANCE OF INTERNATIONAL INDEBTEDNESS. *See* Foreign Investment.

BALANCE OF PAYMENTS (B/P), for a country, a summary of all economic transactions between it and the rest of the world for a given period of time. B/P reflects all payments due and made to the country as well as all liabilities accrued and paid to other countries. All recorded transactions follow the accounting procedure of debits and credits, and the B/P, therefore, always balances. On the U.S. balance of payments, transactions that give rise to foreigners' money claims are debits; transactions giving rise to money claims by Americans on foreigners are credits. Important credits are merchandise exports, interest and dividends on investments abroad, investment by foreigners in America, and foreign travel in the United States. Important debits are merchandise imports, tourist expenditures abroad, shipping services, and investment abroad. The debit items give rise to the demand for foreign exchange; credits give the supply of exchange; the rate of exchange is determined by demand and supply. Whether or not a given rate is an equilibrium rate depends on what transactions are necessary to make B/P balance.

Accounts. Balance of payments generally include the current account, capital account, and gold account. The current account is the "real" side of B/P, comprising transactions in current goods and services, including services being currently rendered by capital but not capital movements themselves. Capital and gold accounts relate to the financial side of B/P. Gold moves to make B/P balance as do short-term capital movements in the capital account—they are balancing items and go "below the line." Long-term capital transactions are generally undertaken independently of other B/P transactions. The presence of balancing items indicates disequilibrium, which im-

BALANCE OF PAYMENTS

For further reading on two very important subsections of the full balance of payments statement, consult the articles on BALANCE OF TRADE and CAPITAL ACCOUNT. The balance of payments also has a bearing on macroeconomic performance. For an especially important interrelationship between international trade and the macroeconomy, see the article on INFLATION.

The student will also find it useful to consult the Subject Map accompanying the article on INTERNATIONAL TRADE THEORY for the position of balance of payments in trade relations.

BALANCE OF PAYMENTS

Millions of Dollars

GOLD STOCK
BALANCE OF PAYMENTS

20,000
15,000
10,000
5,000
0
−5,000
−10,000

1960	1965	1966	1967	1968	1969	1970
−3,901	−1,335	−1,357	−3,544	171	−7,012	−3,848

plies that there is some pressure on exchange rates.

Basic Equilibrium. Current-account exports of goods and services plus long-term capital imports equals current-account imports of goods and services plus long-term capital exports. Capital imports are credits, and capital exports are debits. The absence of gold and short-term capital items shows that B/P is self-financing, not needing international reserves or pressure on the currency. If credits exceed debits, B/P is in surplus disequilibrium, and gold imports or short-term capital exports must finance the surplus. A deficit disequilibrium results from debits exceeding credits, and gold exports or short-term capital imports must finance the deficit.

Gold exports are credits, and gold imports are debits. Short-term capital movements relate to transactions to be completed or reversed within a year and take the following forms: (1) exports through increase in American owned balances abroad or decrease in foreign balances in the United States, and (2) imports through decrease in United States balances abroad or increase in foreign balances in America. These balances are generally demand or time deposits or short-term debt instruments, such as Treasury bills.

America's Payments Deficit. To help in analyzing the United States B/P deficit, which has persisted since the late 1950s, the liquidity and official settlements bases have been developed. Both bases look at net changes in certain liabilities as they relate to net changes in the holdings of international monetary reserves (gold, convertible foreign currencies, and liquid reserves at IMF). The liquidity concept places changes in total short-term liabilities to foreigners (public and private) below the line; the official settlements concept puts only changes in liabilities (both short and long term) to foreign official agencies below the line as only they can command gold. When these changes are greater than changes in international reserves, the deficit has increased. Therefore, the size of the deficit depends on what goes below the line; all foreign liabilities to the United States go above the line, a treatment unique to the United States.

See also Balance of Trade; Capital Account; Devaluation; Exchange Rate; Gold Movement.

Consult (23) Bach, 1971; Board of Governors; Department of Commerce; Snider, 1971.

—John R. Matthews, Jr., *College of William and Mary*

BALANCE OF PAYMENTS, STAGES OF. *See* Stages of a Country's Balance of Payments.

BALANCE OF TRADE, the difference between merchandise exports and imports in a nation's balance of payments. If exports exceed imports the balance of trade is favorable, or in surplus; if imports exceed exports the balance of trade is unfavorable, or in deficit. Mercantilists of the sixteenth and seventeenth centuries had the acquisition of gold and, thus, a favorable balance of trade as a major tenet of commercial policy. David Hume, in his specie-flow analysis, proved that all nations cannot have a favorable balance of trade simultaneously; one nation's gain is another's loss. Hume showed that the income and price effects of gold movements would automatically reverse a favorable or unfavorable balance of trade, and gold would stop flowing when exports and imports were in balance.

Merchandise exports and imports are the two most important entries in the current account of the balance of payments. The difference between them may show an unfavorable balance, but, there will be no disequilibrium in the balance of payments because of other items in the current account. Many countries, such as Great Britain, are noted for unfavorable balances of trade, with the deficit being financed in the current account by such items as shipping and financial services. For many years the United States had a favorable balance of trade, but many of the excess exports were shipped in ships of foreign registry, somewhat mitigating the balance. It is the surplus or deficit relative to the current account, not the balance of trade, that has to be financed by capital movements and gold. In addition, when a country has reached a mature-creditor stage, the balance of trade or the entire current account must be unfavorable for capital to be repatriated.

See also Balance of Payments; Exchange Rate; Terms of Trade.

Consult (23)Bach, 1971; Ingram, 1970; Snider, 1971; Wexler, 1972.

—John R. Matthews, Jr., *College of William and Mary*

U.S. BALANCE OF TRADE
(MILLIONS OF DOLLARS)

	Merchandise exports	Merchandise imports	Balance of trade
1951	14,243	11,176	3,067
1952	13,449	10,838	2,611
1953	12,412	10,975	1,437
1954	12,929	10,353	2,576
1955	14,424	11,527	2,897
1956	17,556	12,803	4,753
1957	19,562	13,291	6,271
1958	16,414	12,952	3,462
1959	16,458	15,310	1,148
1960	19,650	14,744	4,906
1961	20,107	14,519	5,588
1962	20,779	16,218	4,561
1963	22,252	17,011	5,241
1964	25,478	18,647	6,831
1965	26,438	21,496	4,942
1966	29,390	25,463	3,927
1967	30,680	26,821	3,859
1968	33,588	32,964	624
1969	36,490	35,830	660
1970	41,980	39,870	2,110
1971 est	44,308	46,052	−1,744

SOURCE: *Economics Report of the President*, Jan. 1972

BALANCE ON CURRENT ACCOUNT. *See* Balance of Trade.

BALANCE SHEET. The main purpose of the balance sheet is to show both assets and liabilities of a business concern. The balance sheet and the income statement are the two major financial statements of a firm. In practice, total assets should equal total liabilities. For example, if a corporation sells $100 worth of stock, $100 would then be entered under cash on the asset side of the balance sheet, and $100 would be entered under issued stock on the liability side. Thus, assets would equal liabilities. Depending on the individual firm, a balance sheet is usually kept current on a monthly, quarterly, semiannual, or annual basis. During the interim, each transaction of the firm is recorded

ASSETS AND LIABILITIES OF ALL COMMERCIAL BANKS, DECEMBER 31, 1971
(BILLIONS)

ASSETS:		
Cash and due from banks:		
Currency and coin	7.5	
Due from Federal Reserve banks	27.5	
Due from other banks	25.5	
Cash items in process of collection	39.3	99.8
Loans and discounts:		
Commercial and industrial loans	118.5	
Loans to farmers	12.5	
Loans on securities	11.0	
Real estate loans	81.6	
Consumer loans	74.5	
Loans to banks	24.6	
Loans to other financial institutions	16.2	
Other loans	8.0	346.9
Securities:		
U.S. government	64.9	
States and localities	82.4	
Other securities	22.3	169.6
Other assets		24.0
Total assets		640.3

LIABILITIES:			
Deposits:			
Demand:			
Individual and business	192.5		
U.S. government	10.2		
State and local government	17.7		
Interbank	32.3		
Certified and officers' checks	10.1	262.8	
Time:			
Individual and business	242.1		
U.S. government	0.5		
State and local governments	30.4		
Interbank	2.9	275.9	538.7
Borrowings			25.9
Other liabilities			28.5
Total liabilities			593.1
NET WORTH:			
Capital, surplus and undivided profits			47.2
Total liabilities and net worth			640.3

SOURCE: *Federal Reserve Bulletin*

in a journal and referred to as a journal entry. After a designated time period, the journal entries are transferred to either the balance sheet or the income statement.

BALANCE SHEET, BANK. The balance sheet of a bank is identical in principle to any other corporate balance sheet, differing only in the type of items included. The two most obvious differences from, say, a manufacturing corporation, are that almost all of the bank's assets are financial rather than physical and that its liabilities, which greatly exceed its net worth, are almost entirely short-term obligations to depositors: demand deposits and time deposits. A *consolidated balance sheet,* adding together the figures for all 13,783 commercial banks in the United States on December 31, 1971, is shown.

Cash. Cash and due from banks (usually called simply cash) represent funds readily available to meet the demands of depositors. Currency and coin (vault cash) and deposits in the federal reserve banks are basic reserves. Deposits due from other banks are generally considered reserves for state banks that are not members of the federal reserve system. Cash items in process of collection represent checks that have been deposited but not yet collected from the banks on which they were drawn. They will become reserves as soon as they are collected, usually within a day or two. Cash is a liquid asset but produces no income.

Loans and Discounts. Lending is the primary function of commercial banks and represents both their major source of income (interest) and the way by which they provide multiple expansion of the money supply. Commercial loans are made to businessmen most frequently for carrying inventory and for periods of one to three months, though the loans may often be renewed rather than repaid at maturity. Industrial loans are for longer periods, though seldom for more than five years. If their maturity exceeds one year, they are called term loans. Commercial and industrial loans represent about 40% of all loans made by commercial banks.

Mortgage loans are made both on private homes and on commercial property and normally run for 15 to 25 years. They represent another 25% of bank lending activity. Not far behind are other loans to individuals, consisting primarily of consumer installment loans of from one to three years, repaid by monthly payments.

Loans to banks include a small amount of ordinary loans but consist mainly of federal funds, a form of overnight loan in which the lending bank gives the borrowing bank a check drawn on its account with the federal reserve bank of its district in exchange for repayment the following day. The borrowing bank increases its reserves in this way, while the lending bank earns interest on temporarily excess reserves.

Investments. United States government securities, particularly Treasury bills, are secondary reserves bearing a relatively low rate of interest but easily sellable if cash is needed. State and local government securities may bear an even lower interest rate, but this interest is not generally subject to corporate income taxes, so that the net income is higher than it is on taxable issues. Other securities are almost exclusively corporate bonds. Banks may hold a small amount of corporate stock, but normally this type of investment is considered too risky to suit the needs of commercial banks. About half of other assets consists of the bank building, furnishings, and supplies. The rest is quite miscellaneous.

Liabilities. By far the greatest part of a bank's liabilities consists of demand deposits and time deposits owed to its customers, primarily individuals and corporations. Banks borrow primarily from other banks, including the federal reserve banks, for periods up to fifteen days. Banks may also borrow small amounts from the public on capital notes or, more rarely, bonds.

Net worth represents the equity provided by the stockholders of the bank and includes capital, surplus, and undivided profits. Net worth is only 7% of total assets, a very small figure by comparison with almost any other type of corporation.

—Walter W. Haines, *New York University*

BANCOR. *See* Triffin Plan.

BANK FAILURE occurs when a commercial bank or, very rarely, a savings bank is unable to meet the demands of its creditors. Because its primary creditors are its depositors, most of whose claims are payable on demand, a bank fails when it is unable to pay cash to depositors wishing to withdraw funds. More than a third (10,308) of the banks in operation in 1922 failed within a decade. To counteract this avalanche, bank supervision under the federal reserve system and the Comptroller of the Currency was significantly tightened, and the Federal Deposit Insurance Corporation was set up to insure deposits. Since that time failures have seldom exceeded four or five a year, usually due to the theft or criminal manipulation of funds by bank officers or employees.

See also Federal Deposit Insurance Corporation.

BANKING SYSTEM, in a broad sense, all those institutions involved in the business of lending or borrowing money or of dealing in monetary instruments, such as stocks, bonds, mortgages,

THE BANKING SYSTEM

The Subject Maps in the Encyclopedia illustrate the coverage of particular aspects of economics, showing the interrelationships among the articles in twenty-one critical areas of study. Entries in capital letters are subjects for which there are separate articles in the Encyclopedia. Entries in small letters are references to the article immediately above and provide some idea of content.

The Subject Maps are arranged alphabetically in the Encyclopedia under the following titles:

Antitrust Policy
Banking System
Business Cycles
Capital
Circular Flow of Income
Demand Theory
Economic Systems
Factor Markets
Federal Budget
History of Economic Ideas
International Trade Theory
Labor Market
Labor Movement
Market System
Money and Monetary Policy
National Income
Price Level
Regulation
Supply
Theory of the Firm
Wages

BANKING SYSTEM

accounting

BALANCE SHEET, BANK
- consolidated bank balance sheet
- monopoly bank

assets
- RESERVES
  - legal reserves
  - reserve ratio
  - secondary reserves
  - correspondent balances
  - FRACTIONAL RESERVES
  - 100% RESERVES
  - VAULT CASH
- LOANS AND DISCOUNTS
  - CALL LOANS
    - demand loans
- STOCK
- PORTFOLIO
- GOVERNMENT SECURITIES
  - government bonds
  - short-term government bonds
  - long-term government bonds
  - savings bonds
  - treasury bills
  - certificates of indebtedness
  - government notes

liabilities
- DEPOSITS
  - DEMAND DEPOSITS
  - TIME DEPOSITS

structure

FINANCIAL INTERMEDIARIES
- federal savings and loan insurance corp.
- savings and loan associations
- credit unions
- pension funds
- finance companies
- government credit agencies
- intermediation
- disintermediation

FEDERAL DEPOSIT INSURANCE CORPORATION
TREASURER OF THE UNITED STATES
COMPTROLLER OF THE CURRENCY

FEDERAL RESERVE SYSTEM
- board of governors
- open market committee
- interdistrict settlement fund
- float

FEDERAL RESERVE ACT
BRANCH BANK
BANK FAILURE
CENTRAL BANK
MONETARY AUTHORITY, CENTRAL

FEDERAL RESERVE BANKS
- district banks

COMMERCIAL BANK
- NATIONAL BANK
- STATE BANK

MEMBER BANK
- reserve city bank
- country bank
- central reserve city bank

BANKING SYSTEM

Uses of Funds

Government
Consumers
Business
Foreigners

to
directly
through financial institutions in the money and capital markets
made available

Sources of Funds

Savings
provided by
Foreigners
accumulated by
Government
Business
made voluntarily by
Individuals

New money
created by
Commercial banks
Government

or other evidences of debt. In this sense the banking system includes both commercial banks and financial intermediaries. Commercial banks can create money through the issue of demand deposits, an ability they share with no other institution except the federal government, which can create money through the issue of currency. All other financial institutions must obtain savings from individuals or other institutions and cannot lend money that does not exist, as can commercial banks.

Analysis. The banking system, in this broad sense, consists of a multitude of institutions of many types, some highly specialized, some operating with a wide diversity of situations. There is a great deal of overlapping and no overall coordination, so that only loosely can the conglomerate of agencies be thought of as a system at all.

Functions, if not institutions, can be classified in several ways, as by the type of lender, the type of borrower, the form of monetary instrument, or its maturity. In terms of maturity two broad and important markets can be distinguished. The money market consists of institutions and facilities concerned with short-term financial obligations, whose maturities do not exceed one year: Treasury bills, commercial paper, federal funds and so on. The basic operations of commercial banks fall in the money market. The capital market deals with securities with more than one year to run: most bonds, stocks (which are not strictly a credit instrument at all, because they connote ownership rather than loan), mortgages, and other long-term obligations.

The principal function of the banking system is to channel funds from areas with excess money to areas in need of money. The system provides, partly through the great number of institutions involved, a wide variety of terms, maturities, conditions, and interest rates, so that any lender or borrower can presumably find some institution or monetary instrument that closely meets his needs.

The Banking System and Deposits. In a stricter sense the banking system is limited to those institutions that accept deposits repayable on demand or after a specified period of time. Only commercial banks accept demand deposits, but both commercial banks and savings banks accept time deposits. With rare and localized exceptions, no other institution accepts deposits from the general public in the normal course of business, and, hence, no other institution can properly be called a bank in the limited sense. There is a movement afoot to give savings and loan associations the powers of banks, but this alteration would require a substantial change in the law.

Consult (9) Chandler, 1969; Haines, 1966; Shapiro, 1968.

—Walter W. Haines, *New York University*

BANK MERGER ACTS (1960, 1966). The first act, passed by Congress to promote competition among suppliers of loanable funds, required approval from an appropriate administrative agency before bank mergers were to be allowed. This approval was thought to give antitrust exemption to bank mergers under the Celler-Kefauver Act of 1950 and thus remove the uncertainty that had surrounded antitrust coverage. Subsequent decisions of the Supreme Court, however, notably *United States v. Philadelphia National Bank* (1963), held bank mergers to be violations of the Celler-Kefauver Act.

Under the 1966 Bank Merger Act, the appropriate authorities as before were to weigh the anticompetitive effects of a bank merger against the convenience and needs of the public. When the Comptroller of the Currency judged certain mergers of national banks to be permissible under the act, the Department of Justice sued (*United States v. First National City Bank* and *United States v. Provident National Bank*, 1967), and the Supreme Court disallowed the mergers, holding that no proof had been offered by the merging banks that the public interest in the merger outweighed the anticompetitive effects. The net result is that merging banks do not enjoy blanket exemption from antitrust prosecution; rather, both anticompetitive effects and the public interest must be weighed in each merger proposal.

See also Celler-Kefauver Act.

—Thomas O. Depperschmidt, *Memphis State University*

BANK MONEY. *See* Demand Deposits.

BANK MULTIPLIER. *See* Multiple Expansion of the Money Supply.

BANK RESERVES. *See* Reserves.

BARGAINING. For articles on bargaining, *See* Bargaining Unit; Bilateral Bargaining; Collective Bargaining; Industry-Wide Bargaining; Key Bargain; Multi-Employer Bargaining.

BARGAINING UNIT, the group of workers or jobs that the union represents in its bargaining with the employers and to which the contract terms apply. The unit may include all the production workers in a plant or an entire firm, or it may cover one group of workers such as the meatcutters or truckdrivers in a larger work force.

With no standard definition of bargaining units, defining them is one of the highly controversial matters in labor law. When conflict over such definition exists, the National Labor Relations Board is frequently called upon to specify the appropriate scope of the unit.

BARRIERS TO ENTRY, term used to indicate the problems a firm must overcome in order to enter a particular market. The two main types of barriers to entry are natural and artificial.

Natural barriers are built into the nature of the firm. One type of natural barrier exists where the optimum scale of plant is so large compared to the size of the market that entry cannot be profitable. The best examples of this type of barrier occur in the utility and transportation markets, such as telephones and electric companies as well as railroad companies. Another natural barrier occurs in industries where the enormous capital needed to enter the market is almost impossible to obtain. The perfect example of this is the automotive industry.

Artificial barriers include restrictive laws, such as patent rights and licensing laws, such as those in the interstate public transportation field, that limit those who may enter the market.

Another artificial barrier is the price policy of established firms in the industry. For example, existing firms may threaten to undersell any new firms. Other barriers are established product differentiation that discourages the use of "off-brands," and control of strategic sources of raw materials.

See also Entry.

—William D. Wagoner, *Louisiana State University*

BARRIERS TO TRADE. *See* Trade Barriers.

BARTER, direct exchange of goods or services without the use of money. A barter agreement between countries provides for the exchange of specified quantities of goods.

See Balance of Trade; Terms of Trade.

BASE RATE. *See* Rate Base.

BASING-POINT SYSTEM, a pricing arrangement of nominal competitors (especially oligopolists) wherein the price of a product is set as of one or more producing localities or cities ("points") plus an average freight charge to various delivery points so that the price of the delivered product is the same for any delivery. Alternately, the delivered price is a standard base price plus actual freight charged.

An arrangement designating only one production city for purposes of computing the delivery price is called a "single basing-point" system; with more than one it is a "multiple basing-point" system; one where all production cities are basing-points is a "plenary basing-point" system.

See also Cross Hauling; FTC v. Cement Institute; Phantom Freight.

BATOR, FRANCIS MICHEL (1925-), Hungarian-born economist whose major contribution has been in the areas of international relations and welfare economics. He received his Ph.D. in economics (1956) from M.I.T. He is author of *The Question of Government Spending* (1960) and many articles for professional journals and magazines. He has served as senior economic adviser of the Agency for International Development (1963-64), and deputy special assistant to the President for National Security Affairs (1965-67). In 1967 he was named professor of political economy and director of studies at the Institute of Politics at Harvard.

BAUMOL, WILLIAM JACK (1922-), American educator and authoritative writer on economic theory. He graduated from the City College of New York in 1942, and received his Ph.D. in economics from London University in 1949. He won nationwide attention for his co-authorship (with Princeton economist William G. Bowen) of *The Performing Arts—The Economic Dilemma* (1966), the first full-scale study of the financial plight of professional performing artistic activity in the United States. He is chairman of the Economic Policy Council of the State of New Jersey and former vice-president of the American Economic Association. Currently at Princeton University, he is the Joseph Douglas Green '95 professor of economics.

William J. Baumol

BAYESIAN APPROACH. *See* Probability.

BECKER, GARY (1930-), imaginative and innovative modern economist, who has contributed to many new and diverse areas of economics. His analysis of human capital—the concept that, in economic terms, an individual be considered in many ways to have the characteristics of capital (earning power over the individual's lifetime can be capitalized into a present value and this present value can be changed by investing in the individual through education, job training, better health care, and so on)—broadened the scope of economics. Becker's contributions to the economics of crime, his economic analysis of fertility behavior, his work on the economics of discrimination, and his analysis of time in economic theory have also broadened the scope of economics and challenged economists and other social scientists.

See also Human Capital.

BEGGAR-THY-NEIGHBOR POLICY, program of increasing exports or decreasing imports at the expense of other countries. Nations with unemployment have tried at times to increase exports to increase jobs at home. Raising tariffs is one way of creating an export surplus. This has the effect of exporting unemployment to the nation that buys more of your goods and has its exports to you reduced. It usually invites swift retaliation.

Because trucking firms derive greatest benefit from highway use, they pay more heavily for it.

BENEFIT PRINCIPLE, a theory of taxation that holds that tax payments should be in proportion to the benefits the individual receives from government services. It is also referred to as the benefits-received principle or the compensatory principle of taxation.

See also Ability-to-Pay Principle.

BENEFITS, FRINGE. *See* Fringe Benefits.

BENEFITS, STRIKE. *See* Strike Benefits.

BENSON PLAN. Ezra Taft Benson, Secretary of Agriculture during the Eisenhower administration, opposed much of the farm legislation on the books when he took office. He attempted to move in the direction of free markets and away from rigid price supports and production controls. In particular, he favored flexible price supports, a device written into earlier legislation but given little opportunity to operate. Flexible supports provide a sliding scale of support prices—high when supplies are low, low when supplies are large. Since production was large and the government was accumulating surplus stocks, the prospects were that price supports would be low most of the time if supports were flexible. Congress did not put flexible supports into effect, but under the pressure of surplus production, accumulating stocks, and high program costs, price supports on most commodities were lower when Secretary Benson left office in 1961 than when he took office in 1953.

See also Price-Support Programs.

BERGSON, ABRAM (1915-) American economist noted for his application of modern economic analysis to Soviet planning and growth. A graduate of Johns Hopkins University (1933), he received his Ph.D. from Harvard (1940). His publications include *Structure of Soviet Wages* (1944), *Real National Income of Soviet Russia* (1961), and *Essays in Normative Economics* (1966). During World War II he analyzed the Soviet economy for the Office of Strategic Services, and in 1945 he was a member of the U.S. delegation to the reparations conference in Moscow. Bergson is George F. Baker Professor of Economics at Harvard and also a member of the Social Science Advisory Board of the U.S. Arms Control and Disarmament Agency.

BEST FIT

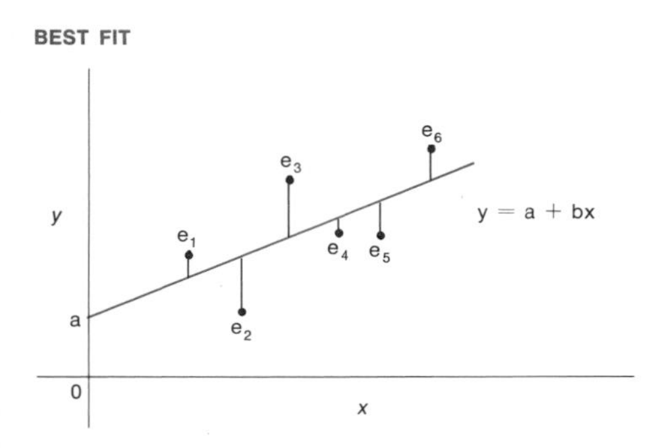

BEST FIT. The curve that best fits a set of data plotted on a scatter diagram is the one which minimizes the sum of squares of error (least squares), where "error" is the difference between the observed and the computed value of the dependent variable. The errors are the e_i in the figure.

See also Curve Fitting; Scatter Diagram.

BILATERAL BARGAINING, situation in which each side represents a monopoly power of sorts. The union representing the bargaining unit is viewed as the single seller (monopolist) of labor services, and the firm, if it accounts for all or most of the employment in the labor market, can be viewed as a single buyer (monopsonist). With this sort of market power on each side of the table, the process, strategies, and outcome may be different from those in other bargaining situations.

BILATERAL MONOPOLY, a market with both a pure monopoly and a pure monopsony, only one seller of the good and only one purchaser of the good. The typical bilateral monopoly occurs when a labor union is selling labor to a single company. The two monopoly powers tend to offset one another, in that the wage rate and compensations may be equal to the value of the output of the worker. In this situation the factor of production will not normally be exploited.

BISSELL, RICHARD MERVIN, JR. (1909-) American economist noted for his work in general economic theory, balance of payments, and international finance. He received his A.B. (1932) and Ph.D. (1939) in economics from Yale. He has served widely in government and industry, and has worked as economic advisor to the Director of War Mobilization and Reconversion (1945-46), executive secretary of the President's Commission on Foreign Aid (1947-48), president of the Institute for Defense Analysis (1962-64), and director of Marketing and Economic Planning, United Aircraft Corporation, beginning in 1964. He has also been on the faculty at M.I.T. and Yale.

BLANKET BOND. *See* Bonds.

BLOCKADED ENTRY. *See* Entry.

BLUE-COLLAR WORKER, a term used to distinguish between those workers who are employed on the administrative end of a firm and those workers who are not. The term originated at a time when factory floor workers wore blue collars and office personnel wore white collars. Blue collar does not imply a skill level. A skilled machinist and the janitor who sweeps the floor are both considered blue-collar workers.

BOARD, MARKETING. *See* Marketing Boards.

BOARD OF GOVERNORS. *See* Federal Reserve System.

BÖHM-BAWERK, EUGEN (1851-1914), Austrian economist and several times minister of finance, his outstanding contribution to the field of economics is his theory of interest, marking a major advance in the understanding of why capital yields profit. Underlying this theory is a combination of the time-preference and marginal-productivity principles; it is derived from the marginal utility theory of value, of which Böhm-Bawerk gave the most comprehensive presentation.

His views were set forth in *Capital and Interest* (1884) and *The Positive Theory of Capital* (1889). The second of these, principally a presentation of Böhm-Bawerk's personal theories, gained much attention for his ideas and stimulated broad controversies even yet unsettled. The argument was constructed thus: (1) people tend to overestimate future resources and underestimate future wants; (2) goods available now will yield goods of higher value in the future; (3) people will then tend to place a higher value on present goods than on future ones of the same kind and quantity; and (4) therefore, to induce them to exchange present for future goods, people must be paid a premium which will make the value of the future good equal to that of the present. The premium is known as interest.

Böhm-Bawerk's critical analysis of the Marxian theorem of the declining rate of profit is also considered a classic. He maintained that socialism's criticism of capitalism was in reality a criticism of the problem of scarcity, which was in fact the central problem of the human condition and with which, therefore, even socialism would eventually have to cope.

Having demonstrated in his early work that interest is a basic component in any rational economic calculation, even noncapitalistic, Böhm-Bawerk developed later in his life a general theory of laws of economic rationality which applies to every type of social order. His work contributed significantly to the development of non-Marxist socialist theory after 1918.

—Clyde A. Haulman, *College of William and Mary*

BOLSHEVIKS, a term (Russian for "men of the majority") used by followers of Lenin in 1903 when they won a temporary majority in the executive committee of the Social Democratic Party. The majority was soon lost to Menshevik (minority) opponents, but the name was retained until 1952.

In 1917 the Bolsheviks provided such leadership that the second (November) revolution was named after them. The party accepted the Marxist revolutionary creed dogmatically and was characterized by highly centralized leadership, tight regime of party discipline, absolutism of party line, intolerance of compromise or disagreement, and an attitude of manipulation relative to mass organization.

See also Lenin, Vladimir.

BONBRIGHT, JAMES CUMMINGS (1891–), American educator. A graduate of Northwestern University (1913), he received his Ph.D. in economics from Columbia (1921). His publications include *Railroad Capitalization* (1920) and *Principles of Public Utilities Rates* (1961). On the faculty at Columbia from 1920, he also served on a number of government commissions.

BOND MARKET. The bond market is not a place but a variety of brokers, dealers, and other institutions that facilitate the purchase and sale of bonds. These agencies are connected by telephone or direct wire so that information can be obtained and transactions completed almost instantaneously. New corporate bonds are usually issued through investment banks. New federal government securities are sold through the agency of the Federal Reserve Banks. Most transfers of already-issued bonds are handled by specialized dealers who buy and sell for their own account, thereby making a continuous market for the general public wishing to sell or buy. Banks and stock brokers will handle orders, or the dealers may trade directly with the public. A few bonds are sold on the stock exchanges.

See also Bond Prices; Open Market Operations.

BOND PRICES. A bond has two different prices. Its par value is the price printed on the face, usually $1,000 or multiples thereof. The bond is normally sold at this price when newly issued. More important, it is the price at which the bond will be redeemed at maturity. Market price is the price at which present bondholders can sell their bonds to prospective purchasers. Unlike par value, market value may fluctuate partly because of changes in the financial condition of the issuer from day to day, though not nearly as much as stock prices, but even more in consequence of a change in the general level of interest rates.

Bond yield is the annual dollar interest paid on a bond divided by its market price and adjusted for appreciation or depreciation to maturity. Every reduction in a bond's market price raises its yield; every increase in price reduces yield. Therefore, as interest rates rise, bond prices fall, and *vice versa.*

BONDS, in finance, interest-bearing certificates issued either by a business firm (corporate bonds) or by a government that promise to pay the bondholder a specified sum of money on a specified date. The main purpose of bond issuance is to raise capital.

There are many different types of bonds. A popular bond issued and guaranteed by the United States government is the *savings bond.* Sold at a discount, it matures to face value after a designated period of time, usually seven or ten years.

A bond issued by a city, county, or

"Come In, Ezra— How's The Weather Out There?"

During the Eisenhower administration (1953–61), Secretary of Agriculture Benson attempted to apply flexible price supports—high when supplies were low, low when supplies were high. Congress did not put his program into effect.

26 THE WALL STREET JOURNAL, Friday, October 6, 1972

New York Stock Exchange Bonds

Thursday, October 5, 1972

Volume, All Issues, $18,620,000

SINCE JANUARY 1

	1972	1971	1970
Total sales	$4,257,810,800	$5,029,151,200	$3,275,576,600

	Foreign Thur	Foreign Wed	Domestic Thur	Domestic Wed	All issues Thur	All issues Wed
Issues traded	4	3	689	712	693	715
Advances	1	1	241	238	243	239
Declines	1	0	232	262	233	262
Unchanged	2	2	216	212	218	214
New highs, 1972	0	0	7	5	7	5
New lows, 1972	0	0	28	30	28	30

Dow Jones Bond Averages

1970 High	1970 Low	1971 High	1971 Low	1972 High	1972 Low		Thursday 1972	Chg.	Thursday 1971	Chg.	Thursday 1970	Chg.
69.73	64.36	73.29	68.62	74.55	73.41	40 Bonds	73.98	+ .02	71.30	+ .08	65.81	....
54.61	45.11	52.63	48.95	54.15	52.67	10 Higher Grade Rails	53.32	− .06	51.08	+ .05	47.61	− .07
69.81	56.53	66.23	59.20	69.01	66.16	10 Second Grade Rails	67.66	+ .01	64.68	+ .01	58.05	− .03
85.67	77.03	89.80	85.50	91.13	89.55	10 Public Utilities	90.48	+ .01	87.12	+ .02	81.20	+ .08
80.86	73.95	84.96	80.22	85.50	84.05	10 Industrials	84.47	+ .12	82.35	+ .27	76.41	+ .03
54.87	44.00	55.21	47.53	55.08	51.67	Income Rails	52.31	+ .06	52.85	....	45.96	− .16

Corporation Bonds

Volume, $18,440,000

A-B-C

1972 High	1972 Low	Bonds	Sales in $1,000	High	Low	Close	Net Chg.
111½	106	AlaPow 9s2000	90	107¾	107½	107½	− ⅜
104	102	AlaPow 7⅞s2002	7	102	101	101	−1
204½	98	Alaska Int cv6s96	63	133	129½	129½	−3½
107¾	79⅞	Allen Grp cv6s87	10	91⅞	91	91⅞	....
105¼	102½	Allied Chm 7⅞s96	5	104½	104½	104½	+1½
96	91	Allied Chm 6.60s93	10	92¾	92¾	92¾	+1
89	83¾	**Allied Chm 3½s78**	29	88¼	88¼	88¼	+ ½
132	100	Allied Str cv4½s81	1	105⅛	105⅛	105⅛	+1⅛
93	78	Allied Str cv4½s92	15	78¾	78¾	78¾	+ ½
73¾	60	AlliedSup cv5¾s87	1	65	65	65	....
102¾	97¾	Alcoa 7.45s96	5	101¼	101¼	101¼	+ ¾
90½	81¾	Alcoa cv5¼s91	125	87	86¾	87	− ¼
83½	79	Alcoa 4¼s82	5	84	84	84	+ ¾
80½	76	Alcoa 3⅞s83	10	77½	77½	77½	....
87	84	AlumCoCan 4½s80	10	85¼	85¼	85¼	....
183	121½	AmAirFilt cv6s90	5	126	126	126	+4½
119	111⅝	AmAirlin 11s88	2	116⅛	116⅛	116⅛	− ⅝
117⅜	112⅜	AmAirlin 10⅞s88	1	114½	114½	114½	....
112⅛	109	AmAirlin 10s89	2	110	110	110	....
119½	77	AmAirln cv4¼s92	163	77	75	75	−2½
89⅛	83¾	Am Brands 5⅞s92	10	87⅝	87½	87⅝	+ ⅞
100	83½	ACenMtg cv6¾s91	5	84½	84¼	84¼	+ ⅛
53¼	17	A Exprt cv5¼s93f	47	20¼	19¾	20	− ¼
101	97½	AmExpCr 6½s77	15	99⅛	99⅛	99⅛	− ½
57½	48	AmForPow 5s2030	15	49	48¼	49	....
59½	48	AmForPw 4.80s87	3	49⅜	49¼	49¼	....
86	75	Am Hoist cv5½s93	7	77	76½	77	− ½
107¼	104½	AmInvest 9½s76	4	105⅝	105⅝	105⅝	− ⅜
102½	85	AmMedicp cv5s97	120	82	80½	80½	−4½
73	69½	Am Smelt 4⅝s88	1	71¾	71¾	71¾	....
75	71⅝	AmSugar 5.30s93	1	73⅞	73⅞	73⅞	+ ⅞
....	....	AmSug 5.30s93reg	2	73	73	73	
112	109¼	AmT&T 8¾2000xw	384	110⅞	110⅝	110⅝	− ¼
111¼	109	Am T&T 8.70s2002	57	110⅞	110½	110½	− ⅜
107⅞	104½	AmT&T 7.75s77	20	106	105	105	−1
99⅞	94⅛	AmT&T 7s2001	176	96¼	96⅛	96¼	+ ⅛
78⅞	76	AmT&T 4⅜s85	59	77¾	76⅞	76⅞	− ⅞
69⅜	66	AmT&T 3⅞s90	5	66⅝	66⅝	66⅝	....
98	95¾	AmT&T 3⅜s73	37	98	97⅛	98	+ ⅞
70½	68⅛	AmT&T 3¼s84	35	69½	69	69	....
63¾	60	AmT&T 2⅞s87	4	61⅞	61⅞	61⅞	+1⅞
91¾	88¾	AmT&T 2¾s75	10	90¾	90¾	90¾	+ ⅛
78⅛	73	AmT&T 2¾s80	40	75¼	75	75¼	+ ¼
62¾	60	AmT&T 2⅝s86	56	60¾	60⅝	60⅝	− ⅜
116	95½	AMF Inc cv4¼s81	14	97½	97½	97½	− ½
111	89	Amfac cv5¼s94	3	88	88	88	−1¼
70½	42	Ampex cv5½s94	34	42½	42⅛	42½	+ ¼
90	85¾	Anheuser 6s92	25	87	87	87	+ ⅜
86	83	Anheuser 5.45s91	3	83½	83½	83½	....
99¾	78	Apco Oil cv5s88	40	97⅛	97	97	−1
108	104⅛	Appal Pw 8⅝s76	5	105½	105⅜	105½	+1⅛
138¼	103½	ARA Svc cv4⅝s96	338	104½	102¼	102¼	−1¼
64¼	43½	ArlansDStr cv6s94	7	45½	45	45	....

1972 High	1972 Low	Bonds	Sales in $1,000	High	Low	Close	Net Chg.
120	111½	Cont Invest cv9s90	1	120	120	120	+ ½
89	77	Cont Mtg cv6¼s90	22	80	79	60	+ ⅞
73	65¾	Cont Oil 3s84	5	70	70	70	....
80½	75	Contrl Data 5½s87	10	81	81	81	+ ½
106	98	Coop Lab cv4½s92	15	100	100	100	− ⅛
81⅜	77	CornProd 4⅝s83	9	79¼	79¼	79¼	....
87	80	CousinMtE 6.50s82	10	82⅛	82⅛	82⅛	− ⅞
89¼	82	Crane Co 7s93	1	84	84	84	+ ⅞
85	81	Crane Co 7s94	13	83½	82½	83½	+1¼
89½	83	Crane Co 6½s92	15	83	83	83	....
109⅛	83	Crane Co cv5s93	15	84½	83	83	−1½
108	104½	CredthftFin 9¾s75	5	106¼	106¼	106¼	+ ¼
100¼	91	CrockNat cv5¾s96	2	94	94	94	....
86	80	CrucibleInc 6⅞s92	1	86	86	86	+ ⅞

D-E-F

1972 High	1972 Low	Bonds	Sales in $1,000	High	Low	Close	Net Chg.
107	89¾	DaycoCp cv6¼96	1	91½	91½	91½	....
114¾	110½	Daytn Hud 9¾s95	17	113	112	112	−1
102	100	Daytn Hud 7¾s94	8	101⅝	101⅝	101⅝	+ ⅝
80	74⅝	Deere Co 4½s83	1	77⅜	77⅜	77⅜	....
47	10½	vjDelLkWn 5s85f	4	10½	10½	10½	−1⅜
12½	1¼	vjDlLkWn inc93f	4	3¼	3¼	3¼	+ ¼
34⅞	6	jvDeLW 4s-6s2042f	4	6⅜	6¼	6¼	....
90	76¼	DelMont cv5¼s94	110	77½	77	77	−1
114½	111	Det Edis 9.15s2000	20	112¼	112⅛	112⅛	....
107½	103½	Det Edis 8.15s2000	20	104¾	104⅛	104⅛	− ⅛
108¼	104¼	Det Edis 8⅛s2001	5	105½	105½	105½	+ ½
93	85¾	Det Edis 6.40s98	5	88⅞	88⅞	88⅞	+1⅞
89	83	Det Edis 6s96	20	84	83¾	84	+ ½
105	100	Dial Finan 8¼s89	3	101	101	101	....
77	64	Dillinghm cv5½s94	25	70	70	70	....
96	76½	Divers Ind 9⅞s91	5	81	80⅞	81	....
70	53¼	Diver Ind cv5⅞s93	35	58½	58½	58½	+ ¾
106	101½	DowChm 7.75s99	5	103⅛	103⅛	103⅛	+ ⅜
100½	100	DowChm 7.40s02	155	100⅜	100⅜	100⅜	....
74⅝	71¼	DowChm 4.35s88	5	73⅞	73⅞	73⅞	+ ⅛
62½	49¼	DPF Inc cv5½s87	68	54¼	54	54	− ½
103½	100½	Duke Pw 7¾s2002	18	103	103	103	....
101¾	99½	Duke Pw 6.85s78	30	100½	100⅜	100½	+ ¾
77	66¾	Duplan cv5½s94	1	68	68	68	− ½
62½	62	DuqsneLt 3½s86	3	65	65	65	+2½
85½	66¾	EastAirLin cv5s92	53	69	68¼	68¼	− ¾
108¾	83	EastAirL cv4¾s93	10	84½	84½	84½	+ ½
122	112¼	ElPaso NG 8½s95	62	113½	112½	113½	+ ⅞
98	88¼	El PasoNG cv6s93	55	89	88¼	88¼	− ½
134	109½	EquityFd cv5½s91	192	112	111	111	−2
12⅞	4	vjErieRR 5s2020f	22	4	4	4	− ¼
11¾	4	vjErie 5s2020f reg	4	4½	4½	4½	....
30⅜	8½	vjErie 3⅛s2000fG	27	9½	8⅞	9½	+ ½
107½	104½	Essex Int 9¼s75	3	104⅝	104⅝	104⅝	− ⅜
114½	99¼	Essex Int cv5⅜s96	55	107	106¾	107	+ ½
132½	110	EvansPd cv6¼s94	8	113	113	113	....
107⅝	91	Extendcre cv6s89	2	91	91	91	− ½
70	58	Fair Ind cv4⅜s92	5	61¾	59	59	−3
109½	105	Family Fin 9½s89	5	108⅝	108½	108½	− ⅛
94	58½	Farah Mfg cv5s94	1	59½	59½	59½	....
109¾	81	Feddrs cv5s96	52	83	82	82	+ ⅛
138½	98¼	FedNMtg cv4⅜s96	76	103	102	102½	+ ⅛
103½	90⅛	FedPacE cv5½s87	87	90⅞	90½	90¾	− ¼

Listing of corporation bond sales shows that day's price fluctuation, year's high and low.

Kenneth Boulding

district government is called a *municipal bond* while state government bonds are simply called *state bonds.* Some municipal bonds are referred to by the purpose for which they are sold, such as *construction bonds* or *bridge bonds.* All of these types are usually secured, or guaranteed, bonds. There are also unsecured bonds, called *debentures,* that are backed only by the credit standing of the issuing agency.

Often, a bond is named for the terms of payment of the interest or the principal. For example, an *annuity bond* has no maturity date; thus the interest is continuing. A *callable bond* is one that must be presented for payment upon due notice to the bond holder. A *continued bond* is one that does not have to be turned in at maturity but may be held indefinitely at the same rate of interest. A *convertible bond* gives the holder the right to exchange his bond for a different type of security, such as stock. Other terms-of-payment bonds include gold bonds, income bonds, installment bonds, and extended and deferred bonds.

Bonds are also named for the way in which they are secured. For example, with an *assumed bond* the principal, or the interest, or both are guaranteed by a corporation other than the one that issued the bond. These bonds are also known as *guaranteed* or *endorsed bonds.* Also, a *blanket bond* indicates a general mortgage pledged as security. Other bonds that fall into this category include a *bottomry bond,* which is secured by a mortgage on a ship, a *collateral trust bond,* a *divisional bond,* and a *sinking fund bond.*

Consult (14) Ludtke, 1967.

—William D. Wagoner, *Louisiana State University*

BOND YIELDS. *See* Bond Prices.

BOOK COST. *See* Original Cost.

BORROWED RESERVES. *See* Free Reserves.

BORROWING. Governments may meet their financial obligations by raising funds through taxation, by creating new money (federal) and by borrowing. The act of borrowing requires that the government, usually through the Treasury Department, issue bonds which may then be offered for sale to private individuals and firms, commercial banks, or the central bank and other governmental agencies. Though the particular certificate will usually bear a stated face value and fixed amount of interest coupons until date of maturity, the actual price paid by the buyer may differ from the face value, depending upon the going rate of interest for low risk investments. Thus, a $1000 bond paying 5% interest for 10 years ($50 per year) will usually sell for something less than $1000 if the buyer is able to earn, say, 7% on alternative investments of similarly low risk. The total of outstanding bonds of various maturities constitutes the gross public debt.

BOTTLENECK INFLATION. *See* Sectoral Inflation.

BOULDING, KENNETH EWART (1910–), a critic of many aspects of modern economics. Having made important contributions to microeconomics, Boulding attacked the failure of economics to be integrated with other social sciences in his *Reconstruction of Economics* (1950). This theme has dominated much of Boulding's work and has reached an eloquent peak in his *Economics As Science* (1970), a series of essays dealing with the larger scientific background of economics. Boulding's additional concern that economists have failed to explain distribution in a macroeconomic sense has led to his important work in considering various aspects of the grants economy.

BOYCOTT, one of the most familiar weapons of labor used to exert pressure on employers. Strikes are not usually considered as coming within the meaning of "boycotts"; rather, the term is used almost exclusively to mean an organized refusal to deal with someone in order to induce him to do something. This is a primary boycott. It may take the form of refusing to patronize a product or refusal to handle certain goods. It may involve only one product, or it may involve a particular store or chain of stores.

Boycotts often become more complicated than strikes because they can involve pressure on a third party. When a third party becomes involved, there is a secondary boycott. In 1947, the Taft-Hartley Act deemed the secondary boycott an unfair labor practice and made it illegal. Unfortunately, in actual cases it is sometimes difficult to determine and prove a secondary boycott.

BRANCH BANK, a commercial bank or, sometimes, a savings bank that maintains at least one branch office in addition to the head office. In the United States, branches may be established only within the state where the head office is located; in twenty-one states, branches are restricted to an even smaller area. Eleven states do not permit branches at all.

BRANNAN PLAN, a plan for supporting farm income proposed in 1949 by Secretary of Agriculture Charles F. Brannan. It differed from earlier policy principally in (1) making extensive use of direct payments to farmers to compensate them whenever market prices for livestock fell below target prices; (2) calculating target prices by a formula that differed from the parity price computation; (3) limiting payments that the larger farmers could receive; and (4) making it possible to require farmers to comply with production controls as a condition for receiving benefits if surpluses appeared. Price support for storable crops was to be continued as before, but for more crops. The plan generated much controversy and was not enacted by Congress.

See also Parity Prices.

BREAK-EVEN POINT, term used in business to designate the exact amount of income required and the number of items that must be sold in order for a firm to meet expenses exactly and be at the position where neither a loss nor a profit is made. For example, if a firm has a fixed cost of $20 and an operating cost of $5 for every item it produces and if the item sells for $10, the break-even point will occur after the fourth item has been sold because the cost to produce the items, $40, equals the income of $40 generated by their sale. A firm must be able to reach the break-even point to justify remaining in business.

In national income analysis, the break-even point is the disposable income at which consumption is 100% of disposable income. It is a useful reference point to compute in solving national income problems.

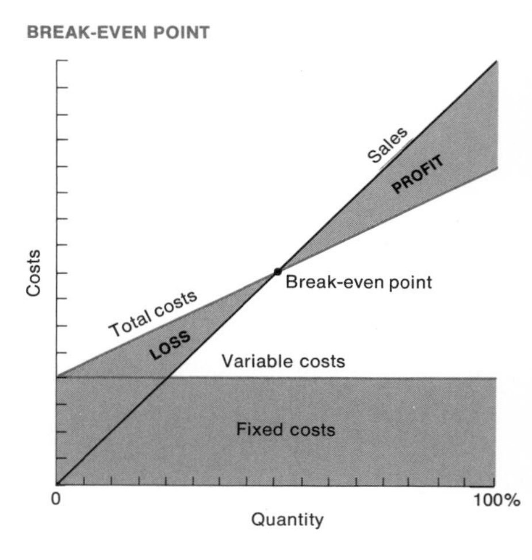

BRETTON WOODS. In 1945 representatives from 40-odd nations assembled at Bretton Woods, New Hampshire, for the purpose of laying plans for an orderly approach to short-run currency and exchange problems and long-run problems of reconstruction and development. Out of this conference came the International Monetary Fund and International Bank for Reconstruction and Development (World Bank) to handle the short-run and long-run problems, respectively.

World Bank grew out of the International Monetary Conference held at Bretton Woods in 1944.

BRIMMER, ANDREW FELTON (1926-), American educator, government official, and expert on monetary policy. He received a B.A. (1950) and M.A. (1951) from the University of Washington and a Ph.D. (1957) from Harvard. He is author of *Survey of Mutual Funds Investors* (1963) and *Life Insurance Companies in Capital Market* (1962), and has been a contributor of articles to various professional journals. Government service includes positions as deputy assistant secretary, Department of Commerce (1963-65), assistant secretary for economic affairs (1965-66), and member of the Board of Governors of the Federal Reserve System, beginning in 1966.

BRITISH FABIAN SOCIETY. *See* Fabian Society.

BRITISH LABOUR PARTY, formed in 1900, stemmed from late nineteenth-century labor unions, the Fabian Society, the Social Democratic Federation, and the Independent Labour Party. It advocates evolutionary socialism within a framework of political democracy.

Believing that private owners can neither meet the necessities of modernization nor bring about growth, steady employment, and a fair distribution of national income, the Labour Party has recurrently urged the nationalization of basic industries. When in power it has imposed controls on finance and investment, furthered government planning or land utilization, put agriculture under national guidance, expanded construction in public housing, and created a system of socialized medicine.

The Labour Party adopted a socialist-oriented constitution in 1918 and won its first national election in 1924. It returned to power in 1929-31. Since then it has won four elections, but it has been out of office since 1970.

See also Evolutionary Socialism; Fabian Society; Nationalization.

Consult (26) Lourks and Whitney, 1969.

BROADCASTING REGULATION. *See* Federal Communications Commission (FCC).

BROWN, DOUGLASS VINCENT (1904-), American economist. He received his A.B. (1925), A.M. (1926), and Ph.D. (1932) in economics from Harvard. His publications include *Economics of the Recovery Program* (1934) and *Industrial Wage Rates, Labor Costs and Price Policies* (1940). Brown was with the advisory commission to the Council of National Defense and Office of Production Management (1940-41), and was a staff member of the Harriman-Beaverbrook mission to Russia (1941), a consultant to the War Department (1942-43), and a member of the National War Labor Board (1943-45). Brown has been Alfred P. Sloan Professor of Industrial Management at M.I.T. since 1946.

BROWN, EDGAR CARY (1916-), American educator noted for his work in the area of fiscal policy (particularly policy lags). He graduated from the University of California at Berkeley (1937) and he received his Ph.D. (1948) in economics from Harvard. His publications include *Financing Defense* (1951), *Effects of Taxation: Depreciation Adjustments for Price Changes* (1952), and *Studies in Economic Stabilization* (1967). He was an economist for the War Production Board (1940-41) and for the Treasury Department (1942-47). Brown has been on the faculty at Berkeley, Harvard, and M.I.T., and he became head of the economics department at M.I.T. in 1965.

BROWN SHOE CO. V. UNITED STATES, 370 U.S. 294 (1962). The merger of Brown Shoe, the nation's fourth largest shoe manufacturer and a retailer as well, and G. R. Kinney, the twelfth largest manufacturer and a major retail chain, provided the first Supreme Court test of the new Section 7 (Celler-Kefauver Act).

In its decision the Court emphasized

BUSINESS CYCLES

For further examination of the major descriptive and analytical considerations of business cycles, see the articles on BUSINESS CYCLES, PHASES; BUSINESS CYCLES, MEASUREMENT; BUSINESS CYCLES, THEORIES; and BUSINESS CYCLES, TYPES. The main problems of the two major phases of the cycle are explored in the articles on INFLATION and UNEMPLOYMENT. The simultaneous occurrence of these two phenomena and the relationship between them is discussed in PHILLIPS CURVE.

The student will also find it useful to consult the Subject Map accompanying this article for further coverage of Business Cycles in the Encyclopedia.

BUSINESS CYCLES

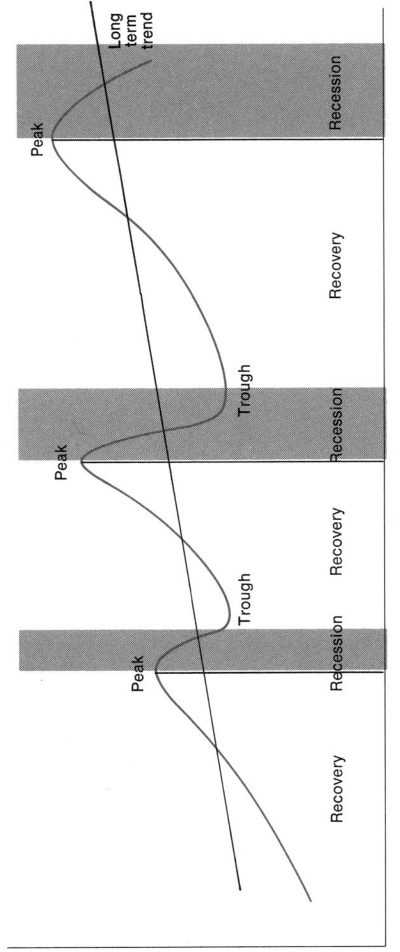

congressional concern with "a rising tide of economic concentration," and the need to halt this trend "in its incipiency." The Court concluded that the vertical aspect of the merger would foreclose competing shoe manufacturers from Kinney's retail outlets, "without producing any countervailing. . .advantages." Such foreclosure, in light of congressional concern and in view of a trend toward concentration and a trend toward vertical integration in the shoe industry, was found to violate Section 7. The Supreme Court also held that the merger would violate Section 7 on horizontal grounds by increasing market concentration in numerous cities in which both Brown and Kinney had retail outlets. The *Brown Shoe* decision presaged a strict standard toward mergers under amended Section 7.

See also Celler-Kefauver Act; Competition; Vertical Merger.

—Peter Asch, *Rutgers University*

BUDGET LINE, CONSUMER, a line in the commodity space representing all commodity bundles whose cost equals the consumer's income. The budget line's slope is negative, and its magnitude equals the ratio of the prices of the commodities in question.

BUDGET LINE, FIRM. If two inputs are plotted on the respective axes, then, for every possible money outlay by a firm, a budget line can be constructed. This line indicates, given factor prices, the locus of points that show varying combinations of inputs available to the firm for a given expenditure. A family of budget lines shows the total cost of every possible factor combination of the inputs in question. Budget lines will be linear and parallel, reflecting the assumption that a firm can purchase all it wishes of the inputs without affecting their prices. If prices do change, the slope of the budget lines will change correspondingly.

BUDGET PROCESS. *See* Federal Budget.

BURNS, ARTHUR FRANK (1904–), Austrian-born economist and educator, and expert on business cycles and macroeconomics. He recieved his A.B. (1925), A.M. (1925), and Ph.D. (1934) in economics from Columbia University. His numerous publications include *Measuring Business Cycles* (1946, with W. Mitchell), *Prosperity Without Inflation* (1957), *The Management of Prosperity* (1966, with Paul Samuelson), and *The Business Cycle in a Changing World* (1969). His public service is wide and varied, including positions as chairman of the President's Council of Economic Advisors (1953–56), chairman of the Advisory Board on Economic Growth and Stability (1953–56), president of the American Economic Association (1959), and chairman of the Board of Governors of the Federal Reserve System.

BUSINESS ACCELERATION AND THE LAW OF DEMAND (1917). *See* Clark, John Maurice.

BUSINESS AGENT, labor unionism, a full-time employee of the local labor union hired to manage the day-to-day affairs of the organization. Often an ex-officer of the union, he provides a variety of services and, while not officially a policy maker, may have a major impact on union policy. He may handle grievances, negotiate contracts, manage the office, collect dues, organize socials, police the employer for contract violations, and in the craft unions he often runs the hiring halls. In the locals, where the elected officers change often, the business agent serves to create a sense of continuity in union policies and affairs.

BUSINESS CYCLES. Economies have proven themselves subject to regularly recurring periods of slump and recovery, particularly since the Industrial Revolution and in England, France, the United States, and other industrialized countries where they are not controlled centrally. Since the beginning of the nineteenth century, culminating in the great depression of the 1930s, the economies of these countries have been subjected to large changes in the levels of income or wealth. In 1815, 1837, 1873, 1893, and 1929 the United States experienced severe depressions, which were interspersed with periods of prosperity, and with milder depressions in 1847, 1857, 1867, 1883, and 1907. Since World War II there have been no real depressions in the United States or other advanced countries, although mild recessions occurred in 1949, 1955, 1958, 1961, and 1970 in the United States. However, most modern governments now intervene in their economic systems, even in so-called free-market economies, distorting the behavior patterns of business cycles that have been established over the last century, so that traditional theories can no longer be expected to apply without considerable variation. President Nixon's New Economic Policy (Phases I and II) is such an example.

The costs of business fluctuations are considerable. Depression and recession result in irretrievable losses of real output and wealth, while creating great hardships for the unemployed, whose number are also increased. The cost associated with such fluctuations explains the interest of economists in the study of business cycles, as well as governmental involvement in moderating wide swings in cyclical activity.

Phases. A typical business cycle characteristically passes through four phases: depression, recovery, prosperity, and recession. Prosperity culminates in a peak, or upper turning point, and depression, on the other hand, eventually reaches a trough, or lower turning point. A recession generally means any mild

BUSINESS CYCLES

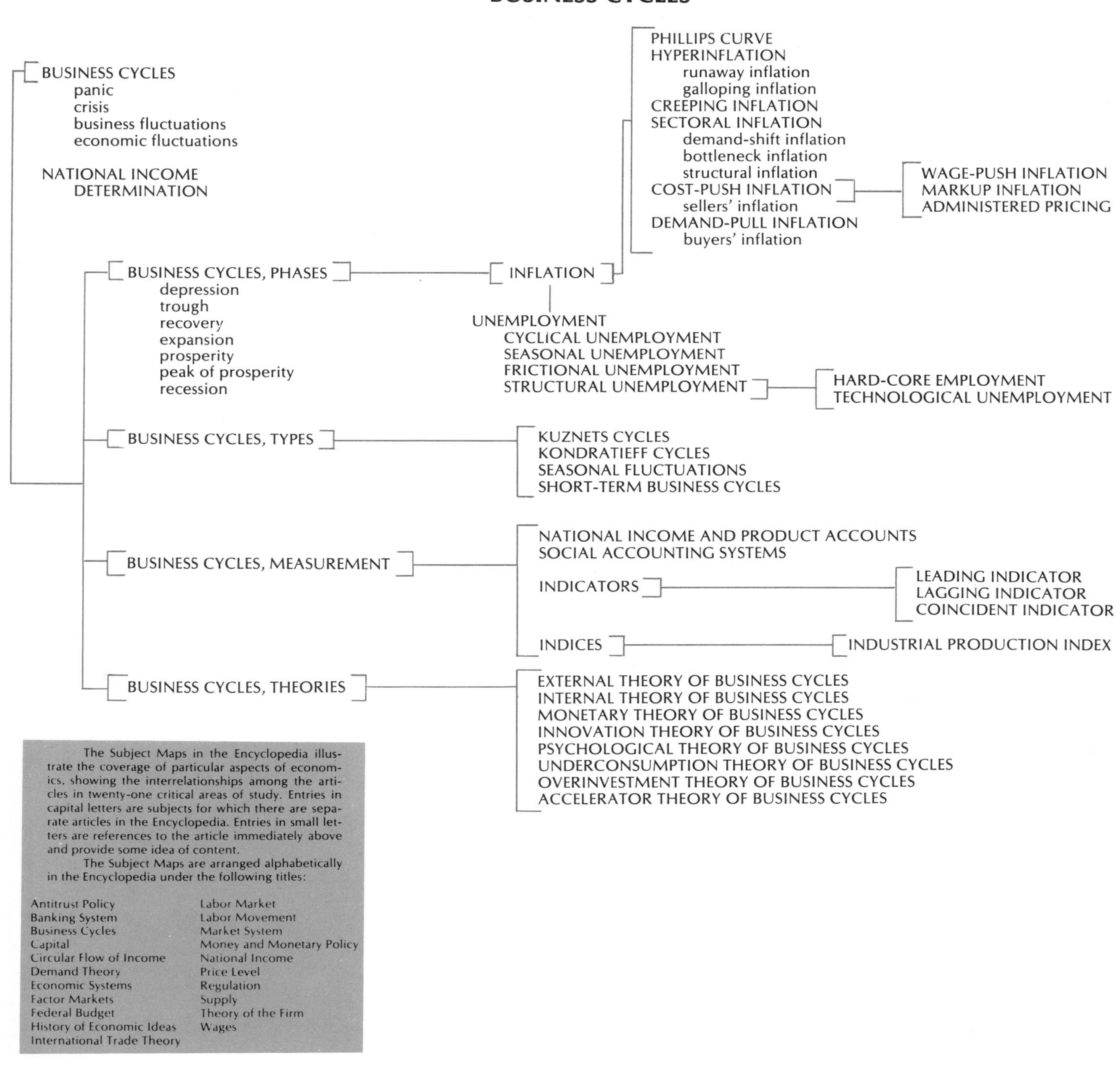

The Subject Maps in the Encyclopedia illustrate the coverage of particular aspects of economics, showing the interrelationships among the articles in twenty-one critical areas of study. Entries in capital letters are subjects for which there are separate articles in the Encyclopedia. Entries in small letters are references to the article immediately above and provide some idea of content.

The Subject Maps are arranged alphabetically in the Encyclopedia under the following titles:

Antitrust Policy	Labor Market
Banking System	Labor Movement
Business Cycles	Market System
Capital	Money and Monetary Policy
Circular Flow of Income	National Income
Demand Theory	Price Level
Economic Systems	Regulation
Factor Markets	Supply
Federal Budget	Theory of the Firm
History of Economic Ideas	Wages
International Trade Theory	

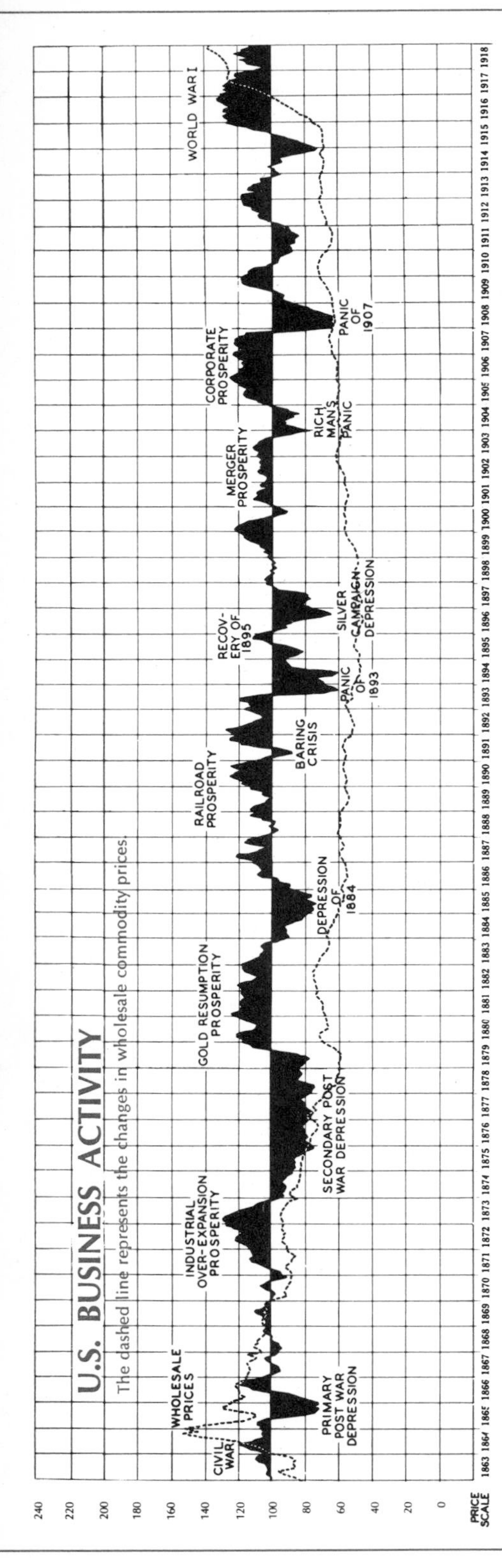

setback in economic growth, while a recovery indicates an upswing from a trough. These are only working descriptions, and it must be remembered that business cycles are not precise and regular, but complex and varying, in pattern, intensity, and duration. They do not follow logical sequences, which causes some economists to refer to them as "fluctuations" rather than "cycles."

The business cycle is enmeshed in other rhythms and patterns of economic activity. There are, for example, seasonal variations in sales, output, and employment; sales are always higher at Christmas and Easter than in nonholiday periods; construction employment is usually higher in the summer than in the winter. Economic activity also tends to expand from year to year. Per capita gross national product, for example, has grown at an average rate of over 2% per annum since 1870. These regularly recurring events and natural expansions, therefore, indicate trends in business activity in addition to the cyclical or fluctuating patterns. The combination of natural expansion and business cycles results in peaks and troughs that are higher in subsequent time periods (see figure).

Alvin Hansen distinguishes between minor cycles associated with variations in inventory investment, lasting 2 to 6 years, and major cycles associated with investment in plant and equipment, averaging 7 to 10 years. In addition to such major and minor cycles, Simon Kuznets has identified and analyzed 25-year fluctuations in the rate of growth, associated with immigrations and natural rates of population growth, railroad building and capital imports, and the growth rate of the money supply. The Russian economist N. D. Kondratieff claims to have identified certain long waves in economic activity lasting 40 to 60 years, which he attributes to changes in technology, new markets, and war and revolution. Finally, certain industries or sectors of the economy have their own cycles, such as the well documented 15- to 20-year cycle in the construction industry. Other individual cycles have been observed in shipbuilding, corn and hog production, and the like.

At any given time, various cycles can interact with one another making clear identification or prediction difficult. If a downturn in a major cycle coincides with a downturn in an individual cycle, such as construction, and a retardation in the rate of growth, the result could be a more severe recession than a major cycle would produce alone.

Business Cycle Theories. Throughout the nineteenth century, economists spent little time researching cycles, holding that Say's law of markets ensured that unemployment was a temporary phenomenon in spite of the recurrence of cyclical fluctuations in incomes and employment. Business and industry previously concentrated on the crises and panics that signaled the end of an expansionary phase rather than planning over the long term. The first study of the business cycle, as a whole, was by Clement Juglar in 1889, since which time many theories of the business cycle have been advanced. Internal theories tend to stress the cumulative, self-generating nature of business cycles, while external theories focus on exogenous factors, such as crop yields and random shocks. Some early endogenous theories emphasized psychological factors, underconsumption, overinvestment, and fluctuations in the supply of credit. Modern business cycle theory, however, is based primarily on Keynesian macroeconomic analysis and the accelerator.

Is the Business Cycle Obsolete? Several institutional changes in the United States have contributed to increasing stability in economic activity. The growth of the service sector relative to manufacturing has tended to stabilize the economy. Workers in the service sector tend to be salaried employees rather than wage earners, and demand for services tends to be stable. The progressive income tax, unemployment insurance, and stable corporate dividend policies also tend to act countercyclically. Finally, the government has declared its intention to prevent widespread unemployment and galloping inflation. The combination of stabilizing institutional changes and progress in economic theory and policy has resulted in an economy that is less apt to experience wide cyclical fluctuations than that which existed prior to 1929.

Although deep depressions may be avoidable through correct monetary and fiscal policy, there will, in all probability, be recessions. The greater problem is turning out to be chronic inflation.

See also Accelerator Theory; Fiscal Policy; Inflation; Multiplier; Say's Law of Markets.

—Carlisle E. Moody, *College of William and Mary*

BUSINESS CYCLES (1939). *See* Schumpeter, Joseph A.

BUSINESS CYCLES, MEASUREMENT. Overall, current business activity in the United States is measured by a wide range of statistical observations: national income and products accounts, industrial production and price indices, and labor force and employment data. Surveys of government, consumer, and business intentions are also used as a gauge of economic activity and are particularly useful in the prediction of future trends.

BUSINESS CYCLES, PHASES. Most economists characterize the four stages through which a typical business cycle passes as depression, recovery, prosperity, and recession.

Depression. The depression phase of the cycle experiences severe unemployment and excess capacity; that is, idle workers, plant, and equipment. Unemployment implies low aggregate demand and income, which, in turn, leads to low levels of production and output. Prices generally fall, and profits become abnormally low or negative. Excess capacity, falling or stagnant consumer demand, and uncertainty contribute to a low level of investment spending. Net investment may be negative as business fails to replace plant and equipment. The lowest ebb of business activity is the trough, or lower turning point. Eventually, through an external or internal force, some element acts to stimulate the economy, and the cycle enters the recovery phase, if the stimulus is strong enough. The stimulus could be an autonomous increase in consumer or government demand or an increase in investment demand.

Recovery. Increased demand leads to increased production and employment, and rising employment implies increasing income and demand through the multiplier, which leads to increases in investment spending for capital goods, and further increases in employment, output, and aggregate demand in a cumulative process. Business attitudes change from the pessimism of the trough to cautious optimism as the expansion gains momentum. As favorable expectations are confirmed, business attitudes become buoyant, and orders are placed for new plant and equipment. Prices and wages begin to rise, although slowly, as previously idle capital and labor is rehired. As the expansion gathers force, the rising price of raw materials places pressure on firms to raise product prices. The combination of rising prices and increasing demand reinforces business optimism and results in further increases until full-scale prosperity or a boom emerges.

Prosperity. As expansion continues, the economy approaches its full-employment output level, and the rate of growth in aggregate demand will begin to slow. Because of the action of the accelerator, there will be an absolute decline in fixed investment. Fixed investment may also fall because of shortages and bottlenecks in the capital goods industries. As the capital goods sector approaches capacity output, its rate of growth of employment and output decline. The action of the accelerator will again ensure an absolute decrease in the level of investment.

Other forces are generated by the boom that can halt the investment boom and set the stage for a contraction. Wage rates will rise rapidly as firms bid against one another for qualified workers, and union wage demands are resisted in the face of high profits and sales. Productivity, or output per capita, will decline due to fatigue, hasty work on rush orders, and employment of less qualified labor. The combination of rising wage and raw material costs with declining productivity causes profits to be squeezed. Also, rising interest rates and construction costs increase the costs of capital goods. Therefore, declining profits, rising capital costs, and decreasing consumer demand cause investment demand to fall, resulting in a downturn into the next stage of the cycle.

Recession. The recession phase is marked by a cumulative contraction in business activity. As investment spending decreases, there is a decline in production and employment in capital goods industries. Consumer demand falls as income declines and unemployment increases. Unless checked, the contraction will continue to gather force until the depression phase is reached, and the cycle begins again.

Considerations. It should be noted, however, that no two cycles are identical, and no cycle will follow the preceding course exactly. Many economists think that the four phases are structured too rigidly, preferring a two-phase scheme (expansion and contraction), or merely discussing the turning points. In any real business cycle, there is not a sharp transition from expansion to contraction; thus economists really discuss turning zones rather than points. At the upper turning zone, or "peak," for example, the forces of contraction are building up faster than the forces of expansion and the predominant force is downward.

However described, not all regions, sectors, or businesses will behave in the same way over the cycle. For example, as the economy reaches the peak of the boom, some firms are already experiencing declines in sales and profits. As the number of firms experiencing contractions begins to outweigh those experiencing gains, the cycle passes its peak and the recession begins. Similarly, even at the bottom of the depression, some firms can be enjoying gains in sales and profits. As this experience spreads to other firms and industries, the recovery phase begins. Thus, contraction begins while expansion is prevalent, and expansion begins while contraction is dominant. The term "cycle," however descriptive, should not lead one to believe that business fluctuations are regular and unvarying.

See also Accelerator Theory; Investment; Multiplier.

Consult (5) Gordon, 1961; Mitchell, 1944; Moore, 1965.

—Carlisle E. Moody, *College of William and Mary*

BUSINESS CYCLES, THEORIES. Many economists have developed theories to explain cyclical fluctuations in income, productivity, investment, and employment. The first study or theory of business cycles, as a whole, was introduced by Clement Juglar in 1889. Many theories have been advanced since that time,

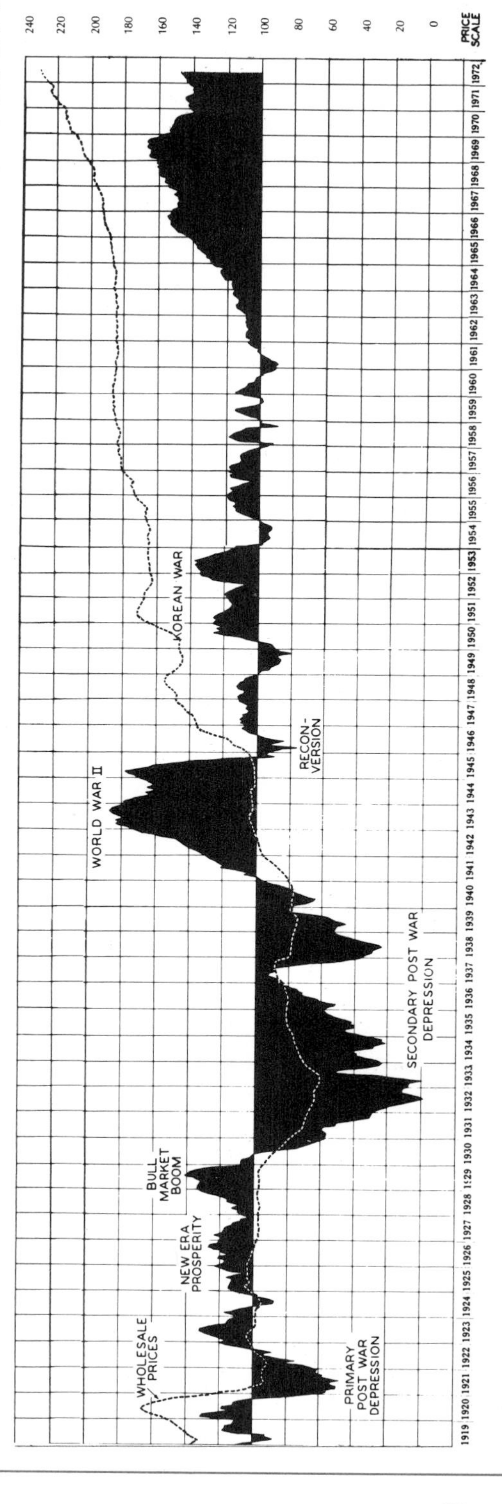

and generally fall into one of two categories: external (exogenous) and internal (endogenous).

External Theories assume that fluctuations in economic activity or business cycles are caused by factors outside the economic system. They include, for example, sunspot cycles (an obsolete nineteenth-century theory), wars and revolutions, and political and social events. Other external factors which lead to fluctuations are the rates of immigration and population growth, discovery of new resources, and scientific and technological innovations. Most of these external elements, although plausible influences, are neither predictable nor controllable over the long run and suggest that business cycles are neither predictable nor controllable either.

Internal Theories acknowledge that certain external factors influence economic activity but contend that, on the whole, the major causes of business cycles are forces within the economic system. Among the endogenous theories are profit motive (psychological), monetary, overinvestment, and underconsumption. Some endogenous theories suggest that mechanisms within the system will naturally generate economic cycles so that, predictably, every expansion will be followed by recession, contraction, and renewed expansion. However, modern governments' interventions in the economy, even in so-called free-market economies, distort expected behavior patterns established over the last century, so that traditional theories can no longer apply without considerable modification.

BUSINESS CYCLES, TYPES, refers to specific cycles of fluctuation in economic activity, each lasting from over a year to upwards of 60 years. In the United States, business cycles last, on an average, about 4 years. There is also cyclical activity associated with specific industries, such as the well documented 15- to 20-year cycle in the construction industry. Seasonal fluctuations over any given year and long-term trends are noncyclical and do not directly affect business cycles.

Some economists distinguish between minor, or short-term, business cycles associated with inventory investment and major cycles triggered by net real investment in plant and equipment. Inventory investment cycles can last from 2 to 10 years, depending upon whether one accepts the theories of Alvin Hansen or those of Joseph Kitchin. Major cycles average 7 to 10 years. On a broader scale, so-called Kuznets cycles, involving fluctuations in the supply trends of resources and the productivity and efficiency with which they are used, last about 25 years. The longest type of fluctuation is called the Kondratieff cycle, named for the Russian economist who identified long waves of price, production, and trade.

Distinction among the types of business cycles is useful for a variety of purposes. However, because they interact, identification and study of each are difficult. A minor downswing in one industry, for example, can coincide with a major downswing in capital formation, thus producing a greater recession than might otherwise be expected. At any given point it is hard to separate the influence of each component on the level of economic activity.

BUSINESS FLUCTUATIONS. *See* Business Cycles.

BUSINESS SAVINGS, which usually total more than half of total gross savings in the United States, come from undistributed profits (retained earnings) and depreciation reserves. Business savings constitute a leakage from the national income stream, since they reduce the economy's marginal propensity to consume. However, they serve a useful function, inasmuch as they are generally reinvested in the businesses themselves for expansion and long-term growth.

See also Personal Savings; Savings.

BUSINESS UNIONISM refers to one of the possible organizational philosophies in the labor movement, and, in contrast to other concepts, stresses the economic goals of the union. Thus, the proponents of business unionism would argue that the role of the union was to get better wages and protect members' jobs from competition, not to act as an agent for social or economic reform. Generally, U.S. unions, particularly the craft unions, have worked within the existing political structure, and have not organized a labor political party. Business unionism is sometimes called "bread-and-butter" unionism.

BUYERS' INFLATION. *See* Demand-Pull Inflation.

BUYERS' MONOPOLY. *See* Monopsony.

CALLABLE BONDS, bonds that must be presented for payment once the issuer has given due notice to the holder of the bond. A callable bond differs from most bonds, because it has no set maturity date but can be called at any time.

CALL LOANS, or demand loans, loans made for a period of one day automatically renewed unless the borrower repays or the lender demands repayment. They are, thus, the most liquid of all loans, because repayment can at any time be required within twenty-four hours. Demand loans are most often made by banks to security brokers against the deposit of stock certificates as collateral.

See also Liquid Assets; Portfolio Balancing.

CAPITAL, durable or long-lasting inputs of a firm, such as machinery, tools, and buildings. Capital, land, labor, and management are the four major factors of production. Unlike the other factors of production, capital goods are secondary factors.

The factor price of capital is the interest rate paid for its use. This interest rate aids in allocating the use of capital goods. Capital formation, because it is future-oriented, necessitates a need for society to forego a certain amount of present consumption to assure future consumption. For example, if a piece of capital machinery that is designed to last five years cost $100, present consumption must be reduced by $100 to invest in this machine.

See also Factors of Production.

CAPITAL, DEMAND FOR. *See* Demand for Capital.

CAPITAL, NET PRODUCTIVITY OF. *See* Net Productivity of Capital.

CAPITAL ACCOUNT, in a balance of payments, records transactions involving paper claims and debts rather than real commodities or services. Purchases and sales of stocks and bonds, lending and borrowing, and changes in bank balances make up the capital account. *Long-term capital movements* (loans and investments with maturities exceeding a year) can finance a new flow of goods and services from lending and investing countries to borrowers and recipients. *Short-term capital movements* primarily serve to finance gaps between payments and receipts relative to transactions in the current account. Unilateral transfers (for example, government grants and immigrant remittances) differ from ordinary capital transactions in that they involve no reciprocal obligations or claims. If the current account in the balance of payments does not balance, the discrepancy is financed by capital movements or gold.

See also Balance of Payments; Capital Movement.

Consult (23) Snider, 1971.

CAPITAL AND INTEREST (1884). *See* Böhm-Bawerk, Eugen.

CAPITAL CONSUMPTION ALLOWANCE (CCA), used in national income accounting, the amount deducted from gross national product (GNP) to obtain net national product, representing the portion of GNP resulting from the value of capital assets consumed or declining in value in the production process. CCA includes capital goods depreciation, accidental losses of capital assets, capital goods bought and consumed in the same period, and such expenditures incurred in finding new resources as oil and mineral exploration costs.

See also Gross National Product; Net National Product.

CAPITAL DEEPENING, a rise in the ratio of capital to both labor and output. Any factor that increases expected returns or lowers the cost of capital will increase investment demand. Growth of new technology and development of new products stimulate the production of new types of capital, and the amount per unit of output would likely increase, thus deepening capital by changing the ratios of it to other factors in the productive mix. A widening of capital results from growth in an economy demanding more capital goods of accustomed types with no change in the capital-output ratio; capital is accumulated in balance with labor.

See also Capital Equipment; Demand for Capital; Technological Change.

Consult (22) Samuelson, 1970.

CAPITAL EQUIPMENT, a man-made factor of production, consisting of the existing stock of machines, plant, and equipment. In the short-run operations of an economy, the supply is fixed, but the stock is diminished each year via production wear and tear; this requires that new capital be produced for replacement. Money spent on equipment beyond that needed for replacement, along with new residential construction and increases in inventory, is net new investment—the most volatile factor in United States economic growth.

See also Capital Deepening; Capital Stock; Demand for Capital; Technological Change.

Consult (22) Lipsey and Steiner, 1969.

CAPITAL FORMATION, the value of net additions to capital stock, such as buildings, equipment, and inventories, excluding repair and maintenance costs. Capital formation is an indirect measure of businessmen's evaluations of anticipated economic growth and profit potential. Capital formation is derived from the gross investment by subtracting estimated depreciation, the decline in value of capital equipment, or fixed assets.

See also Gross Investment; Inventory Investment; Net Investment.

CAPITAL FUNDS, cash or money that is used to carry on a business. This working, or lucrative, capital differs from pure capital, which is the durable inputs of a firm, such as machinery and tools. Capital funds, representing actual cash, can be used for purchasing capital equipment.

The equipment differs, but the Chinese laborers above and the mechanized operation below both represent capital formation—building roads.

CAPITAL

DEMAND FOR CAPITAL

- ROUNDABOUT METHODS OF PRODUCTION
  - indirect production
- TECHNOLOGY
- TECHNOLOGICAL CHANGE

- NET PRODUCTIVITY OF CAPITAL
- MARGINAL EFFICIENCY OF CAPITAL

- PRESENT VALUE
- DISCOUNTED VALUE

- CAPITAL STOCK
- CAPITAL EQUIPMENT

- CAPITAL DEEPENING
  - capital widening

- TIME PREFERENCE

CAPITALISM
CAPITALIST
ENTREPRENEUR
INNOVATOR

UNCERTAINTY
RISK
PROFIT SYSTEM

PROFITS
- EXCESS PROFITS

DIVIDENDS
- distributed earnings
- CORPORATE EARNINGS
- UNDISTRIBUTED PROFITS
- INCOME OF UNINCORPORATED BUSINESS

MONOPOLY PROFITS

INTEREST
- INTEREST RATES
- INTEREST RATE STRUCTURE

The Subject Maps in the Encyclopedia illustrate the coverage of particular aspects of economics, showing the interrelationships among the articles in twenty-one critical areas of study. Entries in capital letters are subjects for which there are separate articles in the Encyclopedia. Entries in small letters are references to the article immediately above and provide some idea of content.

The Subject Maps are arranged alphabetically in the Encyclopedia under the following titles:

Antitrust Policy
Banking System
Business Cycles
Capital
Circular Flow of Income
Demand Theory
Economic Systems
Factor Markets
Federal Budget
History of Economic Ideas
International Trade Theory
Labor Market
Labor Movement
Market System
Money and Monetary Policy
National Income
Price Level
Regulation
Supply
Theory of the Firm
Wages

In addition, they may be used to purchase stocks and other forms of investment securities.

See also Capital.

CAPITAL GAINS TAX. *See* Taxation: *Glossary.*

CAPITAL GOODS, intermediate goods, such as buildings, machinery, trucks, and conveyors, necessary for the production of consumer goods. Primary resources—money, land, and raw materials—are not usually considered capital goods.

CAPITALISM, an economic system based on the right of private ownership of most of the means of production, such as businesses, farms, mines, and natural resources, as well as private property, such as homes and automobiles. Under capitalism the individual has the freedom to engage in economic activities of his choice with limited legal and governmental restrictions. In a capitalistic economy the consumer determines the allocation of scarce resources through the market mechanism of demand. Producers are free to shift resources to meet the demands of consumers expressed via the market mechanism.

Characteristics. Economists are not in agreement as to the exact economic and political characteristics of capitalism. Some of the important characteristics of capitalism are: (1) commercialization of economic life through a market-determined system of wages and prices, (2) the central role of profit in the decision-making process as to the allocation and use of economic resources, (3) technological innovation resulting from a high degree of competition, (4) a significant degree of risk taking and a spirit of entrepreneurship, and (5) a highly developed banking and credit system.

Government plays a relatively minor role in a capitalistic economy, serving primarily to make rules, protect public welfare, and carry on activities avoided by private enterprises as unprofitable.

Origins. As a political-economic system capitalism had its origin in Western European culture and by the eighteenth century had become the dominant system of economic thought in England and the United States. In countries where capitalism was the predominant economic system, societies have achieved high material standards of living for the greatest possible proportion of their citizens. Other terms sometimes used in economic literature as synonyms for capitalism are "private enterprise system," "market system," and "free price system."

See also Economic Systems; Free Enterprise.

Consult (1)Galbraith, 1956.

—Algin B. King, *College of William and Mary*

CAPITALISM AND FREEDOM (1962). *See* Friedman, Milton.

CAPITALISM, SOCIALISM AND DEMOCRACY (1942). *See* Schumpeter, Joseph.

CAPITALIST, a key figure in a market economy, is the private owner or controller of capital equipment and resources, who hires labor to conduct business enterprises; also anyone who provides capital funds through purchase of stocks and bonds.

See also Market Economy; Profit System.

CAPITAL LEVY. *See* Taxation: *Glossary.*

CAPITAL MOVEMENT, liquidation of capital investment of one kind (or in one place) and the reinvestment of the realized funds in another kind of investment (or in another place). Assume a foreign country sells bonds in the United States to get funds to purchase railroad equipment. Assume further that there is a delay in delivering the equipment and the proceeds of the flotation are invested in certificates of deposit (CD) until needed. If three months later the equipment is exported and paid for by cashing the CD's the U.S. balance of payments will have experienced movements in real capital, long-term capital, and short-term capital.

See also Balance of Payments.

CAPITAL OUTPUT RATIO (or Capital Productivity Ratio) is the ratio of marginal capital cost to marginal output, or, phrased differently, the ratio of net investment to the resulting increase in output or productivity. If the ratio is 3:1, then three units of additional capital will yield one additional unit of output.

CAPITAL PRODUCTIVITY RATIO. *See* Capital Output Ratio.

CAPITAL SAVING, the effect of an innovation or invention that lowers the share of capital (inventory, property, or money) relative to the share of labor used in a business or industry. An example of a capital saving device would be the use of leased equipment in a business. Although the total cost of leased equipment over a period of time may be greater than in the case of purchased equipment, the initial capital outlay will be much smaller. In addition, the manufacturer avoids the ever increasing risk that his equipment will become obsolete before its initial cost can be written off against production.

See also Labor Saving.

CAPITAL STOCK, the actual amount of physical capital and inventories in existence at a given time, or, in terms of business organization, a source of funds used for capital. In the latter case capital stock is the common and preferred stock outstanding in the equity section of a firm's balance sheet.

See also Capital Equipment; Demand for Capital.

CAPITAL WIDENING. *See* Capital Deepening.

CARTEL, an agreement (and sometimes the organization) of independently operated business firms in an industry to eliminate price competition among themselves and thereby increase member firms' profits. The agreement typically sets production quotas and market shares so that by output limitation the agreed price can be maintained as if the firm were one entity (in effect, acting as a monopolist would act). The agreement is binding on member firms, with penalties assessed for violations. The cartel is thus a tighter arrangement than a trade association, which may engage in the same practices less formally. Cartels are illegal in the United States (Section 1 of the Sherman Antitrust Act) but legal in most other countries.

See also Antitrust Policy; Restraint of Trade; Trade Associations.

CASH DRAIN. *See* Multiple Expansion of the Money Supply.

Richard Earl Caves

CAVES, RICHARD EARL (1931–), American educator and economist noted for his contribution to international trade theory and market structure. He graduated from Oberlin College (1953), and received his M.A. (1956) and Ph.D. (1958) in economics from Harvard. His numerous publications include *Trade and Economic Structure* (1960), *American Industry: Structure, Conduct, Performance* (1964, with J. S. Bain and J. Margolis), and *Capital Transfers and Economic Policy: Canada, 1951–1962* (1970). Chairman of the department of economics at Harvard from 1966, he has been a consultant to the Council of Economic Advisers (1961), deputy to the special assistant to the president for foreign trade policy (1961), consultant to the Treasury Department (1961–62) and the Bureau of the Budget (1963–64), and a member of the White House Task Force on Foreign Economic Policy.

CCA. *See* Capital Consumption Allowance.

CCC. *See* Commodity Credit Corporation.

CELLER-KEFAUVER ACT (1950), sometimes called the Antimerger Act, amends Section 7 of the Clayton Act, which forbade business mergers through stock acquisitions only. Celler-Kefauver closed a loophole by forbidding mergers effected through asset acquisition.

See also Conglomerate; Merger.

CEMENT CASE. *See* Federal Trade Commission v. Cement Institute.

CENTRAL BANK, a bank of issue, that is, an institution, usually owned by the government, that controls the amount of currency created in the nation. Demand deposits having replaced currency as the most important part of the money supply, the central bank has become increasingly involved in control over commercial banks, the primary creators of demand deposits, in order to achieve a desired monetary policy. The structure, operations, and objectives of central banks differ from country to country. In the United States the federal reserve system acts as the central bank.

See also Monetary Authority, Central.

CENTRALIZATION, the centralized planning and control of economic activities. A basic element in a command economy, central planning also occurs in a capitalist economy in wartime. Whatever the system, centralization involves comprehensive and detailed planning of practically all phases of economic activity in response to planners' sovereignty. Also, resources are allocated primarily by administrative commands in real (physical) terms. Consumer sovereignty is not a major consideration, and markets and prices do not perform their usual roles.

The system's directors make important planning decisions, relay them to operational units by direct commands or directives, and establish a mechanism to assure fulfillment. This mechanism includes: (1) vertical coordination and control, (2) a system of material balances to achieve consistency among the various plans, and (3) "taut planning," to achieve the most rapid mobilization of available resources—maximizing outputs and minimizing inputs and inventory levels. Central planning usually aims at a high rate of economic growth, but planners seem to prefer centralization as such, even at the expense of growth.

See also Command Economy; Consumer Sovereignty; Economic Systems; Nationalism.

—John R. Mathews, Jr., *College of William and Mary*

CENTRALIZED DECISION MAKING. *See* Command Economy.

CENTRAL LIMIT. *See* Sampling Theory.

CENTRAL MONETARY AUTHORITY. *See* Monetary Authority, Central.

CENTRAL PLANNING, the methodology used by government in a controlled economy to determine what goods and services will be produced. Such political-economic systems as socialism, fascism, and communism employ central planning as the means of allocation of economic resources to the major components of gross national product—consumption goods, capital goods, and government purchases. Central planning results in an economic blueprint that details the quantities and sources of each type of goods and services to be produced during a given time period. Under most centrally planned economies the economy is government-directed, and economic decisions are typically based on predetermined national goals.

Problems. As an attempt to substitute bureaucratic planning and coordination for the market system in meeting economic goals and needs, central planning encounters many problems. The most significant are the problems of individual productivity, motivation, and overall coordination. Even with the use of complex input-output tables, central economic planners encounter problems of disallocation, failure to meet quota, and so on, due to complexities of interrelationship of the many economic decisions and events. For example, if a steel mill fails to meet its production quota and is unable to supply a tractor-producing factory with its assigned amount of materials, then the tractor factory is also unable to meet its goals.

Central planners attempt to overcome the problem of coordination by the use of such techniques as planning by negotiation (each major administrative unit in the plan has a chance to review in advance the central committee's master plan and propose changes), reserve stocks (to avoid stock-outs due to unforeseen contingencies), and a priority principle to shift resources from low-priority sectors to high-priority sectors of the economy after bottlenecks occur.

See also Command Economy; Communism; Fascism; Socialism.

—Algin B. King, *College of William and Mary*

CENTRAL RESERVE CITY BANK. *See* Member Bank.

CENTRAL TENDENCY. Given a set (distribution) of data, such as the heights of undergraduate males at a university, we might want to describe the data by using a single summary measure rather than reproducing the entire set. One method of describing a distribution is to find a number that expresses the central, or representative, value of the data set. Such summary statements are called measures of central tendency and serve to locate the distribution.

Suppose that the following set of numbers, the X_i's, are to be described by a single summary measure:

$[X_1, X_2, X_3, \ldots, X_9, X_{10}] = [1, 2, 2, 3, 4, 5, 8, 15, 20, 100]$

Arithmetic Mean. The most commonly used measure of central tendency is the arithmetic mean, or simple average, $\bar{X}$.

$$\bar{X} = \frac{X_1 + \cdots + X_N}{N} = \frac{\sum_{i=1}^{N} X_i}{N} \text{ where } \sum_{i=1}^{N}$$

means to sum all the numbers (X_i) from X_1 to X_N. In our example N=10, as we have 10 numbers.

$$\bar{X} = \frac{\sum_{i=1}^{10} X_i}{10} = \frac{160}{10} = 16$$

So the arithmetic mean is simply the sum of the observations divided by the number of them that we have.

Median. The median is the middle value of a set of numbers arranged in order of magnitude. It is the value that splits a distribution of numbers in two. It has the property that there are as many observations with values above the median as there are observations with values below the median. Where we have an odd number of observations, the median is the middle value. With an even number of observations, the median is the average of the two middle values. In our example, we have 10 observations, so the median is midway between the 5th and the 6th observation and is equal to 4.5.

Unlike the mean, the median is not sensitive to extreme values, such as the value 100 in the example. It is therefore useful for describing income distributions, where a few large incomes could appreciably raise the mean and distort it as a central, or typical, value.

Fractile. A fractile is an observation below which lies a certain proportion of the data. The *median* splits a distribution into two parts. Correspondingly, there are three *quartiles,* which split the distribution in four equal parts; 25% of the observations lie below the first quartile, 50% lie below the second quartile, and so on. We can also divide the distribution into *deciles,* which split the distribution into 10 parts, and *percentiles,* which split the distribution into 100 parts.

Mode. The mode is the most frequently observed value in distribution. In our example, the modal value is 2, as we have observed that value twice. The relationship between the mean, median, and mode is shown in the figure. There are two other more rarely used measures of central tendency: geometric mean and harmonic mean.

Geometic Mean. Economic growth is a multiplicative or compound interest process, rather than an additive process. A description of the "average" rate of growth should take this into account. The appropriate mean for a multiplicative process is the geometric mean:

$$X_G = \sqrt[N]{X_1, X_2, \cdots, X_N}$$

MODE

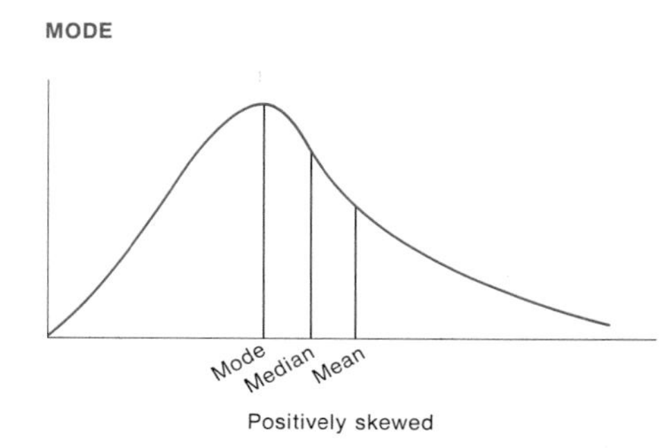

Positively skewed

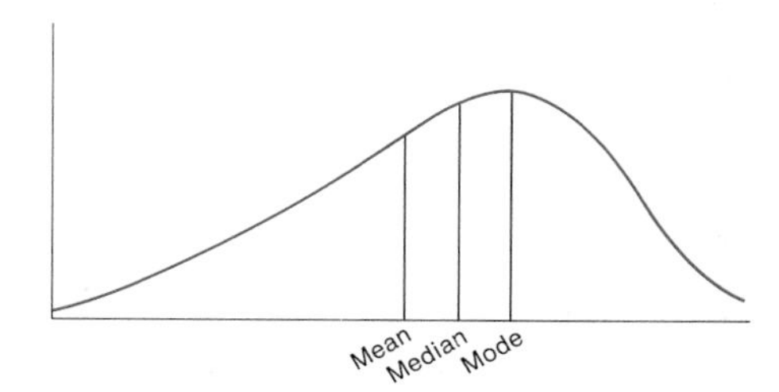

Negatively skewed

The geometric mean is most easily computed using logarithms:
$\log \bar{X}_G = (\log X_1 + \log X_2 + \ldots + \log X_N) / N$.
The geometric mean rate of growth is the only rate that, when applied to each year, will yield the terminal value X_N.

Harmonic Mean. The harmonic mean is the reciprocal of the arithmetic mean of the reciprocal values of our observations:

$$X_H = 1 \Big/ \frac{1}{N} \sum_{i=1}^{N} \frac{1}{X_i}$$

The harmonic mean is most useful for averaging ratios.

Properties. Each of these measures of central tendency has specific properties that are advantageous. The mean, for example, is easy to compute and includes the influence of every observation in the sample. The median and the mode are not affected by extreme values. All these measures are loosely referred to as "averages" and anyone who wishes "to lie with statistics" can choose an average to fit his point.

See also Frequency Distribution; Probability Distribution.

Consult (27)Freund, 1967; Huff, 1954.
—Carlisle E. Moody, *College of William and Mary*

CERTIFICATES OF DEPOSIT. *See* Time Deposits.

CERTIFICATE OF PUBLIC CONVENIENCE AND NECESSITY, a special permit from state or federal agencies that companies desiring to enter certain regulated industries must obtain before they can engage in business, construct facilities, or perform a service. Entry is restricted in this way when it is thought that monopolies will provide better service than competing companies.

See also Public Utilities; Public Utility Entry.

CERTIFICATES OF INDEBTEDNESS. *See* Government Securities.

CERTIFICATION. *See* Representation.

Edward H. Chamberlin

CHAMBERLIN, EDWARD H. (1899–1967), American economist whose most important contribution was *The Theory of Monopolistic Competition* (1933). This work, which appeared a few months before Joan Robinson's *The Economics of Imperfect Competition* (1933), attempted to develop a theory for those market situations which were neither perfectly competitive nor monopolistic.

To construct his model mixing competition and monopoly, Chamberlin used the newly discovered concept of marginal revenue. With a downward sloping demand curve

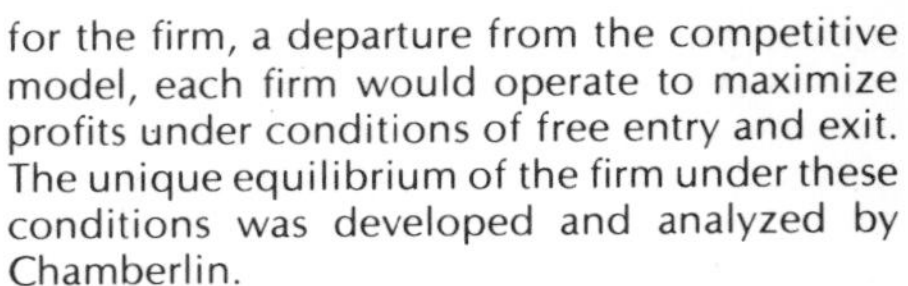

for the firm, a departure from the competitive model, each firm would operate to maximize profits under conditions of free entry and exit. The unique equilibrium of the firm under these conditions was developed and analyzed by Chamberlin.

See also Theory of Monopolistic Competition.

CHANGE, TECHNOLOGICAL. *See* Technological Change.

CHANGES IN POPULATION. *See* Population Growth.

CHANGES IN SUPPLY. Supply has been defined as a schedule of intentions; graphically, it depicts voluntary firm (or industry if that be the case) outputs for varying prices. Changes in supply must therefore, by definition, deal with changes in the schedule of intentions, or, graphically, with changes in curves.

Mathematically we are dealing with the problem of dimensions. For ease of exposition a two-dimensional relationship is portrayed; supply is delineated graphically as a curve showing different quantities supplied at differing prices, *other variables being held constant.* These "other variables" give the clue that the true supply relationship has more than two dimensions. Wage rates, technology, and so on also affect supply. When these so-called parameters change, then supply intentions (and therefore the supply curve) must also change. Thus for every possible wage rate and every possible technological change there exists a possible supply schedule. What is more, there are combinations and permutations for all these potentially important determinants of supply, and the possibilities are manifold.

If we are dealing with industry or market supply then another possibility for a change in supply exists. Since industry supply is the horizontal summation of all the individual supply curves, an increase in the number of firms in the industry due to short-run excess profits or a decrease in the number of firms due to short-run losses will result in an increase or decrease in supply, respectively.

A change in supply implies that quantity supplied will be greater or lesser (depending on the circumstances) at every price than it was previously. Alternately, a change in supply implies that the new circumstances require that price be higher or lower before given outputs will voluntarily be produced and offered for sale.

See also Supply; Supply and Demand, Law of; Supply Curve; Supply Schedule.

—Robert L. Brite, *Louisiana State University*

CHECKING ACCOUNTS. *See* Demand Deposits.

CHENERY, HOLLIS BURNLEY (1918-), American economist noted for his contributions to the theory of growth in less developed economies, with emphasis on investment criteria. He received a B.S. from both the University of Arizona (1939) and the University of Oklahoma (1942), an M.A. from the University of Virginia (1946), and a Ph.D. in economics from Harvard (1950). His publications include *Arabian Oil* (1949, co-author), *Interindustry Economics* (1959), and *Studies in Development Planning* (1971). Professor of economics at Harvard from 1965, he has been an economist for the Economic Cooperation Administration in Paris, (1949-50) and a consultant to the governments of Pakistan, Japan, and Israel (1955-61). Since 1965, he has also been consultant to the Organization of American States, the Agency for International Development, and the World Bank.

CHILD LABOR. Before the twentieth century, no serious attempt had been made to limit or prohibit child labor in the United States. Children were wage earners in the same sense as their parents and no special provisions were made in regard to the number of hours they worked or the amount they earned.

In the 1900s two cases involving child labor were brought to the Supreme Court. The first was *Hammer v. Dagenhart* (1918). The legislation under review denied transportation in interstate commerce to the products of establishments which employed children under a certain age. The court declared the legislation unconstitutional since it attempted to control the conditions of employment within the states.

In *Bailey v. Drexel Furniture Co.* (1922), a federal tax on profits of establishments where children under a certain age were employed was likewise held invalid.

In 1938, Congress succeeded for the first time in getting a law passed to improve the working conditions of children. The Fair Labor Standards Act declared the employment of children under the age of sixteen unlawful in establishments producing goods for interstate commerce. In six particularly hazardous occupations, the minimum age of employment became eighteen. In certain nonmining and nonmanufacturing industries exception to the minimum age is made. State laws covering child labor varies the minimum age anywhere from fourteen to eighteen.

—William D. Wagoner, *College of William and Mary*

CHOICE means to choose between alternative goods, services, uses of resources, and policies. The results of the choice process can be of fundamental importance for all economic activity. Consumers (households) must choose among a variety of goods and services—not all of which can be bought, given a limited budget—between spending now or saving for later, and between hours of work and hours of leisure. Business, in deciding what to produce and how to produce it, must choose among the available resources (land, labor, capital, and entrepreneurial ability). Competition will force each business to combine resources to achieve the highest profits. Government must determine how to best utilize the nation's resources. This must be done on two levels. Government must determine how much resources should be channeled to collective goods and services and national defense. It must also choose a mix of monetary and fiscal policies to control inflation and unemployment. Society as a whole must choose the goods and services that will most satisfy its wants. This choice is made through the aggregate of consumer spending decisions. The composition of spending, as registered through the price system, influences the composition of the nation's total economic output.

CHOICE, CONSUMER. *See* Consumer Choice.

CHOICE UNDER UNCERTAINTY. *See* Expected Utility.

CHRONIC DEFICIT in a nation's balance of payments indicates that structural changes in the economy are in order and/or the exchange rate is overvalued. Overvaluation keeps import prices lower and export prices higher than balance-of-payments equilibrium justifies. The chronic situation also implies that the deficit is financed through use of international monetary reserves, a situation that cannot last forever. Chronic deficits cry out for solutions before all reserves are exhausted.

See also Balance of Payments; Dollar Glut.

CIF. *See* Imports.

CIO. *See* Congress of Industrial Organizations.

CIRCULAR FLOW OF INCOME. The recognition by economists that all economic activity is interrelated has led to the development of numerous theories and hypotheses to explain economic activity and the behavior of various elements of the economic system. One of the most basic and yet most useful of these models of the economic system is the circular flow model.

The model begins with the concept that some relationship exists between the major flows in the economic system. The relationship is one of mutual interdependence. In order to produce goods and services, the producers in the economic system (usually businesses) must obtain the means of production, or resources, from the owners of the resources (usually

CHOICE

Choice is at the heart of economic activity and economic analysis. Its central role in these regards is further explained in the articles on SCARCITY and RESOURCE ALLOCATION. The necessity of choice creates OPPORTUNITY COSTS and compels ECONOMIZING in the economic process. To see how choices are made in an economy such as ours, consult the major article on MARKET SYSTEM as well as the Subject Map accompanying that article.

Not full-fledged miners, these boys had to work the same hours and face the same hazards as adults prior to the advent of child labor legislation.

CIRCULAR FLOW OF INCOME

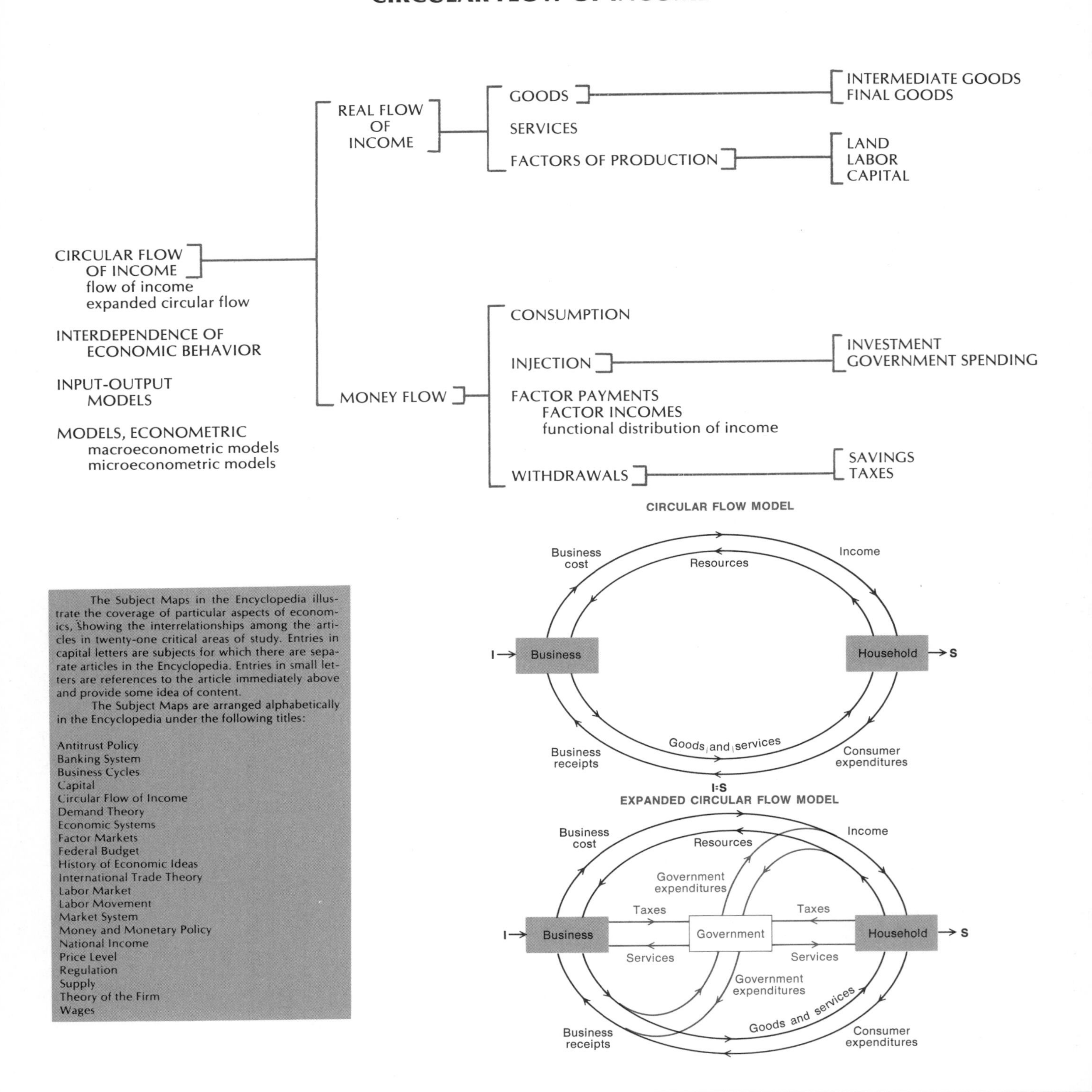

The Subject Maps in the Encyclopedia illustrate the coverage of particular aspects of economics, showing the interrelationships among the articles in twenty-one critical areas of study. Entries in capital letters are subjects for which there are separate articles in the Encyclopedia. Entries in small letters are references to the article immediately above and provide some idea of content.

The Subject Maps are arranged alphabetically in the Encyclopedia under the following titles:

Antitrust Policy
Banking System
Business Cycles
Capital
Circular Flow of Income
Demand Theory
Economic Systems
Factor Markets
Federal Budget
History of Economic Ideas
International Trade Theory
Labor Market
Labor Movement
Market System
Money and Monetary Policy
National Income
Price Level
Regulation
Supply
Theory of the Firm
Wages

households). In exchange for their resources, resource owners gain income. The income generated in such a manner is then spent to purchase goods and services to satisfy the households' demands. The interesting aspect here is that the goods and services that households purchase were produced with the resources that they sold to the producers.

Assuming that households own all resources in the economic system and that businesses produce all goods and services, the major flows are: (1) the flow of resources from owners (households) to users (businesses), (2) the opposite flow of income that occurs when resources are exchanged, (3) the flow of goods and services from producers (businesses) to the consumers (households), and (4) the opposite flow of consumer expenditures that arises from the purchasing of goods and services by consumers. The accompanying figure indicates these basic flows. The first and third are called real flows, because they involve the physical transfer of goods, services, or resources, and the second and fourth flows are considered money flows, because they involve the movement of funds in response to real flows.

Each of these flows depends upon the existence of all the others: if any one were stopped, all would be stopped. For example, if resource suppliers stopped making factors of production available, the income stream would dry and producers would stop production, because they would have no resources available and because without the income stream there would be no effective demand.

The Expanded Circular Flow Model. Several additions to the simple model can provide important insights into macroeconomic relationships. The simple model indicated that all income automatically turns into consumer expenditures. However, many households save a part of their income, thus withdrawing some income from the circular flow, unbalancing the flows, by the amount of saving. At the same time households save, however, businesses spend to purchase capital goods (investment). Thus, an injection of spending exists. If the injection of investment equals the withdrawal of saving, the circular flow remains stable—as in the figure. If the withdrawal and the injection are not equal, changes will occur in the economic system. It is the role of macroeconomic theory to explain how saving and investment can be equal and what happens when they are not equal.

Saving and investment are important withdrawals and injections, but they are not the only ones to consider. When government is added to the basic circular flow model, a number of additional flows develop. The government generally taxes both households and businesses, who in turn receive the public services of government. In addition to these new flows, government spends to purchase both resources and goods and services affecting the existing economic flows. The expanded circular flow figure indicates the impact of including government in the circular flow. If government taxes and expenditures are equal, the circular flow is unaffected. If, however, the government has a surplus or a deficit, the circular flow will be changed. Economic theory again must indicate the effects of unbalanced government budgets.

A final step in expanding the circular flow model is the consideration of the economy's interchange with other economies. The importing or exporting of goods and services, resources, and capital; government foreign-aid programs; and various other foreign transactions affect the circular flow in many, sometimes quite complex manners. The realization that such injections and withdrawals can be vital to an economy is easily demonstrated with a circular flow model.

Limitations. The circular flow model has several limitations. The most important is the lack of detail concerning the various mechanisms that allow the flows to occur in complex economies and the means by which the flows are regulated. The role of microeconomic theory is to explain this detail and to observe and analyze the behavior of individual units rather than the sector analysis of the circular flow model. In addition, the circular flow model ignores intrasectoral flows, which are important elements of the economic system.

See also Money Flow; Real Flow of Income.

—Clyde A. Haulman, *College of William and Mary*

CIVIL AERONAUTICS ACT (1938), the first comprehensive regulation of aviation in the United States. The act created the Civil Aeronautics Administration (CAA) and the Civil Aeronautics Board (CAB). The CAA was responsible for controlling air traffic, enforcing safety rules, investigating air accidents, administering the airport program, and maintaining the airway system. The CAB was responsible for the economic regulation of common carrier airlines.

In 1958, Congress created an independent agency, called the Federal Aviation Administration (FAA), transferred to it the CAA's functions, and also made it responsible for establishing safety rules. In 1967, responsibility for investigating air accidents was transferred to the National Transportation Safety Board.

See also Civil Aeronautics Board; Federal Aviation Administration.

CIVIL AERONAUTICS BOARD (CAB), a semi-independent agency in the Department of Commerce, responsible for economic regulation of commercial air transportation. The board was created by Congress in 1938 with the

John Bates Clark

enactment of the Civil Aeronautics Act and consists of five members appointed by the president for six-year terms.

Economic control of aviation by the CAB extends only to common carriers. The board controls rates and must give its permission for entry into service, abandonment of service, and mergers by such carriers. Because of a "grandfather" clause, carriers in operation when the 1938 act was passed may remain in the industry without such permission. The CAB has a staff of 650 and an annual budget of more than $11,000,000.

See also Civil Aeronautics Act; Grandfather Clause.

CLARK, JOHN BATES (1847–1938), often called the dean of American economists. The first period of his economic thought culminated in his *Philosophy of Wealth* (1885), which sets forth his version of the marginal utility theory of value. It is the product of his second period, however, which constitutes his chief contribution to economics. Clark's *Distribution of Wealth* (1899) contains a detailed statement of the marginal productivity theory of distribution which he developed into a theory which approached a description of the real world and a justification of the social idea "to each what he creates."

CLARK, JOHN MAURICE (1884–1963), son of John Bates Clark, and an important figure in the development of dynamic economic theory. He also attempted to fuse neoclassical and institutional economics. Clark's early article "Business Acceleration and the Law of Demand" (1917) developed the acceleration principle which became a significant element in Keynesian analysis of fluctuations in economic activity.

J.M. Clark's major contributions fall in the area of the relationship of the economic system to the society and human welfare. His *Studies in the Economics of Social Overhead Cost and Social Control of Business* considered (1) that workers, when unemployed, must be maintained, and that this overhead cost to society could be converted to an overhead cost for the employer; and (2) that competition will force business to pursue its self-interest in only the narrowest sense, thus maintaining that social control of business is necessary.

CLASS ANTAGONISMS. *See* Class Conflict; Communism.

CLASS CONFLICT, in Marxian theory, occurs because worker proletariats can only sell their labor to capitalist bourgeoisie for subsistence wages, while the products that they produce sell for more than this. The resulting surplus value provides for further accumulation of capital, with adverse effects on workers who find their plight unbearable. Revolution occurs, and the bourgeoisie is eliminated.

See also Economic Interpretation of History; Marx, Karl; Proletariat.

CLASSICAL ECONOMICS. The period from the publication of Adam Smith's *Wealth of Nations* (1776) until the development of marginalism (1870s) is generally considered the classical period of economic thought. Some of the greatest economists fall into this period. Men such as Smith, Thomas Malthus, David Ricardo, John Stuart Mill, and, in some respects, Karl Marx laid the foundation of modern economics and developed economics into a unified body of theory.

The most distinguishing characteristic of classical doctrine was its reliance upon economic individualism and a harmony of interest. It was generally felt that a free, competitive market would efficiently guide production and distribution in the best interest of society if each individual pursued his own self-interest. In addition, while the government had the responsibility of formulating the framework within which markets would operate, its role was considered one of laissez faire. Under these conditions, classical economists felt that the economy would become a full-employment self-adjusting system.

Another important contribution of classical economics was the development of the abstract, deductive method of analyzing the economic system. Applying this methodology, significant developments occurred in the theory of international trade, price theory, the theory of economic growth and development and many other areas of economic theory.

See also Malthus, Thomas; Mill, John Stuart; Ricardo, David; Smith, Adam; Wealth of Nations.

—Clyde A. Haulman, *College of William and Mary*

CLAYTON ANTITRUST ACT (1914), a companion law to the Sherman Antitrust Act of 1890, with more explicit prohibitions on illegal business behavior, and concerned more with the effect of such behavior, less with intent.

The main provisions of the act prohibit four practices specifically: price discrimination by a seller where the effect may be to injure his competitors (Section 2), amended by the Robinson-Patman Act of 1936 to prohibit injury to buyers; tying contracts and exclusive dealerships where the effect is to lessen competition among potential rivals who might otherwise sell to a buyer (Section 3); acquisition of the stock of a business rival where the effect is to lessen competition substantially (Section 7), amended by the Celler-Kefauver Act of 1950 to prohibit asset acquisition as well; and interlocking directorates among competing firms of a certain size (Section 8). Illegal activities under Sections 2, 3, and 7 require a showing of actual or potential injury to competition, while Section 8 requires evidence that an interlock between competitors would violate some provision of the antitrust laws.

Section 6 seemingly provides agricultural marketing and labor organizations with blanket exemption from antitrust prosecution, but its interpretation by the courts showed otherwise. Substantial exemption to both groups was provided, however, in subsequent legislation and court decisions.

The Clayton Act is enforced jointly by the Federal Trade Commission and the Antitrust Division, Department of Justice.

See also Exclusive Dealership; Merger; Price Discrimination; Substantial Lessening of Competition; Tying Contracts.

Consult (16) Select Committee on Small Business, 1951; Sichel, 1967.

—Thomas O. Depperschmidt, *Memphis State University*

CLOSED SHOP makes union membership a precondition to employment or requires preferential hiring of union members. The Taft-Hartley Act (1947) outlawed the closed shop. However, Taft-Hartley has not been interpreted in a way that forbids de facto closed shops. These are shops in which the matching of workers and jobs normally done through the union hiring hall (as in the building trades and longshoring) leads to the exclusive use of union members. Specific exemptions to the ban on the preferential hiring of union members was afforded the construction industry by the Landrum-Griffin Act in 1959.

See also Landrum-Griffin Act (1959); Open Shop; Taft-Hartley Act (1947).

COALE, ANSLEY JOHNSON (1917-), a demographer and director of the Office of Population Research at Princeton. He received his Ph.D. in economics from Princeton (1947). His publications include *Population Growth and Economic Development in Low Income Countries* (1958, with Melvin Zelnik), *New Estimates of Population and Births in the United States* (1963, with Paul Demeny), and *Regional Model Life Tables and Stable Populations* (1966). In 1961 he became U.S. representative to the U.N. Population Commission. He has been on the faculty at Princeton since 1947.

COBWEB EQUILIBRIUM occurs when the quantity supplied depends upon lagged prices and the quantity demanded depends upon current prices. Assuming there is an initial fluctuation in the price, an oscillation occurs in one of two ways: the price will converge toward the equilibrium or will diverge away from this equilibrium. The two cases are known as stable and unstable equilibrium, respectively.

COEFFICIENT OF CORRELATION. *See* Correlation.

COEFFICIENT OF DETERMINATION. *See* Correlation.

COEFFICIENT OF ELASTICITY OF DEMAND, a measure of the responsiveness of quantity demanded to the impetus provided by a price change, computed by dividing the percentage change in quantity demanded by the causal percentage change in price. The algebraic sign of the coefficient of elasticity will be negative, reflecting the inverse relationship between price and quantity demanded for a typical demand curve. The absolute value of the coefficient provides insight into the behavior of quantity demanded and can range from 0 to infinity.

It can be inferred that a coefficient of elasticity of zero implies that the percentage change in quantity demanded has been 0, in response to a given price change. That is, consumers have not changed their purchases at all in response to a price change (completely inelastic demand). Coefficients of elasticity in absolute value 0-1 mean that the percentage change in quantity demanded is smaller than the percentage change in price (relatively inelastic demand). A coefficient of elasticity equal to 1 implies that a given percentage change in price has evoked the same percentage change in quantity demanded (unitary elasticity). Whenever the absolute value of the coefficient of elasticity is greater than 1, the result of a given percentage change in price has caused a percentage change in quantity demanded that exceeds the change in price (relatively elastic demand). The logical limit to elastic coefficients of demand is negative infinity, where a given percentage change in price has caused an infinite percentage change in quantity demanded.

See also Elasticity of Demand.

—Robert L. Brite, Louisiana State University

COEFFICIENT OF ELASTICITY OF SUPPLY, the numerical result of dividing the percentage change in output by the percentage change in price. This number will normally be positive, since there is a direct relationship between price and quantity supplied: if price rises quantity supplied will normally rise; price reductions normally lead to decreases in quantity supplied. The responsiveness of quantity supplied to price changes can be gauged by the size of the coefficient of elasticity of supply. The larger the coefficient, the greater the out-

Ansley Johnson Coale

put response to price change. Relatively small coefficients (fractions) imply that output response to price change is slight.

See also Elasticity of Supply.

COEFFICIENT OF VARIATION. *See* Dispersion.

COINCIDENT INDICATOR, an economic measurement or time series that experiences peaks and troughs at the same time as total economic activity. Coincident indicators include the Industrial Production Index, GNP in current dollars, and manufacturing and trade sales.

See also Business Cycles, Measurement; Lagging Indicator; Leading Indicator.

COINS, metal tokens accepted by tradition as part of the money supply. Present American coins are copper alloyed with some nickel or zinc. Coins formerly were pieces of metal whose intrinsic value was certified by the stamp on their faces, such as silver dollars or gold pieces.

See also Currency.

COLLECTIVE BARGAINING, a process by which decisions regarding the wages, hours, and conditions of employment are determined by the interaction of workers, acting through their unions, and employers. The term thus applies to the administration as well as the negotiation of contracts. This day-to-day relationship, while often less dramatic than the periodic contract-bargaining process with its publicity and tensions, has come to be recognized as the important "other half" of the labor-management relationship.

Contracts and Impact. There are well over 100,000 collectively bargained contracts in force. Since many of these are multi-year agreements, the number of contracts negotiated each year is nearer 50,000.

The impact of collective bargaining varies from industry to industry. In some of the major mass-production industries, from 80% to 100% of the production employees are covered by contracts, while in others the percentages range downward to quite low levels. For the entire manufacturing sector, an estimated two thirds of production employees are included in recognized bargaining units.

Results and Effects. The results of collective bargaining are difficult to assess. Although approximately 20 million workers belong to unions, there is no conclusive evidence that unionism and collective bargaining have provided higher wages for these workers than they would have received otherwise. Furthermore, collective bargaining has many facets and dimensions that do not lend themselves to quantitative measurement and comparison or to generalization.

However, certain observations are warranted. Collective bargaining has made contributions to both labor and management in stabilizing and professionalizing the relationship between them. To labor it affords a large measure of job and income security, protection from arbitrary treatment, and a sense of self-determination. To management it affords a helpful method for resolving controversies, reducing frictions, and effecting better communications with labor.

Collective bargaining agreement is defined by law. Labor and management, if either so desires, must bargain over matters that the National Labor Relations Board has decided are within the definition of "the terms and conditions of employment." Beyond that, there are matters that are legally bargainable if both parties agree to bargain over them, but over which neither side is compelled to bargain. Last, there are certain matters that are not legally bargainable, usually because an agreement between labor and management in these areas would itself be in violation of the law.

See also Arbitration; Conciliation; Representation.

—Leonard G. Schifrin, *College of William and Mary*

COLLECTIVIZATION. One of the critical tasks that the Soviet regime faced in the 1920s was to determine the best model for rapid industrialization. The key was to design a set of institutions that would generate a large amount of investment funds, ensure food supply, and make agricultural labor available to the urban areas. Stalin decided in 1927–28 that the only solution was to bring agriculture under the central control of the state.

Announced as voluntary, collectivization was in fact coercive. The poor peasants and the urban workers forced the richer peasants (kulaks) from their lands, and many kulaks were killed in the process. The kulaks retaliated by destroying their crops and livestock. Collectivization was so rapid and so disruptive that in 1930 Stalin slowed its pace and reemphasized the voluntary nature of the program, but by the end of 1932 nearly two-thirds of the total sown area was collectivized.

COLLUSION, an agreement or conspiracy, usually secret, among nominal competitors to engage in anticompetitive practices in violation of antitrust laws. The essence of collusion is the avoidance of price competition to ensure that a competitor's price will not ruin a firm's profits.

Identical price policies are not themselves prima facie evidence of collusion. More revealing are the measures taken by the organization to ensure compliance of member firms with its price and output decisions. Thus, the term typically refers to tighter-knit agreements, such as cartels, involving pressure on member firms to comply. Collusion is evident in most price-fixing and market-sharing schemes, but it may refer to conscious parallelism of action in which competitors tacitly comply with the price policies of their rivals.

Collusion is prohibited under the Sherman Act, Section 1, declaring any contract, combination, or conspiracy in restraint of trade illegal. Where evidence of collusion exists, the practices undertaken by competitors to eliminate competition are *per se* illegal. These practices may include limiting production, price discrimination against nonparticipants in the agreements, suppressing technology that may lead to lower costs and prices, preventing entry of new firms into the industry, and abuse of patent rights, such as in cross-licensing and restrictive licensing.

See also Cartel; Conscious Parallelism; Conspiracy Doctrine; Price Fixing; Restraint of Trade.

—Thomas O. Depperschmidt, *Memphis State University*

COMBINATIONS IN RESTRAINT OF TRADE. *See* Restraint of Trade.

COMMAND ECONOMY, an authoritarian socialist economy that has centralized economic decision making as its chief characteristic. This term was originated to describe the Soviet Union's economic system. The economic plan permeates the entire system. Government decisions can be transmitted to the production units by directives that dictate the behavior of the economic units and permit only minimal flexibility at the enterprise level.

A command economy has an ability to generate high levels of investment funds. The Soviet experience has shown that investment levels of 20-30% of gross national product are possible if the center, through its taxation policies, imposes on the population its propensity to save. The center has the power to mobilize resources and to direct them toward such objectives as rapid industrialization. Although the command system has a record of high levels of investment and rapid growth during the early stages of industrialization, its performance is less exemplary when the complexity of the economy increases, and efficiency becomes necessary for maintaining high rates of growth.

—Francis W. Rushing, *College of William and Mary*

COMMERCE COMMISSION. *See* Interstate Commerce Commission.

COMMERCIAL BANK, a financial institution whose basic functions are the receipt, creation, and transfer of demand deposits (checking accounts) for the general public. Originally a commercial bank made short-term (commercial) loans to merchants for the primary purpose of buying inventories that would soon be sold, the proceeds used to repay the loan. Today commercial banks also make substantial amounts of industrial, agricultural, personal, and real estate (mortgage) loans, accept time deposits, provide safe deposit facilities, manage trusts, act as brokers for securities, deal in foreign exchange, underwrite and sell municipal securities, engage in industrial research and security analysis, issue credit cards, and provide many other specialized services.

There are 13,800 commercial banks in the United States, ranging in size from minute institutions in small towns to large city or statewide banks with deposits in excess of $10 billion. One-eighth of all deposits in the United States are held by 12 major New York City banks. In their primary capacity as creator of demand deposits, commercial banks provide the greater part of the money supply and are, therefore, the chief objects of monetary policy.

See also Banking System; Federal Reserve System; Financial Intermediaries; Multiple Expansion of the Money Supply.

—Walter W. Haines, *New York University*

COMMERCIAL PAPER refers either to the promissory notes of businessmen given to a commercial bank to obtain a loan or to large-scale issues of promissory notes sold by prominent corporations to commercial banks or others who have sizeable sums of money to lend for short periods. The latter, usually called open-market commercial paper, is similar to a corporate bond except for a maturity of six months or less. When such commercial paper is sold by personal finance companies or sales finance companies, it is called finance paper.

COMMISSIONS, REGULATORY. *See* Regulatory Commissions.

COMMITTEE FOR INDUSTRIAL ORGANIZATION. *See* Congress of Industrial Organizations.

COMMODITY CREDIT CORPORATION (CCC), the agency within the US Department of Agriculture that handles the money and makes financial arrangements for the department's farm-price and income-support programs and for several lesser activities. It makes or insures commodity loans, makes direct payments to farmers, stores products acquired for price-support purposes, disposes of them, pays export subsidies where authorized, and provides current financing for the P.L. 480 program. It may borrow up to $14.5 billion from the U.S. Treasury, and it is reimbursed for losses by Congressional appropriations.

See also Commodity Loans; Price-Support Programs; Public Law 480.

COMMODITY LOANS, in general, are loans secured by a commodity as collateral. If the loan is not repaid, the lender may take the collateral; and if the value of the commodity is less than the loan, the borrower remains liable for the difference.

Nonrecourse commodity loans are much used by the U.S. government to support market prices of crops. The level at which price is to be supported is the value at which farmers may borrow on stored crops used as collateral. If the market price of the commodity is less than the loan rate at repayment date, the farmer may still turn over the collateral in full as final settlement of the loan. No recourse is available against him for any deficiency between the amount of the loan and the market value of the collateral.

When such a price-support loan is available and the market price is below the loan rate, farmers eligible for the program will ordinarily store some or all of their crops under the loan rather than sell on the market. The reduced market supply raises the price to the vicinity of the loan rate. If the market price rises above the loan rate, farmers may repay their loans, redeem the collateral, and use it as they wish.

See also Commodity Credit Corporation; Price-Support Programs.

—George E. Brandow, *Pennsylvania State University*

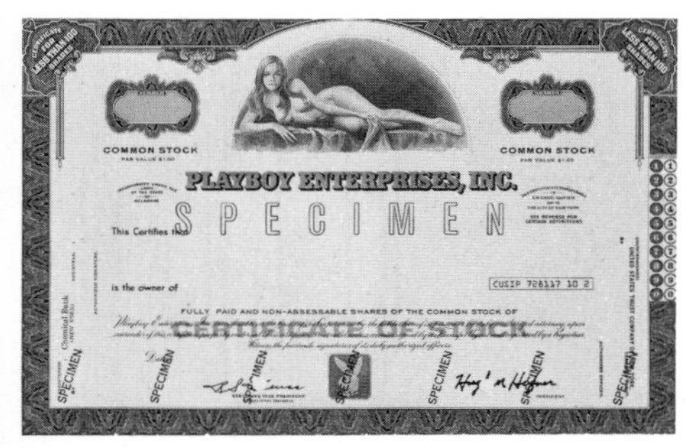

If pleasure is your business, it can be financed like any other enterprise through sale of stock.

COMMON CARRIER, a historical classification encompassing most transportation firms. Under the common law, the carrier is obligated to serve all comers, to deliver goods shipped with reasonable dispatch and in the same physical condition as received, to charge reasonable rates, and to avoid discrimination in price and service.

See also Common Law.

COMMON LAW, in the United States, has come to mean the body of law developed in decisions of English and American courts involving private (nongovernmental) litigants, as contrasted to statutory law or public legislation. Common law draws heavily on the traditional and universal principles developed in the courts, especially regarding property, crime, tort, and contract. Its development is particularly important in the areas of trade-union organization and antitrust policy.

See also Sherman Antitrust Act.

COMMONS, JOHN R. (1862-1945), a much-admired American spokesman for economic and social reform. Born in Ohio, the son of active abolitionists, Commons attended Oberlin College while working part-time as a printer. It was during this time that he became interested in trade unionism. After graduate work at Johns Hopkins University, he taught for ten years at Wesleyan, Oberlin, Indiana, and Syracuse before moving to the University of Wisconsin where his reputation as a student of American labor problems was to grow. It was at Wisconsin that he wrote *A Documentary History of American Industrial Society* and *History of Labour in the United States.*

Commons believed that the trade union movement emerged out of the efforts of individual workmen to protect their job rights against less expensive labor. He claimed that the effectiveness of unions depends on the ability to control conditions within the product market area in which they operate. As a policy maker, Commons helped to make Wisconsin a leader in social and economic reform. He was involved with such issues as legislation for unemployment insurance, workmen's compensation, civil service, and public utility and railroad regulations. In 1915 he became a member of the Industrial Relations Committee under President Wilson.

Among Commons' most famous works are *The Distribution of Wealth* (1893), *Legal Foundations of Capitalism* (1924), and *Institutional Economics* (1934).

COMMON SENSE OF POLITICAL ECONOMY (1910). *See* Wicksteed, Phillip H.

COMMON STOCK, a class of capital stock having certain rights and privileges. If no other type of stock is issued in a corporation, common stock enjoys exclusive claim to the net assets as well as to the profits of the corporation. Common stock is divided into shares issued in the form of stock certificates that are usually transferable by endorsement. These shares of stock may or may not be assigned a par, or face, value. Common stock is also called equity stock or ordinary stock.

See also Stock.

COMMUNICATIONS ACT OF 1934. *See* Federal Communications Act.

COMMUNICATIONS INDUSTRY. *See* Regulated Industries.

COMMUNISM, according to Karl Marx, the last stage of economic development. It is achieved only if and when all class antagonisms are eliminated, the workers have developed attitudes that make them want to perform their social functions, and the state has withered away. Under communism only the proletarian class would exist; socialist organizations would permit the system to produce in abundance, each worker contributing to society according to his ability and receiving according to his needs; the necessity for government having ceased, individuals would enjoy true freedom. Neither Marx nor his ideological successors have described the specific path or the length of time necessary to achieve full communism.

Since World War II the countries of eastern Europe, China, Cuba, and the Soviet Union have been referred to as "communist" countries. The leadership of these countries are followers of the teachings of Marx, but the economies are still in the socialist stage of development.

Consult (26) Dalinky, 1970; Friedman, 1961; Lenin, 1960; Sweezy, 1956.

—Francis W. Rushing, *College of William and Mary*

COMMUNISM, ANARCHISTIC. *See* Anarchistic Communism.

COMMUNISM (PLANNING). *See* Planning (Communism).

COMMUNIST MANIFESTO (1848), a political and economic tract by Karl Marx and Friedrich Engels written to arouse organized political action by the proletariat. The authors felt (1) that property, which is the basis of the bourgeois system, restrained production, and (2) that the system, which could no longer control itself, would be exposed to a constant stream of crises. The solution, according to the authors, lay in a structure involving abolition of property, nationalization of industry, universal education, and a progressive income tax.

COMPANY UNION, one organized by a company for its employees. The concept emerged during World War I with the hope of easing the problems of high labor turnover and labor unrest. Chiefly to dilute the appeal of trade unions, many industries began company unions. Most important of their many drawbacks was that, with the union owing its strength to the company, workers had little bargaining power.

COMPARATIVE ADVANTAGE. Gains from international trade are maximized when each nation specializes in the production of those goods in which its comparative advantage is greatest (or comparative disadvantage least). Assume that with the same composite inputs, Country A provides twice as much of one commodity (X) and three times as much of another commodity (Y) as Country B. Country A has an absolute advantage in both; its productivity is twice that of B relative to X and three times B's relative to Y. Therefore, A will specialize in Y (comparative advantage greatest) and B in X (comparative disadvantage least). Mutually advantageous trade can develop with 1 of X exchanging for no less than 2 nor no more than 3 of Y.

See also Absolute Advantage; International Trade Theory; Specialization; Terms of Trade.

COMPARATIVE DISADVANTAGE. *See* Comparative Advantage.

COMPENSATED PRICE EFFECT. *See* Consumer Equilibrium.

COMPETITION, the ability and opportunity to compete in an economic market. Competition exists in a market in which (1) there are many sellers or buyers, and no one individual or group can influence the market; (2) the sellers or buyers deal with a homogeneous product; (3) there is unrestricted entry to or exit from the market. Each seller and buyer regards the price as given, and in the pursuit of their own self-interests—sellers seeking maximum profits and buyers seeking optimum consumer welfare—the competitive market is cleared (quantities demanded and supplied are equal), and market price is established. Nonprice competition does not apply in a competitive market model.

The marginal principle is important in all economic analysis. In the competitive model, buyers pay what the last unit is worth to them, and producers supply an amount so that the cost of the last unit is equal to the market price: marginal cost equals marginal revenue.

See also Economic Systems; Invisible Hand; Marginal Analysis; Market Economy; Profit System.

COMPLEMENTARY GOODS, goods that are employed jointly in the consumption process. The economic relationship for complementarity between goods necessitates that an inverse relationship exist between the price of one good and the demand curve for another.

COMPTROLLER OF THE CURRENCY, a presidential appointee who acts as administrator of national banks and banks in the District of Columbia. He approves new national banks and branches, consolidations, and mergers and, through his staff, examines each bank at least once a year.

COMPULSORY SAVING. *See* Forced Saving.

COMPULSORY UNION MEMBERSHIP. *See* Closed Shop.

CONCENTRATION. *See* Concentration Ratio.

CONCENTRATION RATIO refers to a share of

Manifest

der

Kommunistischen Partei.

Veröffentlicht im Februar 1848.

London.

Druck von R. Hirschfeld, English & Foreign Printer,

48, Clifton Street, Finsbury Square.

1818.

COMPARATIVE ADVANTAGE

For further discussion of the theory of comparative advantage as the basis for trade between nations, consult the articles on INTERNATIONAL TRADE THEORY, ABSOLUTE ADVANTAGE, and SPECIALIZATION.

some economic variable that is accounted for by the largest or by relatively few of the largest firms in an industry or market. Usually, the degree of concentration in an industry indicates the amount of sales by one or more of the largest firms in that industry as a proportion of total sales. For example, of total sales in the tire and tube industry in 1963, 70% were controlled by the four largest firms, 89% by the eight largest firms, and 99% by the fifty largest firms.

Union leaders George Meany, Walter Reuther hold single gavel as symbol of 1955 AFL-CIO merger.

CONCILIATION, a form of third-party intervention into collective bargaining over new contract terms when the bargaining has broken down or threatens to do so. The conciliator attempts to promote reconciliation and to restore constructive bargaining.

This narrow though often useful function has expanded somewhat through time, and there is now little difference between conciliation and mediation. Both seek to generate agreement between labor and management by skillful and tactful methods that cool tempers, save face, and encourage continued bargaining and compromise.

See also Collective Bargaining; Mediation.

CONFIDENCE INTERVAL, a probability statement concerning the value of an unknown population parameter, based on the sample mean and standard deviation. For example, a 95 percent confidence interval states that 95 times out of 100 a given set of parameter values will contain the true population value.

See also Sampling Distribution.

CONFLICT, CLASS. *See* Class Conflict

CONGLOMERATE, a business firm producing and selling products in more than one market or line of commerce, products usually (though not necessarily) dissimilar to, and therefore not competitive with, each other. The conglomerate typically is formed by multiple mergers of previously independent firms, although the same conglomerate structure could be achieved through diversification internally, without merger. It is the merging of firms producing dissimilar products that distinguishes the conglomerate merger from other types of mergers (vertical and horizontal).

An assessment of the legal and economic implications of conglomerates is pending. The question legally is whether the Clayton Act prohibition on mergers tending to lessen competition can "reach" conglomerates, particularly in their practice of reciprocal dealing among member units. Reciprocal dealing limits the access of outside competitive firms to conglomerate members to the extent that member units deal exclusively with each other for needed goods or materials. From an economic viewpoint, the conglomerate represents a business organization quite different in size and potential market power from the single-product, independent producer portrayed in conventional economic theory.

See also Celler-Kefauver Act; Clayton Act; Diversification; Merger.

Consult (16) Narver, 1967.

—Thomas O. Depperschmidt, *Memphis State University*

CONGRESS OF INDUSTRIAL ORGANIZATIONS (CIO). In 1935, a group of industrial union leaders led by John L. Lewis, vice-president of the American Federation of Labor, met for the purpose of organizing workers within the AFL who were otherwise unorganized. They were successful with such unions as shipbuilding, automobile, rubber, and flatglass, which had had previous problems trying to get charters from the AFL. The AFL, alarmed by the developments of the CIO, ordered the organization to disband but Lewis refused and, instead, resigned his position as vice-president. Two years later the CIO unions were expelled from the AFL.

The CIO meanwhile was in the process of organizing the steel industry and by 1937 the union was so powerful that it could close down Carnegie-Illinois, U.S. Steel's biggest subsidiary, if it decided to strike. For this reason, U.S. Steel agreed to recognize the CIO as a bargaining agent. The CIO also began to make gains in other major industries, namely rubber, automobiles. CIO membership began to grow rapidly and in 1937 and 1938 surpassed the membership of the AFL. After having established themselves in the mass production industries, the CIO received little opposition from the AFL.

In 1938, the CIO set themselves up as a permanent organization. During World War II membership continued to increase and the years following the war saw drastic union gains and wage increases. However, post-war strikes soon got out of hand. Rising wages set off a spiral of rising prices and the economic problem became one of inflation. Public opinion began to go against labor and the result was the Taft-Hartley Act of 1947. This Act curbed labor's rights and, in a sense, repealed much of labor's gains of the Wagner Act of 1932.

In 1955, after much deliberation, the AFL and the CIO merged. At this time it was claiming the six largest unions—which accounted for one-third of all union membership. However, since that time the Teamsters were ousted and the United Auto Workers left the AFL-CIO.

See also Labor Movement.

—William D. Wagoner, *Louisiana State University*

CONSCIOUS PARALLELISM of action, a business practice wherein a firm refrains from price competition with competitors without their overt agreement but knowing that they will do likewise. The result is identical or parallel prices in the market not unlike a conspiracy to fix prices. Conscious parallelism has been treated with some indirection by the courts in this century. The current position is that some overt evidence of agreement is needed to constitute violation of Sherman Act prohibitions against restraint of trade.

See also Collusion; Conspiracy Doctrine; Price Fixing; Restraint of Trade; United States v. American Tobacco.

CONSENT DECREE, negotiated private settlement prior to final judgment in a civil antitrust suit between the prosecuting FTC or antitrust division and a business-firm defendant. After agreement on the terms of the settlement, a district court almost always accepts the terms and issues the decree (court order) incorporating these terms. The decree may include penalties or agreements to take or stop certain actions by the defendant. Between 80% and 90% of all antitrust litigation is settled by consent decree in a typical year.

See also Antitrust Policy.

CONSERVATION RESERVE. *See* Soil Bank.

CONSOLIDATED BANK BALANCE SHEET. *See* Balance Sheet, Bank.

CONSPICUOUS CONSUMPTION, the practice of consuming far beyond one's needs as a display of wealth, power, and success. Thorstein Veblen coined the phrase in his *Theory of the Leisure Class* (1899). He felt that to maintain status in the leisure class (that group which is involved in the predatory seizure of goods without actually working to obtain them), members must avoid productive pursuits and their consumption must be wasteful. Also, because the leisure class is dominant, its outlook is adopted by the other classes of society, so that even the poor indulge in some conspicuous consumption.

See also Veblen, Thorstein.

CONSPIRACIES IN RESTRAINT OF TRADE. *See* Restraint of Trade.

CONSPIRACY DOCTRINE, a common-law principle holding, in its most general form, that an agreement or combination by two or more parties to intend or do injury to a third party is a criminal act. Its use against labor unions in the United States in the late 18th and early 19th centuries reflected the philosophical orientation to natural law of early capitalism. Unions, by seeking higher wages and better working conditions, were accused of upsetting the "natural" balance of a market-oriented economy as well as the price-wage policies of a specific employer. The organization of workers itself was taken as evidence of conspiracy. Subsequently, court decisions and federal legislation in the 20th century removed unions from liability under the doctrine.

Conspiracy in restraint of trade is forbidden to business competitors in the Sherman Antitrust Act. Its use here is premised on the belief that competition is the most satisfactory regulator of activity in a market economy, and that collusive agreements to increase prices artificially by price-fixing or market-sharing agreements destroy the advantages to society of free competition.

See also Clayton Act; Collusion; Market Sharing; Price Fixing; Restraint of Trade; Sherman Antitrust Act.

Consult (16) Millis, 1945.

—Thomas O. Depperschmidt, *Memphis State University*

CONSTANT-COST INDUSTRY, one in which expanded resource use does not lead to increases in resource prices. The resources used by this industry are not specialized and represent only a small part of the aggregate used by all industries. We are dealing with the long run; therefore, we must consider exit and entry of firms. The short-run effects of an increase in demand for this product will include a price rise and increased output and excess profits for existing firms. Now firms with identical cost curves will appear; price falls and the industry supply schedule will be parallel to the axis, at minimum average cost.

CONSTANT FUNCTIONS. *See* Function.

CONSTANT VALUE refers to a national income account adjusted for price changes: what remains is a dollar measure that changes only because of changes in the quantities of goods and services. If, for example, constant-value GNP increases, the quantity of goods and services produced by the economy has increased.

Simple Technique. One technique for calculating constant-value GNP is to use price indexes to deflate GNP: constant-value GNP is the ratio of current-value GNP to a price index for the year multiplied by 100. The constant-value GNP so calculated is denominated in terms of prices prevailing in the base year of the price index. Clearly, if prices are increasing, market-value GNP will be increasing, but so will the price index: both the numerator and the denominator used in the calculation of constant-value GNP will have risen and removed the effect of higher prices.

The difficulty with this approach is that the generality of the price index employed may be sharply limited in comparison to the generality of the goods and services included within GNP. For example, if the Consumer Price Index

What consumers will buy (Mustang, yes; Edsel, no) determines what manufacturers will produce.

CONSUMER EQUILIBRIUM

Consumer equilibrium uses concepts presented in UTILITY and UTILITY FUNCTION. For the theoretical supports behind the concept of consumer equilibrium, see MARGINAL UTILITY and INDIFFERENCE CURVE; and for a general view of its relevance consult DEMAND THEORY.

The relation of Consumer Equilibrium to Demand Theory is clarified in the Subject Map accompanying the latter article.

(CPI) is employed, CPI refers to or characterizes the changes in the prices for consumer goods and services; but GNP includes much more than just consumer goods and services, and the price behavior of these other goods and services may be quite unlike the price behavior of consumer output. The same objection arises if the Wholesale Price Index (WPI) is used instead of CPI.

Refined Technique. Because of these difficulties an alternative technique is used in estimating constant-value GNP. This process involves the calculation of a price index for various components of GNP. Each component is measured in terms of current value and is then deflated by its appropriate price index. The constant-value components of GNP are then added together to obtain constant-value GNP. The value of the GNP deflator, the ratio of current-value GNP to constant-value GNP multiplied by 100, represents a price index that reflects a much broader picture of price change than either CPI or WPI.

—Frank J. Bonello, *University of Notre Dame*

CONSTITUTION, UNION. *See* Union Constitution.

CONSUMER BUDGET LINE. *See* Budget Line, Consumer.

CONSUMER CHOICE exists within an economic system when an individual is free to purchase the goods and services that he desires and for which he has the money. This freedom is sometimes denied during economic and political crises, such as World War II and severe grain shortages. The alternative to consumer choice is rationing, either with coupons or direct allocation of goods.

CONSUMER CREDIT CONTROLS. *See* Installment Credit Controls.

CONSUMER DEMAND. It has long been observed that there is an inverse relation between price and quantity demanded for a consuming household; the quantified expression of the relation is called a demand function for that household for that good. Mere quantification, however, is not a causal explanation.

An initial explanation employs the psychological datum that the more goods and services are consumed, the less is the satisfaction gained by increasing the consumption rate. The last unit consumed will not add as much to a consumer's satisfaction as the previous units added (the theory of diminishing marginal utility). Therefore, the price of a good must fall to induce him to purchase more of it. Furthermore, the result of a price change will induce consumers to alter consumption patterns. That is, when the price of a good falls, a consumer with a given income will be induced to buy more of this good and less of some relatively higher priced good (the substitution effect of a price change). Secondly, when price falls, the consumer's real income (the amount of goods he can purchase with a given money income) rises. He will then be able to purchase more of the good whose price has been decreased. The combined effects of diminishing marginal utility, substitution, and income dictate that a consuming household is increasingly more willing and more able to purchase additional quantities of a good as prices decline.

See also Demand Curve.

—Robert L. Brite, *Louisiana State University*

CONSUMER DETERMINISM, a term for consumer sovereignty used to illustrate the concept that the consumers actually have control of their economic lives in the market economy. The consumer decides which goods to purchase from the total of all goods in existence. As he purchases the good, he is voting for the production of that good. This consumer vote signals the producer in what quantity goods should be produced. The producer must react to the consumer vote to maximize profit.

The producer cannot continue to produce a good that is not in sufficient demand and, on the other hand, he must move into the production of goods that show increases in demand. A decrease in demand shifts the demand curve to the left along the supply curve, giving a lower price and a smaller equilibrium quantity sold and produced. An increase in demand shifts the demand curve to the right, giving a higher market price and a larger equilibrium output.

—Robert L. Brite, *Louisiana State University*

CONSUMER EQUILIBRIUM, a situation in which the consumer allocates his income in the most desirable fashion, purchasing the most preferred bundle within his budget. Because the optimal bundle has the highest level of utility, an equilibrium position is represented by a point on the highest indifference curve within the feasible set.

The Basic Situation. If the consumer has an income of M dollars per period of time, and the prices of X and Y are P^x and P^y, respectively, then the maximum amount of commodity X that the consumer can purchase is M/P^x, and the maximum amount of Y is M/P^y. Points on the line joining M/P^x and M/P^y in Figure 1 represent bundles containing some amount of each good and cost exactly M dollars. The line is called a *budget line.* Points in the shaded triangle in Figure 1 represent bundles whose cost is less than M dollars. The entire triangle, including its boundaries, is called the *feasible set*.

Given the conditions depicted in Figure 1, the highest indifference curve that the consumer can reach feasibly is the curve labeled I, and, therefore, the bundle containing X_1 units of X and Y_1 units of Y represents an equilibrium position. Geometrically, an equilibrium position (except for some special cases) is a point of tangency between the budget line and an indifference curve. At that point, the slope of the indifference curve equals the slope of the budget line. Because the slope of an indifference curve is the rate of substitution in consumption (marginal rate of substitution) between X and Y (RSC_{xy}), and the slope of the budget line equals the ratio of the prices, P^x/P^y, the consumer's equilibrium is characterized by the condition $RSC_{xy} = P^x/P^y$.

Income effects. When his income changes, the consumer adjusts his purchases and moves to a new equilibrium position. Figure 2 illustrates an increase in income from M_1 to M_2. This increase causes the budget line to move to the right in a parallel fashion, thereby increasing the size of the feasible set. Following this change, the consumer moves from his initial equilibrium point E_1 to the new equilibrium at E_2.

When an increase (decrease) in income induces the consumer to purchase more (less) of a good, it is called a *superior good.* When an increase (decrease) in income causes the consumer to purchase less (more) of a good, it is called an *inferior good.* In Figure 2 both X and Y are superior goods. In Figure 3 on the other hand, X is a superior good, and Y is an inferior good.

Price effects. The effect of a change in a price is to change the price ratio P^x/P^y. For example, an increase in P^x increases the ratio, indicating that good X has become more expensive relative to good Y. Because the ratio is also equal to the slope of the budget line, an increase in P^x makes the budget line steeper. Figure 4 illustrates the effect of an increase in P^x from P^x_1 to P^x_2. This change causes the budget line to rotate clockwise around its intercept on the Y axis, thereby reducing the size of the feasible set, and inducing the consumer to move from the initial equilibrium E_1 to the new equilibrium E_2. In this particular example the consumer reduces his purchase of X and increases his purchase of Y. When an increase (decrease) in the price of X causes the consumer to purchase more (less) of Y, then Y is said to be a *substitute* for X. When an increase (decrease) in the price of X causes the consumer to purchase less (more) of Y, then Y is said to be a *complement* for X. Thus, in Figure 4, good Y is a substitute for X.

The example illustrated in Figure 5 shows the effect of a decrease in P^y from P^y_1 to P^y_2. The budget line rotates around its X-intercept, bringing about an increase in the size of the feasible set, and inducing the consumer to move from E_1 to E_2. In this example, good X is a complement for good Y. An unusual feature of this example is the fact that the decrease in P^y makes the consumer purchase less of good Y. Such a phenomenon is referred to as the *Giffen paradox,* and the good in question (good Y in the present case) is called a *Giffen good.* It can be shown that Giffen goods are inferior goods.

Compensated price effects. When the price of a commodity increases, the budget line moves closer to the origin, reflecting the fact that a price increase reduces the consumer's purchasing power, or his *real income.* Thus, a price change affects the consumer's economic conditions in two ways: (1) it changes the relative prices confronting him, and (2) it changes his real income.

It is possible to separate the effects of these two changes by means of a compensated price change, by giving the consumer a compensation in nominal income to offset the loss in real income. If P^x increases from P^x_1 to P^x_2, the budget line rotates around its Y-intercept, as shown in Figure 6. To maintain the consumer's initial purchasing power, his nominal income is increased from M_1 to M_2, where the increase $M_2 - M_1$ is just enough to make the new budget line go through the initial bundle E_1. Thus, the new budget line represents the consumer's market opportunities following an increase in P^x accompanied by a compensating increase in income designed to keep his real income constant. As a response to this compensated price change, the consumer moves from E_1 to E_2, and the changes in quantities demanded are referred to as *substitution effects.* The change in the quantity of X, $X_2 - X_1$, is referred to as the *own substitution effect,* being a change in the quantity of a commodity due to a change in its own price, and the change in the quantity of Y, $Y_2 - Y_1$, is called a *cross-substitution effect.* One conclusion of the theory of consumer behavior is that own substitution effects are always negative; that is, a compensated increase (decrease) in the price of a good always brings about a decrease (increase) in the quantity demanded of that good. This result is also known as the *law of demand.*

See also Utility Function.

Consult (12) Ferguson, 1972; Hadar, 1973; Leftwich, 1970; Stigler, 1966.

—Josef Hadar, *Case Western Reserve University*

CONSUMER GOODS. *See* Goods; Goods and Services.

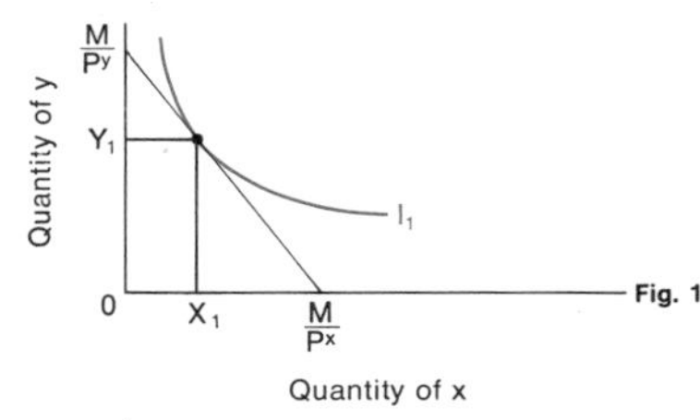

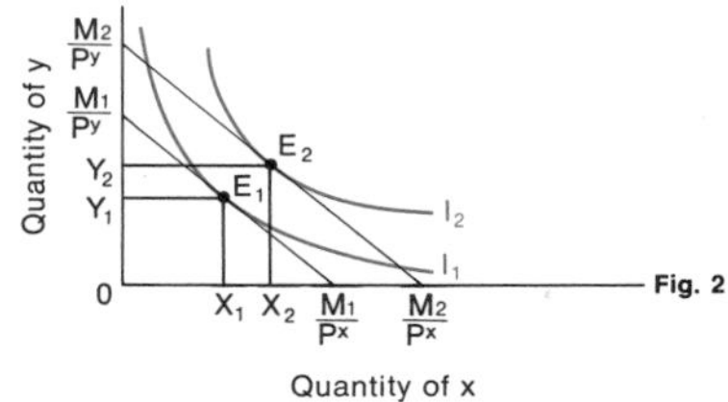

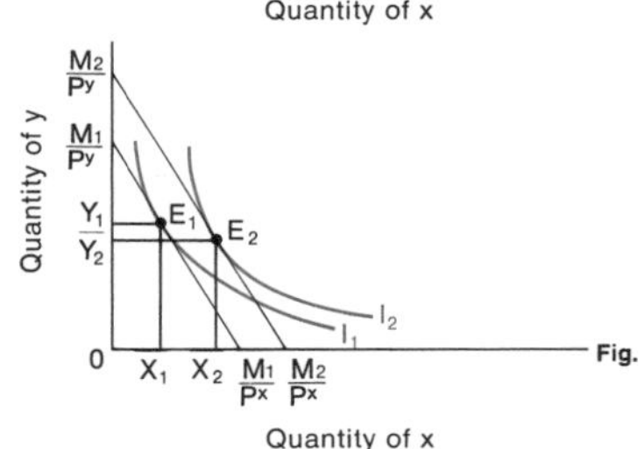

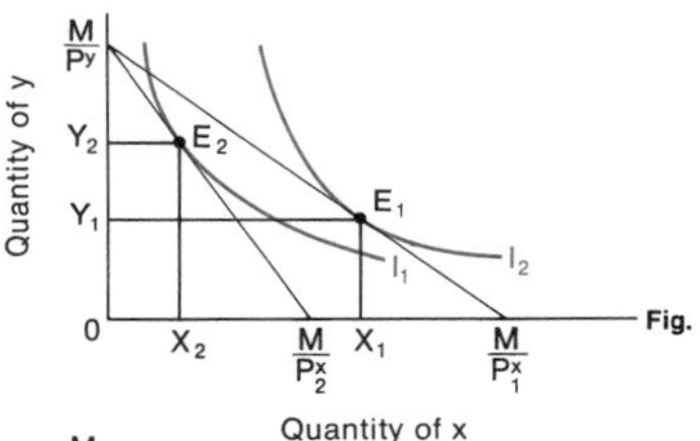

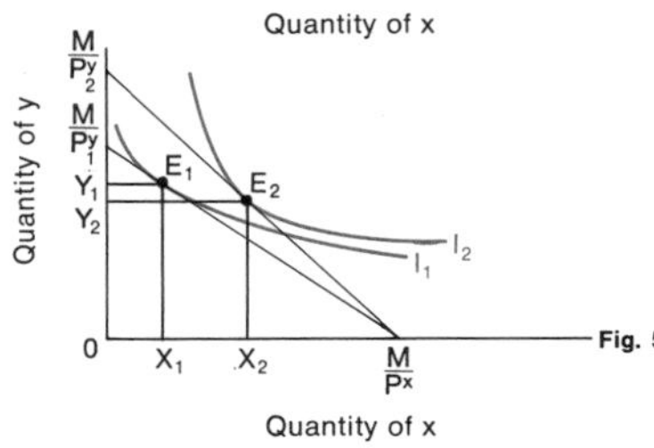

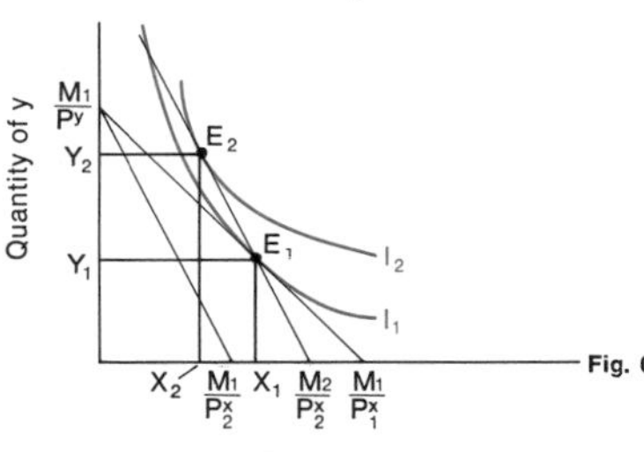

CONSUMER PRICE INDEXES FOR URBAN WAGE EARNERS (1967-100)

Year	CPI All items	Purchasing power of consumer dollar 1967-$1.00
1915	30.4	3.226
1916	32.7	2.890
1917	38.4	2.439
1918	45.1	2.024
1919	51.8	1.764
1920	60.0	1.724
1921	53.6	1.931
1922	50.2	1.980
1923	51.1	1.931
1924	51.2	1.934
1925	52.5	1.862
1926	53.0	1.887
1927	52.0	1.923
1928	51.3	1.949
1929	51.3	1.949
1930	50.0	2.000
1931	45.6	2.193
1932	40.9	2.445
1933	38.8	2.577
1934	40.1	2.494
1935	41.1	2.433
1936	41.5	2.410
1937	43.0	2.326
1938	42.2	2.370
1939	41.6	2.404
1940	42.0	2.381
1941	44.1	2.268
1942	48.8	2.049
1943	51.8	1.931
1944	52.7	1.898
1945	53.9	1.855
1946	58.5	1.709
1947	66.9	1.495
1948	72.1	1.387
1949	71.4	1.401
1950	72.1	1.387
1951	77.8	1.285
1952	79.5	1.258
1953	80.1	1.248
1954	80.5	1.242
1955	80.2	1.247
1956	81.4	1.229
1957	84.3	1.186
1958	86.6	1.155
1959	87.3	1.145
1960	88.7	1.127
1961	89.6	1.116
1962	90.6	1.104
1963	91.7	1.091
1964	92.9	1.076
1965	94.5	1.058
1966	97.2	1.029
1967	100.0	1.000
1968	104.2	.960
1969	109.8	.911
1970	116.3	.860
1971	121.3	.821

CONSUMERISM. *See* Consumer Protection.

CONSUMER PRICE INDEX (CPI), the most frequently quoted price index, often used in discussing the aims and objectives desired for the price level. It is essentially a statistical measure of changes in the prices of items necessary to maintain a certain standard of living for an urban family unit of wage earners. Each listed item is given a weight. This weight is usually determined by its importance in the family budget, noted from consumer spending patterns in the early 1960s. Included in this list are certain types of foods, clothing, rent, and other necessary items for daily living.

The prices of the items are compared to a base year to get an indication of the level and direction of price changes. CPI is compiled by the Bureau of Labor Statistics of the Department of Labor and is reported monthly. CPI is sometimes referred to as the cost-of-living index and is often used to compute pay increases in labor-management negotiations.

See also Price Indexes.

CONSUMER PROTECTION. As a result of the competitive conditions in the modern industrial society and the questionable ethical standards of a segment of the commercial community, the consumer needs protection. Some of the most common areas of abuse against which consumers need protection are:

(1) emergence of monopoly, with its powers over pricing and the amount and quality of product offering;

(2) misleading or false advertising efforts;

(3) misleading or false personal selling practices, such as termite inspections resulting in unneeded home treatment;

(4) excessive interest rates and carrying charges, as when small loan companies or retail stores tack on very high carrying charges by concealing them in the total payback price;

(5) the marketing of harmful products, for example, cosmetics causing skin disorders, or foods packed under unsanitary conditions;

(6) deceptive labeling or packaging of products, such as the failure to inform the consumer of the limitations or potential dangers associated with using the product;

(7) environmental pollution by industries or consumers themselves.

Protecting the Consumer. Local, state and federal governments act as rule makers and policemen, regulating various aspects of business by passing such statutory laws as the Sherman and Clayton Antitrust acts, the Pure Food and Drug Act, and the Truth in Lending Act. In addition, administrative laws and regulations are handed down by agencies such as the Federal Trade Commission and the Pure Food and Drug Administration, which are charged specifically with regulating commercial activities.

Industry's own efforts to protect consumers from questionable business practices are exercised via trade associations, chambers of commerce, and better business bureaus through the adoption of codes of conduct and product standards.

Consumer advocates may study industry practices and product performance to determine if there are abuses against which the consumer should be protected. Their chief weapon is carefully documented publicity that is adverse to a company or a product. Consumer movements are sometimes formalized: delegates meet and attempt to exert pressure for legislation to protect the consumer.

—Algin B. King, *College of William and Mary*

CONSUMER SATISFACTION. *See* Consumer Welfare.

CONSUMERS' COOPERATIVES. *See* Cooperativism.

CONSUMER SOVEREIGNTY occurs when consumers' decisions of which goods and services to purchase affect the quantity and composition of goods and services produced. For example, if increased consumer demand for automobiles results in increased resources allocated to automobile production, then the consumer is sovereign.

CONSUMER'S PREFERENCES, an individual's personal preference for one basket of goods or services over all other alternatives offered, as revealed by his purchases in the markets. An economic system is said to be dominated by consumer preferences when it allocates resources to reflect these tastes.

CONSUMER SURPLUS, the difference between the total utility received from a product and the total market value of that product. The surplus is received by the consumer but not at the expense of the producer. According to the law of diminishing marginal utility, a consumer receives less and less utility from the purchase of identical items; a consumer will purchase items up to that point where he no longer receives any utility. Therefore, he will purchase items until he stops receiving a surplus.

The concept of consumer surplus is very often used in making decisions of a social nature. For example, the decision whether to build a bridge or to build a road may be based on the amount of consumer surplus of each. The item that allows for the most consumer surplus will very often be the one decided upon. If the decision calls for a public vote, each citizen will vote for the item that will give him the most surplus. Although in most cases consumer surplus is very difficult or impossible to measure, consumers are able to relatively price a surplus.

—Robert L. Brite, *Louisiana State University*

CONSUMER WELFARE, an aspect of economics concerned with the maximization of the satisfaction or utility of consumers. An individual can maximize his utility by choosing those items that provide the greatest amount of marginal utility per dollar spent until the marginal utility per dollar spent on each good is equal to the marginal utility per dollar spent on every other good.

CONSUMPTION, the amount spent by households on currently produced goods and services. Consumption refers to *spending* by households, not to the acts of eating or using or wearing out, nor does it refer to the motives of the household in making a purchase. Thus if a household buys an old house or a used car, economists do not call this consumption but the exchange of one asset (money) for another asset (used car) in the "balance sheet" of the family. Similarly, the purchase of a bond or share of stock is not "spending" but the exchange of one asset for another.

Household as a Firm. When a household is both a consuming unit and producing unit—a farm family is an example, or a father-and-son house repair team working out of the basement—economics treats the business aspect of the family's life as a "firm." Thus the receipts of the house repair team would be called "revenues of the firm." Whatever they buy in order to do business is classified as a business outlay (nails—current cost of production; a saw—investment, to be depreciated over the life of the saw). Only the purchases that are not used in production are called household consumption.

Motives for Consumption. Economists, and the theory of income determination, do not deal with motives for consumption other than in the most general way of saying a household chooses its level of consumption (and saving) to maximize its welfare (or utility).

Patterns of Consumption. The theory of income determination focuses on the empirical (statistical) relationship between a household's disposable income, wealth, expectations of future income and wealth, and access to credit, without regard to the individual motives or collective decision-making processes of the household. Consumption spending is closely correlated to (1) current income, (2) wealth, (3) expected future income, (4) expected future wealth, and (5) the availability of credit.

Significance in Income Determination. There are two reasons why the theory defines consumption as "spending by households on currently produced goods and services." First, the considerations and circumstances that cause households to spend and to save (not to consume) are different from the profit motive and opportunities that dominate investment decisions. Thus, household spending and saving intentions do not correspond with business investment intentions, or government's aims in public policy. Second, it is spending on currently produced goods and services that determines how much is produced (GNP), how many are employed, and whether inflation occurs. The focus of the theory is on the *aggregate consumption demand* in money terms, which is the sum of all households' consumption spending.

—Walter C. Neale, *University of Tennessee*

CONSUMPTION, CROSS-SECTION. Studies of the relationship between personal disposable income and consumption (as given by household budget surveys) for households in different income brackets during the same period of time make it possible to draw cross-section consumption functions, which support the assumption that consumption is largely determined by the level of income, and that the marginal propensity to consume is less than 1. High-income households consume more than low-income households, but high-income households also save a larger proportion of income than do low-income households.

CONSUMPTION, TIME-SERIES, the method of examining the relationship between income and consumption by pairing consumption expenditures for previous years with personal disposable income for each of the years to produce a historical consumption function. Such consumption functions show a higher long-run marginal propensity to consume than the short-run MPC shown by cross-section studies.

CONSUMPTION FUNCTION, the relationship between disposable income and consumption, in which it is assumed that the level of disposable income determines the level of consumption, that is, that consumption spending depends on income. Expressed in a table, it is called the *consumption schedule,* and is all possible incomes paired with the consumption spending which would occur at each income. It should be read as a set of "if. . .then. . ." propositions: "if disposable income is $\$Y_a$, then consumption will be $\$C_a$; if disposable income is $\$Y_b$, then consumption will be $\$Y_b$," and so on.

When these values are plotted on a graph, the curve is called the *consumption function.* The consumption function can also

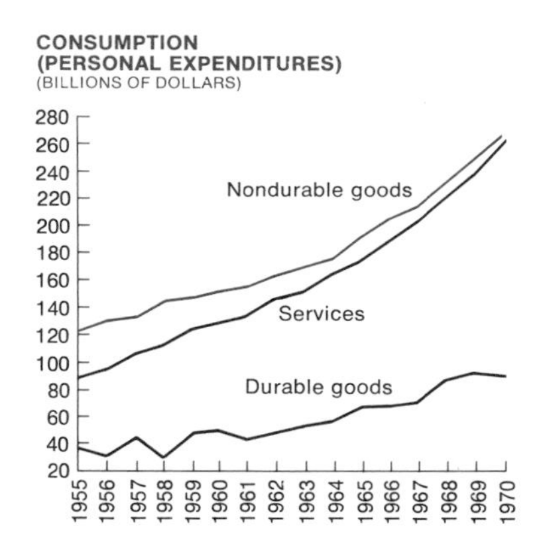

Opposition to English Corn Laws (increasing tariffs on grain imports) played a significant role in the development of free trade theory.

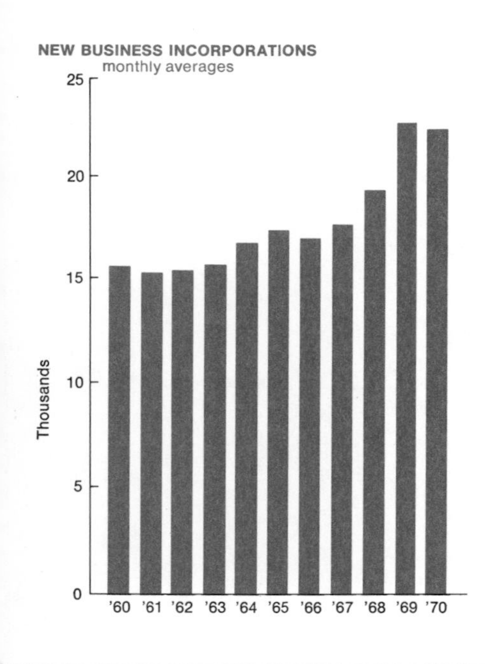

be written as an alegebraic equation; most simply in the form C = C of "Break-even Point" + (MPC) × (disposable income − Break-even Point value of income). More complex equations result if one introduces wealth or other considerations as additional determiners of consumption.

The phrase "propensity to consume" expresses the idea that consumption depends on disposable income and, more broadly, on wealth and expectations about future income, wealth, and prices. When the propensity to consume is put in the form of a specific relationship between income and consumption, it is called a consumption function or consumption schedule. The propensity to consume is an empirical (statistical) relationship and is not a statement about consumers' motives, nor is it a statement about their rationality.

See also Consumption; Consumption, Cross-Section; Consumption, Time Series; Permanent Income Hypothesis; Pigou Effect.

—Walter C. Neale, *University of Tennessee*

CONSUMPTION POSSIBILITY. World production and consumption possibilities are maximized under free international trade. In the absence of trade a nation's welfare is limited by its production-possibilities frontier in the following manner: Country A can produce 10 units of commodity X or 20 units of Y. Country B can produce 10 units of X or 30 of Y. These are the rates at which X can be "transformed" into Y and vice versa in each country. Let trade commence: B reduces output of X by 10 and A increases X output by 10; the quantity of X remains the same. Y output decreases by 20 in A but increases by 30 in B with a net gain of 10. Trade has resulted in no reduction in one commodity accompanied by an increase in the other. All products can increase via specialization and free trade and the world's consumption possibility and welfare increase.

See also Comparative Advantage; International Trade Theory; Specialization.

Consult (23) Snider, 1971.

CONSUMPTION SCHEDULE. *See* Consumption Function.

CONTINUED BOND. *See* Bonds.

CONTINUOUS VARIABLE. *See* Variable.

CONTRACT ARBITRATION. *See* Arbitration.

CONTRACT CARRIERS, highway motor carriers whose services are for hire to individual customers under special contracts covering particular periods of time. These carriers, because they have a contract commitment, often have an advantage in serving an industry's large shippers with special transport requirements. Contract carriers are regulated by the Interstate Commerce Commission.

See also Interstate Commerce Commission; Regulated Industries.

CONTRACT NEGOTIATION. *See* Collective Bargaining.

CONTROLS, QUALITATIVE. *See* Qualitative Controls.

CONTROLS, QUANTITIVE. *See* Quantitive Controls.

CONVENIENCE DEMAND. *See* Liquidity Preference.

CONVENTION, UNION. *See* Union Convention.

CONVERGING EQUILIBRIUM, equilibrium in which price will be restored to the original level if disturbed. In this case the equilibrium price will tend to move toward its initial level.

CONVERTIBLE BONDS, bonds that give the holder the right or option to exchange his bond for a different type of security. Often, this security option is a common or preferred stock. Some convertible bonds can only be converted at maturity, although others can be converted at any time, upon due notice.

See also Bonds.

CONVERTIBLE CURRENCY, currency that can be exchanged for any other currency without loss to the holder and for whatever purpose the holder desires. Under a pure gold standard, currency is freely convertible into gold. Under the initial International Monetary Fund system it was envisaged that all currencies would be convertible into dollars and hence convertible into each other at a fixed rate via the dollar.

See also Exchange Rates; Fixed Exchange Rates; Gold Standard.

COOPERATIVISM, a form of economic organization characterized by the absence of any special capital-providing class. Workers put up the capital in producers' cooperatives. In consumers' cooperatives, historically more successful, the consumer, instead of the nonexistent capitalist, provides the capital and organizational control.

See also Associationism; Fourier, François Marie Charles; Owen, Robert.

Consult (26) International, 1968.

CORN LAWS, English tariffs on the import of grain. In 1815, following the end of the Napoleonic wars, the tariffs were increased to protect English grain prices and economic rent from import competition. The tariffs fostered a great political and economic debate which was most fruitful in the development of the theory of economic rent, free trade, and income distribution. After repeated attempts, the tariffs were repealed in 1846.

CORPORATE BONDS, interest bearing certificates issued by a corporation that promise to pay the bondholder a specified amount of money at a specified date. The main purpose of corporate bonds is to raise money for the corporation. Usually ownership of these bonds can be transferred by endorsement.

See also Bonds.

CORPORATE EARNINGS, corporate profits before taxes. In Gross National Product statistics they comprise about 10% of total earnings. Corporate income taxes are paid on corporate earnings, and what remains is paid out in dividends or kept in the corporation as internal sources of funds. These sources are important, because these funds can be combined with depreciation allowances in a given year to accommodate expansion without having to tap the capital markets or borrow from banks. This practice can have an effect on interest rates, which could also induce expansion.

See also Dividends; Interest Rates; Undistributed Profits.

Consult (22) Samuelson, 1973.

CORPORATE INCOME TAX, a direct levy on the income of corporations, first collected in the United States in 1901. A corporation currently pays 22% on its first $25,000 of income and 48% on the excess. Corporate tax costs tend to be passed on regressively in consumer prices, inasmuch as corporations are subject to virtually double taxation (they pay tax on their profits, and stockholders pay personal income tax on dividends received from the same profits).

CORPORATE STATE. *See* Fascism.

CORPORATION, the most common form of business ownership among large firms, although small firms sometimes use the corporate organization. The corporation is essentially a legal "person," with all the rights of a person. Upon application the state will grant a charter conferring these rights to a firm. Thus, the corporation separates its affairs from that of the owners. The owners are not personally responsible for the legal transactions of the corporation. This exemption is referred to as limited liability of stockholders; that is, stockholders' responsibilities are restricted to the amount invested in stock.

The corporation has the legal advantage of eternal life. Unless it is dissolved, by mutual consent of the owners, it does not die. Thus, it has the advantage of existing without major setbacks even upon the death of an owner.

In large corporations control is by an elected board of directors. The board, in turn, selects the officers of the corporation and decides on the use of profits earned. Profits are usually divided into two categories: distributed profits, which are given to stockholders and undistributed profits, which are usually reinvested.

See also Limited Liability; Partnership.
—William D. Wagoner, *Louisiana State University*

CORRELATION is a concept that refers to the degree of association between variables. We can obtain an exact measure of the relationship between the variables X and Y. We can use the coefficient of correlation, r_{xy}

$$r_{XY} = \frac{\sum_{i=1}^{N}(X_i - \overline{X})(Y_i - \overline{Y})}{\sqrt{\sum_{i=1}^{N}(X_i - \overline{X})^2 \sum_{i=1}^{N}(Y_i - \overline{Y})^2}}$$

We can shorten this formula by using deviations from the mean. Let $x_i = (X_i - \bar{X})$ and $y_i = (Y_i - \bar{Y})$.

$$r_{XY} = \frac{\sum_{i=1}^{N} xy}{\sqrt{\sum_{i=1}^{N} x^2 \sum_{i=1}^{N} y^2}}$$

The coefficient of correlation lies in the range $[+1, -1]$. If Y increases as X increases r_{xy} is positive and close to 1. If Y decreases as X increases r_{xy} is negative and close to -1. If there is no association between X and Y, $r=0$. Standard tests exist to determine whether a coefficient is significantly different from zero.

Coefficient of Determination, a measure of the proportion of the variation of Y explained by the linear influence of X. It is the square of the correlation coefficient (r). Since r_{xy} lies in the range of $[-1,1]$, r^2_{xy} can only take values between zero and one: $r^2 = 0$ implies that none of the variation of Y is explained by X, and $r^2 = 1$ implies that all of the variation of Y is explained by X. One can test if a given r^2 is significantly different from zero.

Rank Correlation Coefficient can be computed from ranked data and has the same interpretation as r.

Partial Correlation, Multiple Determination. A dependent variable can be a function of several independent variables. In $y = f(x_1, x_2)$, y will be associated with both x_1 and x_2. A measure of the association of y with x, holding z constant, is the partial correlation coefficient between y and x computed with the linear influence of z eliminated. The proportion of y explained by the combined effects of x and z is

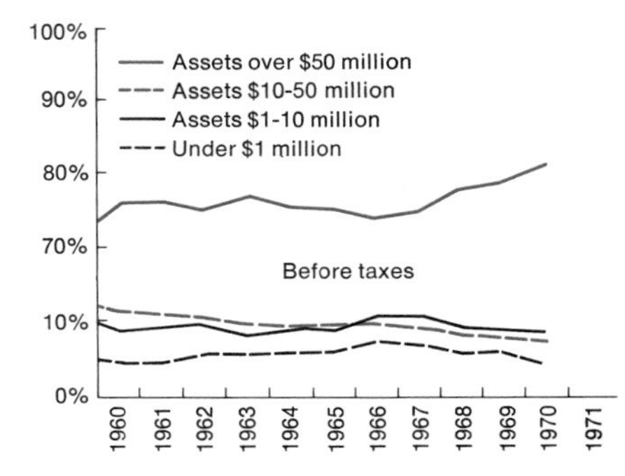

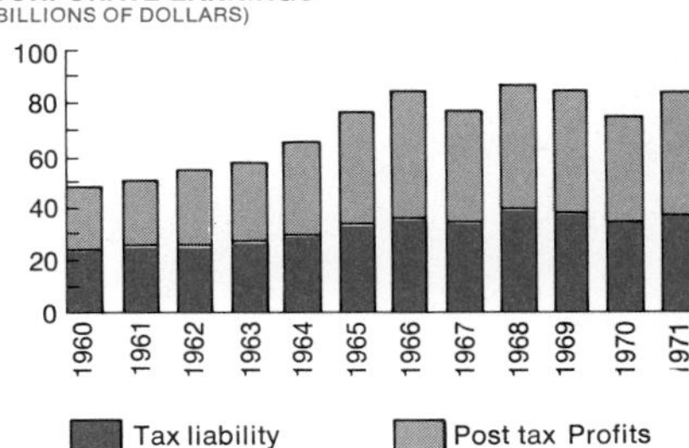

CORRELATION

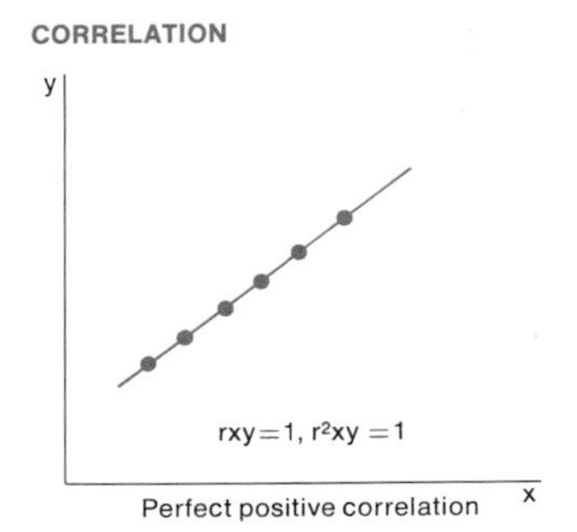

Perfect positive correlation

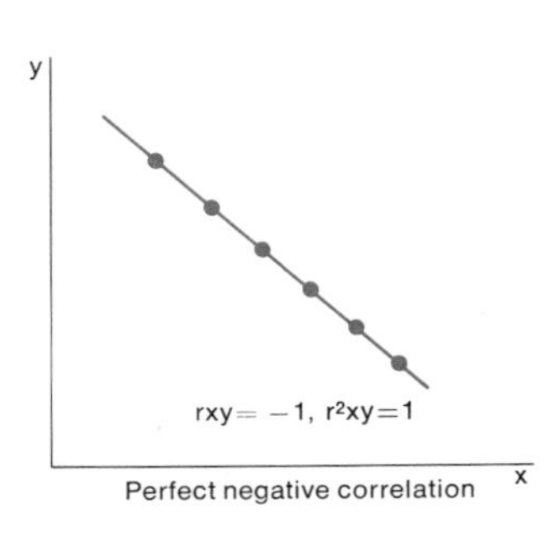

Perfect negative correlation

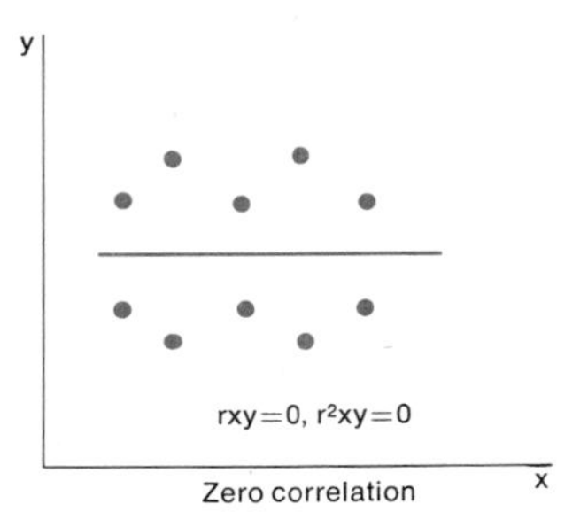

Zero correlation

COST FUNCTION

The cost function of a business firm has many aspects. For the time dimension, see the articles SHORT RUN and LONG RUN. Some of the different cost concepts in the function are explored in the articles TOTAL COST OF PRODUCTION and MARGINAL COST OF PRODUCTION. For a view of the cost function as it bears on decision making in the firm, see PROFIT MAXIMAZATION, EQUILIBRIUM OF THE FIRM, and FIRM SUPPLY CURVE.

The student will also find it useful to consult the Subject Map accompanying the article SUPPLY for further coverage of the Cost Function.

called the coefficient of multiple determination and is denoted R^2.

See also Curve Fitting; Significance.

Consult (27) Spiegel, 1961; Wonnacott, 1972.

—Carlisle E. Moody, *College of William and Mary*

CORRESPONDENT BALANCES. *See* Reserves.

COST. *See* Cost Function.

COST CURVES. *See* Cost Function.

COST FUNCTION. When a producer varies the level of his output (over some fixed period of time), he does so by changing the amounts of the inputs used in the production process, and this causes a change in the cost of production. The relationship between various levels of output and the cost of production is called a cost function. When the planning period is relatively short, certain inputs, such as the physical plant, heavy machinery, and others, remain fixed even when output is changed; other inputs, such as labor and raw materials, vary with the level of output. Consequently, the total cost of production (TC) can be separated into two types of cost: total variable cost (TVC), including all the costs which depend on the level of output, and total fixed cost (TFC), which comprises the costs that are independent of the level of output. These three concepts are related by the basic cost equation TC = TVC + TFC.

The three types of total cost are illustrated by means of the cost schedules in Table 1, showing hypothetical cost figures for the output levels 0 through 10. Input prices are assumed to be fixed, that is, they are not affected by the amounts of the inputs purchased by the producer. It is to be noted that, while TFC remains constant, both TVC and TC increase with output. Furthermore, when the level of output is zero, then TC = TFC, indicating that when no production takes place, the producer still incurs the cost of the fixed inputs—so-called overhead cost.

If the output is capable of continuous variations, then the cost functions can be depicted as continuous curves as shown in Figure 1 in which cost (in dollars) is measured on the vertical axis, and product X on the horizontal axis. TFC is a horizontal line since it is independent of the level of output. According to the diagram, TFC is equal to A dollars. TVC is an increasing function (that is, it has a positive slope), and it goes through the origin; this is so because when output is zero, TVC is also zero. The TC curve lies above the TVC curve, and the vertical distance between them is always equal to TFC, that is, A in the above example. In general, at relatively low levels of output TVC and TC increase at a decreasing rate, while at relatively high levels of output they increase at an increasing rate.

If total cost is divided by the level of output, one obtains an average cost, that is, cost per unit of output. There are three average costs: average total cost (ATC), where ATC = TC/X, average variable cost (AVC), where AVC = TVC/X, and average fixed cost (AFC), where AFC = TFC/X. If both sides of the basic cost equation TC = TVC + TFC are divided by X, one obtains ATC = AVC + AFC. Finally, marginal cost (MC) is defined as the increment in total cost due to a small increase in output. For a discrete increase in output, MC is defined as $\Delta TC/\Delta X$, where Δ denotes "change in." For an infinitesimal increase in output, that is, when cost is represented by a continuous curve, MC is defined as the slope of the TC curve (or slope of the TVC curve). All the seven types of cost are illustrated in the hypothetical cost schedules shown in Table 2.

When output varies continuously, average costs and marginal cost can be represented by continuous curves as shown in Figure 2. These curves have the following general characteristics: (a) In general, ATC, AVC, and MC are U-shaped; (b)AFC has the form of a rectangular hyperbola; (c) ATC lies above AVC; (d) The vertical distance between ATC and AVC is equal to AFC at the respective level of output; (e) MC cuts AVC where AVC has its minimum, and MC cuts ATC where ATC has its minimum; (f) In the range in which MC $<$ ATC (AVC), ATC (AVC) is falling; in the range in which MC $>$ ATC (AVC), ATC (AVC) is rising.

Consult (13) Bilas, 1971; Ferguson, 1972; Hadar, 1973.

—Josef Hadar, *Case Western Reserve University*

COST OF LIVING, a frequently used wage criterion in wage negotiations. The cost-of-living value is usually determined by the consumer price index. The union representatives use rising prices as the basis for justifying wage increases. Because wages are usually fixed from contract to contract, rising prices during the fixed periods reduce purchasing power or real wages. To avoid this, many contracts have automatic cost of living adjustments, called escalator clauses, which specify a precise relationship between changes in the cost of living and changes in the wage rates to be paid employees.

Another type of provision in many bargaining contracts states that the contract may be reopened for negotiations during the term of the contract given a specified increase in the cost of living.

Escalator clauses, the most popular cost of living provision, began in 1948 with a contract between General Motors and the United

Automobile Workers. This contract became so popular, that by 1960 more than three million workers were covered by the cost of living adjustments in labor contracts. However, in the last decade, management has become much less willing to agree to these "open end" increases in wage costs; by the mid-sixties only some two million workers were covered by escalator clauses.

See also Wage Criteria.

—William D. Wagoner, *Louisiana State University*

COST-OF-LIVING INCREASES are provided for in some collective bargaining contracts. This provision, called an escalator clause, specifies an exact relationship between a change in the cost of living during the contract period and the change in the wage rate to be paid covered employees. Because there is an "open-end" to the amount of wages an employer may have to pay, cost-of-living clauses are not very popular with management.

COST-OF-LIVING INDEX. *See* Consumer Price Index.

COST OF PRODUCTION. *See* Cost Function.

COST-PLUS PRICING. *See* Full-Cost Pricing.

COST-PUSH INFLATION, or sellers' inflation, creeping inflation that continues even in periods of deficient aggregate demand. If unions push for wage increases beyond any increases in productivity, firms with a great deal of market power may be able to pass the resulting cost increases on to the consumer. For cost-push inflation to persist, it is necessary either that the firms in question face inelastic demand for their products or that the monetary authorities increase the money supply to prevent decreases in employment and output.

See also Administered Pricing; Markup Inflation; Wage-Push Inflation.

COSTS, EXTERNAL. *See* External Costs.

COSTS, INTERNAL. *See* Internal Costs.

COST SCHEDULE. *See* Cost Function.

COUNTERCYCLICAL POLICY. *See* Monetary Policy.

COUNTERVAILING POWER, a concept developed by John Kenneth Galbraith which holds that economic organizations with original market power bring into being, and eventually are challenged by, organizations on the other side of the market who offset or countervail that original power. Whether buyers or sellers, the theory runs, these holders of original power are prevented by the countervailing sellers or buyers from abusing it.

COUNTRY BANK. *See* Member Bank.

CPI. *See* Consumer Price Index.

CRAFT UNION, an organization of workers that have in common the knowledge of a particular skill. It is the aim of the craft union to create a monopoly for a skill in order to control the market by restricting supply and thus be able to bargain effectively over wages and other benefits.

Usually conservative in nature, the craft union is very much akin to the medieval guilds. An initiation as well as an apprenticeship is usually a prerequisite for membership. Though some unions are open to any person possessing the necessary skill, others limit enrollment considerably. Some, like the Riverboat Pilots, insist that a member must die before a new member can be admitted.

CRAWLING PEG. *See* Exchange Rate.

CREATIVE DESTRUCTION. *See* Schumpeter, Joseph A.

CREDIT [Lat., I trust], the present acquisition of anything of value in exchange for the promise to return its equivalent at some time in the future. Usually credit means either buying goods with payment to be made later or borrowing money. Credit requires that the debtor pay when the debt falls due.

Individual credit is extended by private persons through occasional loans to friends, the purchase of securities, deposits in banks, or loans to other financial intermediaries. *Mercantile credit* is extended by business when it provides goods against a credit card or on open-book account to be paid at the end of the month or on the installment plan. *Finance credit* includes loans by institutions specializing in lending money: banks, finance companies, savings and loan associations, credit unions, life insurance companies, and so on.

Loans may be made to consumers, government, or business. Business loans may be short term (commercial) or long term (investment). Loans may be unsecured, or secured by mortgage or other property depending entirely on the signature of the borrower. One of the most important forms of credit in the United States is the demand deposits of commercial banks, which form the largest part of the money supply.

Credit normally carries an interest charge to reimburse the lender for the costs of carrying on the credit business, the risk of nonpayment, and the reduction of liquidity inherent in holding the debt instead of liquid

COST FUNCTION

Units of output	TC in $	TVC in $	TFC in $
0	24	0	24
1	34	10	24
2	42	18	24
3	48	24	24
4	52	28	24
5	54	30	24
6	60	36	24
7	73	49	24
8	88	64	24
9	105	81	24
10	124	100	24

Table 1

COST FUNCTION

Units of output	TC in $	TVC in $	TFC in $	ATC in $	AFC in $	AVC in $	MC in $
0	24	0	24	—	—	—	—
1	34	10	24	34	24	10	10
2	42	18	24	21	12	9	8
3	48	24	24	16	8	8	6
4	52	28	24	13	6	7	4
5	54	30	24	$10\frac{4}{5}$	$4\frac{4}{5}$	6	2
6	60	36	24	10	4	6	6
7	73	49	24	$10\frac{3}{7}$	$3\frac{3}{7}$	7	13
8	88	64	24	11	3	8	15
9	105	81	24	$11\frac{2}{3}$	$2\frac{2}{3}$	9	17
10	124	100	24	$12\frac{2}{5}$	$2\frac{2}{5}$	10	19

Table 2

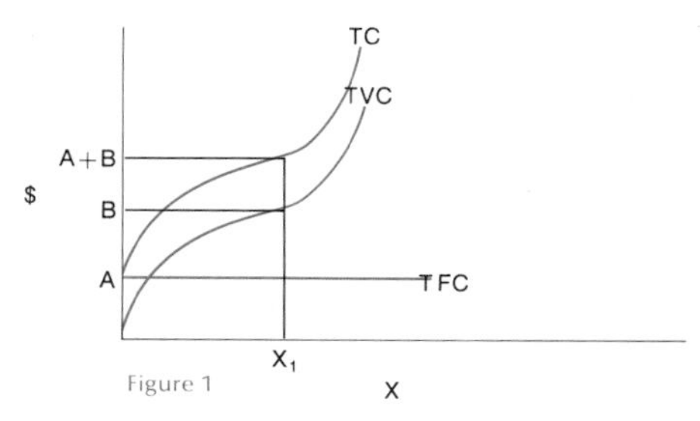

Figure 1

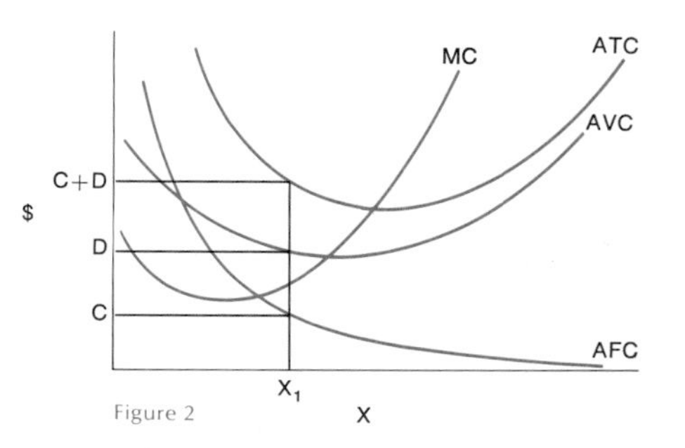

Figure 2

assests. In charge accounts, however, the interest cost is often hidden in the price of the merchandise. Interest rates tend to be higher for small loans, risky loans, and loans with long maturities.

See also Commercial Bank; Demand Deposits; Financial Intermediaries; Liquid Assets; Money Supply.

—Walter W. Haines, *New York University*

CREDIT CONTROLS. *See* Installment Credit Controls.

CREDIT TRANSACTIONS, BALANCE OF PAYMENTS. *See* Balance of Payments.

CREDIT UNIONS. *See* Financial Intermediaries.

CREEPING INFLATION, the phenomenon of persistent price level increases at a relatively low rate (1% to 4% per year). Most advanced industrial countries have experienced creeping inflation since World War II. There is much discussion among economists as to the costs and benefits of creeping inflation. Although it may increase profits and stimulate investment demand and growth, creeping inflation can result in significant redistributions of income. Even at a 3% rate of inflation, the purchasing power of the dollar will be halved in 23 years. The persistence of creeping inflation may require some structural changes in modern economies.

CRISIS. *See* Business Cycles.

CROP RESTRICTIONS have been used in the United States since 1933 in government's efforts to limit production for the purpose of keeping farm prices and incomes higher than they otherwise would be.

Early Restrictions were more commonly put on land devoted to crops than directly on the amounts of crops produced. Historically, acreage allotments for a restricted crop were assigned to farms on the basis of acreages of the crop grown in a prior base period. Efforts were made to get farmers not to exceed some selected percentage of their allotments. Marketing quotas were, in practice, compulsory acreage allotments—growers were permitted to market whatever they produced on permitted acreages. Controls were compulsory on all growers only when growers had first approved them in a referendum where the choice was between (a) price support and crop controls or (b) no price support or only nominal price support and no crop controls. Voluntary controls up to the mid-1950s usually did not attract much farmer participation because inducements for signing up were not attractive.

Another Government Dam Experiment
—Brown in the New York Herald Tribune

An anti-New Deal cartoon of 1935 expresses the fear that crop restrictions would push prices so high as to drown world trade.

Recent Controls. Beginning with the Soil Bank in 1956 and increasingly in the 1960s, government programs offered payments sufficiently high to attract enough participation into compulsory control programs. Variations in yields per acre make total production less controllable than acreage.

In the early 1970s rice, peanut, and tobacco programs used compulsory acreage allotments (for some types of tobacco, poundage quotas were also in force). For feed grains (except oats), wheat, and cotton, producers were asked to hold idle certain proportions of their allotted or base acreages; but no additional limit was imposed on acreages of these crops actually grown. Payments were offered to attract participation and, especially for wheat and cotton, to supplement producers' incomes. No control programs were in effect for hay, soybeans, and oats, the other large-area crops.

In addition to programs annually idling some land on many farms, a few programs have aimed at retiring whole farms of low productivity for several years. The Conservation Reserve of the Soil Bank was the principal example. Later programs were given little or no funding by Congress.

See also Price-Support Programs; Soil Bank.

—George E. Brandow, *Pennsylvania State University*

CROSS-FREIGHTING. *See* Cross-Hauling.

CROSS-HAULING, also cross-shipping or cross-freighting, occurs in a multiple basing-point pricing system where there is no agreement among the firms as to quotas, territorial allocation, or other market sharing. With the delivered price of the product the same at all points of delivery, the normal sales territorial limits are set only by the average rate included in the delivered price. A producer wishing to increase sales volume, however, might ship products outside the normal sales territorial limits, absorbing freight charges because he is shipping a greater distance than the freight-rate portion of the delivered price would warrant. If a producer at another shipping point, under the same delivery-price and average-freight-charge constraint, ships into the first producer's normal sales territory, the same goods are passing each other in transit. Hence, cross-hauling occurs, an essentially uneconomic process, benefiting neither producers nor consumers in the long run.

CROSS-SECTION. Observations on a variable taken at a particular point in time comprise cross-section data. Some examples are observations of consumption expenditures of different families, profits and dividends of different companies, or prices and wages of different cities. Cross-section data is available in official publications, such as the *Census of Population,* or from sample surveys.

CROSS-SECTION CONSUMPTION FUNCTION. *See* Consumption, Cross-Section.

CROSS-SHIPPING. *See* Cross-Hauling.

CROSS-SUBSTITUTION EFFECT. *See* Consumer Equilibrium.

CURRENCY, that part of the money supply consisting of coins and paper bills issued by, or under the authority of, the government. In earlier days, currency included state bank notes, national bank notes, silver certificates, and gold certificates. The only forms of American paper currency now being issued are federal reserve notes and United States notes.

CURRENCY APPRECIATION. *See* Appreciation, Currency.

CURRENCY CONTROLS. Controls are placed over the free exchange of currencies to ensure government supervision of foreign exchange transactions. Reasons may be to curb inflation, prevent speculative flows of capital, and deal with balance of payments problems. All foreign exchange is bought from and sold to an official government agency at prescribed rates. The rate system provides exchange to importers at low rates for those imports desired by the government while those it wishes to discourage are charged higher rates. Exports the government wishes to promote command higher rates in payment for foreign exchange than those offered to exporters shipping goods the government wishes to discourage. Through this mechanism the balance of payments can be kept under control while domestic programs are promoted. Licensing and bilateral trade and payments agreements are other examples of currency controls. All imply inconvertibility of the currency.

See also Balance of Payments; Capital Movement; Exchange Rates.

Consult (23) Wexler, 1972.

CURRENCY DEPRECIATION. *See* Depreciation, Currency.

CURRENT MARKET VALUE. *See* Current Value.

CURRENT VALUE. GNP is normally defined in terms of current market value, or the quantities of various outputs—final goods and services—multiplied by their respective prices and summed together. Thus, GNP may change because of a change in prices, a change in the quantities of goods and services produced, or some combination of the two. This use of current market value is justified on the basis that it is perhaps the easiest and least expensive technique for the measurement of overall economic activity. Once GNP in current value is estimated, various techniques can be employed to remove the impact of price change. One reservation should be made: some items in GNP do not really have a price, for no actual market transaction that yields a price has taken place. Examples of this reservation include the rental value of owner-occupied housing, certain services provided by financial intermediaries, and income in kind.

See also Constant Value.

CURVE FITTING. In economics one postulates many functional relationships among variables, for example, the consumption function, and the demand and supply functions. In many cases even the form of the function is specified by the theory. The consumption function is usually assumed to be linear with a slope (marginal propensity to consume) between 0 and 1. If the assumptions concerning the relationships are true, one would expect that data gathered on income and consumption and plotted on a scatter diagram would lie approximately along a line $C = a + bY$. The process of estimating the parameters a and b in such a way as to approximate the points on the scatter diagram is called curve fitting.

The most common technique used to estimate a functional relationship is least-squares regression. The first step in regression is to transform the data if necessary so as to derive a linear relationship. Any polynomial and many exponential and logarithmic functions can be made linear for estimation purposes. The next step is to choose the estimates of a and b in such a way that the sum of the squared errors is at a minimum. A correlation coefficient will then measure the success of the regression and the validity of the theory.

See also Best Fit; Correlation; Hypothesis; Significance.

Consult (27) Kane, 1968.

—Carlisle E. Moody, *College of William and Mary*

CUSTOM DUTY. *See* Tariffs.

CUSTOMS UNIONS AND FREE TRADE AREAS. Countries form a customs union if they remove all trade restrictions between one another and erect a common tariff against the rest of the world. If the countries retain their individual tariff structures against the outside world, then their grouping is called a free-trade area. The European Economic Community (EEC), also called the Common Market, was established in 1957 uniting France, Germany, Italy, Belgium, the Netherlands, and Luxembourg in a customs union. Examples of a free-trade area are the European Free-Trade Association (EFTA) and the Latin American Free-Trade Area (LAFTA).

CUTTHROAT COMPETITION, an intense type of competition usually engaged in by firms intending to eliminate a business rival, or intending to gain a major portion of the rival's consumers. After the elimination of the rival, the firm may recoup its losses by setting relatively high prices. This type of competition may be used to create a monopoly and may, therefore, be illegal.

CYCLICAL BALANCED BUDGET, budgetary principle advocating the balancing of the budget over the course of a complete business cycle rather than in particular fiscal or calendar years. Over the course of the cycle, tax receipts and expenditures would be equal. Under this principle, a surplus budget is called for during times of prosperity to restrain inflationary pressures and a deficit budget is called for under the condition of cyclical depression in order to stimulate the economy. Ideally, the surpluses and deficits would offset each other over the period of the cycle, thus providing budget balance. The absence of a built-in mechanism to assure a symmetrical cycle is a major obstacle confronting this type of policy.

See also Balanced Budget.

CYCLICAL EXCESS CAPACITY. *See* Excess Capacity.

CYCLICAL UNEMPLOYMENT has become the dominant form of unemployment in our modern economy. It is the result of recurrent fluctuations in business activity which has been called the business cycle. While the business cycle has always existed since American industrial development, mass unemployment of a cyclical nature was not a problem until the Great Depression of the 1930s.

The basic concept of cyclical unemployment is that as business activities begin to rise, unemployment begins to decrease and likewise, as the business cycle declines, unemployment rises.

The effect of cyclical unemployment was felt most severely during the early 1930s but other business cycle troughs occurred in 1949, 1954, 1958, 1961, and 1972 while unemployment rates were at cycle lows in 1948, 1953, 1957, 1960, and 1969.

Although the economy seems less susceptible in recent years to the extreme boom-depression cycle of the 1920s and 1930s, cyclical unemployment still exists.

See also Unemployment of Labor.

Das Kapital.

Kritik der politischen Oekonomie.

Von

Karl Marx.

Erster Band.

Buch I: Der Produktionsprocess des Kapitals.

Das Recht der Uebersetzung wird vorbehalten.

Hamburg

Verlag von Otto Meissner.

1867.

New-York: L. W. Schmidt. 24 Barclay-Street.

In *Das Kapital,* Marx attacked classical economists and stated his own revolutionary theories.

DAS KAPITAL represents the final development of Karl Marx's economics. The first volume was published by Marx in 1867 with the second and third volumes edited and published by Friedrich Engels after Marx's death.

Based upon the labor theory of value and Hegelian philosophy, Marx developed a criticism of classical economics. He felt that classical economists had become apologists for bourgeois interests, and that the profit of the capitalist was derived from the exploitation of labor. Accepting the widely held classical belief in the falling rate of profit, Marx felt that the capitalistic system would lead to a concentration of capital in the hands of a small group who would then be forced to increase the rate of exploitation of labor. As the standard of living of workers declines, they become more willing to revolt and the basis for the end of the capitalistic system comes into being. "The knell of capitalist private property sounds. The expropriators are expropriated."

See also Labor Theory of Value; Revolutionary Socialism.

DEBENTURES are vouchers or certificates that acknowledge a debt owed by the issuer. In finance a debenture bond is an unsecured bond backed only by the general credit standing of the agency that issued it. Bonds that back direct obligations of the government are examples of debentures, because they are secured only by the taxing power of the government. These differ from revenue bonds of the government that are backed by revenue received from a certain project.

DEBIT TRANSACTIONS, BALANCE OF PAYMENTS. *See* Balance of Payments.

DEBREU, GERALD (1921–), French-born educator and economist who has made valuable contributions to mathematical economics and general equilibrium. He received his Doctor of Science degree from the University of Paris in 1956. He is author of *Theory of Value* (1959), and he has been associate editor of the *International Economic Review* since 1959. He was on the faculty at Yale (1955–61) and became professor of economics at the University of California at Berkeley in 1962.

DEBS, EUGENE VICTOR (1855–1926), trade union leader, founder of the Socialist party. Debs was born of immigrant parents in Terre Haute, Ind. A railroad worker at fourteen, he became an officer of his local in 1875, and by 1880 was secretary-treasurer of the National Brotherhood of Railway Firemen.

In 1893 Debs founded the American Railway Union, organized on industrial lines and open to all crafts. In the Pullman strike of 1894, which was broken by violence and the courts, he was jailed six months for violating an injunction. In jail Debs studied socialism, and upon release he worked with Victor L. Berger to consolidate radical factions to form the Socialist party. Debs ran as Socialist candidate for president in five elections, starting in 1900; in 1912 he received 6% of the popular vote.

Convicted in 1918 for speaking against participation in World War I, he was sentenced to ten years imprisonment. He campaigned from inside Atlanta Penitentiary and received 919,801 votes for president. In response to public pressure President Harding commuted Debs' sentence in 1921. After his release and the decline of his party, Debs wrote on prison conditions and edited the socialist weekly *American Appeal.*

DEBT CEILING, a limit set by Congress on the amount of federal debt that may be outstanding during a time period. The debt has grown consistently and often approaches this ceiling. Because the debt ceiling is raised so often, it does not actually limit the federal debt but rather it serves to force periodic reviews of federal finances. Sometimes, when the debt approaches the ceiling, the Treasury uses financing methods which do not increase the debt but which actually cost more than borrowing. This is often cited as an argument against a debt ceiling.

DEBT MANAGEMENT. Management of the federal debt consists of interest payments on current issues of securities, sales of new securities, refunding of old securities when deficit budgets necessitate it, and staggering of maturity dates to avoid excess pressure for refunding.

DECEPTIVE ADVERTISING, that which misleads the consumer in some material respect about a product offered for sale. This current legal position, supplanting the earlier view that deceptive advertising is that which misleads the consumer in any particular, recognizes that while some exaggeration or "puffing" of claims for a product is inevitable, the consumer is entitled to protection against substantial misstatement or intent to deceive.

Deceptive advertising is prohibited in the Wheeler-Lea Act of 1938. It is generally recognized, however, that a less-than-successful enforcement record has resulted from the vastness of business' advertising effort, the limited staff and budget of the Federal Trade Commission (empowered to police interstate advertising), the time consumed in prosecuting one violation of the law, and the deficiency of penalties for deceptive advertising.

See also Antitrust Policy; Federal Trade Commission; Unfair and Deceptive Practices; Wheeler-Lea Act.

DECEPTIVE PRACTICES. *See* Unfair and Deceptive Practices.

DECILE. *See* Central Tendency.

DECREASE IN DEMAND, the shifting downward and to the left on the Cartesian plane of a demand function. This graphical shift indicates that a smaller quantity of a good is being purchased at every price. The position of a demand function depends upon the incomes, tastes and preferences, and expectations of buyers, as well as the prices of related goods. If one of these determinants of a demand function's position changes appropriately, it will result in a new demand function being defined. If the new function shows smaller quantities demanded at each price, demand is said to have decreased.

Decreases in income cause demand curves for normal goods to decrease. Adverse trends in consumer preference will result in decreased demand. Increases in complementary goods' prices and decreases in substitute goods' prices will decrease demand. If a depression in prices were expected by the economic community, it is likely that it would refrain from buying as much of any commodity as was purchased previous to the change in price expectations, causing a decrease in demand.

—Robert L. Brite, *Louisiana State University*

DECREASE IN SUPPLY means that quantity supplied will be smaller at every price than it was previous to the change in circumstances. Graphically, the supply curve shifts backward to the left. If wage rates rise for a firm, technology (and therefore marginal product of labor) remaining constant, then marginal cost will now be greater at any given output than it was previously. The marginal cost curve therefore rises; costs of production have been increased. Due to the increased marginal costs, the firm will require higher prices before it will produce given outputs voluntarily, otherwise profits will fall unnecessarily.

DECREASING-COST INDUSTRY. Since constant-cost industries have supply schedules with zero slope (parallel to the horizontal axis), and increasing-cost industries have supply schedules that are positively sloped, one might expect negatively sloped supply schedules for decreasing-cost industries. However, this is not the case.

If the firm is producing where P=MC, (selling price equals marginal cost of output), then it should be in equilibrium. But if this firm expands, its unit costs will fall, and further and further expansion will result. The first firm to expand will have competitive advantages. Persisting decreasing costs will inevitably lead to the breakdown of perfect competition; either oligopoly or outright monopoly will result.

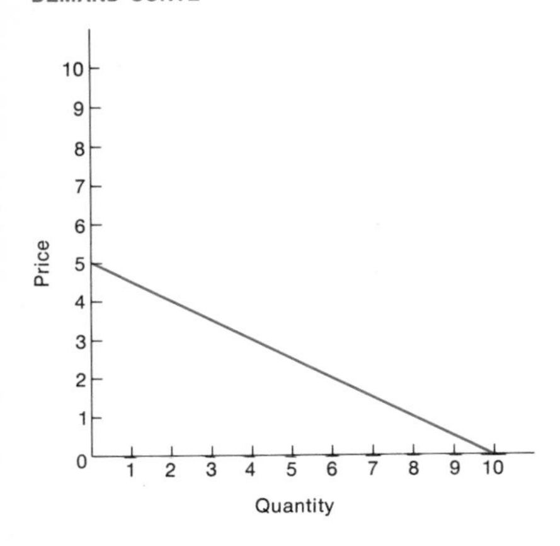

DEMAND

Demand is an essential concept in both macroeconomic and microeconomic analysis. For its macro meaning and significance consult the article on NATIONAL INCOME DETERMINATION. The components of total demand can be examined in the articles on CONSUMPTION, INVESTMENT, and GOVERNMENT SPENDING.

For the micro aspects of demand begin with the articles on CONSUMER DEMAND and MARKET DEMAND. For the expression of demand see DEMAND SCHEDULE and DEMAND CURVE; the conceptual basis for these expressions is explained in DEMAND THEORY.

The Subject Maps accompanying the articles on DEMAND THEORY and NATIONAL INCOME help to clarify the concept of Demand in economic analysis.

DEFICIT BALANCE OF TRADE. *See* Balance of Trade.

DEFLATION, a decrease in the general level of prices or an increase in the value of money in terms of goods and services. In a deflationary period, falling prices are usually accompanied by declining levels of both output and employment caused by a deficiency in the amount of spending in the economy. The main problem with deflation is that as output decreases, people have less goods and services available, and individuals have a greater chance of losing their jobs than in a stable economy.

As with inflation, deflation has a redistribution impact on income in several ways. For example, those people that have fixed incomes, such as pensioners, benefit by a deflationary period, because it raises their real income or purchasing power. Deflation also benefits creditors at the expense of debtors, who pay back money that has more purchasing power than the money originally borrowed. A third distribution effect of deflation is that it increases the value of savings in the same way that it aids creditors.

See also Inflation.

—William D. Wagoner, *Louisiana State University*

DEFLATIONARY GAP. *See* Inflationary Gap.

DEMAND, the relationship between the quantity of a commodity that consumers desire to purchase and the various prices that can exist for the commodity. Individuals desire commodities to achieve progressively higher levels of satisfaction. If all desires were satiable and if resources were unlimited, then the concept of demand would be sterile and academic: to completely satiate himself an individual would merely go to some central distribution point and lay claim to all the goods and services that he could possibly consume. Given the virtual infinity of human desires and the finite nature of the world's resources, such utopian conditions will never be met.

Satisfaction-fulfilling goods being scarce, and human wants being unlimited, a system of individual and community priorities must be developed to allocate goods. In market societies the products are distributed to those persons who are willing and able to purchase them. The price determinant of quantity demanded becomes a rationing device for allocating the scarce goods among their many demanders. The concept of demand applies to all economic societies. Although it is much easier to understand the demand function's application in market societies, even the strictest command societies must heed the concept.

See also Demand Theory.

—Robert L. Brite, *Louisiana State University*

DEMAND, FACTOR. *See* Factor Demand.

DEMAND CHANGE. *See* Demand Shift.

DEMAND CURVE, a graphic representation of the relationship between price and quantity demanded. The construction of a demand curve is accomplished by plotting the number of units of a commodity demanded per unit of time along the horizontal axis (abscissa) of a Cartesian coordinate plane. The vertical axis (ordinate) of the Cartesian plane is used to identify price data. The empirical price and corresponding quantity demanded can then be identified by a point on the plane. A locus of points defines a linear or curvilinear relationship, which is the demand curve.

Demand curves may also be described by a mathematical expression defining the curve (a demand function). The particular form of a demand function is that the quantity demanded of some commodity is a function of the price of that commodity, $q = f(p)$. The linear demand function $q = 10 - 2p$ is shown.

One important characteristic of a demand relationship expressed in functional form is that quantities demanded may be predicted for prices that have not been observed in the construction of the relationship. In the previous example, even if price had never been observed to be $2, a prediction that the quantity demanded would be 6 units per time period at that price could be made. Although, for pedagogic purposes, linear demand curves are most often used in economic examples, demand functions may be used to describe hyperbolic and other curvilinear demand curves when the data so indicate.

—Robert L. Brite, *Louisiana State University*

DEMAND CURVE, FIRM. *See* Firm Demand Curve.

DEMAND DEPOSITS, or CHECKING ACCOUNTS, liabilities of commercial banks that are owed to their customers and payable on demand whenever they write checks. When a person deposits money in his account, the bank obtains a cash asset in exchange for its promise to pay the money back when asked (demand deposit liability). On the other hand, when a borrower obtains a loan from a commercial bank, he gives the bank his promise to repay at the agreed future time and receives a credit to his account, against which he can draw checks just as if he had deposited cash. The bank thus increases its assets (the borrower's IOU) and its liabilities (demand deposits payable to the borrower).

Because people can pay their bills with checks written on their accounts, demand deposits are money, and every time a borrower is given a loan in the form of a deposit credit, the money supply is increased. Thus, commercial banks create money by making loans. Demand deposits account for three quarters of the total money supply in the United States, and payments by check are estimated to account for over 90% of all payments in terms of dollar value.

See also Time Deposits.

DEMAND FOR CAPITAL. Capital as a factor of production is generally defined as durable inputs, such as machinery and buildings, that are used to produce other goods. The demand for factors is derived from the demand for the goods and services they produce. As more of one factor is added while the others remain constant, productivity and returns diminish at the margin: the last unit added increases total output by less than the prior unit, so the revenue added by one more input goes down. If input costs remain the same (or rise), a point is reached when an input costs more than it adds to revenue. Hence, the demand for capital implies a cost-revenue decision.

Return. If a particular unit of capital produces more goods and services than were used to produce the unit itself, there is a positive return. The difference in output has a value in the market for which people are willing to pay; but capital is generally purchased for use over a relatively long period of time, far in advance of any increase in output and revenue. This time interval is important in terms of the opportunity costs involved in tying up funds, and also because the returns being considered are expectations. Therefore, the principal determinant of the demand for the capital is the expected rate of return (in either money or real terms), and the expected rate is subject to diminishing marginal productivity.

See also Discounted Value; Factors of Production; Opportunity Costs; Present Value.

Consult (22) Eckaus, 1972; Fusfeld, 1972; Peterson, 1971; Samuelson, 1973.

—John R. Matthews, Jr., *College of William and Mary*

DEMAND FOR LABOR is derived, as is the demand for other factors of production, from the demand for consumer goods and services. The price of labor (wages) relative to the other factors, and the efficiency of labor relative to the other factors, determine how much labor will be used to fill a given demand for goods and services. Thus, on an overall level, high wages and low interest have encouraged the U.S. employer to substitute capital equipment for workers, while low wages and high interest in certain underdeveloped countries have encouraged the use of human power.

Marginal Productivity Theory. Perhaps the most widely accepted statement explaining the demand for labor is the marginal productivity theory. Given a market, or other fixed wage rate, and assuming that all markets involved are competitive and the other factors of production are fixed in quantity, the employer settles on a level of operation at which the marginal revenue product of labor is equal to the wage rate.

The first point to observe is that the average output varies as the number of workers changes. As more workers are added the average may rise in the early stages, but at some point it must fall. Another way to say this is that the amount added to total output by the last worker hired changes. This amount, called the marginal physical product of labor, multiplied by the price at which the output sells is called the marginal revenue product (MRP) of labor, and this MRP and the wage rate determine the number of workers the employer hires. Thus, if the MRP exceeds the wage rate the employer continues to hire additional workers. If the wage rate exceeds the MRP he must decrease his work force.

Raising Wages. It is often said that any successful attempt to raise wages by governmental action or by union activity can result only in unemployment. That is because if the wage rate is increased by restricting supply or by minimum wage legislation, and if the MRP is not also increased, then the employer must bring the two factors, wages and MRP, back into equality by reducing the number of workers and thus increasing the marginal physical product. The only other way to raise wages without unemployment, would be to raise prices (drop the competitive assumption) or to raise the marginal physical product through better management practices or worker improvement.

See also Labor Market.

Consult (20) Baerwald, 1967; Bloom, 1965; Cohen, 1966.

—William D. Wagoner, *Louisiana State University*

DEMAND FOR MONEY has two meanings. In its literal sense, the desire to hold money for its own sake is liquidity preference and is one of the two basic determinants of interest rates. Demand for money is also used to mean the desire for cash rather than the equivalent in demand deposits. In this sense an increased demand for money results in a cash drain from the banking system and reduces the ability of commercial banks to produce a multiple expansion of the money supply.

See also Multiple Expansion of the Money Supply.

DEMAND FUNCTION. *See* Demand Curve.

DEMAND LOANS. *See* Call Loans.

DEMAND-PULL INFLATION, or Buyers' Inflation, occurs when aggregate demand is greater than the full-employment capacity output of the economy: an inflationary gap exists, and the only way aggregate supply can increase is through rising prices. Even in the absence of active monetary and fiscal policies to reduce aggregate demand, a demand-pull inflation must eventually come to an end if the money supply is not increased. As prices rise, more of the money supply must be used for transactions, making less available for lending at existing interest rates. Interest rates will therefore increase, causing investment demand and aggregate demand to fall off. However, as long as the money supply increases, the inflation can continue, because the same rising product prices that reduce the purchasing power of the dollar increase the money incomes of the workers and owners. The rising money incomes fuel the next round of inflation.

DEMAND SCHEDULE, a table recording the number of units of a commodity demanded per unit of time at various money prices.

The values in this schedule are the result of empirical observation during various time periods. For example, during the first time period when the price of this commodity was $8 per unit, 2 units were purchased. During a subsequent time period, when the price was $4 per unit, 6 units of the commodity were purchased. The presentation of numerical demand data in this tabular form is one of the methods by which economic relationships are quantified. This particular method of quantification transmits demand data in such a way that pricing and output decisions by firms may be made without necessarily relying upon other more intricate methods to quantify the price-quantity relationship.

DEMAND SCHEDULE

Units demanded per time period	Price (in dollars)
2	$8
4	$6
6	$4
8	$2
10	$1

DEMAND SHIFT, alteration of an entire demand function as differentiated from movement along a given demand curve when the number of units of a commodity purchased changes in response to a change in its price, a change in quantity demand. When a specific demand function is identified, certain parameters are held constant: taste, income, expectations of future price changes, and the prices of related commodities. However, in the real world these determinants of demand do change. Consumers come to desire certain products more or less in response to changes in their incomes, personal tastes, or expectations about inflation or deflation. The response of consumption patterns resulting from these changes causes entire demand functions to change. A change in demand for a commodity is evidenced by a different quantity of the commodity being demanded at every price.

DEMAND-SHIFT INFLATION. *See* Sectoral Inflation.

DEMAND THEORY, a plausible explanation of the manner in which purchasers of commodities respond to price changes. It is an empirical fact that consumers purchase more of a good or service at a low price than at a high price. The various demand theories attempt to discover why consumers behave in such a manner.

Assumptions. In order to explain purchasing behavior, it must be assumed that individuals are rational and that they undertake their apparantly uncoordinated economic activities in an attempt to achieve a maximum level of satisfaction. This attempt is subject to various constraints: a person cannot effectively pursue an unfettered hedonistic existence in a world where goods, services, resources, and incomes are limited. The principal constraints affecting an individual's demand behavior are his income, his taste and preference functions, expectations about future price changes, and the market prices of all goods. However, at least in the short run, the principal factor influencing the amount purchased of a given commodity is its price.

If all the other determinants of demand are held constant, the response of demand to a change in price can be quantified. The resultant relationship is the individual's demand function for a given commodity.

Conclusions. One reason a consumer buys more of a good at lower prices than at higher ones lies in his willingness and ability to purchase. Another key to demand behavior is the psychological proclivity to prefer more of the things he has few of and not so many more of the things that he has in abundance: additional units of a good provide smaller additions to total satisfaction than previous units consumed (the law of diminishing marginal utility). So, in order for a consumer to be willing to purchase more of a good, its price must fall. In combination with this willingness to purchase must go the ability to purchase (the real income effect of a price change). If the price of a commodity does fall, a constant level of money expenditure allows the purchaser to obtain more of the good in question: his real income has increased. The net result of this analysis is to provide a logical system to explain the behavior of consumers in allocating their money incomes between competing uses in which they are interested.

—Robert L. Brite, *Louisiana State University*

DEMOCRATIC (LIBERAL) SOCIALISM, an economic system that combines state ownership of at least some of the means of production and a set of democratic political institutions. Significant economic freedom to the consumer is afforded by permitting both consumer choice and some degree of consumer sovereignty.

DEMAND THEORY

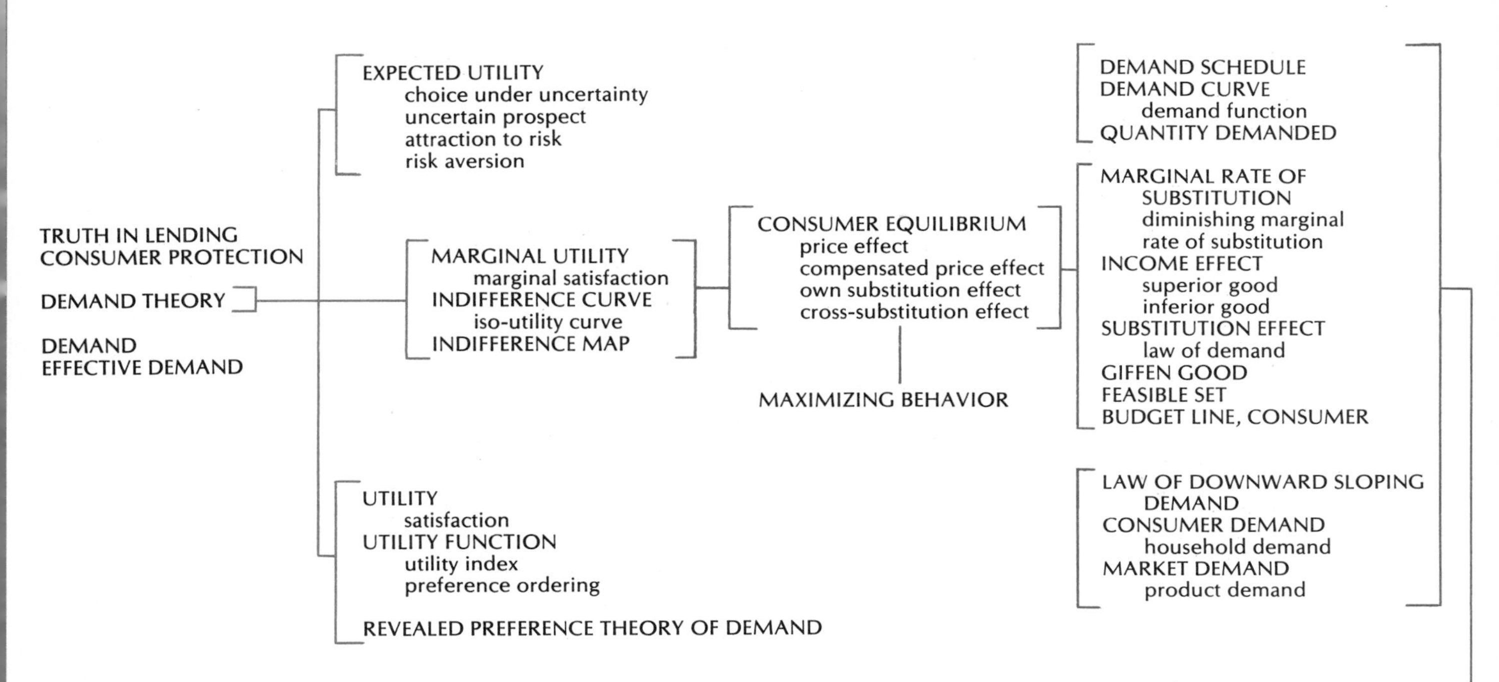

DEMAND SHIFT
- demand change

INCREASE IN DEMAND
DECREASE IN DEMAND

ELASTICITY OF DEMAND
- total-revenue test
- ELASTIC DEMAND
  - relatively elastic demand
  - perfectly elastic demand
  - totally elastic demand
  - infinitely elastic demand
  - horizontal demand curve
- INELASTIC DEMAND
  - relatively inelastic demand
  - perfectly inelastic demand
  - totally inelastic demand
  - VERTICAL DEMAND CURVE
- UNIT ELASTICITY OF DEMAND
- COEFFICIENT OF ELASTICITY OF DEMAND
- INCOME ELASTICITY OF DEMAND
- PRICE ELASTICITY OF DEMAND
  - POINT ELASTICITY
  - ARC ELASTICITY
  - SHORT-RUN ELASTICITY OF DEMAND
  - LONG-RUN ELASTICITY OF DEMAND
- SUBSTITUTE GOODS
- COMPLEMENTARY GOODS

The Subject Maps in the Encyclopedia illustrate the coverage of particular aspects of economics, showing the interrelationships among the articles in twenty-one critical areas of study. Entries in capital letters are subjects for which there are separate articles in the Encyclopedia. Entries in small letters are references to the article immediately above and provide some idea of content.

The Subject Maps are arranged alphabetically in the Encyclopedia under the following titles:

Antitrust Policy
Banking System
Business Cycles
Capital
Circular Flow of Income
Demand Theory
Economic Systems
Factor Markets
Federal Budget
History of Economic Ideas
International Trade Theory
Labor Market
Labor Movement
Market System
Money and Monetary Policy
National Income
Price Level
Regulation
Supply
Theory of the Firm
Wages

Democratic socialism is envisioned as coming about by evolutionary processes, chiefly through the ballot box. Its principal goals are less income disparity (by reduction of private property) and more stable economic growth and employment (by a smoother investment stream).

DEMONSTRATION EFFECT (or Rising Expectations) refers to the effect of the desires and expectations of the peoples, particularly in underdeveloped or poor nations, who have become aware of their poverty and the high standards of the highly developed, wealthy nations. Because of the advances in transport and communications, the horizons of these peoples are no longer limited to their own society. They observe better conditions in other economies and demand the same for themselves, notwithstanding the inability of the economy and society, without extra economic assistance, to satisfy those desires. This effect is also referred to as the phenomenon of rising expectations.

DEPENDENT VARIABLE. *See* Variable.

DEPLETION, reduction in the value of natural resources due to the extraction of natural wealth, such as gas, oil, timber, or minerals.

DEPOSIT CREATION. *See* Multiple Expansion of the Money Supply.

DEPOSITS. *See* Balance Sheet, Bank; Demand Deposits; Time Deposits.

DEPRECIATION, reduction in value, quality, and usefulness of a fixed asset (plant or equipment) because of physical deterioration, destruction, or obsolescence resulting from technological development. The annual amount of depreciation equals the original purchase price less the estimated salvage value divided by the estimated useful life of the fixed asset (straight-line or installment method depreciation). Other methods of calculating depreciation are the diminishing-value method, in which more depreciation is taken at the beginning, when the greatest loss is assumed to occur, and the production method, in which depreciation is charged in proportion to actual use.

DEPRECIATION, CURRENCY. A currency is depreciated when it undergoes a loss of purchasing power, either domestically or internationally. Domestic depreciation is usually related to inflationary increases in prices; international depreciation is reflected in a rise in the rates of exchange on foreign currencies. In the U.S. exchange market an increased demand for a given foreign currency relative to its supply drives up the rate on that currency while that country's rate on the dollar falls. Hence, in terms of the other currency, the dollar is worth less and if the same amount of imports from that country continues it will necessitate larger dollar payments. Conversely, it will cost the other country less to import from the United States.

See also Devaluation; Exchange Rates.

DEPRESSION. *See* Business Cycles, Phases.

DERIVED DEMAND. *See* Factor Demand.

DEVALUATION, a reduction in the gold content of a currency valued in terms of gold. In 1934 and 1972 the United States devalued by raising the dollar price of an ounce of gold from $20.67 to $35.00 in the first instance and to $38.00 in the latter. A major purpose of these moves was to help the balance of payments by increasing the purchasing power of foreigners vis-à-vis the dollar and increasing the dollar cost of imports. Under International Monetary Fund rules all countries except the United States can devalue in terms of the dollar by establishing new parities.

If a country runs a persistent deficit in its balance of payments and meets this deficit by losing international reserves, there is a clear indication that (1) the country's currency is overvalued relative to its international status, or (2) its trading partners have undervalued currencies. To correct this situation, the deficit country can devalue, or the surplus countries can appreciate. Historically, the burden has usually rested on the deficit country. As a solution, devaluation is preferable to inducing a domestic recession; but countries are hesitant to devalue formally, because devaluation generally creates speculative pressures that could necessitate another devaluation.

See also Appreciation; Depreciation; Exchange Rate; Undervaluation.

—John R. Matthews, Jr., *College of William and Mary*

DEVELOPING NATIONS, an expression adopted by the United Nations to refer to underdeveloped countries with poverty-level incomes per capita. Most such countries are located in Africa, Asia, and Latin America and are characterized by illiteracy, disguised unemployment, overpopulation, and reliance on a few export items, generally raw materials. Their economies are predominantly agricultural, although some have well-developed handicrafts.

Economic Growth. In the drive for economic growth, developing nations try to stimulate and encourage private and public capital investments, institute educational and vocational training programs, increase productivity, and, in general, raise their standards of living.

In most undeveloped countries, economic development begins with a high degree of government planning and a large amount of foreign technical and financial aid. The International Bank for Reconstruction and Development (World Bank) provides loans and grants to finance basic development projects, such as dams, communications and transport facilities, and a variety of health and educational programs.

UNESCO, the United States, the USSR, and several other countries maintain a number of technical assistance programs. They are specifically designed to accelerate the pace of industrial development and therefore help to achieve economic independence and make the most effective use of their human and material resources.

See also Less Developed Countries; Stages of Growth; Underdevelopment.

DEVIATION. *See* Dispersion.

DI. *See* Disposable Personal Income.

DICTATORSHIP OF THE PROLETARIAT, a political and economic transition period between capitalism and communism, during which the state, acting on behalf of the proletariat, oppresses and eventually destroys the capitalist class and its institutions. The means of production are no longer in private hands, even though the technology and the organization of production remain very similar to those under capitalism. The worker's pay is determined by his contributions to production; those who do not work are not paid. A Communist society evolves out of the socialistic dictatorship of the proletariat.

DIFFUSION INDEX. *See* Indices.

DIMINISHING MARGINAL PHYSICAL PRODUCTIVITY. As more and more units of a factor are used in the productive process, other inputs being held constant, then eventually the marginal product of the factor will fall, according to the famous law of diminishing returns. In the early stages of production, marginal product may rise, however, due to specialization advantages. The point at which total product ceases to increase at an increasing rate and starts to increase at a decreasing rate (inflection point) is the point of diminishing returns. The diminishing marginal product schedule is the basis for downward sloping factor demand curves.

DIMINISHING MARGINAL RATE OF SUBSTITUTION. *See* Marginal Rate of Substitution.

DIMINISHING MARGINAL UTILITY. *See* Demand Theory.

DIMINISHING RETURNS. *See* Law of Diminishing Returns.

DIRECT INVESTMENT, a term used in international economics for the purchase of land and its natural resources, such as plantations or mines, and the purchase or construction of income-producing real capital, such as oil well rigs or factories in foreign countries. Direct investment results in the ownership and management of land and capital by nationals of one country in another. Direct investment contrasts with portfolio investment, which occurs when nationals of one country buy shares in foreign businesses owned and managed by nationals of another country.

DISABILITY INSURANCE, payments to a worker covered by Social Security who becomes unable to work because of a disability. Payment levels generally coincide with Social Security benefits the worker and his dependents would receive if he were 65.

See also Social Insurance; Social Security.

DISCOUNTED VALUE, the amount that, when accumulated at the given rate over a certain period, equals the final amount. A 90-day $1000 loan from a bank discounted at 7% would net the borrower $983.40, and he would repay $1000. What the bank has done is place a present (capitalized) value on a specific income stream at a given rate.

See also Marginal Efficiency of Capital; Present Value.

DISCOUNT RATE, formerly called the rediscount rate, the interest rate charged by the federal reserve banks on loans to member banks. These loans are sometimes referred to as being made through the "discount window." They are usually made for periods of fifteen days or less.

The discount rate is established by each of the twelve federal reserve banks subject to "review and determination" by the Board of Governors of the federal reserve system. An increase in the discount rate makes borrowing more expensive, thereby discouraging such loans, keeping bank reserves low, and reducing the ability of commercial banks to create a multiple expansion of the money supply. A reduction in the discount rate has the opposite effect, thereby encouraging an expansion of the money supply.

When the federal reserve system was established in 1914, it was thought that discounting would be the normal way for commercial banks to obtain reserves and that changes in the discount rate would be the primary tool of monetary policy. It was also believed desirable that control be localized with each federal reserve bank, thus adjusting monetary policy to the specific conditions of each region. Today banks do very little discounting, and the effect of changes in the rate is almost exclusively psychological, because the banks publicize suggested policies. Further, the nation's monetary markets have been unified to such an extent that local differences are no longer desirable, and changes in discount rates are normally initiated by the Federal Open Market Committee, even though they are still announced by the individual federal reserve banks.

See also Free Reserves.

Consult (10) Anderson, 1966.

—Walter W. Haines, *New York University*

DISCOUNTS. *See* Loans and Discounts.

DISCOUNT WINDOW. *See* Discount Rate.

DISCRETE VARIABLE. *See* Variable.

DISECONOMIES OF SCALE. *See* Economies of Scale.

DISEQUILIBRIUM. *See* Equilibrium.

DISEQUILIBRIUM, BALANCE OF PAYMENTS. *See* Balance of Payments.

DISGUISED UNEMPLOYMENT refers to a situation that occurs when a decrease in aggregate demand, or in the case of less developed nations, no demand, leads to the withdrawal of labor into occupations with little or no marginal productivity. In other words, resources are not employed most effectively, and labor is underemployed. In rural areas and underdeveloped countries where agriculture is predominant, there is a high rate of disguised unemployment because there is little for the people to do during off season. Such people do not appear in the unemployment statistics because they are not seeking work.

This situation also exists in urban areas, where the skilled and educated earn livings in low productivity or low income employment, either by choice or because more constructive, high productivity employment is unavailable. Another example that has received considerable recent attention is the alienation from the economy of the so-called counterculture or subculture. From the economic viewpoint, a society that creates or allows such alienation is underemploying its human resources.

See also Underemployment.

DISINTERMEDIATION. *See* Financial Intermediaries.

DISINVESTMENT, or NEGATIVE INVESTMENT. Net disinvestment occurs when gross investment in fixed capital and in additions to inventories is less than the capital used up during the year. Because there cannot be fewer than no purchases of investment goods, gross investment can never be negative, so disinvestment always refers to net disinvestment. In accounting terms, disinvestment occurs when gross investment is less than depreciation.

DISPERSION. We may be just as interested in finding out how scattered our observations are as we are in finding out what their average value is. We can measure dispersion by looking at the whole range of our observations or we can measure dispersion in relation to some central value. The mean is the central summary measure most often used for the latter type of dispersion measures.

Range. The most simple measure of dispersion is simply the range between the largest and smallest values of our observations, that is [Xmax., Xmin.].

Deviation. The fundamental concept in measuring dispersion is the deviation, or distance between an observation and the mean: $X_i - \bar{X}$, where X_i is the ith observation and $\bar{X}$ is the mean of N values of X. The deviations will tend to be small if the data are bunched together around the mean and large if they are widely dispersed. Since there are as many deviations from the mean as there are observations, it is necessary to reduce this set of measures to a single summary measure.

Since it does not matter, from the point of view of measuring dispersion, whether an observation lies above or below the mean, one can ignore the sign of the deviation and take the mean of the absolute values of the deviations:

$$\textit{Mean Deviation} = \frac{\sum_{i=1}^{N} | X_i - \overline{X} |}{N}$$

Standard Deviation. A more useful and important measure of dispersion is the standard deviation. Squaring the deviations will remove the negative signs just as taking absolute values did. The further the observation is from the mean, the larger will be its squared deviation. The information contained in these squared values can be condensed into a single number by summing:

$$\textit{Variation} = \sum_{i=1}^{N} (X_i - \overline{X})^2$$

The average variation is called the mean-square deviation, or variance, denoted by

$$S^2 = \frac{\sum_{i=1}^{N} (X_i - \overline{X})^2}{N}$$

A problem with this measure is that it is expressed in squared units. Taking the square root expresses the result in original units: the standard deviation,

$$S = \sqrt{\frac{\Sigma (X_i - \overline{X})^2}{N}}$$

Obviously, the standard deviation will be small if the observations are grouped tightly around the mean and larger if the data are more spread out.

Coefficient of Variation. Dividing the standard deviation by the mean, yields the coefficient of variation:

$$V = S/\overline{X}$$

This measure of dispersion has the advantage of being a pure number (a percentage) and, therefore, allows different distributions to be compared with respect to variability.

See also Central Tendency.

Consult (27) L'Esperance, 1971; Spiegel, 1961.

—Carlisle E. Moody, *College of William and Mary*

DISPOSABLE INCOME. *See* Disposable Personal Income.

DISPOSABLE PERSONAL INCOME, or DISPOSABLE INCOME (DI), the total dollar amount individuals have available for personal consumption and personal savings after taxes and other noncommercial fees have been paid to government. DI may also be determined by adding the total amount of personal consumption, net savings, consumer interest payments, and personal transfer payments to foreigners. In the United States since World War II, disposable income has grown more rapidly than most other economic indicators. An important reflector of consumption expenditures, DI is frequently used to measure changes in the national standard of living, after adjustments have been made for changes in population and for inflation.

See also Consumption; Flow of Income; Personal Income.

DISSAVING, spending more than one's income on consumption. Households can dissave by spending previously saved or inherited money, borrowing, or begging. The economy as a whole could dissave no more than the amount of depreciation, if income is thought of as NNP; dissaving is not possible if income is thought of as GNP.

DISSOLUTION, DIVESTITURE, DIVORCEMENT, remedy-penalty provisions a federal court may invoke upon conviction of a firm of antitrust law violations, especially monopolization. There is a technical distinction among the terms, though it is being blurred by the growing use of "dissolution," the most general term, to cover all three actions. Dissolution refers to the breaking up of a firm into separate units, however those individual units were obtained by the firm (internal growth or merger). Divestiture requires the firm to dispose of specific properties or securities, which give it control or undue influence over another firm. Divorcement refers to the breaking off of a merger-acquired unit of the convicted firm.

See also Antitrust Policy; Sherman Antitrust Act; United States v. Standard Oil Company of New Jersey.

DISTRIBUTED EARNINGS. *See* Dividends.

DISTRIBUTION OF WEALTH (1899). *See* Clark, John Bates.

DISTRIBUTION QUESTION. *See* Market Mechanism.

DISTRICT BANKS. *See* Federal Reserve Banks.

DIVERSIFICATION, the process in which a business firm increases the variety of products it produces and sells, either by introducing new products into the same product line or market or by going into new product lines or markets. The firm can diversify either by branching out with existing production processes or by merging with other producers into a conglomerate. Diversification permits the firm to soften geographic or cyclical demand declines in one product by deriving revenue from one or more other products.

See also Conglomerate; Economies of Size.

DIVESTITURE. *See* Dissolution, Divestiture, Divorcement.

DIVIDENDS, earnings distributed to stockholders. Corporations secure capital funds by issuing bonds on which they pay interest—bondholders are creditors. They also issue stock on which they pay dividends—stockholders are owners of a corporation.

Stock has no maturity date, as do bonds, but dividends are not paid unless there are sufficient earnings. In a given year the board of directors decides whether dividends are to be paid, and even then all earnings after taxes are not paid out. Many wealthy stockholders prefer that dividends not be paid in a given year for tax reasons. Undistributed profits (retained earnings) are important sources of internal financing for many corporations, and such retention is reflected in higher values of common stock shares.

See also Corporate Earnings.

Consult (22) Bach, 1971; Eckaus, 1972.

DIVORCEMENT. *See* Dissolution, Divestiture, Divorcement.

Dissolution:
Breakup of CPC into units (Firms) A, B, C and D.
Divorcement:
Plant D must be disposed of.
Divestiture:
Common stock E, or any of plants A, B and C (or possibly D) must be disposed of.

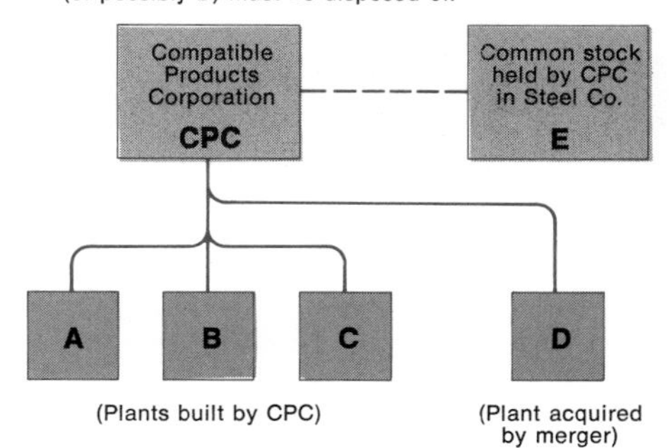

John Thomas Dunlop

DOLLAR GLUT. Since the late 1950s the United States has had a deficit in its balance of payments; it has been paying out more than it has taken in. Since debit items give rise to the demand for foreign exchange (which demand is met by buying exchange with dollars), the size of the deficit is an indication of the excess dollars floating around in the outside world and not being used to purchase U.S. goods and services or financial instruments. A continuing glut of dollars in the exchange markets forces consideration of devaluation. The glut implies an overvalued dollar.

See also Balance of Payments; Dollar Shortage.

DOLLAR SCARCITY. *See* Dollar Shortage.

DOLLAR SHORTAGE. If a nation has a surplus disequilibrium in its balance of payments over a period of time then its currency will become scarce in the outside world. It is through debit items in the balance of payments that a given country makes its currency available to others. For example, when the U.S. imports from abroad this creates a claim for dollar payments. These dollars can be used to buy U.S. exports, etc. There have been two periods of dollar shortage of note in U.S. history: during the Great Depression of the 1930s and from World War II to the 1950s. In the first instance imports from abroad were drastically reduced and capital ceased to flow. In the latter the U.S. market was the only reliable source of supply for goods needed for reconstruction and development.

See also Balance of Payments; Balance of Trade.

DOMAR, EVSEY DAVID (1914-), Polish-born educator and economist, an expert on growth theory. He is the developer of the Domar growth model. A graduate of the University of California (1939), he received an M.A. (1941) from the University of Michigan, and an M.A. (1943) and Ph.D (1947) in economics from Harvard. Domar is author of *Essays in the Theory of Economic Growth* (1957) and was an economist for the Board of Governors of the Federal Reserve System (1943-46). He has been on the faculty at numerous universities, and in 1958 he became professor of economics at M.I.T.

DORFMAN, ROBERT (1916-), American economist and educator noted for his contributions to microeconomic theory. A graduate of Columbia, he received his Ph.D. (1950) from the University of California. His publications include *Linear Programming and Economic Analysis* (1958), *The Price System* (1964), and *Measuring Benefits of Government Investment* (1965). A professor of economics at Harvard since 1957, Dorfman has served as a member of the President's Committee to Appraise Employment and Unemployment Statistics (1962), and as president of the Institute of Management Sciences (1965).

DOUBLE COUNTING. *See* Final Output; Value Added.

DOUBLE TAXATION. *See* Taxation: *Glossary.*

DOUGLAS, PAUL HOWARD (1892-), American educator and former U.S. senator. An expert on wage-theory and a co-developer of the Cobb-Douglas production function, he received a Ph.D. in economics from Columbia (1921). His numerous publications include *Worker in Modern Economic Society* (1923), *The Theory of Wages* (1934), *Ethics in Government* (1952), and *America in the Market Place: Trade, Tariffs, and the Balance of Payments* (1966). He held a seat in the U.S. Senate (1949-67) and was chairman of the President's Commission on Urban Problems (1967-68). In 1969 he was named Chairman of the National Commission on Tax Justice.

DOWNWARD SLOPING DEMAND, LAW OF. *See* Law of Downward Sloping Demand.

DRIVE TO MATURITY. *See* Stages of Growth.

DUNLOP, JOHN THOMAS (1914-), American educator noted for his studies of wage theory and union behavior. He received his Ph.D. from the University of California (1939). His publications include *Wage Determination Under Trade Unionism* (1943), *The Theory of Wage Determination* (1956), and *Programs to Employ the Disadvantaged* (1970). He has been a consultant to the Office of Economic Stabilization (1945-47), the National Labor Relations Board (1948-53), and he was a member of the President's Committee on Equal Employment Opportunity (1964-65). He is David A. Walls Professor of Political Economy at Harvard.

DUPONT CASE. *See* United States v. E.I. duPont and Co.

DURABLE GOODS. *See* Goods.

DUTY. *See* Tariffs.

DYNAMIC EQUILIBRIUM, equilibrium in which time is taken into account. The producers' output plans are determined with a time lag. The dynamic equilibrium shows how planned changes in supply can cause changes in the market price.

EARNINGS, CORPORATE. *See* Corporate Earnings.

EASY-MONEY POLICY. *See* Monetary Policy.

ECKSTEIN, OTTO (1927-), German-born educator and economist noted for his contributions to wage and price theory. A graduate of Princeton (1951), he received his Ph.D. from Harvard (1955). He is author of *Water Resource Development* (1958), *Economic Policy in Our Time* (1963), and *Public Finance* (1963) and is editor of two journals of economics. Eckstein has been technical director of the employment, growth, and price levels study of the Joint Economic Committee of the U.S. Congress (1959-60), a member of the President's Council of Economic Advisers (1964-66), and a member of the President's Commission on Income Maintenance Programs (beginning in 1968). He has been professor of economics at Harvard since 1963.

ECONOMETRIC MODEL. *See* Model, Econometric.

ECONOMIC ACTIVITY, AGGREGATE MEASURES OF. *See* National Income Measurement.

ECONOMIC CONSEQUENCES OF THE PEACE (1919). *See* Keynes, John Maynard.

ECONOMIC EFFICIENCY, in the broadest sense, the absence of waste. If a given commodity can be produced by two available techniques, the technique requiring fewer resources per unit of output is the more efficient.

At a more refined level of economic analysis efficiency is defined as absence of waste, in terms of the satisfactions people derive from consuming goods and services. If by some rearrangement of economic factors it is possible to increase the well-being of one or more persons without diminishing the well-being of any other, it would be wasteful or inefficient not to make the rearrangement.

This concept of economic efficiency is usually attributed to the Italian economist Vilfredo Pareto and referred to as Pareto optimality. The term optimality as used in this context is a bit unfortunate, since "optimum" implies the "best," whereas in economic situations there are generally a multiplicity of positions in which it is not possible to improve one person's lot without diminishing the well-being of someone else. Pareto optimality is unable to make any distinction between such positions, all are equally efficient.

See also Efficient Resource Allocation; Marginal-Cost Pricing; Pareto Optimum.

Consult (14) Boulding, 1952.

—Clarence C. Morrison, *Indiana University*

ECONOMIC FLUCTUATIONS. *See* Business Cycles.

ECONOMIC GOALS, or Economic Objectives, part of the national aspirations that deal with economic issues. The most widely, though not universally, accepted economic goals of most free societies are: (1) full employment, reasonable employment opportunities available to everyone desiring work, (2) a reasonable degree of economic freedom, (3) economic security in old age, (4) control of the harmful, wide, cyclical swings in price levels, inflation and deflation, (5) production in accordance with consumer demands, (6) an equitable distribution of the national income among various segments of society, and (7) a rising standard of living for all members of society, the goal of an increase in the country's output of goods and services.

It should be noted that some of these economic goals are complementary. For example, economic security and equitable income distribution are aided when full employment is achieved. Some goals, however, tend to be in conflict. For example, many excellent economists feel that full employment and price stability are incompatible goals. In view of the fact that any society's resources and energies are limited, and due to the fact that some economic goals are mutually exclusive, society via its government must assign priorities to the achievement of economic goals.

See also Economic Problems.

—Algin B. King, *College of William and Mary*

ECONOMIC INTERPRETATION OF HISTORY sees economic conditions determining the nature of other aspects of society. A central theme in the Marxist view is class conflict, arising from the relationship of the classes of productive factors to the productive process. Historically, mankind passes through tribal communism, slavery, feudalism, capitalism, socialism, and full communism. In the first stage and the last two, means of production are commonly owned, with no class antagonism. The others involve exploitation, because productive factors are owned by small segments, with the majority working for their benefit.

See also Class Conflict; Marx, Karl; Proletariat.

Consult (26) Hunt, 1972.

ECONOMIC NATIONALISM. *See* Nationalism.

ECONOMIC PROBLEMS arise because of unlimited human wants and limited material resources. There are various problems, such as what to produce and which wants to satisfy. A corollary problem in economics is how to produce goods and services once decisions have been made as to what to produce.

Five basic economic problem areas confronting every society are: (1) allocation of percentages of total production to each basic type or class of goods and services; (2) allocation of goods and services to various segments

Otto Eckstein

of the society; (3) methods of production; (4) degree and efficiency of utilization of the country's resources; and (5) maintenance of the economy's capacity to produce goods.

Four specific economic problems could be cited as examples of problem issues currently in public focus: (1) excessive inflation; (2) high unemployment rate; (3) use of government fiscal and monetary policies to achieve national economic goals, such as price stability and full employment; and (4) balance of payments in international trade. Solutions to these four problems are not simple because of the complexities of highly developed industrial economy and because of the lack of agreement of various members of society as to the ordering of priorities.

See also Economic Goals.

Consult (1) Rostow, 1971.

—Algin B. King, *College of William and Mary*

ECONOMIC PROFITS, the amount of total revenue that remains after a firm has paid both explicit and implicit wages, rent, and interest costs as well as a normal profit. Often referred to as pure profits, economic profits can be either positive gains or negative losses. If no economic profits, either positive or negative, exist, the firm is said to have normal profits, the minimum amount of revenue required to sustain a production activity.

Several theories are set forth by economists as to why economic profits might occur. First, entrepreneurs bear certain risks when they undertake a business venture. These risks are uninsurable and stem from both cyclical and structural changes in the economy. Economic profits can then be thought of in part as a reward for the assumption of these risks. A second explanation is related to the possibility of attaining monopoly power. Where firms are able to restrict entry and establish monopoly power, they can restrict output and influence price in such a way as to earn profits. The expectations of economic profits are incentives that encourage investment.

See also Profits.

—William D. Wagoner, *Louisiana State University*

ECONOMIC RENT, any payment to an owner of a productive resource in the long-run period in excess of the minimum payment necessary to keep the resource in its current use. To keep a resource in its current use, a resource owner must receive a minimum return equal to the return available in the best alternative use. Rents are payments in excess of opportunity costs. The nature of economic rents is revealed more clearly by arithmetic example than by words.

Example. Assume that the resource is land, that there are four grades of land, and, to simplify the illustration, that the land has only one use, growing corn. Further assume that once corn is produced, it sells for $4.00 per bushel. The tabulation shows the total cost, total output (q), total revenue (p × q), and rent on 50-acre tracts of various grades of land.

Equal expenditure of $5000 on each grade of land yields varying outputs due to the natural productivity of the different grades. Grade 1 land yields corn valued at $8000 but with a real social cost of $5000. The land itself has zero real cost because it has no alternative use. Rent is the difference between the real cost of the corn and value of the corn produced on the land, $3000. This rent will accrue to the owner of the Grade 1 land. Grade 2 land, being somewhat less productive than Grade 1, receives a lesser rent. Grade 3 is just productive enough so that total revenue is sufficient to cover all cost but not so great as to provide the owner of Grade 3 an economic rent.

If the price of corn were to rise above $4.00 per bushel, rent would accrue to the owners of Grade 3 land. Grade 4 land is not sufficiently productive when corn is priced at $4.00 per bushel to permit the cost of producing 1000 bushels to be covered by revenues from the sale of corn. Not only does rent not occur on Grade 4 land; a rational producer would not spend $5000 to produce corn worth $4000. Either a smaller expenditure would be made on Grade 4 or no expenditure at all.

Elasticity. When a resource is assumed to have no alternative use as in the example above, the resource will have a perfectly inelastic (vertical) supply curve. Such a supply curve represents the classical assumption concerning economic rent. Resources with perfectly elastic (horizontal) supply curves cannot receive rents. Resources with positively sloping supply curves may receive rents if payments to the resource in the current use exceed the value of the resources in the best alternative use.

See also Rent.

—John P. Formby, *University of North Carolina at Greensboro*

ECONOMIC RENT

	Grade of Land			
	#1	#2	#3	#4
Total Cost	$5000	$5000	$5000	$5000
Total Output (q)	2000 bu.	1500 bu.	1250 bu.	1000 bu.
Total Revenue (p x q)	$8000	$6000	$5000	$4000
Economic Rent	$3000	$1000	0	—

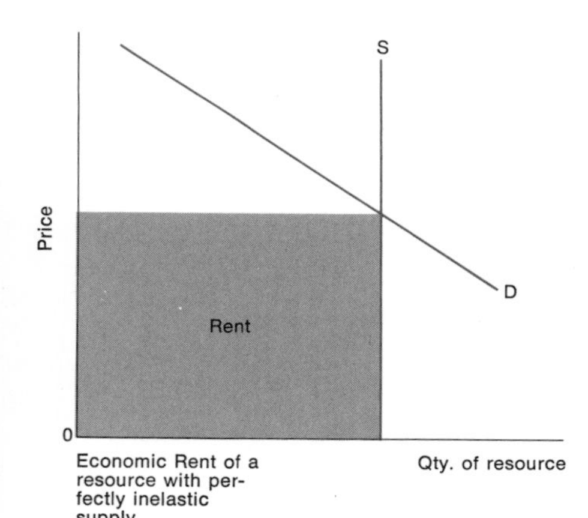

Economic Rent of a resource with perfectly inelastic supply

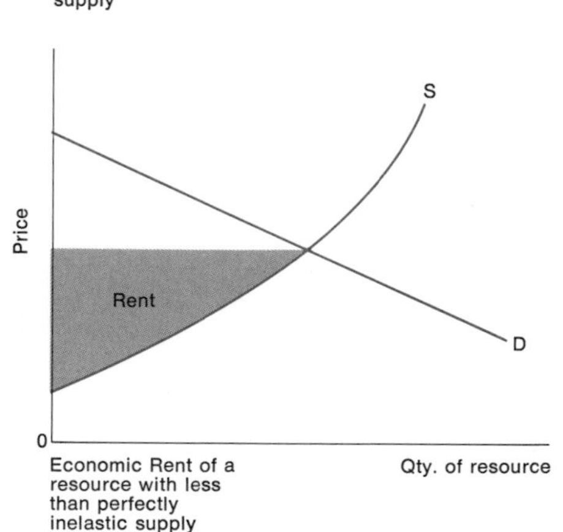

Economic Rent of a resource with less than perfectly inelastic supply

ECONOMICS AS A SCIENCE (1970). *See* Boulding, Kenneth.

ECONOMIC SECURITY. *See* Economic Systems.

ECONOMICS OF CONTROL (1944). *See* Lerner, Abba.

ECONOMICS OF EMPLOYMENT (1951). *See* Lerner, Abba.

ECONOMICS OF IMPERFECT COMPETITION (1933). *See* Robinson, Joan.

ECONOMICS OF WELFARE (1920). *See* Pigou, Arthur.

ECONOMIC STRUCTURE. *See* Economic Systems.

ECONOMIC SYSTEMS. The study of economic systems is now established as a field within the discipline of economics. The world during the 20th century has lost much of the uniformity of its economic structure. The capitalist countries of the 19th century, with their domination of most of the world's territory and all of its commerce, are now only one of many possible alternative systems. The event that most shattered the previous economic order was the 1917 rise to power of the Bolsheviks in Russia. The existence of the USSR destroyed the illusion that only capitalist markets could answer the basic economic questions. Economists are attempting to develop and apply tools of analysis to all economic systems in hopes of gaining insight into the workings of social economics.

Basic Economic Questions. A social economy attempts to obtain its economic goals within the restrictions imposed by scarcity of resources. The economy must be organized to answer these questions:

(1) What is to be produced? What particular mix of goods and services best meets the needs and wants of the economy—both public and private sectors?

(2) How is it to be produced? Given the state of technology, natural resources, and factor endowments, how can production be organized so as to maximize output?

(3) For whom are the goods and services to be provided, and what set of distribution rules is acceptable within the system?

Types of Systems

The economic institutions of a country are influenced by history—economic, social, and cultural—ideology, natural resources and factor endowments, and political structure. These factors are fused together in time to establish an economic system.

The diversity of economic systems is almost as great as the number of countries. The spectrum ranges from the theoretical models of perfect competition, with its heavy emphasis on individualism, to the pure authoritarian systems of socialism with its state orientation. A third model is the competitive socialist model, which attempts to merge the positive features of competitive markets and socialist precepts. None of these models describes any particular country, but they help to analyze economic systems.

Free-Enterprise and Command Systems. Categorization of an economic system should focus on two characteristics—ownership of the means of production and control over the means of production. For example, in the free-enterprise market-system practiced in the United States, individuals own most of the means of production. The citizen enjoys freedom of consumer choice and job choice. The firm is free to dictate its output and its technique of production, of which the consumer is said to be sovereign within the system. The state does exercise some control, through its taxation policy or restrictions on output, illegalizing certain production on the ground that it is either harmful to health or contrary to the people's moral and social conscience.

The antithesis to private enterprise is the command system, in which the plan dictates enterprise activities, determines the pace and direction of growth, and in so doing restricts the output of consumer goods. In the USSR the state owns and controls the means of production. The Soviet citizen does enjoy consumer choice and general freedom of job choice, but the state preferences dominate the system.

The economies of eastern Europe, China, and other "communist" states approximate the organization of the USSR with some deviations for special circumstances. The east European socialist states have recently made some revisions in their organizational structure to move decisions closer to the firm level. This whole bloc of countries seems to be searching for new solutions to the old economic questions. How much divergence from the Soviet model will be permitted by the USSR remains only partially answered after the Soviet invasion of Czechoslovakia in 1968.

Mixed Systems. The categories between the private-enterprise systems (U.S. capitalism) and the authoritarian socialism (USSR command economy) are described as "mixed systems." These systems have both private and state ownership of property, and private and state control of the economic processes. Some countries with a high degree of private ownership, such as Sweden, exert strong central influence on the economy through macroeconomic policies and welfare objectives. A private enterprise authoritarian system (fascism) would best describe the German economy under Adolf Hitler.

Along the spectrum there is a significant group of countries with a strong tradition of private property and individual freedom that for various reasons have nationalized selected industries. The nationalized industries normally function as private corporations in the markets, but their ultimate responsibility is to the state rather than the private stockholder. Planning either does not exist or exists only as targeted aggregate goals of output, employment, prices, and growth. Britain and France are good examples of this category.

The socialist market system is an experiment Yugoslavia is currently making. This system rests on state ownership of means of industrial production, while control resides with the workers themselves. The firms behave as independent entities with only a broad economic plan. Yugoslavia is attempting to

ECONOMIC SYSTEMS

Economic systems include a wide variety of types. For articles relevant to the American system, see CAPITALISM, MARKET SYSTEM, FREE ENTERPRISE, and MIXED ECONOMY. For information on the theories and operation of Socialist-type economies, see the articles on SOCIALISM; COMMUNISM; PLANNING, SOCIALISM; and PLANNING, COMMUNISM. For some broad ideological treatments of alternative types of systems, see MARX, KARL and SMITH, ADAM.

For other entries dealing with comparative economic systems, the student will find it useful to consult the Subject Map accompanying this article.

ECONOMIC SYSTEMS

CAPITALISM
- COMPETITION
  - market price
- LAISSEZ FAIR
  - nonintervention
- INVISIBLE HAND
- PROTESTANT ETHIC
- CONSUMER CHOICE
- CONSUMER SOVEREIGNTY
- CONSUMER'S PREFERENCE
- RESOURCE RIGHTS

SOCIALISM
- EVOLUTIONARY SOCIALISM
  - gradual socialism
- REVOLUTIONARY SOCIALISM
- NATIONALIZATION
  - public ownership
- FABIAN SOCIETY
  - fabian socialism
- DEMOCRATIC (LIBERAL) SOCIALISM
  - liberal socialism
- BRITISH LABOUR PARTY
- SCIENTIFIC SOCIALISM
  - science of human history
- ROBERT OWEN
  - utopian socialism
- PLANNING (SOCIALISM)
- WELFARE STATE
- F.M.C. FOURIER
  - phalanxes
- ASSOCIATIONISM
  - voluntary association
- COOPERATIVISM
  - consumer's cooperatives
  - producer's cooperatives
- PLANNER'S (STATE) PREFERENCES
  - state preferences

COMMUNISM
- ANARCHISTIC COMMUNISM
- SYNDICALISM
  - george sorel
- BOLSHEVIKS
- COLLECTIVIZATION
  - agricultural collectivization
- PLANNING (COMMUNISM)
  - five-year plans
  - one-year plans
- NEW ECONOMIC POLICY (NEP)
- REVISIONISM
- GOSPLAN
  - state planning committee (USSR)
- GOVERNMENT-CONTROLLED ECONOMY
  - state-controlled economy
- DICTATORSHIP OF THE PROLETARIAT
  - socialist dictatorship
- KARL MARX
  - ECONOMIC INTERPRETATION OF HISTORY
  - PROLETARIAT
    - propertyless class
  - SURPLUS VALUE
  - CLASS CONFLICT
- VLADIMIR LENIN
- JOSEPH STALIN
- MAO TSE-TUNG

The Subject Maps in the Encyclopedia illustrate the coverage of particular aspects of economics, showing the interrelationships among the articles in twenty-one critical areas of study. Entries in capital letters are subjects for which there are separate articles in the Encyclopedia. Entries in small letters are references to the article immediately above and provide some idea of content.

The Subject Maps are arranged alphabetically in the Encyclopedia under the following titles:

Antitrust Policy
Banking System
Business Cycles
Capital
Circular Flow of Income
Demand Theory
Economic Systems
Factor Markets
Federal Budget
History of Economic Ideas
International Trade Theory
Labor Market
Labor Movement
Market System
Money and Monetary Policy
National Income
Price Level
Regulation
Supply
Theory of the Firm
Wages

decentralize decision making with a prominent role for the marketplace in directing resources.

Most of the developing countries of Africa, Asia, and South America have been strongly influenced by their former relationships with the colonial powers. Since World War II these countries have been searching for their own paths to growth and development, and economists find it difficult to categorize them as particular systems. In fact, economists have become increasingly aware that the tools of economic analysis appropriate for industrialized states may be only partially adequate for the developing world.

Evaluating Economic Systems

In order to evaluate an economic system it is necessary to establish a set of criteria. The criteria below are broad in scope but helpful in analyzing a country's performance.

Economic Wealth and Rate of Growth. The wealth of a country reflects its past economic performance. Gross national product (GNP) tells how productive an economy is in one year, while GNP per capita relates how much each individual would receive if output were distributed equally to all citizens in the country.

The leadership of most nations has attempted to design economic policies in order to promote economic growth. A rising GNP per capita increases the economic alternatives available to a country. It has the potential of raising the standard of living and enhancing the political and economic power of the state.

Stability. Economic stability is a criterion of great concern to economic policy makers of any system. Their objective is to promote growth without generating wide and frequent cyclical movements in employment, output, and the price level. A critical question is whether the fluctuations are inherent in the system. If so, policies should be designed to neutralize the problem. Some disequilibrium in a growing system is necessary. Change frequently causes instability, and the magnitude and consequences of instability require evaluation.

Efficiency. An economy is said to be efficient if it has maximized its output by utilizing its inputs in the most effective way possible to achieve the objectives of the system. Then it cannot increase the output of any one product without reducing the output of another. The efficiency criterion is difficult to apply, since the production capabilities of a system are continuously changing. Thus, an economy must constantly adjust its economic allocations to achieve efficient operation.

Security. How well an economic system provides for security is a critical measure of the well-being of its population. People are concerned about security—security of a job, security from the burden of medical bills, security from lack of adequate income during a period of disability or old age, and security for the family at death. Too much security, however, may have detrimental effects on productivity and motivation.

Economic Freedom. This criterion helps to analyze (1) the extent to which the individual consumer and the firm or enterprise are free to make basic economic decisions, and (2) the influence each has on resource allocation. Such freedoms are freedom of consumer choice, freedom of job choice, freedom of firms to make their basic allocation and production decisions, and consumer sovereignty.

Equality. A system can be evaluated by the extent of economic and social discrimination based on sex, race, or nationality. Discrimination may take such forms as different wage levels for the same job, or using a criterion other than personal capabilities for filling a position.

Application of Criteria. Any analysis of economic systems requires certain cautions. First, theoretical models must be compared with theoretical models, and functioning economies with other existing systems. Secondly, a set of evaluation criteria will require a value framework for judgments. For instance, if personal freedom is considered a basic right of man, then within this value framework, authoritarian systems would seem to be inferior to more liberal systems. Thirdly, countries should be evaluated within the context of their own set of objectives. If growth is the goal of a society, then to say it does not achieve static equilibrium is to make an observation but not a pertinent evaluation.

Consult (26) Bornstein, 1969; Grossman, 1967; Loucks and Whitney, 1969; Snavely, 1969.

—Francis W. Rushing, *College of William and Mary*

ECONOMIES, EXTERNAL. *See* Externalities.

ECONOMIES OF SCALE. Economies or diseconomies of scale refer to the effects on unit costs of a firm as it increases its scale or plant size over the long run. Economies of scale imply decreasing unit costs as plant size increases; diseconomies imply increasing unit costs concomitant to increases in plant size.

Economies of scale may be reaped due to increased scope given to specialization and division of labor. Small plant size often requires that one man handle several jobs; time is lost in changing jobs, tools, and so on.

Technological factors may account for lower unit costs as scale increases. Larger machines which increase output by some multiple of smaller machines do not ordinarily require proportional increases in space or in labor to operate. Qualitative as well as quantitative changes occur with increased plant size. Advanced technology often requires large output before it is economically feasible.

Financial advantages can also be reaped with increased scale size. Unit costs will correspondingly fall. Discounts are often given to large buyers of resources, and the comparatively large firms with high sales volumes have greater access to cheaper credit markets.

Diseconomies are alleged to arise as the firm expands its scale of operations to extremely large sizes. Presumably these are mostly managerial problems. More and more red tape becomes necessary; control and coordination problems become much more important. More and more decisions have to be delegated to others and informational gaps may well arise. In a sense, this problem may be viewed as the inability of the management system to increase along with the scale of operations. These diseconomies may eventually offset and even surpass the advantages, or economies, referred to above. When diseconomies offset economies the net result will be increased unit costs.

The classic example of diseconomies due to great size is supposed to be U.S. Steel. Whether this is true or whether U.S. Steel's problems were in part due to aggressive antitrust policy is debatable.

—Robert L. Brite, *Louisiana State University*

ECONOMY, COMMAND. *See* Command Economy.

ECONOMY, MARKET. *See* Market Economy.

ECONOMY, SUBSISTENCE. *See* Subsistence Economy.

EFFECTIVE DEMAND involves the desire and the ability to purchase a certain number of units of a commodity at a given price. In order for potential demand (willingness to buy) to be translated into effective demand, the money to finance the desired transaction must be obtainable.

EFFICIENCY, how effectively an economy's scarce resources are allocated in meeting consumer demands for goods and services. Economic analysis concerns itself with the question of efficiency under different market conditions. Measures of efficiency in macroeconomic theory deal with the distribution of goods and services, the utilization of resources, and economic growth. Efficiency analysis is used in examining the production processes of the firm seeing, for example, if it has combined inputs in the most technologically correct proportions. Other examples of efficiency applications for the firm's production process would be reducing cost, increasing output, and qualitatively improving output.

EFFICIENT RESOURCE ALLOCATION, allocation that satisfies the criterion of Pareto optimality (any situation in which it is impossible to make one individual better off without making someone else worse off).

Competition. Intermediate and advanced economic theory constructs a model representing an entire economy and demonstrates in the context of this model that Pareto optimality requires that firms be operated competitively, pricing output so that its unit cost to customers is equal to the price of any productive factor divided by its marginal physical product. The marginal product of a factor is the increase in output that results from employing an additional unit of that factor while holding all other factors constant.

If market price for the output of the firm is set equal to marginal cost, the consuming public has direct and efficient access to the productive process. With such access, it is reasonable to assume that individual consumers will allocate their incomes in a manner most satisfactory to themselves and, thus, eliminate the possibility of making someone better off without making someone else worse off: where all markets are competitive (where firms price at market cost), the market allocation of resources is Pareto optimal.

Monopoly. The foregoing explains the classical indictment of monopolistic market structures. Although one would expect monopolistic firms to be internally efficient, their prices place an economic barrier between consumers and the productive process. Frequently it is argued that in some cases monopolies operate at a more efficient scale than do competitors, and, therefore, it is not certain that monopolistic elements always result in higher prices; but even where this possibility exists, economic theory indicates that there is some possible reorganization, involving marginal cost pricing, that would move toward a Pareto optimum. This conclusion is the basis of the argument that natural monopolies should be nationalized and directed to price at marginal cost.

See also Economic Efficiency; Marginal Cost Pricing; Pareto Optimum.

Consult (14) Lerner, 1947.

—Clarence C. Morrison, *Indiana University*

ELASTIC DEMAND. A typical demand curve will contain the total spectrum of elasticities. That is, a downward sloping demand curve will have an elastic range, a point of unitary elasticity, and an inelastic range. If, however, prices tend to stay within a limited range, it is possible to identify the demand as relatively elastic.

For example, if the ordinary range of prices for some good is between P_1 and P_2, and if the percentage change in quantity demanded between those two prices is always greater than the percentage change in price, then the demand curve is said to be elastic over the relevant range of price changes.

The demand curves for some specific commodities can be horizontal at a specific price, implying that an infinite number of units of the commodity will be demanded at the going price, and that sellers cannot increase sales by lowering the price. Furthermore, if sellers attempt to raise the price of the commodity, no units will be sold. This type of demand curve characterizes a market with perfect competition where a large number of perfect substitutes are available for the product in question. Such a demand curve is said to be infinitely or totally elastic.

—Robert L. Brite, *Louisiana State University*

ELASTICITY OF DEMAND, the degree of response that occurs in quantity changes as a result of a change in price.

Range of Elasticity. If quantity demanded changes by a relatively large amount when price changes by a small amount, the demand function between the two points in question is said to be elastic. Conversely, if large price changes are necessary to evoke even small changes in quantity demanded, then demand is said to be relatively inelastic between the two points. If a given relative change in price causes quantity demanded to change by the same relative amount, then demand is said to be of unitary elasticity. Typical demand curves display varying ranges of elasticity. For example, a downward sloping linear demand curve will be relatively elastic at high-price and low-quantity-demanded combinations, and the degree of elasticity will decline as lower-price and higher-quantity-demanded combinations are attained. As the elasticity of demand for a given demand curve passes from the relatively elastic range to the relatively inelastic range, a point is passed at which demand will be of unitary elasticity.

Coefficient of Elasticity. It is useful to identify the various ranges of elasticity of demand by making reference to a coefficient of elasticity, which is computed by dividing the percentage change in quantity demanded by the causal percentage change in price. The resulting coefficient will have a negative algebraic sign, which reflects the negative relationship between price and quantity demanded. It is the absolute value of the coefficient, however, which is of importance in identifying the degree of elasticity possessed by the demand function. If the absolute value of the coefficient is greater than 1 the demand is elastic. If the absolute value of the coefficient is less than 1, the demand is inelastic. If the absolute value of the coefficient is equal to 1, demand is said to be of unitary elasticity at that point.

Total-Revenue Test. One useful test to indicate whether demand is elastic or inelastic at some point is the total-revenue test for elasticity. Starting from a given price-demand relationship, price is allowed to change. If the change in total sales revenue resulting from the price change is in the opposite direction from the price change, then demand is relatively elastic. That is, if price increases from some point and the resulting total revenue (the product of price times quantity sold) decreases, demand is said to be relatively elastic between the two points in question. If price and total revenue change in the same direction then demand is said to be relatively inelastic over the range in question. Whenever, as occasionaly happens, price changes by some very small amount, and the total revenue remains the same as before the price change, demand is said to be of unitary elasticity.

—Robert L. Brite, *Louisiana State University*

ELASTICITY OF SUPPLY. The law of supply tells us that as price increases quantity supplied will also rise. The slope of the supply curve would generally tell us "by how much?" but when we try to discuss responsiveness to price changes across differing commodities, we have a units problem. The concept of elasticity is introduced as a meaningful way, free of units of measurement, to compare responsiveness of quantity changes to price changes. Elasticity is defined as the *percentage* change in quantity divided by the *percentage* change in price.

Elasticity of supply deals with the responsiveness of producers to change in price. Do slight changes in price lead to large percentage changes in output, or does it take relatively large percentage changes in price to lead to even mild percentage changes in output? The former is referred to as relatively elastic supply, the latter as relatively inelastic supply.

It should be emphasized that although economists often, for convenience, infer elasticity from the *slope* of a curve, this is not precise. Even along a linear function, which of course has a constant slope, elasticity changes importantly. It is for this reason one should refer to *point* elasticity; elasticity should be treated in a calculus type manner—when dealing with very small changes. Thus, to be precise, one should talk about elasticity over given (small) ranges rather than "the" elasticity of supply of some commodity.

The elasticity of supply of agricultural products is usually considered to be inelastic; in the short run the crops have already been

UNEMPLOYMENT OF MILITARY VETERANS AND NONVETERANS (20-29)

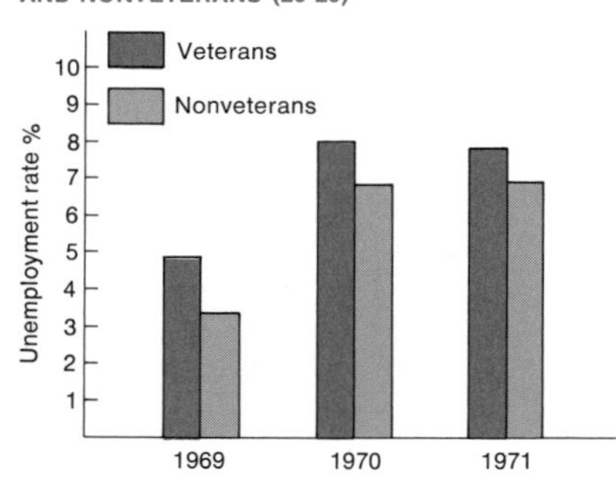

planted and the ultimate yield will be more a function of weather conditions than it will be of price. However, even here, if prices are very low, farmers have the option of feeding the crops to their livestock, plowing under, and so on.

—Robert L. Brite, *Louisiana State University*

ELASTIC SUPPLY. The supply of a product is said to be elastic, over some small price range, when the computed coefficient of elasticity is greater than one. Theoretically all coefficients greater than 1, up to positive infinity, would be described as elastic. Of course the greater the coefficient the more elastic is supply. The implication is that over given price ranges and for certain commodities some firms (or industries) are better able to react to price changes; rising costs due to diminishing returns do not immediately and significantly appear. It would be safe to say that manufacturing goods are characterized by greater elasticity of supply than are agricultural commodities.

ELEMENTS OF PURE ECONOMICS (1874-77). *See* Walras, Leon.

EMERGENCY STRIKES, work stoppages that are especially harmful to the public interest. Most strikes impose an inconvenience on consumers and sometimes they cause serious economic damage. But economic harm alone does not create an emergency. Rather, if a strike seriously jeopardizes the public safety and well-being, an emergency situation results, and the strike becomes an "emergency strike."

Examples. Emergency strikes in the public sector may occur, for example, by refusals to work by firemen, policemen, sanitation workers, or nurses, and in the private sector by food and fuel delivery men. But strikes by school teachers or auto and steel workers generally would not constitute emergencies.

See also Mediation.

EMPLOYEE COMPENSATION, all present and deferred remuneration an employee is eligible to receive from his employer. It is the sum of straight wages and fringe benefits, such as bonuses, stock options, pension plans, life and unemployment insurance, discounts on merchandise, and profit-sharing plans.

EMPLOYMENT, as related to the labor force, describes the condition of people working in exchange for monetary payment. There are several types of employment. Full employment exists when about 96% of the labor force is employed; this usually indicates a prosperous economic condition where jobs are available to almost anyone seeking work. In the state of the economy in which there is less than full-employment, there are people who are actively seeking work, but jobs are unavailable. The proportion of these people in the labor force who are unable to find work represent the unemployment rate.

A third type of employment, known as underemployment, represents the condition in which workers, though employed, are not used to their full capacity. This is also known as disguised unemployment. Examples of this type of employment are often found in agriculture where more people are working an amount of land than is necessary. This usually represents an inefficiency problem.

It has been the goal of the United States since the Employment Act of 1946 to work toward achieving full employment of labor, and it has so directed its policies.

See also Unemployment of Labor.

Consult (20) Bloom, 1965.

—William D. Wagoner, *Louisiana State University*

EMPLOYMENT, AGGREGATE. *See* National Income Determination.

EMPLOYMENT ACT OF 1946, legislation passed as a result of the economic conditions in the United States prior to and expected after World War II. The act authorizes federal government economic activity to favorably influence aggregate economic performance. The goal of high employment is directly specified by the act; the goal of price stability is clearly implied. In recent years, the interpretation of the Employment Act has been broadened to include the economic growth objective and the objective of improvement in the nation's balance of international payments. The act also established the Council of Economic Advisors to assist and advise the President on economic matters.

ENDOGENOUS THEORY OF BUSINESS CYCLES. *See* Internal Theory of Business Cycles.

END RESULT DOCTRINE. *See* Hope Natural Gas Case (1944).

ENFORCEMENT OF COMPETITION. *See* Antitrust Policy.

ENTREPRENEUR, one whose role is to see the opportunity to make a profit from a new product, new process, or unexploited raw material and then take the organizational risks to promote the opportunity by bringing together the requisite raw materials, manpower, and capital. His specialty is innovation, not management.

See also Innovation; Profit System; Risk.

Consult (22) Schumpeter, 1962.

ENTRY, the relative ease with which firms can enter a particular market. Free entry is a characteristic of purely competitive markets and implies an ease of entry that is not blocked by any major barriers. Unlike the purely competitive markets, oligopolistic and monopolistic markets usually have one or more major barriers that make entry into the industry difficult or impossible. These are of two main types: natural barriers and artificial barriers.

Natural barriers are usually characteristics of certain monopolistic industries. Built into the nature of the firm, they give it a natural advantage over other firms. For example, the exclusive rights to resources is a major advantage of the utility companies and forms a natural barrier. A second natural barrier is the need for an amount of capital so large that profits could not be obtained. To enter competitively into the automotive industry would be almost impossible because of the large amount of capital, manpower, and knowledge needed.

Artificial barriers include patent and licensing laws, the pricing policies of existing firms that have the ability to undersell new firms, and product differentiation of existing firms that make "off-brands" difficult to market.

See also Barriers to Entry; Free Entry.

—William D. Wagoner, *Louisiana State University*

ENTRY UNEMPLOYMENT occurs when a worker tries to enter the job market for the first time or tries to enter a new trade or skill. Entry unemployment is heaviest among students and housewives who have little or no work experience, because they very often are competing with much more experienced people. In addition, workers changing trades experience entry unemployment because, even though they have worked before, they lack proper experience. The severity of unemployment of this nature depends on the economic conditions of the country. When labor is scarce, entry unemployment is minimal.

ENVELOPE CURVE. *See* Long-Run Average Cost Curve.

EQUALIZING WAGE DIFFERENTIALS are those wages paid to individuals to compensate for the non-money differences among jobs. For example, if two workers perform the same duties at the same plant, one working the day shift, the second the night shift, the one on night shift is usually given a wage differential to compensate for the inconvenience of night work. Wage differentials are also used to induce people to work at less attractive or more dangerous occupations.

EQUATION, a statement of equivalence between two sets of symbols: $47 = 3$; $ax^2 + bx + c = 0$; $y = f(x)$. Equations can be solved to yield the implied values of the variables. Thus, we can only solve for as many variables as we have equations; one equation can be solved for one variable, two equations can be solved simultaneously for two variables, and so on.

EQUATION OF EXCHANGE, a mathematical statement of the fact that the market value of goods sold is equal to the amount of money paid for them, normally written $PQ = MV$, where, in terms of income, P is (roughly) the retail price level, Q is the physical quantity of goods sold to ultimate users (mostly consumers), M is the money supply, and V is the velocity of circulation of money, or the number of times during a year that money changes hands between one income recipient and another. In this form PQ is approximately the same as the monetary value of goods produced, that is, national income. The equation is useful in examining broad trends within the economy, for if any factor of the equation changes, some other factor must also change. If people hoard more (reducing V), then unless the money supply rises, either fewer goods will be sold (Q falls) or prices drop.

Quantity Theory of Money. The quantity theory of money, developed by Irving Fisher, says that normally both V and Q remain constant, so that a rise in the money supply will cause an exactly proportional increase in the price level, the sole cause of inflation. Historical statistics show that the assumption is false. Transactions (and production) have risen continually over time, while velocity has varied unevenly, so that the relation between money and prices is not simple. Nevertheless, the importance of the money supply as one basic factor in price changes is implied in the equation of exchange itself and is accepted by most economists. Modern quantity theorists, led by Milton Friedman, are inclined to say that the money supply is the most important factor in inflation; this group, known as the monetarists, believes that strict control of the quantity of money is the most important policy action needed to stabilize the economy.

Consult (8) Fisher, 1911; Friedman, 1956.

—Walter W. Haines, *New York University*

EQUILIBRIUM, a state of balance or rest. In order to give the concept a more formal definition, it is convenient to introduce the idea of a system. A system may be thought of as, or described by, a set of *variables* (that is, entities capable of variation), and a set of *forces* acting on the variables, thereby causing them to assume certain values (positions). If the forces that act on each variable are exactly balanced, so that no variable will change its value (posi-

EQUILIBRIUM

Equilibrium applies to virtually all economic units in the economy, to the relationships among them, and to the economy as a whole. Building upward from the individual role-players in the economy to the economy as a whole—all viewed in the microeconomic framework—consult CONSUMER EQUILIBRIUM, EQUILIBRIUM OF THE FIRM, and EQUILIBRIUM OF THE INDUSTRY. Then, in regard to the interplay of buyers and sellers, see MARKET EQUILIBRIUM, EQUILIBRIUM PRICE, and EQUILIBRIUM QUANTITY.

For an understanding of macroeconomic equilibrium, see the major article on NATIONAL INCOME DETERMINATION; and in relation to international trade, see BALANCE OF PAYMENTS.

The Subject Maps accompanying the articles on DEMAND THEORY, MARKET SYSTEM, and THEORY OF THE FIRM are also useful in clarifying the interrelationships among the various economic units.

tion), then the system is said to be in equilibrium.

In economics, equilibrium positions occur in three levels of economic analysis—analysis of individual decision makers, market analysis, and analysis of an entire economic system.

Individual Analysis. A typical problem of a firm is to purchase various inputs (factors of production), transform them into one or more outputs (products), and sell these outputs on the market to maximize profit. When the firm chooses levels of inputs and outputs that yield a maximum profit, the firm is in a state of equilibrium; so long as environmental conditions remain the same, the firm has no reason for changing its plan of action. Analogously, an individual consumer is in equilibrium when he allocates his income among the available commodities to attain the highest level of satisfaction from his purchases.

Market Analysis is concerned with the determination of market price (if the market is competitive) and quantity exchanged. Under competitive conditions the market price reacts to the forces of supply and demand; an excess of demand over supply drives the price up, and vice versa. A graphical representation of a competitive market is shown in which the curve D is the market demand function, showing the quantities that buyers are willing to buy at different prices. The curve S is the market supply function, showing the quantities that sellers are willing to supply. If the market price is p_1, quantity demanded (x_2) exceeds quantity supplied (x_1), and, therefore, the existence of excess demand ($x_2 - x_1$) will push the price up. Such a situation is referred to as disequilibrium. Similarly, at prices above $\bar{p}$ there exists an excess of supply over demand (a negative excess demand), resulting in disequilibrium. When the market price is $\bar{p}$, excess demand is zero, which means that the forces of supply and demand are evenly balanced: the price $\bar{p}$ and the quantity $\bar{x}$ represent an equilibrium position.

EQUILIBRIUM

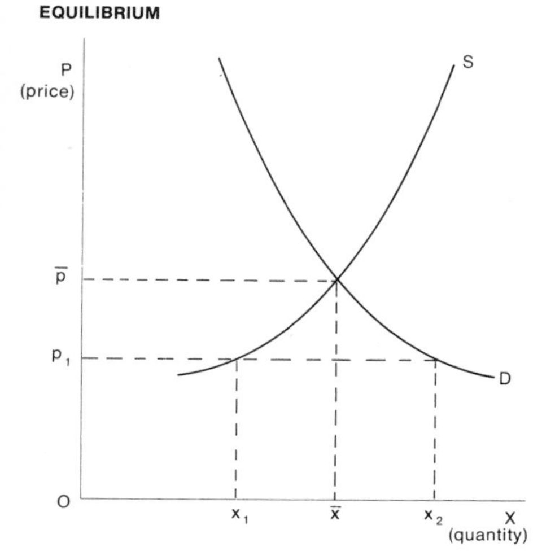

General Analysis. An entire economic system may be represented by a set of markets, one market for each product. Since in the analysis of such a system the concept of equilibrium occupies a central position, it is referred to as general equilibrium analysis. In such a system, an equilibrium occurs when all the constituent markets attain an equilibrium position simultaneously.

—Josef Hadar, *Case Western Reserve University*

EQUILIBRIUM, BALANCE OF PAYMENTS. *See* Balance of Payments.

EQUILIBRIUM LEVEL OF INCOME. *See* National Income Determination.

EQUILIBRIUM OF THE FIRM. Equilibrium for a system is the situation in which the forces associated with the system are in a state of balance. The forces associated with the firm are the various factors that affect its profitability. As a first approximation, economic theory assumes that the goal of the firm is to make profit, and the term "profit maximization" describes both the motive force in the model and the equilibrium state of the model. When there is no possibility for increasing the firm's profits, the forces associated with the firm are in balance, and the firm is in equilibrium.

Most economists think that insights into the workings on an economy can be gained by deducing the equilibrium properties of its component parts. Implicit in this approach is the belief that economic units are equilibrium seekers or equilibrators and that equilibrium positions are important in determining their behavior regardless of whether equilibrium states are actually achieved.

Static Equilibrium. Generally in the formal study of economics it is the concept of static equilibrium that is first encountered. Static analysis deals with states of rest relative to the passage of time, while dynamic analysis deals with nonstationary time paths. In static analysis the only significant role that time plays is in furnishing a basis for measurement. Inputs and outputs are thought of as flows which are measured in terms of number of units of input or output per basic unit of time: one speaks of the hourly, daily, or weekly, output of a machine or process. If a machine used by the firm is powered by an internal-combustion gasoline engine, then gasoline is one of the inputs of the firm. Similarly, sales can be measured in terms of units of output sold per unit of time. Static equilibrium of the firm involves balancing all of the flows of this type so that profit, measured as a flow, is a maximum.

Short Run v. Long Run. Frequently, input flows are the direct consequence of having access to stocks of objects that are physically durable. A machine shop owning a drill press would have its services (a flow) during a given time period, but the drill press itself would not be used up during that period. The distinction between the long run and short run hinges on durability, but in the theory of the firm the distinction is in terms of economic durability (or variability) rather than physical durability. Although a drill press might have a physical durability of ten years, a firm does not necessarily commit itself to ten years of drill press services when it purchases the machine (as long as there is a market for used drill presses). Further, an alternative to owning the machine might be to lease it, and the same machine would have different economic durabilities for different lease terms: if leasable on a six-month basis, it is less durable from an economic point of view (furnishes a more variable factor of production) than when leasable only on an annual basis.

Static short-run analysis of the firm assumes that, within the span of the basic time period, the factors in one set are variable and the factors in a second set are not. The cost of the variable factors (variable cost) is found by simply multiplying their respective market prices by the number of units employed. The costs of the nonvariable (fixed) factors (fixed cost) must also be stated in terms of the basic time period and may be thought of as the depreciation on those factors and the interest that the firm could have obtained on the funds tied up in them. Long-run analysis assumes that the maximal number of factors are variable (as they are from the entrepreneur's viewpoint whenever he considers varying the scale of his operation) and does not explicitly account for any fixed cost. Although this analytical scheme implicitly suggests that there are only two economic durabilities when, in fact, there are many, it serves well as a first approximation.

Dynamic Equilibrium. Dynamic analysis deals with time paths, and the firm is in dynamic equilibrium when it is on the time path that the entrepreneur finds most profitable in terms of his conception of what the future holds. One case of dynamic equilibrium corresponds to static equilibrium: where the entrepreneur has stationary expectations with respect to the "givens" in the model, the static equilibrium continues through time, generating stationary time paths.

See also Equilibrium of the Firm, Short-Run; Equilibrium of the Firm, Long-Run.

Consult (14) Allen, 1967; Samuelson, 1943.

—Clarence C. Morrison, *Indiana University*

EQUILIBRIUM OF THE FIRM, LONG-RUN, the situation that would maximize the firm's profit with all inputs in the production process variable.

See also Equilibrium of the Firm.

EQUILIBRIUM OF THE FIRM, SHORT-RUN. In the short-run the firm adjusts those inputs which are variable so as to maximize profit. This involves equating short-run marginal cost and short-run marginal revenue, since if they are unequal it is possible to increase revenue more than cost by either increasing or decreasing output.

See also Equilibrium of the Firm.

EQUILIBRIUM OF THE INDUSTRY. Equilibrium may be defined as a situation in which there is no tendency to move. Therefore, equilibrium of an industry occurs when the conditions within it are such that no firm, either already in the industry or outside it and potentially an entrant, sees any reason to alter existing arrangements. Thus, equilibrium of an industry can occur only when certain conditions are met, and these conditions are more easily considered in the pure competition case.

Allowing the firms enough time to make basic alterations in plant size, to build new plants, to leave the industry or for new firms to enter the industry (the long-run period), the conditions under which no one would decide to change the present scale and scope of operations must satisfy the conditions of both short- and long-run equilibrium.

The long-run conditions for equilibrium in the industry exist when only normal profits are being earned by the individual firms. Thus, the price charged by the firms must be just equal to the long-run average cost of production. A price above or below this would create either greater than normal or less than normal profits, and would encourage firms to enter or exit the industry. If this condition of price equality with long-run average costs is met, then one requirement of industry equilibrium is achieved.

However, even if this condition is met, one or more firms already in the industry may find it profitable to change the level of production by more or less intensive utilization of existing plant and equipment. Therefore, the second condition for industry equilibrium is that each firm in the industry be operating at its equilibrium output. This level of output occurs when, for each plant, marginal cost equals marginal revenue, the profit maximization position. When this condition exists in the short run, and the long-run conditions are met, then long-run average cost equals short-run marginal cost and short-run marginal revenue.

When the individual firms and industry are operating under equilibrium conditions, then, for the moment, equilibrium of the industry exists. This condition, assuming it can ever develop, is a brief one, for changes in technology, in demand, or in other areas, can and will upset it. The safest statement is that a tendency toward this equilibrium is always present in competitive industry.

See also Equilibrium; Theory of the Firm.

Consult (14) Leftwich, 1970.

—William D. Wagoner, *Louisiana State University*

EQUILIBRIUM PRICE, or MARKET PRICE, the price at which the quantity of a good offered by the producer is exactly equal to the quantity of a good that will be demanded by the consumer for a particular period of time. This equilibrium price represents a compromise of the producer and the consumer. The producer would like to achieve as high a price as possible for his good to maximize his profit. The

EQUILIBRIUM OF THE FIRM

Closely related to the concept of EQUILIBRIUM OF THE FIRM is the article on PROFIT MAXIMIZATION. Equilibrium of the firm applies both to the short and long run; accordingly, see the articles on EQUILIBRIUM OF THE FIRM, SHORT RUN and EQUILIBRIUM OF THE FIRM, LONG RUN. Closely related to the latter of these concepts is EQUILIBRIUM OF THE INDUSTRY. For the broader context in which this concept appears, see the major article on THEORY OF THE FIRM as well as the Subject Map accompanying that article.

EQUILIBRIUM PRICE

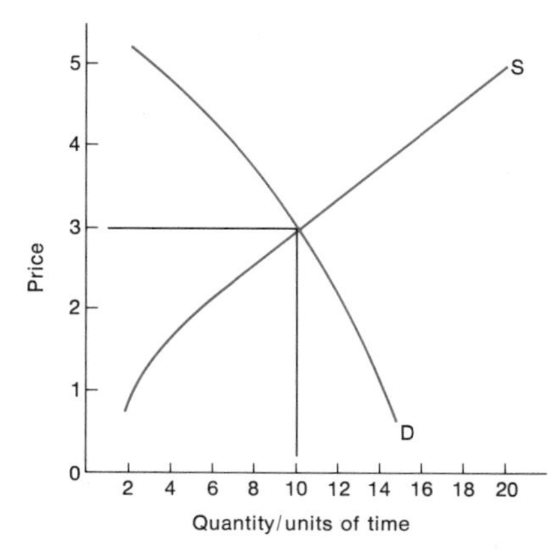

P	Q_D	Q_S
$5	3	20
4	7	15
3	10	10
2	12	5
1	14	2

consumer would like to pay as low a price as possible for the good to allow the purchase of other consumer goods.

If the price were above equilibrium, the producers would produce a larger quantity of the good than consumers would be willing to accept at that price, glutting the market and forcing prices down. If the price were below equilibrium, consumers would attempt to purchase a larger quantity of the goods than were being produced at that price, bidding the price up. Of course, this price movement assumes that there is no government control of prices. If there are price controls of any kind, there is always the possibility of a black-market bypassing the normal market channels.

See also Market Equilibrium.

Consult (11) Ferguson, 1968.

—Robert L. Brite, *Louisiana State University*

EQUILIBRIUM QUANTITY, the quantity of a good that the producers are willing to supply and the consumers are willing to purchase at a given price. In equilibrium the quantity supplied is equal to the quantity demanded. This situation will occur at only one market price. At higher prices the quantity that producers are willing to supply will exceed the quantity demanded, and at lower prices the quantity that producers are willing to supply will be smaller than the quantity demanded. Thus, only at the equilibirum price is the equilibrium quantity achieved.

EQUIPMENT, CAPITAL. *See* Capital Equipment.

EQUITIES. *See* Stock.

EQUITY, as a term, has several connotations, the most common being ownership in part or in whole of a firm. An example of equity is common stock issued by a corporation to secure capital. Equity carries with it risks of ownership, that is, possible gains or losses. The term equity is also used to describe the capital structure of a firm, for example, equity capital (from stock issues) as opposed to debt capital (from bond issues). In corporate financial evaluation equity is defined as the net value of a business derived by subtracting all liens and/or charges against it from its total value.

In welfare economics, equity is used to describe fairness, a method of judging the performance of a firm or the effect of a particular type of market structure on the consumer. Under certain market structures, such as a monopoly, the fairness criteria are not fulfilled, and the consumer may be exploited by the single producer.

EQUITY STOCK. *See* Common Stock.

ESCALATOR CLAUSE. *See* Cost-of-Living Increases.

ESCAPE PERIOD. *See* Maintenance of Membership.

ESSAY ON POPULATION (1798). In a reply to the unbounded optimism of Godwin and Condorcet, Thomas Malthus challenged their belief in man's perfectibility. He then postulated that (1) food is necessary, and (2) sexual passion will not diminish. Based upon these postulates, Malthus concluded that "the power of population is indefinitely greater than the power in the earth to produce subsistence for man," because population grows at a geometric rate, while food increases only at an arithmetic rate. When population presses against food supplies, the checks of vice, misery, and a higher death rate will prevent further population growth.

While the prediction of the first edition of the *Essay* was quite pessimistic, later editions, beginning with the second in 1803, added a third check—moral restraint—which allows man a further means of checking population growth in addition to vice, misery, and death.

See also Malthus, Thomas.

ESSAY ON THE NATURE AND SIGNIFICANCE OF ECONOMIC SCIENCE (1932). *See* Robbins, Lionel.

ESSAYS IN POSITIVE ECONOMICS (1953). *See* Friedman, Milton.

ESTATE TAX. *See* Taxation: *Glossary.*

EURODOLLARS, deposits denominated in dollars held in banks and/or financial institutions outside the United States. Though held mostly in England and Western Europe they can be held anywhere. There is a ready market in these holdings with demand and supply establishing interest rates conducive to regular investment as well as speculation. The use of the dollar as a "vehicle currency" in international transactions was an important factor in the creation of the Eurodollar.

See also Balance of Payments; Dollar Glut; Foreign Investment.

EUROPEAN COMMON MARKET. In a free-trade area, restrictions on the free movement of goods and services among members are eliminated, but each country retains its own restrictive devices with the rest of the world. In a customs union all restrictions are removed between members, and a common external tariff (CET) is established on goods entering the union from outside. A common market is the next higher degree of economic integration beyond the customs union; in addition to free trade among members and a CET, national restrictions on the movement of labor and capital among members are removed.

The European Economic Community (EEC), or Common Market, was established by the Treaty of Rome (1957), and was more or less an extension of the European Coal and Steel Community, created in 1953. EEC's present membership is West Germany, France, Italy, Belgium, The Netherlands, Luxembourg, Great Britain, Ireland, and Denmark. In addition to the provisions indicated above, the Treaty of Rome provided for: (1) prohibition of cartels and similar restrictive devices (unless they enhanced goals of the Community), (2) common agricultural policy, (3) two investment funds to channel capital from advanced to less developed regions in Europe, and associated overseas territories, and (4) a social fund to help relieve economic injuries to workers resulting from movement toward integration.

See also Customs Unions and Free-Trade Areas.

—John R. Matthews, Jr., *College of William and Mary*

EUROPEAN ECONOMIC COMMUNITY. *See* European Common Market.

EUROPEAN RECOVERY PROGRAM. *See* Marshall Plan.

EVOLUTIONARY SOCIALISM, the idea of socialism via gradual change rather than revolution. Most socialists agreed that capitalism had to be replaced; the evolutionaries believed that government could be an instrument of reform to reorganize society. A leading spokesman for gradualism was Eduard Bernstein of Germany (1850–1932), who called for a revision of Marxian theories, because many had proved incorrect and because the Marxian revolution was impracticable. The evolutionary approach was adopted in other countries, its supporters favoring such measures as increasing government control of business, gradual expansion of national and municipal ownership of productive enterprises, use of taxation to reduce inequality, and extension of free social services.

See also Nationalization; Fabian Society; Revisionism; Revolutionary Socialism.

Consult (26) Spiegel, 1971.

EXCESS CAPACITY refers to that scale of plant over and above that needed to produce enough goods to meet aggregate market demand. Often referred to as redundant capacity, excess capacity adds to the costs of production while adding nothing to the value of the product. For example, if a firm invests money in a plant capable of producing 1000 units, when only 500 units of the item are demanded, it is said to have excess capacity. If the firm had invested only enough money for a plant large enough to produce only 500 units the plant would be fully utilized and production costs would be less (equipment that has become obsolete due to technological innovations is not considered to be excess capacity.)

Excess capacity has a high incidence in the manufacturing industries, very often reflecting the seasonal nature of products. In addition, manufacturing industries, especially those producing durable goods, are greatly affected by fluctuations in the business cycle. Therefore, these industries are considered to have "cyclical excess capacity."

It is very difficult for industries, as well as individual firms, to determine just how much capacity will be needed at any specific time, because the demand for products in most industries is influenced by fluctuations in the economy. For example, from 1946 to 1956, the steel industry operated at nearly 100% utilization of capacity. In 1956, however, a minor business recession lowered utilization in that industry to less than 60%.

—William D. Wagoner, *Louisiana State University*

EXCESS DEMAND for a commodity occurs when its price is below the equilibrium. The equilibrium price clears the market by equating supply and demand. When the good's price is less than equilibrium, consumers demand a larger quantity of the good than producers are willing to supply, creating a shortage. Consumers will bid up the price to equilibrium. If there is government interference, a black market may result.

EXCESS PROFITS, in accounting, a base upon which an extra tax beyond the normal income tax can be levied (generally during war). In an economic sense, the term is synonymous with economic profits.

Normal profits are imputed returns sufficient to prevent owners from withdrawing from the industry in which they are earned. They are opportunity costs to the economist and are, therefore, included in the average total unit cost of the producer. Should products command a price higher than this unit cost, excess profits appear. These are signals for new firms to enter, whereupon the increased supply tends to reduce market price (production costs may also rise) until the excess profits—economic profits—are eliminated. If there are barriers to entry, such as occur in monopolistic markets, excess profits can remain.

See also Monopoly; Opportunity Cost; Profit System.

Consult (22) Eckaus, 1972; Lipsey and Steiner, 1969.

Idle equipment, like other forms of excess capacity, continues to run up production costs.

Foreign Exchange

Thursday, October 5, 1972

Selling Prices, New York Market

	High	Low	Final	Wednesday's Final
STERLING	$2.4251	$2.4215	$2.4215	$2.4248
CANADA	101.75	101.66	101.70	101.71
GERMANY	31.30½	31.23½	31.23½	31.23½

EUROPE

	Thursday	Wednesday	Week Ago	Year Ago
STERLING — No effective par value established yet.				
Spot	$2.4215	2.4248	2.4229	2.4895
90 days'	2.4071	2.4093	2.4076	2.5015
AUSTRIA—4.2918 cents a schilling. (4.198—4.3884).				
Spot	4.33	4.33	4.34	4.20
BELGIUM—2.23135 cents a franc. (2.18245—2.28310).				
Spot	2.2675	2.2650	2.2675	2.1280
DENMARK—14.3266 cents a krone. (14.0115—14.6563).				
Spot	14.48	14.51	13.95	13.78
FRANCE—19.54717 cents a franc. (19.1168—19.9980).				
Spot	19.98	19.96	19.96	18.11
GERMANY—31.0318 cents a mark. (30.3490—31.7460).				
Spot	31.23½	31.23½	31.22¾	30.17½
90 days'	31.48	31.50½	31.48¾	30.25½
ITALY—0.171969 cent a lira. (0.168180—				
Spot	0.1720	0.1718½	0.1719	0.1634
NETHERLANDS—30.8195 cents a guilder. (30.1432—31.5217).				
Spot	30.92	30.90½	30.91	29.74
NORWAY—15.0480 cents a krone. (14.7169—15.3866).				
Spot	15.20	15.15	15.12	14.63
PORTUGAL—3.6693 cents an escudo. (3.5894—3.7518).				
Spot	3.73	3.73	3.74	3.71
SPAIN—1.55102 cents a peseta. (1.151689—1.58672).				
Spot	1.59	1.59	1.59	1.47
SWEDEN—20.7775 cents a krona. (20.3202—21.2558).				
Spot	21.13	21.14	21.10	19.95
SWTZERLAND—26.0417 cents a franc. (25.-4680—26.6418).				
Spot	26.36	26.36	26.30	25.25½
90 days'	26.56	26.56	26.65	25.62½

OTHER COUNTRIES

	Thursday	Wednesday	Week Ago	Year Ago
AUSTRALIA—$1.2160 an Australian dollar. (1.1886—.11934).				
Spot	1.1940	1.1940	1.1940	1.1630
CANADA—No effective par value established yet.				
Spot	101.70	101.71	101.70	99.48
90 days'	102.72	101.75	101.72	99.63
NEW ZEALAND—$1.2160 a New Zealand dollar. (1.1887—1.2017).				
Spot	1.2020	1.2020	1.2020	1.1660
SOUTH AFRICA—$1.3383 a rand.				
Spot	1.2440	1.2440	1.2500	1.4110

FAR EAST

	Thursday	Wednesday	Week Ago	Year Ago
HONG KONG—17.87 cents a Hong Kong dollar. (17.48—18.28).				
Spot	17.80	17.80	17.80	17.18
INDIA—13.7376 cents a rupee. (13.4353—14.0538).				
Spot	12.98	12.98	13.07	13.45
JAPAN—0.324675 cents a yen. (0.317531—0.332149).				
Spot	0.3325	0.3322½	0.3325	0.3025
PAKISTAN—9.09 cents a rupee.				
Spot	9.20	9.20	9.20	21.50

Exchange rate listing tells how much of foreign currencies a dollar will buy.

EXCESS RESERVES. *See* Multiple Expansion of the Money Supply.

EXCESS SUPPLY of a commodity occurs when its price is above the equilibrium. The equilibrium price is defined as the price that clears the market by making supply equal demand. If the price of the good exceeds equilibrium, producers will tend to supply a quantity in excess of the amount demanded by consumers, creating an excess supply. From this price there will be an automatic tendency for the price to decline as producers' inventories build up.

EXCHANGE ARBITRAGE. *See* Arbitrage.

EXCHANGE RATE, the domestic price of a unit of foreign currency. This price is set by demand and supply and is derived from the demand and supply of goods and services. Claims of foreigners on the United States give rise to demand for exchange in this country; American claims on foreigners give rise to supply. If demand exceeds supply, the exchange rate rises; if supply increases with no change in demand the rate falls; it is in equilibrium when there is no pressure to change. The overall situation in a nation's balance of payments determines whether or not the rate will change. The rate can be manipulated, and such manipulation, or lack of it, has given rise to several exchange rate systems.

Freely Fluctuating rates vary with demand and supply without limits. Adjustment is automatic; rising rate makes imports more costly and increases exports (a rise in English pounds in the United States means a decline in the pound rate on dollars, and United States goods are cheaper). If the rate change is one of a series in the same direction, there will be destabilizing operations.

Fixed Rates, such as the pure gold standard, move over a narrow range, with the upper and lower points known. Adjustment is automatic, but unlike the freely fluctuating system, the fixed rate places the burden on the domestic economy rather than the balance of payments.

Flexible Rates allow the market to set rates within prescribed limits, with government intervention when those limits are reached. Exchange is supplied when demand would drive the rate too high; exchange is purchased when supply would push the rate too low. This system allows for automatic adjustment but relieves the domestic economy of the burden. This system is used by the International Monetary Fund in that each member agrees to peg its currency, within limits, to the dollar. Resources for pegging may be obtained when necessary from IMF. Problems arise when a nation has to intervene on only one side of the peg and a new official rate has to be established.

Floating Rates are employed as temporary measures; rates are allowed to seek their own level in the market to establish what the new official rate should be. This system does not rule out intervention, but there is no official limit. On a more permanent basis the adjustment problem requires a mechanism for changing parities with less delay than the present system of large and infrequent changes; a crawling (or sliding) peg is one such mechanism: changes would be made often and in small amounts, either up or down, based on some accepted criterion, which would operate automatically or discretionarily until equilibrium is achieved.

Exchange Control rates are set by the government, which has direct control over both demand and supply. A multiple rate system is often concomitant with rates being set in line with a specific government program.

See also Devaluation; Fixed Exchange Rates; Gold Standard; International Trade Theory.

Consult (23) Ingram, 1970; Krause, 1971; Snider, 1971; Wexler, 1972.

—John R. Matthews, Jr., *College of William and Mary*

EXCHANGE RATE EQUILIBRIUM. *See* Exchange Rate.

EXCISE TAX, a type of sales tax which is narrow-based, that is, applied to one or a few commodities. In addition to providing revenue, excise taxes may be imposed on "luxury" goods for the purpose of income redistribution, or on "undesirable" commodities, such as liquor and tobacco, to discourage consumption. The tax is likely to be borne by the consumer of the taxed product.

EXCLUSIVE DEALERSHIP, an agreement in which a producer of a line of products stipulates that a retailer may sell those products only if he does not handle the products of a rival producer. Such agreements, clearly anticompetitive in their limitation of a rival's opportunity to sell, are prohibited by the Clayton Act (Section 3) where their effect tends to lessen competition substantially.

EXIMBANK. *See* Export-Import Bank.

EXIT of a firm from an industry usually occurs when normal profits cannot be made. This means that total revenue received by the firm is less than total costs in the long run and the firm is operating at a loss. The decision to exit is often very difficult for the individual firm, especially if there has been a heavy capital investment and its fixed cost factor is large.

EXOGENOUS THEORY OF BUSINESS CYCLES. *See* External Theory of Business Cycles.

EXPANDED CIRCULAR FLOW. *See* Circular Flow of Income.

EXPANSION. *See* Business Cycles, Phases.

EXPECTED UTILITY, or CHOICE UNDER UNCERTAINTY. Choice under certainty means that the outcome of a particular choice is known in advance. For example, in the standard theory of consumer behavior, the consumer chooses a bundle of commodities, and he knows exactly how much of the various commodities is in each bundle before he makes his choice. Choice under uncertainty, on the other hand, is a situation in which the outcome of a particular choice is not known in advance. Often the nature of the uncertainty can be specified in probabilistic terms. In such circumstances for each possible choice the consumer knows the complete set of all potential outcomes, and to each potential outcome he can attach the probability of its occurrence. Thus, with each possible choice there is associated an uncertain prospect, or probability distribution. One important aspect of the theory of choice under uncertainty is the determination of the decision maker's preference ordering for uncertain prospects.

Two Payoffs. The problem is illustrated for choices whose outcomes are monetary payoffs. The simplest uncertain prospect is one that has only two possible payoffs, say x_1 and x_2. If, for example, the probability of x_1 is $\frac{1}{3}$, and that of x_2 is $\frac{2}{3}$, then the mean of this probability distribution, also called the expected payoff, and denoted by $\bar{x}$, is given by the weighted average $\bar{x} = \frac{1}{3}x_1 + \frac{2}{3}x_2$. The two payoffs and the expected payoff are marked on the horizontal axis in Figure 1. The expected payoff divides the interval between the two payoffs into two segments whose lengths are proportional to the two probabilities:

$$\frac{\bar{x} - x_1}{x_2 - \bar{x}} = \frac{2/3}{1/3} = 2$$

Also shown on the diagram is the decision maker's total utility curve (utility function), which assigns a utility to every possible payoff x.

Under conditions of uncertainty the actual outcome is not known in advance, and the consumer has no way of knowing with certainty which level of utility he will attain if he chooses a particular uncertain prospect. However, it is possible to compute the expected utility of any uncertain prospect, which for the above example is defined as the weighted average $\bar{u}_3 = \frac{1}{3}u_1 + \frac{2}{3}u_2$. Expected utility can be thought of as the utility level that the decision maker would attain on the average if he chose the same prospect time after time. The value of expected utility $\bar{u}_3$ can be found on the vertical axis at a point two-thirds the distance from u_1 to u_2. It can also be located by drawing a horizontal line from point C to the vertical axis.

Expected utility is the criterion for ordering uncertain prospects. For any two uncertain prospects, the prospect with the higher expected utility is preferred. Thus, in the theory of choice under uncertainty, expected utility plays the same role as the utility index in choice under certainty. A choice between two uncertain prospects is illustrated in Figure 2, which in part reproduces the conditions of Figure 1. A second uncertain prospect is introduced with the same payoffs as the first one, but in which the probability of the payoff x_1 is greater than $\frac{1}{3}$. Consequently, the expected payoff of the second uncertain prospect, denoted by x_4, is less than $\bar{x}_3$. Therefore, the expected utility $\bar{u}_4$ of the second uncertain prospect is also less than that of the first prospect; the first prospect is preferred to the second one.

Another example is illustrated in Figure 3, which involves two uncertain prospects A and B. The payoffs of prospect A are x_2 and x_3, and its expected payoff is $\bar{x}_A$; prospect B offers payoffs x_1 and x_3, and its expected payoff is $\bar{x}_B$. Because $\bar{u}_A > \bar{u}_B$, prospect A is preferred. Unlike in Figure 2, the expected payoff of the preferred prospect is smaller than the expected payoff of the other prospect. Thus, to determine preference between uncertain prospects, it is in general not enough to compare the expected payoffs of the prospects under consideration.

Risk Aversion. Decision makers operating under uncertainty often exhibit a type of behavior known as risk aversion. By definition, a person is averse to risk if he prefers a sure prospect of, say, x dollars to an uncertain prospect whose expected payoff is x dollars. If the individual's utility function is concave, then he is a risk averter, as illustrated in Figure 4. The uncertain prospect under consideration consists of the two payoffs x_1 and x_2, and its expected payoff is $\bar{x}$. If the individual is asked to choose between $\bar{x}$ dollars for sure and the above uncertain prospect, he will choose the sure prospect, because the utility u′ of the sure prospect is higher than the expected utility $\bar{u}$ of the uncertain prospect.

If the individual is offered a choice between x_3 dollars for sure and the uncertain prospect represented in Figure 4, he will be indifferent between the two choices—both have the same level of utility. The payoff x_3 is therefore referred to as the certainty-equivalent of the above uncertain prospect. If the sure prospect that is offered as an alternative to the uncertain prospect is less than x_3, then the individual will choose the uncertain prospect. The quantity $\bar{x} - x_3$ is called the insurance premium, or risk premium, of the uncertain

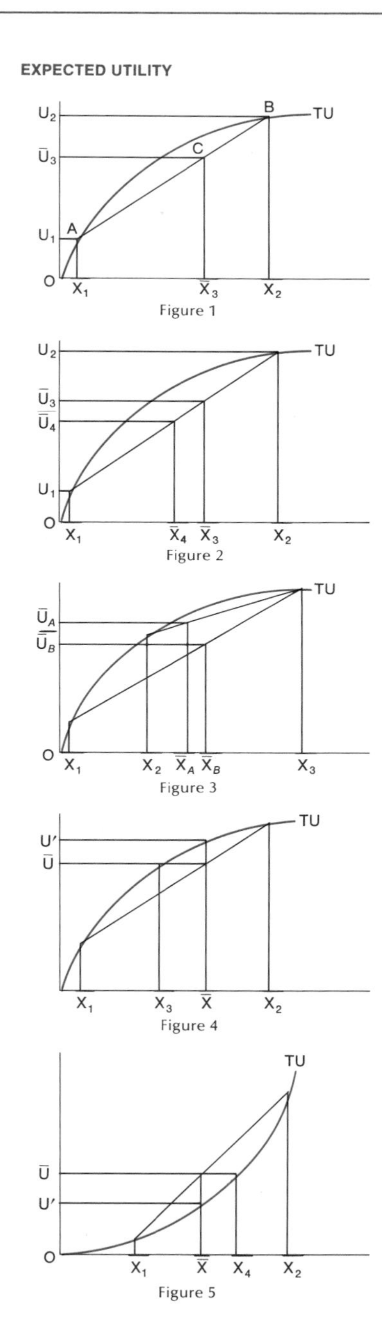

Figure 1

Figure 2

Figure 3

Figure 4

Figure 5

Automobiles are an export of several countries; these U.S.-made cars are arriving in Japan.

prospect. This premium may be interpreted in either one of two ways: (1) it may be thought of as the maximum amount of dollars the individual is willing to forgo in order not to be exposed to risk; (2) it may also be thought of as the minimum premium the individual has to be paid to expose himself to risk by switching from the sure prospect to the uncertain prospect. A typical manifestation of risk aversion is the purchase of insurance.

Attraction to Risk is the opposite of risk aversion. By definition, an individual is attracted to risk if he prefers an uncertain prospect with an expected payoff of x dollars to x dollars with certainty. Attraction to risk occurs when the utility function is convex, as in Figure 5. As before, the uncertain prospect is specified by the payoffs x_1 and x_2, the expected payoff being $\bar{x}$. Because the expected utility $\bar{u}$ of the uncertain prospect is higher than the utility u' of the sure payoff $\bar{x}$, the individual prefers the uncertain prospect. If instead of being offered $\bar{x}$ dollars for sure, the individual is offered x_4 dollars for sure, then he is indifferent between the sure prospect and the uncertain prospect. Thus, x_4 is the certainty-equivalent of the uncertain prospect. If the sure prospect exceeds x_4, the individual prefers the sure prospect to the uncertain prospect. It is to be noted that the risk premium $\bar{x} - x_4$ is negative. Rather than demanding insurance, a person who is attracted to risk is willing to pay a certain amount to be exposed to risk. In the above example the amount $x_4 - \bar{x}$ is the maximum amount the individual is willing to forgo to assume the risk associated with the uncertain prospect. A typical manifestation of attraction to risk is participation in games of chance.

See also Utility Function.

Consult (12) Hadar, 1973.

—Josef Hadar, *Case Western Reserve University*

EXPLOSIVE EQUILIBRIUM, an equilibrium in which the price and quantity of a commodity move away from the initial equilibrium rather than converge toward it after an initial disturbance. The explosive equilibrium is associated with the cobweb model.

See also Cobweb Equilibrium.

EXPORT-IMPORT BANK. The Eximbank was established in 1934 as a District of Columbia banking agency; in 1945 it was reincorporated as an independent government agency. It extends credits to foreign purchasers of U.S. goods and so aids the export segment of the economy. Its loans are "tied" in that the proceeds must be spent in the lending country. In addition the Eximbank provides guarantees against credit and political risks. Though most of its operations are related to financing U.S. exports it also extends long-term development loans in maturities from 8 to 20 years. Many such loans have been made to countries in Latin America and the Eximbank is considered a source of development finance. When these loans are used to finance basic industrial and public utilities projects, U.S. exports of heavy machinery and equipment are benefitted. Loans have also been made to underdeveloped countries with balance of payments difficulties to enable them to maintain their level of U.S. imports. The Eximbank provides little technical assistance to developing nations; its basic interest is the promotion of U.S. exports.

Consult (23) Wexler, 1972.

EXPORTS, the credit item in the balance of trade, and a major credit item in the current account in a nation's balance of payments. Exports of goods and services include all the credit items in the current account. The capital account in the balance of payments includes both short and long-term capital exports, which unlike merchandise exports, are debits. When a nation exports merchandise, there is an impact on the domestic economy: the immediate result is an increase in incomes to exporters and a concomitant fall in the supply of goods and services. Therefore, exports have an expansionary impact in the economy of the exporting nation.

The gross national product is composed of personal consumption, domestic investment, government purchase, and net exports. The last component is the difference between gross exports and imports and the reason for recording it on the net basis is to preclude double-counting—the other components include imports as well as domestic goods. Hence any change in net exports has the domestic income multiplier applied to it and is most important in the determination of the foreign trade multiplier. Combined exports and imports for the United States have never exceeded 10% of GNP. Other countries, such as Great Britain, have to trade to live. Underdeveloped nations are constantly trying to develop an export base as a means of obtaining foreign exchange to purchase imports necessary for development.

See also Balance of Payments; Balance of Trade; Foreign Trade Multiplier; Visible Goods and Services.

Consult (23) Ingram, 1970; Snider, 1971; Wexler, 1972.

—John R. Matthews, Jr., *College of William and Mary*

EXTERNAL COSTS, those costs of the production process, such as water and air pollution, that are not borne by the producing unit and, therefore, are not taken into account by that unit in making its economic decisions. Under pressure from environmental groups and others, government has recently begun to force producers to internalize a number of costs that were previously externalities. For example, laws passed in some localities requiring deposits on all beverage containers require consumers and bottlers, rather than the local government, to bear the cost of container disposal.

See also Internal Costs.

EXTERNAL DEBT, the condition where the borrowing unit (the government) acquires money from some lending unit or units outside of the nation itself. There is therefore an outside or external claim against American productive resources and against the income and output which these resources can create. Such borrowing actually transfers real goods and services from the debtor nation to the creditor nation.

See also Internal Debt.

EXTERNALITIES (External Economies) arise when producers are not paid the full value of their production or when consumers do not pay the full value of their consumption. Their existence implies a situation in which a producer (a firm or an individual) can not appropriate the full value of his output, or in which society cannot appropriate a full value of its services to a firm or an individual.

In a Less Developed Country (LDC), for instance, the establishment of a new firm often "produces" labor training by taking inexperienced workers, adapting them to an industrial environment and factory discipline, and perhaps teaching them new skills. But in most societies (where slavery or apprenticeship are illegal), these workers are then free to move on to other jobs, and the industry must constantly train new laborers. In addition to its normal output, for which it is paid, the firm produces labor training at a loss; the value of production to society exceeds the price that the society must pay. Because there is no mechanism to pay the firm for its extra output, too little will be produced; because of its reduced profits the firm may not expand as rapidly as it should, or it may not be able to operate at all.

Diagram Explanation. This type of externality may be demonstrated in the figure. The firm is willing to supply its normal output (say cloth) and the associated labor training according to the supply curve S. Consumers, who individually demand only the cloth, operate along the demand curve D, and thus the equilibrium price and quantity are P_2 and Q_1 respectively. Society, however, values both the cloth and the labor training and would thus be willing to pay more than individual consumers at any given level of cloth and labor training consumption. Society's demand curve is then above D_1 at D_2, and the social equilibrium is at point Q_2, P_3. Yet without some mechanism for transforming society's extra demands into market demands, the firm will continue to produce too little cloth and too little labor training (Q, rather than Q_2) because at the output the market price, P, will be below value of the output to society, that is, its shadow price, P_4. Indeed, the firm may not even be able to operate at all at the market price P_2, whereas at the shadow price, P_4, or the social equilibrium price and quantity, P_3, Q_2 production might well be profitable.

This is an example of an external economy. External diseconomies arise when society pays more, in terms of increased pollution for example, than the value of output produced.

The solution to externalities is to "internalize" them, and this may be done in at least two ways. The first is to pay producers for the full social value of their output and to charge consumers for the full social value of their consumption. For example, the firm training labor may be given a subsidy equal to the value of its labor training and a polluting firm may be required to pay for the value of the clean air and water it consumes (pollutes). In the labor-training case diagram this would involve society's giving a subsidy to the firm equal to the vertical distance between D_2 and D_1, making D_2 the market demand curve facing the firm and eliciting the output Q_2.

The second solution is to have society participate directly in the decision-making process of the firm, perhaps by forcing it to produce at the socially optimal output. This may involve losses for the firm if, for instance, consumers pay only P_1 (see diagram) for the output. If the firm refuses to produce the social optimum, it may be nationalized.

See also Infrastructure; Planning for Growth.

—Charles Staelin, *University of Michigan*

EXTERNALITIES

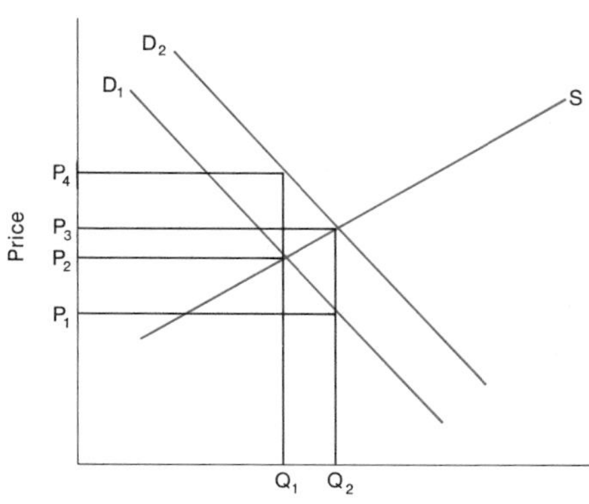

EXTERNAL (or EXOGENEOUS) THEORY OF BUSINESS CYCLES assumes that fluctuations in economic activity are caused by factors outside the economic system. External explanations include, for example, wars and revolutions; politics; and sunspot cycles, a now disused nineteenth-century theory. Other external factors include the rates of immigration and population growth, discovery of new resources, and scientific and technological innovations. An innovation, for example, encourages business to invest in the same or similar technology. Exogenous theories, because they seem to indicate that business cycles are neither predictable or controllable, generally lack favor among economists.

See also Business Cycles, Theories.

FABIAN SOCIETY, British organization committed to the gradual improvement of society in every legal and ethical way. Founded in 1884, it was named after a Roman general who fought his enemies in a variety of ways without going into battle. The Fabians actively sup-

Fabian George Bernard Shaw.

ported labor unions, public education, and the consumer cooperative movement and were politically involved with social and economic reforms. Initial leaders in this form of evolutionary socialism were George Bernard Shaw and Sidney and Beatrice Webb.

See also British Labour Party; Evolutionary Socialism; Nationalization.

FABRICANT, SOLOMON (1906-), American economist. He is a graduate of the City College of New York (1929) and he received his Ph.D. in economics from Columbia (1938). His numerous publications include *Employment in Manufacturing* (1942), *Trends of Government Activity Since 1900* (1952), *Economic Progress and Economic Change* (1954), and *Primer on Productivity* (1969). He has been director of research at the National Bureau of Economic Research (1953-65), and a consultant to the Bureau of the Census (1945-50), the Bureau of the Budget (1946-52) and the National Security Resources Board (1948-49).

FACT FINDING, a form of third-party intervention into collective bargaining impasses. In public interest disputes or emergency strikes, fact finding by a government-designated board may be an influential force in bringing about a settlement, particularly if the board's conclusions and recommendations bring public opinion to bear on labor and management, or if the parties have agreed to abide by such recommendations. In disputes not seriously affecting the public well-being, the parties are free to agree among themselves to use fact finding as an aid to reaching agreement.

See also Collective Bargaining; Emergency Strikes.

FACTOR COMPLEMENTARITY. *See* Joint Demand.

FACTOR DEMAND, the demand for a factor of production. Factor demand differs somewhat from the demand for a commodity, which reflects the satisfaction or utility that consumers receive.

Factors and Commodities. When businessmen demand a factor, they do so because the input can produce commodities that ultimately generate revenues to the firm by sales to households. Therefore, indirectly, factors are desired for the satisfactions they produce: factor demand is a derived (indirect) demand. Another difference between commodity and factor demands is that the commodities are purchased outright (by a consumer); factors are hired as a service to be used for a period of time (by businesses). However, the demand for a factor parallels the value theory of commodities; in the final analysis, supply and demand per unit of time determine the market prices of factors.

Demand Schedules. Because the demand for a factor of production depends on that factor's ability to produce goods and services, ultimately the demand schedule of an input reflects the input's productivity according to the law of diminishing returns. It can be demonstrated that in a barter economy the demand curve for a variable factor is the same as that factor's marginal product curve. If, say, the going rate for a factor is 10 bushels of wheat per year in a barter economy, input buyers will hire up to the point where the factor's marginal (extra) product equals 10 bushels. Units of a factor that have marginal product less than 10 bushels will not voluntarily be hired. This result can easily be generalized to a money economy: an input will be hired up to the point where its cost (market price) equals its marginal revenue product (marginal physical product times commodity selling price, under pure competition). A firm will not voluntarily hire an input if it produces goods worth less than the firm has to pay for the input itself. Advanced treatments indicate that a factor's marginal product schedule (physical or value) is, in fact, the factor demand schedule only when the factor is the only variable input. If several factors may be varied, then their respective demand schedules can be theoretically derived, but they are somewhat more complicated.

—Robert L. Brite, *Louisiana State University*

FACTOR EARNINGS, payments made to the factors of production for their use as inputs. The four factors of production are land, labor, management, and capital.

See also Factor Payments.

FACTOR EMPLOYMENT, the usage of any of the four factors of production—land, labor, capital, and entrepreneurship. The employment of land refers to its use either as a primary productive unit, as in agriculture, or as a secondary means of production, such as the groundwork for the construction of a building. The employment of labor refers to the hiring of workers in the labor force for productive purposes. Capital employment is the use of durable items, such as machinery, tools, and buildings, that are used as inputs in the production process.

See also Factors of Production.

FACTOR INCOMES, that proportion of total payments to factors of production which go to any one factor. They include wages, rent, interest, and profit as payments to labor, land, capital, and entrepreneurial ability, respectively. The distribution of income among factors (the functional distribution of income) isolates the income paid to the various factors rather than payments received by those who supply the factor. A factor supplier may supply several factors, such as his own labor, land he owns, and so forth. His income is the sum of the income he receives from each source. Thus, measuring the total income of individuals tells nothing about the amount of income generated by each factor. Economists feel it is important to know both the distribution of income among individuals and among factors of production.

See also Circular Flow of Income; Factor Payments.

FACTOR INPUTS. *See* Factors of Production.

FACTOR MARKETS, the markets for land, labor, capital, and management. A market is a closely interrelated group of buyers and sellers. In the factor markets the buyers and sellers are all concerned with a specific input of production. The buyers, which are usually individual firms, purchase the inputs for production from the sellers for a price, usually determined by the intersection of market supply and market demand curves.

The market for land is based upon three major items, its availability, desirability, and cost of use (rent). If both the buyer and the seller of land agree on a price, land is then used as an input to production.

The labor market consists of individual firms (purchasers of labor) and members of the labor force (sellers of labor). The price of labor (wages) is determined by the supply of and demand for each type of labor. There are many types of labor, depending upon such attributes as skill, training, and experience levels.

The capital market is mainly the market for capital funds that can be used for investment. Capital is the accumulation of durable goods used in the production process, such as machinery, tools, and buildings. The main determinant of the allocation of funds in the capital market is the interest rate. The interest rate is the price paid for the use of money. The sellers in the capital market are normally investors, and usually they will invest where they expect to get the highest rate of interest.

See also Factors of Production; Market Mechanism.

Consult (11) Ferguson, 1968; Leftwich, 1970; Liebhafsky, 1968.

—William D. Wagoner, *Louisiana State University*

FACTOR MOBILITY refers to the relative freedom with which the factors of production are able to move among alternative uses. These factors are land, labor, capital, and entrepreneurship.

Factors are mobile to the extent that they are free of restraint. For this reason, factor mobility is greatest in purely competitive market structures because, in monopolistic market structures, such things as large investments and few firms inhibit free movement of production factors. For example, if a man is trained to install telephones, he may not be free to take his knowledge to another telephone company without relocating. Hence, factor mobility is restrained.

FACTOR PAYMENTS, the prices paid for the inputs of production, the costs of a firm. The four factors of production are land, labor, entrepreneurship, and capital. The cost of land usually comes in the form of rent paid for the use of land. Factor payments to labor and entrepreneurship are in the form of wages and salaries. Wages are paid to workers to compensate them for their services. Payments for the use of capital are in the form of interest.

FACTOR PRICES in a competitive market structure are determined by the supply and demand conditions existing in the market, as are the prices of other commodities. Thus, if the labor supply curve shifts to the right, showing an increase in supply, then the price of labor (wages) falls, and the quantity demanded subsequently increases. Other shifts in market conditions, shown by movements of the demand or supply curves, would cause other wage and quantity changes, depending upon the direction of the particular shift.

FACTOR PRODUCTIVITY, the ability of a factor to produce goods and services of value to consumers. The productivity of a factor underlies the demand for it by businesses. When discussing factor productivity, one has to distinguish clearly between physical productivity and value productivity.

The physical productivity of a factor is a purely technological phenomenon. As such, a factor's physical productivity (in terms of the various physical product schedules of an input) depends on: (1) the state of the arts (technology), (2) the amounts of other factors used in the productive process (increases in one factor will lead to increased productivity for other factors), and (3) the law of diminishing returns.

The value productivity schedule also depends on the above three considerations. In addition, marginal value schedules are determined by the market price of the commodity produced. The market price reflects the value that society places on the commodity. If consumer preferences change in favor of this commodity, prices will rise, and the value productivity schedules will increase. If tastes change against this commodity, prices will fall, and the value productivity schedules will shift backward, essentially a reduction in the demand for that factor. Thus, the price of a factor depends on the selling price of the commodities it produces.

The obvious factor of production here is labor; implicit are the tools used, the building in progress (capital), and the land occupied.

FACTOR MARKETS

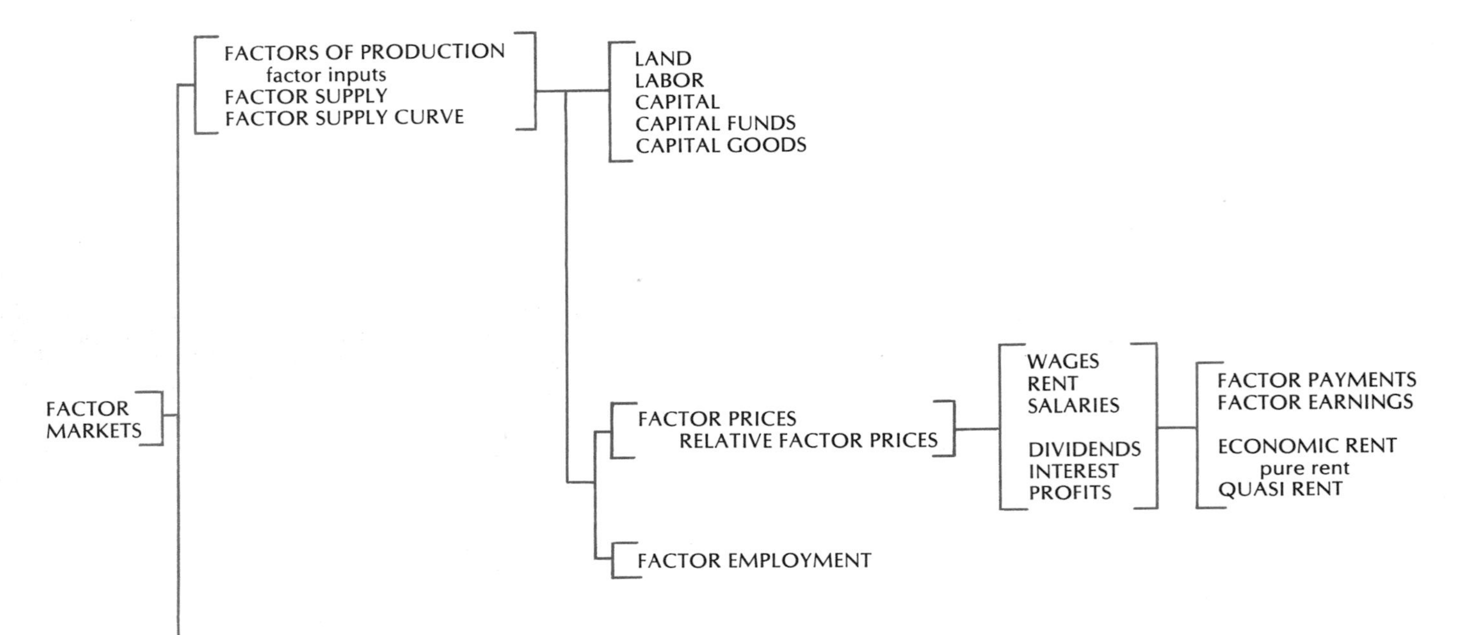

FACTOR DEMAND
derived demand
FACTOR PRODUCTIVITY
value productivity
PHYSICAL PRODUCTIVITY
MARGINAL PHYSICAL PRODUCTIVITY
DIMINISHING MARGINAL PHYSICAL PRODUCTIVITY

FACTOR SUBSTITUTION
JOINT DEMAND
factor complementarity
FACTOR PROPORTIONS

ISO-PRODUCT CURVE
isoquant
equal-product curve
BUDGET LINES, FIRM

The Subject Maps in the Encyclopedia illustrate the coverage of particular aspects of economics, showing the interrelationships among the articles in twenty-one critical areas of study. Entries in capital letters are subjects for which there are separate articles in the Encyclopedia. Entries in small letters are references to the article immediately above and provide some idea of content.

The Subject Maps are arranged alphabetically in the Encyclopedia under the following titles:

Antitrust Policy
Banking System
Business Cycles
Capital
Circular Flow of Income
Demand Theory
Economic Systems
Factor Markets
Federal Budget
History of Economic Ideas
International Trade Theory
Labor Market
Labor Movement
Market System
Money and Monetary Policy
National Income
Price Level
Regulation
Supply
Theory of the Firm
Wages

The price of other factors of production will affect marginal value. If the price of labor rises, then to the extent that the other inputs can substitute for labor in the productive process, the demand for the other factors will rise. Similarly, a reduction in the price of capital will lead to a reduction in the demand for labor and other competing inputs.

—Robert L. Brite, *Louisiana State University*

FACTOR PROPORTIONS. Variable proportions imply that factors of production are substitutes for each other. A given product is produced by different techniques—or a given quantity of output is produced several ways—by changing the proportions, or ratios of the factors. Fixed proportions imply that there is only one way to produce a given product—or that a given quantity of output can be produced in only one way. Fixed proportions fit the layman's notion of production, but very few examples of fixed proportions actually exist.

FACTOR SERVICES, the financial services of a person or institution (a factor in this context) who lends a business money on the security of its inventory or accounts receivable. Factor services are typically utilized in industries, such as textiles, so fragmented that the individual businesses are of insufficient size and stature to obtain loans on their own credit.

FACTORS OF PRODUCTION, the inputs that a firm uses to produce units of output. The amounts of each input needed for a specified output vary with the product, the production technique, and the degree of substitutability of the inputs. There are four major factors of production: land, labor, capital, and management (entrepreneurship). The higher the degree of substitutability of these inputs is, the cheaper will be the factor costs of the firm, because as the price of one factor rises, the firm can substitute an input with a lower price.

Land, as a factor of production, refers to any land used for purposes of producing an output. Land is a primary factor when it is cultivated or used for grazing in the agricultural industry. Land is a secondary factor when it is used, for example, as the ground on which a building is built. Rent is payment for the use of land.

Labor, as a factor of production, is usually calculated on the basis of man-hours, the number of hours of actual labor needed. The inputs of labor are employed by hiring qualified workers from the labor force, which is made up of individuals who are willing and able to work. The factor payment to labor is in the form of wages and salaries.

Capital, as an input, is the accumulation of wealth that is invested in durable items for the purposes of production. Capital often takes the form of machinery, tools, and buildings that are made to last a certain period of time. The factor payment for the use of capital is in the form of interest.

—William D. Wagoner, *Louisiana State University*

FACTOR SUBSTITUTION. Much of what is interesting in the economics of production depends on factor substitutability. The fact that factors compete with each other in the productive process implies that there are at least several ways that a given product or output can be produced. The profit-maximizing firm must take the substitutability of factors into consideration.

Factor substitution implies that the amount of a given factor that will be used depends on its price and on the prices of the other factors as well. The elasticity of substitution, which measures the ability of businesses to alter factor ratios, due to relative factor price changes, ultimately determines factor shares (functional distribution of income). If wage rates rise and capital cannot be easily substituted, labor's share of income will rise.

FACTOR SUPPLY, a functional relationship that specifies the determinants of the conditions under which varying amounts of a factor will voluntarily be offered. The factors usually analyzed in elementary economic studies are labor and land.

Some of the potential determinants of the supply of labor, in general, include wage rates, population, and work-ethic notions of the society. Potential determinants of the supply of labor to an industry include relative working conditions and ease of mobility into the industry. Mobility may be restricted by natural requirements (intelligence, skill, strength), transportation costs, or union restrictions.

Land is a special case; the supply of land is generally considered to be in constant supply. Some extreme methods may increase or decrease land, but existing land prices preclude most of them. The uses to which land can be put may be highly responsive to price.

FACTOR SUPPLY CURVE, a two-dimensional graphical representation of the conditions under which various quantities of a factor will be offered per unit of time. Factor price is usually plotted on the vertical axis against quantity supplied. Changes in other determinants of quantity shift the supply curve. If group notions change to more highly prize leisure, a reduction in supply will occur and the supply curve of labor will shift backward to the left. Normally, except for land, factor supply curves are positively sloped; higher prices are required before additional quantities of a factor will be offered.

FACTORS OF PRODUCTION

For the general role of factors of production in a market economy, see the article on the *CIRCULAR FLOW OF INCOME. Details of this role are to be found in the articles on *FACTOR MARKETS, FACTOR DEMAND, FACTOR PRICES, and FACTOR PAYMENTS. For still more specifics, see the articles on *LABOR MARKET, LABOR FORCE, LABOR SUPPLY, and DEMAND FOR CAPITAL. For the specific forms of factor incomes, see *WAGES, RENT, DIVIDENDS, and INTEREST.

The articles preceded by an asterisk (*) above are each accompanied by a Subject Map which further illuminates the interrelationships of the various Factors of Production to other articles in the Encyclopedia.

FACTORS OF PRODUCTION

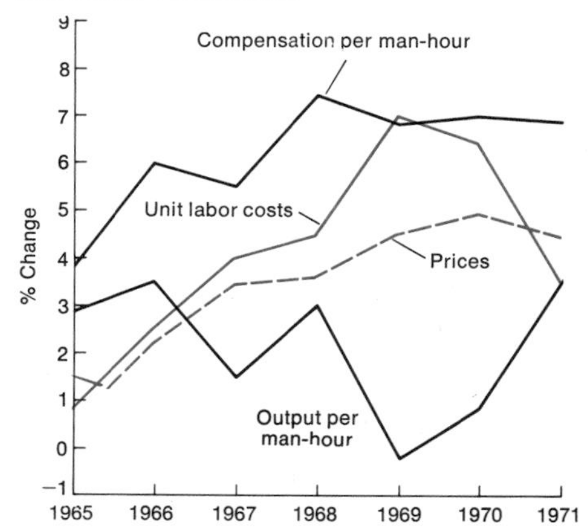

FAIR LABOR STANDARDS ACT (FLSA) (1938), also known as the Wage and Hour Law or the Minimum Wage Law, an important part of the wide-ranging economic reform legislation of the 1930s. The original act set a minimum wage of $.25 per hour in covered employments and provided for time-and-a-half pay for hours beyond 44 per week. Stair-step increases in the minimum wage to $.40 were provided for, and the regular work week was scaled down to 40 hours.

Numerous amendments to the FLSA have expanded its coverage, dramatically raised the minimum wage level, specified overtime pay for hours beyond 8 per day as well as beyond 40 per week, and added the "equal pay" and several other protections against sex discrimination in employment. The expanding coverage of the federal law now comprises almost 80% of all workers in the private sector. For the rest, state minimum wage laws may apply, but a relatively small percentage of the labor force is protected by them, and fewer still are actually affected.

—Leonard G. Schifrin, *College of William and Mary*

Italian Fascist dictator Benito Mussolini.

FAIRNESS. *See* Equity.

FAIR RETURN ON FAIR VALUE, the general standard established by the U.S. Supreme Court in *Smyth v. Ames* (1898) to be used in determining rates in a regulated industry. To substitute an administrative device for the impersonal market mechanism, some standard (guideline) has to be determined for regulatory commissions. The Supreme Court established this standard because rates too low would confiscate property without due process in violation of the 5th and 14th amendments; rates too high would be "unjust and unreasonable." Hence a utility is constitutionally guaranteed the right to recover its operating expenses plus an opportunity to earn a fair return on a fair value. Interpretation of what is "fair" is obviously judgmental.

See also Hope Natural Gas Case (1944); Smyth v. Ames (1898).

FAIR-TRADE LAWS permit contracts between the manufacturer and the retailer of a branded product setting a minimum price below which the retailer agrees not to sell. Such fair-trade contracts ostensibly are violations of Section 1 of the Sherman Act, prohibiting restraints of trade. Since individual states govern intrastate commerce, the first trade laws were state laws, having neither validity in interstate commerce nor exemption from the Sherman Act. The Miller-Tydings Act ('37) enabled firms selling in interstate commerce to sell into those states having state fair-trade laws, an exemption reaffirmed in the McGuire-Keogh Act (1952). At one time or another, all but four states (Alaska, Missouri, Texas, and Vermont) have passed fair-trade laws. They are now considered effective in about 20 states.

See also McGuire-Koegh Act; Miller-Tydings Act; Resale Price Maintenance.

FAMILIES WITH DEPENDENT CHILDREN, AID TO. *See* Aid to Families with Dependent Children.

FAMILY ASSISTANCE. *See* General Assistance.

FAMILY PLANNING. *See* Population Growth.

FARM BUREAU FEDERATION, AMERICAN (AFBF) began in one county in 1911 and became a national federation in 1920. By 1971 AFBF had 2,058,000 members, most of America's farmers, and was the largest of the several national farm organizations. AFBF actively works for agricultural policy it favors. Until about 1950 it usually supported government farm programs; since then it has emphasized individual freedom and free markets and has generally sought to reduce the role of government in agriculture. Numerous affiliates engage in the cooperative purchase of farm supplies and in providing various kinds of insurance. The American Agricultural Marketing Association organizes bargaining associations of farmers to negotiate terms of sale with buyers.

FARMERS ORGANIZATION, NATIONAL (NFO), the newest and probably the smallest of the four national farm organizations. It was formed in the Midwest in 1955 in reaction to low prices. Its principal aim is to organize farmers into sufficiently large blocs to exercise strong bargaining power in the sale of their products. NFO has organized a number of "withholding actions" to keep products from the market. Too limited in most instances to have much effect on prices, the actions have succeeded in publicizing the purposes of the organization.

FARMERS UNION, NATIONAL (NFU), begun in 1902 as the Farmers Educational and Cooperative Union. Apparently ranking third in size among farm organizations, NFU is strongest in the Great Plains and Minnesota. It endorses parity prices and the family farm as farm policy goals and favors a wide range of government programs to achieve them. Among its affiliates are farm supply and marketing cooperatives and the Grain Terminal Association (GTA), a large elevator and grain-marketing organization.

FASCISM, an authoritarian, free-enterprise system with private ownership of the means of production, essentially the same income distribution as in private enterprise, and ostensibly the same economic freedoms. Economic ideas implied in the system are: (1) the state alone has the right to determine what national interests, defined by the totalitarian leader, require; (2) conflicting interests of all economic participants, including the state, are unified in the corporation, operating under public control; (3) strikes and lockouts are forbidden; and (4) experts take precedence over politicians. This corporate state substitutes class collaboration for class conflict. It is controlled capitalism within the framework of a self-acknowledged totalitarian state and generally occurs in advanced industrial societies. The best known examples of fascism have been Italy under Mussolini and Germany under Hitler.

See also Centralization; Nationalism.
Consult (26) Dillard, 1967.

FAVORABLE BALANCE OF TRADE. *See* Balance of Trade.

FDIC. *See* Federal Deposit Insurance Corporation.

FEASIBLE SET, the set of choices available to a decision maker. In consumer theory it represents the set of all commodity bundles whose cost is equal to or less than the consumer's income.

See also Consumer Equilibrium.

FEATHERBEDDING, the enforcement by a union of work rules or practices that management deems inefficient and obsolete but which the union considers important to the workers' job security and to the union itself. Forms of featherbedding are: preserving older methods despite technological change; requiring workers to perform unnecessary work; keeping unneeded workers on the job; imposing limitations on the amount of work permissible per worker within a set time.

FEDERAL ANTI-INJUNCTION ACT. *See* Norris-LaGuardia Act (1932).

FEDERAL AVIATION ADMINISTRATION (FAA), formerly the Federal Aviation Agency, a regulatory commission created by the Federal Aviation Act of 1958. It was transferred to the Department of Transportation in 1967. The FAA is principally a rule-making and operating group as distinct from a regulatory commission. It has physical control of the U.S. airways and operates and manages the nation's air space. Safety, airway control, research and development, and airport improvements are some of the major functions. It has over 50,000 employees and an annual budget in excess of $1 billion.

See also Civil Aeronautics Act.

FEDERAL BUDGET. The federal government spends at an annual rate of about $250 billion, close to one-fourth of GNP. Less than half the total is for federally supplied goods and services. The remainder is in the form of transfers to individuals (social security, veterans' pensions, interest), loans and subsidies to business, and grants in aid to state and local governments, foreign governments, and international agencies.

Some expenditures are financed by earmarked taxes and channeled through special trust funds. The most important are Social Security benefits and federal highway expenditures. The remainder, about 75 percent of the total, is financed through general revenues and appropriated for specific uses by Congress.

Budget Process. The federal budget process encompasses program planning and operation by the executive branch, appropriation of funds by Congress, evaluation by both branches, and audit by the General Accounting Office (GAO), which reports to Congress. It is, thus, an integral and continuous part of the operation of the federal government.

The budgeting process in the executive branch centers on preparation of the executive budget presented to Congress by the president each January. It contains detailed spending proposals for all departments and agencies for the upcoming fiscal year.

In January preparation of the budget for the fiscal year beginning some 18 months later begins. Within each department or agency the individual subunits begin to plan their programs and expenditure needs in accordance with guidelines from the Office of Management and Budget (OMB), an agency in the Executive Office of the President that represents him on budgetary matters. By May the initial recommmendations are collected and reviewed by the department for initial review by OMB during July and August. Economic forecasts for the next fiscal year (still nearly 12 months away) are provided to assess the total fiscal impact of the budget on the economy.

The president examines the OMB recommendations and issues guidelines to departments for preparation of final requests due in September. The final OMB review occurs in October and November, at which time departments may present appeals for changes to the OMB or even to the president.

During November and December the president receives the recommendations of the OMB along with updated economic forecasts and gives final approval to the budget document that goes to Congress in January.

Appropriations. In Congress, program proposals are examined by congressional committees. Hearings are held, representatives of executive departments and other interested parties testify, and eventually the various ex-

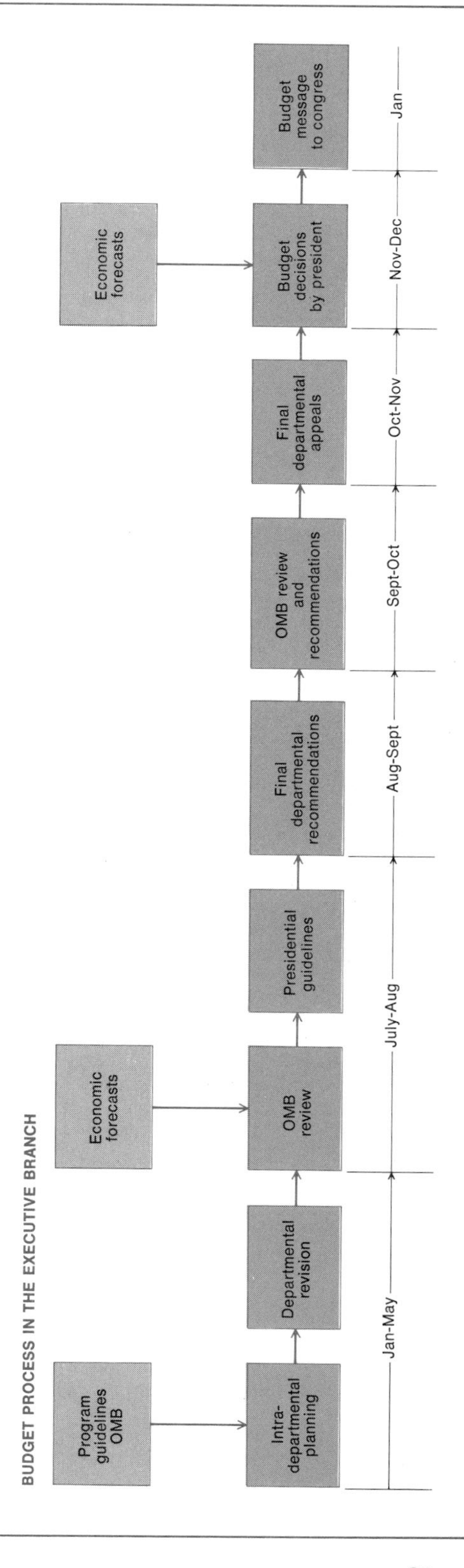

FEDERAL BUDGET

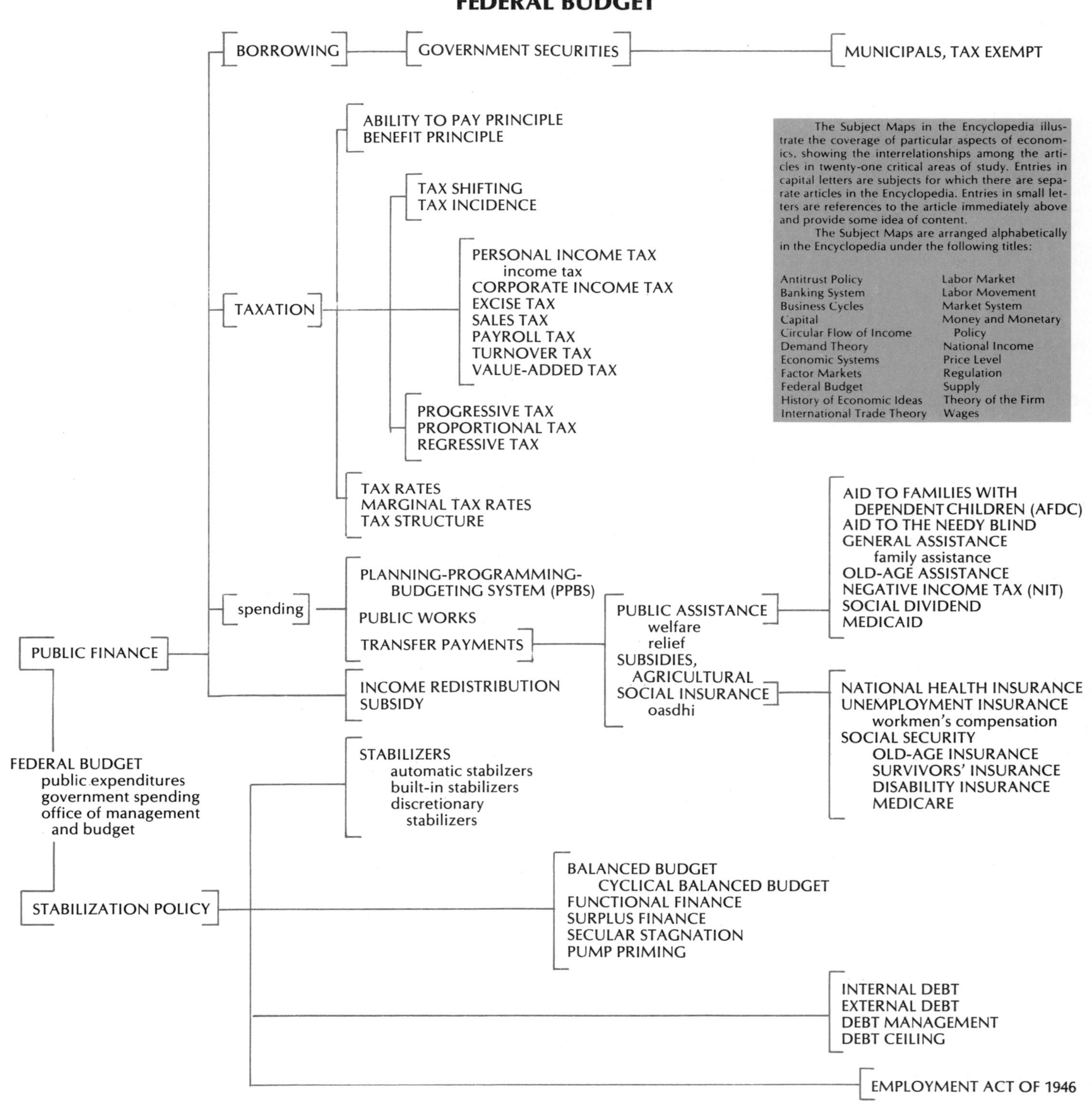

ecutive programs are authorized, usually after congressional alteration. Before programs can be funded, however, Congress must also appropriate the money. Appropriations for specific programs are made after hearings and examination, most of which is handled by subcommittees of the House and Senate appropriations committees.

About 15 appropriations bills pass Congress each year. The president, lacking item-veto power, must accept the whole package contained in each bill—or veto the whole thing—even if he dislikes parts of it. Appropriations for ongoing programs are often made for more than one year, so that in any given fiscal year sizeable appropriations are carried over from past years.

See also Planning-Programming-Budgeting System; Public Finance.

—Charles W. Meyer, *Iowa State University*

FEDERAL COMMUNICATIONS ACT, also known as the Communications Act of 1934, created an independent agency, the Federal Communications Commission (FCC), to regulate the communications industry. This industry consists of two diverse groups: the communication carriers (telephone and telegraph) and the broadcasters (radio and television). The act states that interstate and foreign communication carriers are common carriers, that is, they must furnish service on request, and gives the FCC the authority to control entry into service, discontinuance of service, combinations, and rates. The act stated that broadcasters are not common carriers, and it empowered the FCC to allocate radio spectrum space and to grant licenses to broadcasters.

See also Federal Communications Commission; Regulated Industries.

FEDERAL COMMUNICATIONS COMMISSION (FCC), independent federal agency that regulates radio and television broadcasting and interstate and foreign telephone and telegraph services. Created under the Communications Act of 1934, the commission is composed of seven members appointed by the president for seven-year terms. Because of limited space on the radio spectrum, broadcasters are required by the 1934 act to obtain licenses from the FCC. The FCC also controls the entry of common carriers by wire (telephone and telegraph companies) to the communications industry. This control is intended to prevent the elimination of essential services through destructive competition. In addition, the commission regulates the rates and services of common carriers by wire. A staff of 1500 works with a budget of $18,000,000 annually.

See also Federal Communications Act; Regulated Industries.

FEDERAL DEPOSIT INSURANCE CORPORATION (FDIC), an agency wholly owned by the United States government, whose primary function is to insure the depositors of commercial banks and savings banks. Each participant bank pays to the FDIC an annual premium of 1/12 of 1 percent of its total deposits, in exchange for which the FDIC insures each deposit up to a maximum of $20,000 against loss due to failure of the bank. The FDIC also supervises banks to help prevent failures and assists in the liquidation of banks that do fail.

See also Bank Failure.

FEDERAL OPEN MARKET COMMITTEE. *See* Federal Reserve System.

FEDERAL POWER COMMISSION (FPC) ,independent federal agency that controls the construction and operation of hydroelectric projects on navigable streams and regulates the interstate transmission and sale for resale of electricity and natural gas. It is composed of five members appointed by the president to serve five-year overlapping terms.

Since the 1960s the commission has been active in ordering reductions in the interstate wholesale rate for electricity. However, the largest share of the FPC's attention is given to regulation of the natural gas industry. Over the years, the commission has ordered substantial reductions in the rates charged by gas pipeline companies. Since a Supreme Court decision in 1954 (*Phillips Petroleum Co. v. Wisconsin*), the commission has also controlled the gas field market prices of natural gas producers. The FPC has a staff of 1200 and an annual appropriation of $15,000,000.

See also Phillips Case (1954); Regulated Industries.

FEDERAL RESERVE ACT (1913) created the federal reserve system, originally passed in response to the succession of financial crises in the United States, culminating in the crisis of 1907, which almost paralyzed the financial markets of the country. The act was the second attempt to unify the banking system of the country, the first having been the National Bank Act (1863). The Federal Reserve Act provided for the first time a national check-clearing system, a source of credit for the banking system, a flexible currency in the form of federal reserve notes, and central control over a large part of the banking system. The act failed, however, to provide a completely unified system, because many state banks decided not to participate.

See also Federal Reserve System.

FEDERAL RESERVE BANKS, the operating arms of the federal reserve system, which is the central bank of the United States. There are

Banks displaying this emblem have bought insurance protecting depositors against bank failure.

Preparation of federal budget for fiscal year starting July 1, 1973 started 18 months before.

twelve federal reserve banks, each serving a federal reserve district. Although each bank is a separate corporation, the policy of the twelve is closely coordinated through the Board of Governors of the federal reserve system in Washington. The federal reserve banks act as bankers' banks, serving the needs of district member banks and carrying out the monetary policy of the federal reserve system.

A federal reserve note is backed by government securities held by the federal reserve banks.

FEDERAL RESERVE NOTES are issued by the twelve district federal reserve banks, are printed by the US Bureau of Printing and Engraving, and constitute almost the entire amount of paper currency in the country. They are currently issued in denominations of $1, $5, $10, $20, $50, and $100; larger denominations of up to $10,000, formerly used, are no longer being printed. The notes are backed by United States government securities held by the federal reserve banks.

See also Money; Money Supply.

FEDERAL OPEN MARKET COMMITTEE. *See* Federal Reserve System.

FEDERAL RESERVE SYSTEM, a coordinated group of financial agencies that at its highest level, acts as the central bank of the United States, issuing paper currency, supervising the commercial banks of the country, and implementing monetary policy. The Federal Reserve Act established the system (1914) and its structure has been extensively modified since, particularly by the Banking Acts (1933, 1935). As presently constituted, the system is composed of three levels: the member banks, the federal reserve banks and branches, and the Board of Governors. The organizational structure and functions are shown in the figure.

Member Banks. It was hoped in the beginning that all commercial banks would join the system, so that it would be a single unified association covering the whole commercial banking structure. All national banks are required to join, but state banks have the option of joining, and most have decided not to. Thus, of the 13,800 commercial banks in the United States, only 5,700 are members, of which 4,600 are national banks and 1,100 are state banks. These banks, however, account for 83% of the commercial banking business of the country, indicating that it is the small banks that have not joined, being unable to meet the minimum capital requirements of membership.

Member banks have the right to hold deposits in the federal reserve bank of their district, to borrow from it when appropriate, to use federal reserve facilities for check clearing and transfer of funds, to receive information and advice, and to elect directors of the district federal reserve bank. Members' obligations include purchase of stock of their federal reserve bank, maintenance of legal reserves in an amount prescribed by the Board of Governors, compliance with the regulations of the system, and subjection to examination and general supervision by the federal reserve authorities.

Federal Reserve Banks. Unlike any other central bank in the world, the federal reserve includes twelve nominally separate regional banks, each responsible for a specific federal reserve district. These banks (identified by the number of their respective districts) are located in: (1) Boston, Mass., (2) New York, N. Y., (3) Philadelphia, Pa., (4) Cleveland, Ohio, (5) Richmond, Va., (6) Atlanta, Ga., (7) Chicago, Ill., (8) St. Louis, Mo., (9) Minneapolis, Minn., (10) Kansas City, Mo., (11) Dallas, Tex., and (12) San Francisco, Calif. In the larger territories there are branches in addition to the head office of the bank, each branch serving a part of the larger district. The total number of branches is 24.

Each Federal Reserve bank is a legal corporation whose stock is owned exclusively by the member banks of the district in an amount equal to 6 percent of the individual member's capital and surplus, although only one-half of this amount has been paid in. This stock ownership gives members the right to elect six of the nine directors of their federal reserve bank. The other three directors are appointed by the Board of Governors, which is analogous to a corporate board of directors. Although the federal reserve banks are separate institutions, owned and controlled by the member banks of their district and responsive to local needs, the twelve banks are coordinated in terms of national policy. Since their founding, the predominance of this overall coordination has increased markedly.

Each federal reserve bank operates a banking business for its customers, primarily member banks, in much the way that an ordinary depositor deals with an ordinary bank. The banking activities of the system are indicated in the aggregate balance sheet of the twelve federal reserve banks added together.

Assets. The federal reserve banks hold cash and can also create federal reserve notes to meet the needs of their depositors. The banks also hold the international monetary reserves of the United States in the form of gold certificates (representing the actual gold stored in Fort Knox) as well as special drawing rights, a form of international money created by the International Monetary Fund.

The Federal Reserve banks make loans to member banks in temporary need of funds to meet their reserve requirements. Usually these loans are for periods not to exceed fifteen days. Reserve banks buy bank acceptances, partly to put money into the market and partly to encourage the use of these instruments. The

ORGANIZATION AND FUNCTIONS OF THE FEDERAL RESERVE SYSTEM

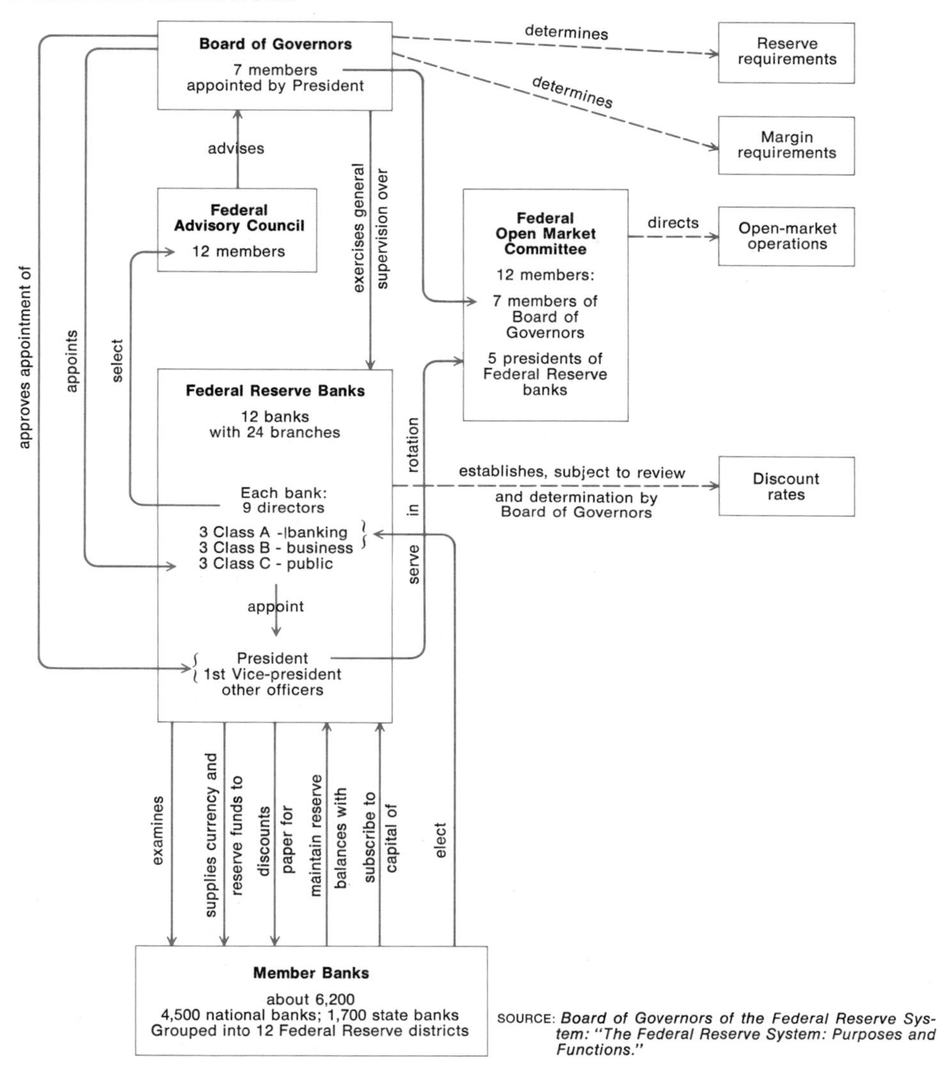

SOURCE: *Board of Governors of the Federal Reserve System: "The Federal Reserve System: Purposes and Functions."*

STATEMENT OF CONDITION OF THE 12 FEDERAL RESERVE BANKS COMBINED, 1971

(IN MILLIONS OF DOLLARS)

ASSETS:		
International reserves:		
Gold certificate account	9,875	
Special Drawing Rights certificate account	400	10,275
Cash on hand:		
Federal Reserve notes of other banks	1,135	
Other cash	261	1,396
Loans and securities:		
Loans	39	
Bank acceptances	261	
Federal agency obligations	586	
U.S. Government securities	70,218	71,104
Cash items in process of collection		15,680
Bank premises		150
Other assets		918
Total assets		99,523

LIABILITIES:		
Deposits:		
Member bank reserves	27,780	
U.S. Treasurer	2,020	
International Monetary Fund	144	
Other foreign	294	
All other	1,237	31,475
Federal Reserve notes		54,954
Deferred availability cash items		10,963
Other liabilities		647
Total liabilities		98,039
NET WORTH:		
Capital paid in	742	
Surplus	742	1,484
Total liabilities and net worth		99,523

SOURCE: *Federal Reserve Bulletin.*

federal reserve banks buy obligations of various federal agencies to provide a market that will make such obligations more attractive to prospective buyers. The banks' major lending activity, however, is through the open-market purchase and sale of large quantities of government securities, primarily for the purpose of implementing monetary policy.

Liabilities. The federal reserve banks accept deposits, primarily from members, but also from certain nonmembers for whom they have agreed to act as clearing agents, from the federal government, and from foreign central banks and governmental institutions. Because these banks hold deposits for the majority of commercial banks in the country, the federal reserve provides a very effective clearing mechanism by which checks that are deposited in a bank other than the one on which they are drawn can be presented for payment. The bank in which the check is deposited merely deposits it in turn in its federal reserve bank account, thus receiving a deposit credit and increasing its reserves. The federal reserve then charges the account of the bank on which the check was drawn, which loses reserves at the same time that it deducts the amount of the check from the account of the depositor who wrote it. When checks must go from one federal reserve bank to another, the transfer of funds between them is handled by similar deposit entries in the gold certificate account held by all federal reserve banks in the Interdistrict Settlement Fund in Washington. Because the federal reserve banks hold deposits of the federal government, all government checks are written on these accounts, and so the system clears the vast number of federal checks directly on its own books.

Like central banks throughout the world, the federal reserve is a bank of issue, distributing the major portion of the nation's currency in the form of federal reserve notes, which are fundamentally promissory notes of the banks that issue them. Thus, they appear as liabilities in the same way that deposits do. The quantity of these notes in circulation is determined by the desire of the public to hold cash: the notes are paid out only when requested by a member bank, which obtains them by writing a check against its reserve account.

Float. The two least readily understandable items on the balance sheet are "cash items in process of collection" and "deferred availability cash items". These entries arise from the check clearing process and are of little individual significance; for the most part they offset each other. The difference between them (float) is a form of loan by the federal reserve banks to their members, representing credit to these banks for checks that the federal reserve banks have not yet collected.

Profit. The federal reserve banks make a substantial profit from their operations, primarily through the receipt of interest from government securities held. A small portion of this profit is plowed back into surplus, an equivalent amount is paid to member banks in the form of a 6% dividend on the stock they hold, and the remainder, the greater part by far, is paid to the US Treasury.

Control Functions. Among the control responsibilities of the individual federal reserve bank, the most important is its right to change the discount rate charged on loans to members, but even this responsibility is subject to "review and determination" by the Board of Governors. The federal reserve banks also select the twelve members of the Federal Advisory Council, a group of bankers that makes suggestions to the Board of Governors.

Board of Governors. At the top of the system stands the Board of Governors of the Federal Reserve System, a group of seven members appointed by the President of the United States for fourteen-year terms, not subject to reappointment. The Board of Governors (at first called the *Federal Reserve Board*) was originally thought of as a rather weak coordinating agency for the twelve district banks. Over time it has been given more and more power until, on paper at least, the board is the center of power, and the federal reserve banks are the operating arms of the system, carrying out the directives of the board.

In reality, however, the center for major policy decisions is the Federal Open Market Committee. This committee consists of the seven governors plus five presidents of federal reserve banks. The president of the Federal Reserve Bank of New York is a permanent member, and the other presidents serve in rotation. In practice all twelve presidents normally attend the meetings of the committee, usually held every three weeks, and participate in the discussions, although only the five official members can vote.

Legally the only significant function of the Open Market Committee is to determine at what time and in what amounts the system shall engage in open-market operations to carry out monetary policy. The Board of Governors has the sole responsibility for setting reserve requirements, and the individual federal reserve banks establish discount rates. Because both the board and the banks are represented on the Open Market Committee, and because it is desirable that the various activities of the system be coordinated, it is hardly surprising that they are all discussed by the committee, which makes recommendations to both the board and the banks with respect to policies generally agreed to by the committee as a whole. It is unusual for either the board or the banks to ignore the advice of the committee, which has thus become the real center of authority of the federal reserve system.

Consult (9) Board of Governors, 1963; Federal Reserve Bank of Philadelphia, 1964; Procknow, 1960.

—Walter W. Haines, *New York University*

FEDERAL SAVINGS AND LOAN INSURANCE CORPORATION. *See* Financial Intermediaries.

FEDERAL TRADE COMMISSION (FTC) shares responsibility for enforcement of antitrust and related laws with the Antitrust Division, Department of Justice. Headed by a five-man governing body, it includes a nationwide network of staff and local agencies.

FTC's function to counter deceptive acts and practices and anticompetitive behavior by businesses is carried out in research and investigation of specific industries, publication of findings, prosecution of violators, and promotion of voluntary compliance with the laws, especially the Clayton and Federal Trade Commission Acts. To provide a preventive ingredient in administration of these laws, the commission renders advisory opinions on the legality of proposed business practices; writes advisory trade-practice rules (indicating specific practices which violate laws administered by the commission); and develops trade regulation rules which are binding on entire industries.

See also Antitrust Division, Department of Justice; Antitrust Policy.

—Thomas O. Depperschmidt, *Memphis State University*

FEDERAL TRADE COMMISSION V. CEMENT INSTITUTE (1948), one of the Federal Trade Commission's several major challenges to basing-point pricing. FTC charged (1) that identical pricing of cement by producers as a group lessened competition and constituted an unfair trade practice under Section 5 of the FTC Act, and (2) that the phantom freight and freight absorption entailed by the cement basing-point system constitutes price discrimination, violating Section 2 of the Clayton Act.

See also Basing-Point System.

FELLNER, WILLIAM JOHN (1905–   ), Hungarian-born economist noted for his work in macro-economic theory and the theory of the firm. He received his B.S. from the Federal Institute of Technology, Zurich (1927) and his Ph.D. from the University of Berlin (1929). His publications include *Monetary Policy and Full Employment* (1947), *Emergence and Content of Modern Economic Analysis* (1960), and *Probability and Profit* (1965). Fellner served as consulting expert to the U.S. Treasury Department (1945, 1949–52), as a consultant to the National Security Resources Board (1948–49), and as president of the American Economic Association (1969). He has been at Yale since 1959.

FIAT MONEY, paper currency that is issued under government decree without any metallic or other valuable backing and is not convertible into anything with intrinsic value. When first issued, United States notes were fiat money.

FINAL GOODS, those goods purchased for final use and not for resale or further processing. It is the sum of the value of these final goods that is used in the determination of the national income accounts. Intermediate goods are not included, because to do so would mean double counting and an overstatement of gross national products. Double counting would occur because the purchase price of the final good includes the purchased price of any intermediate goods utilized plus processing and distribution charges. Thus, if both final goods and intermediate goods were counted, the national income accounts would be exaggerated.

See also Goods; Intermediate Goods.

FINAL OUTPUT. Output flows to four sectors of the economy: consumers, government, business, and the rest of the world. Purchases of output by consumers almost by definition represent purchase of final output; such purchases are made for the gratification of the purchaser. Government and the rest of the world appear much in the same way: there is no attempt at resale for economic gain, and such purchases can be treated as sale of final output.

Some expenditures of business, such as the purchase of plant and equipment or increases in inventory, can be characterized as purchase of final output, because the commodities will remain within the firm and are not intended for resale at a profit. Other business expenditures do not involve final goods. The flour purchased by a baker is intended to be part of the commodity that the baker sells to obtain revenues. The flour is a purchase of an intermediate good, rather than the purchase of a final good. The distinction between intermediate and final output purchases of business firms is not unambiguous. The necessity of distinguishing between the two types of purchases arises because the inclusion of intermediate output as final output will grossly overstate—in effect, double count—the magnitude of goods and services produced.

—Frank J. Bonello, *University of Notre Dame*

FINANCE COMPANIES. *See* Financial Intermediaries.

William John Fellner

SIZE OF MAJOR FINANCIAL INTERMEDIARIES

Institution	Size ($billion)
Commercial banks (time deposits, 1971)	275.2
Mutual savings banks (deposits, 1971)	81.4
Savings and loan associations (share capital, 1971)	174.5
Credit unions (share capital, 1970)	15.4
Life insurance companies (policy reserves, 1970)	167.6
Property and liability insurance companies (assets, 1970)	55.0
Private noninsured pension funds (trust funds, 1970)	95.9
Old age and survivors insurance (trust funds, 1970)	32.5
Other federal government funds (trust funds, 1970)	9.0
State and local government retirement funds (assets, 1967)	39.3
Trust accounts in commercial banks (trust funds, 1964)	155.8

SOURCES: *Federal Reserve Bulletin, Statistical Abstract of the United States, Life Insurance Fact Book, National Banking Review.*

FINANCE PAPER. *See* Commercial Paper.

FINANCIAL INTERMEDIARIES, institutions that assemble the funds of one group of persons (savers) to lend to a second group (borrowers) at interest covering the cost of operation. Although savers could lend directly to borrowers, as when a man finances a mortgage for his neighbor, borrowers and lenders generally find it more convenient to use intermediaries because they (1) constitute a visible market readily accessible to all, (2) minimize risk, partly by superior knowledge, but primarily by portfolio diversification as a result of their larger size, and (3) accommodate the desires of savers—who frequently want to invest small sums for short periods—with those of borrowers—who are likely to want larger and longer loans. Thus, consumers may each put $10 in a savings bank, knowing that they can get it out when they want it, and the bank can accumulate these small sums in order to make a $20,000 mortgage loan for 20 years. The table shows pertinent financial information for a number of the major financial intermediaries.

Savings Banks are mutual institutions operated solely in the interest of their depositors by trustees who are closely supervised by state authorities. Savings banks exist in only eighteen states, primarily in the northeast, but in the areas where the banks operate their frequently higher interest rates attract more time deposits than do commercial banks. Savings banks lend primarily on mortgages on homes, apartments, and business buildings but also hold small amounts of government and corporate securities. Although many savings banks are insured by the Federal Deposit Insurance Corporation (FDIC), failure is extremely rare. When commercial banks create demand deposits, as is usually done when making loans, the banks are not intermediaries, since the money so created did not come from someone else, but when they lend funds entrusted to them in the form of time deposits, the banks are acting just like savings banks.

Savings and Loan Associations are found throughout the United States, though they are smaller in the aggregate than savings banks. They may be chartered by federal or state governments, and many associations are insured by the Federal Savings and Loan Insurance Corporation (FSLIC), which is similar to the FDIC. Unlike savings banks, they do not normally accept deposits but sell stock to customers in any fractional amount desired, entering the amount in a pass-book much as if it were a deposit. When a customer (since he buys stock, he is actually an owner) wants to withdraw his money, he sells the stock back to the association at par. These associations lend almost exclusively to members on home mortgages but also hold a small amount of government securities as liquid assets. Federal associations and those state associations insured by FSLIC are supervised by the Federal Home Loan Bank Board, an agency patterned after the federal reserve system but limited in operation to those institutions specializing in home mortgages.

Credit Unions may also be either federally or state chartered, but they are limited to operating among an already established group, such as a labor union, church, or lodge. They also obtain their funds by sale of stock in fractional amounts and make loans only to members, usually on a short-term installment basis. Most credit unions are members of the Credit Union National Association, which is an affiliate of the Cooperative League of the United States of America.

Life Insurance Companies are financial intermediaries, because they must set aside a substantial part of their premiums to meet future claims. These legal reserves represent the cash value of each policy, which accumulates over its lifetime and which belongs to the policy-holder, who can borrow against it or withdraw it at any time by lapsing the policy. Life insurance companies invest heavily in mortgages but also hold large quantities of government and corporate bonds. Even property insurance companies (fire, automobile, and so on) are intermediaries, because they also build up large cash reserves from their premiums. These companies' primary investments are in corporate stocks and bonds.

Pension Funds are a large and rapidly growing source of investment money, as they accumulate and hold regular contributions from employers and employees until disbursement is due. Pension funds may be operated by life insurance companies, federal, state, or local governments, corporations, or labor unions. The largest pension fund in the United States is the old age and survivors insurance fund of the social security system. Commercial banks and, to a lesser extent, individuals act as trustees for pension funds and for trusts set up by individuals in living trust agreements or wills. The aggregate size of such trust funds is very large.

Other Savings Institutions. Mutual funds and the similar closed-end investment companies sell their own stock to the general public and use the funds thus obtained to buy stocks or bonds of other corporations. Other institutions that channel savings into the financial markets include charitable foundations and even such nonprofit institutions as colleges, which have endowment funds to invest.

Finance Companies. Personal (consumer) finance companies obtain funds from the issue of stock and by fairly continuous borrowing from commercial banks or from the capital market through the sale of commercial paper. They make installment loans to individuals to enable them to purchase household goods. Sales finance companies obtain their funds in much the same way but specialize in financing the sale of merchandise, primarily automobiles, either from the manufacturer to the dealer (in which case the dealer is the borrower) or from the dealer to the consumer.

Governmental Credit Agencies obtain funds either from general tax revenues or from the issue of their own bonds. These agencies include the Banks for Cooperatives, Federal Land Banks, Commodity Credit Corporation, Urban Renewal Administration, Federal National Mortgage Association, Veterans Administration, Small Business Administration, and Export-Import Bank of Washington. The intent of all of these agencies is to provide funds to particular groups of borrowers on better terms than in the general market. States and sometimes even cities have also set up funds to finance small businessmen, college students, or others.

Service Agencies are not strictly intermediaries, because they do not actually borrow or lend. Several agencies facilitate the transfer of funds by providing facilities or services to intermediaries. The stock market provides a place where buyers and sellers of stocks can meet; stock brokers handle the actual transactions; investment banks (not really banks at all) underwrite (guarantee) and sell new issues of stocks and bonds; mortgage companies process mortgages for institutional lenders; commercial paper houses find buyers for open market commercial paper; and acceptance dealers provide a market for bank acceptances, a form of bank obligation used primarily in financing international trade.

Intermediation, the function of a financial intermediary, interposes one step between the borrower and lender of funds. To meet its costs, the intermediary introduces a spread between the interest the borrower pays and the interest the lender receives. When lenders feel that they can do without the services or the fees of the intervening institution, funds are removed from intermediaries to be invested directly. Such disintermediation occurs, for instance, when savers withdraw money from savings banks to buy government securities.

Consult (9) Goldsmith, 1958; Robinson, 1960.

—Walter W. Haines, *New York University*

FIRM, a business concern usually involved in production. It may be a sole proprietorship, a partnership, or a corporation, and may produce one or more products. Usually, however, only one product or one type product is produced, for example, cars or steel.

A firm often belongs to a specific industry (General Motors belongs to the automotive industry). In addition, a firm very often consists of more than one plant, the physical facility where work is done.

See also Industry; Plant.

FIRM, THEORY OF THE. *See* Theory of the Firm.

FIRM DEMAND CURVE. A firm's demand curve represents the quantities of the firm output that consumers wish to buy at various specified prices (not to be confused with the curve representing the quantities the firm wishes to sell—its supply curve). In the absence of price discrimination the firm's demand curve is also its average revenue curve.

FIRM EQUILIBRIUM. *See* Equilibrium of the Firm.

FIRMS, CLASSIFICATION OF. *See* Theory of the Firm.

FIRM SUPPLY CURVE, a graphic delineation of the profit maximizing outputs under differing prices, per unit of time, other variables constant. This curve will be upward sloping, reflecting increased marginal cost of output. If a firm is unable to affect price by its own actions it will maximize profits by producing up to the point where the marginal cost of an additional unit of output equals selling price. An increase in price will call forth greater output. Therefore, comparing the marginal cost curve with the profit maximizing output curve reveals that the firm's supply curve under pure competition is actually its marginal cost curve.

FISHER, IRVING (1867–1947), mathematical economist and early developer of econometrics, best known for his work with the quantity theory of money. His *The Purchasing Power of Money* (1911) presented the now famous equation of exchange $MV = PT$, where M = quantity of money; V = velocity of circulation; P = average price level; and T = total number of transactions. This quantity theory of money, given the assumption of a constant velocity, indicates the importance of the money stock in the determination of prices and the level of economic activity.

In addition, Fisher felt that business cycles were not inherent in the economic system but were the result of monetary instability. His solution was a system of 100% reserves, whereby banks would no longer be able to create or destroy money, thus eliminating a large source of monetary instability.

FITZGERALD ACT. *See* Apprenticeship.

FIVE-YEAR PLAN. *See* Planning (Communism).

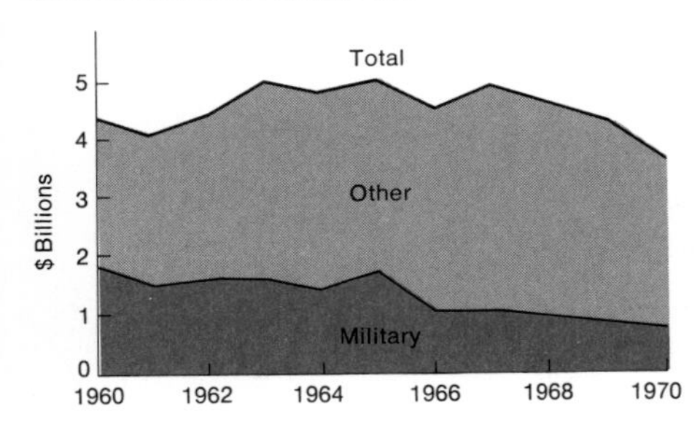

FIXED COST OF PRODUCTION. *See* Total Fixed Cost of Production.

FIXED COST PER UNIT. *See* Average Fixed Cost of Production.

FIXED EXCHANGE RATES. Each country on a pure gold standard defines the gold content of its monetary unit (mint par) and this is the rationale for an official rate of exchange among countries. If the British pound has 2.5 times more gold than the dollar then the rate on the pound in the United States is $2.50. If it costs $.02 to ship the gold equivalent of one British pound between the two countries the rate in the United States will never go above $2.52 nor below $2.48 per pound. Dealers in the U.S. will supply all exchange demanded at $2.52 (export point). They will demand all exchange supplied at $2.48 (import point). The exchange rate is fixed within narrow limits.

International Monetary Fund members have a fixed rate in the short-run via pegging of currencies in a 4.5% band around the official parity.

See also Exchange Rates; Gold Standard.
Consult (23) Ingram, 1970.

FLEXIBLE EXCHANGE RATE. *See* Exchange Rate.

FLOAT. *See* Federal Reserve System.

FLOATING EXCHANGE RATE. *See* Exchange Rate.

FLOATING PRIME RATE. *See* Prime Rate.

FLOW OF INCOME. *See* Circular Flow of Income.

FOB. *See* Imports.

FOGEL, ROBERT WILLIAM (1926-   ), American educator, economist, and expert on railroads. He is a graduate of Cornell University (1948), receiving his A.M. from Columbia (1960), and his Ph.D. from Johns Hopkins (1963). His publications include *The Union Pacific Railroad: A Case in Premature Enterprise* (1960), and *Railroads and American Economic Growth: Essays in Econometric History* (1964). Fogel has been a professor of economics at the University of Rochester since 1968.

FOOD FOR PEACE. *See* Public Law 480.

FORCED SAVING, a decreased consumption because of inflation's reduction of real incomes. Forced saving occurs during full employment in inflation, when business or governments bid resources away from production of consumption goods, leaving fewer, higher priced consumer goods. Compulsory saving requires people to lend to the government, as the British did through the tax collecting system during World War II.

FOREIGN AID, government-to-government transfers of resources, capital, and technology for development, usually from advanced to less advanced nations. It is a relatively recent phenomenon, such transfers traditionally having been handled by private investors. The goals of governmental aid range from thinly disguised bribery—to insure the friendship of potentially unfriendly nations—to the realization that world stability depends in part on the stability and growth of the "third world," to, occasionally, humanitarianism. Bilateral (direct government-to-government) aid serves the first of these goals while multilateral aid (channeled through such international organizations as the United Nations) is designed to serve the last two. Bilateral aid is by far the largest component of the total.

Aid implies a transfer of resources leading to a balance-of-trade deficit in the recipient country. This deficit allows the importation of either investment goods to promote growth directly, or consumption goods and raw materials with which to finance domestic saving and domestic production of investment goods.

Yet, aid may not lead to investment and growth if imports are simply used to generate increased consumption rather than savings and investment. The fear of such squandering of aid has led most donors to prefer project aid—tied either to specific investment projects such as dams and steel mills or to specific products such as food stuffs and industrial raw materials. Most recipients, however, prefer program aid, a grant or loan of foreign exchange to ease the balance of payments and domestic budget deficits, as this can be spent more flexibly to meet the recipient's needs and desires.

Aid Controls. Fear of aid misuse has also led donor countries to prefer lending rather than granting funds, on the theory that borrowed money will be used more wisely and profitably. But loans can be considered as aid only to the extent that they are "softer" (made on more concessionary terms with lower interest rates and longer pay-off periods) than "hard" loans made at non-subsidized commercial terms. Development programs seldom generate the profits expected of them, and repayment has become a serious burden for many countries. Furthermore, the flow of aid has not increased substantially, and some receiving countries find their net aid inflow (the difference between new aid inflows and the outflows of interest and amortization of old loans) dwindling.

Finally, balance of payments deficits in donor countries have inspired the tying of aid to purchases in the donor country, so increased aid is balanced by increased exports.

The price of goods purchased from the donor country is often higher than the prices available elsewhere in the world, and the value of tied-aid is consequently reduced.

Aid Goals. A United Nations conference set as a goal the transfer of 1% of the gross national product of advanced nations to less developed countries (LDC's) in the form of aid. There is a limit, however, to the rate at which LDC's can absorb money, and the shortage of managerial, planning and entrepreneurial resources endemic to most LDC's places a limit on the amount of money that any LDC government can manage effectively. Since most reach their absorption limit quite rapidly, increasing attention has been paid to technical assistance—the training of managers and civil servants in modern techniques, the development of new techniques of planning and development administration, and the development of new production technologies more amenable to the LDC environment—in order to improve the absorptive capacity of LDC's.

See also Less Developed Countries.

Consult (24) Bhagwati and Eckaus, 1970; Ohlin, 1966.

—Charles Staelin, *University of Michigan*

FOREIGN ASSISTANCE ACT OF 1948. *See* Marshall Plan.

FOREIGN EXCHANGE RATES. *See* Exchange Rate.

FOREIGN INVESTMENT is accomplished through movements of capital between countries. At a given moment the net investment position of a country can be ascertained that will reflect the total value of its outstanding investments abroad and of outstanding foreign investments made in it. Foreign assets are matched against liabilities to foreigners. If foreign assets exceed obligations, the country is a net international creditor; in the opposite case it is a net debtor. This *balance of international indebtedness* reflects the net results of past transactions on a country's capital position; the balance of payments shows international transaction over a given period of time. If a country is a net creditor on long-term capital account but a net debtor on short-term account (lending long and borrowing short) the liquidity position in its balance of payments will come under strong pressure.

See also Balance of Payments; Capital Account; Capital Movement.

Consult (23) Wexler, 1972.

45° LINE, also aggregate supply curve or Z curve, a line that bisects the right angle at the origin of a graph or diagram of the relationship of consumption, investment, government spending, and net exports to aggregate income. Along the line, (aggregate) income equals the sum (aggregate) of its components (C, I, G, X−M).

FOUNDATIONS OF ECONOMIC ANALYSIS (1947). *See* Samuelson, Paul.

FOUNDATIONS OF POLITICAL ECONOMY (1871). *See* Menger, Carl.

FOURIER, FRANÇOIS MARIE CHARLES (1772-1837), an eccentric utopian socialist who early in his working career was ordered to destroy a stack of goods in order to maintain its market price. He concluded that a better system could be devised than the wastefulness of a free-market economy. His objective was the harmonious development of human nature, free from restrictions imposed by law and convention.

To attain this, Fourier projected and planned in minute detail communities, called phalanxes, that were to operate on a cooperative basis. After abundant subsistence had been provided, the output of the phalanx was to be divided into 12 shares; 5 to labor, 4 to capital, and 3 to the managers (talent reward). Machinery would keep work to a minimum. Fourier's appeal for financing by capitalists was unheeded, but many phalanxes were organized by his followers. The best known in the United States was Brook Farm, near Boston.

See also Association; Cooperativism; Owen, Robert.

Consult (26) Heilbroner, 1961.

François Marie Charles Fourier

FRACTILE. *See* Central Tendency.

FRACTIONAL RESERVES typify the basic principle by which commercial banks create money. The reserves(cash or its equivalent) held by a commercial bank are less than (that is, a fraction of) its demand deposits. If a bank had to maintain 100% reserves, it could not lend money and, hence, could not increase the money supply. By keeping only a fraction of the total, the bank can lend the rest and expand the money supply. If the bank did not have to keep any reserves at all, it could expand the money supply without limit.

See also Monetary Policy; Reserve Requirement.

FREE, FLUCTUATING, FLOATING EXCHANGE RATES. *See* Exchange Rate.

FREE ENTERPRISE, commonly, a microeconomic concept referring to a business firm privately owned and operated for a profit motive. In the free-enterprise system most of the goods and services are provided by the private sector. The free-enterprise firm is one of the basic units of the economic system, along with the other basic units, such as household, government, and labor union. The major-

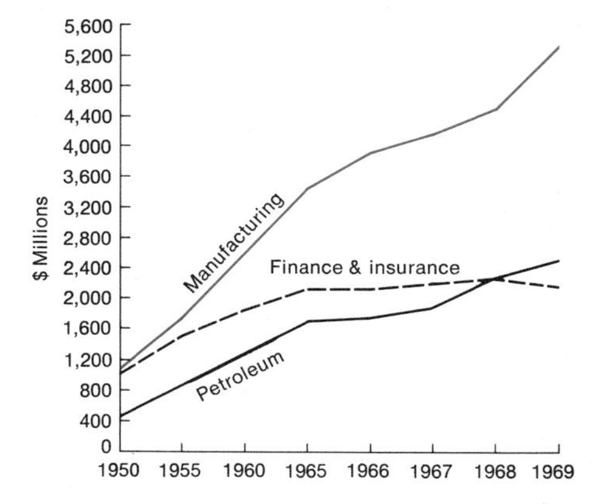

ity of goods and services consumed in the United States are produced and distributed by over 7 million private firms.

See also Capitalism.

Consult (1) Newman, 1954; Smith, 1963.

FREE ENTRY means that a firm is free to enter a market or industry because there are no major barriers that would prohibit entry. Free entry is a characteristic of pure and perfectly competitive markets. Industries that are purely competitive usually have a large number of small firms, making it easy for an individual firm to begin operation without larger and more powerful firms forcing it to close.

Free entry is much more difficult in oligopolistic and monopolistic markets where large investments are needed, and older, more established firms have control of the market.

See also Barriers to Entry; Entry.

FREE MARKET PRICES, prices established in the market without intervention by government, as distinguished from prices established or at least directly influenced by government price supports or production controls. In the early 1970s, prices of wheat, feed grains, cotton, rice, tobacco, peanuts, milk, and some other farm products were not free market prices, but prices of beef cattle, hogs, poultry, eggs, and a number of fruits and vegetables were essentially free. Even so, prices of livestock products were indirectly affected by price support for feed grains. Though price support has been the principal form of farm market intervention by government, price ceilings are also exceptions to free market prices.

See also Price-Support Programs.

FREE RESERVES are excess reserves of commercial banks minus borrowings at the federal reserve banks. They therefore indicate what excess reserves would be if banks repaid the reserves that they had borrowed, and they represent the basic potential of the banking system to create money.

If free reserves are negative, that is, if borrowings exceed excess reserves, they are called *net borrowed reserves.* Under these conditions the banking system is under pressure to reduce the money supply.

See also Discount Rate; Multiple Expansion of the Money Supply.

FREE-TRADE AREAS. *See* Customs Unions and Free-Trade Areas.

FREQUENCY DISTRIBUTION, a way of organizing observations to show the number of times a certain result or class of results was observed. It may be presented as a table, a bar graph (histogram), or a line graph (frequency polygon). Dividing the frequency of a class by the total number of observations yields the relative frequency distribution. By the law of large numbers, the relative frequency distribution is an approximation of the probability distribution.

See also Probability; Probability Distribution.

FRICTIONAL UNEMPLOYMENT is the loss of work that occurs from time lost changing jobs. No matter what the economic situation, from full employment to depression, there will always be frictional unemployment because there will always be mobility. People change jobs for such reasons as better opportunity, health, or family problems, and very often this involves relocation which is time consuming. In addition, workers who have been fired or laid off must usually spend time finding new jobs. The fortunate thing about frictional unemployment is that it usually is temporary.

See also Unemployment of Labor.

Milton Friedman

FRIEDMAN, MILTON (1912-). A member of the Chicago school in the tradition of Irving Fisher and Frank Knight, Milton Friedman is among the most controversial and prolific contemporary economists. His support of the quantity theory of money and the position that monetary rather than fiscal policy is the most effective means of controlling the level of economic activity have caused economists to reevaluate their positions and stimulated one of the most important discussions of modern economics. In addition, Friedman has been an outspoken critic of the federal reserve system and its use of monetary policy.

His *A Monetary History of the United States 1867-1960* (1963), written with Anna Schwartz, is one of the most important modern works in monetary economics. Friedman has also made significant contributions to the theory of consumption, the methodology of economics, and price theory. *A Theory of the Consumption Function* (1957) presents Friedman's hypothesis that the difference found by Kuznets between long- and short-term consumption behavior can be explained by the division of income into permanent and transitory elements.

In *Essays in Positive Economics* (1953) Friedman suggests that to operate effectively, economics must analyze and present alternative policies free of any normative judgments. He also discusses the Marshallian demand curve and makes a case for free exchange rates. Finally, Friedman's *Capitalism and Freedom* (1962) presents his suggestions for changing many current governmental programs and minimizing the role of the government in the economy. His suggestions include a negative income tax, changing public education, and many more.

—Clyde A. Haulman, *College of William and Mary*

FRINGE BENEFITS, a labor cost to employers for payment to labor beyond regular wages and salary. Fringes usually include: time off with pay (holidays, vacations, sick leave); deferred payments (retirement pensions, supplemental unemployment benefits); and various types of insurance benefits (life, hospitalization, medical care).

To be classified as a fringe, the benefit must be paid for by the employer but not for something required by law, such as the employers' share of the social security tax, the payroll tax to finance unemployment insurance, or the provision of workmen's compensation insurance. Fringes may be required of the employer in the collective bargaining contract or be provided voluntarily.

FULL-COST PRICING, a pricing policy used in some imperfectly competitive market structures. Under this type of pricing policy, a profit rate is usually predetermined by the firm. Price is then set equal to the average cost of the product plus the established profit rate.

Also sometimes referred to as cost-plus pricing, full-cost pricing is often used in those industries that compete for government contracts.

Under certain circumstances when full-cost pricing is used, price is set equal to average cost, allowing only for normal profits.

FULL EMPLOYMENT, the availability of employment opportunities for all workers, has been a fundamental objective of the United States since the Employment Act of 1946. Full employment is sometimes said to have been reached when at least 96% of the labor force is employed. The reason that 100% employment is not necessary is that there will always be some frictional unemployment due to mobility of the labor force, technological changes, and growth. Much of this unemployment is temporary and does not represent serious problems.

See also Frictional Unemployment; Labor Mobility.

FULL-EMPLOYMENT EQUILIBRIUM, level of income that satisfies the equilibrium conditions and at which 96% to 97% of the labor force is employed. Unemployment of 3% to 4% is regarded as normal in any economy where people quit jobs or are fired. The labor force consists of people employed or looking for jobs. Severe labor shortages such as those caused by World War II may bring more people, such as housewives, into the labor force; higher wages may also have the same effect. However, except in such special cases, the labor force is not likely to change size rapidly.

Up to the full-employment level of income, employment increases (decreases) in direct proportion to the level of income (employment is a result of, or a function of, income). At and above the full-employment level of income, employment cannot increase further because the labor force is fully employed.

Full-employment equilibrium is important for two reasons: (1) it is the highest level of GNP obtainable without inflation or changes in productive capacity. (2) It is the most desirable level of income, because the economy is producing as much as it can without inflation, and there is no unemployment, other than frictional and structural unemployment. The full-employment level of income is seldom an equilibrium level of income. Aggregate demand may be too high or too low to result in an equilibrium income that is also the full-employment income.

See also Frictional Unemployment; Production Possibility Frontier; Structural Unemployment; Underemployment of Productive Capacity.

—Anne Mayhew, *University of Tennessee*

FULL EMPLOYMENT GNP. *See* Full Employment Equilibrium.

FULL EMPLOYMENT INCOME. *See* Full Employment Equilibrium.

FULL EMPLOYMENT OF LABOR. *See* Full Employment Equilibrium.

FULL-LINE FORCING, an extension of the tying contract, promoted by a multiproduct firm, whereby a retailer who obtains a preferred (perhaps heavily advertised) product must agree to carry all products in that producer's line.

See also Clayton Act; Exclusive Dealership; Tying Contract.

FUNCTION, a relationship or correspondence between variables such that each value of one is associated with a single value of the other. In $y = f(x)$, to be read "y equals f of x," the function $f(x)$ states a rule by which values of x are transformed or mapped into values of y. The result is a set of ordered pairs of values of x and y, which can be graphed on the rectangular coordinate system. Because the value of y depends on the chosen value of x, y is called the dependent variable and x the independent variable.

There are several standard operations or rules by which x is transformed into y. Some are: constant functions ($y = 7$); linear functions ($y = a + bx$); quadratic functions ($y = a + bx + cx^2$. Other common functional forms are rational functions (formed by taking ratios), such as $y = a/x$, and transcendental functions, such as the exponential ($y = e^x$), logarithmic ($y = \log x$), and trigonometric ($y = \sin x$). Finally, a single dependent variable can

Henry George

John Kenneth Galbraith

be a function of several independent variables: $y = g(x_1, x_2)$. The function g is then a set of ordered triples (x_1,x_2,y) in three-dimensional space.

See also Variable.

—Carlisle E. Moody, *College of William and Mary*

FUNCTIONAL DEPENDENCE. *See* Functional Relationship.

FUNCTIONAL DISTRIBUTION of income in the United States is distribution according to the resource classes into which resources are divided: (1) compensation of employees, (2) business and professional proprietors' income, (3) farm proprietors' income, (4) rental income, (5) interest, and (6) corporate profits.

See also Factor Incomes.

FUNCTIONAL FINANCE, budgetary principle that calls on the government to determine appropriate fiscal measures according to the way these measures function, disregarding the balancing of the budget. Promotion of the macroeconomic goals of low unemployment, stable prices, and growth are the primary concerns of functional finance. This principle rejects the balanced budget or any other established budget policy; it is more concerned with aggregate economic performance and economic growth objectives. It has its base in Keynesian economic theory.

FUNCTIONAL RELATIONSHIP, an association between a dependent and one or more independent variables. For one variable it is written in the general form $y = f(x)$. A statement of functional dependence is a statement of causality, an assumption that x determines y. In some cases the function can be inverted to yield $x = f^{-1}(y)$ so that y becomes the independent variable. The notion of causality remains, but the direction is reversed. Some common functional relationships in economics are the consumption function $C = f(Y)$, where C is consumption and Y is disposable income, and the demand function $Q = f(P)$, where Q is quantity demanded and P is price.

See also Function; Variable.

GALBRAITH, JOHN KENNETH (1908–   ), professor of economics at Harvard. He has served as ambassador to India and has been Chairman of the Americans for Democratic Action. Galbraith is best known for three books, which have all created substantial controversy. His *American Capitalism: The Concept of Countervailing Power* (1956) suggested that the existence of large producers in some industries generated the development of large buyers and large unions to counteract their power. *The Affluent Society* (1958) attacked the conventional wisdom of traditional economics and suggested that the development of a large and active public sector is necessary if America is to solve its problems.

Finally, *The New Industrial State* (1967) suggests that the businessman discussed by traditional economic theory has been replaced by a technostructure of specialists because of the complexities of modern economic organizations. The evolutionary approach of Galbraith's work places him as a descendant of the institutionalists, and while many economists do not completely accept his views, he has raised important questions and challenged many aspects of modern economics.

—Clyde A. Haulman, *College of William and Mary*

GALLOPING INFLATION. *See* Hyperinflation.

GAME THEORY, the study of situations in which the outcome depends jointly on the actions of each of the participants. The simplest and most completely analyzed game is the two-person zero-sum game, in which there are two players and the loser must pay the winner. Game theory has been applied to a number of situations. A simple business example is the decision to introduce a costly new product line, which will depend on whether or not a competitor intends to introduce one.

The optimum strategy (or mix of strategies) is determined by the minimax principle: list the worst possible results that an opponent could inflict, and find the strategies that realize the best outcome from this list. When both players have found their optimum strategies, the game is solved.

Consult (27) Baumol, 1965; Ellsberg, 1956.

GATT. *See* General Agreement on Tariffs and Trade.

GENERAL ACCOUNTING OFFICE (GAO). *See* Federal Budget.

GENERAL AGREEMENT ON TARIFFS AND TRADE (GATT), an organization composed of most countries outside the Communist world and including all the important industrial and trading countries of the West. Since 1947, tariff negotiations involving all members of GATT have been held periodically. Their basis is the most-favored-nation principle: any tariff reduction (called a tariff concession) that one member grants to another must be extended on an equal basis to all other members. The most important negotiations in the GATT series were those conducted in 1962–67, and called the Kennedy Round. The basis for United States participation was the Trade Expansion Act (1962), giving President Kennedy the authority to reduce any United States tariff by up to 50% of its existing level. In fact the Kennedy

Round resulted in decreases in tariffs averaging about 35% among GATT members.

GENERAL ASSISTANCE, a program of assistance or relief to needy recipients who fail to qualify for the federally subsidized categorical programs (for the aged, blind, and dependent children). Because there is no federal subsidy or supervision, the support levels are generally lower, especially in the poorer states.

GENERAL THEORY OF EMPLOYMENT, INTEREST AND MONEY (1936), by John Maynard Keynes, stands with Adam Smith's *The Wealth of Nations* as a milestone in the development of economics. In his work Keynes emphasized the importance of full employment and stable prices as the goal of public policy and constructed a system using many analytical tools which he developed to indicate the means of obtaining such a goal.

Keynes' contribution in the *General Theory* can be divided into three parts. (1) Keynes considered the relationship between saving and investment, concluded that the two must be equal in equilibrium, and analyzed the forces which create a macroeconomic equilibrium. (2) The consumption function with its propensities was analyzed, and the multiplier relationship was made an integral part of the system. (3) The investment function as determined by the marginal-efficiency-of-capital schedule was discussed and included as an important element of the system. The theoretical developments presented in the *General Theory* provided the basis for much of modern macroeconomic theory.

See also Keynes, John Maynard.

—Clyde A. Haulman, *College of William and Mary*

GEOGRAPHIC MOBILITY OF LABOR. *See* Labor Mobility.

GEOMETRIC MEAN. *See* Central Tendency.

GEORGE, HENRY (1839–97), American economist who authored *Progress and Poverty* (1879), in which he proposed a single tax on land. George understood the Ricardian classical land-rent theory and observed that westward expansion in the United States led to rapid increases in the value of strategically located land. These rising land values he attributed to the general process of economic growth. George's single tax proposal rested upon two principles: (1) the land rents could be taxed away without changing the allocation of land into its various uses, and (2) it was unfair and inequitable for land owners who made no productive contribution to receive great wealth while many Americans remained poor.

George believed that a single tax on land would be sufficient to finance all governmental expenditures. George's idea became immensely popular and spawned single-tax political movements in a number of countries. Today, a tax of the sort envisioned by Henry George would raise far less revenue than is needed to finance governmental expenditures.

—John P. Formby, *University of North Carolina at Greensboro*

GERSCHENKRON, ALEXANDER (1904–), Russian-born economic historian. He received his doctoral degree from the University of Vienna in 1928. His publications include *Bread and Democracy in Germany* (1943), *Economic Backwardness in Historical Perspective* (1962), and *Europe in the Russian Mirror: Four Lectures* (1970). He served as a staff member of the Board of Governors of the Federal Reserve System (1944–48) and was president of the Economic History Association (1966–68). He has been a professor of economics at Harvard since 1948.

Alexander Gerschenkron

GIFFEN GOOD, a good of which more (less) is demanded as its price rises (falls).

See also Consumer Equilibrium; Price Effects.

GIFT TAX. *See* Taxation: *Glossary.*

GLUT. *See* Excess Supply.

GNP. *See* Gross National Product.

GNP DEFLATOR, officially called the Gross National Product Implicit Price Deflator, measures changes in the overall price level of all final purchases of goods and services in all sectors of the economy. It is calculated by combining several indexes, including components of the Wholesale Price Index and the Consumer Price Index, into one index and applying this index to GNP in current dollars to get a GNP figure in constant dollars, using a base year.

See also Price Indexes.

GNPIPD. *See* GNP Deflator.

GOLD, long preferred as a basic form of money, because it was desirable but scarce (hence, valuable), easily transported, divisible into small units, and rather widely available. Used as early as ancient Greece, gold replaced silver in the nineteenth century as the most popular form of coin. Today gold coin no longer circulates in any country. Although gold bullion (bars worth about $15,000 each) is still used to settle balances between countries in international trade, it will probably soon no longer be used even for that purpose.

See also Gold Standard; International Monetary Fund.

John Maynard Keynes, whose *General Theory of Employment, Interest and Money* was a milestone in the development of modern economics.

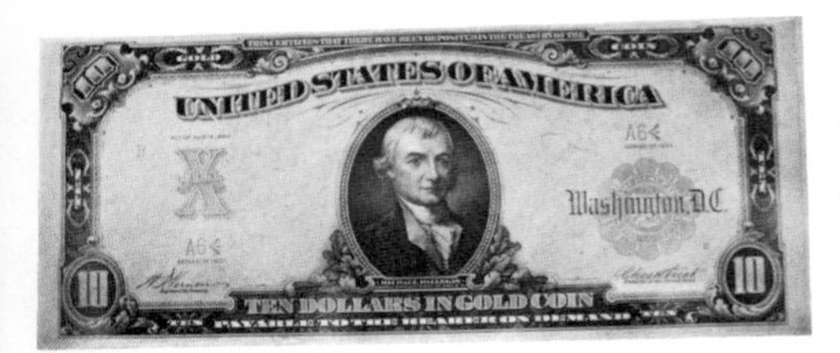

Gold certificates, recalled in 1933, are now museum pieces, illegal for use as exchange.

GOLD AND THE DOLLAR CRISIS (1960). *See* Triffin, Robert.

GOLD ARBITRAGE. *See* Arbitrage.

GOLD BULLION MARKET. *See* Gold Movement.

GOLD CERTIFICATES, paper bills issued by the government as a receipt for an equal quantity of gold held in its vaults. The certificates were first issued by the United States in 1866 to save wear on gold coins and became the most important type of currency between 1910–20. The certificates were recalled in 1933. They are now held by the federal reserve banks as nominal title to the gold stock in Fort Knox, but it is illegal for a private citizen to use the certificates as money.

The Treasury is the sole owner of gold and buys and sells at a fixed price when transactions are permitted. The Treasury maintains deposit balances at federal reserve banks and draws on these accounts to pay for gold imports. These checks are deposited in commercial banks and clear through federal reserve banks via increasing commercial bank deposits and decreasing Treasury deposits. The Treasury can restore these balances by issuing gold certificates to the reserve banks, whose assets of gold certificates increase as Treasury deposits rise. If no certificates are issued, the import is "free gold." The reverse of the above occurs with a gold export. Prior to 1968 a certain percentage of gold certificates were required as backing for U.S. currency.

See also Gold Movement; Gold Standard.

GOLDEN AGE OF AGRICULTURE, a nostalgic term for the five years 1910–14, a favorable period for farming, which more or less by accident became the base period for parity price calculations. The period followed two decades of gradual inflation, the closing of the frontier, and slow improvement in the relation of farm product prices to other prices. Technological advances that were soon to start a long-term decline in the number of farms and farmers had not yet appeared. Farm people were one-third of the population and politically powerful. But rural health and educational services were poor, much farm work was sheer drudgery, and the per capita purchasing power of farm people probably was not more than one-third that of 1970.

See also Parity Prices.

GOLD-EXCHANGE STANDARD. *See* International Monetary System.

GOLD MARKET. *See* Two-Tier Gold System.

GOLD MOVEMENT. Gold is treated as a short-term asset in the same vein as short-term capital assets—as a balancing item in the balance of payments. Under a pure gold standard, gold is the primary financing item moving in response to imbalances in the trade or current account. Since the 1930s a gold-bullion or gold-exchange standard has been in vogue and now gold moves primarily to settle international balances between governments and central banks. Most official movements of gold among countries of the western world take place within the Federal Reserve Bank of New York; an export of gold to Germany could be accomplished by transfer from the U.S. vault to that of Germany. There is a bullion market in London and several countries in Western Europe where demand and supply determines gold price; this price exists alongside of the official price for a two-tier system.

See also Capital Account; Fixed Exchange Rates; Gold Standard.

GOLD POINTS. If under a gold standard the rate on the British pound in the United States is $2.50, the pound contains 2½ times more gold than the dollar. If the cost of shipping gold between the two countries, including crating and loss of interest enroute, is $.02 per pound the rate on the pound in the United States can never rise above $2.52 nor fall below $2.48 because gold can be shipped. The upper point is the export point, the lower is the import point.

See also Balance of Payments; Exchange Rates; Gold Standard.

GOLD POOL. *See* Two-Tier Gold System.

GOLD STANDARD, a monetary system under which a country (1) defines its currency as a given weight of gold, (2) provides a mechanism by which anyone can exchange any form of domestic currency and gold at that official value, and (3) does not interfere with domestic or international movements of gold. Britain was the first nation to adopt the gold standard (1821), and the last countries in the world to abandon the system did so in 1936. Although some countries still define their currencies in terms of gold, no country converts its currency into gold: the gold standard is of purely historical significance.

David Hume's famous specie-flow analysis accounts for the standard's abandonment. When a country has a favorable balance of trade, gold flows in to pay for the excess of exports over imports, and the gold import expands the domestic money supply, which drives up prices and incomes. The price increases make exports more costly to foreigners and exports drop; the income increase brings in more imports for two reasons: there is increased purchasing power, and foreign goods are relatively cheaper via loss of gold. In addition, interest rates fall in the country gaining gold and rise in the nation losing gold, causing capital to flow to the latter. Although these automatic results ensure that the trade balance will be quickly restored and the rate of exchange will fluctuate little, the cost of external stability is drastic domestic fluctuation in prices, incomes, interest rates, and other major variables.

See also Exchange Rate.

GOMPERS, SAMUEL (1850–1924), London-born American labor leader who believed in the policy of conservatism in labor unions, was an advocate of autonomous craft unions, and vehemently opposed the more militant characteristics of the Knights of Labor and the Industrial Workers of the World.

After only four years of elementary school, Gompers became an apprentice to a cigar maker, then with his family in 1863 sailed to New York City and became a member of the Cigar Makers' International Union. He aided in the development of Local 144 of the union, was elected president in 1874, but was ousted seven years later by socialist opponents.

Gompers helped to found the Federation of Organized Trades and Labor Unions, and was a leader in the movement to organize a national federation of labor unions. In 1886 the AFL was formed and Gompers became its president. He held this position, with the exception of one year when he lost to a socialist, until his death in 1924, when he was succeeded by William Green.

During World War I Wilson appointed Gompers as a member of the Advisory Commission to the Council of National Defense. In 1919, at the Versailles Peace Treaty, he served as Chairman of the Commission of International Labor Legislation.

Samuel Gompers

GOODS are the tangible products of the economic system that possess the ability to satisfy human wants or desires. Because the term can be applied in so many different ways, economists attempt to classify goods in several manners.

Durable or Nondurable. At one level goods are classified as either durable or nondurable, a durable commodity providing use to its purchaser over extended periods of time or performing a particular function repeatedly. An automobile is a durable good and an orange is a nondurable good. The distinction between durable and nondurable is not always precise. Clothing is classified as a nondurable good, although it may provide use for as long as an automobile.

Consumer or Producer. At another level, goods are classified as consumer or producer. A consumer good is a commodity purchased by an economic unit for its personal gratification; a commodity purchased by an economic unit for economic gain is a producer good. Because producing and consuming units are distinguished on the basis of their motivation, the classification depends on the motivation of the purchaser of a particular good. An automobile purchased by an individual for his own pleasure is a consumer good, but it is a producer good if purchased for use by his firm. The categories are often combined: consumer durables, consumer nondurables, producer durables, and producer nondurables.

—Frank J. Bonello, *University of Notre Dame*

Final or Intermediate. Another means of classifying goods involves their position in the production process. If the good is purchased for final use so that no further processing is to be done or so that the good is not to be resold, it is called a final good. If, however, further processing of the good is needed before it reaches its final form or if it is being purchased for resale purposes, it is called an intermediate good.

Necessities or Luxuries. Economists also classify goods by whether they are necessities or luxuries. In addition, the income elasticity of demand is used to indicate whether goods are inferior, normal, or superior. If, as income increases, consumers purchase proportionally less of a good, it is considered inferior. When income increases and consumers purchase proportionally more of the good, it is considered superior. If the proportion of income spent on a good remains the same as income changes, that good is considered a normal good.

Problems. While placing goods within these various classifications can be quite useful, some problems arise. Goods considered luxuries fifty years ago may be necessities today. A final good in some situations may require further processing in others. Thus, economists must be careful when classifying goods and should be prepared to change the classification when the situation dictates.

See also Real Flow; Services.

—Clyde A. Haulman, *College of William and Mary*

Consumption goods.

GOODS/SERVICES refers to tangible and intangible commodities capable of satisfying human wants. Goods are the tangible commodities and include, for example, cars, food, and clothing. The intangibles, such as catering, chauffeuring, and banking, are called services.

See also Goods; Services.

GORDON, KERMIT (1916–), American economist. He is a graduate of Swarthmore College (1938) where he also received his L.L.D. (1963). He is author of *Agenda for the Nation* (1968) and has served on the board of editors of the *American Economic Review* (1958–60). Gordon has been a member of the Council of

Lincoln Gordon

OWNERSHIP OF THE PUBLIC DEBT, 1971
(BILLIONS OF DOLLARS)

U.S. government agencies and trust funds			106.0
Federal Reserve banks			70.2
Private investors:			
Commercial banks		65.3	
Mutual savings banks		2.7	
Insurance companies		6.6	
Other corporations		12.6	
State and local governments		20.4	
Individuals:			
Savings bonds	54.4		
Other securities	23.0	77.4	
Foreign and international		46.9	
Other*		16.0	247.9
Total gross public debt			424.1

*Savings and loan associations, nonprofit institutions, corporate pension trust funds, and dealers and brokers.

SOURCE: *Federal Reserve Bulletin.*

Economic Advisers (1961-62), director of the Bureau of the Budget (1962-65), and vice president (1965-67) and later president (beginning in 1967) of the Brookings Institution in Washington. He has also been on the faculty at Swarthmore, Harvard, and Williams College.

GORDON, LINCOLN (1913-), American educator and expert on Latin America. He is a graduate of Harvard (1933) and received his doctoral degree from Oxford (1936). His publications include *International Stability and Progress: U.S. Interests and Instruments* (1957, editor) and *A New Deal for Latin America* (1963). His government service is wide and varied, including offices as U.S. Ambassador to Brazil (1961-66), and Assistant Secretary of State for Inter-American Affairs (1966-67). Gordon has been on the faculty at Harvard, and he was president of Johns Hopkins University 1967-72.

GORDON, ROBERT AARON (1908-), American economist noted for his contributions to macroeconomic theory. He is a graduate of Johns Hopkins (1928), and received a Ph.D. from Harvard (1934). His publications include *Business Fluctuations* (1952) and *The Goal of Full Employment* (1967). A professor at the University of California at Berkeley since 1947, Gordon has served on the board of directors of the National Bureau of Economic Research (beginning in 1961), and as Chairman of the President's Commission on Employment and Unemployment Statistics (1961-62).

GOSPLAN, the state planning committee of the Soviet Union, responsible for designing, disseminating, administering, and evaluating the economic plans based on the directives given to it by the government's council of ministers.

See also Planning (Communism).

GOVERNMENTAL AID. *See* Foreign Aid.

GOVERNMENT BONDS. *See* Government Securities.

GOVERNMENT-CONTROLLED ECONOMY, a system in which the state controls economic activity. Economies may be evaluated in terms of the degree of preference given the consumer in relation to that given the state. In a laissez-faire economy there is consumer's preference only, and in a dictatorship model of communism, state preference only; between are varying degrees of government control and influence.

In mixed economies of regulated capitalism, there is influence but not control except during crisis. In market socialism, as in Yugoslavia, there is control, but consumer preferences exert influence. In centrally-planned command economies, as in the USSR and Communist China, state preferences have priority. In these latter examples and in fascism the government owns and/or controls productive factors and centrally plans their use to meet state preferences.

See also Centralization; Command Economy; Fascism.

Consult (26) Drewonowski, 1969.

GOVERNMENT CREDIT AGENCIES. *See* Financial Intermediaries.

GOVERNMENT EXPENDITURES. *See* Government Spending.

GOVERNMENT NOTES. *See* Government Securities.

GOVERNMENT REGULATION. *See* Public Utilities; Regulated Industries; Regulation.

GOVERNMENT SECURITIES, promissory notes issued by the government to those sources from whom it borrows money. In this country the term, often shortened to "governments," normally refers to obligations of the federal government. State and local governments (cities, school districts, and so on) also issue bonds, tax anticipation notes, and other forms of debt, usually termed "municipals."

Government Debt and Deficit. When the government spends more than it receives in taxes, the difference (government deficit) must be financed by borrowing. When taxes exceed expenditures, the surplus may be used to repay part of the debt. Deficits are very common during wars, when expenses rise rapidly and taxpayers are unwilling to bear the cost. Deficits may also be deliberately incurred as a matter of fiscal policy to raise national income and employment, but surpluses, whose function is to restrain inflation, are harder to achieve, primarily for political reasons: elected officials are more likely to want to cut taxes than to raise them and to increase expenditures than to reduce them.

Types. The kinds of securities that the federal government issues to finance its deficits come in a wide variety of forms. The best-known securities are *savings bonds,* sold only to individuals and nonprofit organizations on a discount basis. As interest rates have risen, Congress has reduced the maturity, rather than increasing the discount, to make the effective interest rate almost 5½%. If savings bonds are held beyond maturity, interest continues to accumulate at the same rate and is added on to the maturity value. These bonds cannot be sold, but they may be redeemed at the Treasury through any bank. Easily cashed, they serve as near money. The other nonmarketable securities, as well as convertible bonds, are special issues sold to rather limited groups of investors under special conditions and frequently on a one-time basis; these securities are not normally available to the general public.

Marketable securities cannot be redeemed prior to maturity, but they may be sold to anyone at a price agreeable to both parties. The minimum denomination is $1000; more frequently the securities are sold in amounts of $25,000 to $1,000,000.

Treasury bills are short-term marketable securities most commonly with a maturity of 91 days, but sometimes of 182 days or a year. Treasury bills are sold every week at auction. Bids are accepted from the highest downward until the sum of the accepted bids equals the amount the government wishes to sell. Because they are repayable in a short time and can be sold on the market for a price that tends not to deviate very much from their face value, Treasury bills are liquid assets and are held in sizeable quantities by commercial banks as secondary reserves.

Government notes are intermediate-term securities, with maturities of one to five years. Traditionally, notes bear a stated rate of interest, which is paid semi-annually. A few have recently been sold at auction like Treasury bills.

Government bonds are long-term securities, with maturities of more than five years, usually around twenty years. These certificates also bear a fixed interest rate, payable every six months on presentation of the appropriate coupon, which is attached to the bond. Marketable bonds, often thought of as the typical government securities, are a rather small part of the total debt.

At one time the government also issued *certificates of indebtedness,* short-term securities with maturities of about a year, frequently issued to fall due on tax dates. These securities have now been replaced by the longer issues of Treasury bills.

Ownership of the Debt. Government securities are owned by individuals and almost all types of organizations. Government agencies themselves hold substantial sums of government securities, primarily in the form of special issues that are not available to the public, but also including some marketable issues. The biggest official holder is the Social Security Trust Fund, and other trust accounts similarly invest their available funds in governments.

The federal reserve banks are another semi-governmental group that holds large amounts of these securities, purchased in the open market (not directly from the Treasury) to expand the money supply and help stimulate the economy. More than half of the federal reserve holdings are short-term securities, maturing within one year.

Commercial banks themselves hold large quantities of government securities of various maturities, thus providing not only income but also liquidity, because they can be sold at any time in an active market and with a minimum of risk. Other financial institutions hold them for similar reasons, as do ordinary corporations when they have excess funds to invest.

Individuals hold more securities than either the federal reserve banks or the commercial banks, primarily in savings bonds and other long-term bonds. The large holdings of foreigners and international institutions is primarily the result of the recent dollar glut. Foreigners have acquired large quantities of dollars, which earn interest on government securities.

Consult (9) Abbott, 1953; Federal Reserve Bank of Cleveland (1970).

—Walter W. Haines, *New York University*

Seven-year maturity makes Series E U.S. Savings Bonds among the most popular of guaranteed bonds.

GOVERNMENT SPENDING, expenditures by government at federal, state, and local levels on services and currently produced goods. Transfer payments, such as interest on national debt or unemployment insurance, are listed as expenditures in government budgets as they are usually presented; but in the theory of national income determination, government spending does not include transfer payments, because they are not demands upon productive capacity, requiring the employment of labor, production of goods, and consequent payment of incomes, although transfer payments will affect the disposable incomes of households and, thus, consumption spending.

GRADUAL SOCIALISM. *See* Evolutionary Socialism.

GRAIN TERMINAL ASSOCIATION. *See* Farmers Union, National.

GRANDFATHER CLAUSE, found initially in the Motor Carrier Act of 1935, is often included in legislation that provides for regulatory control of an industry. Such a clause attempts to preserve the rights of firms in operation before enactment of the law by exempting these firms from certain provisions of the law.

See also Motor Carrier Act (1935).

GRANGE, NATIONAL. The Grange began in 1867 as the Patrons of Husbandry and was a vigorous part of the populist movement opposing trusts, the railroads, and hard money policies in the latter part of that century. At present, the Grange is strongest in a bloc of states east and north from Ohio and on the West Coast. It apparently ranks second in size among general farm organizations but is much smaller than the American Farm Bureau Federation, the largest. The Grange has several affiliates engaged in providing various types of insurance.

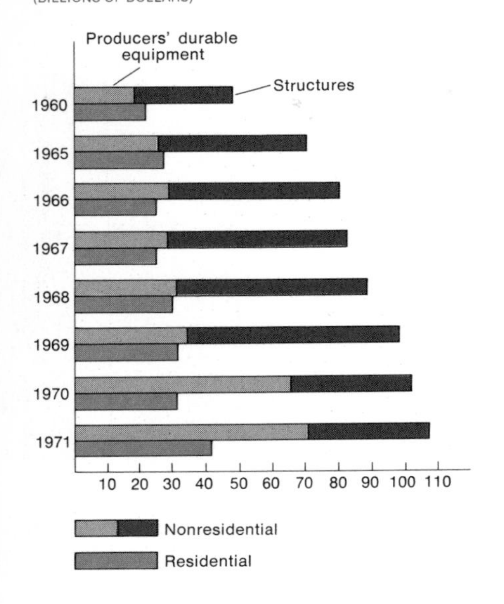

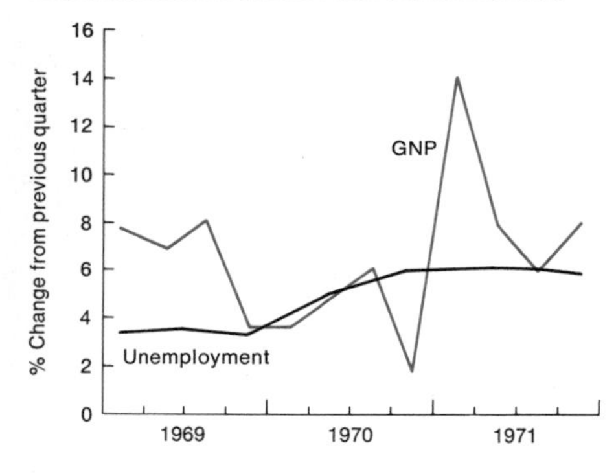

GREEN REVOLUTION (green denoting agriculture) refers to the introduction of improved farming methods, often accompanied by dramatic increases in farm production, in a substantial part of the underdeveloped world since the mid-1960s. The new technology essentially represents the application of agricultural and biological science developed in the advanced nations. New varieties of wheat in combination with fertilizer and controlled water supply have been a prominent part of the green revolution, as have similar innovations in rice cultivation. Initial production advances are being followed by "second generation" problems—for example, developing marketing systems, stabilizing prices, and dealing with social problems arising from modernization of agriculture and uneven distribution of benefits among the people.

GRIEVANCE ARBITRATION is very often the final step in the grievance procedure. If a worker's grievance cannot be settled through the normal procedure, both union and management may agree to submit the matter to an outside neutral party, an arbitrator, for settlement. The arbitrator's power is confined to the specified agreements of either the collective bargaining contract or the contract between the arbitrator and the parties involved. The arbitrator's decision is usually abided by unless he exceeds his authority, or is found guilty of fraud, misconduct, or unfairness.

Arbitration, being more flexible and less expensive than court proceedings, is usually preferred by both labor and management. Arbitrators are usually chosen from the American Arbitration Association, the Federal Mediation and Conciliation Service, or an agency of the federal, state, or city government.

GRIEVANCE PROCEDURE, a provision in the collective bargaining contract or company rules that is used to settle disputes without the use of a strike when issues arise concerning problems of interpretation of the contract or implementation of certain clauses.

The grievance procedure provides the means whereby a worker with a complaint or problem involving management is assigned a representative who is responsible for protecting his rights as well as bringing the grievance to the attention of management. It thus acts as a communication channel between labor and management and protects the worker against having to go through the supervisor who is responsible for his grievance in order to make himself known.

By keeping communication open, the grievance procedure often helps to ward off major problems and is therefore useful to both workers and management. Most grievance procedures provide for a series of discussions, if needed, at all levels of management.

GRILICHES, HIRSCH ZVI (1930–), Lithuanian-born educator and economist who has gained recognition for his work in econometrics and statistical methods and the economics of technological changes. He received a B.S. (1953) and M.S. (1954) from the University of California at Berkeley, and an M.A. (1955) and Ph.D. (1957) from the University of Chicago. He is author of *Price Indexes and Quality Change: Studies in New Methods of Measurement* (1971) and various journal articles. Griliches has been research associate of the National Bureau of Economic Research (1959-60), and a consultant to the Rand Corporation, Brookings Institution, Board of Governors of the Federal Reserve System, the Ford Foundation, and the National Science Foundation. He became professor of economics at Harvard in 1969.

GROSS INVESTMENT, or GROSS PRIVATE DOMESTIC INVESTMENT, a comprehensive measure of all nongovernmental spending for new buildings, machinery, vehicles, and inventories. Gross investment, a major component of GNP, tends to fluctuate from year to year depending on whether the private sector of the economy expects economic expansion or contraction.

GROSS NATIONAL PRODUCT (GNP), the sum of the values of all goods and final services produced by Americans in any given year. Final services, such as a barber's or a lawyer's, are included explicitly as part of GNP. Services of workmen who help produce products need not be explicitly included, because the value of their services is already counted as part of the goods that they help to produce. GNP is composed of three broad types of goods: (1) private consumer goods, (2) private investment goods, including producers' buildings, machines, and materials, and (3) government goods, such as postal services, national defense, and education.

Computation. The expenditures approach measures the expenditures by Americans on consumer, investment, and government goods. The total of these three expenditures is not quite GNP, because it measures Americans' production rather than their expenditures. Some goods (imports) are purchased by Americans but are produced by foreigners. Other goods (exports) are produced by Americans but are not purchased by them. GNP is, therefore, the sum of expenditures plus net exports (exports minus imports).

The income approach computes GNP by measuring the stream of income derived from the production of the total product. For each dollar of product produced, the producers have certain expenses: wages, rent, interest, indirect business taxes, and depreciation charges. Profits are what is left after expenses. GNP is the sum of the values of the products produced by all producers, or expenses plus profits.

Significance. Because GNP measures a nation's total product, it is, in some sense, a measure of the nation's economic well-being during any given year. Furthermore, comparisons of a country's GNP over the years measure the national rate of economic growth. International comparisons of economic growth may also be made by comparing GNP trends for various nations. Because the output of a nation at any given moment varies closely with its level of employment, GNP statistics may be used to throw light on employment levels and trends. A group of related concepts, such as net national product, national income, and disposable income, are also very useful for many analytical purposes. Recently there has been some criticism because GNP does not take account of "bads" (that is, environmental pollution and resource exhaustion) in addition to the production of goods.

See also National Income Measurement; Net National Product.

—Allan B. Mandelstamm, *Michigan State University*

GROSS NATIONAL PRODUCT IMPLICIT PRICE DEFLATOR. *See* GNP Deflator.

GROSS PRIVATE DOMESTIC INVESTMENT. *See* Gross Investment; National Income Determination.

GROUP PROFIT MAXIMIZATION. *See* Joint Profit Maximization.

GROWTH, the greater and greater amounts of output that a country produces. There are several ways in which a country can grow. First, labor power can be improved through education and training, which aids both the quantity and the quality of production. Second, improvements in productive techniques allow for greater output with given quantities of resources. In addition, the accumulation of capital is an investment into the production possibilities for future consumption and growth. Lastly, the price mechanism plays an important part in growth by channeling resources into alternate uses.

GROWTH, BALANCED. *See* Balanced Growth.

GROWTH, POPULATION. *See* Population Growth.

GROWTH, SELF-SUSTAINED. *See* Self-Sustained Growth.

GROWTH PLANNING. *See* Planning for Growth.

GUARANTEED ANNUAL WAGE, an assurance by an employer to his employees of a certain amount of wages for a certain number of weeks (usually forty or more) in a year. Therefore, any employee forced to work less hours or weeks is still guaranteed a certain amount of money. The amount of money and number of weeks guaranteed are decided through the collective bargaining process.

Collective bargaining for guaranteed annual wages began in the 1890s with the wallpaper industry, was slowly negotiated in several other industries, but died with the depression of the 1930s. In the 1950s the United Automobile Workers sought to bargain with Ford Motor Company for a guaranteed annual wage. Although the UAW did not succeed in getting the guarantee, they did get the alternative of supplemental unemployment benefits. However, subsequent collective bargaining contracts are moving closer and closer to the concept of a guaranteed annual wage.

Everett Einar Hagen

HAGEN, EVERETT EINAR (1906-   ), American economist noted for his work in economic growth and development. A graduate of St. Olaf College (1927), he received his M.A. (1932) and Ph.D. (1941) from the University of Wisconsin. His publications include *Economics and the Emerging Nations* (1961), *On the Theory of Social Change* (1962) and *The Economics of Development* (1968). He has served as chief fiscal analyst of the Bureau of the Budget (1946-48), and as economic advisor to the governments of Burma (1951-53) and Japan (1956). He has been a professor of economics since 1953, and a professor of political science since 1964, at M.I.T.

HALM, GEORGE NIKOLAUS (1901-   ), German-born educator noted for his work in international monetary relations and comparative economic systems. He received his doctoral degree from the University of Munich in 1924. His publications include *Economics of Money and Banking* (1961) and *Economic Systems: A Comparative Analysis* (1968). Halm has been on the faculty at the University of Munich, the University of Wurzburg, Germany, and Tufts University. He has been a professor of economics of the Fletcher School of Law and Diplomacy since 1944.

Alvin Harvey Hansen

HANSEN, ALVIN HARVEY (1887-   ) is best known for his interpretations of Keynes' *General Theory* and his efforts to gain general

Walter W. Heller

Training programs can help overcome a key cause of hard-core unemployment: lack of wanted skill.

acceptance of Keynes' theory in the United States. Expanding and refining various elements of the Keynesian system, Hansen's work provided the foundation for a generation of American economists.

Hansen's most original contribution was his discussion of the problem of secular stagnation in a mature economy. While he has been greatly criticized for his position that only governmental action could stop the drift of a free-enterprise system toward stagnation, Hansen's discussions opened the consideration of population growth and resource availability in the economic growth process.

See also Secular Stagnation.

HARBERGER, ARNOLD CARL (1924-), American economist and expert on taxation. He received his Ph.D. (1950) from the University of Chicago. He is author of *Project Evaluation: Collected Papers* (1971), and editor of *Demand for Durable Goods* (1960) and *The Taxation of Income from Capital* (1968). Chairman of the economics department at the University of Chicago since 1964, Harberger has served as a consultant to various organizations and the U. S. government, including the International Monetary Fund, the Treasury Department, and the Department of State.

HARD-CORE UNEMPLOYMENT, a term used to describe the unemployment problem of a certain group of workers who, due to problems of an emotional, physical, or mental nature, cannot secure employment even when jobs are available. These people usually are handicapped by such problems as a lack of any type of education or skill, an emotional inability to handle a job, or a physical disability. Often the hard core are from poor socio-economic backgrounds and are members of minority groups. Special provisions were made for the hard-core unemployed in the Manpower Development and Training Act of 1962, to help train or retrain this group so that their employment opportunities may increase.

See also Unemployment of Labor.

HAYEK, FRIEDRICH VON (1899-) has made important contributions, in the tradition of the Austrian school, to the history of economic thought, the theory of business cycles, and capital theory. Most significant are (1) the overinvestment hypothesis of the cause of downturns in economic activity during the business cycle; and (2) the introduction of a production period to the theory of capital.

Hayek's later career has been characterized by an adherence to laissez-faire and the belief that the impersonal nature of the market is preferable to any form of governmental intervention. In *The Road to Serfdom* (1944) Hayek also attacked growing statism on the political grounds that totalitarianism was the inevitable outcome.

See also Overinvestment Theory of Business Cycles.

HEALTH INSURANCE, NATIONAL. *See* National Health Insurance.

HELLER, WALTER WOLFGANG (1915-), American educator, and expert on fiscal policy, noted for his work on the concept of revenue sharing between different levels of government. A graduate of Oberlin College in 1935, he received both his M.A. (1938) and Ph.D. (1941) in economics from the University of Wisconsin. His books include *New Dimensions of Political Economy,* 1966, *Revenue Sharing and the City,* 1968 (with Richard Ruggles), and *Perspectives on Economic Growth,* 1968. As chairman of the Council of Economic Advisors from 1961-1964, Heller was involved in the development of New Frontier and Great Society economic policies. He is currently regents' professor of economics at the University of Minnesota.

HICKS, JOHN R. (1904-), one of the most important contributors to modern microeconomic theory. In *Value and Capital* (1939), Hicks attempted to reconstruct demand theory based upon indifference curves. While many of his developments did not fundamentally alter the theory, his emphasis upon the general equilibrium analysis of Leon Walras and Vilfredo Pareto, and upon its extension to capital and interest, has seriously challenged Marshall's partial-equilibrium analysis. In addition, the concepts of complementarity and substitution were developed by Hicks.

Hicks' *Theory of Wages* (1932) was a refined statement of a marginal-productivity theory, and his "Mr. Keynes and the 'Classics'" (1937) was one of the earliest attempts to reconcile the work of Keynes with the Neoclassical system.

HIGH MASS CONSUMPTION. *See* Stages of Growth.

HIRSCHMAN, ALBERT OTTO (1915-), German-born economist, expert on the economic development of less developed countries, and advocate of unbalanced growth. He received a diploma from the Institut de Statistique, Sorbonne (1935) and his doctoral degree from the University of Trieste (1938). His publications include *National Power and the Structure of Foreign Trade* (1945), *The Strategy of Economic Development* (1958), *Exit, Voice, and Loyalty* (1970), and *Bias for Hope: Essays on Development and Latin America* (1971). Hirschman was named Littauer professor of political economy at Harvard in 1967.

HISTORICAL CONSUMPTION FUNCTION. *See* Consumption, Time Series.

HISTORICAL SCHOOL. Beginning with the works of Friedrich List and Wilhelm Roscher in the middle of the nineteenth century, the Historical school continued until the early part of the twentieth century making important changes in the study of economics. The most significant aspect of the school was its evolutionary approach: that economics as an area of study must be considered in conjunction with other social phenomena.

The school was generally critical of the abstract, deductive methods of classical economists and marginalists, feeling that inductive studies of society dealing with a mass of information were a more fruitful approach. This difference led to the famous methodological debate between historicist Gustav Schmoller and marginalist Carl Menger. The outcome of the debate is the generally held position that economists must consider both methods, accumulating information and developing methods to analyze the information.

See also Sombart, Werner; Weber, Max.

HISTORIC COST. *See* Original Cost.

HISTORY, ECONOMIC INTERPRETATION OF. *See* Economic Interpretation of History.

HISTORY OF ECONOMIC ANALYSIS (1954). *See* Schumpeter, Joseph A.

HITCH, CHARLES JOHNSTON (1910–), American educator and expert on defense economics. He studied at the University of Arizona and Oxford and received a doctoral degree in commerce from Drexel Institute of Technology (1963). His publications include *America's Economic Strength* (1941), *Economics of Defense in the Nuclear Age* (1960), and *Decision Making for Defense* (1965). He served as chief of the economics division and chairman of the research council at the RAND Corporation (1948–60), and as assistant secretary of defense (1961–65). He was named president of the University of California at Berkeley in 1968.

HOFFA, JAMES RIDDLE (1913–), one of the most controversial of America's contemporary union leaders. Born in Indiana, the son of a coal driller, Hoffa quit school at the end of the seventh grade to go to work. In 1932 he became a union official for the Teamsters and its president in 1957. In 1964 he was sent to prison on the charge of jury tampering. He was paroled in 1972.

HOLDING COMPANY, a single firm which owns other companies for the express purpose of exercising control over their management. A holding company is usually formed when the managers of several firms find it more advantageous to cooperate closely with each other without giving up their firm's individual identity. The holding company will then control all of the companies.

HOPE NATURAL GAS CASE (1944), case in which the Supreme Court abandoned its previous efforts to review specific formulas for determining fair return on fair value, such as original cost or reproduction cost, and adopted the "end result doctrine." The court promised to henceforth concern itself only where the end result of regulation failed to cause the firm to (1) operate successfully, (2) maintain financial integrity, (3) attract capital, or (4) compensate investors for risks assumed. Regulatory commissions were to ascertain if these standards were met, with potential court review, hence restoring much commission latitude.

See also Fair Return on Fair Value; Original Cost; Rate Base; Reproduction Cost; Smyth v. Ames (1898).

HORIZONTAL DEMAND CURVE. *See* Elastic Demand.

HORIZONTAL MERGER, a combination of firms on the same plane or level of competition, that is, firms producing and selling in the same market. A horizontal merger has more direct adverse effect on competition than other forms (conglomerate, vertical), since it immediately reduces the number of independent producers of similar or identical products.

See also Celler-Kefauver Act; Clayton Act; Conglomerate; Merger.

HOURS OF WORK is a problem of only minor consideration today, but has been a major concern in the past. As far back as 1840 efforts were made to limit the number of hours that women and children could be allowed to work. In the early 1900s wage earners averaged from 54 to 60 hours a week. In the early 1930s state governments began to enact protective labor legislation in regard to working hours, and in 1938 Congress passed the Fair Labor Standards Act which established the 40-hour work week. From this emerged the concept of overtime pay, pay at more than a worker's normal wage rate.

HOUSEHOLD, a statistical concept that refers to a living unit functioning as an economic unit. It can consist of a single person living alone, a married couple, or a complete family, but whatever its composition, each such unit will have a source of income and responsibility for its disposal. Thus, the concept can be used to measure, estimate, or predict the quantitative economic consequences of such disposal.

Charles Johnston Hitch

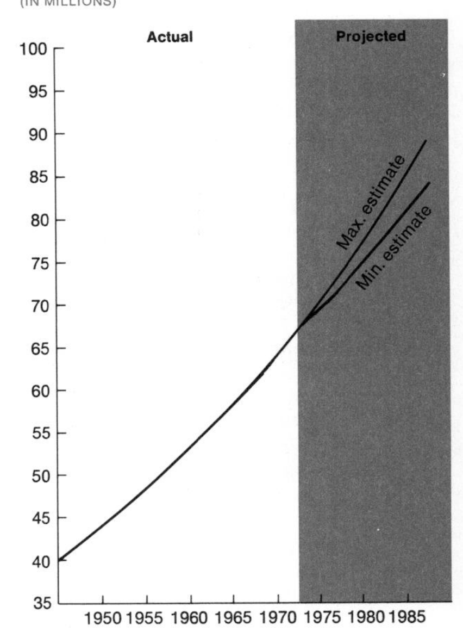

HISTORY OF ECONOMIC IDEAS

PHYSIOCRATS
- FRANCOIS QUESNAY
  - TABLEAU ECONOMIQUE (1758)

MERCANTILISM

CLASSICAL ECONOMICS
- ADAM SMITH
- LAISSEZ FAIRE
  - WEALTH OF NATIONS (1776)
  - theory of moral sentiments (1759)
- THOMAS MALTHUS
  - ESSAY ON POPULATION (1798)
- DAVID RICARDO
  - principles of economics and taxation (1817)
- JOHN STUART MILL
  - principles of political economy (1848)

NEOCLASSICAL ECONOMICS
- MARGINALISM
- WILLIAM JEVONS
- CARL MENGER
  - foundation of political economy (1871)
- FRIEDRICH VON WIESSER
  - karl marx and the close of his system (1896)
- EUGEN VON BOHM-BAWERK
  - capital and interest (1884)
  - positive theory of capital (1889)
- JOHN BATES CLARK
  - philosophy of wealth (1885)
  - distribution of wealth (1899)
- LUDWIG VON MISES
- FRIEDRICH VON HAYEK
  - road to serfdom (1944)

- LEON WALRAS
  - elements of pure economics (1874-77)
- VILFREDO PARETO
- JOHN R. HICKS
  - theory of wages (1932)
  - value and capital (1939)

- PHILIP H. WICKSTEED
  - common sense of political economy (1910)
- ALFRED MARSHALL
  - principles of economics (1890)
- ARTHUR C. PIGOU
  - economics of welfare (1920)
- LIONEL ROBBINS
  - essay on the nature and significance of economic science (1932)
- JOHN MAYNARD KEYNES
  - economic consequences of the peace (1919)
  - treatise on money (1930)
  - GENERAL THEORY OF EMPLOYMENT, INTEREST AND MONEY (1936)

HISTORICAL SCHOOL
- WERNER SOMBART
  - protestant ethic and the spirit of capitalism (1904-05)
- MAX WEBER

SOCIALISM
- PRE-MARXIAN SOCIALISM
  - utopian socialism
  - analytical socialism
  - ricardian socialism
- KARL MARX
  - COMMUNIST MANIFESTO (1848)
  - LABOR THEORY OF VALUE
  - DAS KAPITAL (1867)
- SIDNEY AND BEATRICE WEBB
  - lord and lady passfield

INSTITUTIONALISM
- THORSTEIN VEBLEN
  - CONSPICUOUS CONSUMPTION
  - theory of the leisure class (1899)
- JOHN MAURICE CLARK
  - business acceleration and the law of demand (1917)
- JOHN KENNETH GALBRAITH
  - AMERICAN CAPITALISM: THE CONCEPT OF COUNTERVAILING POWER (1956)
  - THE AFFLUENT SOCIETY (1958)
  - THE NEW INDUSTRIAL STATE (1967)

united states
- FRANK H. TAUSSIG
  - tariff history of the united states (1888)
  - international trade (1927)
- IRVING FISHER
  - purchasing power of money (1911)
- FRANK H. KNIGHT
  - risk, uncertainty and profit (1921)
- ALVIN HANSEN
- JOSEPH A. SCHUMPETER
  - creative destruction
  - theory of economic development (1912)
  - business cycles (1939)
  - capitalism, socialism and democracy (1942)
  - history of economic analysis (1954)
- JOAN ROBINSON
  - economics of imperfect competition (1933)
- EDWARD H. CHAMBERLIN
  - THEORY OF MONOPOLISTIC COMPETITION (1933)

PAUL A. SAMUELSON
- foundations of economic analysis (1947)

SIMON KUZNETS
- national income and its composition 1919-1938 (1941)
- national product since 1869 (1946)

MILTON FRIEDMAN
- essays in positive economics (1953)
- theory of the consumption function(1957)
- capitalism and freedom (1962)
- monetary history of the United States 1867-1960 (1963)

KENNETH E. BOULDING
- reconstruction of economics (1950)
- economics as a science (1970)

ABBA P. LERNER
- economics of control (1944)
- economics of employment (1951)

WASSILY LEONTIEF
- structure of american economy (1941)

FRITZ MACHLUP
- international trade and the national income multiplier (1943)

GEORGE J. STIGLER
- production and distribution theories (1947)
- theory of price (1952)

ROBERT TRIFFIN
- gold and the dollar crisis (1960)

GARY BECKER

JAMES TOBIN

HISTORY OF ECONOMIC IDEAS

An examination of the historical development of economic doctrines provides an appreciation of the background of the current state of economic theory and demonstrates the ability of economics to respond to what have been continual challenges. In addition, the need for constant challenging of the mainstream of economic thought is evident when we consider how important critical appraisal has been to the evolution of economic doctrines.

This Subject Map shows the Encyclopedia's coverage of the history of economic ideas. Subjects for which there are separate articles are shown in capital letters. Entries in lower case are cross references. Other Subject Maps in this volume include:

Antitrust Policy
Banking System
Business Cycles
Capital
Circular Flow of Income
Demand Theory
Economic Systems
Factor Markets
Federal Budget
International Trade Theory
Labor Market
Labor Movement
Market System
Money
National Income
Price Level
Regulation
Supply
Theory of the Firm
Wages

For example, the number of households can be of value in predicting the scope of the market for a new consumer durable good. The estimated net increase in the number of households (household formation) enables the economist to forecast the demand for new housing, schools, and health facilities, as well as the sales potential for existing consumer goods, among other things.

HOUSEHOLD CONSUMPTION. *See* Consumption.

HOUSEHOLD DEMAND. *See* Consumer Demand.

HOUSEHOLD FORMATION. *See* Household.

HOUTHAKKER, HENDRIK SAMUEL (1924-), Dutch-born educator, noted for his contributions to the theory of consumer behavior. He received a doctoral degree in economics from the University of Amsterdam in 1949. His publications include *The Analysis of Family Budgets* (1955, with S. J. Prais) and *Consumer Demand in the United States, 1929–70* (1966). He has served as senior staff economist of the Council of Economic Advisers (1967-68) and as consultant to the Treasury Department, beginning in 1961. Houthakker became professor of economics at Harvard in 1960.

HUMAN CAPITAL refers to the expenditures that improve the individual in the system in order to increase his worth to the society. For the advanced economies of the Western world the expenditure is normally in the form of educational programs designed to prepare one for employment.

Generally, the greater the investment in human capital made by society the more wealthy the society. The simple relationship between educational expenditures and per capita incomes is strikingly clear. One study has suggested that this investment is growing much more rapidly than investment in physical capital in the United States.

The underdeveloped nations face their most troublesome problems in this area. The human resource, in both the educational and physical aspects, is often unsuited for work in a fast moving industrial job. Yet, capital to develop this important resource is often difficult to find: steel mills are easier to find, or finance, than schools.

HUMAN RESOURCES. The resources available to a society that may be used to further the goals of that society include the size and the abilities of its population. While natural resources are valuable and necessary, more and more attention has been given to the quality and quantity of the human resource. For this reason, both the developed and the underdeveloped nations of the world are concerned with the development of the human resource factor in economic growth.

A number of studies have shown the value of investment in human resources, and most point up clearly the return to be gained from such an expenditure. One study indicates that a nation poor in natural resources but rich in human ones can develop, while none poor in human but rich in natural resources have done so. Japan, perhaps the classic case in point, has become an advanced, industrial, wealthy nation by extensive development of its human resources. Lacking most of the natural resources many other wealthy nations take for granted, Japan has given a great deal of attention to its human resource and has earned its position among the advanced nations.

—William D. Wagoner, *Louisiana State University*

HYPERINFLATION, or GALLOPING INFLATION, a condition in which prices rise faster and faster: people rush to get rid of money before it buys even less. Eventually, the system can break down entirely, with people resorting to barter. Examples are Germany in 1920–23 and Hungary in 1946. Hyperinflation occurs only in countries whose governments have lost the power to tax. Raising taxes sufficiently chokes the excess aggregate demand. Hyperinflation is not likely in peacetime.

HYPOTHESIS, a stated belief concerning a statistical population, such as, that mean family incomes are different in Philadelphia and in Atlanta. Statistical inference can be used to test such an hypothesis to determine whether any observed difference is reasonably attributable to chance.

The testing procedure begins with a null hypothesis and an alternative hypothesis. For example, the null hypothesis is that the true mean incomes are equal and the alternative is that they are not equal. When we reject the null hypothesis we accept the alternative.

See also Inference; Significance; Population, Statistical.

IBRD. *See* International Bank for Reconstruction and Development.

IMPERFECT COMPETITION occurs in those markets that are characterized by barriers that affect the free flow of goods and services found in pure and perfectly competitive markets. There are essentially three types of imperfectly competitive markets: monopolistic competition, oligopoly, and monopoly.

Under monopolistic competition there are only a few things that impede pure competition. The main difference is that product differentiation occurs. By means of advertising and variations in the quality and design of a

Hendrik Samuel Houthakker

HUMAN RESOURCES

For concepts closely related to that of human resources, see the articles on HUMAN CAPITAL and LABOR SUPPLY. To pursue some of the problems bearing on the human factor of production, consult the articles on UNEMPLOYMENT OF LABOR, and STRUCTURAL, TECHNOLOGICAL, and HARD-CORE UNEMPLOYMENT. Some of the programs for developing human resources are described in MANPOWER POLICY, RETRAINING, and MANPOWER DEVELOPMENT AND TRAINING ACT.

The relationships of these and other articles pertaining to human resources may be seen in the Subject Map accompanying the article on LABOR MARKET.

At food or other specialty shops, consumers can choose among imports from dozens of countries.

product, a seller can persuade buyers that products essentially the same in nature are really very different. This occurs often in the food processing and clothing industries.

Oligopoly refers to a market with only a few sellers, where the actions of one firm almost always affect all other firms in the industry. Thus, because there is a certain amount of interdependence among the sellers, oligopolistic industries have a direct influence on price. Informal collusion, though illegal, sometimes occurs in industries of this nature.

The purely monopolistic market consists of only one firm that has supreme control over the product and, therefore, the selling price.

All of these imperfectly competitive markets lack one or more of the conditions of a purely competitive market: product homogeneity, smallness of individual firms in relationship to the market, freedom of exit from and entry into the market, and mobility of both resources and goods and services to move among alternative uses. If any of these conditions is not met, there is imperfection in the market, and the pricing mechanism then relies on other means than simply demand and supply.

Consult (14) Leftwich, 1970; Leibhafsky, 1968.

See also Perfect Competition.

—William D. Wagoner, *Louisiana State University*

IMPLICIT COSTS. *See* Imputed Costs.

IMPLICIT RENT. Economic rent is rather difficult to identify in practice. The payment to a resource may be labeled as wages, profits, or interest and yet some portions of the payment may be in excess of the minimum necessary return to keep the resource in the current use in the long run and, hence, be an economic rent. Implicit economic rent is the portion of wages, profits, and interest which is, in fact, an economic rent, even though it is not so designated. Almost all economic rent is implicit rent.

The future rents of physical capital and land may be capitalized in the market-place so that current values of these assets reflect future expected implicit rents.

—John P. Formby, *University of North Carolina at Greensboro*

IMPORT QUOTAS. *See* Quotas.

IMPORTS, debit items in the balance of payments of a nation. Imports are deducted from exports to give a favorable or unfavorable balance of trade. Imports of goods and services include all debit items in the current account. Unlike other imports, capital imports, both short and long term, are credits in the balance of payments.

When a nation imports from abroad, domestic income earned from adding to the supply of domestic goods is spent on goods manufactured in another country, and the supply of domestic goods available for purchase is increased. These effects act as contractive forces on the domestic economy: imports have the same effect as savings; both are treated as leakages in the domestic and foreign trade multipliers. Increases in income call forth increased savings and increased imports, depending on the marginal propensity to save and the marginal propensity to import: national income growth is dampened as part of any increase is siphoned off from the income stream. Imports are easy to understand as leakages, because the value added by manufacture (increase in GNP) accrues to the exporting country; imports can be an effective anti-inflationary measure.

Trade patterns among countries, especially import and export consideration, are readily available in published statistics. World trade data show imports exceeding exports, exports being recorded FOB (free on board at port in the exporting country) and imports being recorded CIF (cost, insurance, and freight paid by importers and due upon arrival in the importing country). Insurance and freight are important elements of income to the nations providing them ("invisible" services on its balance of payments). The United Nations and the International Monetary Fund are important sources of information on world trade.

See also Balance of Payments; Balance of Trade; Exports; Foreign Trade Multiplier; Visible Goods and Services.

—John R. Matthews, Jr., *College of William and Mary*

IMPUTED COSTS, or IMPLICIT COSTS, refer to payments for internally owned factors of production. Payments to factors external to the firm, such as wages to laborers or rent to landowners, are explicit costs. Economists maintain both kinds of cost are important. If an owner of a business fails to consider his own time and effort, or that he is foregoing interest on the money originally invested, he is neglecting imputed (implicit) wages and interest, respectively. These must, in the long run, be considered if the business is to make a rational decision regarding continued operation.

INCENTIVE PAY is a form of wage payment related not to the amount of time worked but to the amount of output produced by a worker. This type of pay is common in the apparel and textile industries. Piece work, where a worker is paid for each piece of work done, is a principal type of incentive pay. A second type is the group incentive plan where bonus payments are given to individual groups for special accomplishments. This is sometimes done on a plant-wide basis to keep competition alive. In sales, the incentive payment is usually in the form of commission.

INCOME, PERSONAL. *See* Personal Income.

INCOME EFFECT, the change in the quantity demanded of a commodity as a result of a change in the consumer's income. If the income effect is positive, the respective good is said to be superior, or normal; if the effect is negative, the good is said to be inferior.

See also Consumer Equilibrium; Giffen Good.

INCOME ELASTICITY OF DEMAND, the responsiveness in the quantity demanded of a product to the income changes of the purchasers, measured by a coefficient that is calculated by dividing the percentage change in quantity demanded by the percentage change in income. The commodity in question may be classified as either income elastic or income inelastic according to the value of the coefficient. Income elasticity coefficients for normal goods will be positive, indicating that as income rises quantity demanded rises. However, some income elasticities are negative, which indicates that the quantity demanded moves in a different direction from income changes. Commodities with negative income elasticities of demand are called inferior goods.

INCOME MAINTENANCE. During the Great Depression there were no government programs to help people maintain some form of income. Therefore, legislation of the 1930s was aimed at helping essentially four groups of people to maintain an income. These groups were the aged, the unemployed, the disabled, and the children of poor families without fathers.

The most important legislation for these groups was the Social Security Act of 1935. Its compulsory Old Age, Survivors, and Disability program (OASDI) provides income to retired or disabled workers and to the survivors of a deceased worker. In addition, the worker receives an income (unemployment compensation) if he loses his job through no fault of his own.

Relief or income maintenance funds are provided through programs sponsored by federal, state, and local governments. In addition to government insurance programs such as OASDI, many welfare programs assist the poor, such as Aid to Families with Dependent Children.

—William D. Wagoner, *Louisiana State University*

INCOME OF UNINCORPORATED BUSINESS, income from individual proprietorships and partnerships—farmers and other self-employed individuals and professionals. A good deal of their income is return for land, labor, and capital they provide for their own business, but national statisticians treat it as profit.

See also Profit System.

Consult (22) Eckaus, 1972.

INCOME REDISTRIBUTION. In a pure market economy with no taxes or transfer payments, the income of each household would be wholly from earnings of factors of production. Thus, distribution of income would be determined by the distribution among households of owned income-producing property and labor skills. Households with insufficient factor endowments would have to rely on private charity or face starvation. Society may choose to guarantee a socially determined minimal standard of living for all households through money transfers (public assistance and social insurance) or transfers in kind (food, free medical care, and subsidized low-income housing).

Since roughly 30% of U.S. income is collected as taxes, the tax structure can be designed to alter considerably the distribution of income. By adopting progressive taxation, the percentage of income paid in taxes will rise as income rises. High-income households will thus bear a disproportionate share of the tax burden, and the relative gap between families with high and low income will be less after taxes than before.

Income redistribution caused by inflation occurs because inflation changes the real income, or purchasing power, of individuals. For example, people with fixed incomes, such as pensioners, are penalized by inflation, because they cannot buy as many goods and services as before inflation began. Inflation benefits debtors at the expense of creditors, lessening the power of the money paid back from its value when borrowed. Inflation also lessens the value of savings.

See also Public Assistance; Taxation.

—Charles W. Meyer, *Iowa State University*

INCOMES POLICY, any policy that has an effect on the real income, the purchasing power of individuals' money incomes. For example, if a man makes $2.00 an hour and can buy a loaf of bread for $.20, he has a purchasing power of 10 loaves of bread for every hour he works. If, however, the price of bread rises to $.25 a loaf and there is no increase in salary, his real income has decreased to only 8 loaves of bread an hour.

Real income is essentially a function of the money wages and the general price level. A change, in either direction, of one of these factors, without a corresponding change in the second factor, changes real income. Therefore,

INCOME DISTRIBUTION

The term "income distribution" is used to describe both a process and the pattern of its results. For additional understanding of the income distribution process, see particularly the articles on FACTOR MARKETS, FACTOR INCOMES, and FACTOR PRODUCTIVITY.

The results of the process by which household income is determined are also called the resulting "income distribution" or "distribution of income." For one method of showing this distribution, see LORENZ CURVE; and for some of its implications, see POVERTY LINE. For other facets of the distribution of income, consult the articles on FUNCTIONAL DISTRIBUTION OF INCOME and INCOME REDISTRIBUTION.

The Subject Maps accompanying the articles on CIRCULAR FLOW OF INCOME, FACTOR MARKETS, PRICE LEVEL, and WAGES show many other articles touching on the subject of Income Distribution.

INCOMES POLICY

For aspects of economic stabilization closely related to incomes policy, consult the articles on WAGE-PRICE GUIDEPOSTS and WAGE-PRICE CONTROLS. For the broad context in which an incomes policy becomes relevant, see the articles on INFLATION and STABILIZATION POLICY.

The student will also find it useful to consult the Subject Map accompanying the article on PRICE LEVEL for other entries related to Incomes Policy.

policies that affect wages or prices are incomes policies. Two incomes policies that have been used on the national level to help curb inflationary pressures have been wage-price guideposts and wage-price controls.

Wage-price guideposts are voluntary guidelines for changes in wages and prices. There are no penalties for violation. The first national guideposts were set up in 1962 during the Kennedy administration and proved to be very effective. In 1969 and 1970, with inflationary pressures beginning to mount, new wage-price guidelines were established under President Nixon. However, these guideposts did not meet with the same success as the earlier ones, and in August 1971 Nixon announced a ninety-day freeze, which held all wages and prices constant in the hope of relieving some of the pressures of inflation.

Consult (7) Levitan, 1972.

—William D. Wagoner, *Louisiana State University*

INCOME STATEMENT, a condensed account of the operations of a business firm over a certain specified period of time, usually one year. It is one of two major financial statements of any business, the other being the balance sheet. This statement, also referred to as a profit-and-loss statement, is a record of all income received and all expenses incurred. Non-cash items, such as depreciation, are also considered an expense in most businesses. The results of the statement indicate either a profit or a loss for the business, depending on which figure (income or expenses) is greater.

See also Balance Sheet.

INCOME TAX. *See* Taxation; Taxes.

INCREASE IN DEMAND, the shifting outward and to the right on the Cartesian plane of a demand curve. A given demand function is constructed under ceteris-paribus conditions. However, when demand functions are examined over time, it becomes apparent that the determinants (income, tastes, prices of related commodities, expectations) of the position of a given demand curve do not, in fact, remain constant; techniques for deriving subsequent demand functions are necessary.

For example, for normal goods an increase in consumer income will cause demand to increase: a new demand function will be defined with larger amounts of the commodity being purchased at every existing price. If a product becomes more fashionable, there will be an increase in demand. If the price of a substitute good rises, the demand for X will increase. If the price of a complementary good falls, the demand for X will increase. Finally, if purchasers anticipate future increases in the price of a commodity, then they tend to increase their current purchases, causing the demand to increase.

See also Consumer Demand; Decrease in Demand; Demand Curve.

—Robert L. Brite, *Louisiana State University*

INCREASE IN SUPPLY means that quantity supplied will be greater at every price than it was previous to the change in circumstances. Graphically, the supply curve shifts outward to the right. If a technological change occurs for a firm, then conceivably the marginal product of labor will not be higher for every man. Given constant wage rates, marginal cost will now be lower at every output. Hence the marginal cost curve (supply) falls; costs of production have been lowered. Due to the decreased marginal costs the firm will willingly, and profitably, offer a given output at a lower price than it would have previously.

INCREASING-COST INDUSTRY, one in which expanded resource usage leads to increases in resource prices. Either the resources used by this industry are specialized or this industry is extremely large relative to others. An increase in the demand for the product will, in the short run, cause prices to rise, and individual firms will increase output and receive excess profits. Entry will bid resource prices up for old as well as new firms. The industry cost curves will rise; entry will cease when all firms have a minimum average cost equal to the new price. The supply schedule for this industry will therefore be positively sloped.

INDEPENDENT VARIABLE. *See* Variable.

INDEXES, PRICE. *See* Price Indexes.

INDEX NUMBER, a percentage or ratio of two observations, the denominator being the base item in a cross section or the base period in a time series. The observations could be prices, quantities, or values. If average annual earnings in manufacturing are $4946 and $5221 for 1958 and 1959, then the 1959 index of manufacturing earnings with base 1958 (100) is $5221/$4946 X 100 = 105.56. Thus, one can tell at a glance that average earnings rose over 5.56% from 1958 to 1959.

Some commonly used index numbers are the Consumer Price Index and the Index of Industrial Production. These are composite indexes, made up of a variety of objects. The Consumer Price Index, for example, summarizes the price movements in approximately 400 items. To construct a composite index we must decide what items to include and measure their relative importance. A weakness of such index numbers is their inability to allow for quality changes.

INDEX OF INDUSTRIAL PRODUCTION. *See* Industrial Production Index.

INDICATORS are statistical time series, or groups of series, used by economists to predict future economic activity. Although there are multitudinous time series covering most components of the economic system, most indicators may be categorized as coincident, lagging, or leading.

Leading indicators are indispensable to economic forecasts and public and business decisions. However, during expansion, they tend to turn downward several months before a true peak has been reached, while in a recession, leading indicators tend to turn upward a month or two before the aggregate economy. *Lagging indicators* show probable movement of certain economic components and tend to be slightly more predictable. *Coincident indicators* generally move in agreement with the aggregate economy and are useful approximations of the present state of the economy. In order to obtain a reasonably complete picture of the stage of the business cycle, one must compare the three types of indicators.

See also Business Cycles, Measurement.

INDICES are series of statistical observations used as measurements of specific economic activities. In the United States the majority of indices are published, monthly or quarterly, by the U.S. Department of Commerce. The function of these indices is to measure the current levels of inflation, unemployment, investment, consumption, and output.

Among the most widely used and discussed indices are the Industrial Production Index, the Wholesale Price Index, and the Consumer Price Index. Other important indices are New Business Starts, Construction Contract Awards, and Department Store Sales. Specifically, the Industrial Production Index is a monthly measurement of total physical output based on manufacturing, mining, and the utilities industries. The Wholesale Price Index is a monthly measurement of price changes for a representative group of 2,000 commodities from agriculture and industry. The Department Store Sales Index is a monthly measurement of sales volume and indicates the consumer's extreme sensitivity to changes in the general business situation.

In addition to indices for major economic activities, there are indices for individual items, product classes, industries, and industrial groups.

See also Business Cycles, Measurement.

INDIFFERENCE CURVE, or ISO-UTILITY CURVE, the locus of points in the commodity space representing bundles with equal utility. Any two points on the curve represent bundles between which the consumer is indifferent. An indifference curve has a negative slope.

See also Utility Function.

INDIFFERENCE MAP, a diagram containing several indifference curves for bundles with various amounts of commodities X and Y. Indifference curves are negatively sloped, and they do not intersect or touch one another. The farther an indifference curve is from the origin of the map, the higher is its level of utility; thus, $U_3 > U_2 > U_1$. The convexity of the indifference curves shows the principle of diminishing marginal rate of substitution.

See also Utility Function.

INDIFFERENCE SET. *See* Indifference Curve.

INDIRECT BUSINESS TAXES, federal, state, and local levies that are usually collected from corporations and unincorporated businesses and are partially or entirely shifted to someone other than the original taxpayer. Examples of such taxes include excise taxes, real (business and rental) property taxes, and import duties, but not personal or corporate income taxes. For purposes of national income accounting, the National Income is determined after the indirect business taxes are subtracted from the Net National Product.

INDIRECT DEMAND. *See* Factor Demand.

INDIRECT PRODUCTION. *See* Roundabout Methods of Production.

INDIRECT TAXES. *See* Indirect Business Taxes.

INDIVIDUAL CONSUMPTION. *See* Consumption.

INDUCED INVESTMENT, investment that occurs because demand is expected to exceed current productive capacity. High current levels of demand will not induce investment unless they are expected to continue for long enough to make the investment profitable; conversely, expectations of higher future demand will induce investment even when current levels of demand are low. Thus, induced investment depends more on belief than on actuality.

See also Autonomous Investment.

INDUSTRIAL INFRASTRUCTURE. *See* Infrastructure.

INDUSTRIAL MOBILITY OF LABOR. *See* Labor Mobility.

INDUSTRIAL PRODUCTION INDEX, a monthly measurement of physical output,

INDUSTRIAL PRODUCTION INDEXES (1967-100)

	Total industrial production	Manufacturing	Mining	Utilities
1929	21.6	22.8	44.4	7.2
1930	18.0	18.7	38.5	7.4
1931	14.9	15.3	33.0	7.1
1932	11.6	11.8	27.6	6.6
1933	13.7	14.0	31.5	6.5
1934	15.0	15.3	33.0	6.9
1935	17.3	18.0	35.8	7.5
1936	20.4	21.5	41.2	8.5
1937	22.3	23.4	46.4	9.3
1938	17.6	18.0	40.2	9.4
1939	21.7	21.5	43.4	10.4
1940	25.4	25.4	48.2	11.5
1941	31.6	32.4	51.2	13.0
1942	36.3	37.8	52.8	14.6
1943	44.0	47.0	54.0	16.1
1944	47.4	50.9	57.9	17.1
1945	40.6	42.6	56.8	17.4
1946	35.0	35.3	55.8	18.1
1947	39.4	39.4	63.1	19.6
1948	41.0	40.9	66.3	21.9
1949	38.8	38.7	58.8	23.3
1950	44.9	45.0	65.7	26.5
1951	48.7	48.6	72.1	30.3
1952	50.6	50.6	71.5	32.8
1953	54.8	55.1	73.4	35.6
1954	51.9	51.5	71.9	38.3
1955	58.5	58.2	80.2	42.8
1956	61.1	60.5	84.4	47.0
1957	61.9	61.2	84.5	50.2
1958	57.9	56.9	77.5	52.5
1959	64.8	64.1	81.1	57.8
1960	66.2	65.4	82.7	61.8
1961	66.7	65.6	83.2	65.3
1962	72.2	71.4	85.6	70.2
1963	76.5	75.8	89.0	75.1
1964	81.7	81.2	91.1	81.9
1965	89.2	89.1	93.9	86.9
1966	97.9	98.3	98.4	93.6
1967	100.0	100.0	100.0	100.0
1968	105.7	105.7	103.9	109.4
1969	110.7	110.5	107.2	119.5
1970	106.7	105.2	109.7	128.5
1971	106.5	104.9	106.9	135.3

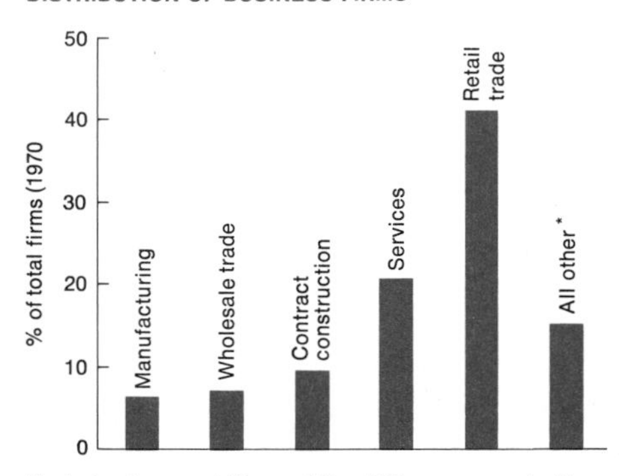

*Includes transportation, public utilities, communications, finance, insurance, real estate, and mining.

INFERENCE

For statistical concepts closely related to inference, see the articles on PROBABILITY and SAMPLING; and for more specific details, consult POPULATION, STATISTICAL; FREQUENCY DISTRIBUTION; SAMPLING DISTRIBUTION; HYPOTHESIS; and SAMPLING THEORY.

compiled and published by the Board of Governors of the Federal Reserve System. The Index covers approximately 35% of total U.S. output and includes a representative group of over 200 products from manufacturing, mining, and public utility industries. This index, which fluctuates more widely than most other measures of economic activity, expresses current output as a percentage of annual production levels during the 1957–1959 base period.

See also Business Cycles, Measurement; Indices.

INDUSTRIAL UNION. Because of the mass production technology of American industry, it has often become necessary to break down what were formally highly skilled operations into somewhat minute tasks. Workers therefore often develop expertise in tasks that, although important in a particular industry, may be useless in other industries. For this reason, these workers often organize on an industry-wide basis for bargaining purposes.

Because industrial unions often have the power to literally shut down an industry's operations, they usually are very powerful in negotiations over wages and other benefits. Two examples of powerful industrial unions are the United Automobile Workers and the International Brotherhood of Teamsters.

INDUSTRIES, REGULATED. *See* Regulated Industries.

INDUSTRY, in price theory, the term most often used to identify a certain segment of productive enterprise, such as the steel industry or the aluminum industry. The word industry usually implies such productive enterprises as manufacturing or services that employ huge amounts of capital and labor. Individual business firms that produce the same or similar products are grouped under the collective heading of an industry. In addition, each firm has one or more plants or physical facilities where work is actually done.

See also Firm; Plant.

INDUSTRY SUPPLY. *See* Market Supply.

INDUSTRY-WIDE BARGAINING occurs when a union represents the bulk of the workers in a particular industry and bargains simultaneously with all of the employers. There are few examples of complete (national) industry-wide bargaining, although multi-employer bargaining is common and there are many cases of "industry-wide" bargaining for a particular geographic sector.

Employers may prefer industry-wide bargaining because it reduces the possibility of competitive disadvantage resulting from dissimilar individual contracts. Unions may like it because it leads to wage uniformity among workers in different firms and possibly to higher settlements by "taking the wage out of competition."

See also Multi-Employer Bargaining.

INELASTIC DEMAND. Demand for a downward sloping linear demand curve is said to be relatively inelastic if within the ordinary range of price changes the percentage change in quantity demanded is less than the percentage change in price.

Demand curves for some isolated commodities may display characteristics that differ from the typical demand curve. A demand curve for a commodity may intersect the quantity axis at some positive quantity demanded and proceed to rise from that quantity with an infinite slope. That is, the demand curve will appear vertical, implying that a given quantity of the good will be demanded regardless of price. An example of a vertical demand curve is an essential medication, such as insulin, required to sustain life regardless of the price. No substitute is available for a good with a perfectly vertical demand curve. The elasticity implication for this class of demand curves is that any percentage change in price will evoke no percentage change in quantity demanded. This demand curve is hence said to be perfectly, or totally, inelastic.

See also Demand Curve; Elastic Demand; Elasticity of Demand.

—Robert L. Brite, *Louisiana State University*

INELASTIC SUPPLY. The supply of a product is said to be inelastic, over some small price range, when the computed coefficient of elasticity is less than one. Theoretically all coefficients less than one, down to negative infinity, would be described as inelastic. Of course, the smaller the coefficient the less elastic is supply. The implication of the term is that over given price ranges for certain commodities the firms in question (or the industries) are better able to react to price changes due to changes in demand. Certain characteristics of the firm or industry imply that an increase in output will cause significant diminishing returns and marginal cost will rise rapidly.

INFANT INDUSTRY. If an industry has large potential economies of scale, prices and costs are much higher when the industry is small than they will be later, if growth can occur. Hence, latecomers to the industry may need tariff protection in the early stages of growth until they can compete with established foreign rivals.

INFERENCE, in statistics, refers to the process of estimating the true population values on the basis of experimental or sample values. To find the mean income of nonwhite families living in Boston, for example, we could poll every such family and compute the mean income. This could be expensive or simply impossible. Alternatively, we could select a sample of a few such families and from the sample mean infer the population mean income.

See also Population, Statistical; Sampling.

INFERIOR GOOD. *See* Income Effect.

INFINITE ELASTICITY. *See* Perfect Elasticity.

INFINITELY ELASTIC DEMAND. *See* Elastic Demand.

INFLATION, a continuously rising general price level, resulting in a loss of the purchasing power of money.

Redistributive Effects. The problem of inflation lies in its redistribution of income and wealth. For example, people such as pensioners and salaried employees, whose incomes are fixed in money terms, will be worse off than workers whose wages keep pace with inflation. Also, inflation redistributes income from creditors to debtors as debts are repaid in dollars whose purchasing power has declined. Because the elderly depend most heavily on monetary assets, savings, and pensions for income, there is a redistribution from the old to the young in inflation. Further, because real estate prices tend to rise with the general price level, there is a redistribution of income from renters to homeowners, from the poor to the less poor.

The Record. During the nineteenth century and even up to World War II, periods of inflation alternated with periods of deflation, lending support to the observation that prices were stable in the long run. However, since World War II, prices have been rising continuously in almost every country. In the U.S. the Consumer Price Index has doubled since 1946.

Causes and Cures. There are essentially three types of inflation: demand pull, cost push, and sectoral, or demand shift. In demand-pull inflation aggregate demand exceeds full employment output, and prices rise: the cure is to reduce aggregate demand by increasing taxes, reducing government spending, reducing the money supply, or some combination of monetary and fiscal policy. Cost-push inflation arises when oligopolistic firms pass on union wage or other cost increases in the form of higher prices: the appropriate policy seems to be "jawboning" (presidential coercion-persuasion), guidelines, or actual wage-price controls. Sectoral inflation occurs when prices are inflexible downward but flexible upward. Shifts in demand cause prices to rise in the sectors whose demand has increased, while prices fail to decline in the sector where demand has fallen off. Sectoral and cost-push inflation do not seem responsive to the usual monetary and fiscal controls.

When several types of inflation occur simultaneously, it is difficult for policy makers to determine the appropriate response. This problem is compounded by the observed tendency of prices and unemployment to move in opposite directions: slowing the rate of inflation may mean increases in the level of unemployment, a dilemma.

Consult (5) Lindauer, 1968; Peterson, 1962.

—Carlisle E. Moody, Jr., *College of William and Mary*

INFLATIONARY GAP, the amount by which intended investment, intended consumption, intended government expenditure, or any combination thereof must decrease to achieve full employment at stable prices. For example, if the full-employment stable-price level of income is $900 and the marginal propensity to consume is .75 (and, therefore, the multiplier is 4), and if at that level households spend $700, investment demand is $40, and government demand is $180—all totaling $920—there will be an inflationary gap of $5. That is, a first-stage reduction of $5 in any component of aggregate demand will lead, because of the multiplier, to a fall in income of $20 to the full-employment stable-price income of $900.

Similarly, the deflationary gap is the amount by which intended investment, intended consumption, intended government expenditure, or any combination thereof would have to increase to achieve full employment at stable prices. In the example above, the deflationary gap would be $10, if the full-employment income were $960, rather than $900.

See also Aggregate Demand; Marginal Propensity To Consume; Multiplier; National Income Determination.

—Walter C. Neale, *University of Tennessee*

INFRASTRUCTURE can refer to a broad range of enterprises, with perhaps two general characteristics: (1) the goods or services they produce augment the productivity of other industries and (2) they are usually undertaken by public bodies.

Some infrastructure industries are virtually required for other production to take place; roads, railroads, electricity, water, and sewage supply are prime examples. Others, particularly the service industries, such as public health, urban transportation, education, and even housing, merely contribute to the productivity of other industries, often through an

INFLATION

Inflation is a major concept related to many other terms and concepts in macroeconomics. For the closest of these, see PRICE LEVEL, BUSINESS CYCLES, and BUSINESS CYCLES, PHASES. For some of those aspects of inflation most relevant to the present time, see PHILLIPS CURVE and SECTORAL INFLATION. For methods of dealing with inflation, see STABILIZATION POLICY, MONETARY POLICY, and INCOMES POLICY.

The Subject Maps accompanying the articles on BUSINESS CYCLES, FEDERAL BUDGET, MONEY, and PRICE LEVEL show many other articles touching on Inflation.

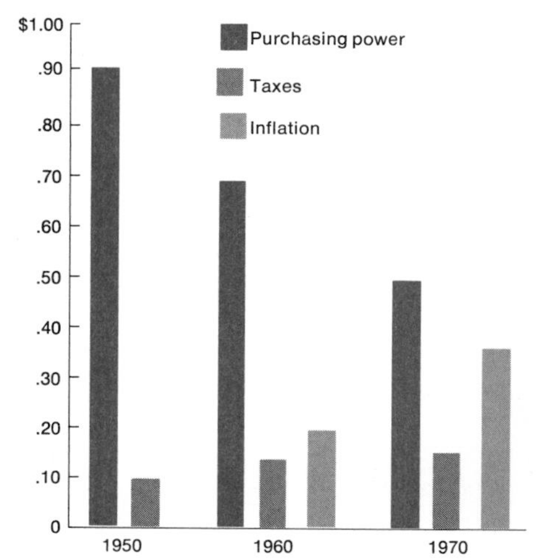

increase in the productivity of labor. The crucial role played by infrastructure in allowing other industries to operate has placed them high in developmental investment priorities. Yet the role is passive, not formative: they allow other industries to exist but they do not bring them into existence.

Role of Public Bodies. Infrastructure falls normally under the responsibility of public bodies for two major reasons. The first is the existence of externalities. Often, a private firm could not afford to make all consumers pay the full value of the services consumed. This may simply be due to physical constraints, such as the impossibility of collecting tolls from all users of all roads, or to the impracticality of determining precisely how much each person benefits from a service (such as law enforcement and public health services) where collective benefits accrue to everyone.

The second is the existence of economies of scale and the indivisibility of large projects, such as hydroelectric dams, where the minimum efficient size of a private firm is so large that it invites monopolies, and government regulation or ownership is thus required.

See also Externalities; Economies of Scale.

Consult (24) Nurkse, 1961.

—Charles Staelin, *University of Michigan*

INJECTION refers to businesses (which ordinarily take some money out of the circular flow of income through business savings) placing money back into the income stream through transfer payments, investment spending, and increased production. Injections directly increase personal income and, therefore, consumption. The injections, based on future expectation, usually occur well ahead of the expansionary phase of the business cycle and can contribute to its upturn.

INJUNCTION, LABOR. Opposed bitterly by labor, the injunction is a legal technique developed in equity courts to provide relief against continuing injury where recovery in the form of monetary damages does not suffice. If it can be proved that "irreparable damage" might occur to the requesting party unless certain acts of the defendant are stopped, an order can be issued by a judge enjoining continuation of the acts. A refusal by the defending party may result in fines or imprisonment.

In the past, in cases of a union strike against management, an injunction could tie union hands while leaving employers free to discharge union members and otherwise act to destroy union organization before the union could be heard in court. Often before the court date the employer could defeat the union. Such injunctions were effectively outlawed by the Norris-LaGuardia Act in 1932.

INNOVATION THEORY OF BUSINESS CYCLES states that scientific and technological inventions and new methods of production have a significant impact on the level of economic activity. Although external to the economic system, innovation is vital to economic growth and provides the incentive that business needs to invest in research and products in the hope of reducing costs and increasing profits. Major innovations—for example, railroads, electric power, the transistor, and nuclear power—have been observed to provide important stimulants to economic activity, causing significant increases in investment which, in turn, result in cyclical upswings.

See also Business Cycles, Theories.

INNOVATOR. *See* Innovation Theory of Business Cycles.

INPUT, a concept associated with the production process. Certain factors, such as raw materials, semi-manufactured goods, labor skills, and machine capability, are fed at one end into the production system, and some product emerges at the other end. The most common classifications of inputs are land, labor, and capital. Land inputs include all primary products, such as land, iron ore, or crude oil. Labor inputs encompass all human services, such as an individual's manual skills, or a person's knowledge of proper market action. Inputs of capital include all man-made aids to production, for example, a fork-lift truck, or a drill press. In complex production there may be hundreds of specific inputs entering into the output of a product, such as an automobile.

INPUT-OUTPUT MODELS represent an attempt to quantify and isolate the important intersectoral flows of the economic system. Influenced by the work of François Quesnay and the general equilibrium analysis of Leon Walras, Wassily Leontief constructed a basic input-output model. Leontief divided the economy into various industries and considered the outputs, or production, and the inputs, or consumption, of each industry. Sectors such as households, government, and foreign trade were considered to be industries with their own inputs and outputs. For example, the inputs to the household sector consist of final goods and services obtained from other industries, and the outputs of this sector consist of labor and capital.

Closed Model. Leontief's basic, or closed, model assumed that all outputs of sectors became inputs of other industries. Thus, no final demand exists. Also the model assumes fixed techniques of production. This means that a fixed relationship exists between the inputs and outputs of industries so that if inputs are varied, output will vary accordingly.

Open Model. A more general, or open,

input-output model divides the economy into two parts. The first part includes all industries that are functionally related in that they purchase from and sell to each other various intermediate goods and services. The second part of the open model includes the sectors where the industries sell their final goods and services and where those industries obtain their primary inputs, or factors of production. The open model, thus, allows economists to isolate the relationships among producers in the first part of the model and to view the relationship between producers and those who supply resources and purchase the final output (household, governments, and the rest of the world). Like the closed model, the open model also assumes fixed production techniques.

Uses. For economic planners the information and relationships demonstrated by the models are important. For satisfying a given or planned level of demand, the necessary inputs can be isolated. Also the models can be quite useful for regional planning where the region may have different techniques of production or consumption behavior than the nation as a whole. However, input-output models can only be used in industrial nations; their assumption of fixed production techniques ignores technological change, and the mass of data needed to prepare the model may be difficult to obtain.

See also Model, Economic.

—Clyde A. Haulman, *College of William and Mary*

INSTALLMENT CREDIT CONTROLS (consumer credit controls) prescribe the minimum down payment and the maximum repayment period on installment loans to consumers in order to reduce the amount of borrowing by consumers. These controls were established by the Board of Governors of the Federal Reserve System under the War Powers Act (1941) and the Defense Production Act (1950) and published as Regulation W. They were discontinued in 1952.

INSTANTANEOUS EQUILIBRIUM. *See* Momentary Equilibrium.

INSTITUTIONALISM. One of America's early original contributions to economic thought, the institutional school studied the economy as a whole with the emphasis upon institutions and their role in the economic system. The inductive methodology of institutionalism was adopted from the Historical school but was generally more liberal and democratic. The institutionalists were also concerned with income and wealth distribution and considered that disequilibrium was the normal state of the economy rather than the equilibrium conditions discussed by neoclassical theory.

Major early figures of the school were Thorstein Veblen, first of the institutionalists, and Wesley Mitchell, instrumental in the founding of the National Bureau of Economic Research and in the use of inductive statistical studies. While much of institutionalism has been incorporated into the mainstream of economics, modern economists, such as Gunnar Myrdal and John Kenneth Galbraith, are in many ways descendents of Veblen.

See also Historical School.

INTENDED INVESTMENT. *See* Investment Schedule; Marginal Efficiency of Capital.

INTERDEPENDENCE, OLIGOPOLISTIC. Because in oligopoly market structures there are only a few firms selling, the actions of each firm affect every other firm in the industry, resulting in oligopolistic interdependence. Therefore, if one firm decides to lower its price below the established market price, all other firms must lower their price in order to retain their share of the market. This also holds true in regard to output. If, for example, in the automotive industry, one firm decides to offer air-conditioning as a standard feature, other firms must also offer this feature to remain competitive. Because of this interdependence, a certain amount of collusion usually exists in these markets.

INTERDEPENDENCE OF ECONOMIC BEHAVIOR. Modern market economies have developed because societies have found that there are advantages from the division of labor, and that if the society is to benefit from advancing technology, the economic system must maximize the division of labor. Thus, most economic systems have evolved to the point where there are a multitude of economic units all involved in one or more aspects of production, distribution, or consumption. Although the various economic units in the system do not always appear to be related, all economic activity affects all other activity in some manner. For example, every consumer purchase of goods affects the demand for these goods, which in turn affects, in however small a manner, the industry's or firm's decision of how much to produce and, thus, the decision on the amount of inputs to purchase. All economic decisions have similar impacts.

Eighteenth Century. The realization that the economic system is composed of individual units, that these units can be grouped into sectors, and that all economic units and sectors are interdependent is the framework for the various theories and hypotheses that are central to the study of economics. The interdependence of economic behavior was first recognized by the French physiocrats in the middle of the eighteenth century. François Quesnay's *Tableau èconomique,* a three-sector economic

INTEREST RATES

To examine other aspects of the meaning and function of interest rates in their microeconomic capacity, see the articles on INTEREST and INTEREST RATE STRUCTURE. For an understanding of interest rates as payments to providers of capital, consult the articles on TIME PREFERENCE and RISK.

The major macroeconomic facets of interest rates are explained in the article on MONETARY POLICY. Closely related concepts are described in PRIME RATE, DISCOUNT RATE, and OPEN MARKET OPERATIONS.

The Subject Map accompanying MONEY displays the interrelated articles on Interest Rates.

INTEREST RATES

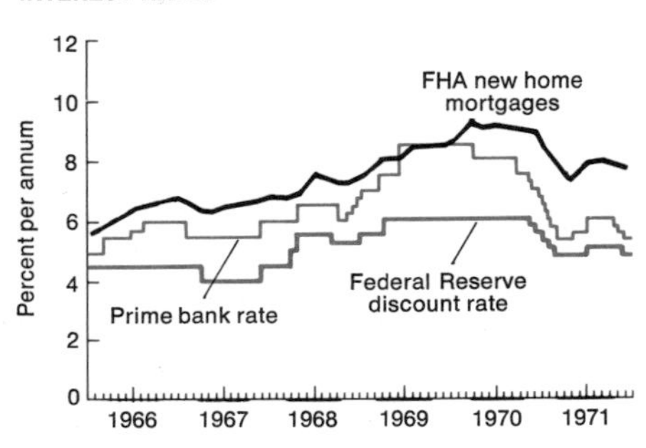

flow model, was the culmination of early thought on the interdependence of economic activity and a forerunner of the modern circular flow model. The classical statement of economic interdependence was Say's law, which, in its simplest terms, states that in supplying goods and services, the economy also creates demands for this output.

Nineteenth and Twentieth Centuries. The most important manifestation of the interdependence concept in economic theory, however, appeared in the late nineteenth century with the work of Leon Walras and Vilfredo Pareto concerning general equilibrium analysis of the economic system. This analysis attempted to consider the situation in which all units in the economic system are in simultaneous equilibrium and the adjustments necessary to reach this state. Although much consideration has been given to general equilibrium theory, the complexities of modern economies do not lend themselves to empirical general equilibrium analysis. Input-output models have come closest to such analysis. The realization, however, that such interdependence exists and the attempt to take into account those relationships known to exist greatly improves the validity of economic analysis.

See also Circular Flow of Income; Input-Output Models.

—Clyde A. Haulman, *College of William and Mary*

INTERDISTRICT SETTLEMENT FUND. *See* Federal Reserve System.

INTEREST, a payment for the use of money or credit. It is both income and cost in the supply and demand framework. Before capital goods can exist, resources that could have gone toward consumer goods creation must be made available. The time preference-abstinence theory says interest is compensation to those who refrain from current consumption for the sake of more or better consumption in the future. If new capital investment is to occur, entrepreneurs must expect revenues to exceed the cost of replacing the capital equipment plus the interest; the rate of return is the marginal efficiency of capital.

Liquidity Preference. The liquidity preference theory looks at motives for holding cash (transaction, precautionary, speculative) rather than investing. Prices of financial assets and demand for money (liquidity) vary inversely with the rate of interest: when interest rates are high, investors will depart from liquidity to buy low-priced bonds, and vice versa.

Discounting and Compounding. Interest relates goods over time through discounting (translating future income into present value) and compounding (present amount into future value). The use of these procedures with concomitant monetary and fiscal policy implications facilitates economic decision- making, even in the Soviet Union, which views interest as a capitalistic phenomenon.

See also Demand for Capital; Interest Rates; Interest Rate Structure; Present Value; Roundabout Methods of Production; Time Preference.

Consult (22) Eckaus, 1972; Fusfeld, 1972; Samuelson, 1973.

—John R. Matthews, *College of William and Mary*

INTEREST-RATE ARBITRAGE. *See* Arbitrage.

INTEREST RATE CEILINGS are established by the Board of Governors of the Federal Reserve System to limit the interest rate that may be paid by commercial banks on demand deposits and time deposits. No interest is permitted on demand deposits. The ceiling on time deposits is changed from time to time and varies according to the form of the deposit and its maturity. These ceilings are published as Regulation Q.

INTEREST RATES, the price paid for the use of money. Because the use takes place over time, interest must be expressed as a rate per unit of time, customarily one year. Thus, if a borrower pays $1 in interest for the use of $100 for one month, the interest charge is 1% per month, but the interest rate is 12% per year. If he pays $12 interest in advance (a discount rather than a loan), he actually has the use of only $88: although the discount rate is 12%, the interest rate is 12/88, or 13.6%. Furthermore, if he repays the $100 in monthly installments of $8.33, he does not have the use of $88 for a year, but only for one month, then $79.67 for the next month, and so on. The true interest rate in this case is more than twice the nominal rate of 12%.

Structure. There is no single interest rate at a given time, but rather a large variety of rates for different types of loans and securities. Generally speaking, interest rates are higher for long-term loans than for short-term, for small loans than for large, for risky loans than for safe, and for specialized loans than for standard market instruments. Thus, the interest rate on Treasury bills may be 2% and the charge for a $100 personal finance-company loan may be 36%.

Determination. Interest rates, like other prices, are determined by the supply of and demand for capital or credit, but equilibrium in credit markets may be brought about more by changes in national income than in fluctuation of the interest rate. When many borrowers (corporations, governments, and consumers) are in the market for funds, they tend to push interest rates up. On the other hand, a large volume of loanable funds from personal and business savings, banks, and other intermediaries tends to lower interest rates. The government cannot determine interest rates, but it has a sizeable influence in the market on both sides. The federal government is usually a large borrower and, therefore, has a substantial impact on the demand for funds. On the other hand, the federal reserve system can affect the quantity of funds that commercial banks are able to lend and, hence, can increase or reduce supply as a matter of monetary policy.

Consult (10) Conrad, 1959; Homer, 1963.

—Walter W. Haines, *New York University*

INTEREST RATE STRUCTURE, rates existing in different types of income-earning assets at a given time. Influencing this structure are credit risk, administrative and credit investigation costs, tax treatment, and differences in maturity. This maturity aspect alone could explain different yields even if the other factors were the same for all types of securities. It is from the maturity structure that yield curves are derived: Curve (1) shows that lenders and borrowers expect long-term rates to rise; in (2) they are expected to fall. Switching between securities of different maturities is unimpeded here; if the different markets are segmented, then demand and supply in each segment determine the rate there and the resulting yield curves.

See also Interest; Interest Rates.

Consult (22) Eckaus, 1972.

INTEREST RATE STRUCTURE

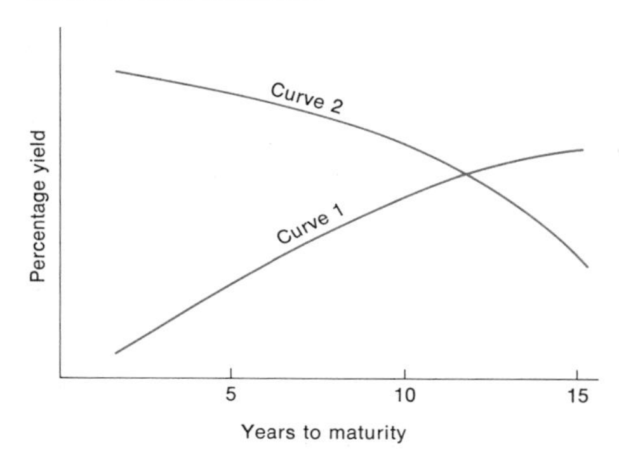

INTERLOCKING DIRECTORATE, business practice in which a member of the corporate board of directors of one firm is a member of at least one other firm. While many forms of "interlocks" exist, only one form is prohibited, that where the director sits on boards of firms of a certain size in direct competition with each other. This prohibition, in the Clayton Act (Section 8), is based on the concern that an interlocking directorate among competitors would facilitate price and output limitation agreements and other anticompetitive actions. Even this limited prohibition is not effective, however, since officers other than directors may serve on a competitor's board, and indirect interlocks are legal (as when directors of two competitors serve together on a third firm's board).

See also Antitrust Policy; Clayton Act.

INTERMEDIATE GOODS, those goods that have not completed the manufacturing process, that are being purchased for modification before final use, or that are being purchased for resale. Many intrasectoral transactions involve intermediate goods. For example, when General Motors purchases a truck engine from Detroit Diesel, the engine will be changed little, if at all. However, it is not a final good, because GM will combine the engine with other parts to make a truck to be sold as a final good. The engine, while complete at the point of sale from Detroit Diesel to GM, is an intermediate step in the production of the final good—a truck.

See also Final Goods; Goods.

INTERNAL COSTS, those costs of the production process that are borne by the producing unit and, therefore, must be taken into account by that unit in making its economic decisions. Businesses have been forced by society to internalize a number of costs that were previously externalities, such as water and air pollution.

See also External Costs.

INTERNAL DEBT, a situation where the borrowing unit (the national government) acquires funds from within its domestic economy. If the gross federal debt of the United States were financed totally by the sale of securities to American governmental agencies, financial institutions, businesses, and individuals, the debt would be purely an internal debt. No claims against the borrowing unit would arise from outside the country. All interest and debt repayment would involve transfers from the nation as a whole (taxpayers) to those who hold the debt within the same nation.

See also External Debt.

INTERNAL (or Endogenous) THEORY OF BUSINESS CYCLES acknowledges that certain external factors influence economic activity, but contends that the major cause of business cycles is attributable to factors or forces within the economic system. Among the endogenous theories are profit-motive (psychological), monetary, overinvestment, and underconsumption. Some internal theories suggest that mechanisms within the system will naturally generate economic cycles so that, predictably, every expansion will be followed by recession, contraction, and renewed expansion. Psychologically, this type of self-generation can be attributed to waves of optimism and pessimism in response to political, social, and economic occurrences which induce businesses to invest and expand, or cut back and save.

See also Business Cycle, Theories.

INTERNATIONAL BANK FOR RECONSTRUCTION AND DEVELOPMENT (IBRD), or World Bank, came into being in 1944 as a specialized agency of the United Nations. Its central activity consists in making loans to less developed member countries. The funds used by the bank are raised largely through bond issues in private capital markets. No loans can be made unless there is reasonable assurance that the borrower can repay and meet service charges. Also, the funds must be used for specific approved projects.

Thus, the World Bank is guided by bank-

INTERNATIONAL TRADE

The Subject Maps in the Encyclopedia illustrate the coverage of particular aspects of economics, showing the interrelationships among the articles in twenty-one critical areas of study. Entries in capital letters are subjects for which there are separate articles in the Encyclopedia. Entries in small letters are references to the article immediately above and provide some idea of content.

The Subject Maps are arranged alphabetically in the Encyclopedia under the following titles:

Antitrust Policy
Banking System
Business Cycles
Capital
Circular Flow of Income
Demand Theory
Economic Systems
Factor Markets
Federal Budget
History of Economic Ideas
International Trade Theory
Labor Market
Labor Movement
Market System
Money and Monetary Policy
National Income
Price Level
Regulation
Supply
Theory of the Firm
Wages

INTERNATIONAL TRADE THEORY

- ABSOLUTE ADVANTAGE
- COMPARATIVE ADVANTAGE
  - comparative disadvantage
- TERMS OF TRADE
- SPECIALIZATION
- CONSUMPTION POSSIBILITY
- BARTER

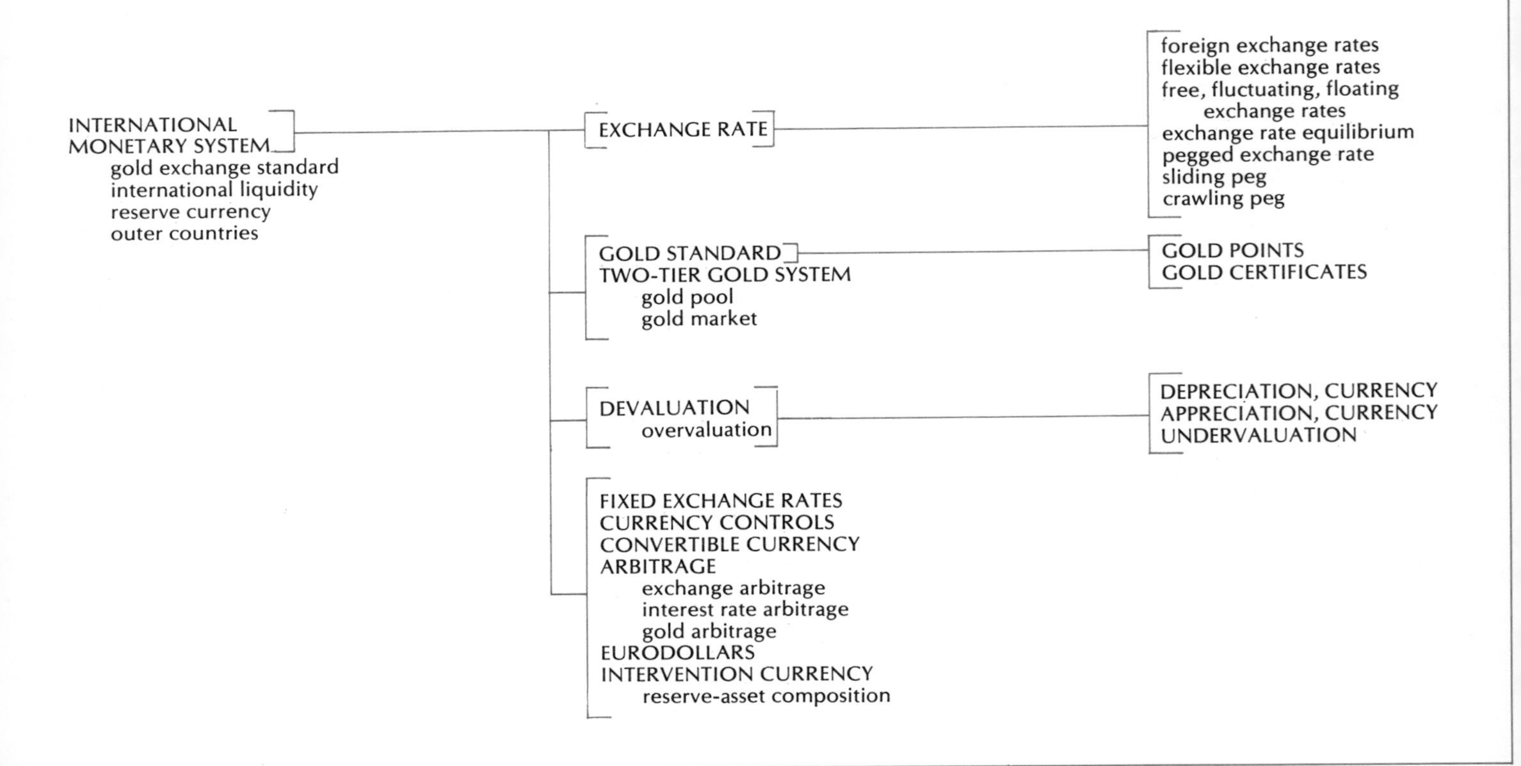

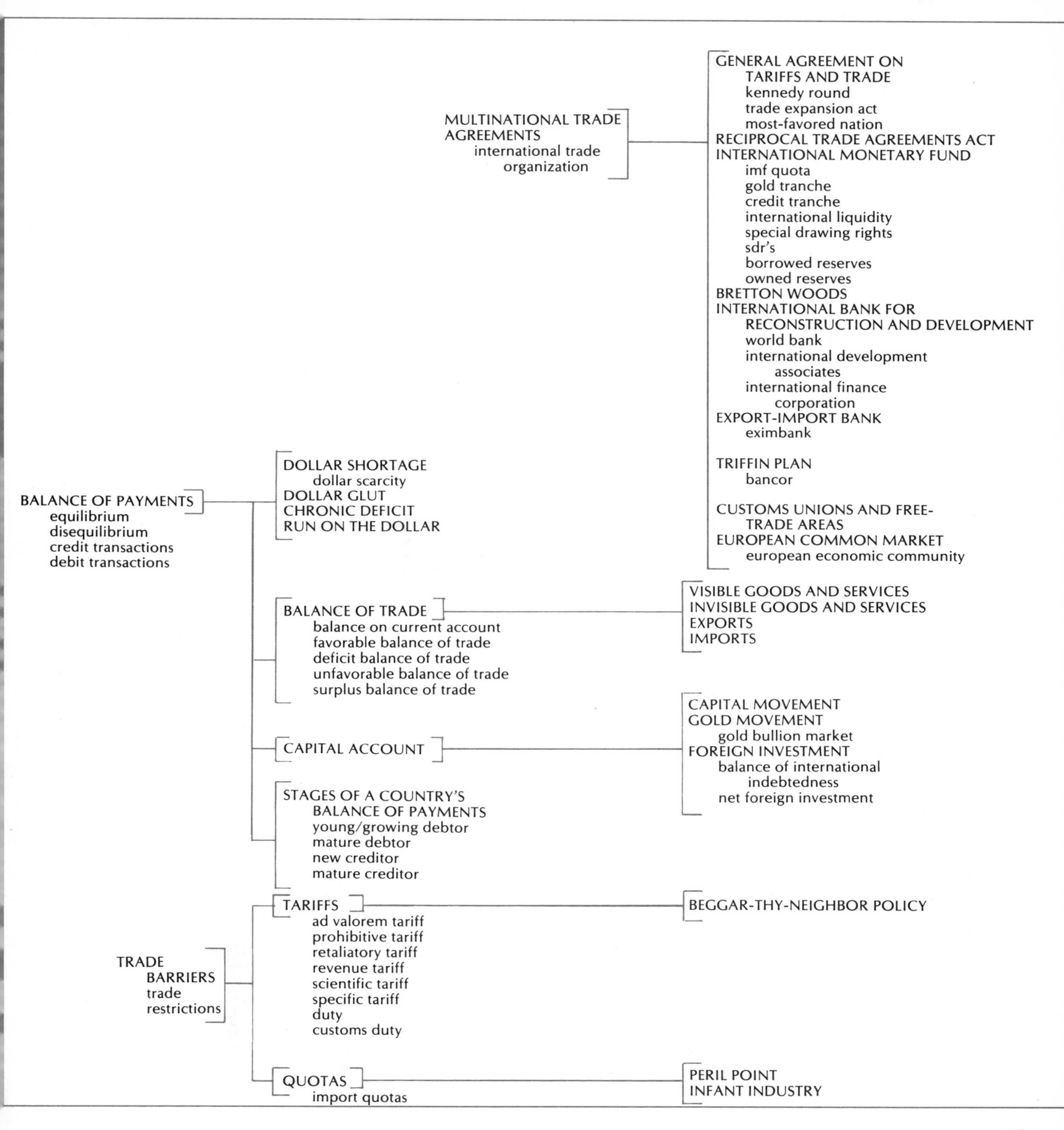

MULTINATIONAL TRADE AGREEMENTS
international trade organization
GENERAL AGREEMENT ON TARIFFS AND TRADE
kennedy round
trade expansion act
most-favored nation
RECIPROCAL TRADE AGREEMENTS ACT
INTERNATIONAL MONETARY FUND
imf quota
gold tranche
credit tranche
international liquidity
special drawing rights
sdr's
borrowed reserves
owned reserves
BRETTON WOODS
INTERNATIONAL BANK FOR RECONSTRUCTION AND DEVELOPMENT
world bank
international development associates
international finance corporation
EXPORT-IMPORT BANK
eximbank
TRIFFIN PLAN
bancor
CUSTOMS UNIONS AND FREE-TRADE AREAS
EUROPEAN COMMON MARKET
european economic community
BALANCE OF PAYMENTS
equilibrium
disequilibrium
credit transactions
debit transactions
DOLLAR SHORTAGE
dollar scarcity
DOLLAR GLUT
CHRONIC DEFICIT
RUN ON THE DOLLAR
BALANCE OF TRADE
balance on current account
favorable balance of trade
deficit balance of trade
unfavorable balance of trade
surplus balance of trade
VISIBLE GOODS AND SERVICES
INVISIBLE GOODS AND SERVICES
EXPORTS
IMPORTS
CAPITAL ACCOUNT
CAPITAL MOVEMENT
GOLD MOVEMENT
gold bullion market
FOREIGN INVESTMENT
balance of international indebtedness
net foreign investment
STAGES OF A COUNTRY'S BALANCE OF PAYMENTS
young/growing debtor
mature debtor
new creditor
mature creditor
TRADE BARRIERS
trade restrictions
TARIFFS
ad valorem tariff
prohibitive tariff
retaliatory tariff
revenue tariff
scientific tariff
specific tariff
duty
customs duty
BEGGAR-THY-NEIGHBOR POLICY
QUOTAS
import quotas
PERIL POINT
INFANT INDUSTRY

Washington, D.C. headquarters of the International Bank for Reconstruction and Development.

ing criteria and countries not meeting these do not have access to its facilities. To help overcome these limitations the International Development Associates (IDA) was formed to provide soft loans to less developed countries (terms more favorable than World Bank and with longer periods). The International Finance Corporation, which together with the IBRD and IDA form the World Bank Group, was formed to further economic development in less developed member countries by investing directly in private enterprises in association with private investors.

See also International Monetary Fund.

INTERNATIONAL BROTHERHOOD OF TEAMSTERS, chartered by the AFL in 1899 as the Team Drivers International Union, organized the drivers of horse-pulled vehicles. Headquarters were set up in 1903 in Indianapolis and the present name was adopted.

In 1907 Daniel J. Tobin became president and in his 45-year reign brought the union from a membership of less than 40,000 to one of over a million with assets of nearly $30 million. In 1952 Dave Beck became the Teamsters' president but his term was short lived. In the 1957 McClellan Committee investigations, Beck took the Fifth Amendment and gave up his position to James Hoffa. In that same year, the AFL-CIO's Ethical Practices Committee voted to expel the Teamsters.

The government continued its attack on the Teamsters and on Hoffa. The charges involved allegations of financial malpractice, and the resort to undemocratic procedures, racketeering and violence. In 1964 Hoffa was found guilty of jury tampering. Frank Fitzsimmons succeeded him as president of the Teamsters, whose current membership is just under 2,000,000.

INTERNATIONAL DEVELOPMENT ASSOCIATES. *See* International Bank for Reconstruction and Development.

INTERNATIONAL FINANCE CORPORATION. *See* International Bank for Reconstruction and Development.

INTERNATIONAL LIQUIDITY. *See* International Monetary System.

INTERNATIONAL MONETARY FUND (IMF, also called simply the Fund) functions as the regulator of foreign exchange rates and as a source of international liquidity. Each member country, upon joining the IMF, receives a quota (its IMF quota) based on its economic size. (Thus, the United States has by far the largest quota.) A country is required to deposit one quarter of its quota in gold and the remainder in its domestic currency with the IMF. These deposits constitute the country's quota subscription. In return, the country has the opportunity to borrow any foreign currency from the Fund.

Provisions. The loan is in reality a purchase-and-resale agreement in which the borrowing country sells its own currency to the Fund for the desired foreign exchange, agreeing to reverse the transaction in three to five years. There is an interest cost (called a service charge).

A country has an unconditional right to borrow until the IMF holds domestic currency equal to 100% of its quota (that is, the 75% it deposits and the 25% it exchanges for other currencies). The amount of foreign exchange it can borrow unconditionally is called its gold tranche, and is equal to 25% of its quota. Beyond the gold tranche a country has the privilege, not the right, of borrowing four successive credit tranches, each equal to 25% of its quota. The credit tranches may be borrowed only at the discretion of the Fund. They are borrowed reserves, as distinct from the country's gold tranche and its holdings of gold and dollars, all of which are owned reserves. When the IMF holdings of a country's domestic currency reaches 200% of its quota—that is, the country has borrowed its gold tranches and its four credit tranches—the country has reached the limit of its borrowing power.

SDRs. At discrete intervals international liquidity is increased by increasing countries' quotas with the IMF, the increased quotas again in proportion to a country's current economic size. Moreover, in 1967 the members of the IMF agreed to establish a new form of international reserves, called *Special Drawing Rights (SDRs).* Each country receives an SDR allocation (SDR balances) in proportion to its IMF quota. SDRs were allocated in three installments—on January 1 in each of 1970, 1971, and 1972.

A country may use its SDRs to purchase another country's currency, thus acquiring foreign exchange, in which case the first country's SDR balances are reduced and those of the second country increased by the amount of the transaction. SDRs are owned reserves in the sense that they may be used fully without permission of the IMF. However, they resemble borrowed reserves because of the existence of a reconstitution provision: a country must retain at least 30% of its SDR allocation unused as a daily average over the base period.

See also Exchange Rates; Multinational Trade Agreements.

—Lawrence H. Officer, *Michigan State University*

INTERNATIONAL MONETARY SYSTEM, the framework within which balance-of-payments deficits and surpluses are settled between countries. *International liquidity* (also called international reserves or reserve assets or reserve holdings or simply reserves) are assets held by governments for the purpose of financing balance-of-payments deficits, in which case their reserve holdings increase. The international monetary system of the 19th century was the gold standard, in which gold was the only reserve asset. The present international monetary system is known as the *gold-exchange standard,* because both gold and foreign exchange (the so-called hard currencies, chief among which is the dollar) are used as reserve assets. Thus, the dollar is a reserve currency, and the United States is a reserve-currency (or key-currency) country.

INTERNATIONAL TRADE (1927). *See* Taussig, Frank W.

INTERNATIONAL TRADE AND THE NATIONAL INCOME MULTIPLIER (1943). *See* Machlup, Fritz.

INTERNATIONAL TRADE ORGANIZATION. *See* Multinational Trade Agreements.

INTERNATIONAL TRADE THEORY explains why nations trade. David Ricardo and John Stuart Mill are associated with the classical theory of international trade; Alfred Marshall and Frank Taussig were later neoclassicals; prominent names in the modern theory are Heckscher and Ohlin. International trade is based on the law of comparative advantage: each nation should produce those goods and services that its resource endowment and technology indicate it can produce better and cheaper than other nations; it then trades these products for goods and services that it finds more costly to produce. Prices differ, therefore, between countries, but behind absolute prices lie differences in relative prices based on the pretrade situation.

In pretrade isolation each country has a production-possibility frontier embodying its full potential with all resources fully employed. At full employment the real cost to the economy of more of a good is the value of other goods not produced as a result (opportunity cost). If these opportunity costs for a given good differ between countries, relative cost and price comparisons may be made. These pretrade relative differences are translated into absolute differences via rates of exchange—domestic price of a unit of foreign currency. Exchange rates determine exports and imports; each country exports products with lower comparative costs before trade and imports products whose comparative costs are higher. Trade is beneficial when the opportunity cost of importing is lower than the opportunity cost of producing: the production-possibility frontier is pushed outward.

See also Comparative Advantage; Exchange Rate; Terms of Trade.

Consult (23)Bach, 1971; Ingrams, 1970; Massel, 1965; Snider, 1971; Wexler, 1972.

—John R Matthews, Jr., *College of William and Mary*

INTERNATIONAL UNIONS. *See* National Unions.

INTERSTATE COMMERCE ACT (1887), enacted by Congress after shippers—especially Midwest farmers—had complained for two decades that railroad rates were being set at monopoly levels and were discriminatory. The law, formally the Act to Regulate Commerce, created the Interstate Commerce Commission and required that interstate rail rates be reasonable and just. In addition, the law forbade arrangements among competing railroads for sharing traffic and earnings, required that rates be published and adhered to, and limited rate discrimination. The commission's regulatory authority has since been expanded to include oil pipeline, motor carrier, and water carrier companies.

See also Interstate Commerce Commission.

INTERSTATE COMMERCE COMMISSION (ICC), first federal regulatory commission, established in 1887, which served as a pattern for subsequent state and federal commissions. Presently there are 11 commissioners, no more than six from one political party, appointed by the president with the consent of the senate for staggered terms of seven years each.

The ICC has jurisdiction over most domestic interstate surface transportation, including railroads, motor carriers, inland water transportation, freight forwarders, express companies, rate bureaus, and other transportation firms. It is organized into three divisions (operating rights; rates, tariffs, and valuation; finances and services), four "offices," and five "bureaus," and has a staff of 1800 persons and an annual appropriation over $28 million.

Been Rolling a Little too High.

The rail industry received greatest initial attention of the Interstate Commerce Commission.

INTERVENTION CURRENCY, the currency with which member governments of the International Monetary Fund (IMF) intervene in foreign-exchange markets. A country will accumulate dollars (buy dollars) when its exchange rate is at the lower support point and lose dollars (sell dollars) when its exchange rate is at the upper support point. Until August 1971 governments could replenish dollar holdings by selling gold to the United States. Alternatively, governments could increase gold holdings by selling dollars to (buying gold from) the United States. Either transaction involves changing the country's *reserve-asset composition:* the ratio of dollar holdings to gold in its reserves, or, in general, the ratio of any one reserve asset (gold or dollar holdings) to the country's total reserves.

INVENTORY INVESTMENT CHANGES
(1962=0)
(BILLIONS OF CONSTANT DOLLARS)

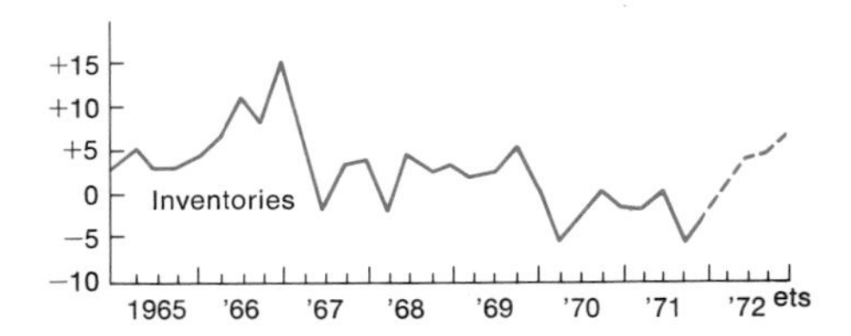

INVESTMENT
(1962=0)
(BILLIONS OF CONSTANT DOLLARS)

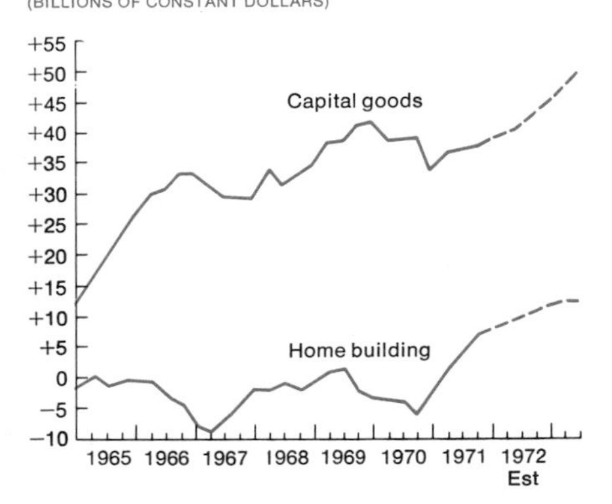

INVESTMENT

For an explanation of the macroeconomic significance of investment see the major articles on NATIONAL INCOME DETERMINATION and BUSINESS CYCLES, THEORIES. Other macroeconomic facets of investment are found in the articles on INJECTION, MARGINAL EFFICIENCY OF CAPITAL, and INTEREST. And for more narrowly defined terms, see DIRECT INVESTMENT, AUTONOMOUS INVESTMENT, INDUCED INVESTMENT, and INVENTORY INVESTMENT.

The Subject Map accompanying the article on NATIONAL INCOME shows the interrelationships of these and other investment concepts.

INVENTORY ACCUMULATION, the voluntary or involuntary buildup of goods when production is running ahead of consumption. Accumulation also occurs when merchants, particularly in an economic upswing, overestimate their needs in acquiring stock in an attempt to accommodate anticipated sales.

See also Inventory Investment.

INVENTORY DECUMULATION, the reduction of business inventories. It can occur when consumption exceeds production or, by design, during downswings when businesses want to divest themselves of inventory.

See also Inventory Investment.

INVENTORY INVESTMENT, the market value of all raw materials, supplies, and finished goods purchased by manufacturers, wholesalers, retailers, and farmers. The rate of inventory investment depends on technological innovation, anticipated economic expansion, and the state of the economy, as measured by the quantity of money, credit, and interest rates.

In years of upswing, businesses seek to build their stocks to accommodate a rise in sales. Conversely, in a downswing, businesses cut back production, reduce inventory, and lay off men, all of which are ultimately registered in a geometric drop in Net National Product. Waves of optimism and pessimism in the business and financial communities, usually generated by political policies and activities, also cause fluctuation in inventory investment.

To attenuate cyclical fluctuation in inventory accumulation and decumulation, most businesses have short- and long-term investment plans for purchases of new plant and equipment.

INVESTMENT, in national income accounting and development economics, spending by businesses on currently produced capital goods (I); and in finance, the purchase of stocks, bonds, and other titles to property.

The Income Stream. Investment is spending that contributes to the income stream when that spending is on currently produced goods. When spending is for titles to property rights (real or intangible), it does not contribute to the aggregate demand for goods and services. When spending is for previously produced goods, it makes no demands upon productive capacity—the demand for already produced goods does not require production and, hence, causes no income payments to be made to the factors of production. It is only when new goods are demanded that factors must be employed and paid.

Terminology. In physical terms capital goods themselves are thought of as fixed capital and as inventory. Fixed capital includes all structures, machinery, or equipment used in further production of goods and services for sale. Capital goods are determined by virtue of this criterion of further production for sale and not by virtue of their physical characteristics.

Governments, of course, purchase capital goods to be used in producing other goods and services and often sell the products, but because the reasons for and processes of political decisions to buy these goods are different from the profit motive of businesses, government purchases of capital goods are classified as government expenditure, G. By definition, in national income theory and national income accounting only businesses invest.

Inventories—materials awaiting processing or products awaiting sale—are the real (as opposed to monetary or financial) working capital of firms. An increase in total inventories is a net investment, because the increase requires suppliers to hire additional labor to provide materials; a decrease is a negative investment, because suppliers of materials, supplying less, will lay off workers. When inventories remain constant, they neither increase nor decrease the stock of goods; the materials supplied and used in production are accounted for as products in the final goods produced. If inventories are maintained at the same level, there is no change from year to year in spending.

Theoretical Structures. In national income theory, spending is divided into the categories of consumption (C), investment (I), government (G), and net exports (F), because the motive for each is different. Investment, which occurs when profits are anticipated and finance can be had, has a leading role in the theory of income determination, because I fluctuates more rapidly than C, G, or F. Investment spending is volatile, because expectations about profitability change more quickly than do consumers' standards and tastes, government policy, or the reasons why Americans buy from foreigners (imports: M) and why foreigners buy from Americans (exports: X). Furthermore, it is far more difficult for policy and administration to change expectations of profitability than it is for them to affect disposable income or government spending; and the monetary authorities can limit or encourage investment in ways that cannot be applied to consumption and government spending.

In the study of economic development, investment is defined in the same way, but its role in theories of development is different. In these theories investment is the addition to the stock of capital in the country and is often symbolized by ΔK (for change in capital). The importance of investment in these theories is that over time the additions to capital stock increase the productive capacity of the country. In the poorer countries the problem is frequently not that aggregate demand is too low to employ the whole labor force; rather, there is not enough equipment for the labor force to use. The focus is on capacity rather than on demand.

See also Actual Investment; Aggregate Demand; Autonomous Investment; Induced Investment; Investment Schedule; National Income Determination.

—Walter C. Neale, *University of Tennessee*

INVESTMENT, GROSS. *See* Gross Investment.

INVESTMENT, INVENTORY. *See* Inventory Investment.

INVESTMENT, NET. *See* Net Investment.

INVESTMENT, PERSONAL. *See* Personal Investment.

INVESTMENT FUNCTION. *See* Investment Schedule.

INVESTMENT SCHEDULE, a schedule of the amounts that would be spent on investment (capital) goods at each possible level of income (most realistically GNP in this case). When the relation of investment to income is plotted on a graph or expressed as an algebraic equation it is called the *investment function.* The schedule of that portion of investment which is autonomous would show only one amount whatever the level of income; on a graph it would plot as a horizontal line (investment plotted on vertical axis, income on horizontal axis). The schedule of *induced investment* will show greater investment at higher incomes, an upward sloping function, most likely showing zero or negative net investment at low incomes. The total investment schedule, the sum of the two, will show higher investment at higher incomes and be upward sloping.

The investment schedule is also the schedule of *planned investment.* Planned investment, also called *intended investment,* is the amount that businesses expect to invest, based on anticipated GNP. The planned investment schedules are based upon the expectation of profits from buying and using the investment goods.

See also Autonomous Investment; Induced Investment; Investment; Marginal Efficiency of Capital.

—Walter C. Neale, *University of Tennessee*

INVISIBLE GOODS AND SERVICES. All items in the current account of a balance of payments other than merchandise exports and imports are classified as invisibles. These include services, which cannot be seen or touched, such as freight handling, and insurance, tourist expenditures, and interest on investments abroad (or due foreign investors).

INVISIBLE HAND, theory that individuals free to pursue their own self-interests will automatically promote the interests of society, as if by an "invisible hand." The concept, first advanced by Adam Smith in the *Wealth of Nations* (1776), of the market as an "invisible hand" that channeled individual selfish actions into socially useful activities supported a doctrine of laissez faire in which the primary function of government would be to support and encourage profit making. According to Smith, a purely competitive market—characterized by small and numerous economic units, homogeneous products, market knowledge, and mobility—would be a safeguard against misuse of economic self-interest.

See also Competition; Laissez Faire; Market Economy; Profit System.

Consult (26) Cole, 1969.

INVOLUNTARY INVESTMENT. *See* Disinvestment.

IRON LAW OF WAGES, an outgrowth of the thinking of the classical economists, especially Thomas Malthus and David Ricardo, in the early nineteenth century. As a wage theory, the Iron Law of Wages states that a rise in real income of a worker is self-defeating because, as income rises, family size begins to increase substantially and thus the number of workers eventually increases. This was especially true before the advent of child labor laws. This increase in population will cause food prices to rise so that the initial increase in real wages is cancelled out by the increase in food prices.

The idea of a positive relationship between food prices and population was first presented by Malthus in his *An Essay on the Principle of Population,* published in 1798. The Iron Law of Wages eventually gave way to more progressive theories and by the twentieth century was generally considered erroneous.

ISOPRODUCT CURVE, or ISOQUANT, the locus of points in the input space representing the varying combinations of inputs that can produce a given output of some commodity. Isoquant analysis assumes that inputs can substitute for each other in the productive process: hence, a given output quantity can be produced in several ways, for example by using much labor and little capital, or much capital and little labor.

Ideally the curve will be continuous, implying that the same output can be produced by making very small substitutions, and that many combinations of inputs are able to produce a given output quantity. A family of isoproduct curves may be plotted with two factors on the respective axes. Higher isoquants represent larger outputs. Isoquants slope downward and do not intersect.

See also Production Function.

George Katona

ISOQUANT. *See* Isoproduct Curve.

ISO-UTILITY CURVE. *See* Indifference Curve.

JEVONS, WILLIAM STANLEY (1835-82). English economist who, with Carl Menger and Leon Walras, laid the foundation for the development of neoclassical economics and developed an important element of modern microeconomic theory. Building upon the base of Bentham Utilitarianism, Jevons combined the marginal concept with utility, using a mathematical approach. He then applied the marginal utility concept thus developed to individual consumer decisions, constructing a theory of value which provided the basis of modern demand theory. This analysis was also extended to considerations of exchange. In addition, Jevons made significant advances in the use of index numbers and is also remembered for his hypothesis that business cycles were the result of sunspots.

JOHNSON, HARRY GORDON (1923-), Canadian-born economist who has gained recognition for his contributions to the theory of international trade and monetary theory. He holds degrees from Cambridge, the University of Toronto, Manchester University, and Harvard. His publications include *International Trade and Economic Growth* (1958), *Money, Trade, and Economic Growth* (1962), and *Essays in Monetary Economics* (1967). He served as a member of the U.S. Review Committee on Balance of Payments Statistics (1963-65), and became a professor at the London School of Economics and Political Science in 1966.

JOINT DEMAND. Factors are not very productive unless they cooperate with other factors. Labor, by itself, can produce only negligible output. This fact is the origin of the endless quarrels by owners of factors as to which factor is the most important in the productive process. More importantly, the necessarily joint demand for factors of production sets the stage for an important economic riddle: if land, labor, and capital jointly produce a given output, how can one measure the individual contributions. This important question, which is related to the distribution-of-income problem, is answered by long-run marginal productivity theory.

JOINT PROFIT MAXIMIZATION, a method of determining a market price of an industry by adjusting all output and prices to that point which will produce the largest aggregate of profit to all firms combined. Joint profit maximization is most often found in oligopolistic market structures because there are only a few sellers in these industries and, therefore, collaboration is relatively easy. When all firms in an industry join in this type of price determination, the industry is able to achieve much the same effect as a monopolistic industry.

JORGENSON, DALE WELDEAU (1933-), American educator and econometrician, noted for his contribution to the theory of capital and productivity change. A graduate of Reed College (1955), he received his Ph.D. from Harvard (1959). He is author of *Optimal Replacement Policy* (1967, with J.J. McCall and R. Radner) and journal articles. He has been a consultant to the RAND Corporation since 1959 and a professor of economics at Harvard since 1969.

JOURNAL ENTRY. *See* Balance Sheet.

JURISDICTION, UNION. Each union claims a group or groups of employees and asserts its claim as the only union to organize these workers. Thus, the jurisdiction of the Teamsters, as the union views it, includes at least twenty different groups of workers, in a number of occupations. Often other unions claim the same workers, and a jurisdictional dispute, that is, a conflict between two or more unions, occurs.

JURISDICTIONAL DISPUTES, conflicts between unions as to which one shall represent a certain group of workers. Such disputes were common in the period of organizing rivalry between unions of the Congress of Industrial Organizations (CIO) and the American Federation of Labor (AFL) before the two federations merged in 1955. CIO unions were mainly industrial, with jurisdictions defined by industry boundaries, while AFL unions generally defined their jurisdictions by skill or craft boundaries. Overlap and hence competition and conflict resulted.

As unions evolved into more loosely-defined heterogeneous organizations, the boundaries became blurred, but the quest for growth continues to generate jurisdictional disputes. These now tend to be settled within the labor movement or by the National Labor Relations Board, rather than through overt actions between rival unions or by pressures they put on the employer.

KARL MARX AND THE CLOSE OF HIS SYSTEM (1896). *See* Weiser, Friedrich von.

KATONA, GEORGE, (1901-), Hungarian-born social scientist, who received his Ph.D. from the University of Goettingen, Germany in 1921. Included among his publications are: *Price Control and Business* (1945), *Consumer Attitudes and Demand* (1953), *The Mass Consumption Society* (1964), and *Consumer Response to Income Increases* (1968). Through detailed interviews with about 1400 heads of households every quarter, Katona surveys consumer attitudes in order to predict purchasing patterns. His most recent book, *Aspirations and Affluence,* offers interesting contrasts between American and European consumers. He is currently professor emeritus of economics at the University of Michigan, and has been the director of the economic behavior program at the University's Survey Research Center.

KAYSEN, CARL (1920-), American economist noted for his contributions to business regulation. A graduate of the University of Pennsylvania (1940), he received his Ph.D. from Harvard (1954). His publications include *American Business Creed* (1956, co-author), *Anti-Trust Policy* (1959, co-author) and *Higher Learning: The Universities and the Public* (1969). Kaysen served as deputy special assistant to President Kennedy for national security affairs from 1961-63. He has been a professor of economics at Harvard, and he was named director of the Institute for Advanced Study at Princeton in 1966.

KENNEDY ROUND. *See* General Agreement on Tariffs and Trade.

KEY BARGAIN, agreement that sets an industry precedent. Unions that engage in multi-employer bargaining often negotiate first with the most prominent firm in the industry, and the features of that bargain in relation to wage increases, work rules, pensions, and other matters tend to become those the union seeks to establish in contracts with other firms. The contract that sets the pattern is the "key contract" and is the result of the "key bargain."

See also Collective Bargaining.

KEYNES, JOHN MAYNARD (1883-1946). The best known and one of the most important figures in economics, English monetary expert Keynes was responsible for the development of much of the framework of modern macroeconomic theory. A prolific writer, Keynes published a number of books, each of which had important impact. His *Economic Consequences of the Peace* (1919) eloquently presented the controversial view that the problems of World War I could be attributed to the peace settlement, not to those who had caused the war. *A Tract on Monetary Reform* (1923) and *The Economic Consequences of Mr. Churchill* (1925) were also policy-oriented works. The first suggested that the gold standard which had existed prior to World War I was no longer workable; the second attacked the restoration of the gold standard by Winston Churchill as Chancellor of the Exchequer.

Keynes' most important works on economic theory appeared later in his career. The two-volume *A Treatise on Money* (1930) was a complete treatment of monetary theory and policy. In these volumes Keynes made important contributions to (1) the theory of the demand for money and other financial assets; (2) the analysis of the relationship between saving and investment; and (3) the theory of the return on capital. In *The General Theory of Employment, Interest and Money* (1936), Keynes refined many of the concepts developed in his *Treatise on Money* and presented a theory of macroeconomics which has become known as the Keynesian system. While the initial reaction to the *General Theory* was many times unfavorable and, while economists agree that the system has many problems, Keynes did change the direction of economics to the extent that most economists agree that "today we are all Keynesians."

See also General Theory of Employment, Interest and Money.

—Clyde A. Haulman, *College of William and Mary*

John Maynard Keynes

KINDLEBERGER, CHARLES POOR (1910-), American economist and expert on international trade. A graduate of the University of Pennsylvania (1932), he received his Ph.D. from Columbia (1937). His publications include *Economic Growth in France and Britain, 1851-1950* (1964), *International Economics* (1953-68, editions) and *Power and Money: The Politics of International Economics and the Economics of International Politics* (1970). Kindleberger was a research economist for the Federal Reserve Bank of New York (1936-39) and the Bank for International Settlements (1939-40). He also served on the Board of Governors of the Federal Reserve System (1940-42) and in the Office of Strategic Services, Washington D.C. (1942-44, 1945). He has been a professor of economics at M.I.T. since 1948.

KINKED DEMAND CURVE, an analytical approach, using certain assumptions to explain price rigidity in oligopolistic markets. The assumptions are, first, that the industry is mature and has certain established prices. Second, if one firm attempts to lower prices, all other firms will follow in order to retain their share of the market. Third, the demand curve assumes that firms will not follow a price rise. Therefore, the kinked demand curve shows that if a firm prices above an established price it will lose its share of the market, and if it prices below the established price, since each firm will follow, it will merely retain its share of the market, but at a lower revenue.

KNEESE, ALLEN V. (1930-), American economist, who has published prolifically on economics and the environment, water resources and water quality, measuring social and economic change, and technology and growth in a world of limited resources. He received his Ph.D. in economics from Indiana University in 1956. His books include *Economics and the Environment: A Materials Balance* (1970), *Wa-*

Allen V. Kneese

Frank Hyneman Knight

Simon Kuznets

Tjalling Charles Koopmans

ter Pollution: Economic Aspects and Research Needs (1964), and *Water Resources Development and Use* (1959). He has been a visiting professor at Berkeley and the University of Mexico, and is presently director of the Quality of the Environment Program with Resources for the Future, Inc. in Washington, D.C.

KNIGHT, FRANK HYNEMAN (1885-), a prolific economic thinker, best known for his *Risk, Uncertainty and Profit* (1921). In this work, Knight stressed the manner in which the entrepreneur entered the decision-making process. According to him, true profit was the result of uncertainty, and a high rate of return to an entrepreneur for undertaking a risky venture was merely a premium for uncertainty.

In addition, Knight discussed problems of demand theory, felt that the traditional division of factors into land, labor, and capital was unnecessary, debated problems of capital theory with a production period, and expressed an abstinence theory of interest.

KNIGHTS OF LABOR, formed in 1869, represented the first serious attempt to organize labor on a national basis in the United States. It was conceived as a coalition of a large number of local unions and labor organizations. The organization, unlike the later trade unions, tended toward the system of industrial unionism, trying to organize all workers in an industry regardless of skill. Also, it concerned itself with demands for a fundamental reform of the economic structure.

The Knights reached their peak in 1886 after a strike on the Wabash, Missouri-Kansas-Texas, and Missouri Pacific railroads forced Jay Gould, the financier who controlled these railroads, to grant recognition. From 100,000 the previous year, membership rose to 700,000. Its decline, however, was as rapid as its ascent. The loss of several strikes and the separation of skilled men into a rival organization turned the tide. In 1893 membership was down to 75,000, and the organization was dissolved in 1913.

KONDRATIEFF CYCLES are economic fluctuations, named for the Russian economist N.D. Kondratieff, which last from 50 to 60 years. Each cycle consists of a series of long waves in prices, production, and trade. Kondratieff suggested that such changes as technological innovation, new markets, and war and revolution—rather than random occurrences—were the most important factors affecting these variables.

KOOPMANS, TJALLING CHARLES (1910-), Dutch-born economist, noted for his contributions to the development of mathematical methods of economic analysis. He received an M.A. (1933) from the University of Utrecht, and a Ph.D. (1936) from the University of Leiden. His publications include *Statistical Inference in Dynamic Economic Models* (1950, editor), *Activity Analysis of Production and Allocation* (1951, editor), and *Three Essays on the State of Economic Science* (1957). Director of Yale's Cowles Foundation for Research in Economics from 1961-67, he has been a professor of economics at Yale since 1955.

KUH, EDWIN (1925-), American educator and econometrician noted for his work in macroeconomic theory. He is a graduate of Williams College (1949) and he received his Ph.D. from Harvard (1955). His publications include *Capital Stock Growth: A Micro-Econometric Approach* (1963) and *The Brookings Model, Some Further Results* (1969). Kuh served as a staff member of the President's Materials Policy Commission (1951), and as a consultant to the U.S. Treasury (1959-60). He has been a professor of management and economics at M.I.T. since 1962.

KURTOSIS is a measure of how peaked or pointed a distribution is. The fourth moment about the mean measures kurtosis, but the concept is seldom used.

KUZNETS, SIMON SMITH (1901-), a Russian-born American economist, considered the father of the current national income accounting system. Working in the National Bureau of Economic Research, Kuznets studied the problem of measuring the level of aggregate economic activity and its composition. His *National Income and Its Composition 1919-1938* (1941) presented estimates of national income for the United States. However, while Kuznets had developed the concept of national income during the 1930s, it was not until after World War II that an effort was made to construct a systematic framework of national income accounts with Kuznets' earlier work providing the foundation. Kuznets has also estimated national income in the United States for the last half of the nineteenth century in his book *National Product Since 1869* (1946).

In that book, Kuznets also estimated consumption functions. He found that the long-term relationship between income and consumption was proportional, rather than the nonproportional relationship found in short-term functions and used in the Keynesian system. This finding, further supported by Goldsmith, has led to numerous attempts to reconcile the contradiction between long- and short-term consumption behavior including Friedman's permanent-income hypothesis and the life-cycle hypothesis.

Finally, in his *Modern Economic Development* (1966), Kuznets had discussed the growth process and isolated the major sources of economic growth. For his efforts, Kuznets was awarded the Nobel Prize in Economics (1971).

—Clyde A. Haulman, *College of William and Mary*

KUZNETS CYCLES, economic fluctuations which average from 15 to 25 years. They were identified in 1930, and named for Simon Kuznets, who suggested these cyclical variations were associated closely with immigration and natural rates of population growth, railroad building and capital imports, and the growth rate of the money supply.

See also Business Cycles.

LABOR, as a factor input, involves demand and supply relationships. Early economists believed wage rates were determined exclusively by labor's productivity (demand), but modern economists recognize the importance of supply, too. Modern derivations of labor supply make use of indifference curves; an individual decides the optimal trade between leisure and income for various wage rates. Some individuals may work less as wage rates rise, but it is generally agreed that group supply is upward sloping; if labor purchasers are to attract greater quantities, there must be higher wage rates.

It is proper to visualize supply and demand operating in many labor markets, rather than just one. Thus, different labor skills would lead in equilibrium to different wage rates even if there were no unnatural barriers to entry across industries. Moreover, even for a given quality of labor, wage rates may in equilibrium vary across occupations due to different working conditions (equalizing differences). The demand for labor, of course, is a function of its productivity. The interaction of supply and demand for labor in more or less segmented markets accounts for wage differentials.

—Robert L. Brite, *Louisiana State University*

LABOR FORCE, all members of the working-age population who are either employed or seeking or awaiting employment. The size of the labor force is one of the three main dimensions of the aggregate supply of labor to the market sector of the economy. (The length of the average workweek and the average intensity of work are the other two.)

The labor force consists of the employed and the unemployed. According to the current official definitions in the United States the employed are persons aged 16 and over who worked for pay or profit or worked in a family business or on a family farm during the preceding week, plus those who were absent from their jobs because of illness, vacations, labor disputes, bad weather, or personal reasons. The unemployed are persons 16 and over who looked for work during the past four weeks, or who were on layoff from their present jobs and waiting to be recalled, or who were waiting to start a new job within 30 days. Persons in the Armed Forces are also counted in the total labor force but not in the civilian labor force. Persons 16 and over not in the labor force include those who have retired or who are unable to work, inmates of institutions, the voluntarily idle, many seasonal workers during their "off season," many housewives and students, and persons who would like to have a job but are not looking for one because they believe no work in their line is available. The latter group is often called the "hidden unemployed."

Size. The size of the labor force depends on the size of the working-age population and the percentage of this population that is in the labor force. The labor force is subject to seasonal variations and tends to be somewhat larger, other things being equal, when unemployment is low than when it is high.

Comprehensive labor force statistics in the United States are gathered each month by the Bureau of the Census from a scientifically selected sample of about 47,000 households in all parts of the country. The most closely-watched statistic is the seasonally-adjusted overall unemployment rate (the percentage of the civilian labor force that is unemployed), which is an important measure of the health of the economy and a key guide to economic policy.

Current labor force statistics are presented monthly by U.S. Department of Labor in *Employment and Earnings.* Labor force developments in the preceding year are analyzed in the annual *Manpower Report of the President.* Special reports on the labor force appear in the *Monthly Labor Review,* also published by the Department of Labor.

See also Labor Force Participation Rate; Labor Supply; Unemployment.

—T. Aldrich Finegan, *Vanderbilt University*

LABOR FORCE PARTICIPATION RATE (LFPR), the percentage of a population group that was in the labor force during a specified period of time. These rates vary across countries and across groups within countries; they have also changed markedly over time.

In 1971 the average LFPR for the total noninstitutional population aged 16 and over in the U.S. was 61%. But these were rates for selected groups: men aged 25 to 54, 96%; men 18-19, 69%; married women under 65, 44%; and men over 64, 26%.

From 1947 to 1971, the overall LFPR in the U.S. changed very little, but the rate for

LABOR FORCE BY AGE AND SEX (1970)

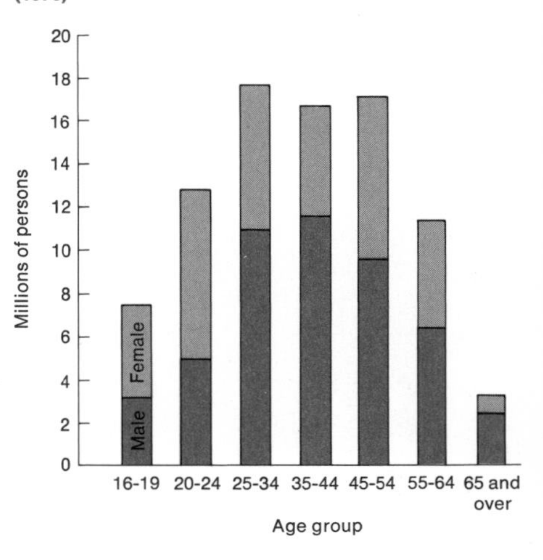

LABOR FORCE PARTICIPATION RATES
PERCENT OF TOTAL POPULATION IN THE LABOR FORCE, 1970

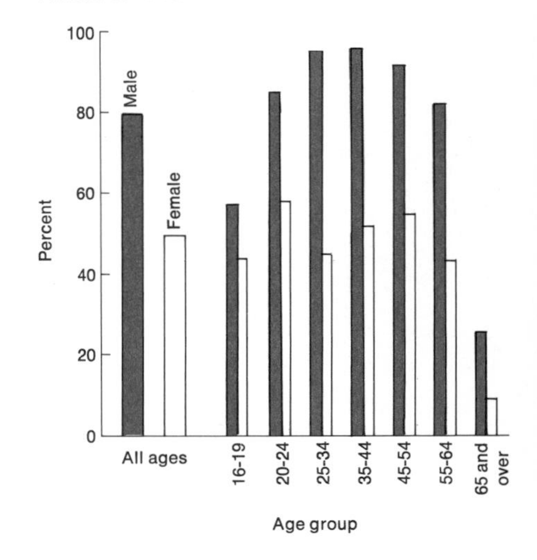

LABOR FORCE

For additional articles closely related to the labor force, see LABOR SUPPLY and HUMAN RESOURCES. The relationship between the labor force and the population as a whole is discussed in LABOR FORCE PARTICIPATION RATE. For the role of the labor force relative to the demand for labor, see the article on the LABOR MARKET. Definitions of the two components of the labor force are presented in the articles on EMPLOYMENT and UNEMPLOYMENT. And for the extent and patterns of unionism in the labor force, see LABOR MOVEMENT.

These and other interrelated concepts are displayed on the Subject Maps accompanying the articles on LABOR MARKET, LABOR MOVEMENT, and WAGES.

LABOR MARKET

To see the labor market in the context of the resource allocation process of the economic system, consult the articles on the CIRCULAR FLOW OF INCOME, FACTOR MARKETS, and LABOR. To understand more fully the two counter-forces in the labor market, see the articles on DEMAND FOR LABOR, LABOR SUPPLY, and LABOR SUPPLY CURVE. For the results of labor market operation, see EMPLOYMENT, WAGES, SALARIES, and INCOME DISTRIBUTION.

The Subject Map accompanying this article, and the Maps with the FACTOR MARKETS and WAGES articles, display a major portion of the Encyclopedia's coverage of the Labor Market.

married women more than doubled while the rate for elderly men (over 64) fell by almost one half.

Consult (20) Bowen, 1969; Mincer, 1968.

LABOR INJUNCTION. *See* Injunction, Labor.

LABOR-MANAGEMENT RELATIONS. *See* Collective Bargaining.

LABOR-MANAGEMENT RELATIONS ACT OF 1947. *See* Taft-Hartley Act (1947).

LABOR-MANAGEMENT REPORTING AND DISCLOSURE ACT. *See* Landrum-Griffin Act (1959).

LABOR MARKET, hypothetical meetingplace for employers who need workers and employees who need jobs. The market is as broad as the two groups involved decide to make it.

Most universities have agencies that assist graduates in finding jobs. Such an agency, if it does its assignment well, should list openings in the various occupations from all over the country. None could carry all possible job listings, but a typical placement office might list openings for engineers, say, in twenty states, with employers representing all areas of industry and government. Students in Maine, California, or South Dakota may learn of and apply for the same job, and two roommates in any one of these states may accept positions thousands of miles apart. Thus the market in this case is national, or even international, and exists in many places.

At the same time, the labor market for some occupations may be very narrow and well defined. Employers and employees in the market may decide to operate through some type of hiring hall, and both may meet there on a regular basis to make arrangements for employment. On some docks, for example, a market in the more normal sense of the word seems to exist, with workers and employers physically meeting to settle on jobs. A worker needing a job shows up to offer his services, and employers needing men send representatives to this employment area. There, in noise and confusion, the market works.

These represent two extreme market conditions, one narrow and one broad. Each, in its own way, works to bring employer and employee together. Most people operate in some in-between situation, where the market may be the city or even the state. The limits of the market determine for the individual what jobs may be available, and how much competition there will be for them.

Limitations. In a "tight" labor market the employer may broaden his market, and you may see ads in the paper that a firm from another state is hiring carpenters to move to his place of operation. In a market where jobs are hard to find, the employee may attempt to look in areas he normally would not consider, and thus expand his market.

In some situations the market is limited by formal or informal regulations of one or more types. Some cities, for some positions, hire only from the city population, and anyone outside is not considered. Some states, for some occupations, require a state license to be eligible for jobs, and sometimes a person can be licensed only by attending a school within that state. A public school teacher, for example, usually is "certified" by the state, and often, except in temporary situations, one who is uncertified is unemployable. In other situations customs have grown up in a market limiting employment to individuals with certain ethnic, racial, or sexual qualifications.

Generally, the individuals who must sell their labor services know the characteristics of the market in which they operate, and can find employment. The dock worker may view with amazement the "paper work" associated with the college graduate's job search; so may the student view the practices on the dock. Yet, both are markets, and both, however imperfectly, work.

See also Labor Force; Labor Supply.

Consult (20) Baerwald, 1967; Bloom, 1965; Levitan, 1972.

—William D. Wagoner, *Louisiana State University*

LABOR MOBILITY. The freedom to move from job to job has always been a normal and important characteristic of the American worker. The United States has the most mobile labor force in the world. Labor mobility has always gone along with the American dream that, regardless of a person's origin, he can move up the ladder of success; that anyone who works hard can improve his job, his prestige, and his income. For this reason, it is no surprise that few people hold only one job during their lifetimes. Rather, it is common to change not only jobs, but industries and locations as well.

Several major types of labor mobility common to the United States are occupational, geographical, and industrial.

Occupational Mobility is the most common. This simply means that a worker moves from one job to another, either with the same or another employer. Although there are numerous reasons why workers change jobs, usually the move involves an upward mobility; that is, a change that improves the worker in some way (better income, more responsibility, etc.). The logic behind this is that the economic and social costs involved with changing jobs usually means that only improvement will attract the worker to a new position.

LABOR MARKET

The Subject Maps in the Encyclopedia illustrate the coverage of particular aspects of economics, showing the interrelationships among the articles in twenty-one critical areas of study. Entries in capital letters are subjects for which there are separate articles in the Encyclopedia. Entries in small letters are references to the article immediately above and provide some idea of content.

The Subject Maps are arranged alphabetically in the Encyclopedia under the following titles:

Antitrust Policy
Banking System
Business Cycles
Capital
Circular Flow of Income
Demand Theory
Economic Systems
Factor Markets
Federal Budget
History of Economic Ideas
International Trade Theory
Labor Market
Labor Movement
Market System
Money and Monetary Policy
National Income
Price Level
Regulation
Supply
Theory of the Firm
Wages

LABOR SUPPLY

- HUMAN RESOURCES
- HUMAN CAPITAL
- LABOR SUPPLY CURVE
- BACKWARD BENDING SUPPLY CURVE

- RESTRICTION OF NUMBERS
- APPRENTICESHIP
  - national apprenticeship act
  - fitzgerald act
- LABOR FORCE
- LABOR FORCE PARTICIPATION RATE (LFPR)

- WHITE-COLLAR WORKER
- BLUE-COLLAR WORKER
- MOONLIGHTING
- NONCOMPETING GROUPS

DEMAND FOR LABOR
- marginal revenue product of labor

LABOR MARKET

- MANPOWER POLICY
  - RETRAINING
  - MANPOWER DEVELOPMENT AND TRAINING ACT (MDTA)
- COLLECTIVE BARGAINING
- LABOR MOBILITY
  - geographic mobility
  - occupational mobility
  - industrial mobility
- EMPLOYMENT
  - FULL EMPLOYMENT
  - CHILD LABOR
    - UNEMPLOYMENT OF LABOR
      - SEASONAL UNEMPLOYMENT
      - FRICTIONAL UNEMPLOYMENT
      - CYCLICAL UNEMPLOYMENT
      - STRUCTURAL UNEMPLOYMENT
      - TECHNOLOGICAL UNEMPLOYMENT
      - HARD-CORE UNEMPLOYMENT
      - TRANSITIONAL UNEMPLOYMENT
      - ENTRY UNEMPLOYMENT
    - UNEMPLOYMENT INSURANCE
      - unemployment compensation
    - PUBLIC EMPLOYMENT SERVICE
      - wagner-peyser act
- WAGES
  - HOURS
  - PAID HOLIDAYS
  - VACATIONS
  - WORKING CONDITIONS
    - WORK RULES
    - LAYOFF
    - RECALL
    - GRIEVANCE PROCEDURE
    - GRIEVANCE ARBITRATION

Geographical Mobility involves relocation, either within a county, or from one county or state to another. Every year in the United States, about eight and one-half million people move across state lines while twice as many more move across county lines. If the people who move within counties are taken into consideration, mobility of Americans involves about one in every six people. Historically, geographic mobility has been the farm-to-city migration or European immigration. However, it now entails also the newer city-to-suburb move.

Industrial Mobility is the movement from one industry to another. Usually, to distinguish this from occupational mobility, this implies staying with the same type of job or trade but changing the industry, such as a machinist who moved from the automotive industry to the steel or plastics industry.

—William D. Wagoner, *Louisiana State University*

LABOR MOVEMENT may be viewed as consisting of those actions taken by groups of workers in a society to improve their economic or social position, or the economic or social position of their children. Generally, in the United States, these actions have been directed at improving the economic position of the wage earner. The worker has apparently accepted the political, economic, and social system of the country, and the main thrust of the labor movement has been to provide a better life style for the individual. Only a small portion of the American movement has been devoted to an overthrow of the system.

Beginnings. The beginnings of the U.S. labor movement are, perhaps, lost forever. Almost any date from the arrival of the *Mayflower* may be cited as the first evidence of organized action by workers. Certainly, the movement was observable during the colonial period, and by the time of the Revolution, strikes had occurred. Toward the end of the century, organizations of workers on a planned permanent basis were created. These early unions were generally found among the better-trained workers—the shoemakers, printers, carpenters, and tailors. Their demands, phrased in polite language of the day, were for better pay, shorter hours, and a right to the jobs for members of the organization.

The employers responded with court actions, and the courts, bringing English common law to the cases, found the unions guilty of criminal conspiracy. From 1806 to 1842 any group of workers acting in concert to improve their condition of employment could well face fines or other punishment. The years were not totally wasted, however, for in several states the movement, continuing to fight for the legal right to exist, secured through political action, full public education, some relaxation of the imprisonment-for-debt laws, and other gains as citizens, including the right to vote for some improvements. After the court restricted the use of the criminal-conspiracy doctrine in 1842, organization continued.

Experiments. In the middle 1800s a number of experiments were tried. The unions were trying to organize on a larger scale, and the national union concept arose. The first of these failed, and others were attempted, but the national was not really successful until late in the century. The movement turned to other methods of attaining goals, and several attempts were made to improve the position of the worker through communal societies, producer and consumer cooperatives, and opening of public lands to settlement. None worked, and the movement turned again to economic action.

In 1866 the National Labor Union was organized as a combination of labor groups, farmer organizations, suffragettes, and other reform movements. Described by one writer as labor leaders without members, farmers without land, and women without husbands, NLU turned to the eight-hour day as a goal. After some success it turned to monetary reform and cooperatives. The unions withdrew, and the movement failed.

As NLU was declining, the Knights of Labor (1869) was organized. The Knights turned to reform as well as economic action and admitted as members everyone except a few specified groups on an occupational basis. After 1879 the organization grew very rapidly. Riding on a few successful strikes, membership rose to over one-half million. Its decline was soon to follow, perhaps speeded by strike losses. However, the most important cause of its failure was its organizational framework. It took in too many members too fast with too few common interests and without a common philosophy. The trade unions could not accept the reform philosophy, and the division of interests broke the back of the movement.

The AFL. The most valuable contribution of these two organizations was negative—they showed what not to do in the labor movement. Samuel Gompers learned the lesson well and in 1886, when he formed the American Federation of Labor, these negative contributions were very visible. Thus, the AFL was created as an economic union, not as a reform body. Based on the philosophy that unions are for skilled workers, that every skilled worker should be in a union with others of his trade, that power should rest in the locals and the nationals, that the job of the union is to secure for its members better current conditions for employment, that the union is a responsible organization that will honor its contracts, and that the proper role of the union is to bargain with employers, the AFL grew slowly and solidly.

LABOR MOVEMENT

LABOR MOVEMENT

AFL-CIO
AMERICAN FEDERATION OF LABOR
CONGRESS OF INDUSTRIAL ORGANIZATIONS
KNIGHTS OF LABOR
UNITED AUTO WORKERS
INTERNATIONAL BROTHERHOOD OF
    TEAMSTERS

NATIONAL UNIONS
    international unions
LOCAL UNION
CRAFT UNION
INDUSTRIAL UNION
COMPANY UNION

BUSINESS AGENT
BUSINESS UNIONISM
UNION CONVENTION
UNION CONSTITUTION

TRUSTEESHIP
JURISDICTION, UNION
INJUNCTION, LABOR
YELLOW-DOG CONTRACT
UNION LABEL
STEWARD

SENIORITY
BOYCOTT
    primary boycott
    secondary boycott

COMMONS, JOHN
DEBS, EUGENE VICTOR
COMPERS, SAMUEL
HOFFA, JAMES
LEWIS, JOHN L.
MEANY, GEORGE
PERLMAN, SELIG
REUTHER, WALTER
WOODCOCK, LEONARD

COLLECTIVE BARGAINING
    labor-management relations
    contract negotiations
    BILATERAL BARGAINING
    FEATHERBEDDING
    FRINGE BENEFITS
    KEY BARGAIN
    UNION SECURITY
        worker-union relations
    RECOGNITION
    INDUSTRY-WIDE BARGAINING
    MULTI-EMPLOYER BARGAINING
        whipsaw tactics
    CLOSED SHOP
        compulsory union membership
    OPEN SHOP
    UNION SHOP
        right-to-work laws
    AGENCY SHOP
    MAINTENANCE OF MEMBERSHIP
    BARGAINING UNIT
    REPRESENTATION
        certification

    MEDIATION
        third-party intervention
    ARBITRATION
        contract arbitration
        grievance arbitration
    CONCILIATION
    FACT FINDING

STRIKE
    sit-down strike
    LOCKOUTS
    WILDCAT STRIKES
        unauthorized work stoppage
    EMERGENCY STRIKES
    WORK STOPPAGE
    PUBLIC INTEREST DISPUTES
    STRIKE NOTICE
    STRIKE BENEFITS
        union benefits
    JURISDICTIONAL DISPUTES

    REFUSAL TO BARGAIN
    UNFAIR LABOR PRACTICES

    PICKETING

LABOR LAW
    RAILWAY LABOR ACT (1926)
        national mediation board
        railroad adjustment board
    NORRIS-LAGUARDIA ACT (1932)
        federal anti-injunction act
    SOCIAL SECURITY ACT (1935)
        retirement pensions
    WAGNER ACT (1935)
        national labor relations act
    NATIONAL LABOR RELATIONS BOARD
    FAIR LABOR STANDARDS ACT (1938)
        wages and hours law
        minimum wage law
    TAFT-HARTLEY ACT (1947)
        labor-management relations act
    LANDRUM-GRIFFIN ACT (1959)
        labor management reporting
        and disclosures act

The Subject Maps in the Encyclopedia illustrate the coverage of particular aspects of economics, showing the interrelationships among the articles in twenty-one critical areas of study. Entries in capital letters are subjects for which there are separate articles in the Encyclopedia. Entries in small letters are references to the article immediately above and provide some idea of content.

The Subject Maps are arranged alphabetically in the Encyclopedia under the following titles:

Antitrust Policy
Banking System
Business Cycles
Capital
Circular Flow of Income
Demand Theory
Economic Systems
Factor Markets
Federal Budget
History of Economic Ideas
International Trade Theory
Labor Market
Labor Movement
Market System
Money and Monetary Policy
National Income
Price Level
Regulation
Supply
Theory of the Firm
Wages

AFL-CIO organizing drive to extend West Coast representation wins clothing workers' support.

The AFL was attacked from both sides. On the right the employers fought this rising union structure and, in many ways were successful. On the left the Industrial Workers of the World cursed the conservatism of the AFL. IWW, perhaps the only really radical movement in U.S. labor history, apparently opposed the AFL almost as much as it did the employer or the system.

These attacks may have resulted in some reduction in the growth rate, but the AFL continued to grow until 1920, when it had about 4 million members. In the 1920s the organized labor movement actually lost membership in a period of prosperity. By 1930 almost 2 million members of labor unions had been removed from the rolls. The loss continued into the depression of the 1930s. However, in this decade the government came out for the union, and legislation was passed making organization easier.

The Wagner Act. The most important gain was the Wagner Act (1935), which granted to workers the right to be members of labor organizations and placed a duty to bargain on the employer. If the employees wanted a union, the employer could not oppose them.

Perhaps the most important result of the Wagner Act was the effect on those employees ignored by the AFL, the industrial workers. Under the rights granted by the act, workers in steel, automobiles, and other mass-production industries showed an interest in organization. A group of AFL leaders formed the Committee for Industrial Organization. Opposed by the AFL, in 1938 their unions were expelled from the federation, and a new labor group, the Congress of Industrial Organization (CIO) was created. These two rival organizations dominated the labor movement until 1955, when they finally united.

Another result of the Wagner Act was a rapid growth in union membership. From 1935 to 1945, membership grew from over 3 million to over 14 million. Although some of this increase was due to the increased employment resulting from World War II, much of the growth came from the easy organization under the act.

Postwar Problems. By the end of the war the favorable treatment of labor was attacked, and Congress again turned its attention to the movement. In 1947 the Taft-Hartley Act placed restrictions on the union. Still the most important piece of labor legislation, the act proscribed a series of unfair labor practices for unions, abolished the closed shop, made state right-to-work laws legal, and set forth a procedure for national emergency strikes. Passed over President Truman's veto, the law was bitterly resented by labor leaders.

In the 1950s the progress of the labor movement slowed down, and membership grew very slowly. As a percentage of the labor force, membership actually declined. The major unorganized groups in the country remained unorganized—the Southern worker, the female worker, the white-collar worker, and the employees of small firms. It seemed as though these groups were rejecting the union, and nothing the unions did seemed to improve the situation.

Also during the 1950s, Congress again looked at the labor movement and did not like what it saw. Some unions seemed corrupt, seemed to be involved with organized crime, and did not appear to be furthering the interest of their members. Congress, in the Labor-Management Reporting and Disclosure Act (1959), attempted to resolve some of these problems.

This law, popularly known as the Landrum-Griffin Act, represented a major attempt to correct some of the flaws, as Congress viewed them, in labor union practices. Financial practices, elections, officers, constitutions, member rights, and more came under the law, and the unions were required to be more responsive to the membership. Thus, the unions entered the 1960s under fire, with some public and official suspicion, and seemingly unable to come to grips with the problems of the day. The nonunionized worker was still hesitant to join, and while membership began to increase, the rate of growth was still very slow.

Outlook. The problems the unions faced may have been related to the changing value system in the society, to the youth revolt on civil rights, and, later, to the attitudes on the war and on pollution. In these areas, as the young groups often saw it, the labor movement was not relevant, and thus the younger worker was apt to view the union as part of the establishment.

It has been suggested that what future success the movement will have will be related to its ability to change. If it cannot adapt to the younger worker, to the white collar, to the minority worker, or to the female employee, it will continue to fade. Perhaps the most hopeful sign for the unions is the success the government employees' unions have had in the 1960s. Here all the groups above have joined to form a successful structure in a very difficult situation. The other unions would be well advised to examine this most recent success.

See also Collective Bargaining; Strike; articles on individual labor unions and acts of labor legislation.

Consult (21) Baitsell, 1964; Bloom, 1965; Cohen, 1966; Dulles, 1966.

—William D. Wagoner, *Louisiana State University*

LABOR PRACTICES, UNFAIR. *See* Unfair Labor Practices.

LABOR SAVING, the decrease in the share of labor, relative to the share of capital, used in a business or industry, achieved through innovation or by a plan. When an electronics manufacturer substitutes printed circuits for conventional circuitry, he is reducing the amount of labor previously necessary for assembly of conventional models. Steady increases in wage rates have induced many employers to introduce labor saving devices in order to reduce their overall costs and maintain reasonable profit margins in relatively inelastic markets.

See also Capital Saving.

LABOR SUPPLY is the amount of labor available to a society, expressed as a fraction of the population size or the percentage of the population who are in the labor force. The labor force in the United States, at any point in time, includes those who are at work or who are looking for work. Countries vary in the groups included in this labor force, and their variation alters the labor supply among the populations of the world. A society may exclude from its work force children below a certain age, it may encourage older people to retire, it may exclude or discourage females from entering the labor force, or it may take other actions to affect the number of its people who can work.

At a point in time in a particular society, given the possible labor force size, the supply of labor may be related to the wage rate. The exact relationship is not always clear. One firm can get more employees by raising wages, but a wage increase may actually decrease the number of individuals in the total market. An increase in the wages of parents may send more children to school for more years. On the other hand, a wage decrease may force individuals who are now out of the market into it to maintain family income. The supply curve may bend backwards at some point.

Over a number of years the supply of labor would seem more flexible. Given a rising wage level the labor force may well increase in twenty years, the time necessary to bring children to maturity. The short run seems to be inelastic, however, and the major cause of changes in labor supply may be the number of hours the individual is willing to work.

See also Labor Force.

Consult (20) Baerwald, 1967, Cohen, 1966.

—William D. Wagoner, *Louisiana State University*

LABOR SUPPLY CURVE, a graphic representation of the labor supply and the wage rate at a certain point in time. The supply curve is upward sloping due to the generally positive relationship between wages and available workers. That is, as wage rates rise, more and more labor enters the market; as wages decrease, fewer hours of labor are offered.

LABOR THEORY OF VALUE, the theory that the value of a good is determined by the amount of labor necessary to produce that good. Suggested by numerous pre-classical economists as one of several alternative value theories, it emerged in the late classical period as the central value theory of economics. Karl Marx based his economic analysis upon the labor theory of value, and its use led to the position that labor was exploited, because the owners of capital obtained a return (profit) for which they had no claim.

The labor theory of value, however, lacked generality, because it could not explain value in situations where little or no labor was used. This theory was eventually replaced by the marginalists' analysis in which scarcity and utility determine the value of a good.

See also Das Kapital.

LABOR UNIONS. *See* Labor Movement.

LABOUR PARTY. *See* British Labour Party.

LAGGING INDICATOR, an economic measurement or time series of one aggregate of the economy which follows or trails a change in total economic activity. Lagging indicators include the value of manufacturing or trade inventory, labor cost per unit of output, and bank rates on short-term loans.

See also Business Cycles, Measurement; Coincident Indicator; Leading Indicator.

LAISSEZ FAIRE ("let them do"), a concept of nonintervention by government developed by the 18th-century French physiocrats in reaction against mercantilism, and incorporated into classical economic writings by Adam Smith and others. They believed the market mechanism in a free-enterprise competitive economy coordinates production and distributes income in a self-adjusting manner which tends toward full employment without government intervention.

The intervention allowed by the classical economists (just enough to assure that the adjustment will take place) was probably based more on concern with individual freedom than with efficient operation of the economy. Laissez faire in the form described does not exist today.

See also Competition; Invisible Hand; Market Economy; Mercantilism.

Consult (26) Grossman, 1967.

LAMPMAN, ROBERT J. (1921-   ), American educator whose work in the area of poverty has led to new policies concerning the distribution of income. He received a B.A. (1942) and a Ph.D. in economics (1950) from the University of Wisconsin. His publications on the subject of poverty, economic growth, and transfer payments include *Ends and Means of Reducing*

Robert J. Lampman

Income Poverty (1971). Currently a professor of economics at the University of Wisconsin, he is also a staff member of both the Institute for Research on Poverty and the Health Economics Research Center, and editor of the *Journal of Human Resources.*

LAND, generally considered to be a factor fixed in supply. At some very high prices for land, it might be feasible to drain swamps and parts of rivers, but, as a practical matter, land is fixed.

Graphically the supply of land will be parallel to the vertical axis. Regardless of price, the same quantity will be offered for productive use. Higher prices are impotent to induce greater quantities of land; lower prices will not lead to withdrawal from markets, because owners prefer something to nothing. This interesting result implies that land or any fixed input will be price-determined; the prices of commodities do not depend on land's value. This latter point is true when one's viewpoint is society as a whole. An individual or industry that uses land must pay for its service and include rent as a long-run cost factor; fixed factors viewed this way are commodity price-determiners.

LAW OF SUPPLY AND DEMAND

The law of supply and demand is an inclusive concept, related to virtually all other concepts in the broad area of the MARKET SYSTEM; other articles covering many of the same points are ALLOCATION, MARKET EQUILIBRIUM, and MARKET MECHANISM. To see that economic questions can be answered by societal mechanisms not structured around the law of supply and demand, consult the articles on SOCIALISM, COMMAND ECONOMY, and COMMUNISM.

The Subject Map accompanying MARKET SYSTEM displays many of these and other relationships.

LAND REFORM, normally, the redistribution of agricultural land from landlords to peasants, primarily to transfer income from the rich to the poor, but hopefully to increase agricultural productivity as well. Occasionally, as in India, attempts have been made to consolidate splintered land holdings to raise productivity through economies of scale.

Where land is transferred from absentee landlords to peasants, the cultivator's security of ownership is apt to induce him to improve the land and his farming techniques and thus increase output. The fragmentation of large, well-run plantation-type holdings into small plots, however, is likely to lower output unless cooperatives can be formed to replace the equipment, working capital, and expertise, both managerial and agronomic, formerly provided by the old landowners.

See also Economies of Scale.

Consult (24) Carroll, 1961; Raup, 1967.

LAND RENT. *See* Rent.

LAW OF SUPPLY AND DEMAND

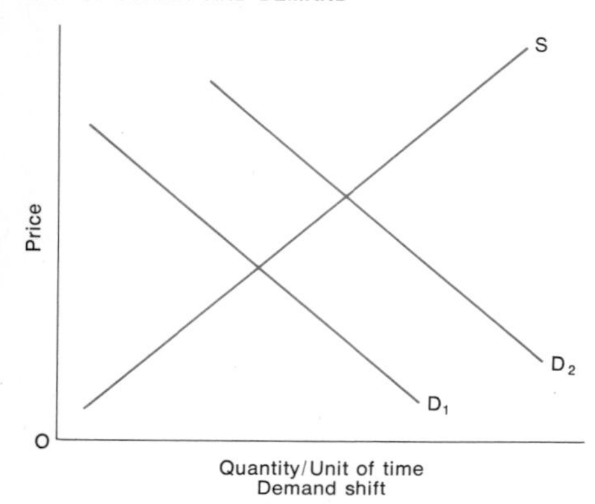

LANDRUM-GRIFFIN ACT (1959), also known as the Labor-Management Reporting and Disclosure Act. Its passage resulted from (1) disclosures, during Congressional hearings in the late 1950's, of corruption and lack of internal democracy in unions; (2) continued feelings that union power and practices needed further curbs; and (3) dissatisfaction with certain features of the existing laws. The act covers several different areas: democratic reforms in union operations; restrictions on Communist party members and persons convicted of certain felonies in regard to union office; and amendments clarifying and strengthening provisions of the Taft-Hartley Act (1947). It also makes picketing under certain circumstances an unfair labor practice by unions and has provisions on the eligibility of striking workers to vote in representation elections.

The Landrum-Griffin Act has a decided anti-union tone. Like the Taft-Hartley Act it makes the basic assumption that neither unions and employees nor unions and their own members are synonymous, then spells out limitations on unions in regard to their relationships with employers, members, and the public.

See also Taft-Hartley Act.

—Leonard G. Schifrin, *College of William and Mary*

LAW OF DEMAND. *See* Substitution Effect.

LAW OF DIMINISHING RETURNS, a property of a production process which states that when one input is given successive increments, all other inputs being held constant, then a point will be reached beyond which the increments in output will diminish. Geometrically, diminishing returns to an input occur in a range in which the total product curve of that input is concave.

See also Production Function.

LAW OF DOWNWARD SLOPING DEMAND, an overwhelming fact that more of a given commodity is purchased at lower prices than at higher prices. Furthermore, the major causative factor in changing the quantity purchased of a good is a change in its price. The theory of downward sloping demand achieved its transformation into law by the weight of overwhelming empirical evidence. The behavioral aspects in the theory of demand need not even be explored for the law of demand to be accredited. It is a statistical fact that the price of a commodity is inversely related to the quantity of the commodity demanded.

LAW OF LARGE NUMBERS. *See* Probability.

LAW OF SUPPLY AND DEMAND states that, other things being equal, price and demand vary inversely (the law of demand), and price and supply vary directly (the law of supply). The demand curve shows the relationship between price and quantity, and the supply curve relates price and supply.

A change in demand will also occur if there is a change in the price of related goods, or consumer income, or consumer tastes and preferences. Such a change in demand will shift the entire demand curve to the right or the left. The quantity of a good supplied also varies with changes in the cost of production, due to changes in technology, changes in the wage rate, or numerous other reasons. Such a change in supply will shift the entire supply curve to the right or to the left. Although there are exceptions to the law of supply and demand, these exceptions are few, and the basic laws cover most circumstances. Together, supply and demand curves can be used to determine market equilibria.

Consult (11) Leftwich, 1970.

—Robert L. Brite, *Louisiana State University*

LAYOFF, a term used when employees lose their jobs not for cause, but due to a necessary cut-back in the number of workers needed by a company. In keeping with seniority rights, when a layoff becomes necessary, the last person hired by the company is the first person to be laid off.

LDC. *See* Less Developed Countries.

LEADING INDICATOR, an economic measurement or time series of one aggregate of economic activity which precedes a change in total economic activity. Leading indicators include new durable goods orders, average weekly state unemployment insurance claims, and new building permits.

See also Business Cycles, Measurement; Coincident Indicator; Lagging Indicator.

LEAKAGE. *See* Multiple Expansion of the Money Supply.

LEAST-COST FACTOR COMBINATION. If labor is plotted on the vertical axis and capital is plotted on the horizontal axis, then a family of isoquants can be derived for some commodity, given the level of technology. These downward sloping nonintersecting isoquants have the property that the absolute value of the slope decreases as one moves down a given isoquant. Suppose the slope is taken at some point and its absolute value is found to be equal to m: a unit increase in capital requires m units of labor to be released with output constant. The absolute value of the slope is numerically equivalent to the ratio of the marginal product of capital to labor. Moving down an isoquant, capital is substituted for labor, implying that the marginal product of capital will fall and the marginal product of labor will rise. Thus, the decreasing absolute value of the slope of an isoquant is economically justified.

Budget lines may be plotted on the same coordinate system discussed above. The absolute value of the slope of these linear budget lines, it can easily be demonstrated, is equal to the ratio of the price of capital to the price of labor. Economic theory suggests that the least cost of producing a given output will be where the constant sloped budget line is tangent to the varyingly sloped isoquant. Because the slopes must be equal at the point of tangency, the ratio of the marginal products will be equal to the ratio of the factor prices. It should be noted that the least-cost combination is not necessarily equilibrium, which depends on both demand and cost.

See also Isoproduct Curve.

—Robert L. Brite, *Louisiana State University*

LEAST SQUARES. *See* Curve Fitting.

LEGAL RESERVES. *See* Reserves.

LEGAL TENDER, any form of money that the law requires a creditor to accept in payment of debt. All currency in the United States is legal tender, but checks are not.

See Currency; Money.

LENIN, VLADIMIR ILICH (1870-1924), Russian Communist leader. Lenin met revolution at 17, with his brother's execution for plotting to assassinate the Tsar, and his own arrest and expulsion from the University of Kazan. He obtained a law degree in 1891, was exiled to Siberia from 1896 to 1899 for revolutionary activities, and went to Switzerland in 1901 to help found a Marxist newspaper. Thereafter, many travels, mostly involuntary, marked the intertwining of his life with that of the Russian Revolution. He organized the Bolsheviks in 1903 (from London), and the party started publishing *Pravda* ("Truth") in 1912. Lenin's classic study, *Imperialism, the Highest Stage of Capitalism,* was published in 1916.

Economic Thought. The growth of finance capitalism and large business assets at home caused capitalists to look abroad, delaying the fulfillment of Marx's predictions. But Lenin, deeming imperialism the last stage of capitalism, indicated that imperialists would face two forces—domestic proletariat and colonial proletariat abroad—in inevitably violent confrontation. Russia, though not industrialized, was the first country to experience revolution, explained Lenin, because it was the weakest link in the imperialistic chain.

See also Bolsheviks; Class Conflict; Marx, Karl; Proletariat.

Consult (26) Dillard, 1967; Griesbrecht, 1972; Gruchy, 1966; International, 1968; Marshall, 1967.

—John R. Matthews, Jr., *College of William and Mary*

LEONTIEF, WASSILY (1906-). The concept of mutual interdependence among economic sectors dates back to François Quesnay and the *Tableau èconomique.* While the theoretical concept was extended by Leon Walras and Vilfredo Pareto, it was not until Wassily Leontief developed the input-output table that an effective means of handling the empirical data

Vladimir Ilich Lenin

Wassily Leontief

of general equilibrium was available. Leontief's *The Structure of American Economy, 1919-1929* (1941) presented the first input-output table, which isolated flows of goods and services between various economic sectors and measured the inputs and outputs of each sector. Thus, the table allows an economist to view the source of the inputs in any given sector and the uses of that sector's output.

The input-output table is an important tool for the purposes of economic planning and can be extremely useful for underdeveloped and socialist economies.

See also Input-Output Models; Quesnay, François.

LERNER, ABBA (1903-), author of works dealing with socialistic economics, welfare economics, employment theory and international trade theory. His *Economics of Control* (1944) supports a mild form of collectivisim and provides a guide for the effective operation of a socialist economy. In *The Economics of Employment* (1951) and *Essays in Economic Analysis,* Lerner contributes to many areas of economic theory.

Lerner is also responsible for the Marshall-Lerner condition, which requires that the sum of a trading country's demand elasticities be greater than one if depreciation of its currency is to improve the balance of payments.

LESS DEVELOPED COUNTRIES (LDC), nations, primarily in Africa, Asia, and Latin America, characterized by poverty income levels, little or no savings, high rates of population growth, labor forces primarily employed in agriculture, extensive underemployment, illiteracy, and reliance on a few export items. They are also known as underdeveloped, or low-income countries. The governments of most such countries are either controlled or influenced by a small, wealthy elite, religious leaders or tribal chieftains.

Less developed countries, as designated by the United Nations, include Indonesia, India, Kenya, Syria, Brazil, Turkey, and Ecuador. These countries try to develop their economies through UN-initiated technical cooperation and assistance programs and various bilateral financial and technical aid programs.

See also Developing Nations; International Bank for Reconstruction and Development (World Bank); Underdevelopment.

LESSENING OF COMPETITION. *See* Substantial Lessening of Competition.

LET THEM DO. *See* Laissez Faire.

LEVERAGE, a term used to refer to the substitution of low-cost, fixed-charge securities (bonds) in place of common equity (stock) to obtain capital. This substitution is often made when fluctuations in security markets intensify speculative effects on a firm's common stocks. Individuals sometimes prefer to receive a fixed amount of income and interest rather than participate in the risks of common stocks. This process is also called trading on the equity, a term that indicates that an exchange has been made between the classes of securities.

LEWIS, BEN WILLIAM (1900-), American educator and expert on business regulation. He received his A.B. (1922), M.B. (1923), and Ph.D. (1926) from the University of Michigan. His publications include *British Nationalization and Planning* (1952), *Economics by Admonition, A.E.A. Proceedings* (1959), and *The Duty of a Public Utility, Land Economics* (1959). Lewis has been on the faculty at the University of Michigan and Oberlin College, and he was named program adviser of the Middle East-Africa Program, International Division of the Ford Foundation, in 1967.

John Llewellyn Lewis

LEWIS, JOHN LLEWELLYN (1880-1969), son of an Iowa coal miner, climbed to prominence as head of the United Mine Workers. In 1909, AFL President Samuel Gompers appointed him legislative agent for the United Mine Workers, and in 1911 he became an AFL organizer. A year later he became UMW vice-president, in 1920 president.

In 1935, in an effort to sponsor industrial unions, Lewis led the Committee for Industrial Organization within the AFL and in 1938 he became president of the Congress of Industrial Organizations outside the AFL. He remained UMW head until he retired in 1960.

In 1947 he became the subject of a nation-wide controversy when he was fined $10,000 by a Federal court because of his defiance of a restraining order issued under the Taft-Hartley Act directing the miners to end a strike. Lewis directed the miners back to work but became a bitter foe of the Taft-Hartley Act.

In 1964 he received the U.S. presidential medal of honor.

LFPR. *See* Labor Force Participation Rate.

LIABILITIES OF THE BANKING SYSTEM. *See* Balance Sheet, Bank.

LIBERAL SOCIALISM. *See* Democratic Socialism.

LIMITED LIABILITY, the legal condition that exists when individuals purchase the stocks of a corporation. They are thus assured that their losses can only amount to the purchased price of the stocks. They are not held responsible for any debts or other liabilities of the corporation.

The purpose of limited liability is chiefly

the promotion of capital accumulation for industrial endeavors. When investors are assured that their involvement in a corporation is limited to the amount of their investment, more people are willing to buy stocks. Thus, large firms can gather huge amounts of capital with a minimum of risk for their stockholders.

See also Corporation.

LINEAR CORRELATION. *See* Correlation.

LINEAR FUNCTIONS. *See* Function.

LINTNER, JOHN VIRGIL JR. (1916-), American economist and educator noted for his contribution to the theory of the firm under conditions of uncertainty. He received an A.B. (1939) and an M.A. (1940) from the University of Kansas, and an M.A. (1942) and a Ph.D. (1946) from Harvard. His publications include *Mutual Savings Banks in the Savings and Mortgage Markets* (1948), *Corporate Profits in Perspective* (1950), and *Effect of Taxation on Corporate Mergers* (1951, with J.K. Butters and W.L. Cary). Lintner has served as a consultant to various government agencies, private foundations, and businesses, and he has been a professor at the Graduate School of Business Administration at Harvard since 1956.

LIQUID ASSETS, assets that can be turned into cash rapidly and with little loss of value. Liquidity is relative. Money is 100% liquid. Near money is almost as liquid as cash. Government securities, and to an even greater extent corporate bonds and stocks, have a ready market but fluctuating values and hence are much less liquid than cash. Commodities, such as houses, are not liquid at all.

See also Liquidity Preference; Portfolio Balancing.

LIQUIDITY PREFERENCE, the desire to hold money (currency and demand deposits) rather than equivalent amounts of interest-earning assets, such as bonds or a saving account. Money can always be used at any time to buy goods, but an earning asset must be sold before the proceeds can be spent. Such a sale may take time or yield less than the book value of the asset, or both. There are four basic motives affecting the desire to hold money.

Transactions demand is the desire to have money readily available to meet regular or anticipated day-to-day purchases. The need to have cash for this purpose arises from the fact that income is usually sporadic (weekly or monthly) and payments are continual. Transactions demand depends primarily on the level of income.

Precautionary demand is the desire to have emergency funds to meet unexpected expenditures, whether as a result of accident, emergency, or unusual opportunities. Precautionary demand depends primarily on the amount of wealth.

Speculative demand is the desire to hold money because of the expectation that it will rise in value or that prices will fall. The expected decline may refer to goods (a falling price level) or to securities (a rising interest rate). If prices are expected to rise, speculative demand disappears or becomes negative, which implies borrowing. Speculative demand depends primarily on interest rates.

Convenience demand is the proclivity to hold money because of the trouble involved in acquiring earning assets.

See also Bond Yields.

—Walter W. Haines, *New York University*

LIVING STANDARDS. *See* Standard of Living.

LOANABLE FUNDS, money available for lending. There are two sources of loanable funds: savers and commercial banks. Savers include individual consumers; corporations, which save both by depreciation allowances and reinvested earnings; and governments, which save when they have a surplus of tax receipts over expenditures. Savings become loanable funds only if they are actually offered on the market and not hoarded. Savers may make their funds available directly to borrowers or through financial intermediaries. Commercial banks simply create the money they lend and, hence, are limited in the loanable funds they can provide by their reserve requirement.

See also Demand Deposits; Loans and Discounts; Monetary Policy.

LOANS AND DISCOUNTS. A loan is money lent by one person or institution to another, usually for a specified period of time and at a given rate of interest. A discount is a loan on which the interest is deducted in advance. Thus, with an ordinary loan of $1000 for three months at an interest rate of 6 percent, the borrower would receive $1000 and repay $1015 (6 percent of $1000 being $60 a year, or $15 for one-quarter of a year). On a discount of the same terms the $15 would be deducted in advance, so that the borrower would get $985 and repay $1000. When merchandise is bought on credit, the transaction is sometimes also referred to as a loan of the value of the goods by the merchant to the customer.

LOCAL UNION, an organization of workers that exists independently of any employer, based rather on some other mutual interests. Usually a local union is made up of members of a particular craft or industry. The local is controlled by the vote of the members, and payment of dues and observation of the local's rules usually keep a member in good standing.

Through authorized agents, the local

SELECTED LIQUID ASSETS HELD BY THE PUBLIC, 1946-71
(BILLIONS OF DOLLARS, SEASONALLY ADJUSTED)

End of Year or month	Total	Demand deposits and currency	Time deposits		Postal savings system	Savings and loan shares	U.S. Government savings bonds	U.S. Government securities maturing within 1 year
			Commercial banks	Mutual savings bank				
1960	399.2	138.4	73.1	36.2	.8	61.8	47.0	41.9
1961	424.6	142.6	82.5	38.3	.6	70.5	47.4	42.6
1962	459.0	144.8	98.1	41.4	.5	79.8	47.6	46.8
1963	495.4	149.6	112.9	44.5	.5	90.9	49.0	48.1
1964	530.5	156.7	127.1	49.0	.4	101.4	49.9	46.1
1965	573.1	164.1	147.1	52.6	.3	109.8	50.5	48.6
1966	601.5	168.6	159.3	55.2	.1	113.4	50.9	53.9
1967	650.4	180.7	183.1	60.3	—	123.9	51.9	50.5
1968	709.6	199.2	203.8	64.7	—	131.0	52.5	58.5
1969	731.7	206.8	197.1	67.3	—	134.9	52.4	73.2
1970	786.1	207.6	234.8	71.5	—	145.7	52.7	73.8
1971	879.7	222.3	274.9	81.2	—	173.5	55.1	72.7

negotiates with employers the terms of the employees' work agreement, handles grievances, and helps to influence wages.

LOCKOUTS, the management counterpart of strikes. To enforce its bargaining position, to show firmness, or to put pressure on the workers and the union, management may refuse to continue production without a labor contract, even if the union is willing to do so.

Although the resulting work interruption is the employer's doing, not the union's, it is as permissible a tactic in the bargaining of a new contract as a strike and is part of the strategy and maneuvering brought into play at the bargaining table.

See also Strike.

LOGARITHMIC FUNCTIONS. *See* Function.

LONG RUN

An understanding of the economic meaning of the long run is aided by also consulting the article on the SHORT RUN. Other articles that relate to or help define this concept are EQUILIBRIUM OF THE INDUSTRY; EQUILIBRIUM OF THE FIRM, LONG RUN; LONG-RUN AVERAGE COST CURVE; and LONG-RUN MARKET EQUILIBRIUM. For a specific difference between the short and long run, consult the article on TOTAL FIXED COST.

The Subject Maps accompanying the articles on SUPPLY and THEORY OF THE FIRM show the interrelationships of these and other concepts.

LONG RUN, a period of time long enough for all the factors of production to be variable. It is not so long, however, that the basic technology in use can be changed. In the long run, labor and raw materials are variable, and capital equipment may be increased or decreased, but decisions on the future of the operation must be made under the assumption of fixed technology. Within any long-run period there will be a number of short-run periods in which labor is the variable factor of production, with plant size and capital equipment fixed. Under the assumption of fixed plant size, the output or capacity utilization of that plant may be varied.

See also Short Run.

LONG-RUN AVERAGE COST CURVE the "envelope" of all the short run curves for the firm. Production always takes place in the short run, and along short-run curves. The long run may be viewed as a planning horizon for the firm; it decides on the best way to combine inputs to produce the most profitable output. Given technology, and holding input prices constant, the long-run average cost curve indicates the minimum average cost possible (by varying all inputs) to produce any given output.

The actual long-run average cost curve depends, in the final analysis, on the extent of economies and diseconomies that accompany increases in scale size. Another determinant of the shape of the curve is whether the firm (or industry) can expand and cause input prices to rise as a result.

Assume that initially, as the firm expands its scale of operations, some economies of scale accrue due to specialization possibilities, technology, or financial matters. What this implies is that if inputs are increased by some proportion, output will increase by a *greater* proportion. Given fixed resource prices, average cost (total cost divided by output) must have fallen; total cost will have increased by less than the output increase. The new short-run average cost curve will be to the right of the old, and *its* minimum point will be lower.

After all the economies have been reaped and diseconomies now emerge, the firm will find that increasing its inputs by some proportion will cause total output to rise less than that proportion. Given constant input prices, minimum average cost for the new short-run curve will be higher than the old. The envelope will show a U-shaped long run average cost curve. Its precise shape will depend on the magnitudes of economies and diseconomies.

—Robert L. Brite, *Louisiana State University*

LONG-RUN COST AND SUPPLY. In the long run, which really is a planning horizon, the firm has the option of varying *all* inputs to produce the most profitable output. The long-run cost curve for the firm depends on the extent of its economies (reduction in unit costs as firm size increases due to specialization, technological, and financial advantages) and diseconomies (increases in unit costs as firm size increases, due to increased management problems). Another crucial curve is the effect on resource prices as the firm size increases.

The shape of the long-run average cost curve of the firm tends to affect the long-run supply curve of the industry. In addition one must consider the effect on resource prices as the industry expands. This latter consideration depends largely on whether the industry in question is a relatively large buyer of the resources used. The supply curve of the industry shows the conditions under which the firms in a given industry will voluntarily produce different outputs. Of course, another consideration with industry supply must be the entry and exit of firms in response to abnormal and subnormal profits.

Persisting decreasing costs due to economies will lead to the breakdown of competition and the industry supply schedule will be difficult to establish. Normally some economies will appear as a firm expands, then some diseconomies will arise; the long-run average cost curve will be U-shaped. If resource prices remain constant throughout, then the industry supply schedule will be a horizontal line at the minimum average cost, parallel to the X axis. If resource prices rise as the industry expands, average cost will tend to rise for the old as well as the newly entered firms. Before the industry will voluntarily increase output, therefore, price must rise; the supply schedule will be upward sloping.

See also Economies of Scale.

—Robert L. Brite, *Louisiana State University*

LONG-RUN ELASTICITY OF DEMAND measures the responsiveness of consumer purchases initiated by price changes over a time period sufficiently long that changes in the shape and position of the demand curve for the good in question can occur. This change in shape and position of demand curves occurs because of changing incomes, tastes, expectations, and prices of related goods. Evidence tends to support the claim that the elasticity of demand for a good increases in the long run, primarily because of the increasing number of available substitute goods.

LONG-RUN ELASTICITY OF SUPPLY refers to a firm's or industry's ability to react to demand changes in the long run, in which capital is also a variable factor of production, so that the firm has the option of increasing plant size and equipment. Assuming the industry is relatively small so that expansion will not dramatically increase input prices, the firm can take on more labor and capital simultaneously, thereby offsetting diminishing returns and increasing costs somewhat. We would expect, therefore, that long-run elasticity of supply should be considerably greater than short-run elasticity. Changes in demand are reflected mostly in *price* changes in the short run, mostly in *output* changes in the long run.

See also Elasticity of Supply.

LONG-RUN EQUILIBRIUM OF THE FIRM. *See* Equilibrium of the Firm, Long-Run.

LONG-TERM CAPITAL MOVEMENT. *See* Capital Account.

LONG-TERM GOVERNMENT BONDS. *See* Government Securities.

LOOSE-KNIT ASSOCIATIONS. *See* Trade Association.

LORENZ CURVE, a device for representing the distribution of income among groups. The cumulated percent of the population is shown on the horizontal axis, the cumulated percent of income on the vertical axis. If all members of the population had equal incomes, then the first 20% of the population would account for 20% of the income, and so on. The curve would lie along the diagonal AC. If the first 20% received less than 20% of the income, the curve would lie below the diagonal. As the inequality of income distribution increases, the Lorenz curve is bowed further away from the diagonal.

LOSS MINIMIZATION is a special case of profit maximization, where the maximum profit is negative. This case arises in the short run where the firm is obliged (explicitly or implicitly) to pay for certain fixed factors of production regardless of whether they are utilized. If the firm can generate revenue in excess of its variable cost, it will pay the firm to continue operation until such time as it can free itself of its fixed obligations—even if there is no way to show a positive profit. If an unprofitable firm were to cease operation prior to this time, it would incur a loss equal to the full amount of its fixed cost. If the firm can cover variable cost, it will minimize its loss by maximizing its negative profit.

See also Profit Maximization.

LOW INCOME COUNTRIES. *See* Less Developed Countries.

McGUIRE-KEOGH ACT (1952) re-establishes the validity of the "non-signers" clause in fair-trade contracts executed by firms selling goods in interstate commerce. The Miller-Tydings Act of 1937 permitted individual states to pass resale price-maintenance (or fair-trade) legislation, under which firms selling in these states could contract with retailers to set a minimum resale price and be exempt from prosecution under the antitrust laws.

A significant feature of these contracts was the non-signers clause, by which any retailer selling the product in a state could be bound by the provisions of a resale-price-maintenance contract executed with any other seller in the state.

In the *Schwegmann v. Calvert Corp.* decision (1951) the Supreme Court rendered the non-signers clause invalid, holding that it was not a part of the Miller-Tydings Act. Thus, only those contracts voluntarily entered into would be binding on a retailer. The McGuire-Keogh Act in effect reverses the *Schwegmann* decision and re-establishes in law the validity of the non-signers clause in fair trade pricing.

See also Fair-Trade Laws; Miller-Tydings Act; Resale Price Maintenance.

—Thomas O. Depperschmidt, *Memphis State University*

MACHLUP, FRITZ (1902–), a specialist in international economics, one of the first to consider the international trade aspects of the Keynesian multiplier. Machlup's *International Trade and the National Income Multiplier* (1943) used a period analysis to consider the impact of trade upon the multiplier process. Much of the current knowledge of foreign trade multipliers is the result of Machlup's work. In addition, Machlup provided an excellent discussion of foreign exchange in his article "The Theory of Foreign Exchanges." Machlup has also been an important figure in analyzing various plans for reforming the international exchange system.

MACROECONOMICS, a study of economics using a total or aggregate approach. Such economic factors as total ouput of goods and services, total income, total employment, and

Fritz Machlup

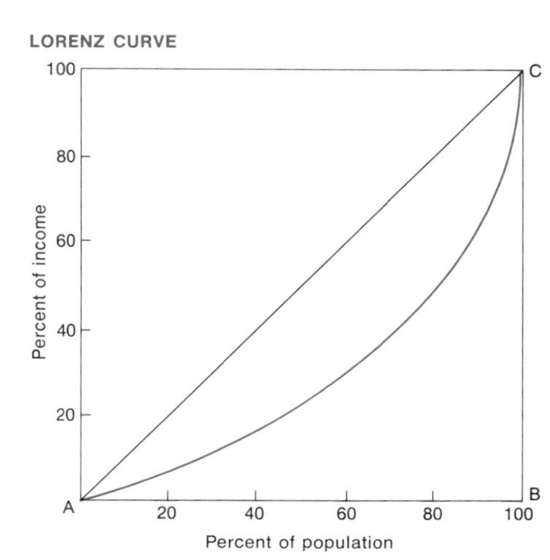

U.S. GROSS NATIONAL PRODUCT, 1970
(CURRENT DOLLARS)

Components	In Billions
Consumer purchases	$616
Business investment expenditures (including foreign)	139
Government purchases	219
Total	974

U.S. NATIONAL INCOME, 1970
(CURRENT DOLLARS)

Source of Income	In Billions
Total	$796
Wages and salaries	602
Net income of unincorporated business*	67
Corporation profits	71
Interest	33
Rental income	23

*Mainly farmers and professional men in business for themselves.

average level of prices are analyzed. For example, the study of the aggregate expenditure patterns of all consumers or the total output of all firms is a macroeconomic approach. Out of this aggregate approach have developed what are commonly referred to as macroeconomic theory, Keynesian economics (after the British economist John Maynard Keynes), or national income theory.

Concepts. The more important concepts employed in macroeconomics are gross national product, net national product, national income, total savings, total investment, total personal consumption expenditures, government purchases of goods and services, total employment, the multiplier, transfer payments, and balance of payments. Macroeconomic theory has developed a system of national accounts in which the relationship of the aggregate or macrovariables is established and analyzed.

Concerns. Macroeconomics concerns itself with the effects of changing one macrovariable on another variable and on the economy of the country. Such analyses are helpful to federal, state, and local governments in formulating sound fiscal and monetary policies, and in developing other legislation to meet national economic goals. An example of fiscal policy is the employment of the rediscount rate to affect interest rate levels. Another example of government action was the imposition of direct price and wage controls in 1971 to help curb inflation. Another major area of concern in macroanalysis is the determination of the flow of income. In an effort to get a better insight into the workings of an advanced industrial economic system, macroeconomics theorists have developed a basic theoretical structure or model that depicts a circular flow of income.

—Algin B. King, *College of William and Mary*

MAINTENANCE OF MEMBERSHIP, provisions in collectively bargained contracts that require those union workers to remain so, although non-members may not be required to join. Frequently an "escape period" is provided, during which workers may terminate their union membership. If they do not, they must remain members until another escape period occurs.

MALTHUS, THOMAS ROBERT (1766–1834). Best known for the theory of population in his *Essay on Population* (1798), the Reverend Malthus of England also made significant contributions to classical economics in his *Principles of Political Economy* (1820) and in his correspondence with David Ricardo.

The most significant economic doctrine which Malthus developed was his contention that it was possible to have a general overproduction (or underconsumption) of goods. While Malthus introduced this concept, most of his contemporary economists, particularly Ricardo, argued against the possibility, and it was not until the Keynesian development a century later that such a consideration again entered the mainstream of economic thought. Malthus also made important contributions to the theories of rent, wages, and the returns to capital.

See also Essay on Population.

MANPOWER DEVELOPMENT AND TRAINING ACT, (MDTA) enacted in 1962, designed to allocate funds (about $14.5 million a year) to programs to retrain the unemployed. It provided for an income for the trainees during the time they were involved in the program. The original act was designed mainly for the retraining of mature, experienced family heads who had been displaced due to economic or technological changes. In 1963, the act was amended to include youth—as much as one fourth the number in the training program. In addition, the program was expanded to encompass basic education. In the first two years following the MDTA some 5,000 institutional projects were approved and over 1500 on-the-job training programs went into operation. The trainees numbered about 320,000. By the end of 1969 nearly two million people had been enrolled in MDTA programs.

The most successful projects under MDTA have been the on-the-job training programs. In 1969, for example, of the 65,000 persons completing OJT projects, 82% were employed upon completion. Of the institutional programs, about 75% of the trainees in 1967 and 1968 secured employment—usually at a higher wage than before training. Median hourly wages for the trainees after training increased to $2.04 as compared with $1.55 before training.

In 1966 MDTA provided guidelines for training to meet skill shortages, and also sought to improve the linkages between various manpower programs.

The MDTA also required the *Manpower Report of the President* to be published annually.

—William D. Wagoner, *Louisiana State University*

MANPOWER POLICY. Although there has always been considerable emphasis on the development, training, and efficient use of manpower resources, it was not until the 1960s that the United States developed a major national manpower policy.

When President Kennedy took office in 1961, there were nearly five million people unemployed, the largest number since before

World War II, and concern was growing over the problem. By the end of 1962 unemployment had reached 5.5% and federal spending did not seem to be aiding in reducing this percentage. In 1962, Congress passed the Manpower Development and Training Act (MDTA), providing nearly $15 million annually for programs to retrain the unemployed. Originally, the act only provided for the retraining of mature, experienced, family heads who had been displaced by technological and economic changes. However, amendments later provided for the training of youth, also provided for in the Vocational Education Act of 1963.

The basic theme behind the manpower policy of the sixties was that education and training were the prerequisites to employment. In 1965, the Higher Education Act provided special federal funds to higher education, and the Elementary and Secondary Education Act provided federal assistance for schools in poverty stricken areas. In that same year, two acts were passed for concentrated redevelopment of depressed areas. These were the Public Works and Economic Development Act and the Appalachian Regional Development Act.

As a result of the acts passed in reference to manpower policies, many types of programs went into effect in the sixties. The institutional training programs included Job Corps, the Concentrated Employment Program (CEP), and the Work Incentive Program. On-the-job training programs included JOBS, Public Service Careers, and Jobs Optional. Programs dealing with work experience and work support were the Neighborhood Youth Corps, In-School and Summer programs, Out-of-School programs, Operation Mainstream, and Foster Grandparents.

The manpower programs of the sixties had many failures, but there seem to have been successes also. By 1969, the unemployment figure was down to 3.5%. However, one of the lessons learned from the programs was that it is well to aid people to be better prepared for jobs, but there must be jobs available for these people if employment is to be achieved.

See also Manpower Development and Training Act; Retraining.

Consult (20) Levitan, 1972.

—William D. Wagoner, *Louisiana State University*

MAO-TSE-TUNG (1893–), Communist leader of China, who helped found the Chinese Communist Party in 1921. In 1926 he staged an unsuccessful peasant revolt and in 1931 established a short-lived "soviet republic." Emerging as the leader of Chinese communism, Mao became both party chairman and chief of state when the communists took over in 1949, but resigned the latter position in 1959. The rift between China and the USSR and the tactics of the Red Guards are indicative of Mao's revolutionary philosophy.

Peasant-emphasis and nationalism are China's posture. When the Communist movement originally led by urban industrial workers was crushed, Mao drew support for his guerrilla movement from the peasantry, indicating that revolutionary possibilities are far better in poor agricultural countries. Mao also believed that capitalists of developed, industrialized nations are exploiting the peasants in the underdeveloped world more than the traditional industrial proletariat. He was nationalistic in trying to secure for China the role in world affairs to which he believed it was entitled.

See also Nationalism; Revisionism; Revolutionary Socialism.

Consult (26) Griesbrecht, 1972; Oser, 1970.

—John R. Matthews, Jr., *College of William and Mary*

MARGINAL ANALYSIS, an analytical technique frequently used in economics in which small increments in quantities are examined. As an illustration, assume the total cost of producing 10 units of product is $100, and the total cost of producing 11 units of product is $132. From the total cost data we may easily compute the average costs by dividing the total costs by the number of units of product. Thus, the average costs for 10 and 11 units would be $10 ($100 ÷ 10 units) and $12 ($132 ÷ 11 units), respectively. The marginal cost of the eleventh unit is $32, that is, the total cost of producing 11 units ($132) minus the total cost of producing 10 units ($100). The preceding is merely illustrative of marginal analysis. Economists use many other marginal concepts in addition to the concept of marginal cost.

Thomas Robert Malthus

Marginal Utility. The first widely accepted application of marginal analysis came in the 1860s when marginal utility became an important tool for economists. Prior to this time Adam Smith in his famous book *An Inquiry into the Nature and Causes of the Wealth of Nations* (1776) had noted that diamonds sold for a high price even though they were less useful than water, which had a very low price. Smith failed to solve this paradox of value, but in 1862 the English economist Stanley Jevons explained that the price of a good is not determined by the total satisfaction (or total utility) obtained from the good. Rather, the good's marginal utility (the additional satisfaction obtained from a small increment of the good) determines its value. The total satisfaction we gain from water is greater than that received from diamonds. On the other hand, one drop of water added to the universe would produce virtually no additional satisfaction (marginal utility) because of the large quantity

Most successful of various MDTA-funded programs have been those providing on-the-job training.

MARGINAL ANALYSIS

The marginal analysis can be applied usefully to many aspects of economic behavior. For its application to consumer behavior, see the articles on CONSUMER EQUILIBRIUM and MARGINAL UTILITY; in regard to the theory of the firm, see PROFIT MAXIMIZATION and LEAST COST FACTOR COMBINATION. For application of the marginal analysis in a macroeconomic frame of reference, see MARGINAL EFFICIENCY OF CAPITAL and CONSUMPTION FUNCTION.

of water already existing. A small increment of diamonds, however, would give more marginal utility because of their greater relative scarcity; so, their price is greater.

At about the same time that Jevons was writing in England, three influential Austrian economists, Carl Menger, Friedrich von Wieser, and Eugen von Böhm-Bawerk, and the famous French economist Leon Walras were utilizing marginal analysis. By the mid-1880s the new methodology had swept the economics profession.

Equilibrium. The neoclassical school of economics (1880–1940), with its British leader, Alfred Marshall, used the law of diminishing marginal utility to explain the slope of the demand curve for almost all individual goods. Within a given period of time if a person receives more and more and more units of one particular good, the marginal utility of each new unit of the good would decline; for example, the tenth suit of clothes received in one year's time adds less utility than the first. Because of this law, each person could be induced to buy additional suits only if the price were lowered: it follows that the lower the price, the more suits buyers would stand ready to buy. Marshall and the other neoclassical economists used this analysis together with a new treatment of supply to demonstrate the determination of the equilibrium price and the equilibrium quantity traded for each commodity. Much of this analysis remains as part of current economic theory.

Resource Allocation. Modern economics also uses marginal utility as a tool in teaching proper resource allocation. A resource is properly allocated when the marginal utility derived from it in each of its uses is equal. In other words, so long as there is greater marginal product from a resource when it is producing product A rather than product B, the resource should be transferred from B to A, but as more of A is produced, its marginal utility declines, and as less of B is produced, its marginal utility increases. There is less and less additional satisfaction from resources transferred to A and more and more satisfaction lost from resources taken from B. So long as the gain exceeds the loss, the transfer should continue, but eventually the marginal utility of labor when used to produce A will equal the marginal utility of labor when used to produce B. At that point the transfer should stop.

The same type of marginal analysis can be applied to many specific resource allocation decisions, such as whether to devote more resources to public goods, like dams, or private goods, like refrigerators. Cost-benefit analysis helps make allocation decisions on the basis of the marginal returns versus the marginal costs. Economists also analyze the behavior of the business firm by assuming that it will decide to produce a unit of product only so long as its marginal revenue (that is, the additional revenue to be received as a result of the production and sale of the unit of product) is greater than its marginal cost.

In 1936 the distinguished economist John Maynard Keynes introduced several new marginal concepts, among which were the marginal propensity to consume and the marginal propensity to save. These concepts refer to the percentages of an increment of income utilized for additional consumption and additional savings, respectively. If, for example, the government reduces taxes to stimulate demand for goods, the extent of the increase will depend on the values of the marginal propensities to consume and save. Among the marginal concepts used as part of the analytical framework of economics are marginal efficiency of capital, marginal product, marginal revenue product, and marginal rate of substitution. All of these concepts focus attention on additional units in analyzing important economic questions.

See also Consumption Function; Equilibrium; Marginal Cost; Marginal Revenue; Marginal Utility.

—Allan B. Mandelstamm, *Michigan State University*

MARGINAL COST measures the rate at which total cost changes as output is varied; it can be thought of as the difference in total cost between producing or not producing an additional unit of output.

See also Average Cost; Total Cost.

MARGINAL COST OF PRODUCTION (MC), the increment in total cost (TC) resulting from a small increase in output. For a discrete increase in output X, MC is defined as $\Delta TC/\Delta X$ (or $\Delta TVC/\Delta X$), with Δ signifying "change in." If the TC function is differentiable, then MC is defined as the derivative of TC.

See also Cost Function.

MARGINAL-COST PRICING, a particular concept of economic efficiency. A rigorous development of this concept involves complex mathematics, but an intuitive idea of what is involved is easy to grasp if one reasons by analogy. An efficient firm maximizes its profit by equating marginal revenue and marginal cost: it expands output as long as additional units of output add more to revenue than to cost. If society could define social benefit and social cost, an efficient society would maximize benefit by equating marginal social benefit and marginal social cost. Where exchange is voluntary, many economists find it persuasive to take market price as measuring marginal social cost, and accordingly advocate pricing goods and services (especially those goods and services produced by government) at marginal cost. The most notable attempt at implementing this social theory is the production and pricing of electricity in France.

—Clarence C. Morrison, *Indiana University*

MARGINAL EFFICIENCY OF CAPITAL (MEC) or Marginal Efficiency of Investment, the rate of return expected from expansion of the capital stock, the rate of return expected from additional investment. The rate of return on a possible specific new investment would be computed by taking the value of the additional annual output and deducting the other additional annual costs necessary to put the new equipment to work, and dividing this figure by the cost of the equipment.

Diminishing Returns. In the narrowest, least realistic sense, MEC would be the value of the output added annually by the capital without the use of any other additional inputs (in which case there would be no deductions: one would divide the value of the additional output per year by the cost of the equipment to compute the rate of return). In this case one would have the exact conditions for the application of the law of diminishing returns: one input (the new capital equipment) increasing, while all other inputs remain constant. One would therefore expect that increasing investments would be accompanied by smaller rates of return: the MEC curve would slope down to the right, as a demand curve. Since the reason for investment is profits, and since the rate of return measures them, MEC is the demand for capital.

In a more realistic world one would expect possible investments to have different expected rates of return, so that if only a few investments were undertaken, they would be the most profitable ones, and that if more investments were undertaken, they would have lower rates of return. For this reason, too, one would expect the MEC curve to slope downward, even if the the full requirements for the law of diminishing returns were not met, and more of other inputs were used.

Capital Supply and Demand. In Keynes' original treatment the quantity of investment that will occur equates MEC with the rate of interest, the intersection of the demand and supply curves for capital. The supply of and demand for money result in an interest rate; equating MEC with the interest rate results in a specific amount of investment spending; investment and consumption spending result in a specific level of income and employment.

Realistically, the rate of interest is not the operative limit to investment. Most businesses expect the investments they plan to make to have a rate of return appreciably higher than the rate of interest. In addition, bankers and other suppliers of capital want a margin or cushion for error. A realistic MEC demand curve would, then, be the expected value added by the investment project less all additional input costs other than the costs of the capital, and a realistic supply curve would be what bankers were persuaded was safe to lend.

—Walter C. Neale, *University of Tennessee*

MARGINAL EFFICIENCY OF INVESTMENT. *See* Marginal Efficiency of Capital.

MARGINALISM. The extension of the marginal principle to all areas of economic theory must stand as one of the most significant developments in economic theory. The idea that economic decisions generally are made in terms of a little more of this or a little less of that, rather than in all-or-nothing terms, made possible the fruition of the theory of market in Alfred Marshall's scissors of supply and demand. The acceptance of the marginal principle allowed the concept of equilibria, and introduced the possibility of expanding economic theory through the use of differential calculus. The development of marginalism is unusual in that the concept was developed simultaneously but independently by William Jevons, Carl Menger, and Leon Walras.

See also Jevons, William Stanley; Menger, Carl; Neoclassical Economics; Walras, Leon.

MARGINAL PHYSICAL PRODUCTIVITY, or MARGINAL PRODUCT, of a factor is the extra output obtained by using one more unit of that factor, other factors of production being held constant. The marginal product of a factor can be calculated by taking the slope (first partial derivative) of the total product curve, if it is differentiable.

MARGINAL PRODUCT. *See* Marginal Physical Productivity.

MARGINAL PRODUCTIVITY OF LABOR. *See* Wage Theories.

MARGINAL PROPENSITY TO CONSUME (MPC). *See* Consumption Function.

MARGINAL PROPENSITY TO IMPORT, the proportion of an increase in income that will be spent on imports. Imports are leakages from the income stream, because the payments go to foreigners and, therefore, do not maintain domestic money incomes.

MARGINAL PROPENSITY TO SAVE (MPS), the ratio of the change in savings resulting from a change in income to the change in income,

1.00 minus the marginal propensity to consume. Either MPS or MPC can be used to compute the multiplier, which tells the ultimate effect of a change in spending on national income.

See also Consumption Function; Marginal Propensity To Consume; National Income Determinations.

MARGINAL RATE OF SUBSTITUTION, the rate at which one commodity must be substituted for another to keep utility constant. Geometrically, the rate is the slope of an indifference curve.

See also Indifference Curve; Utility Function.

MARGINAL RATE OF TECHNICAL SUBSTITUTION, the rate at which one input must be substituted for another so as to keep the level of output constant. Geometrically, it is the slope of an isoquant.

See also Production Function.

MARGINAL REVENUE is the rate at which total revenue varies as sales quantity varies and can be thought of as the difference in revenue between selling an additional unit and not selling that unit.

MARGINAL REVENUE PRODUCT OF LABOR. *See* Demand for Labor.

MARGINAL SATISFACTION. *See* Marginal Utility.

MARGINAL TAX RATE, the rate applied to discrete increments or brackets of a tax base, usually income. This marginal tax rate varies according to whether the tax rate is progressive, regressive, or proportional. Progressive tax rates have marginal tax rates which increase with additional increases in the tax base, and proportional tax rates have marginal tax rates that remain constant for increases in the tax base.

See also Taxation; Tax Rates.

MARGINAL UTILITY, the rate of increase in utility due to a small increase in the amount of one commodity. If the utility function is differentiable, the marginal utility of X is defined as the first partial derivative of the utility function with respect to X.

See also Utility Function.

MARGIN REQUIREMENT refers to legal limits on the amount of money that can be borrowed for the purpose of buying or continuing to hold securities (stocks or bonds). *Margin,* in this context, means the percentage of the price of the security that the purchaser puts up in cash. A 100% margin requirement means that the buyer must pay the whole price in cash. A 60% margin requirement means that a loan may be obtained for not more than 40% of the sales price. Margin requirements are set from time to time by the Board of Governors of the federal reserve system and published as Regulations T (covering brokers and dealers) and U (covering banks). They are intended to prevent too much money from being diverted from productive loans into the stock market in times of tight money.

See also Monetary Policy.

MARKET ANALYSIS. *See* Equilibrium.

MARKET CLEARING occurs when the market price of a commodity is such that the quantity demanded by consumers equals the quantity supplied by producers. The market will not clear at any other price.

MARKET CONCENTRATION, the control of a large proportion of total sales by a small absolute number of firms in an industry. For example, of total sales in the transformer industry in 1963, 68% of these sales were controlled by the four largest firms in that industry, while 79% were controlled by the eight largest firms and 93% by the twenty largest firms. Considering the fact that there were 144 firms in that industry, the transformer industry could be said to have a high degree of market concentration.

Concentration of control of US business corporations seems to be very heavy. The very large corporations are relatively few in number but they control a high majority of all corporate assets. For example, in 1962, about 1% of the number of US corporations controlled over 76% of all corporate assets. In addition 94.2% of the number of all corporations controlled only 11% of all corporate assets.

Because a few large corporations control the bulk of employment, sales, and assets, competition is lessened. In addition, each very large corporation can centralize within its management a considerable amount of economic power. In spite of the growing concern over market concentration, statistics indicate that concentration of control by a relatively few giant corporations has actually declined somewhat since the early 1930s.

See also Concentration Ratio.

—William D. Wagoner, *Louisiana State University*

MARKET DEMAND for a product is represented by a schedule showing the various amounts of the good demanded at the various possible prices. These market demand curves are the functions facing the firms producing for sale in a particular market. Markets will absorb additional output only at lower prices, and higher prices paid will result from restricted quantities of output. The law of demand applies to markets. The market demand curve is constructed by horizontally summing the demand curves of all individuals constituting the market. The resulting demand curve shows that the market will absorb only the aggregate quantity of goods that all individuals will demand at various prices.

MARKET ECONOMY, one in which the basic questions of what, how, and for whom goods shall be produced are answered by market forces in a system of interrelated markets involving exchange of large quantities of goods and services. Markets are defined in terms of time, area, and types of product. Prices are set by demand and supply of buyers and sellers, respectively.

In the diagram, P_E is the equilibrium price and Q_E the equilibrium quantity; the market is cleared. This tendency to automatic adjustment of consumers' preferences, reflected in demand, and producers' costs, reflected in supply, is the result of a competitive market in which (1) factors of production are privately owned and (2) production is carried out through the initiative of private enterprise. Resources are allocated via prices, as consumers and producers aim toward maximizing their economic gains with no restrictions on their capacity to participate. This allocative function can be modified by governments or by the exercise of monopoly powers in markets where competition does not prevail.

See also Allocation; Command Economy; Competition; Evolutionary Socialism; Invisible Hand; Laissez Faire; Market Clearing.

Consult (26) Halm, 1968.

—John R. Matthews, Jr., *College of William and Mary*

MARKET ECONOMY

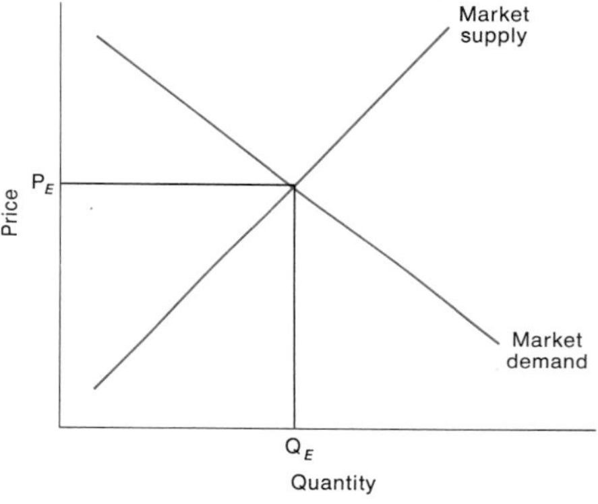

MARKET EQUILIBRIUM is determined through supply and demand. The demand curve for a commodity represents the various quantities that the consumer would purchase at various prices. The supply curve for a commodity represents the various quantities that producers would be willing to supply at various market prices.

Theory. The individual quantity that is demanded is, of course, dependent upon the market price, the income of the consumer, the price of related goods, complements and substitutes, and consumer taste and preferences. A change in any one of these variables would cause a change in the amount of the good demanded. The supply curve is dependent upon the price of the commodity and the cost of producing that commodity. Together the supply and the demand curves determine the equilibrium price and quantity. Equilibrium avoids excess supply and excess demand.

The schedule shows equilibrium at market price where the quantity supplied is exactly equal to the quantity demanded: consumers are willing to purchase exactly the amount that producers are willing to produce. This price is the market equilibrium price. At higher prices the producers would like to supply a larger quantity than consumers are willing to purchase, and at lower prices the consumers would like to purchase a larger quantity than producers are willing to supply. Graphically, the intersection of the supply and demand curves is at market price $3 and equilibrium quantity 7 units per unit of time as shown.

Significance. If price is above equilibrium and there is excess supply, the inventory of producers tends to build up and the producers will lower price toward the equilibrium to clear their inventories. If price is below the equilibrium, then consumers will demand a larger quantity of the good than is being produced and will bid up the market price toward the equilibrium. Once this market equilibrium is established, there is no tendency to move away from it unless there is a disturbance in either the market's supply or demand curves.

See also Market Structure.

Consult (11) Cohen, 1965; Leftwich, 1970.

—Robert L. Brite, *Louisiana State University*

MARKET EQUILIBRIUM

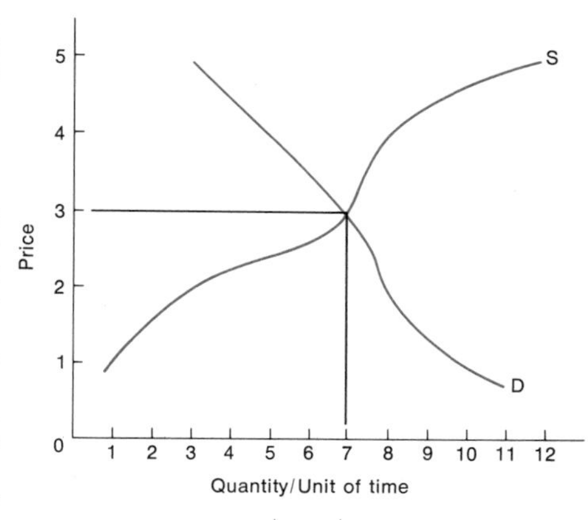

P	Q_D	Q_S
1	10	1
2	8	3
3	7	7
4	5	8
5	3	12

MARKET FORCES. *See* Market Mechanism.

MARKETING BOARDS, governmental or semigovernmental bodies, usually with a monopsony in the purchase (from local producers and traders) of selected agricultural products and a monopoly in their subsequent wholesale and export marketing. They are designed to reap economies of scale in the purchase, transport, and wholesaling of the crop. In addition, they often regulate consumer sales of important food crops, stabilize prices and supplies through the use of buffer stocks or funds, provide extension and research services for the farmers with whom they deal, and earn profits for use in development expenditures.

See also Economics of Scale.

Consult (24) Helleiner, 1964.

MARKETING ORDERS, AGRICULTURAL, are economic regulations, enforced by federal or state governments and intended to benefit producers, that apply to all sales of particular farm commodities in specified areas. Almost all milk produced under sanitation conditions making it eligible for consumption in fresh form is sold under orders regulating large metropolitan markets or areas containing smaller cities. All such orders establish minimum prices to be paid to producers for milk actually sold for fresh consumption (Class I) and for extra milk diverted to manufacturing uses (Class II). Some state orders also establish minimum wholesale and retail prices.

Numerous marketing orders for particular fruits and vegetables, mostly for fresh consumption, are also in effect in California, Florida, and elsewhere. Among the provisions sometimes included in such orders are minimum standards for quality and size, requirements for diverting products to processing uses under some conditions, rate-of-shipment regulations, and assessment of producers to provide funds for research or advertising.

See also Price-Support Programs.

MARKET MECHANISM, a device that blends the interactions of supply, demand, prices, competition, and communications in a market economy. Through the market mechanism the diverse desires of millions of consumers are made known to businesses, and the millions of economic decisions and actions of buyers and sellers are coordinated. The market mechanism is often referred to as the invisible hand regulating the everyday economic processes and activities in a market economy. In a market system the market mechanism is the key instrument that enables the system to solve the three basic economic problems confronting any society: what economic goods to produce, how to produce them, and how to distribute the economic goods to the members of society.

There are four basic components of the market mechanism which enable consumers to signal effectively to businesses that they wish more beef and less chicken, or more furniture and less clothing; X type car, Y type TV set, etc. These four components are: (1) demands of consumers translated into demand schedules for each type or class of goods; (2) available supply as furnished by businesses at a given time, usually referred to as a supply schedule for each type or class of goods; (3) price, which serves as a linking and coordinating device; and (4) competition, a component ensuring that proper efforts are made by businesses to supply goods and services in forms desired by the public, in proper quantities and at times when consumers want them.

Supply and Demand Schedules. A demand schedule is an aggregate of consumer demand for any brand or class of products at a given price or at several price levels. A supply schedule is an aggregate of the amounts of any given brand or class of products that producers are willing to supply at a given price or at several price levels. A combination supply and demand schedule for black-and-white, twelve-inch portable televisions appears in the table.

Market Mechanism

$ Prices	Quantity Demanded Millions Per Quarter	Quantity Supplied Millions Per Quarter	Pressures on Prices
$ 120.	1.5	6.0	Declining
$ 105.	2.3	4.8	Declining
$ 99.	3.2	3.2	Equilibrium State
$ 85.	4.5	1.9	Increasing
$ 79.	5.7	1.0	Increasing

Price and Competition. In a money economy everyone receives money for what he sells and in turn purchases what he wants with money. If consumers want more of a good than is currently being offered, in process of bidding against each other, they will cause the price to rise and, thereby, induce producers to produce more. Conversely, if supply exceeds demand, competition will force prices down, and producers will not produce as much of the good as before. Thus, supply and demand will gradually move to an equilibrium state through the mechanisms of price and competition.

Equilibrium State. As a result of the operation of the market mechanism, there evolves a state of equilibrium in which the amount of a product demanded by consumers and the amount supplied by producers are equal. The interactions of the four components bring supply and demand together at a given price. The equilibrium state is shown for twelve inch portable televisions. For this particular type of television set supply and demand are at equilibrium at a price of $99 and a volume of 3.2 million sets. The market mechanism works in an impersonal but effective way to supply consumers with what they want and are capable of purchasing.

Imperfections. The components of the market mechanism can operate in the manner discussed only under the conditions of perfect competition. Actions and effects are often modified under other market conditions, such as oligopoly, monopolistic competition, and monopoly. For example, under oligopoly the normal downward pull on prices of excess supply may not be fully realized, because there are so few suppliers involved that they control most of the available supply: through gentlemen's agreements they can immediately withhold goods from the market and not reduce prices in response to a drop in demand. It is not uncommon to find some degree of administered pricing under oligopoly market conditions especially where one or a few powerful labor unions or companies constrain the effects of the market mechanism. Although only partially effective in successfully coordinating consumers' demands with supply in the most efficient economic manner when modified by reality, it is, nevertheless, a powerful force.

See also Market Structure; Market System.

Consult (11) Cohen, 1965; Leftwich, 1970; Maxwell, 1970.

—Algin B. King, *College of William and Mary*

MARKET PRICE. *See* Competition; Equilibrium Price.

MARKET SHARING is the division of a market or sales territory by agreement among producers so that price competition among them is minimized or eliminated. This division may be geographic or by product class. Market sharing is a regular accompaniment of price-fixing plans, since agreements not to compete leave pricing to the one producer with "selling rights" in that area. Market sharing is inherently (*per se*) illegal under the Sherman Act.

See also Collusion; Per Se Illegality; Restraint of Trade.

MARKET STRUCTURE. There are a number of different market structures in any economy. They range from pure competition to pure monopoly. In between the two extremes lie oligopoly and monopolistic competition.

An assumption of pure competition is that the industry contains many firms producing a homogeneous product. There is free entry and exit of these firms from the industry and a situation where no one firm can affect the market price. That is, any one firm is so small relative to the total market that its increasing or decreasing output cannot influence the market price.

On the other extreme there is monopoly, an industry of only one firm. This firm obviously controls the industry's output and has a number of advantages. A monopolistic firm will normally produce a smaller output and charge a higher market price than a number of firms (pure competition) producing the same total industry output.

Between the two extremes there is oligopoly, an industry of only a few firms. It is closer to pure monopoly than it is to pure competition. The other type of industry is monopolistic, or imperfect, competition, where several firms produce a similar output. The major difference between monopolistic competition and pure competition is that under monopolistic competition there is product differentiation: all firms in the industry are not producing identical products. Under monopolistic competition there is free entry and exit whereas under either monopoly or oligopoly, entry is difficult.

See also Competition; Monopolistic Competition; Monopoly; Oligopoly.

Consult (11) Cohen, 1965.

—Robert L. Brite, *Louisiana State University*

MARKET SUPPLY. The market (or industry) supply curve shows the conditions under which *all* the firms in an industry will voluntarily offer varying outputs. As such, it shows the total amounts that will be forthcoming to markets at various prices, per unit of time, other variables held constant.

Graphically the market supply curve is the horizontal sum of all the individual firm supply curves (recall that quantity supplied is on the horizontal axis). This schedule will have the important property ascribed to an individual firm's supply schedule—it will be upward sloping. The interaction of the market supply schedule and the group demand schedule determines the market price of a given commodity.

MARKET SYSTEM, an economic system that relies predominately on a market mechanism to determine allocation of scarce resources, production techniques, pricing, distribution of goods and services to members of society, and so on. Under a market system, economic activity is highly organized via a system of markets, through which buyers and sellers interact. Common synonyms for a market system often used in the literature are "price system," "free enterprise system," and "capitalism."

The Invisible Hand of the Market. Because they have virtually unlimited economic wants, consumers must choose how to spend their incomes. Consumers' decisions are translated into a demand schedule communicated to businesses in the market places. In developing supply schedules, the business decision maker tries to supply goods and services demanded by consumers in quantities that will maximize firm profits. Consumers are relatively assured that their demands as to type and quantity of goods and services will be met through the market mechanism of competition. Firms that produce what consumers want are patronized, and vice versa. Business firms compete for consumer dollar votes and will shift economic resources, such as labor and capital, to synchronize production choices with consumer choices. To a substantial degree the market economy similarly governs how resources are to be allocated among specific industries and how resources will be combined to maximize profits efficiently. Technological innovation is encouraged to achieve competitive advantage.

The Distribution of Goods and Services in a market system is based on the consumer's ability to pay the equilibrium price for any particular good or service. Ability to pay is a function of current income, accumulation of wealth, or both. Income and wealth distribution under the market system is impersonal, being predicated on the premium placed by society on the skills and talents each individual has to contribute to society. Inequalities of income distribution among individuals or households is common in a market system. The distribution is not based upon needs.

Imperfections. The market system's major controlling mechanism, competition, weakens over time, leading to great concentrations of economic power in a few hands, finally stifling the system's virtues of innovation, responsiveness to consumer wants, and ease of market entry. Over time the concentration of wealth in a relatively small segment of society can be excessive, and, thus, the system fails to provide a desirable allocation of economic goods to a large part of society. Furthermore, the price system is incapable of registering social or collective wants satisfactorily. Critics contend that some goods and services, such as education, highways, and national defense, cannot be economically purchased in household-unit demand but can only be consumed economically on a collective basis. Finally, there are failures to adjust rapidly to drastic

MARKET STRUCTURE

For the various characteristics that determine market structure, see PRODUCT DIFFERENTIATION and MARKET CONCENTRATION. To follow up on the various types of market structure, see PERFECT COMPETITION, IMPERFECT COMPETITION, MONOPOLISTIC COMPETITION, OLIGOPOLY, MONOPOLY, MONOPSONY, and BILATERAL MONOPOLY. And for a view of some of the underlying factors that influence the characteristics of markets see ENTRY, BARRIERS TO ENTRY, and ECONOMIES OF SCALE.

The Subject Maps accompanying MARKET SYSTEM and THEORY OF THE FIRM show these and other interrelationships.

MARKET SYSTEM

To see the market system in its role as but one of many possible types of economic systems, consult ECONOMIC SYSTEMS. In that regard, also consult COMMUNISM, SOCIALISM, CENTRAL PLANNING, and PLANNING for alternative forms of economic organization.

For the specific functioning of the market system, also see the articles on PRICE THEORY, MARKET MECHANISM, and MARKET EQUILIBRIUM. And for an approach toward evaluating the performance of the market mechanism see WELFARE ECONOMICS and PARETO OPTIMUM.

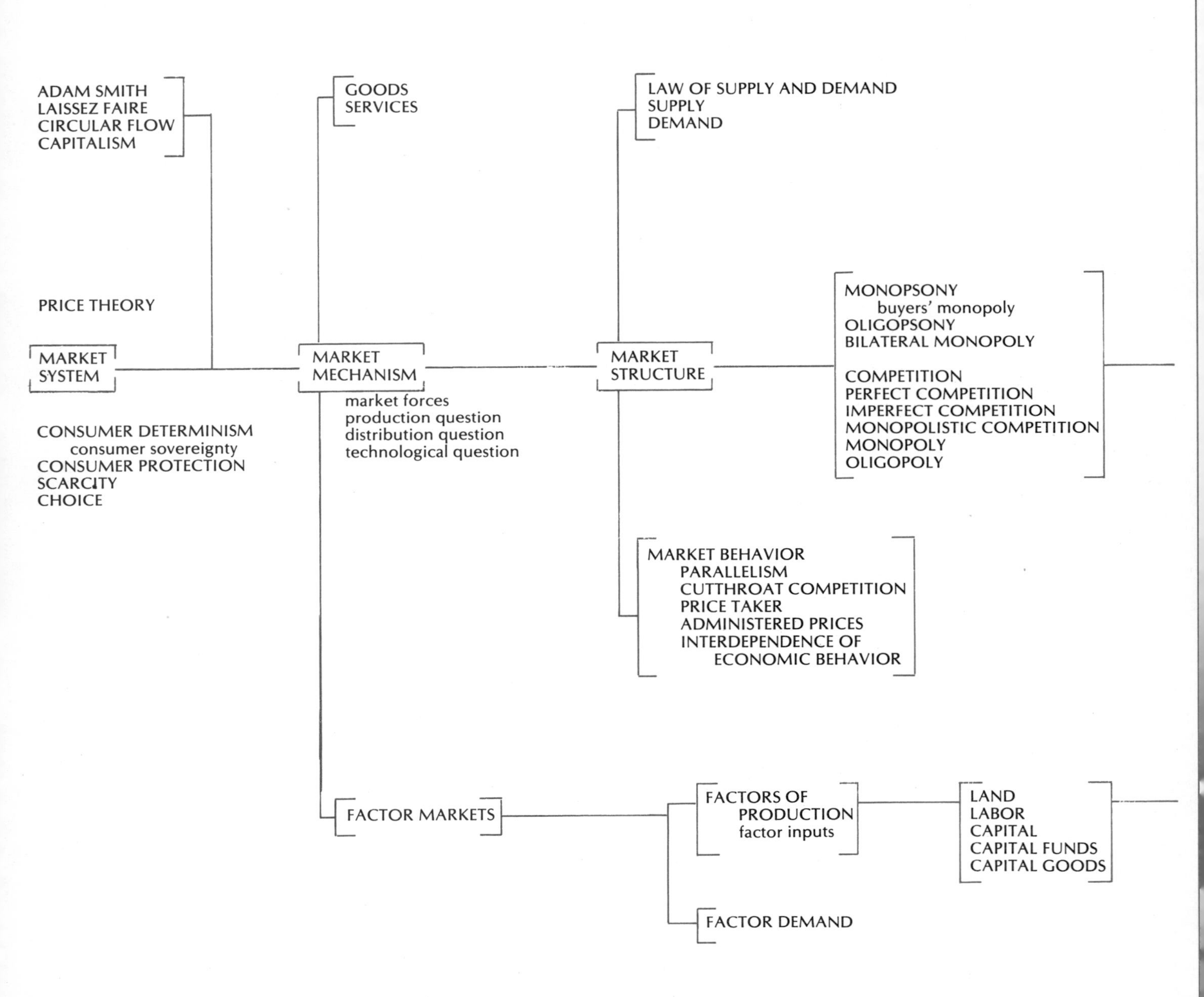
ADAM SMITH
LAISSEZ FAIRE
CIRCULAR FLOW
CAPITALISM
PRICE THEORY
MARKET SYSTEM
CONSUMER DETERMINISM
consumer sovereignty
CONSUMER PROTECTION
SCARCITY
CHOICE
GOODS
SERVICES
MARKET MECHANISM
market forces
production question
distribution question
technological question
FACTOR MARKETS
LAW OF SUPPLY AND DEMAND
SUPPLY
DEMAND
MARKET STRUCTURE
MONOPSONY
buyers' monopoly
OLIGOPSONY
BILATERAL MONOPOLY
COMPETITION
PERFECT COMPETITION
IMPERFECT COMPETITION
MONOPOLISTIC COMPETITION
MONOPOLY
OLIGOPOLY
MARKET BEHAVIOR
PARALLELISM
CUTTHROAT COMPETITION
PRICE TAKER
ADMINISTERED PRICES
INTERDEPENDENCE OF ECONOMIC BEHAVIOR
FACTORS OF PRODUCTION
factor inputs
FACTOR DEMAND
LAND
LABOR
CAPITAL
CAPITAL FUNDS
CAPITAL GOODS

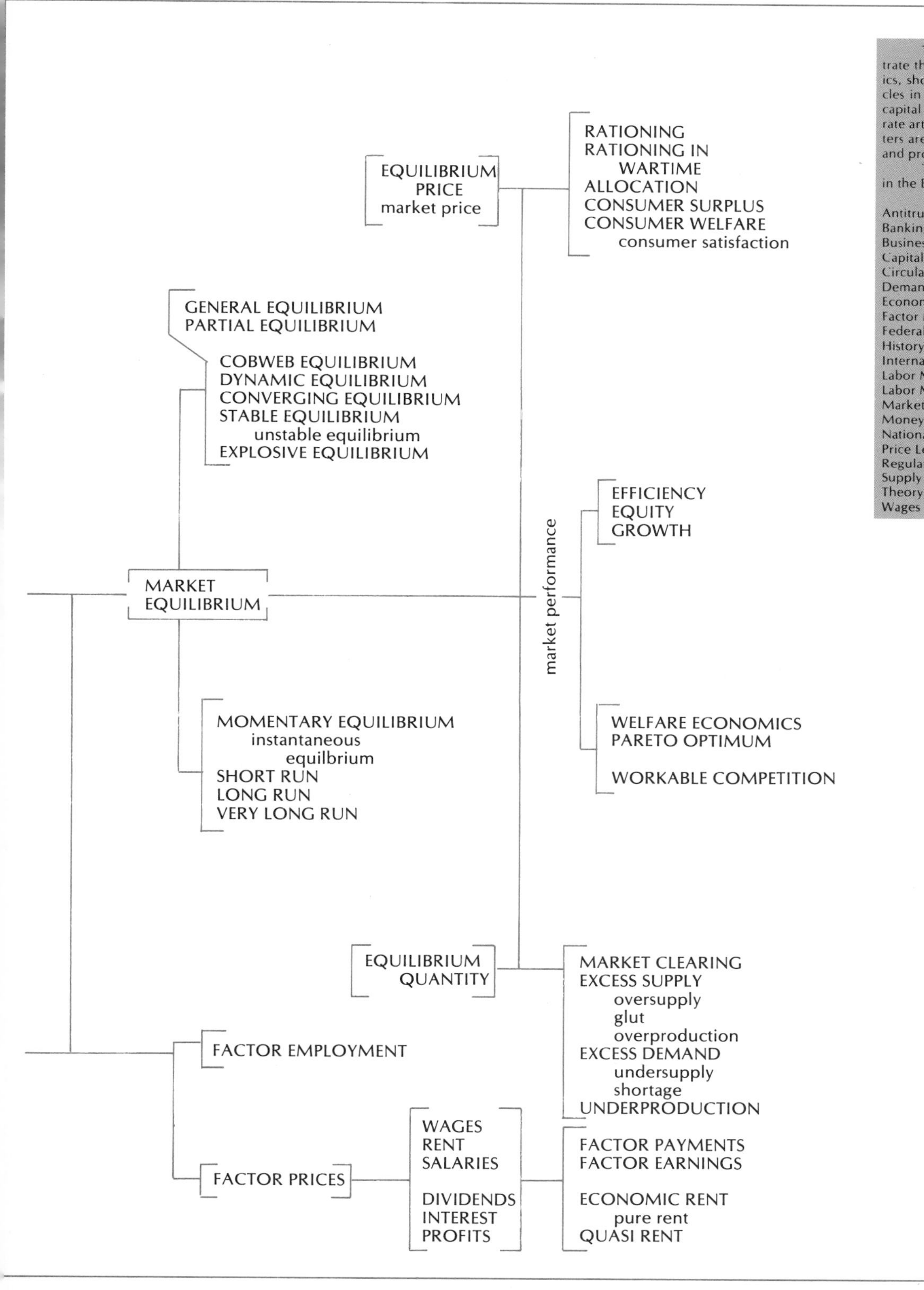

The Subject Maps in the Encyclopedia illustrate the coverage of particular aspects of economics, showing the interrelationships among the articles in twenty-one critical areas of study. Entries in capital letters are subjects for which there are separate articles in the Encyclopedia. Entries in small letters are references to the article immediately above and provide some idea of content.

The Subject Maps are arranged alphabetically in the Encyclopedia under the following titles:

Antitrust Policy
Banking System
Business Cycles
Capital
Circular Flow of Income
Demand Theory
Economic Systems
Factor Markets
Federal Budget
History of Economic Ideas
International Trade Theory
Labor Market
Labor Movement
Market System
Money and Monetary Policy
National Income
Price Level
Regulation
Supply
Theory of the Firm
Wages

Karl Marx, 19th-century German philosopher and writer, advocate of revolutionary socialism.

Alfred Marshall

changes desired by society, such as a shift from peace to war.

America's Economy could be characterized as a modified market economy. Three important modifications can be cited. First, in some major product and resource markets a few giant firms dominate, thus modifying the pure market-economy model. Second, the giant and powerful labor unions frequently distort the type of market mechanism discussed in the model. Third, the role of government is much more active and significant in the United States than is envisioned in a pure capitalistic system.

—Algin B. King, *College of William and Mary*

MARK-UP INFLATION, a version of cost-push inflation where firms are assumed to set price by applying a markup over average cost. A cost-push inflation could occur without a wage push if some firms increased their markups.

MARK-UP PRICING refers to the pricing policy of a business firm in regard to the rate of profit that it establishes. Mark-up pricing usually entails a certain percentage increase over the cost of the item. For example, if the mark-up pricing policy of a firm is 40%, any item that costs the firm $1 will be priced at $1.40, or 40% more than cost. Mark-up pricing is used most frequently in noncompetitive market structures where some individual control over price is present. In purely competitive industries, mark-up pricing is seldom used because prices are usually set by the market.

MARSCHAK, JACOB (1899-   ), Russian-born educator and expert on the economics of information and decision making. He received his Ph.D. from the University of Heidelberg in Russia in 1922. His publications include *Income, Employment, and the Price Level* (1951), and *Economic Theory of Teams* (1969, with Roy Radner). He has been professor of economics and business administration at the University of California at Los Angeles since 1960, and director of the Western Management Science Institute since 1965.

MARSHALL, ALFRED (1842-1924). The most important and influential of the Neoclassical economists, Marshall stands with Adam Smith, David Ricardo, and John Maynard Keynes as one of the greatest of modern economists. His *Principles of Economics* (1890) was a synthesis of classical and marginalist economics.

Demand, according to Marshall, is based upon diminishing marginal utility and the balancing of marginal utilities among goods, while supply is determined by the cost of production. Both are schedules or curves, and it is the interaction of the desires of consumers and the willingness of producers which determines the market price or economic value of goods. Marshall's discussions of elasticity, his concept of the short run, with its variable and fixed cost, and his long-run concept were other important additions to economic theory.

The use of the concept of the representative firm, increasing and decreasing long-run cost, internal and external economies of scale, and a marginal-productivity theory of distribution characterized Marshall's economics. These, combined with Marshall's use of partial equilibrium analysis and the ceteris paribus assumption, provided a complete treatment of microeconomic theory, some elements of which are the foundation of economics as it exists today.

See also Partial Equilibrium; Theory of the Firm.

MARSHALL PLAN, a foreign-aid program intended to rebuild the European economy after World War II. Also known as the European Recovery Program, it was passed as the Foreign Assistance Act of 1948.

Aims and Results. For his role in its development, Secretary of State George C. Marshall received the 1953 Nobel Peace Prize. The program arose from the desire of the United States to (1) reestablish the commercial ties from which both the United States and Europe had long profited and (2) contain the spreading influence of communism and the USSR, which had been aided by the post-war economic and political demoralization of most European nations.

Between April 1948 and June 1951, when the Marshall Plan was superseded by the Mutual Security Program, approximately $12 billion in grants and loans were made available for European recovery by the United States, much of it used for the purchase of U.S. exports by European nations.

MARX, KARL (1818-83), the founder, with Friedrich Engels (1820-95), of "scientific" socialism and leader of the revolutionary movement to overturn capitalism. Born in Prussia, Marx studied at universities in Bonn, Berlin, and Jena, receiving a doctorate in philosophy at 23. With university positions closed to him because of his radicalism, he turned to journalism. Expelled from Germany for his writings, he went to Paris, studied French socialism and English political economy, served as a New York *Tribune* correspondent, and met Engels. Expelled from France and Belgium, he finally settled in London. Much of his life was spent in poverty and ill health, causing him at times to borrow funds at exorbitant interest rates and to accept financial support from Engels.

In 1848, Marx and Engels wrote the

Communist Manifesto as a call to revolution. It contains the concept of the dialectical process—thesis, antithesis, and synthesis—of the philosopher Hegel and an economic interpretation of history in which Marx saw each stage containing the seeds of its own destruction. Feudalism (thesis) had been destroyed by capitalists (antithesis), and capitalism had its antithesis in the proletariat. As thesis and antithesis struggle, there emerges a synthesis that becomes the thesis for the subsequent stage until the final synthesis of communism, when all classes but the proletariat have been eliminated. Marx's thoughts were further developed in *Das Kapital,* the first volume of which was published by Marx in 1867; the second and third, by Engels after Marx's death.

Marxian Economics. The economics of Marx employ the labor theory of value, assuming that goods exchange on the basis of labor of average skill and intensity using modern means of production and producing commodities that are in demand. The exchange value of labor itself is determined by the labor time needed to produce the means of subsistence for laborers. The difference between the wage paid and the revenue from the product is surplus value, or profit, which the capitalist keeps for himself. The value of the commodity thus consists of constant capital (depreciation and raw materials), variable capital (labor), and surplus value. Only labor produces surplus value, but with technological advances more constant capital is used with less surplus value resulting. Increased use of machinery makes some labor superfluous, creating a reserve army of unemployed with downward pressure on wages, which reduces the consuming power of the masses even though productive potential in the economy has risen. However, with greater unemployment, profits increase, more capital is accumulated, and more labor is demanded.

Therefore, periodic crises are inherent in the capitalistic system. In each crisis real wages and the standard of living fall; the smaller capitalists are eliminated; the proletariat grows. The existing property relations imply antagonistic conditions of distribution, leading to inadequate demand relative to production. Therefore, the seeds of social revolution are a part of the capitalistic system, and socialism will emerge to fill the void resulting from capitalism's demise.

See also Economic Systems; Revolutionary Socialism.

Consult (26) Cole, 1969; Halm, 1968; Heilbroner, 1961; Hunt, 1972; Marshall, 1967.

—John R. Matthews, Jr., *College of William and Mary*

MASON, EDWARD SAGENDORPH (1899-), American economist who has made numerous contributions to the study of economic development. He is a graduate of the University of Kansas (1919), and he received his Ph.D. from Harvard (1925). Mason has served as deputy to the assistant secretary of state in charge of economic affairs (1945), economic counselor to the Department of State (1946-47), chief economic adviser to the Moscow Conference (1947), and chairman of the advisory committee on economic development for the Agency for International Development. He became a professor of economics at Harvard University in 1937.

Edward Sagendorph Mason

MATURE CREDITOR. *See* Stages of a Country's Balance of Payments.

MATURE DEBTOR. *See* Stages of a Country's Balance of Payments.

MAXIMIZATION OF PROFIT. *See* Profit Maximization.

MAXIMIZING BEHAVIOR, a basic assumption in economics that each individual will maximize his total satisfaction subject to certain external and internal constraints. The principal external factors influencing maximizing behavior are the income of the individual and the price of the goods he purchases. Internal constraints include his preference functions and his expectations concerning future price changes.

The rational consumer takes all of these constraints into consideration when he determines his expenditure pattern for all the goods and services that he purchases. Assuming that an individual's purchases can be sequentially separated, his first purchase will yield him the greatest amount of satisfaction per dollar's worth of expenditure. He will continue to purchase additional units of the most important item (the item that yields the greatest satisfaction per dollar) until the increase in satisfaction yielded by one more unit of the given item per dollar is less than the increase in satisfaction he would achieve if he transferred the dollar to buy another good. The rational economic man will pursue, by his expenditure pattern, the goal of achieving the greatest possible total satisfaction within the income price structure.

This goal of maximization of total satisfaction is reached whenever the consumer has optimally allocated his income among all of the goods and services, and the income budget is exhausted. He may, of course, save from his income, but the act of saving in itself yields some measure of satisfaction. The consumer has maximized satisfaction when he cannot achieve any increase in satisfaction by spending one dollar less on any good or one dollar more on any other good. Maximization of

AFL-CIO's George Meany was among labor leaders who met with President Nixon to discuss what steps would follow 90-day wage-price freeze.

Prominent labor mediator Theodore Kheel.

satisfaction occurs whenever the marginal utility per dollar's worth or expenditure is the same for each good or service purchased.
—Robert L. Brite, *Louisiana State University*

MAXIMUM PROFIT OUTPUTS. *See* Profit Maximization.

MDTA. *See* Manpower Development and Training Act.

MEAN. *See* Central Tendency.

MEAN DEVIATION. *See* Dispersion.

MEANY, GEORGE (1894–   ), was born in New York City, educated in the public school system, served a brief apprenticeship and became a journeyman plumber in 1915. Seven years later, he was elected business representative of Plumber's Union Local 463, and in 1934 he was elected president of the New York State Federation of Labor.

In 1940, he began working for the American Federation of Labor acting as treasurer. During World War II he was a member of the National War Labor Board. In 1952, after the death of William Green, Meany was elected president of the AFL. In 1957 he served as U.S. delegate to the United Nations.

In 1955, after the American Federation of Labor merged with the Congress of Industrial Organizations, forming the AFL-CIO, Meany was chosen to be its president, a position he still holds.

MEASURES OF ECONOMIC ACTIVITY. *See* National Income Measurement.

MEC. *See* Marginal Efficiency of Capital.

MEDIAN. *See* Central Tendency.

MEDIATION is an important and often effective form of third-party intervention in the bargaining process, particularly in an "emergency strike" situation. Unlike an arbitrator, who renders a decision after hearing labor's and management's positions, the mediator endeavors mainly to keep the bargaining from breaking down and to seek paths to an agreement. By clarifying the issues, defining and containing areas of disagreement, offering suggestions, and serving as an intermediary, the mediator can contribute substantially to a settlement.

See also Collective Bargaining; Conciliation; Emergency Strike.

MEDICAID, a federally subsidized, state-administered program to pay for medical and hospital costs of low-income families. Recipients of public assistance qualify automatically, and other low-income families may be eligible for at least partial coverage.

See also Medicare; Public Assistance.

MEDICARE, a program which pays a portion of the hospital costs for persons over 65. It is financed in part from the Social Security trust fund, but coverage is not limited to elderly in the Social Security program. In addition, the elderly are granted an option of buying federally subsidized medical insurance at a rate of $5.60 per month. The hospital insurance covers most of the cost of up to 90 days in the hospital, plus additional time in an extended-care facility, and home visits by nurses. Medical insurance covers 80 percent of the cost of physicians' fees (above $50 per year) and a variety of related medical services.

See also Social Insurance; Social Security.

MEDIUM OF EXCHANGE. *See* Money.

MEMBER BANK, a commercial bank that has accepted membership in the federal reserve system. All national banks must join, and state banks may join if they wish and if they can fulfill the requirements of membership, including a minimum amount of capital. All member banks must be insured by the Federal Deposit Insurance Corporation. Only 40% of commercial banks have joined the system, but they conduct 80% of the banking business. Those member banks located in some 50 of the largest financial centers (reserve city banks) are subject to somewhat higher reserve requirements than other banks (country banks). At one time, banks in the financial districts of New York City and Chicago were classified separately as central reserve city banks, but this class has been absorbed into the reserve city designation.

MEMBERSHIP MAINTENANCE. *See* Maintenance of Membership.

MENGER, CARL (1840–1921), a leading Austrian economic theorist, chiefly notable as the originator of the Austrian school's explanation of economic phenomena. Menger's principal work is *Foundations of Political Economy* (1871), a study in which he demonstrated, through the use of very basic terminology and illustrations, how the utility principle connects use-value with scarcity. Further, he stressed how fundamental a role marginal utility plays in determining economic value.

The 1870s revolution in the theory of value used to explain income and price formulation was in large part stimulated by Menger's development in this area, along with similar developments by Jevons and Walras. Menger subsequently employed the marginal-utility principle in studies of money and its value. The chief distinction between Menger and the other marginalists lies in his approach, which was outside the utilitarian tradition. For him, economizing man, rather than pursuing maximization of pleasure, seeks to satisfy his needs by the most efficient means.

See also Marginalism.

MERCANTILISM. As Western civilization emerged from the Middle Ages and economic activity shifted from the feudal community to a system of merchant capitalism, economic thought developed its first meaningful doctrines. These doctrines existed in many countries at many different times from as early as the sixteenth century to as late as the middle of the eighteenth. However, whether we consider English mercantilism with writers such as Munn, French mercantilism under Colbert, or the later German cameralists, several common themes appear.

The most distinguishing feature of mercantilism was its view of a nation's wealth in terms of its treasury of gold and silver. The earliest manifestations of this view were the bullionist policies of a nation's participating in international trade only if the transaction increased the nation's wealth, that is, its holdings of precious metals. As trade increased, this position was modified to consider the overall balance-of-payments aspect of a transaction. Thus, gold could leave a country if by doing so more gold eventually came into the country.

The mercantilist view of wealth and the emphasis upon international trade led to a number of policies which, it was felt, would promote trade and increase the nation's wealth. Policies such as (1) extensive colonization and the exploitation of the colonies' raw materials, (2) strong government participation in the economy, including establishing trade monopolies, and (3) strong nationalism were all developed and supported by mercantilist thought.

Later mercantilist thinkers, such as Sir William Petty, David Hume, and Richard Cantillon (some would call them transitional between mercantilism and the Physiocrats) anticipated many of the doctrines which would appear in later works and were surprisingly modern in many of their concepts.

See also Balance of Payments; Balance of Trade; International Trade Theory.

—Clyde A. Haulman, *College of William and Mary*

MERGER, a contractual joining of the assets of one hitherto independent business firm with another. Since the merged firms become one business entity, the merger is the surest method of providing identity of interests among firms (as compared to various forms of intercorporate stockholding, community of interests, overt or tacit agreements). Mergers are undertaken for a variety of reasons: diversification of product line, credit availability, acquisition of managerial talent, acquisition of patents or research capabilities. But the ultimate reason is financial gain to one or both of the merging firms.

From the point of view of economic structure, mergers fall into one of three categories: (1) horizontal, combining firms on the same plane or level of competition; (2) vertical, combining firms at different stages of a productive process; (3) a conglomerate, combining firms in dissimilar product lines.

Mergers are accomplished through one of two methods (and sometimes both). In stock acquisition, the acquiring firm secures controlling interest of voting stock in another firm and then votes absorption of that firm into the acquiring firm. In asset acquisition, the acquiring firm directly purchases the assets of another firm. (Often acquisition of some voting stock is preliminary to asset acquisition.)

Mergers which may tend to lessen competition substantially have been prohibited since the Clayton Act of 1914. It barred mergers by stock acquisition only, however; not until the 1950 Celler-Kefauver Act was a similar prohibition placed on asset acquisition.

See also Conglomerate; Horizontal Merger; Vertical Merger.

Consult (16) Bock, 1965.

—Thomas O. Depperschmidt, Memphis State University

MEYER, JOHN ROBERT (1927-), American educator noted for contributions to investment theory, transportation economics, and economic history. A graduate of the University of Washington (1950), he received his Ph.D. from Harvard (1955). His publications include *The Investment Decision: An Empirical Inquiry* (1957), *The Urban Transportation Problem* (1965) and *The Economics of Slavery and Other Essays on the Quantitative Study of Economic History* (1965). Meyer became president of the National Bureau of Economic Research in 1967 and professor of economics at Yale University in 1968.

MICROECONOMICS, the study of the individual business firm—what it is; how it works; how it allocates various resources inputs; how it prices goods and services; how it reacts to competitive pressures; and the various types of competitive environments and their ramifications on it. A second major focus of microeconomics deals with an analysis of individual or single-family consumption behavior, particularly as it relates to demand schedules, allocation of income in consumption, and effects of price variation on demand and on product

TYPES OF MERGERS

C Typewriter producer

D Motion picture producer

E Leather goods producer

(Supplies)

A Shoe producer

B Shoe producer

(Supplies)

F Retail shoe store

Examples:

Horizontal merger:
If Shoe producers A and B merge.

Veritcal merger:
If Shoe producer B merges with Leather goods producer E ("backward integration") and/or Retail shoe store F ("forward integration").

Conglomerate merger:
If Shoe producer B merges with Typewriter producer C and/or Motion picture producer D.

John Robert Meyer

substitution. Among the more important concepts in microeconomics analysis are demand and supply schedules, price elasticity, variable costs, fixed costs, marginal utility, marginal costs, short-run analysis, long-run analysis, equilibrium condition, marginal revenue, total revenue, and profit maximization.

Analytic Tools. To better understand firm behavior, the economist uses analytical concepts of general types of market conditions: pure competition, monopoly, monopolistic competition, and oligopoly. For example, the firm will price its products and services at the point that will maximize profits if it is operating under monopoly market conditions, but if it is operating under conditions of pure competition, pricing will be set by the market forces of supply and demand. In microeconomic analysis dealing with the individual consumer or family unit, such concepts as individual demand schedules, diminishing marginal utility, shift in the demand curve, elastic demand, inelastic demand, unit elasticity, and supply curves are useful.

Analytic Goals. The purpose of the analytical and conceptual tools is to enable the business firm to determine what to produce (the types of goods and services the consumer wants), how to best combine scarce economic resources (land, labor, and capital) to minimize costs and economic waste and thus maximize the efficiency of economic processes of an individual firm in meeting the economic needs of the consumer and society.

Consult (14) Liebhapsky, 1968.

—Algin B. King, *College of William and Mary*

John Stuart Mill

MILL, JOHN STUART (1806-73), political philosopher and last of the important classical economists. His *Principles of Political Economy* (1848) stands as the ultimate statement of the classical system.

Mill's most important contribution to economics was in his extension of international trade theory. Based upon Ricardo's concept of comparative advantage, Mill completed the system by using the concept of reciprocal demand to determine the exact terms of trade. In doing this, he also became aware of the concept of demand elasticity and developed one of the few analytical arguments favoring tariffs.

Beyond Natural Law. Mill's work also contains a number of other important economic concepts. In his *Principles,* Mill makes a distinction between production, which he felt was governed by natural laws beyond man's control, and distribution, which he felt was in part institutionally determined. While he failed to see that the two processes are also interrelated, the freeing of distribution from the bonds of natural law provided a challenge to existing economic theory which became the basis for many future developments.

The Wages Fund. Mill's wage theory replacing Ricardo's subsistence theory was the basic wages-fund doctrine: that wages are determined by the number of workers and a predetermined portion of capital set aside to pay the workers—a wages fund. While this theory was used extensively before the development of the marginal-productivity theory of wages, it is basically incorrect because there is no set amount of capital which must go to labor.

Based upon a falling rate of profit, a concept present in the works of all important classical economists, Mill felt that the accumulation of capital would eventually stop and a stationary state would result. The stationary state, however, would not be reached in the near future, and if population were checked, it could be a state free from the problems and pressures of increasing production.

Finally, Mill made no contribution to value theory because he felt that "the theory of the subject is complete."

See also Classical Economics; International Trade.

Consult (25) Rima, 1967; Spiegel, 1971.

—Clyde A. Haulman, *College of William and Mary*

MILLER-TYDINGS ACT (1937), the first national legislation enabling firms selling in interstate commerce to engage legally in so-called "fair-trade" pricing, which is the establishment of a minimum resale price for a nationally branded product by contract between manufacturer and retailer. The act was enabling legislation: if individual states passed fair trade laws, firms selling into those states would be exempt from prosecution under the Sherman Act for price fixing and under the FTC Act for unfair trade practices when they entered into the resale price-maintenance contracts.

An important feature of these contracts was the "non-signers" clause, whereby retail firms selling the branded product were bound by a contract executed by any other seller of the same product in that state not to sell the product below the price minimum set in that contract. The non-signers clause was rendered invalid in the case of *Schwegmann Brothers v. Calvert Corp.* (1951) but was re-established as law by the McGuire-Keogh Act of 1952.

See also Fair-Trade Laws; Resale Price Maintenance; McGuire-Keogh Act.

—Thomas O. Depperschmidt, *Memphis State University*

MINIMAX PRINCIPLE. *See* Game Theory.

MINIMIZATION OF LOSS. *See* Loss Minimization.

MINIMUM WAGE LAW. *See* Fair Labor Standards Act (1938).

MINIMUM WAGES. In an effort to keep people out of poverty, minimum wage laws have been enacted on both federal and state levels. The federal government, after several laws involving minimum wages in particular industries, finally passed a comprehensive wage law, the Fair Labor Standards Act, in 1938. At that time, minimum wages were set at $.25 an hour; this figure increased over the years to keep up with the rising cost of living. In 1971 the minimum wage was $1.60.

The law covers most workers in the United States, but still excepts several types, including proprietors and other self-employed persons, outside salesmen, apprentices, handicapped persons, domestic servants, and most employees in agriculture, forestry, and fisheries.

MISES, LUDWIG VON (1881-), an advocate of political individualism, who has continued the tradition of the Austrian school to the extreme. Much of Mise's work has been directed toward criticizing economic socialism, which he feels is unworkable because it contains no effective pricing system. In addition, Mises believes that any governmental intervention in the economic system places the system in danger. His dogmatic and unyielding position has placed him on the conservative perimeter of economics.

MIXED ECONOMY, an economic system with some characteristics of capitalism and some characteristics of socialism. The political-economic spectrum may be characterized as follows: At one end of the spectrum is laissez-faire capitalism—a system in which almost all economic means are privately owned and almost all economic processes are market-determined. At the other end of the spectrum is socialism, a system in which almost all the means of production are owned and controlled by government. Somewhere between these extremes lies the mixed economy. The primary reasons for the emergence of the so-called mixed economy are: (1) social goals have been given higher priorities by society through democratic governmental processes; and (2) the private sector did not want to provide certain goods or services.

In a mixed economy the private sector produces many of society's goods and services, but a significant amount of goods and services are under direct government ownership. An example of a mixed economy would be that of the United Kingdom. Many of its basic industries, such as transportation, steel, and coal, are owned or operated by government, but a large portion of goods and services are still produced by private enterprise. In the United States' economy the current peacetime economic output mixture is approximately 80% private and 20% government.

—Algin B. King, *College of William and Mary*

MOBILITY, FACTOR. *See* Factor Mobility.

MOBILITY, LABOR. *See* Labor Mobility.

MOBILITY, RESOURCE. *See* Resource Mobility.

MODE. *See* Central Tendency.

MODEL, ECONOMETRIC. Econometric models are empirical statements of economic theory. Rather than merely being content with abstract a priori reasoning, econometric models place the relationships that such reasoning indicates exist in mathematical form and, using a host of analytical techniques, attempt to measure or estimate these various economic relationships. Econometric models combine economic theory with the reality of economic events, providing a means of validating economic theories and isolating exact relationships.

The information needed to create econometric models may be difficult or impossible to obtain. Often, detailed information on a wide range of economic variables is needed. While much of these data are supplied by governments and other institutions, some must be generated by economists to fit a particular need.

Some econometric models are essentially microeconomic, concerned with measuring economic relationships that influence individual units in the economy. Estimating supply and demand relationships, measuring the degree of industrial concentration, and explaining individual consumer behavior are examples of microeconometric models. Macroeconometric models, on the other hand, are concerned with estimating aggregate economic relationships. Models of various sectors of the economy, growth models, and large models of the entire economy are examples. Both microeconometric and macroeconometric models use data that comes from the actual performance of the economy rather than from controlled experiments.

See also Model, Economic.

—Clyde A. Haulman, *College of William and Mary*

MODEL, ECONOMETRIC

To compare econometric models of the economy with other types, see the articles on INPUT-OUTPUT MODELS, NATIONAL INCOME DETERMINATION, and CIRCULAR FLOW OF INCOME, as well as the Subject Map accompanying this last article.

Holland's Jan Tinbergen, whose work with econometric models earned him a share of the first Nobel prize awarded in economics (in 1969).

MODEL, ECONOMIC, a construct embodying a particular economic theory. The core of a model is a set of *assumptions* concerning the factors, or variables, that are believed to be relevant to the phenomenon, and the relationships between these factors. From the assumptions of a model, one deduces certain conclusions in the form of statements, or *hypotheses,* about various aspects of the phenomenon. These derived hypotheses constitute the essence of the theory embodied in the model. Thus, a model may be thought of as a medium for the construction of a theory.

A theoretical model may be stated in the form of a set of mathematical equations or specifications, and often may be depicted graphically. Sometimes a model is represented as a three-dimensional physical construct, like models of a molecule.

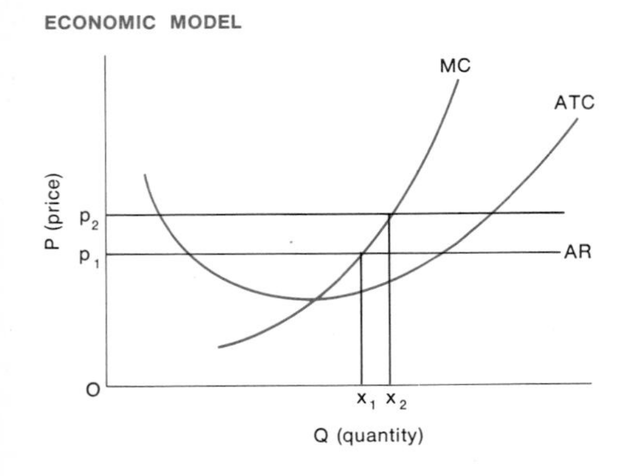

Economic models are found on all levels of analysis and in most branches of economics, such as the theory of the firm, consumer behavior, market or industry analysis, regional analysis, general equilibrium analysis, and economic relations among nations. Economic phenomena being manifestations of the actions of decision makers, the assumptions incorporated in economic models can usually be identified as assumptions about the *environment* in which the decision maker operates, or assumptions about the *objectives* (or goals) of the decision maker.

An example of an economic model of a competitive firm is shown in the figure. The ATC (average total cost) curve shows the unit cost of production, and the shape of this curve embodies certain assumptions about the technological environment of the firm. The MC (marginal cost) curve is derived from the ATC curve and shows the increments to total cost of small increases in output. The AR (average revenue) line represents the economic environment of the firm, indicating that it can sell any amount of its product at the current market price p_1. The assumption about the firm's objective is that it wants to maximize total profit in each period of time. Then, according to the model, the firm will produce x_1 units of its product in each period (the output at which MC = AR). One of the hypotheses generated by the model is that when the market price rises, the firm will increase its production. As may be seen in the diagram, if the market price rises to p_2, the firm increases output to x_2.

—Josef Hadar, *Case Western Reserve University*

MODEL OF THE FIRM. *See* Theory of the Firm.

MODIGLIANI, FRANCO (1918–), Italian-born economist who has achieved recognition for his contributions to the understanding of macroeconomic policy and his work on the Federal Reserve-MIT econometric model. He received doctoral degrees from the University of Rome (1939) and The New School for Social Research (1944). His publications include *National Incomes and International Trade* (1953), *Planning, Production, Inventories and Work Forces* (1960), and *The Role of Anticipations and Plans in Economic Behavior and Their Use in Economic Analysis and Forecasting* (1961). Modigliani served with the Institute for World Affairs in New York City from 1945–48 and became professor of economics and finance at M.I.T. in 1964.

MOMENTARY EQUILIBRIUM, an instantaneous equilibrium in which the quantity supplied by producers per unit of time equals the quantity demanded by consumers per unit of time. The equilibrium position is normally instantaneous due to the fact that other variables, which are assumed to be constant, may vary over time. The quantity demanded is a function of consumer income, price of related good, and consumer tastes and preferences. If any of these variables change throughout the period of the analysis, there is a shifting of the demand curve, giving a new equilibrium position. On the supply side, if costs vary during the period of analysis, the supply function will shift. Because all of the variables are changing over time, the equilibrium position is constantly moving.

MOMENTS, of a probability distribution, are a set of parameters which summarize or describe that distribution. Some important moments are the mean and variance, which measure central tendency and dispersion. Higher moments measure skewness and kurtosis.

See also Central Tendency; Dispersion; Kurtosis; Skewness.

MONETARY AUTHORITY, CENTRAL, the agency or group of agencies whose function is to implement monetary policy through the control of the money supply or other monetary aggregates or indicators. This may be done directly through the issue of currency or indirectly through such market influences as interest rates or the conditions under which loans may be made by commercial banks (thus affecting the volume of demand deposits) or financial intermediaries (thus influencing the wider financial markets). In most countries the central bank is the primary monetary authority, frequently in conjunction with the national treasury and, sometimes, with the help of other agencies, such as an exchange stabilization fund. In all cases a parliament or congress establishes the rules under which these agencies work and, hence, holds the ultimate authority over monetary matters.

MONETARY HISTORY OF THE UNITED STATES 1867–1960 (1963). *See* Friedman, Milton.

MONETARY POLICY, all activities of the federal government intended to produce changes in the money supply, the availability of loanable funds, or the level of interest rates to influence general economic activity. Monetary policy is one of the two major forms of governmental action designed to stabilize the economy; the other control, fiscal policy, covers measures concerned with governmental receipts, expenditures, and debt management. The objective of both these policies is to provide countercyclical forces to reduce the severity of business cycles by stimulating the economy in depression and calming it during inflation.

Some forms of monetary policy have been used for this purpose for at least a hundred years, but they have become increasingly significant as the economy has become more complex. The financial panic of 1907 led to the Federal Reserve Act, and the great depression of the 1930s forced a substantial strengthening of controls to prevent a repetition of the catastrophe.

Objectives. In terms of its countercyclical policy the objectives of the federal reserve are normally stated as full employment (absense of depression) and a stable price level (absence of inflation). In the last two decades two additional objectives have been added: a high and sustainable level of economic growth, and an external stability of the exchange value of the dollar. Currently however, these additions have been questioned: rapid growth may raise more problems than it solves, in terms of pollution, exhaustion of natural resources, and dehumanization of life. On the international side the long series of deficits in the United States balance of payments has been more than monetary policy alone can cope with, and the world is now embarking on a new form of monetary standard that will not require as much stability in international exchange rates as was formerly thought desirable. Thus, the stability of the dollar is no longer pursued as strongly as it once was.

Full employment and stable prices still stand as basic objectives. During depression there is a tendency for employment to fall, along with production, prices, income, and general well-being. Maintaining high employment levels is not only desirable for its psychological effect on the individual worker and its stabilizing effect on society, but at the same time it is one basic element in maintaining production, consumption, incomes, and prices. As depression turns to prosperity, all these factors tend to rise, and although increased employment, income, and production are desirable, the rise in prices (inflation) causes undesirable social changes in the distribution of income and wealth, and maladjustments in the productive process that tend to bring on a later recession. If prices are kept stable, these undesirable consequences are prevented.

Tight Money and Easy Money. Monetary policy acts primarily on the level of production by making it easier or harder for businessmen to obtain loans to expand facilities or to pay for labor and materials. Under a tight-money policy, loans are made more difficult to get by restricting the money supply, raising interest rates, or putting pressure on banks to retrench. Under an easy-money policy, businessmen are encouraged to borrow by increasing the money supply, lowering interest rates, or inducing banks to expand.

The Locus of Monetary Control. The authority primarily responsible for executing monetary policy is the federal reserve system, although other agencies may also contribute. The U.S. Treasury may reduce the effective money supply by shifting funds from its tax and loan accounts in commercial banks to its account in the federal reserve banks; it may increase the money supply by shifing back. These movements are usually quite small. The treasury also affects interest rates by the form and timing of its borrowing from the public, although Congress determines the ultimate amount of borrowing by its tax and expenditure policy. At this point monetary and fiscal policy overlap. When the government is operating at a substantial deficit and must borrow large sums of money, it is impossible to produce tight money conditions without driving interest rates extremely high, denying funds to legitimate borrowers.

The many government lending agencies also affect both the supply of loanable funds and the interest rate. Indeed, the agencies' main purpose is often to make money available to certain groups of borrowers at especially advantageous rates. State governments have control over nonmember state banks, although the states are usually passive or follow the major actions of the federal reserve.

Instruments of Federal Reserve Policy. The central bank, however, has ultimate control over the money supply, and if Congress allows the bank sufficient independence, it can make almost any policy effective. The tools that the federal reserve has are numerous.

Quantitative controls, which directly affect the amount of banks' excess reserves, include *open-market operations,* the most important and flexible tool, used almost continuously; *changes in discount rate,* occurring on the average about twice a year and used primarily for psychological effect; and *changes in reserve requirement,* used quite infrequently, because they have relatively drastic effects.

Qualitative controls over the size or maturity of specific kinds of loans to discourage such loans more than others make use of *margin requirements,* specifying the maximum amount that can be borrowed for the purchase of securities; *installment credit controls* and *mortage lending controls* to restrict the volume of loans made to consumers, used during past war periods but not now in effect; and *interest rate ceilings,* regulating the amount that banks can pay on deposits.

Moral suasion, designed to obtain voluntary compliance with monetary objectives, includes *bank examination and visitation, publicity, and voluntary credit restraint,* another wartime measure no longer used.

Operation. The primary basis of monetary controls is the equation of exchange which says that as long as the velocity with which money circulates is unchanged (and there is very little the government can do to alter it), an increase in national income (the monetary value of physical output) can occur only if the money supply increases. Thus, to cure a depression, more money is needed. If prosperity develops into inflation, however, national income rises more rapidly than production because of the rise in prices, which can be discouraged if the money supply is restricted to a slower rate of expansion or, in rare cases, is forced to contract.

Because commercial banks are the major source of the money supply through their creation of demand deposits, monetary policy concentrates on the banks' ability or willingness to create deposits through loans. Quantitative controls on excess reserves determine the ability of banks to expand. Qualitative controls and moral suasion affect the willingness of banks to lend. In addition, a scarcity of loanable funds drives up interest rates, which makes borrowers more reluctant to borrow. There are three prongs of monetary policy: money supply, availability of funds, and interest rates.

Effectiveness. Some economists, such as Milton Friedman, think that monetary policy does not work. Most economists, however, admitting that it certainly does not work perfectly, believe that the increasing complexity of industrial, commercial, and financial interrelations could not have been handled without serious breakdown in the absence of monetary policy. At the very least, the United States has not suffered the severity of a great depression for forty years, and unemployment levels since the 1930s have not approached the rate of 25%, which was reached in those years. On the other hand, inflation has been almost continuous since 1933, partly because of expansionary fiscal policy during most of this period. It is extremely difficult for monetary policy to restrain inflation when the government operates at a large deficit.

Another problem arises from the changing nature of the economy. The earlier pattern of business cycles was such that unemployment and falling prices went hand in hand, as did high employment and rising prices. Thus, the goals of full employment and stable prices normally called for the same kind of action, both in depression and in prosperity. In the early 1950s, however, and again in the late 1960s a new phenomenon has developed: a high level of unemployment has occurred while prices are rising fairly rapidly. One important ingredient, the wage-price spiral, is probably intensified by the insistence of labor unions on pay increases even in periods of slack business activity.

Whatever the cause, high unemployment calls for expansionary monetary policy, and inflation calls for contraction. Under these circumstances the monetary managers have been perplexed as to what kind of policy to pursue. For the most part they have decided that unemployment was the greater evil. Their attempt to raise employment when prices were already rising has added fuel to the fire of inflation, in turn aggravating the dollar crisis in international trade. Both price and wage controls and devaluation of the dollar are results of the inability of monetary policy to achieve its objectives as effectively as could be wished.

See also Equation of Exchange; Fiscal Policy.

Consult (10) Carson, 1972; Jacoby, 1964; Lee, 1966; Mayer, 1968.

—Walter W. Haines, *New York University*

MONETARY THEORY OF BUSINESS CYCLES attributes fluctuations in economic activity to the expansion and contraction of money, credit, and interest rates. The quantity of money and the rate of interest are dependent on the decisions of monetary authorities, such as central banks in European countries or the U.S. Federal Reserve Board. The rate of interest and the level of income (or wealth), determined both by the authorities and by demand conditions, influence the level of investment which, through the multiplier, determines aggregate income. Thus, when interest rates and credit conditions are favorable, they encourage business to borrow (invest and spend). In a downswing, banks usually restrict credit by making less money available and increasing interest rates, because they are beginning to deplete their reserves and additional funds are not being extended. On the whole, contraction of the quantity of money is an internal factor influenced significantly by external forces which contribute to the cyclical process.

See also Business Cycles, Theories; External Theory of Business Cycles; Internal Theory of Business Cycles.

MONETARY UNIT. *See* Money.

MONEY, anything that is accepted as a means of payment at a given time and place. There is no single thing that universally serves as money. In primitive societies, money consisted of such valuable commodities as cattle, shells, or beads. The American colonies used wampum, tobacco, and beaver skins. More com-

MONEY

For further information on the money supply, see the articles on DEMAND DEPOSITS, NEAR MONEY, and MONEY SUPPLY. To see the theoretical basis behind the money supply, consult FRACTIONAL RESERVE. For views of the monetary and financial systems as a whole, refer to BANKING SYSTEM and FINANCIAL INTERMEDIARIES; some additional macroeconomic aspects are discussed in MONEY FLOW and MONETARY POLICY.

The Subject Maps accompanying this article and the article on BANKING SYSTEM show the relation of MONEY to other articles in the Encyclopedia.

MONEY AND MONETARY POLICY

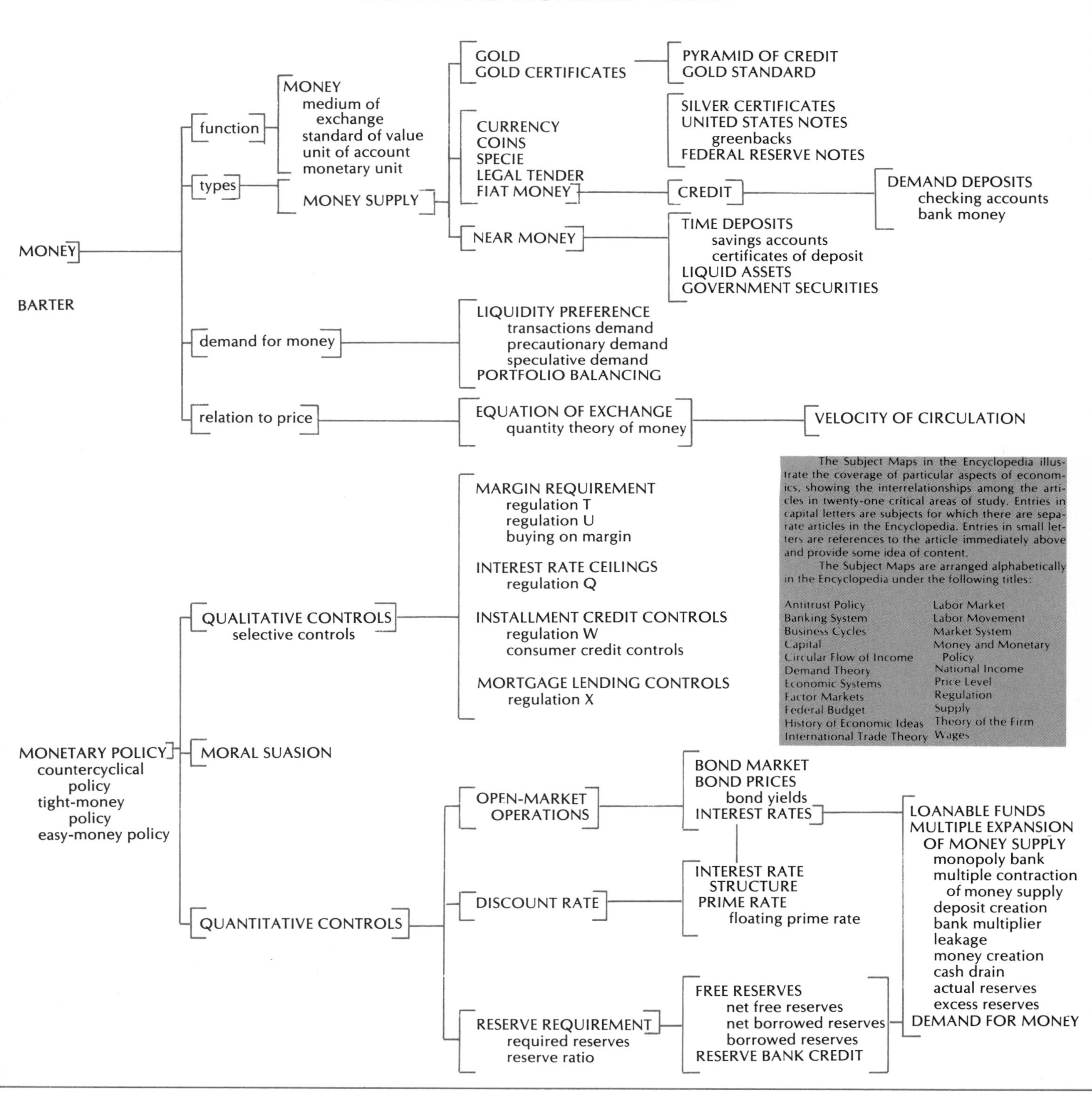

"Then it's agreed. Until the dollar firms up, we let the clamshell float."

Shells or silver, if exchangeable for goods or labor it's money, worth only what it can buy.

monly, nations have concentrated on gold and silver coin. Indeed, prior to the Civil War the United States government issued no money except coins and refused to receive taxes in anything except specie. Gold and silver certificates were basically warehouse receipts for an equal amount of specie in the Treasury's vault. As people became accustomed to the use of paper, they cared little about the backing, and other forms of paper currency became common. More recently, the extensive use of checks for payment of bills has made demand deposits of commercial banks the most common form of money.

The creation of money is traditionally a function of national sovereignty. The yen, for instance, is money in Japan but not in the United States. In international transactions, gold has been the traditional money, but today it is being replaced by special drawing rights (SDRs), a form of bank credit issued by the International Monetary Fund. Thus, in international as in domestic trade, money is rapidly becoming a ledger entry rather than a commodity even in token form. As long as people will accept it, the form that money takes is not important.

Medium of Exchange. Money as a medium of exchange developed naturally as a result of the disadvantages of barter as a means of trade. Barter requires a double coincidence of wants: one must want what the other fellow has and have what he wants in equal value. It is difficult to trade shoelaces for a horse, but by selling shoelaces to enough people for money, one can finally get the price of a horse. Only in a well developed money economy, where money wages can be spent for the hundreds of different products that workers want, is it possible to develop the specialization of labor that lies at the heart of economic efficiency and high productivity. Money that can be spent anywhere provides freedom of choice of goods, freedom of choice of jobs, as well as freedom of movement.

The Monetary Unit of a country is its standard of value, or unit of account. If a business has $10,000 in assets, the things it owns have that much value in terms of the monetary unit. In the United States the monetary unit is the dollar, defined as 12 12/19 grains of fine gold (which is the same as saying that gold is priced at $38 an ounce).

In the days of commodity money, when rice was money, for instance, its value depended on supply and demand, how much rice there was in comparison with the community's desire for rice; that is, if there was an abundant harvest, the value of rice (money) fell, and the rice-price of everything else rose. Although money no longer has any intrinsic value and can be produced in any quantity desired, its value still depends on supply and demand. The demand for money is essentially the sum total of things that money will buy, the output of the country in a given period. If the demand is given, any increase in the supply of money will lower its value, which is almost the same thing as a price increase. Inflation (a general rise in prices) is nothing more than much money chasing few goods. If there are 100 units of goods produced in a period when the available money supply is $100, the price of goods will be $1 each. Double the money supply, and prices rise to $2. It is for this reason that the quantity of money needs to be controlled by some form of government regulation, and in the United States this control is undertaken principally by the federal reserve system.

See also Banking System; Liquidity Preference; Money Flow; Monetary Policy; Money Supply.

Consult (8) Angell, 1929; Jevons, 1896; Ritter, 1970; Robertson, 1948.

—Walter W. Haines, *New York University*

MONEY CREATION. *See* Multiple Expansion of the Money Supply.

MONEY FLOW. The exchange of goods, services, and factors of production among various sectors of the economy would be difficult without the use of money as a medium of exchange to facilitate these real flows. Thus, in money-using economies, money flows develop in amounts equal to the value of real flows and in opposite directions. The money has no real value, in that it cannot be used to produce goods and services and it cannot be consumed. However, the money does represent a claim and as such enables real flows to occur more efficiently.

See also Circular Flow of Income; Real Flow.

MONEY SUPPLY. A nation's money supply consists of the immediately available purchasing power in the hands of the general public. In the United States at the present time the money supply consists of currency (coins and paper money) and demand deposits. In statistical terms the money supply is defined as currency outside banks plus demand deposits adjusted (the adjustment subtracts interbank and government deposits). The money supply so defined is often referred to as M_1. The change in both the amount and the composition of the United States money supply in the twentieth century is shown in the accompanying table.

The table shows that from a heterogeneous assortment of currency the money supply has been consolidated into minor (token) coins, federal reserve notes, and demand deposits. The table also shows that the money supply has multiplied by forty times in 71 years, an average rate of growth of 5.29 percent per year.

Alternative Measures of the Money Supply. Although near money is not immediate purchasing power, consumers frequently think of it as if it were, since they can withdraw funds from their savings accounts to make purchases. Some experts, therefore, believe that near money has almost the same effect on the economy as money itself and should be included in the concept of the money supply. An alternative concept of money, M_2, is defined as M_1 plus time deposits at commercial banks (but not including time certificates of deposit of more than $100,000). A third concept, M_3, adds in addition the deposits of mutual savings banks as well as shares of savings and loan associations.

See also Gold; Monetary Policy; Money; Near Money.

Consult (8) Federal Reserve Bank, 1967.

—Walter W. Haines, *New York University*

MONEY WAGES are the amount of money received for services rendered, hence, the price paid for labor. Money wages are usually paid an individual in the form of a wage rate per unit of time. They differ from real wages insofar as they do not consider the purchasing power of the money.

MONOPOLISTIC COMPETITION, one of four major markets that characterize the American economy, the other three being pure competition, oligopoly, and monopoly. Monopolistic competition is characterized by relatively many sellers in a market where the product of each seller is similar in nature, but differentiated in other ways. Examples of monopolistically competitive products are most clothing items, such as shoes and dresses, and various food products, such as frozen foods and canned foods. Because there are many sellers, no one seller has much influence over price and, therefore, must differentiate its product in order to gather a larger share of the market.

Demand Curve. With the exception of product differentiation, monopolistic competition has many of the characteristics of pure competition. There is usually relative ease of entry into a monopolistically competitive market. In addition, resources as well as goods and services in these markets are considerably mobile. And, as mentioned above, each seller has little, if any, influence over price because of the large number of firms in these markets. For these reasons, the demand curve of these markets is relatively elastic; that is, there can only be small variations in price, justified by product differentiation, if a seller wants to remain in the market, because the substitutability of these products is very great.

However, an exact representation of a demand curve for a monopolistically competitive product is very difficult because product differentiation can make similar products quite different. For example, toothpastes and toothpowders are virtually the same things in nature, but different in product. The same is true between fresh milks and powdered milks. Because of these minor distinctions the monopolistically competitive markets can allow for some restriction of output and increase in prices that cannot be allowed for in purely competitive markets. For this reason, marginal revenue is usually less than price, and output is usually short of that point where marginal cost equals price.

Market Structure. In discussing any market structure, a distinction must be made between short run and long run. The short run is that time span in which the firm is unable to change its scale of plant and, also, in which new firms do not have sufficient time to enter the market. For this reason, it is often possible for firms to achieve economic as well as normal profits in the short run. In the long run, however, if entry is not blocked and firms are free to enter and exit the market, there are no economic profits. The reason for this is that the entry of new firms shifts the demand curves faced by individual firms downward and cost curves of the firms upward, causing profits to decrease. New firms will continue to enter the market until the point where all pure profits have been eliminated.

The main advantage of monopolistically competitive markets to the consumer is that he is given a wide range of products, styles, and brands from which to choose.

Consult (14) Leftwich, 1970; Liebhafsky, 1968.

See also Imperfect Competition; Market Structure; Perfect Competition

—William D. Wagoner, *Louisiana State University*

MONOPOLISTIC PROFITS refer to those returns to input that are over and above the firm's total costs after a normal profit has been taken out. Monopolistic profits are called economic or pure profits and are found in industries that are less than perfectly competitive. Usually the fewer the number of firms in an industry, the greater the amount of monopolistic profits. For example, monopolistically competitive industries are expected to earn less monopolistic profits than oligopolistic or monopolistic industries.

Purely monopolistic industries are able to earn economic profits because their marginal revenue curve lies below their demand curve. For this reason, a monopoly firm can set

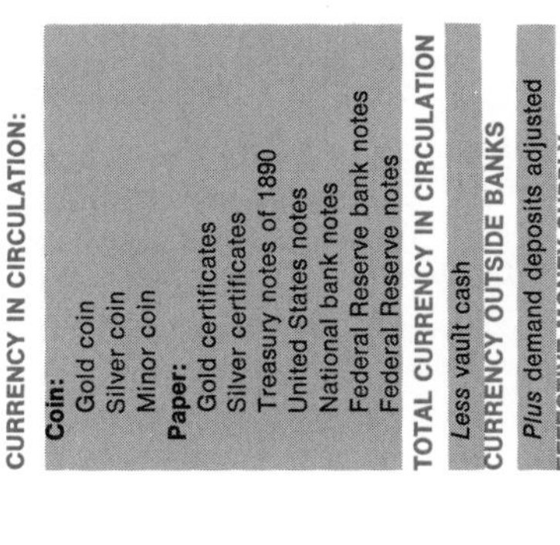

EFFECTIVE MONEY SUPPLY FOR SELECTED YEARS

(FIGURES FOR JUNE 30, IN MILLIONS OF DOLLARS)

CURRENCY IN CIRCULATION:	1900	1914	1929	1933	1945	1960	1971
Coin:							
Gold coin	611	325	81	34	0	0	0
Silver coin	142	230	328	285	913	1,789	482
Minor coin	26	57	115	113	292	549	5,990
Paper:							
Gold certificates	201	1,026	935	265	52	30	*
Silver certificates	408	479	387	361	1,652	2,128	296
Treasury notes of 1890	75	2	1	1	1	1	*
United States notes	318	338	262	269	323	318	321
National bank notes	300	715	653	920	120	56	*
Federal Reserve bank notes	0	0	4	126	527	100	*
Federal Reserve notes	0	0	1,693	3,061	22,867	27,094	51,304
TOTAL CURRENCY IN CIRCULATION	2,081	3,172	4,459	5,434	26,746	32,065	58,393
Less vault cash	750	1,639	820	673	1,649	3,765	7,393
CURRENCY OUTSIDE BANKS	1,331	1,533	3,639	4,761	25,097	28,300	51,000
Plus demand deposits adjusted	4,420	10,082	22,540	14,411	69,053	107,800	172,700
EFFECTIVE MONEY SUPPLY	5,751	11,615	26,179	19,172	94,150	136,100	223,700

*Included in the figure for silver certificates. All of these forms of currency are in the process of retirement.

ALTERNATIVE MEASURES OF THE MONEY SUPPLY

(FIGURES FOR JUNE 30, IN BILLIONS OF DOLLARS)

	1964	1971
M	154.2	223.7
M_2	261.3	449.1
M_3	403.1	687.1

MONOPOLY

For further consideration of monopoly as one type of market structure, see the articles on PERFECT COMPETITION, IMPERFECT COMPETITION, OLIGOPOLY, MONOPOLISTIC COMPETITION, and MONOPSONY. One of the numerous factors contributing to monopoly is discussed in BARRIERS TO ENTRY.

For an examination of the legal definition and status of monopoly, consult the relevant statutes and some of their most notable applications: The major statutes are examined in the articles on the SHERMAN ACT, CLAYTON ACT, and CELLER-KEFAUVER ACT; notable applications are described in UNITED STATES v. ALUMINUM CO. OF AMERICA, UNITED STATES v. STANDARD OIL CO. OF NEW JERSEY, and UNITED STATES v. E.I. duPONT AND CO. Additional details on legally prohibited and permissable actions are explained in RESTRAINT OF TRADE, PRICE FIXING, MONOPOLIZING, COLLUSION, MERGER, and RULE OF REASON.

An economically and socially defensible type of monopoly is explained in the article on PUBLIC UTILITIES.

The Subject Map accompanying the articles on ANTITRUST POLICY and REGULATION display the interrelations of these and other articles in the Encyclopedia.

Typical of monopolies developed from the need for economies of scale are public utilities.

its output at that point where marginal costs equal marginal revenue, but instead of setting its price at this point, it can set a higher price because of the position of the demand curve. This higher price results in pure or economic profits.

In an oligopolistic industry, an industry with only a few firms, output is again set at that point where marginal costs equal marginal revenue. However, again, the demand curve lies above the marginal revenue curve and a higher price can be set. Because of the unusually kinked demand curve that occurs, caused by the interdependence of the firms in an oligopolistic industry, all firms usually sell at the same price, producing a monopolistic effect. Because economic profits must be shared among the firms in the industry, these profits are usually less for each firm than they would be if the firm were a monopoly.

In monopolistically competitive markets, some, but relatively little, economic profits, occur. The reason is because the demand curve is less than perfectly elastic and causes the marginal revenue curve to fall somewhat below it.

See also Monopoly Profits; Profits.

Consult (14) Leftwich, 1970.

—William D. Wagoner, *Louisiana State University*

MONOPOLIZING, or MONOPOLIZATION, is the intent or attempt on the part of a business firm or firms to acquire a position of monopoly in a market by damaging or eliminating competitors. To the extent that oligopolists behave as one firm, have similar motives, and take similar actions against rivals, they can also monopolize.

There is an essential difference between monopoly, a type of market structure in economic analysis in which there is but one firm setting price and output for a product, and monopolizing, a legal concept describing the illegal behavior (predatory practices, sales below cost, local price discrimination) of one or more firms designed to damage economic rivals. In law (Sherman Antitrust Act, Section 2) a firm may be a monopoly without having monopolized (if it can show that "monopoly was thrust" upon it); a firm may have monopolized without achieving a monopoly. The act's prohibition clearly is against monopolizing. For while the result (monopoly) threatened by monopolizing is feared, the legal proscription of monopolizing looks to the anticompetitive effects of a monopolizing firm's behavior toward rivals. Thus, interpretation of the Sherman Act has emphasized the acquisition and use of economic power against actual or potential rivals rather than the structure of markets.

See also Collusion; Monopoly Thrust Upon a Firm; Oligopoly; Predatory Practices; United States v. Aluminum Company of America; United States v. U.S. Steel Corp.

Consult (16) Sichel, 1967; Wilcox, 1971.

—Thomas O. Depperschmidt, *Memphis State University*

MONOPOLY, a market structure in which there is only one seller in the industry and there are no perfect substitutes for the product. Thus, the firm has no rivals or competition, a condition that can only persist if entry into the industry is blocked. This is done in several ways. For example, a natural monopoly can exist when the economies of scale are so pronounced that competition is impractical, inconvenient, and unworkable. A second block to entry occurs when the government reserves exclusive rights of production to itself, or to firms that it designates by means of a license. A third, but less effective, bar to entry is the patent right.

Economies of scale are an important factor in monopolies, because most monopolies require huge investments and, to be profitable, the firm's average cost scale must decline over a wide range of output. Public utilities, such as American Telephone and Telegraph, having high investment costs, are perfect examples of this need for economies of scale. In addition, it can easily be seen that duplication of certain utility lines, such as telephone and gas lines, cannot be profitable.

Monopoly price determination is almost always on a profit maximizing basis, although in special cases, the price set is a socially optimum one. A monopoly, like all other market structures, produces output to the point where marginal cost equals marginal revenue. However, instead of charging the price indicated at that point, the monopolist can charge a higher price because of lack of competition.

Regulation. There are two main reasons why some economists feel that monopoly should be minimized. First, in any situation where price is higher than marginal cost there is a misallocation of resources. Second, monopoly tends to lower the incentive for cost reducing technology and for the development of new and better products. Because of the "restraints of trade" that a monopoly imposes on the public, the government has attempted to curtail monopoly power by law. The Sherman Antitrust Act of 1890 and the Clayton Antitrust Act of 1914 make any attempt to monopolize trade a criminal offense against the federal government. The Federal Trade Commission was also set up in 1914 and given the power to investigate unfair business practices and to take legal action if required.

Consult (14) Leftwich, 1970; Liebhafsky, 1968.

See also Imperfect Competition.

—William D. Wagoner, *Louisiana State University*

MONOPOLY BANK. *See* Multiple Expansion of the Money Supply.

MONOPOLY PROFITS. There are several types of profit that a firm can reap. Firms in purely competitive industries enjoy what is called normal profits. A monopoly firm also enjoys normal profits, but in addition, receives economic or pure profits. Normal profits are simply the minimum return to inputs (capital and labor) necessary to maintain a given production level. Therefore, when a firm receives a price that is set at the point where its marginal cost is equal to the marginal revenue it earns normal profits.

Pure Profits, however, are the returns to a production level over and above all cost, both implicit and explicit, or that amount of revenue left over after all costs have been covered.

A monopoly industry is able to earn pure profits because its marginal revenue curve lies below its demand curve. Therefore, a monopoly sets its output at that point where marginal costs equal marginal revenue, the point at which a competitive firm or industry would also set price. However, because of the placement of the demand curve of a monopolist, he is able to charge a higher price and in this way earn pure profits.

The pure profits of a monopolist represent a misallocation of resources, however, and often a certain amount of inefficiency in the industry.

See also Monopolistic Competition; Profits.

—William D. Wagoner, *Louisiana State University*

MONOPOLY THRUST UPON A FIRM describes a defense plea to a charge of monopolizing under Section 2 of the Sherman Antitrust Act. It means that a firm, having obtained dominance or monopoly in a market, argues that it achieved its position through normal, benign, and legal business practices, without intent or attempt to monopolize. The plea has legal status, but has not been employed with much success, for the firm using it must be free of virtually all semblance of wrongdoing in its relations with competitors.

See also Antitrust Policy; Monopolizing; Predatory Practices; United States v. Aluminum Co. of America.

MONOPSONY, a market in which there is only one buyer. An example of a monopsony would be a single firm in an industry purchasing the factors of production for that industry. The monopsony is commonly known as a buyers' monopoly. In the labor market the monopsonist is able to pay a wage lower than the value of output produced by the marginal worker (exploitation of labor). A typical monopsony is the telephone industry, where the telephone company is the only employer of telephone operators.

MONTIAS, JOHN MICHAEL (1928-), French-born educator noted for his work in comparative economics. He received his B.A. (1947), M.A. (1949), and Ph.D (1958) in economics from Columbia University. His publications include: *Institutional Changes in the Postwar Economy of Poland* (1955, with W. Stankiewicz), *Central Planning in Poland* (1962), and *Economic Development in Communist Rumania* (1967). He was a United Nations economic officer from 1950-53 and he has been an adviser to a panel on East-West trade of the Committee on Economic Development. He is currently professor of economics and chairman of the Council on Russian and East European Studies at Yale University.

John M. Montias

MOONLIGHTING, the taking on of an additional job by workers who are employed at a regular full-time job. The term originated because these second jobs are very often night jobs. Workers who moonlight are predominantly men, between the ages of twenty-five and forty-four, with growing family responsibilities. The primary reason for moonlighting is financial pressure, with 40% of all moonlighters working to meet regular expenses and 10% working to pay off debts. One-sixth of moonlighters are women.

MORAL SUASION refers to pressure exerted on the banking system or the public by the federal reserve system in an attempt to achieve specific objectives of monetary policy, but without compulsion. The most important forms of moral suasion are: (1) suggestions made during bank examination with respect to the volume, kind, or safety of the bank's various loans and investments; (2) discussions with banks under a program of informal visitation for the purpose of explaining federal reserve objectives and policies; and (3) publicity directed toward the general public, including information and statistics concerning the present state of the economy, explanations of the nature of federal reserve operations and objectives, and admonitions with respect to current policy.

During the Korean War the federal reserve encouraged and coordinated voluntary agreements among financial institutions to restrain the inflationary expansion of that period. The program was suspended in 1952 as inflationary pressures eased.

See also Monetary Policy.

"Boys—Please—Are You Listening To Me?"

6/30/57

Even if coercive measures are available, leadership may first try moral suasion to gain objectives.

MORTGAGE LENDING CONTROLS prescribe the minimum down payment and the maximum repayment period on mortgage loans. Such controls were established by the Board of

Coca-Cola in Amharic

Coca-Cola in Bengali

Fanta in Amharic

Fanta in Bengali

Sprite in Amharic

Coca-Cola in Chinese

Coca-Cola in Arabic

Fanta in Chinese

Coca-Cola in Cyrillic

Coca-Cola in Japanese

KOKA-KOΛA
Coca-Cola in Greek

Coke in Japanese

Coca-Cola in Hebrew

Fanta in Japanese

Coca-Cola in South Korean

Sprite in Japanese

Sprite in Thai

Coca-Cola in Thai

Coca-Cola in Turkish

Fanta in Thai

A multinational company must often cope with a wide variety of work customs and even languages.

Governors of the federal reserve system under the Defense Production Act of 1950 and published as Regulation X. They were discontinued in 1953.

MOST-FAVORED NATION. *See* General Agreement on Tariffs and Trade.

MOTOR CARRIER ACT (1935), the basic law regulating motor transportation and a portion of the Interstate Commerce Act. It has six basic parts. Carriers are classified as common carriers, contract carriers, private carriers, brokers, and exempt carriers. Entry is controlled by use of certificates of public convenience and necessity and permits by a grandfather clause. Rates are controlled in the same manner as railroad rates, consolidations and mergers are controlled, and securities and accounts are supervised. Finally, a series of innovational regulatory devices such as exemptions, joint boards, and insurance controls are utilized. It is essentially a modification of railroad regulation imposed on trucks and buses.

See also Common Carrier; Grandfather Clause; Interstate Commerce Act.

MPS. *See* Marginal Propensity to Save.

MULTI-EMPLOYER BARGAINING occurs when a union representing workers in several or all firms in an industry enters into contract bargaining with a number of employers simultaneously. It is likely to result when either party considers uniform contract provisions desirable and individual bargaining wasteful, difficult, or undesirable. Employers may favor this type of bargaining in an attempt to protect themselves from "whipsaw" tactics (playing one employer against another).

See also Collective Bargaining.

MULTINATIONAL COMPANY, a firm based in one country with operations in one or more additional countries. In 1972, about 60% of multinational companies were American-based.

Some controversy surrounds the legal status of American-based multinational companies. Proponents argue that they tend to break down trade barriers and promote cooperation among countries. Opponents, especially in labor groups, contend that domestic unemployment is increased, and that these firms enjoy unfair tax advantage over smaller domestic companies and aggravate the balance-of-payments problem.

MULTINATIONAL TRADE AGREEMENTS. In a conference at Havana in 1948 a charter for an International Trade Organization (ITO) was approved by representatives of 54 countries. The United States failed to ratify the charter and the ITO never came into existence. However, many provisions of the charter are embodied in the General Agreement on Tariffs and Trade (GATT). Significant characteristics of GATT, based in Geneva, are its general provisions, which constitute a code of commercial policy, and the multilateral approach to negotiations. Among the general provisions of GATT are unconditional most-favored-nation treatment, elimination of quantitative restrictions, and the obligation to negotiate tariff reductions at the request of a member. The 70-odd members of GATT have met at least once a year since 1948. Between sessions work is carried on by a Council of Representatives (delegates from participating nations). In addition, major tariff negotiating conferences are held when deemed desirable by a consensus of member countries. There have been six bargaining conferences thus far: 1947, 1949, 1951, 1956, 1962, 1964. Prior to 1964, the United States attended on the basis of the Reciprocal Trade Agreements Act; the Trade Expansion Act of 1962 gave the nation new bargaining areas and the call for the conference led to the "Kennedy Round." GATT deals with underdeveloped nations under the aegis of UNCTAD—United National Conference on Trade and Development.

See also General Agreement on Tariffs and Trade.

—John R. Matthews, Jr., *College of William and Mary*

MULTI-PLANT FIRM, a business unit with more than one production facility, or plant. Typically, economic analysis distinguishes between the firm, as the organizational-administrative-financial aspect of a business unit, and the plant, as the physical production unit. Most major, national, goods-producing firms are multi-plant in nature.

MULTIPLE CONTRACTION OF THE MONEY SUPPLY. *See* Multiple Expansion of the Money Supply.

MULTIPLE DETERMINATION. *See* Correlation.

MULTIPLE EXPANSION OF THE MONEY SUPPLY, the power of commercial banks to increase the money supply through the creation of demand deposits on the basis of a fractional reserve system. Because demand deposits are considered by the public to be money (they can be spent at any time by writing a check), any increase in such deposits represents an increase in the money supply. Because they are simply liabilities of the bank, representing the amounts the bank has promised to pay to depositors against their checks, a bank can increase its deposits at any time by crediting a customer's deposit account.

Loans. Banks increase their deposits by accepting cash or checks for the account of the depositor (primary or deposited deposits) and by creating a deposit for a borrower in exchange for his promissory note (derivative or created deposits). Thus they create money whenever they make a loan. The limits to a bank's ability to lend are determined by its reserve requirement compared to the *actual reserves* held in the form of cash, deposits with a federal reserve bank, or other assets normally acceptable as reserves. More precisely, any commercial bank may make loans equal to its *excess reserves,* which are computed by subtracting *required reserves* (either legal reserves or the amount of reserves the bank feels that it is necessary to set aside to meet normal withdrawals) from its actual reserves. Thus, if a bank has $100 million in deposit liabilities, $20 million in actual reserves, and a reserve requirement of 18%, its required reserves are $18 million, and its excess reserves are $2 million. This $2 million is the amount of new money the bank can create by making loans.

To take a simpler illustration, if a customer deposits $100 in cash in a commercial bank A, and bank A has a reserve requirement of 20%, only $20 must be kept in reserves, and the bank may lend the other $80, usually by simply crediting the borrower's deposit account so that he can write checks in the amount of the loan. Thus, the bank has increased the money supply by $80, or 80% of the original deposit. Normally the borrower does not keep this money on deposit: he borrowed it to pay a bill of some kind. If he writes a check against his account for the full $80 and gives it to his creditor, who deposits it in bank B, bank B now has an additional $80 of deposits and reserves. If this bank also has a reserve requirement of 20%, $16 must be reserved and $64 may be lent. This process can continue through a long chain of banks, as shown in the table.

Bank Multiplier. If nothing occurs to interrupt the process, the total monetary expansion of the whole banking system is a multiple (in this case, 5) of the initial deposit. That is, total deposits are $500.00 ($100.00 by cash and $400.00 by check), or 5 times the initial deposit of $100.00. The total loans made are $400.00, or 5 times the initial increase in excess reserves of $80.00. The bank multiplier is, thus, the reciprocal of the reserve requirement. A high reserve requirement inhibits expansion, and a low reserve requirement encourages expansion.

Leakages. The bank multiplier applied to an initial figure for excess reserves for the banking system as a whole shows the maximum possible expansion of the money supply. Leakages are apt to occur to reduce the actual expansion below this amount. The most common leakage is a cash drain, which is when depositors withdraw their funds in cash. This amount of reserves is lost to the banking system. Funds may be diverted from commercial banks to savings banks, which are unable to create money, because checks cannot be written against their deposit accounts. It is unlikely that banks will lend exactly the amount of their excess reserves, and if business is slow, banks may lend a great deal less than the maximum possible.

Multiple Contraction of the Money Supply. It is clear that multiple expansion of money supply depends on the existence of excess reserves. If the monetary authorities wish to reduce the money supply they can force a contraction by reducing excess reserves to a negative figure. For instance, if a bank has $100 million in deposit liabilities, $20 million in actual reserves, and a legal reserve requirement of 20%, it is "loaned up" and cannot expand at all. If the legal reserve is then raised to 21%, the bank's required reserves rise to $21 million, of which it has only $20 million. It must acquire more reserves by selling securities or borrowing (which are likely to be short-run solutions), or it must reduce the volume of its loans and deposits (usually by letting loans "run off," accepting payment for matured loans while not making new ones). At maturity the borrower pays his loan by writing a check against his account, thereby reducing the total deposits of the bank by the amount of the payment. Just as $1 million in excess reserves with 20% reserve requirement permits an expansion of $5 million in loans and deposits, a deficiency of $1 million in reserves requires a contraction of $5 million in deposits. The process is exactly the reverse of the one already described.

Consult (10) Federal Reserve Bank of Chicago, 1961; Haines, 1966.

—Walter W. Haines, *New York University*

MAXIMUM POSSIBLE EXPANSION OF THE MONEY SUPPLY ON THE BASIS OF A NEW DEPOSIT OF $100 AND A UNIFORM RESERVE REQUIREMENT OF 20 PERCENT

	Increase in actual reserves		Increase in required reserves	Increase in excess reserves	Loans made
	by cash deposit	by deposit of check drawn on preceding bank			
Bank A	$100.00		$20.00	$80.00	$80.00
B		$80.00	16.00	64.00	64.00
C		64.00	12.80	51.20	51.20
D		51.20	10.24	40.96	40.96
E		40.96	8.19	32.77	32.77
F		32.77	6.56	26.21	26.21
G		26.21	5.24	20.97	20.97
H		20.97	4.19	16.78	16.78
I		16.78	3.36	13.42	13.42
J		13.42	2.68	10.74	10.74
First 10 banks	$100.00	$346.31	$89.26	$357.05	$357.05
All remaining banks		53.69	10.74	42.95	42.95
Total, all banks	$100.00	$400.00	$100.00	$400.00	$400.00

MULTIPLIER, the ratio of the ultimate increase in income caused by an original increase in spending to that original increase; or the process by which the original increase in spending gives rise to the ultimate increase in income. In early expositions of national income determination the original change was an increase (or decrease) in investment, partly to show that the fluctuations in national income could occur quite independently of government policy, and partly because spending on investment goods is considered the least stable component of aggregate demand and, hence, the most important in accounting for the business cycle. However, the original change in spending can equally well be in consumption (upward or downward shift in the consumption function), in government spending, or in net exports (purchases by foreigners).

The Process. As a process, the multiplier is the sequence of consumption spendings set off by the original increase in spending. The original increase, being new, will add to the incomes of some people, who will spend a

MULTIPLIER

The basic theoretical concept underlying the multiplier is explained in the article on the CIRCULAR FLOW OF INCOME. The significance of the multiplier is shown in the articles on the INFLATIONARY GAP and NATIONAL INCOME DETERMINATION (especially those parts dealing with changes in the level of national income.)

Gunnar Myrdal

Richard A. Musgrave

portion of their new incomes on consumption, in turn adding to the incomes of other people, who will then spend, and so on. Since the marginal propensity to consume (MPC) is less than 1.00, each stage in the series will be smaller than the previous one, in a declining series. As a ratio, the multiplier equals 1/(1 − MPC).

Tax-reduction and transfer-payment multipliers are one less than the investment, government spending, consumption spending, and net export multipliers, because the first stage (leaving people with larger disposable incomes by not taking from them or giving them more) is not a payment for services rendered, and does not involve tangible spending.

The balanced budget multiplier, where all additional government spending on goods and services is exactly balanced by increased tax revenues, is 1.00; because, on the one hand, the additional government spending sets off an upward multiplier process while, on the other hand, the increase in taxes sets off a downward multiplier effect by reducing the disposable income of consumers. In the latter, downward process, the first stage is not a reduction in spending, but causes a "second stage" reduction in spending of (MPC) × (Change in after-tax income). One can view the balanced budget multiplier either as a full upward multiplier effect minus a tax increase multiplier (the same as a negative tax reduction multiplier), or as a full multiplier of the net effect of increase in government spending minus the decrease in consumption spending.

—Walter C. Neale, *University of Tennessee*

MUNICIPAL TAX EXEMPT BONDS. The interest on state and local government bonds is not subject to federal income taxation. Originally, based on the doctrine of intergovernmental tax immunity ("the power to tax is the power to destroy"), this provision now provides an important source of tax avoidance for investors and at the same time enables state and local governments to sell their securities at less than market interest rates.

MUNN v. ILLINOIS (1877), the original Supreme Court decision upholding the legal right of the public to regulate business "affected with the public interest." Using ancient common law precedents, the court upheld the public's right to regulation of special categories of business where "clothed with the public interest."

MUSGRAVE, RICHARD ABEL (1910-), German-born educator and authority on fiscal policy and taxation. He received a diploma from the University of Heidelberg in 1933, and earned both his M.A. (1936) and Ph.D. (1937) in economics from Harvard University. His major publications include *The Theory of Public Finance* (1958), *Fiscal Systems* (1969), and *The Shifting of the Corporation Tax* (1963, co-authored with M. Krzyzaniak). Musgrave has consulted with the governments of Colombia, Burma, Japan, and Puerto Rico in the fields of fiscal policy and planning, and with Chile, Taiwan, and Colombia in the field of tax reform. He is currently the Harold Hitchings Burbank professor of political economy at Harvard University and professor of economics at Harvard Law School.

MYERS, CHARLES ANDREW (1913-), American economist and expert on industrial relations. A graduate of Pennsylvania State College (1934), he received his Ph.D. from the University of Chicago (1939). His publications include *Labor Problems in the Industrialization of India* (1958), *Education, Manpower and Economic Growth* (1964, with Frederick Harbison), and *Personnel Administration* (1969, with Paul Pigors). Myers has been a member of the federal advisory council on employment security (1957-59) and president of the Industrial Relations Research Association (1962). He became Sloan Fellows professor of management at M.I.T. in 1967.

MYRDAL, GUNNAR (1898-). An outstanding Swedish economist and social thinker, Myrdal has made important contributions to economic theory in the areas of economic development, international trade, and macroeconomic theory and policy and has addressed questions such as the use of the scientific method and the racial problem in the United States.

Myrdal is probably best known for his study of the race problem in *The American Dilemma* (1944). However, his early work on the saving-investment relationship and his discussions of the problems of development are more important from an economic standpoint.

He feels that the gains to underdeveloped nations which international trade theory predicts will result from trade with developed countries do not really exist. In addition, Myrdal feels that the gap between the rich nations and the poor nations is widening and traditional economic policies are unable to cope with the problem. The governments of underdeveloped countries, therefore, must play a larger role in the implementation of economic planning to promote progress. These plans should include a more equitable distribution of income, the volume and distribution among sectors of investment, and the control of foreign trade. Myrdal takes this stand on the role of government in underdeveloped countries because he feels that such countries function in an institutional framework that operates against their interest.

—Clyde A. Haulman, *College of William and Mary*

NATIONAL APPRENTICESHIP ACT. *See* Apprenticeship.

NATIONAL ASSOCIATION OF SECURITIES DEALERS. *See* Stock Market.

NATIONAL BANK, a commercial bank that chooses to obtain a charter from the federal government under the National Bank Act (1863) as amended, particularly by the Federal Reserve Act (1913). National banks are chartered by the Comptroller of the Currency and are under his supervision and that of the federal reserve system, of which they must be members, and that of Federal Deposit Insurance Corporation, which they are required to join. Subject primarily to federal law, they are also subject to the law of the state in which they operate, and they cannot carry on a public banking business in more than one state. Although only one-third of the commercial banks in the United States are national banks, they hold two-thirds of the deposits.

NATIONAL DEBT, INTEREST. In order to carry a national debt, a nation must pay interest, which is the price of borrowing money. Interest payments on the national debt depend upon the size of the outstanding debt and the market rate of interest on federal securities. The actual interest rate on comparable securities influences the interest rate the government must pay to borrow money. Tax revenues finance the interest payments. Keeping these payments low reduces the amount of tax revenues needed. But during recessionary periods, this can cause instability in the economy. Higher interest rates and the growth of the federal debt have caused interest payments to increase in recent years. At present, total interest payments made by the federal government amount to approximately $21 billion.

NATIONAL FARMERS ORGANIZATION. *See* Farmers Organization, National.

NATIONAL FARMERS UNION. *See* Farmers Union, National.

NATIONAL GRANGE. *See* Grange, National.

NATIONAL HEALTH INSURANCE. Many countries operate some form of comprehensive program of compulsory health insurance that provides coverage for all residents. Programs may be financed by special taxes earmarked for the purpose, funded from general tax revenues, or a combination of the above. Personnel in the health services industry (including physicians) may be employees of the government or may be in private practice and receive partial or total reimbursement of fees. Patients may be free to choose their physicians or may be assigned them by a government agency. The plan may cover in part or in full the cost of dental service, drugs, and devices such as eyeglasses, crutches, and wheel chairs. A national health insurance program, even if comprehensive, need not preclude continuance of private practice for clientele willing to pay.

See also Social Insurance.

NATIONAL INCOME may refer either to a specific accounting measure or to a general concept of the total value of goods and services produced in an economy during a particular period, such as a year.

As a specific measure national income is defined as Net National Product (that is, Gross National Product less depreciation) minus indirect business taxes and is a measure of the total cost of factors of production used in the production of the NNP, or of total incomes earned in producing the GNP. Indirect business taxes are part of the price or total value of output but are not payments to a factor of production.

As a general concept and as commonly used in the theory of national income determination, however, the term refers either to a gross or net value of an economy's output, or expenditures for that output. National income (or "Y," its usual symbol) is thus defined as the sum of C (consumption) + I (investment) + G (government expenditure for goods and services) + (X − M) or net exports. In the theory of national income determination this definition is sufficient.

Specific Measures. For calculating a country's national product or income a number of specific measures and procedures known as national income accounts and accounting have been developed. National income does *not* refer to the total wealth of a country. The total wealth would include the value of all the capital, land, and natural resources, and every other material thing of value.

See also Capital; Gross National Product; National Income Measurement.

—Anne Mayhew, *University of Tennessee*

NATIONAL INCOME, CHANGES *See* National Income Determination.

NATIONAL INCOME ACCOUNTING. *See* National Income Measurement.

NATIONAL INCOME AND ITS COMPOSITION 1919–38 (1941). *See* Kuznets, Simon.

NATIONAL INCOME
(BILLIONS OF DOLLARS)

	Total	Compensation of employees	Business and professional income	Income of farm proprietors	Rental income of persons	Corporate profits and inventory valuation adjustment	Net interest
1960	414.5	294.2	34.2	12.0	15.8	49.9	8.4
1961	427.3	302.6	35.6	12.8	16.0	50.3	10.0
1962	457.7	323.6	37.1	13.0	16.7	55.7	11.6
1963	481.9	341.0	37.9	13.1	17.1	58.9	13.8
1964	518.1	365.7	40.2	12.1	18.0	66.3	15.8
1965	564.3	393.8	42.4	14.8	19.0	76.1	18.2
1966	620.6	435.5	45.2	16.1	20.0	82.4	21.4
1967	653.6	467.2	47.3	14.8	21.1	78.7	24.4
1968	711.1	514.6	49.5	14.7	21.2	84.3	26.9
1969	763.7	565.5	50.3	16.8	22.6	78.6	29.9
1970	795.9	601.9	51.0	15.8	23.3	70.8	33.0
1971	850.8	641.8	52.1	16.3	24.3	80.7	35.6

NATIONAL INCOME

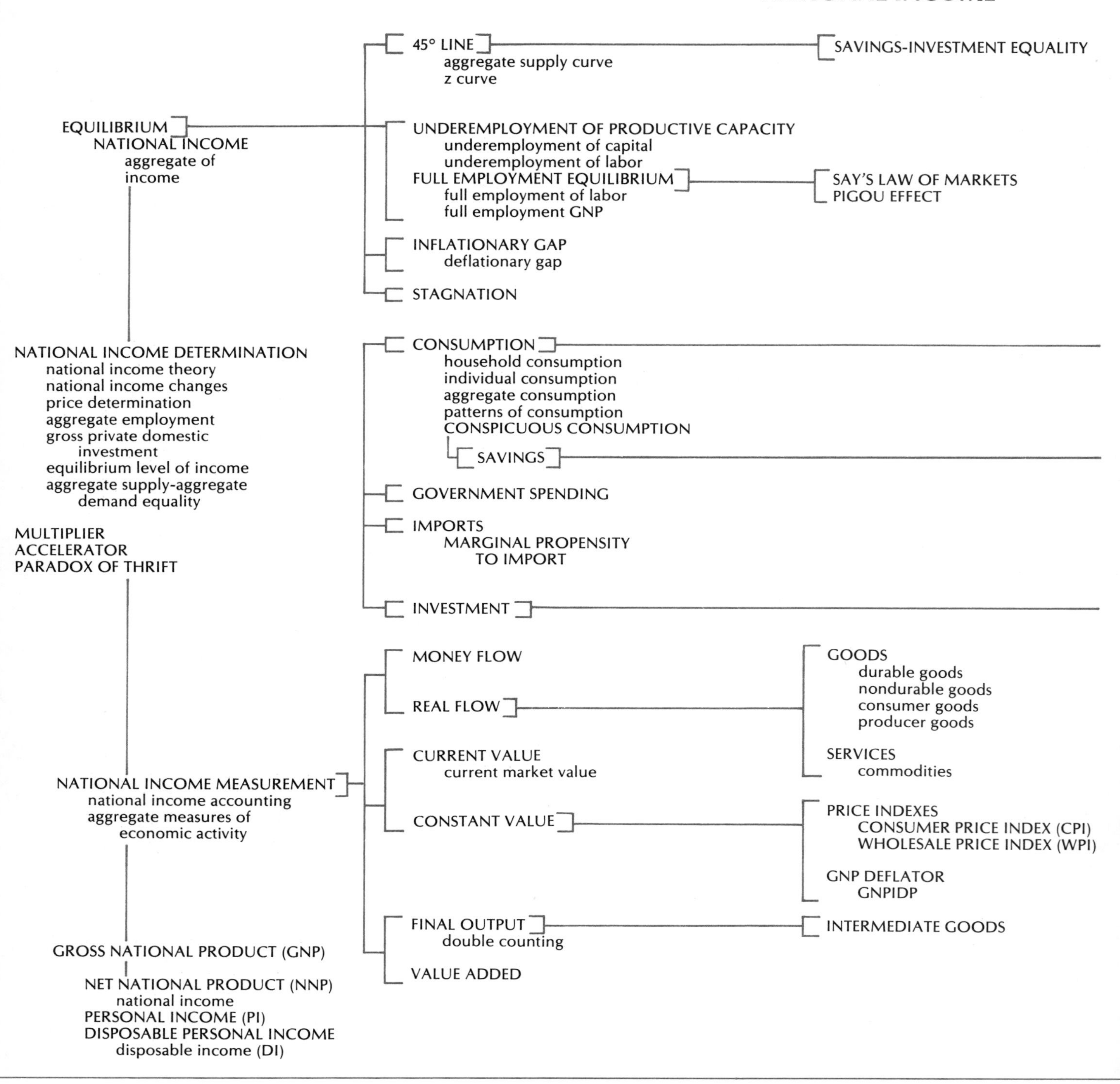

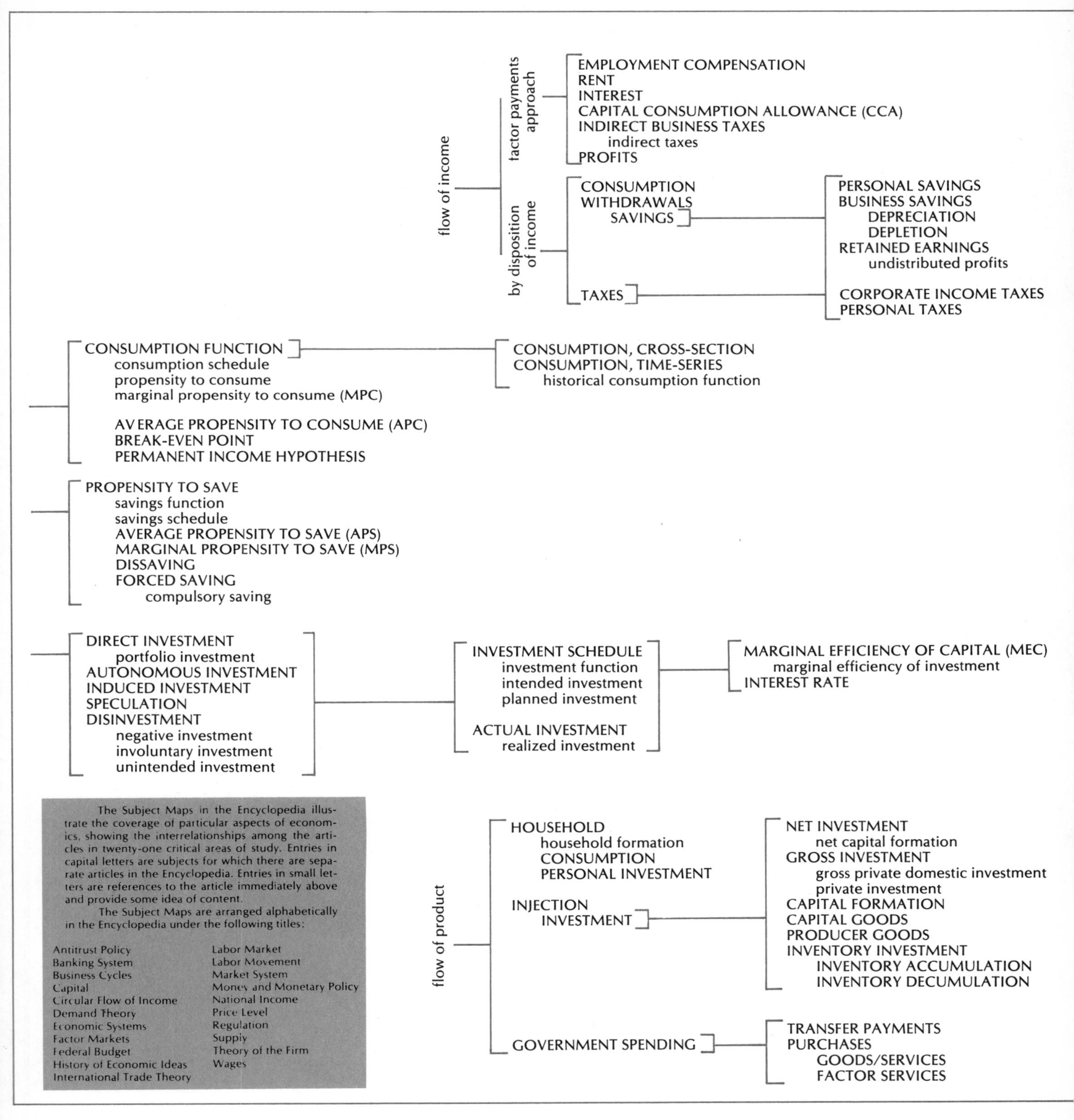
flow of income
factor payments approach
EMPLOYMENT COMPENSATION
RENT
INTEREST
CAPITAL CONSUMPTION ALLOWANCE (CCA)
INDIRECT BUSINESS TAXES
indirect taxes
PROFITS
by disposition of income
CONSUMPTION
WITHDRAWALS
SAVINGS
PERSONAL SAVINGS
BUSINESS SAVINGS
DEPRECIATION
DEPLETION
RETAINED EARNINGS
undistributed profits
TAXES
CORPORATE INCOME TAXES
PERSONAL TAXES
CONSUMPTION FUNCTION
consumption schedule
propensity to consume
marginal propensity to consume (MPC)
AVERAGE PROPENSITY TO CONSUME (APC)
BREAK-EVEN POINT
PERMANENT INCOME HYPOTHESIS
CONSUMPTION, CROSS-SECTION
CONSUMPTION, TIME-SERIES
historical consumption function
PROPENSITY TO SAVE
savings function
savings schedule
AVERAGE PROPENSITY TO SAVE (APS)
MARGINAL PROPENSITY TO SAVE (MPS)
DISSAVING
FORCED SAVING
compulsory saving
DIRECT INVESTMENT
portfolio investment
AUTONOMOUS INVESTMENT
INDUCED INVESTMENT
SPECULATION
DISINVESTMENT
negative investment
involuntary investment
unintended investment
INVESTMENT SCHEDULE
investment function
intended investment
planned investment
ACTUAL INVESTMENT
realized investment
MARGINAL EFFICIENCY OF CAPITAL (MEC)
marginal efficiency of investment
INTEREST RATE
The Subject Maps in the Encyclopedia illustrate the coverage of particular aspects of economics, showing the interrelationships among the articles in twenty-one critical areas of study. Entries in capital letters are subjects for which there are separate articles in the Encyclopedia. Entries in small letters are references to the article immediately above and provide some idea of content.
The Subject Maps are arranged alphabetically in the Encyclopedia under the following titles:
Antitrust Policy
Banking System
Business Cycles
Capital
Circular Flow of Income
Demand Theory
Economic Systems
Factor Markets
Federal Budget
History of Economic Ideas
International Trade Theory
Labor Market
Labor Movement
Market System
Money and Monetary Policy
National Income
Price Level
Regulation
Supply
Theory of the Firm
Wages
flow of product
HOUSEHOLD
household formation
CONSUMPTION
PERSONAL INVESTMENT
INJECTION
INVESTMENT
NET INVESTMENT
net capital formation
GROSS INVESTMENT
gross private domestic investment
private investment
CAPITAL FORMATION
CAPITAL GOODS
PRODUCER GOODS
INVENTORY INVESTMENT
INVENTORY ACCUMULATION
INVENTORY DECUMULATION
GOVERNMENT SPENDING
TRANSFER PAYMENTS
PURCHASES
GOODS/SERVICES
FACTOR SERVICES

THE NATIONAL INCOME ACCOUNTS FOR 1970
(CURRENT DOLLARS)

	In Billions	
Gross national product		$974
Deduct: Capital consumption allowances (mainly business depreciation allowances)	$ 88	
Net national product		886
Deduct: Indirect business taxes	93	
National income		793
Deduct: Corporation profits	71	
Social security taxes	56	
Add: Transfer and interest payments	112	
Dividends	25	
Personal income		803
Deduct: Personal taxes	115	
Disposable personal income		688
Of which: Consumer outlays		634
Personal saving		54

NATIONAL INCOME AND PRODUCT ACCOUNTS, a generic term used in national accounting, refers to series of statistical statements of aggregate national output or income, published regularly, usually monthly or quarterly, by the US Department of Commerce. These statistics are used by economists in every sector—business, industry, and government—to determine the present level of productivity, and as a base from which to forecast future economic growth and expansion.

The economic measurements, indices, and components used to determine national income were developed by the National Bureau of Economic Research, which began its studies in this area during the 1920s and 1930s. The Congress directed the preparation of national income accounts in 1932, and a few years later the Department of Commerce began issuing its regular statistical statements. The monthly personal income series was initiated in the late 1930s. During World War II, the development of the Gross National Product (GNP) series was accelerated because of its value in planning the war effort and in instituting controls.

During the postwar period, the accounts were extended beyond the original scope of measuring the size and composition of national output. Today, they include not only the GNP and personal income series, but Net National Product and disposable income series, as well as the following individual indices: consolidated business income and products accounts, construction contract award data, gross savings and investment accounts, import and export statistics, and a variety of other data, such as consolidated government receipts and expenditures, and new business starts and business failures.

This statistical information is augmented regularly by the Department of Commerce breakdown of national income by industry, listing the income in terms of dollars and as a percentage of the country's total output.

The diversity of the data that contribute to the make-up of national income and product accounts, when combined into a unified statistical statement, provides a picture of the total volume of production of goods and services over a specific period.

See also Business Cycles, Measurement.

NATIONAL INCOME DETERMINATION (National Income Theory). According to modern, or Keynesian, theory, national income, the value of an economy's output during a year, is determined by a country's productive capacity *and* the demand for that output. Pre-Keynesian economics emphasized the productive capacity, or ability to supply output, as the determinant of the level of national income. The ability of an economy to produce goods and services limits the level of real national income, but within this limit it is the level of total (aggregate) demand for currently produced goods and services that determines how much will be produced.

Aggregate Demand. Total, or aggregate, demand is divided into four categories: (1) the demand of households for consumption goods and services, or consumption (C); (2) the demand of businesses for capital goods, or investment (I); (3) the demand of governments for goods and services, government expenditure (G); and (4) the net foreign demand for goods and services (exports minus imports: X−M, or F). So, aggregate demand and, therefore, national income (Y) are equal to C + I + G + F. Aggregate demand is divided into these four categories because the reasons for spending are different in all four cases.

Households spend to keep the family alive and happy. In national income theory it is assumed (fairly accurately) that consumption is determined by households' disposable income. If one ignores taxes and transfer payments and that part of national income retained by businesses as depreciation allowances and retained earnings, consumption may be said to be a function of national income. Savings, that part of disposable income not spent on consumption, is, therefore, also a function of income.

Business firms spend to earn profits from investment. Investment demand is assumed to consist of two parts: (1) autonomous investment demand, which is not determined by the current level of income; and (2) induced investment, which does vary with the level of income. In national income theory investment is frequently called gross private domestic investment because (1) it is the total expenditure for goods currently produced in the country that is of concern, and whether those goods are purchased to replace equipment or to add to the stock of capital goods is not important in determining the level of total demand; and (2) although governments buy capital goods, these public expenditures are included in government expenditures.

Governments spend to carry out public policies of all kinds, ranging from economic stabilization to defense to public education. Government demand for goods and services is assumed to be autonomous, not related to or determined by the level of income, except insofar as counter-cyclical policy is a response to the level of income and employment.

Foreign goods are purchased by households, businesses, and governments when they prefer foreign goods or find them cheaper, and foreigners purchase American goods for the same reasons. United States imports will increase as income increases, and the demand in other countries for goods and services produced in the United States will increase as income increases in those countries. Of course, the demand for imports and exports depends upon a number of things other than income, such as relative prices and tariff policies. In national income theory it is assumed that these other factors do not change—and if they do change, the results can be expressed as a change in the marginal propensity to import. So, imports are a function of income, and exports are autonomous.

Net exports—exports minus imports—are added to total demand, because spending by foreigners on American goods (American exports: X) is demand for goods and services currently produced by Americans, and the imported components (American Imports: M) of C, I, and G are not demand for American production and employment, but for foreign production and employment. Imports are, therefore, along with savings and taxes, leakages from the income stream. If exports exceed imports, the foreign balance ($X - M$) is positive, which is to say foreign trade adds to the demand for goods and services produced during the year. If imports exceed exports, the foreign balance is negative, which is to say that the net effect of foreign trade has been to reduce the demand for goods and services produced during the year.

Since imports and exports are a fairly small percentage of GNP in the United States, the foreign balance is often ignored and the economy is assumed, in order to make the analysis simpler, to be a "closed economy"—an economy with no foreign trade.

Equality of Aggregate Supply and Aggregate Demand. National income is determined by the total demand for goods and services: $Y = C + I + G + F$. Of course, during any period of time national output is also the total value of goods and services produced during that period, and the question arises as to what happens if this dollar quantity is not equal to the dollar amount of aggregate demand. Because the decisions about how much to produce during any period of time are made independently of the decisions about how much to purchase, the producers (businesses) may be unable to sell all they had planned to, or may be able to sell more than they had planned.

Businesses produce what they hope to sell plus what they want to add to inventories. If households, governments, foreigners, and other businesses do not want to purchase as much as a firm produces, the firm will find itself with more inventories than it wants to hold. Since inventories are part of Investment, if businesses as a whole produce more than they can sell, total actual investment will exceed total planned investment. Thus actual aggregate demand, which may include some unintended demand by businesses in excess of what they planned to demand, will equal aggregate supply, even though planned aggregate demand did not equal planned aggregate supply.

National Income Changes. If businesses are producing more than is being demanded, they will cut production and so buy or hire fewer inputs. Both aggregate supply and the incomes paid to produce it will fall. As households receive less income, they will spend less, and incomes will fall still further. The total amount by which income falls depends on how much households' demand decreases as income decreases (the multiplier). Incomes will continue to fall until the total (aggregate) planned spending by households, businesses, governments, and foreigners equals the value of the amount being produced. The income at which this equality exists is the *equilibrium level of income*.

At the equilibrium level of income planned investment plus planned government expenditures plus exports will equal savings plus taxes plus imports. All of the output supplied and not consumed by households will be demanded by businesses, governments, or foreigners. If planned total demand is greater than planned aggregate supply, aggregate supply and the national income it generates will rise to the point where the amount that households, businesses, governments, and foreigners want to buy is equalled by the amount being supplied. National income will rise as businesses expand output, to satisfy demand for goods and services, and consequently purchase more inputs—which will become increases in household income and lead to further increases in consumption. As in the previous case of declining income, the amount by which income will rise depends on the multiplier, which itself depends on the marginal propensity to consume.

National income will also change as a result of changes in any component of aggregate demand. If businesses decide to increase investment, national income, will rise by the amount of the increase in investment plus the amount by which consumption will increase as a result of the change in income. Thus, income will eventually rise by the amount of the initial change in income (the change in investment) times the multiplier. If households decide to save more and consume less, aggregate demand and national income will fall. National income will also change if government demand for goods and services changes or if net foreign demand changes. Of course, if businesses increase investment and governments decrease their expenditure for goods and services by the same amount there will be no net change in aggregate demand, and national income will not change.

Reality of Constant Changes. In reality, businesses and households do not make plans for a year and then wait to alter them. Produc-

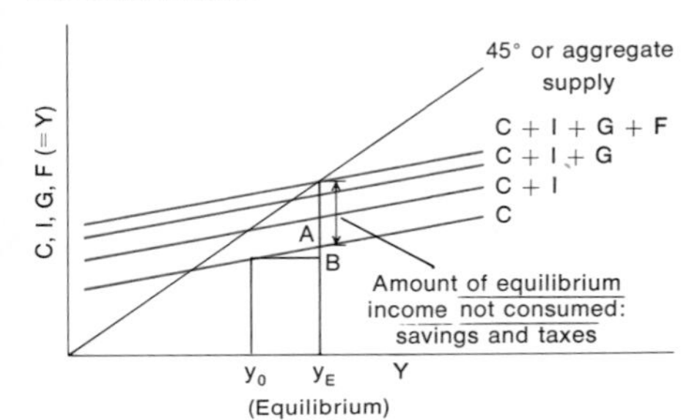

tion plans and spending plans are altered as often as households and firms see that significant changes have occurred in the economic conditions they face. And, in reality, the full effects of any one change in aggregate demand are not fully worked out before another change is made. This means that we do not achieve an equilibrium level of income nor can we say that any particular level is an equilibrium level. What we can say is that a particular level is too high or low for equilibrium, meaning that given the plans of households, businesses, governments, and foreigners to purchase goods and services, income will rise or fall.

Graphic Analysis. The determination of national income and changes in national income are frequently explained by use of a graph.

The 45° line, or aggregate supply curve, shows the dollar amount that will be supplied at the levels of income measured on the horizontal axis. For each level of income the associated aggregate demand is measured on the vertical axis: first C, then I added to it, then G added to that, then F to all of them, giving the aggregate demand curve. The equilibrium level of income—the level at which planned aggregate supply is equal to planned aggregate demand—will be that level at which the aggregate demand curve intersects the aggregate supply curve. The slope of the consumption curve is the marginal propensity to consume and shows how much consumption will change as income changes. If income increases from Y_o to Y_e, consumption will increase by the amount measured by the distance AB and the marginal propensity to consume—$\Delta C/\Delta Y$—is $AB/(Y_e - Y_o)$. As drawn here, investment, government spending, and net exports are assumed to be independent of income: they are the same at all the levels of income shown on the horizontal axis. This means that the C, C+I, C+I+G, and C+I+G+F lines are parallel. In using this diagram, F is usually ignored and aggregate demand is C + I + G. The difference between the level of consumption at any level of income and the aggregate supply curve represents savings plus taxes: that part of income, or total supply, that is not consumed. For any level of income to be the equilibrium level, governments, businesses, and foreigners must plan to take this amount of the total output.

National Income, Employment, and the Price Level. In national income theory it is assumed that both the total level of employment (aggregate employment) and the level of prices are related to the level of national income. Employment, the percentage of the labor force employed, is assumed to increase in proportion to increases in national income up to the level of income at which the labor force is fully employed and there can be no further increases in employment. Equilibrium income may be too low for full employment to be achieved, and there will be unemployment. Thus, cyclical unemployment can be said to result from insufficient aggregate demand, and the remedy for cyclical unemployment is, therefore, to increase aggregate demand.

The level of prices in the economy (the rate at which some average of all prices changes) is related to the level of national income. If aggregate demand is higher than the full-employment aggregate supply, the price level will rise. If the economy is at a full employment level, but households, businesses or governments attempt to increase their purchases, output cannot increase, but the prices or output can and will increase. Thus, money national income (national income expressed in current dollar value) can increase beyond the full-employment level of income, but real national income (actual products measured by money national income adjusted for price increases) cannot increase. This increase signals inflation, a state in which the general price level is rising. It follows that inflation is a consequence of excess aggregate demand and that the cure for inflation is to reduce aggregate demand. Many economists would argue that inflation may be caused by things other than excess aggregate demand. Inflation as described here is called "demand-pull inflation." For a description of how inflation may result from conditions other than excess demand see Cost-push Inflation.

In the simplest models of the economy, prices are assumed to remain constant up to that income at which full employment is achieved and then to rise if income rises beyond this point. In more realistic models, prices are assumed to begin to rise as the full-employment level of income is approached and as shortages of particular inputs become more common, and the prices for those inputs and the prices of the outputs begin to rise in response to the shortages.

Consult (4) Dillard, 1948; Hansen, 1953; Keynes, 1936; Klein, 1966.

—Anne Mayhew, *University of Tennessee*

NATIONAL INCOME MEASUREMENT. The Department of Commerce undertakes the difficult task of estimating national income data. These data take the form of national income accounts, which represent measurements of various aspects of aggregate economic activity. Through its efforts the Department of Commerce hopes to provide some understanding of the nature and level of current economic activity, the basic structure of the economy, and the nature and extent of changes taking place within the economy over time.

The National Income Accounts are estimates and, as such, lack the precision of hard count enumerations, which are physically difficult and financially prohibitive. The estimates are generated in different ways, including sample surveys and trend projections, but care is taken to ensure that the estimating techniques are statistically sound.

GNP. Although there are many national income accounts, the gross national product or expenditure account seems to have the widest currency. GNP may be defined in various ways; two definitions employed by the Department of Commerce are: (1) "GNP is the market value of the output of goods and services produced by the nation's economy, before the deduction of depreciation charges and other allowances for business and institutional consumption of durable capital goods," and (2) "GNP comprises the purchase of goods and services by consumers and government, gross private domestic investment and net exports."

These two definitions emphasize different facets of GNP. The first highlights the meaning of "gross" in the term GNP: market value of goods and services produced before the deduction of items that represent a reduction in the productive capability of the economy. The second indicates the four sectors that purchase the goods and services produced. The four sectors and the official title of their purchases are: consumers (personal consumption expenditures), government (government purchases of goods and services), business (gross private domestic investment), and the rest of the world (net export of goods and services).

Analysis. Aside from the definition of the term, there are several important characteristics of GNP. First, GNP is the broadest of the national income accounts. Second, GNP is a flow variable and, thus, must be expressed in terms of a time dimension, say, for a quarter or a year. Third, because GNP is a market value concept—the sum of quantities of various goods and services multiplied by their respective prices—it may change without a change in the quantities of goods and services produced by the economy. Fourth, GNP is a crude measure of the economic well-being of the country; a better measure would be GNP adjusted for price and population changes.

See also Gross National Product; National Income and Product Accounts.

—Frank J. Bonello, *University of Notre Dame*

NATIONAL INCOME THEORY. *See* National Income Determination.

NATIONAL INDUSTRIAL RECOVERY ACT (NIRA) (1933). A major part of the New Deal program of the 1930s was directed to general business recovery from the Great Depression. While economists of the traditional school were counseling a cautious recovery program (balance the budget, limit government intervention in the private economy), the Roosevelt administration undertook more aggressive measures. The National Industrial Recovery Act (NIRA) was based on the belief that the general business depression was traceable to two principal causes: disorderliness of markets leading to excessive price competition, and insufficiency of consumer demand.

The NIRA sought to accomplish price stabilization by allowing agreements among firms of an industry on most aspects of business practice, including output and price. By limiting price competition leading to lower prices, the squeeze on profits would be reduced. Under the aegis of government, nearly 900 industry codes containing these and other agreements were written. Cooperating firms were allowed to display the "Blue Eagle," the symbol of the recovery program.

Stimulation of consumer demand was to be accomplished indirectly by setting minimum wages and by permitting laborers to organize and bargain collectively through their own trade unions. This legislation (Section 7) marked the first positive recognition and encouragement by the national government of workers' rights to organize into unions. The higher wages (thus purchasing power) accompanying unionization were expected to boost consumer demand. At the same time, prices would be stabilized through the code provisions (hopefully, price increases to cover the wage increases would be deferred), leading to more sales, more employment, and eventually economic recovery.

The effect of the program was to suspend the antitrust laws regarding restraint of trade. In 1935, the Supreme Court rendered the NIRA unconstitutional in *Schechter Brothers v. United States,* on the grounds that (1) violations charged were mostly of a local nature, had only an indirect effect on interstate commerce, and hence were outside the power of Congress to regulate and, (2) Congress had delegated powers to the President excessively.

See also Competition; Sherman Antitrust Act.

Consult (16) Corwin, 1936.

—Thomas O. Depperschmidt, *Memphis State University*

NATIONALISM, intense loyalty and devotion to the national state, expressing itself in such varied ideological forms as democracy, fascism, or communism. Each form is conditioned by social structure, intellectual traditions, cultural history, and geographic location. Economic nationalism is usually directed toward self-sufficiency for a group or area, with indus-

NATIONAL INCOME MEASUREMENT

A fuller analysis of the way aggregate economic activity is measured is presented in the article on NATIONAL INCOME AND PRODUCT ACCOUNTS. Some of the more commonly used measures are discussed in GROSS NATIONAL PRODUCT, PERSONAL INCOME, CONSUMPTION, and INVESTMENT. A full discussion of all facets of national income can be found in the article on NATIONAL INCOME DETERMINATION. The interrelationships of these and other articles are displayed on the NATIONAL INCOME Subject Map.

The NRA blue eagle symbolized one of New Deal's key efforts to help business out of depression.

trialization as a goal, and is often coupled with fear or envy of other nations. The Mercantilists were extremely nationalistic, as are the underdeveloped countries today, with Communist China a prime example.

See also Mercantilism.

Consult (26) Spiegel, 1971.

NATIONALIZATION, the process of achieving public ownership in desired areas of the economy. At a minimum it covers industries such as coal, electricity, gas, transportation, iron and steel, with some control over central banking. Under socialism, nationalization tends to be complete; in countries such as the United Kingdom, France, and Italy there are varying degrees, with compensation implied when there is a change from private to public ownership.

See also British Labour Party; Fabian Society.

Consult (26) Gruchy, 1966.

NATIONAL LABOR RELATIONS ACT. *See* Wagner Act.

NATIONAL LABOR RELATIONS BOARD (NLRB), independent, regulatory agency empowered under the Wagner Act (1935), the Taft-Hartley Act (1947) and the Landrum-Griffin Act (1959). The NLRB is made up of five members appointed by the president for five years and a general counsel appointed for four years. The board performs quasi-judicial and quasi-legislative functions aimed at preventing and remedying unfair labor practices by employers or by union organizations and at protecting fair union representation. In disputes it supervises secret-ballot union elections. The general counsel brings cases and complaints before the board for a ruling, and most are settled by voluntary action.

The board maintains 31 regional and several subregional offices. The NLRB has been crucial in formulating and altering national labor policy since the 1930s. It is the single agency most responsible for ending violent labor/management confrontations. A strong pro-labor reputation earned by the NLRB for its early and forceful action guaranteeing employees' rights to strike and to organize has been mitigated by forceful NLRB application of subsequent legal strictures on the unions.

NATIONAL LABOR UNION. *See* Labor Movement; National Unions.

NATIONAL MEDIATION BOARD. *See* Railway Labor Act (1926).

NATIONAL PRODUCT SINCE 1869 (1946). *See* Kuznets, Simon.

NATIONAL UNIONS. Approximately 200 unions in the United States are national or international organizations. "National" suggests that the union has members in several states, while "international" normally means one or more locals in Canada. The national or international may have fewer than one hundred members, or more than a million.

As an organization, the national union stands between the locals and the federations, and usually includes members from a specific work group. For example, the Steelworkers' Union includes almost all blue-collar employees of the steel industry, and the Carpenters organize individuals who work as carpenters in any industry. The AFL-CIO, the largest of the federations, is an organization of national unions.

NATIONS, DEVELOPING. *See* Developing Nations.

NATURAL GAS. *See* Hope Natural Gas Case (1944); Natural Gas Pipeline Case (1942); Phillips Case (1954).

NATURAL GAS ACT (1938). *See* Phillips Case (1954).

NATURAL GAS PIPELINE CASE (1942), decision in which the Supreme Court began abandoning its traditional role of reviewing the procedure by which fair return on fair value was calculated and became concerned with the overall effect of regulation rather than the procedure or formula. The court specifically indicated that it would not be bound to a given formula for rate-making purposes and also established the concept of a "zone of reasonableness" for "fair return" rather than a specific numerical figure.

See also Regulated Industries.

NATURAL MONOPOLY, an industry in which the economies of scale are particularly pronounced and in which competition is impractical and almost unworkable, because of the natural barriers to entry and the high financial investment needed.

The best examples of natural monopoly are the public utilities industries, including the electric and gas companies, the transportation services such as railroads, and the water supply and communication facilities. To duplicate telephone lines or man-made water facilities would be unfeasible. Thus, these industries are sanctioned monopolies due to natural causes.

Natural monopolies are usually given rather exclusive franchises by the government, which usually reserves the right to regulate these monopolies to prevent abuses or restraints of trade. Even more so than most other types of monopolies, natural monopolies have heavy fixed cost and, therefore, have decreasing cost of production.

A natural monopoly can also be established by obtaining exclusive rights to, or ownership of, raw materials. For example, the United States retained its monopoly position in the aluminum industry for many years by controlling the basic sources of bauxite.

Consult (14) Leftwich, 1970.

—William D. Wagoner, *Louisiana State University*

NEAR MONEY, assets with a specified monetary value readily redeemable. Time deposits and, particularly, savings accounts are the primary form of near money. Series E savings bonds, also, can be cashed in at any time. Sometimes other government securities are classed as near money because they have an active market, but only treasury bills, because of their short maturity, are relatively safe from market fluctuations. Near money is a close substitute for money.

See also Liquidity Preference; Money Supply.

NEGATIVE INCOME TAX (NIT), an income maintenance scheme that would provide a guaranteed minimum income for eligible families with no other income and a supplement for families with incomes below a predetermined level. A variety of plans have been proposed, but all contain the same basic elements. They include the basic allowance (B), which varies with family size and provides a guaranteed minimum; the marginal rate (t) at which B is reduced as income from other sources (Y) rises; and breakeven income (Yb), above which NIT transfers cease.

Total payment (P) is determined by the formula $P = B - tY$ and breakeven income is reached when $Y = B/t$. To illustrate, if $B =$ \$2,000, $t = 0.5$, and family income, Y, is \$2,000, the family will receive a supplement of \$1,000. NIT supplements will cease if family income exceeds \$4,000.

See also Income Tax; Public Assistance; Social Dividend.

NEGATIVE INVESTMENT. *See* Disinvestment.

NEOCLASSICAL ECONOMICS. Criticism of the classical economic system by Marx and others generated attempts by those favorable to the classical school to eliminate some of the more important errors. The development of marginalism in the 1860s and 1870s provided the basis for restructuring the classical system with the emphasis upon the theory of individual units and their decision-making process. While the neoclassical school is generally considered to have reached a peak by World War I, the bulk of present day microeconomic theory can be traced directly to developments of this school. In addition, important developments in interest theory and some aspects of macroeconomic theory have been made by economists following neoclassical traditions.

See also Marginalism.

NEP. *See* New Economic Policy.

NERLOVE, MARC L. (1933–), American educator, econometrician, and microeconomic theorist. A graduate of the University of Chicago (1952), he received his Ph.D from Johns Hopkins University (1956). His publications include *The Dynamics of Supply* (1958), *Distributed Lags and Demand Analysis* (1958), and *Estimation and Identification of Cobb-Douglas Production Functions* (1965). Nerlove has been on the faculty at the University of Minnesota, at Stanford, and at Yale, and has been a professor of economics at the University of Chicago since 1969.

NET BORROWED RESERVES. *See* Free Reserves.

NET CAPITAL FORMATION. *See* Net Investment.

NET FOREIGN INVESTMENT. *See* Foreign Investment.

NET FREE RESERVES. *See* Free Reserves.

NET INVESTMENT, or NET CAPITAL FORMATION, the amount of net private domestic spending by business, industry, and agriculture for new capital goods and net increases in inventory. Net investment occurs only when additional real capital is created and is equal to gross private domestic investment less depreciation, the capital consumption allowance. An important component of Net National Product, net investment tends to remain relatively stable. As a whole, it is influenced by autonomous elements, such as new population, new territory, innovations, and other growth elements, rather than anticipated returns and economic expansion.

See also Net National Product.

NET NATIONAL PRODUCT (NNP), the dollar value of all goods and services produced by an economy in a given year. NNP includes net production of all goods and services available for current consumption and, thus, reflects personal consumption expenditures, government purchases, and net exports.

Computation. In the flow-of-product approach to national accounting, NNP may be computed by adding all personal consumption expenditures, net private investments, and all government purchases. The same result can be obtained by first calculating GNP and then deducting capital depreciation (CCA), which is the approach utilized by most governments.

From the flow-of-income or costs approach, NNP is the total of wages and salaries, interest, rents, corporate profits, income from unincorporated businesses, and indirect business taxes. Another way of looking at NNP is through the value-added approach. By carefully calculating the value added to a good at each stage of production, and subtracting expenditures or intermediate goods, the value of the final product is derived. Therefore, the sum of all final products from which wages, rent, interest, and profits have been deducted equals NNP.

Significance. NNP is often used interchangeably with GNP, as they differ little more than a twelfth. NNP is also used as a point of departure for figuring national income, personal income, and disposable personal income. It should be noted that the calculations for NNP do not allow for inflation and deflation. Therefore, to compare one year's NNP to another's requires multiplication by an official price index number. The result, NNP expressed in constant dollars, is called real NNP. Currently, the United States government is using 1958 as the base year.

See also Gross National Product.

NET PRODUCTIVITY OF CAPITAL, the net return from capital investment. Capital equipment is expected to provide an income stream over its useful life by producing a saleable output. After allowing for depreciation, capital has a net productivity that can be expressed as a yearly rate.

See also Capital Equipment; Marginal Efficiency of Capital.

Consult (22) Fusfeld, 1972; Peterson, 1971.

NET REPRODUCTION RATE (NRR), the average number of females who will be born to a new-born female during her lifetime. If the number is one, population is stationary; if it is less than one, population is declining; and if greater than one, population is growing. The NRR for the United States during the 1960's was above one, and higher than most other advanced nations, but appears to be declining during the 1970s. Some demographers estimate that the United States will reach Zero Population Growth (NRR = 1) during the late 1970s.

See also Zero Population Growth.

NEW CREDITOR. *See* Stages of a Country's Balance of Payments.

NEW ECONOMIC POLICY (NEP), instituted in the USSR by Lenin in 1921 in an attempt to speed the country's recovery from World War I and the civil war and to reestablish popular support for the Communist Party, particularly among the peasants. The NEP restored a high degree of capitalism in agriculture and the trade sectors, while the state controlled heavy industry, transportation, the credit system, and international trade. It was terminated with the introduction of the First Five-Year Plan in 1928.

NEW INDUSTRIAL STATE (1967), by John Kenneth Galbraith, concentrates on the private sector of the American economy, examining how industry has obtained power and how this power is corrupting the U.S. economy.

Galbraith's theme is that industry has reached such an influential level in American society that it now concentrates on using this influence to further increase its power. This has occurred because the influence of unions has declined, the dramatic increase in college education has made the white collar worker more dependent upon industry for employment, and the use of advertising to influence demand has increased significantly.

With the power that industry possesses, it has developed systematic plans for the future. These plans are necessary because the size of investment and the time period necessary to realize it have become very large. The complexities of the plans and problems of successfully completing them have led to the development of a technostructure which has replaced the entrepreneur. Because industries are led by the technostructure, the profit maximizing goal which is the center of conventional economic theory is no longer applicable. Thus traditional economic analysis is no longer valid for contemporary American industry.

In order to correct the situation, Galbraith suggests, many reforms must take place, the most important being to reduce the prevalent U.S. belief that anything the market does is good. This will involve not only breaking down the now powerful private sector but also building up a new more powerful public sector.

—Clyde A. Haulman, *College of William and Mary*

NFO. *See* Farmers Organization, National.

NFU. *See* Farmers Union, National.

NHI. *See* National Health Insurance.

NIT. *See* Negative Income Tax.

NNP. *See* Net National Product.

NONCOMPETING GROUPS, a term that originated in the nineteenth century to distinguish between different categories of labor that are not in direct competition with one another. The theory is that because noncompeting groups are only partial, not perfect, substitutes for each other, wage differentials are justified.

For example, an engineer may be a highly skilled and well-trained individual. However, he cannot compete for a job that requires the skills of a heart surgeon. Thus, engineers and heart surgeons belong to non-competing groups.

NONDURABLE GOODS. *See* Goods.

NON-EQUALIZING WAGE DIFFERENTIALS are differences in money wages that have no real basis for existence. Unlike equalizing wage differentials which compensate for differences among jobs, non-equalizing wage differentials are the result of imperfections in the labor market. Such things as unions, monopolies, and lack of perfect knowledge of the market all add to the uneven wage distribution of workers.

NONINTERVENTION. *See* Laissez-Faire.

NON-PRICE COMPETITION, a means of attracting a larger part of the market for a product without changing price. The main form of non-price competition is called product differentiation, and is carried out by advertising and by variations in the quality and design of the product.

See also Product Differentiation.

NONRATIONAL WAGE DIFFERENTIALS are those based on illogical reasons such as historical accidents, unessential peculiarities of places and practices, and on the relative skill of different groups in gaining wage increases. For example, members of powerful unions, because of their tremendous bargaining power, very often make much more money than members of the same trade who do not belong to a union. In addition, women and minority groups often receive lower salaries than their white, male counterparts.

NONRECOURSE COMMODITY LOANS. *See* Commodity Loans.

NON-SIGNERS CLAUSE. *See* Miller-Tydings Act.

NORMAL PROFITS, that return to input that a firm needs in order to remain in a competitive industry. It is that point where the total costs of a firm equal its total revenue and there are no economic profits. Normal profits differ from economic profits insofar as there is only one point where a firm achieves normal profits, but economic profits can be either positive (gains) or negative (losses).

In a perfectly or purely competitive market in the long run, the only profits that individual firms can achieve are normal profits because all economic profits are used up when new firms enter the market. Also, in the long run, any firm entering the market that cannot achieve normal profits is forced to leave the industry because it would be operating at a loss. Therefore, it can be said that a firm must achieve that point where firms achieve normal profits in order to remain in the competitive market.

See also Profits.

NORRIS-LAGUARDIA ACT (1932), also known as the Federal Anti-Injunction Act, the first of numerous laws passed by the federal government during the 1930s directly favorable to organized labor and collective bargaining. It contains a turning-point declaration of public policy in support of workers' freedom to unionize and bargain collectively, free of employer interference. To promote this freedom, and to maintain the government's neutral role in labor-management relations, the act severely restricted the availability to management of one of its most potent anti-labor weapons, the injunction granted by federal courts. No comparable legal devices had been available to labor.

In essence, the act denied management the use of these injunctions to restrain labor in its pursuit of lawful organizing activity or in labor disputes, except under very limited and well defined circumstances. Tangentially, the law also made unenforceable in court the "yellow-dog" contract, under which workers, in order to obtain or keep jobs, must promise not to join unions.

See also Injunction, Labor; Yellow-Dog Contract.

—Leonard G. Schifrin, *College of William and Mary*

NOURSE, EDWIN GRISWOLD (1883-), American economist and expert on agricultural economics. A graduate of Cornell, he received his Ph.D. from the University of Chicago in 1915. He has published numerous volumes including *American Agriculture and the European Market* (1924), *Price Making in a Democracy* (1944), and *Economics in the Public Service* (1953). Active in public service, Nourse has been vice president of the Brookings Institution in Washington (1942–46) and chairman of the Council of Economic Advisers (1946–49). He has served on the faculty at the University of Pennsylvania, the University of South Dakota, The University of Arkansas, Iowa State College, and Pennsylvania State University.

NRR. *See* Net Reproduction Rate.

NULL HYPOTHESIS. *See* Hypothesis.

OASDHI. *See* Social Insurance.

OCCUPATIONAL MOBILITY OF LABOR. *See* Labor Mobility.

OFFICE OF MANAGEMENT AND BUDGET (OMB). *See* Federal Budget.

OLIGOPOLY

To view oligopolistic industries or markets in relation to other types, see the articles on MONOPOLY, MONOPOLISTIC COMPETITION, PERFECT COMPETITION, and OLIGOPSONY. Closely related to the concept of oligopoly is MARKET CONCENTRATION, as measured in CONCENTRATION RATIO.

For two concepts of importance in the theory of oligopolistic behavior see KINKED DEMAND CURVE and JOINT PROFIT MAXIMIZATION. And for some aspects of oligopolistic pricing and market behavior, see CARTEL, CONSCIOUS PARALLELISM, PRICE LEADERSHIP, and QUALITY COMPETITION. Three of the numerous factors that contribute to the existence of oligopoly are explained in ECONOMIES OF SCALE, BARRIERS TO ENTRY, and MERGER.

The Subject Maps accompanying the articles on ANTITRUST POLICY and THEORY OF THE FIRM display the interrelationships of these concepts.

OPPORTUNITY COST

Additional concepts related to the principle of opportunity cost are discussed in the article on NORMAL PROFITS. The basic idea of opportunity costs derives from the fact of SCARCITY and the necessity of CHOICE. Consult these articles for an understanding of these relationships. For one application of the opportunity cost concept, see the article on PRODUCTION POSSIBILITY FRONTIER.

OFFICE OF PRICE ADMINISTRATION. *See* Wage-Price Control.

OIL, GAS, AND ELECTRICITY INDUSTRIES. *See* Regulated Industries.

OKUN, AUTHUR MELVIN (1928-), American macroeconomist. He received his A.B. (1949) and Ph.D. (1956) from Columbia. His publications include *The Battle Against Unemployment* (1965, editor), and *The Political Economy of Prosperity* (1970). He has also been a contributor of articles on economic forecasting, potential output, and fiscal and monetary policy in professional journals. Okun served on the Council of Economic Advisers (1964–69), has been a member of the advisory committee of the Bureau of the Census, a senior fellow at the Brookings Institution in Washington, and was on the faculty at Yale (1952–67).

OLD AGE ASSISTANCE, a federally subsidized categorical public assistance program for indigent persons over 65. It is administered by state and local welfare agencies. Beneficiaries include the declining number of indigent elderly not included in the social security program and, in some cases, social security recipients whose benefits fall short of state-designated minimum standards.

See also Public Assistance.

OLD-AGE INSURANCE, a monthly payment for retired persons, financed out of the social security trust funds. Payments vary with past contributions to the system and with number of dependents. An eligible worker may retire on partial benefits at age 62, full benefits at 65. Beneficiaries under 72 years of age lose some or all benefits if earnings exceed certain levels. Additional benefits are paid for dependents.

See also Old-Age Assistance; Social Insurance; Social Security.

OLIGOPOLY, a market that consists of relatively few sellers. Because there are only a small number of firms in the market, the actions of each individual firm usually affect all the other firms in the industry and the sellers are interdependent.

The firms in oligopolistic markets usually have similar products that are distinguished from one another only by means of product differentiation, a non-price mechanism used to increase the firm's share of the market by differentiating its product from that of the other firms. The two major means of product differentiation are advertising and variations in the quality and design of the product.

An oligopolistic market, of which the automotive industry is a prime example, is faced with what is known as kinked demand curve. This demand curve is an analytical tool used in explaining why oligopolists have fairly rigid prices. The kinked demand curve assumes that, first, if one firm lowers its price below the existing market price, all other firms in the industry will follow in order to keep their relative shares of the market.

Second, it assumes that firms will not follow a price rise. Using these assumptions, it is easy to see why oligopolistic firms tend to stay with the established market price. If a firm raises its price, it prices itself out of the market and, if a firm lowers its price, it tends to keep the same share of the market, but at a lower income.

Oligopolistic markets often relied on collusion to set the established price. However, collusion is now illegal and not usually practiced openly.

See also Interdependence, Oligopolistic; Kinked Demand Curve; Product Differentiation.

—William D. Wagoner, *Louisiana State University*

OLIGOPSONY, a market in which a few buyers dominate the market. In a wage oligopsony the buyer is able to avoid paying a wage rate equal to the value of the output of the marginal worker. In the American automobile and steel industries there are only a few firms purchasing labor input.

OMB. *See* Federal Budget.

100% RESERVES, the name of a proposal that would require each commercial bank to hold in reserves every cent of its demand deposits so that it could pay to its depositors instantly the total amount owed them. Such a proposal would make it impossible for banks to create money though fractional reserves, by which loans of commercial banks produce multiple expansion of the money supply.

See also Monetary Policy; Money Supply; Reserve Requirement.

ONE-YEAR PLAN. *See* Planning (Communism).

ON THE PRINCIPLES OF POLITICAL ECONOMY AND TAXATION (1817). *See* Ricardo, David.

OPEN MARKET COMMITTEE. *See* Federal Reserve System.

OPEN MARKET OPERATIONS, the purchase or sale of government securities (or sometimes other securities) by the federal reserve banks to implement monetary policy. Buying such securities puts money into the economy, stimulates business, and tends to reduce unemployment. Selling securities removes money from the economy and reduces the pressure toward inflation.

The decision as to how many securities shall be bought or sold is made by the Federal Open Market Committee of the federal reserve system. The actual purchase or sale is carried out by the Federal Reserve Bank of New York as agent for all twelve federal reserve banks. The federal reserve buys from (or sells to) government-bond houses, some twenty private corporations that specialize in creating a market for government securities (bills, notes, and bonds) by standing ready to buy and sell them at all times.

The figure illustrates a purchase of securities. The federal reserve finds which government-bond house will sell at the lowest price, orders the bond, and pays the bond house by means of a cashier's check drawn on itself. When the bond house deposits this check, in its commercial bank, it has more money (demand deposits) than it had before (and fewer earning assets). Then the bank deposits the check in its account with the federal reserve bank and increases its reserves.

The effects of the purchase are (1) to increase the money supply in the hands of the public (so far represented by the bond house) and (2) to increase the reserves of commercial banks so that they are thereby permitted to launch a multiple expansion of the money supply. The bond house, finding its inventory of securities reduced, will try to replenish it by offering a higher price for such securities. This rise in bond prices is a fall in bond yields, lowering interest rates.

See also Monetary Policy; Quantitative Controls.

Consult (10) Federal Reserve Bank of New York, 1963.

—Walter W. Haines, *New York University*

OPEN SHOP, situation in which the employer is free to hire without considering applicants' status as members of a union and in which the workers are under no compulsion to join a union as a condition of job retention. The open shop thus affords no security to the union, which must seek out the workers and recruit them on a voluntary basis.

See also Closed Shop.

OPPORTUNITY COST, or ALTERNATIVE COST, the value of the benefit that is given up to produce one economic good as opposed to another.

The concept of opportunity cost is crucial to all economic activity, because all resources are limited. Steel used to produce girders cannot be used to produce locomotives; labor services used to produce shoes cannot be used to build houses. Therefore, in order to ascertain the cost of choosing one alternative use of a given set of limited resources rather than another, the economist uses the opportunity cost concept. He measures the "real" cost of doing business by its opportunity cost, not by its explicit, or outlay, cost. The real cost of producing nails, for example, is the value of another product, say rails, that might have been produced from the same amount of resources.

In utilizing the opportunity cost concept, however, it is not sufficient simply to compare the values of different products that can be produced by utilizing a given set of resources in more or less the same manner. To illustrate, assume that a man has a farm and has invested his life savings in land and equipment, with all of which he grows alfalfa. The opportunity cost of such economic activity might be the difference between the value of alfalfa and the value of some other crop that he could also produce. He could have put his self-owned, self-employed resources to entirely different uses, however. By using his resources as he has, he has forgone the opportunities of (1) lending his savings and receiving interest on that investment, (2) renting his land and receiving income therefrom, (3) working for someone else for wages. If the total return from such alternative uses of his resources were greater than the return from the production of any other crop that he might grow, it is that return that is the measure of the opportunity cost to him of growing alfalfa.

From the point of view of economics, the most rational use of resources is that use which produces the greatest return. Although opportunity cost is the true measure of the cost of one use of a given set of resources as compared with any other use, the most rational use is that which produces the greatest return. Therefore, the economically relevant opportunity cost of a given activity is the difference between the value of the benefit it produces and the value of the benefit that would have been produced by the most rational alternative use of the resources concerned.

—Josef Hadar, *Case Western Reserve University*

ORDINARY STOCK. *See* Common Stock.

ORGANIZED EXCHANGE. *See* Stock Market.

ORIGINAL COST, one way to determine the fair value of a regulated firm. The procedure is to calculate the original cost of the physical plant used (and useful to the public), less accumulated depreciation, plus additions and betterments. Sometimes called historic cost, book cost, or actual cost.

See also Fair Value; Regulation.

OUTER COUNTRIES. *See* International Monetary System.

OUTPUT, the goods and services that emerge

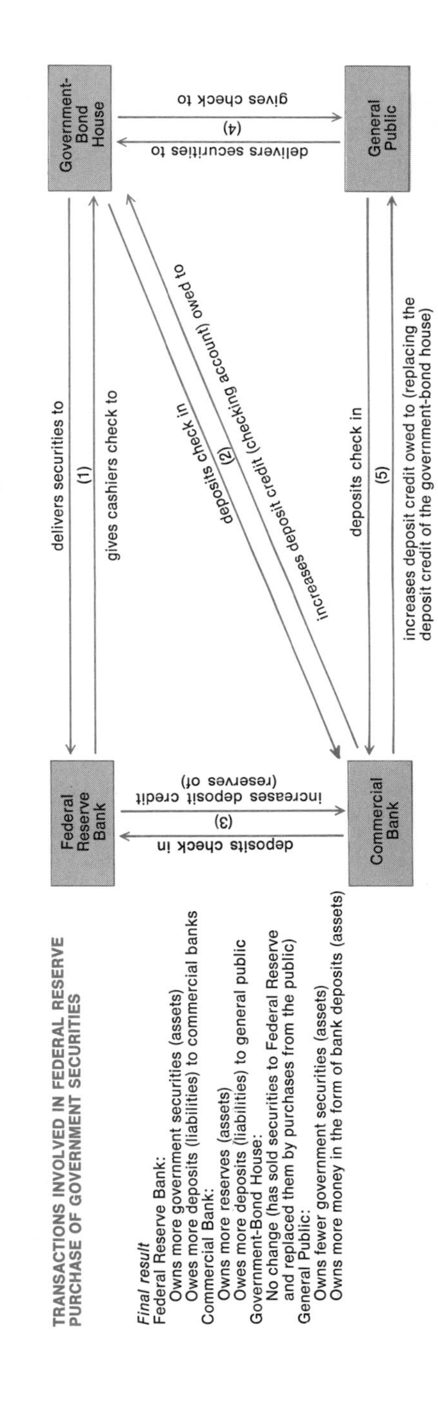

TRANSACTIONS INVOLVED IN FEDERAL RESERVE PURCHASE OF GOVERNMENT SECURITIES

Final result
Federal Reserve Bank:
Owns more government securities (assets)
Owes more deposits (liabilities) to commercial banks
Commercial Bank:
Owns more reserves (assets)
Owes more deposits (liabilities) to general public
Government-Bond House:
No change (has sold securities to Federal Reserve and replaced them by purchases from the public)
General Public:
Owns fewer government securities (assets)
Owns more money in the form of bank deposits (assets)

Robert Owen

as a result of the production process. Output is viewed in either a micro (a single firm) context or a macro (an entire economy) context. Output is one of the most significant variables in the production process. In economic analysis of the firm, comparisons between levels of inputs and resulting levels of outputs are the basis for measurement of profit and productivity; different levels of output for a firm will directly affect its unit costs of producing a product. Aggregate output is an important device to compare the growth rates of a nation's economy and to determine a nation's relative state of health, its general productivity level, its output per manhour, and so on.

See also Input.

OUTPUT EXPANSION PATH, the locus of all the points of tangency between a family of isoquants and a series of budget lines. It defines the long run total cost curve for a firm; the firm purchases *all* inputs in the least cost combinations so as to minimize total cost. The long run average cost envelope curve can also be derived from the output expansion path. Each point on the curve is a paired combination of total cost and quantity produced. Dividing total cost by output defines average cost for that given output.

OUTPUT RATIO. See Capital/Output Ratio.

OVERINVESTMENT THEORY OF BUSINESS CYCLES attributes cyclical downswings or recessions to too much rather than too little investment. This internal theory holds that business overinvests to meet anticipated rises in demand and then sharply curtails such investment if, and when, it realized that such enthusiasm was unwarranted. This type of investment behavior is said to be one of the primary forces responsible for initiation of cyclical activity within the economy.

See also Business Cycles, Theories; Internal Theory.

OVERPRODUCTION. *See* Excess Supply.

OVERSUPPLY. *See* Excess Supply.

OVERT COLLUSION. *See* Collusion.

OVER-THE-COUNTER MARKETS. *See* Stock Market.

OVERVALUATION *See* Devaluation.

OWEN, ROBERT (1771–1858), most famous of the founders, in about 1800, of utopian socialism. His basic premise was that human nature is molded by environment and that the way to produce better people is to produce better conditions. To prove this Owen converted the New Lanark Mills into a model community and, in the process, developed the largest and best spinning mills in Scotland while making a profit. Reforms included a minimum work age, shorter work day, high wages, social insurance, abolition of fines and punishments, free schools, comfortable housing, and recreational facilities.

Owen believed his "villages of cooperation" would bring producers and consumers together and hence eliminate the competitive system and capitalism. The New Harmony Venture (Indiana, 1825) failed; the Rochdale Pioneers (England, 1844), however, was highly successful.

See also Associationism; Cooperativism; Evolutionary Socialism.

Consult (26) Oser, 1970.

OWN SUBSTITUTION EFFECT. *See* Consumer Equilibrium.

PAID HOLIDAYS are days for which employees receive wages but do not work or, if required to work, receive extra pay or compensatory time off at a later date. Besides national holidays such as Christmas and New Year's Day there are holidays limited to certain regions, states, or individual companies. The average number of paid holidays in the United States annually is eight.

PANIC. *See* Business Cycles.

PARADOX OF THRIFT, the apparent contradiction that as households try to save more, they may find that they are only saving the same amount out of a smaller total income, or even saving less than they were originally. The explanation of the paradox is that a decrease in consumption, which is the obverse of an increase in savings, causes income to fall by the amount of the decrease in consumption times the multiplier. A new equilibrium level of income will be reached only when income has fallen to that level where saving is again equal to investment. If investment does not decrease as income decreases, income will fall to that point where the same amount is being saved out of the new smaller level of income as was previously being saved out of the larger income. If investment decreases as income decreases, income will fall to a point where both savings and investment are smaller than they were previously.

PARALLELISM, a market condition under which two firms run parallel or in the same direction, possibly toward a monopoly or a cartel situation. Under normal circumstances a cartel is often illegal, but parallelism is regarded as innocent coincidence, because one firm does not know the activities of the other firm.

See also Cartel.

PARAMETERS, or PARAMETRIC CONSTANTS, are the constants written in a general equation, for instance a and b in the equation $y = a + bx$. Changing a parameter generates a whole family of curves.

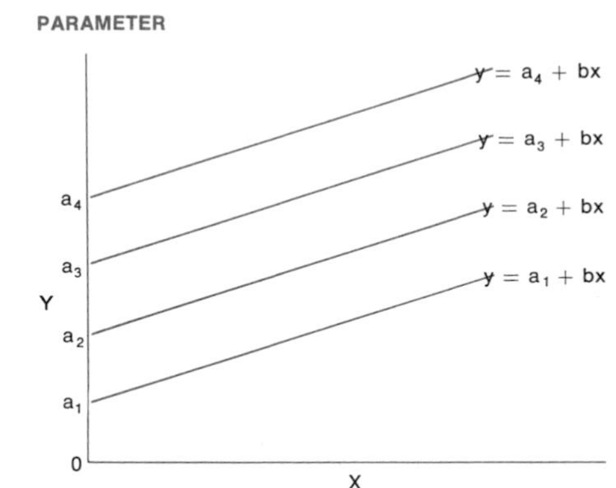

PARAMETRIC CONSTANT. *See* Parameters.

PARETO, VILFREDO (1848–1923), Italian economist and sociologist who, like Walras, made extensive application of mathematical analysis to economic problems, in particular, expanding the concept of general equilibrium and its implications. In continuing the Walrasian mathematical approach to political economy, Pareto introduced concrete matter, made distinction between abstract reasoning and empirical inquiry, and employed not only competitive but also monopolistic and collectivist assumptions in examining and analyzing economic systems.

Pareto also paved the way for the changeover from utility analysis to indifference curve analysis by stripping the indifference curve principle of its utility content, making it instead an ostensibly empirical observation about combinations of goods equally acceptable to the consumer. In this, Pareto followed Edgeworth's interpretation of the utility of a good as a function not of the quantity of that one good but of the quantities of all goods under the control of the individual.

See also Indifference Curve; Pareto Optimum.

—Clyde A. Haulman, *College of William and Mary*

PARETO OPTIMUM, a situation in which no action can be taken to benefit some members of society without hurting someone else. Any social action that benefits some members of society without hurting anyone is desirable. The Italian economist, Vilfredo Pareto (1848–1923) pointed out, however, that if a social action hurts some persons while helping others, one cannot clearly say that it is desirable, since it is impossible to compare the damage to some people with the benefit to other people.

There are, of course, a large number of situations that are Pareto optimal. Unfortunately, the criterion provides no basis for choosing among the situations; for example, a transfer of goods or income from a rich man to a poor man could not be evaluated. All that can be said is that if a society is not at a Pareto optimum, at least one other situation is better, in that some individuals would benefit at no one's expense.

PARITY. *See* Parity Prices.

PARITY PRICES represent an effort to define fair prices for farm products. The method in use in the 1970s traces back to the early 1920s, when there was an intuitive appeal in saying that a fair price for a farm product was one that had changed from the pre-war level exactly as much as had an index of prices paid by farmers. The idea was retained as time passed and was written into the Agricultural Adjustment Act of 1933 as the parity price formula.

Farm prices collectively are at parity when the index of prices received by farmers, on a 1910–14 base, is the same as the index of prices paid by farmers (called the Parity Index), also on a 1910–14 base. The parity ratio is computed by dividing the first index by the second and multiplying by 100.

Until 1950, parity prices of most individual farm commodities were computed simply by multiplying the 1910–14 average farm price of the product by the parity index and dividing by 100. Now the parity price for an individual commodity is computed by (1) dividing the average farm price during the most recent 10 years by the average index of prices received by farmers (1910–14 base) during the same 10 years and (2) multiplying by the current value of the parity index (1910–14 base). The revised method has the effect of increasing the parity prices of those commodities that have been high priced in relation to other farm commodities during the past 10 years and of reducing parity prices of commodities that have been relatively low priced.

The proposition that parity prices are fair prices is hard to support, especially today. A principal reason is that techniques of agricultural production have been revolutionized since 1910–14. In tacit recognition of the lack of realism of parity prices, legislation aims at different percentages of parity for different products. For example, in 1972 the corn loan plus direct payment was required to be not less than 70% of parity, while milk was to be supported between 75% and 90% of parity.

See also Golden Age of Agriculture; Price-Support Programs.

Consult (15) USDA, 1970.

—George E. Brandow, *Pennsylvania State University*

PARTIAL CORRELATION. *See* Correlation.

PARTNERSHIP, the result of an agreement between two or more people to own and operate a business together. Each individual assumes full personal liability for the debts of the joint endeavor. A partnership can be a verbal agreement between two individuals or a very detailed legal entity.

Partnerships are a common practice and are very often most successful among professional people, such as doctors, lawyers, and accountants. Advantages include the ability to share both facilities and staff as well as the opportunity to share knowledge and consultation.

United States Patent [15] **3,691,943**
Boyd [45] **Sept. 19, 1972**

[54] **TRASH COMPACTION SHELTER INCORPORATING A REMOVABLE CONTAINER**
[72] Inventor: **John A. Boyd,** 3314 Holloman Road, Falls Church, Va. 22042
[22] Filed: **June 4, 1971**
[21] Appl. No.: **150,060**

[52] **U.S. Cl.** ....**100/215,** 100/218, 214/16 B, 214/75 H
[51] **Int. Cl.** **B30b 15/30**
[58] **Field of Search**.100/218, 229 A, 215; 214/75 H, 214/16 B

[56] **References Cited**

UNITED STATES PATENTS

3,093,252	6/1963	Cahill	214/16 B
3,355,044	11/1967	Nelson	100/218
3,358,590	12/1967	Howard	100/218
3,424,078	1/1969	Boyd et al.	100/215 X
3,517,608	6/1970	Tezuka	100/218 X
3,557,683	1/1971	Boyd	100/218
3,572,513	3/1971	Tantlinger et al.	214/75 H
3,597,927	8/1971	Hemphill	100/215 UX
3,583,164	6/1971	Sherrill	100/218 UX

FOREIGN PATENTS OR APPLICATIONS

176,621	9/1961	Sweden	100/218

Primary Examiner—Billy J. Wilhite
Attorney—Roylance, Abrams, Berdo & Kaul

[57] **ABSTRACT**

A shelter structure in the form of a building having outside walls and an access door. Trash or other material can be introduced into a trash compactor contained within the structure through either an outside wall chute door or by entering the structure through the access door and placing the trash or other material inside the compactor. The compactor functions to compress the materials into bales which are moved by a suitable transportation means into a container. The container has at least one side which forms an integral part of the outside wall of the structure and the container is adapted for easy removal by a front end loading rubbish disposal truck.

9 Claims, 5 Drawing Figures

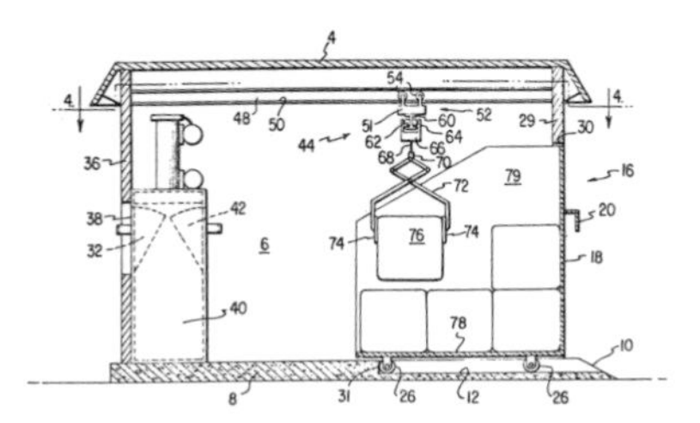

A U.S. patent grants an inventor the right to exclude others from making, using, or selling an invention for a period of 17 years.

PERFECT COMPETITION

For comparison and contrast between perfect competition and other types of markets, begin with the article on MARKET STRUCTURE, which sets forth the characteristics by which markets are classed as to structural "type." To compare perfect competition with other of these types, consult the articles on IMPERFECT COMPETITION, MONOPOLISTIC COMPETITION, OLIGOPOLY, MONOPOLY, MONOPSONY, and OLIGOPSONY.

For the historical roots of the concept, and some its present policy implications, see LAISSEZ FAIRE, PARETO OPTIMUM, FREE ENTERPRISE, CAPITALISM, and CLASSICAL ECONOMICS.

The Subject Map accompanying the article on MARKET SYSTEM displays the relationships of these and many other concepts.

However, when there is a clash of opinion, decision making is often difficult. In addition, the individual owners of the partnership, unlike the corporation, are personally responsible for any debts or other legal matters incurred by the partnership. If one individual takes action under the partnership's name, the other partners are legally responsible.

See also Corporation; Proprietorship.

PASSFIELD, LORD AND LADY. *See* Webb, Sidney J., and Beatrice Potter.

PASSIVE BENEFICIARY OF MONOPOLY. *See* Monopoly Thrust Upon a Firm.

PATENT, a form of property right giving an inventor of a new product, design, or process (or the owner of the patent, if sold) the sole legal right to use, not use, or dispose of the invention. Patents in the United States are issued for a period of 17 years by the U.S. Patent Office, with renewal possible after significant modification of the original design.

A patent has importance in economic analysis and antitrust policy because it provides a monopoly to the owner. Especially troublesome is the extension of such inherent monopoly power to pricing and output policies of the patent-holding firm or a licensee. Patent rights might also be misused (1) as the basis for tying contracts; (2) in the hoarding or monopolization of patents by one firm; (3) in cross-licensing and patent pools, which tend to reserve technology to a few dominant firms in an industry.

See also Antitrust Policy; Monopolizing; Restraint of Trade.

PATRONS OF HUSBANDRY. *See* Grange, National.

PATTERN BARGAINING, attempt by a union, in bargaining with various firms in an industry, to attain with each a set of terms comparable to those established in a key bargain. To the extent that comparable terms are achieved, an industry-wide pattern or similarity results. Deviations from the pattern often occur, largely due to economic differences among the firms.

See also Key Bargain.

PATTERNS OF CONSUMPTION. *See* Consumption.

PEAK OF PROSPERITY. *See* Business Cycles, Phases.

PEASANT ECONOMY. *See* Subsistence Economy.

PEGGED EXCHANGE RATE. *See* Exchange Rate.

PENSIONS are periodical allowances to workers or their wives and children, received from the time of retirement. The first major legislation dealing with pensions was the Social Security Act of 1935 which provided a worker with an income after age 65 if he retired. However, social security payments could not keep up with the cost of living and, as a result, many private pension plans have come into existence.

The development of the bargained pension dates from the early 1900s but did not get any major attention until 1946, when John L. Lewis won a health and welfare fund for coal miners. After that, major pension plans were added in steel companies and automotive industries. By the mid-sixties, 36% of the labor force were covered by industrial pension plans.

There are two major types of pension plans. In contributory plans, the employee usually pays the greater share of the costs; in noncontributory plans, the employer pays the cost. In addition, there are non-funded pension plans under which the employer pays the cost of the pension as it is incurred. The type of plan, benefits paid and received, and eligibility for retirement are almost always agreed upon through a bargaining process.

—William D. Wagoner, *Louisiana State University*

PER CAPITA REAL INCOME, individual personal income, mostly wages, stated in noninflationary monetary units. It is calculated by dividing net national income, adjusted to eliminate the effect of inflation or deflation, by population. It represents a national average.

It does not reflect the unequal distribution of income that exists to some degree in most countries due, among other things, to regional differences in the mix of industries and between industry and agriculture, or the fact that higher wage levels are more prevalent in large cities than in small towns and rural areas. In many underdeveloped countries, the per capita real income during the early 1970s was approximately $100 annually, whereas the U.S. figure was well over $3,000.

See also Net National Income.

PERCENTILE. *See* Central Tendency.

PERFECT COMPETITION suggests a purely competitive market with the addition of the condition that all economic units of the market have perfect knowledge of all relevant facts. For example, if one seller has a price different from existing market price, all buyers will know of this price and purchase accordingly. Under this assumption, no one would sell above or below the market price.

In addition to perfect knowledge of the market, there are four other conditions that must be met in order for a market to be perfectly competitive.

First, there must be product homogeneity. This means that the product sold by each individual seller in the market is identical to that same product sold by all other sellers. This condition must be met in pure competition so that product differentiation cannot play a part in the decisions of buyers.

A second condition of perfect competition is that each individual seller has such a small share of the entire market that he cannot influence price. In addition, there must be many buyers so that no one buyer can influence price.

Third, there can be no artificial restraints that would influence price. In this way, prices can freely fluctuate with changing conditions in the market. This implies no government price fixing or other administered prices, such as union wages.

The final condition of pure competition is that of mobility. Firms must be free to enter and exit the market and resources must be free to move among alternative uses.

When these conditions are met there is a market where only one price, the market price, prevails in the long run. There are, however, some fluctuations in the short run. Although there may be no perfectly competitive markets, the concept of one is valuable when discussing the less-than-perfect models more relevant to the real world.

See also Imperfect Competition.

Consult (14) Leftwich, 1970; Liebhafsky, 1968.

—William D. Wagoner, *Louisiana State University*

PERFECT ELASTICITY, or INFINITE ELASTICITY, of supply is a theoretical, polar extreme of elasticity coefficients. The coefficient approaches positive infinity in the limit; an infinitely small change in price elicits an infinitely large output response. When discussing perfect or infinite elasticity one usually is referring to the long-run supply schedule for some relatively small industry characterized by constant returns to scale. This supply schedule would be parallel to the horizontal axis.

In the case of perfect elasticity of supply for some industry, an increase in the demand for the product will result in no change in price; the total response to the demand change would appear as a quantity change.

PERFECT INELASTICITY, or TOTAL INELASTICITY, of supply is a theoretical, polar extreme of the set of elasticity coefficients. In the limit the elasticity coefficient approaches zero; very large changes in price lead to infinitely small changes in quantity supplied. Normally one is involved in the very short run when discussing perfectly inelastic supply. This supply curve would be parallel to the vertical Y axis.

In the theoretical case of perfect inelasticity of supply, an increase in demand will theoretically lead to no change in quantity supplied; the total response would be a price change. Price is said to be demand-determined.

PERFECTLY ELASTIC DEMAND. *See* Elastic Demand.

PERFECTLY INELASTIC DEMAND. *See* Inelastic Demand.

PERIL POINT. In tariff-reducing negotiations a country will consult with interests likely to be affected by potential cuts. Out of these consultations emerges an idea of a point beyond which tariff cuts will imperil domestic industries. This peril point sets the floor for tariff cutting in bargaining for reciprocal cuts from other nations.

See also Reciprocal Trade Agreements Act; Tariffs.

PERLMAN, SELIG (1888–1959), Polish-born American educator remembered for his pro-union attitudes as well as his excellence as a teacher.

After study in Poland and Naples, Perlman went to the United States in 1908, obtained his doctorate from the University of Wisconsin and joined the faculty there. In 1928 he published *A Theory of the Labor Movement.*

Perlman's interests were in specific attitudes and group behavior rather than general economic principles. He was very much a believer in labor unions and was convinced that negative results would occur if unions were suppressed.

PERMANENT-INCOME HYPOTHESIS, the hypothesis that consumption is more closely related to what people expect their average income to be over future years than to actual income during any particular period. Households, it is believed, save most of any increase in income that they do not expect to continue and try to maintain previous levels of consumption in the face of what are thought to be temporary declines in income.

The hypothesis explains why consumption of groups, such as farmers, with large annual variations in income does not show corresponding fluctuations. The hypothesis also fits the observation that, over a fairly long period of time, consumption rises at almost as rapid a rate as income, whereas, in the shorter run, households are known to increase their consumption much less rapidly than the rate at which their income rises. If consumption is related to permanent income rather than current income, the multiplier effects of changes in current income will be smaller than they would be if current income were the dominant influence.

Perfect competition requires a multiplicity of buyers with equal knowledge and opportunity, like these bidders at Chicago Board of Trade.

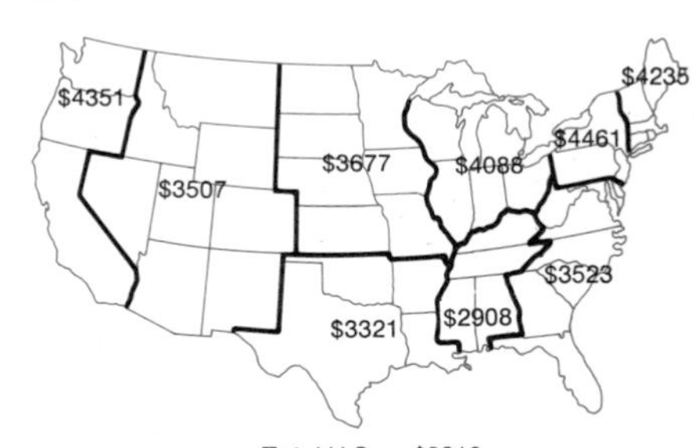

PERSONAL SAVINGS
(BILLIONS OF DOLLARS)

	Personal income	Disposable personal income	Personal savings	Savings as % of disposable personal income
1950	227.6	206.9	13.1	6.3%
1955	310.9	275.3	15.8	5.7%
1960	401.0	350.0	17.0	4.9%
1965	538.9	473.2	28.4	6.0%
1967	629.3	546.3	40.4	7.4%
1968	688.7	591.2	40.4	6.8%
1969	748.9	631.6	37.6	6.0%
1970	801.0	684.8	50.2	7.3%

Form 1040 US Department of the Treasury / Internal Revenue Service
Individual Income Tax Return 1971
For the year January 1–December 31, 1971, or other taxable year beginning .... 1971, ending .... 19 ....

Please print or type
First name and initial (If joint return, use first names and middle initials of both) | Last name | Your social security number
Present home address (Number and street, including apartment number, or rural route) | Spouse's social security number
City, town or post office, State and ZIP code | Occupation | Yours | Spouse's

Please attach Copy B of Form W–2 to back

Filing Status—check only one:
1 ☐ Single
2 ☐ Married filing jointly (even if only one had income)
3 ☐ Married filing separately and spouse is also filing. Give spouse's social security number in space above and enter first name here ▶
4 ☐ Unmarried Head of Household
5 ☐ Surviving widow(er) with dependent child
6 ☐ Married filing separately and spouse is not filing

Exemptions — Regular / 65 or over / Blind — Enter number of boxes checked
7 Yourself . . . . . ☐ ☐ ☐
8 Spouse (applies only if item 2 or 6 is checked) ☐ ☐ ☐ ▶
9 First names of your dependent children who lived with you .... Enter number ▶
10 Number of other dependents (from line 33) . . . ▶
11 Total exemptions claimed . . . . ▶

Income
12 Wages, salaries, tips, etc. (Attach Forms W–2 to back. If unavailable, attach explanation) . 12
13a Dividends (see pages 6 and 11 of instr.) $ .... 13b Less exclusion $ .... Balance . ▶ 13c
(If gross dividends and other distributions are over $100, list in Part I of Schedule B.)
14 Interest. [If $100 or less, enter total without listing in Schedule B] [If over $100, enter total and list in Part II of Schedule B] 14
15 Income other than wages, dividends, and interest (from line 40) 15
16 Total (add lines 12, 13c, 14 and 15) 16
17 Adjustments to income (such as "sick pay," moving expense, etc. from line 45) 17
18 Adjusted gross income (subtract line 17 from line 16) 18

● See page 3 of instructions for rules under which the IRS will figure your tax.
● If you do not itemize deductions and line 18 is under $10,000, find tax in Tables and enter on line 19.
● If you itemize deductions or line 18 is $10,000 or more, go to line 46 to figure tax.

Tax, Payments and Credits
19 Tax (Check if from: ☐ Tax Tables 1–13, ☐ Tax Rate Sch. X, Y, or Z, ☐ Sch. D, ☐ Sch. G or ☐ Form 4726) 19
20 Total credits (from line 54) 20
21 Income tax (subtract line 20 from line 19) 21
22 Other taxes (from line 60) 22
23 Total (add lines 21 and 22) 23
24 Total Federal income tax withheld (attach Forms W–2 or W–2P to back) . . 24
25 1971 Estimated tax payments (include 1970 overpayment allowed as a credit) . 25
26 Other payments (from line 64) 26
27 Total (add lines 24, 25, and 26) 27

Write soc. sec. no. on Check or Money Order. Attach here

Bal. Due or Refund
28 If line 23 is larger than line 27, enter BALANCE DUE Pay in full with return. Make check or money order payable to Internal Revenue Service ▶ 28
29 If line 27 is larger than line 23, enter OVERPAYMENT . . . . ▶ 29
30 Line 29 to be: (a) REFUNDED Allow at least six weeks for your refund check . . . ▶
(b) Credited on 1972 estimated tax . . . . ▶

Foreign Accounts
31 Did you, at any time during the taxable year, have any interest in or signature or other authority over a bank, securities, or other financial account in a foreign country (except in a U.S. military banking facility operated by a U.S. financial institution)? If "Yes," attach Form 4683. (For definitions, see Form 4683.) . . . . . . ▶ ☐ Yes ☐ No

Under penalties of perjury, I declare that I have examined this return, including accompanying schedules and statements, and to the best of my knowledge and belief it is true, correct, and complete.

Sign here
▶ Your signature | Date
▶ Spouse's signature (if filing jointly, BOTH must sign even if only one had income)
▶ Signature of preparer other than taxpayer, based on all information of which he has any knowledge. | Date
Address

The personal income tax form.

PER-SE ILLEGALITY, a phrase denoting those violations of antitrust law which are inherently illegal: if evidence of the practice exists, there is no defense that it was "reasonable" in effect or result. Among practices held by federal courts to be *per se* illegal under various antitrust laws are price fixing and market sharing, the execution of a tying contract by a monopolist, and various predatory practices by a monopolizing firm designed to damage severely or eliminate a business rival from competition.

See also Collusion; Predatory Practices; Price Fixing; Rule of Reason; Tying Contract.

PERSONAL INCOME (PI), the aggregate amount of current income received by all individuals in a given year. This figure includes all wages and salaries; unincorporated business and nonprofit institutional income; rental income; dividends and interest; transfer payments from government and business, such as social security benefits, pensions, and unemployment insurance; and nonmonetary income, such as the estimated value of food consumed on farms and the estimated value of homes occupied by their owners.

Personal income is usually derived from the National Income (NI) because of the difficulty in estimating such components of PI as nonmonetary income and unincorporated business income. Undistributed profits and direct corporate taxes are deducted from NI, and transfer payments are added to the remaining figure to arrive at PI. Transfer payments are not a part of NI because they do not reflect any current production.

Personal income is often used interchangeably with disposable income as an indication of standard of living or individual spending because PI is the actual amount people have to spend, save, and pay taxes.

See also Disposable Personal Income; Transfer Payments.

PERSONAL INCOME TAX, a tax on the income of individuals. "Taxable Income" may be broadly defined as the sum of (1) an individual's expenditures for consumption goods and services, whether from "factor" or "transfer" sources, (2) the estimated monetary value of his nonmarket consumption, plus (3) any change in the individual's net worth. In the United States, the personal income tax base is generally looked upon as a current flow of wealth to a family spending unit in the form of monetary receipts or factor earnings. In 1971, this net tax yielded over $86 billion to the federal government.

PERSONAL INVESTMENT, individual spending of disposable personal income for consumer durable goods, new securities and bonds, and other potentially profitable ventures. Personal savings are not a part of personal investment.

The rate of personal investment depends on such noneconomic elements as technology, politics, and expectations and, thus, is extremely variable.

See also Consumption; Disposable Personal Income.

PERSONAL SAVINGS, the amount of disposable personal income not spent on consumption. Personal savings is influenced by the size of family income and future expectations. As the amount of disposable income increases, the marginal propensity to save usually increases. On the other hand, there is less motivation to accumulate savings when anticipated future income appears stable, regardless of its size.

See also Savings.

PERSONAL TAXES, federal, state, and local levies on personal income to finance governmental expenditures and to redistribute income. These direct taxes include income, property, estate (inheritance), and gift taxes. Indirect taxes, levied on goods and services, are not considered personal.

See also Taxes.

PHALANXES. *See* Fourier, François Marie Charles.

PHANTOM FREIGHT. In a system of basing-point pricing, the price of a commodity is made the same at various delivery points by adding the averaged freight charge to the base price (that prevailing at the production city). Those products sold at delivery points nearer the basing-point therefore carry a higher freight rate than actual freight costs would be. The difference is called "phantom freight" and is borne by the buyer.

See also Basing-Point System; FTC v. Cement Institute.

PHILLIPS CASE (1954), key decision in which the Supreme Court concluded that the Federal Power Commission (FPC) has "jurisdiction over the rates of all [sales for resale]. . . of natural gas in interstate commerce . . . whether occurring before, during, or after transmission by an interstate pipeline company." The decision negated part of the Natural Gas Act of 1938, which provided for FPC regulation of the interstate transmission of natural gas and its sale for resale and specifically exempted the production and gathering of gas from FPC control. As a result of this decision, the FPC expanded the scope of its activities to include the regulation of the prices of natural gas producers.

See also Federal Power Commission; Regulated Industries; Regulation; Regulatory Commissions.

Consult (17) Kitch, 1968; MacAvoy, 1971.

PHILLIPS CURVE, the statistical relationship between the rate of change of money wage rates and the level of unemployment first described by British economist A. W. Phillips. A generalized Phillips curve is shown. The shape of the curve corresponds to what one may expect from simple economic theory. As demand for any commodity increases, its price rises, and conversely. Thus, if unemployment is low, any increased demand for labor will result in rising wage rates. If unemployment is high, wages will rise less rapidly and may even fall.

The original Phillips curve related the rate of wage increase to the level of unemployment. A similar relationship can be derived between increases in the general price level and unemployment. For example, suppose productivity (output per worker) is growing at 3% per year. According to the figure, if unemployment is 5.5%, then wages will rise by 3%. However, because productivity is also up by 3% there is no increase in labor costs to the firm and, therefore, no pressure on prices. Policies that encourage rapid productivity growth, labor mobility and the acquisition of skills can shift the Phillips curve to the left and mitigate the terms of the trade between inflation and unemployment.

—Carlisle E. Moody, Jr., *College of William and Mary*

PHILOSOPHY OF WEALTH (1885). *See* Clark, John Bates.

PHYSICAL PRODUCTIVITY, as distinguished from value productivity, is a purely technological phenomenon. The physical product schedules usually analyzed in economics are total, average, and marginal. These schedules, calculated for the short run, reflect the law of diminishing returns.

The total product schedule defines the maximum output, given the quantities of other factors and the state of the arts, that can be obtained by varying a given factor of production. As labor increases, over broad limits, total product rises.

The average product schedule is derived by dividing total product by the quantity of the relevant factor used to produce that output. Average product is plotted against factor quantities.

The marginal product schedule is derived by dividing the change in total product by the increment in the factor necessary to effect the change. Marginal product is plotted factor against quantity.

See also Factor Productivity.

—Robert L. Brite, *Louisiana State University*

PHYSIOCRATS, a group of economic writers influential in France in the middle of the eighteenth century. Led by François Quesnay, they attempted to discover the general or natural laws which direct economic activity and to refute the doctrines of mercantilism. Their abstract reasoning marks the first step toward the development of economics as a discipline. The major contributions of the Physiocrats were (1) the broadening of the concept of wealth, from the mercantilists' treasure to goods produced with nature's aid, and (2) the development of the concept of interdependent sectors in the economic system and the importance of intersectoral flows.

See also Quesnay, François; Tableau économique.

PI. *See* Personal Income.

PICKETING, the advertising of a labor dispute on signs carried by people (usually striking workers) walking past the plant gate, store entrance, or work site. The dispute may be over the employer's unwillingness to recognize a union or new contract terms.

Picketing has long been a controversial activity. Besides advertising the dispute, it encourages customers, other workers, or other unionists to "respect" (not cross) the picket line. Because it thus threatens or actually imposes economic harm on the employer, courts sympathetic to management, long after legal recognition of unions, continued to prohibit or enjoin picketing. Further opposition was based on the possibly intimidating presence of the picketers, or their potentially violent opposition to strike breakers crossing their lines and entering the plant.

With the turn to more favorable attitudes toward labor in the 1930s, picketing became legal if it was done peacefully, and was not obstructionist, threatening, or used to enforce an illegal demand.

PIECE WORK describes the payment of wages for each unit of work accomplished rather than for each unit of time worked. Since earnings become a function of output, this is an incentive form of pay that provides a direct stimulus to the worker. It is most common in the apparel and textile industries.

PIGOU, ARTHUR CECIL (1877–1959), was the most important neoclassical economist, after Alfred Marshall, and the father of welfare economics: *Economics of Welfare* (1920). Concerned with unemployment and other social problems, Pigou attempted to use money as a measure of the economic welfare of society. He considered the size, distribution and stability of income as measurable welfare criteria and developed a distinction between social and private cost and benefits. The concept of social cost, in particular, has been used extensively in the economic analysis of pollution and other aspects of economic activity.

PHILLIPS CURVE

The basic concepts involved in the Phillips curve "trade-off" are discussed in the general articles on INFLATION and UNEMPLOYMENT OF LABOR; more specific aspects of the trade-off are presented in the articles on CYCLICAL UNEMPLOYMENT and STRUCTURAL UNEMPLOYMENT. Central to many of the policy proposals designed to improve the attainable combinations of price-level stability and high employment are labor force and labor market programs, discussed in the articles on MANPOWER POLICY, HUMAN RESOURCES, and LABOR MOBILITY. See also the Subject Map accompanying the article on WAGES.

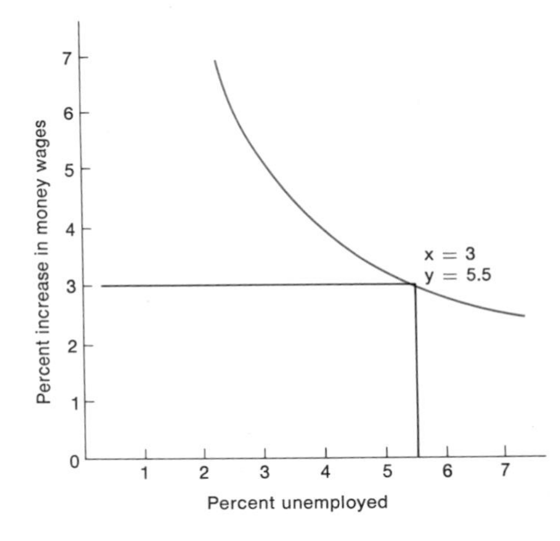

Pigou also suggested an alternative to the Keynesian argument that the economic system contained no mechanism for restoring full employment after a depression. The "Pigou effect" suggests that as prices and wages decline, the value of money-holding will increase, thus causing an expansion in consumer spending. While the Pigou effect has theoretical validity, it does not appear to be a powerful enough influence to bring an economy out of a depression situation.

PIGOU EFFECT, the effect named after its formulator, A.C. Pigou, an English economist, of falling prices on the real value of liquid assets and, thus, on saving and consumption. As prices fall, the real value (purchasing power equivalent) of financial assets of fixed money value increases. According to Pigou, this causes an increase in consumption (an upward shift in the consumption function) if, as Pigou postulated, the increase in the value of these assets achieves some part of the objectives of the savers. The Pigou effect (of falling prices) reduces fluctuations in consumption and, therefore, in incomes and employment.

PLANNED INVESTMENT. *See* Investment Schedule; Marginal Efficiency of Capital.

PLANNER'S (STATE) PREFERENCES, the particular quantities of goods and services that the planners (central planning board) prefer to have produced over all feasible alternatives. Planner's preferences can be revealed *ex ante* (beforehand) through the announced plan and *ex post facto* (after the fact) through the actual governmental expenditures.

An economy is said to be dominated by planner's preferences when a large portion of resources are directed by the administrative plan rather than by consumer behavior in the free markets (consumer preferences). Most economies have their resource allocation influenced by both consumer's and planner's preferences.

ECONOMIC ORGANIZATION OF THE SOVIET COMMAND ECONOMY

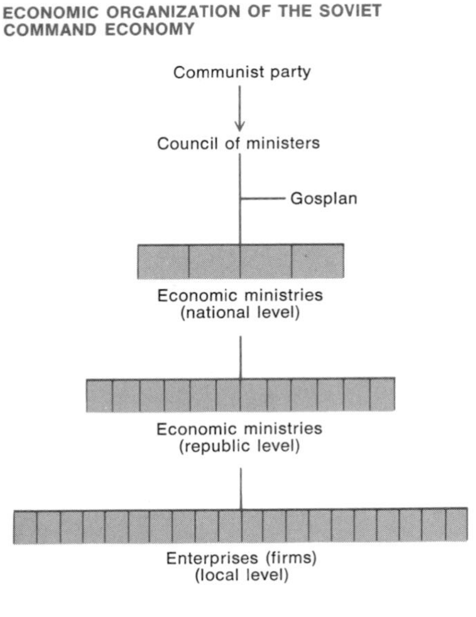

PLANNING (COMMUNISM). Economic planning is the institution established by the communist states to achieve their long-term goals of economic growth and development. The Communist Party establishes the broad economic objectives for the state and these are incorporated into a five-year plan, whose goals are broken into annual plans that provide the economic units with their operating instructions. The annual plan permits the state to incorporate revisions in its long-term objectives when conditions warrant.

Operation. The first stage of the process is for Gosplan, the state planning committee, to take the broad objectives of the government and design a tentative plan, with control figures, to achieve these goals. Meanwhile, the ministries and firms are assessing their capabilities and categorizing their needs. The control figures are broken down by the ministries and the enterprise is informed of the level of operation necessary to obtain the economic goals. This is generally accomplished by May. During the next few months the production enterprise negotiates for alterations in the plan to accommodate specific circumstances at the firm level. These modifications are aggregated as the plan retraces its steps to Gosplan, usually by sometime in October.

Gosplan now has the monumental task of assuring that the plan is consistent and feasible and will accomplish the government's objectives. This is done by a method known as "material balances." The size and complexity of the economic system guarantees that the plan is "balanced" in name only. The priority system is necessary to have flexibility in the program.

Once the plan is as nearly balanced as the system and time will permit, the government approves it, and it is broken down once again. In this manner, the state firms receive their operating instructions for the next year, hopefully before the calendar year begins.

See also Gosplan.

Consult (26) Campbell, 1966; Davies, 1969; Montias, 1962; Spulber, 1969.

—Francis W. Rushing, *College of William and Mary*

PLANNING (SOCIALISM). Under socialism the market mechanism is superseded by varying degrees of planning. In some cases public ownership of productive factors and central planning are retained, but there is freedom of consumer choice. A planning board stimulates the market process by setting prices and by establishing rules for plant managers that are geared to bring the same result as in a competitive, free-enterprise economy. In addition full-employment is assured via planned investment. In other cases, prices as planning tools are eliminated through input-output analysis, which involves direct determination of physical quantities to be produced if there is to be a consistent overall plan without bottlenecks or superfluous inventories.

See also Centralization; Government-Controlled Economy; Market Economy.

Consult (26) Loucks and Whitney, 1969.

PLANNING FOR GROWTH, the optimal allocation of resources, particularly capital investment, among the various sectors of the economy so as to promote development.

The need for planning springs from several sources. The vital role of government in the typically small Less Developed Country (LDC) economy as an important (if not the most important) employer of labor, a major saver (through taxes) and investor in infrastructure, and the recipient and allocator of foreign aid, gives government the ability and the responsibility to investigate and regulate the impact of its actions on development. Secondly, the often important externalities associated with individual investments in LDC's require that investments be coordinated.

In addition, market imperfections in LDC's lead to incorrect market prices and may lead, possibly, without government planning and intervention, to improper resource allocation by private investors. Social and other goals frequently override optimal economic goals (Pareto Optimum), requiring government intervention and planning even in a perfect market system. The tools of planning are many, as are the methods of implementation—from tax/subsidy intervention in the market to direct control through fiat or government ownership (nationalization).

See also Allocation; Infrastructure; Less Developed Countries; Nationalization; Subsidy.

Consult (24) Johnson, 1962; Waterson, 1965; Watson and Dirlan, 1965.

—Charles Staelin, *University of Michigan*

PLANNING - PROGRAMMING - BUDGETING SYSTEM (PPBS), system of federal budgeting introduced in the Defense Department during the early 1960s and extended throughout the executive branch in 1965. It is designed to promote more efficient allocation of resources among governmental programs. Each federal agency is required to state explicitly the output of each program (measured in dollars where quantification is possible) and to state explicitly the relationships among similar programs including those of other agencies. Outputs must be related to inputs with evidence that the least-cost method of achieving a given output is being used. Agencies are required to engage in long-range planning and to evaluate results of on-going programs.

See also Federal Budget.

PLANT, the smallest whole entity in a firm or industry, that physical facility of a firm where workers are employed. The plant belongs to an individual firm and the firm is usually a part of an industry. There may be only one, or there may be several plants belonging to one firm. A plant may take the form of a factory or any actual building, or it may be any place where operations of the firm take place as coal mines, oil fields, or drilling rigs in the ocean.

See also Firm; Industry.

POINT ELASTICITY, the value of price elasticity of demand at a given point on a demand curve. The concept of elasticity of demand, however, implicitly requires that changes in quantity demanded result from changes in prices: technically a demand curve possesses elasticity only between two points. This problem is circumvented whenever estimates of point elasticity are made by allowing price to change only very slightly and recording the resultant change in quantity demanded. When the change in price from a certain value is very small, then the ensuing change in quantity demanded will likely also be small, and the resulting coefficient of elasticity can be said to refer to the elasticity of demand at a given point on the demand curve. Strictly, point elasticity is the reciprocal of the slope of the curve times the ratio of price to quantity.

POINT FOUR PROGRAM, a U.S. technical assistance program for less developed countries, first put forward as the fourth point of President Truman's inaugural address of 1949. It envisaged "a bold new program for making the benefits of our scientific advances and industrial progress available for the improvement and growth of underdeveloped areas" and resulted in the Act for International Development of 1950 and the establishment of the Technical Cooperation Administration—forerunner of the present Agency for International Development (AID). Early programs concentrated primarily on technical assistance in such areas as agriculture, education, public health, and transportation and were accompanied by limited financing of related infrastructure.

See also Foreign Aid; Infrastructure.

POPULATION, STATISTICAL. In statistics, population refers to the totality of phenomena under investigation. It is the reference set, the set of all possible observations or outcomes from which we can select samples. Populations can be hypothetical (the results of an infinite number of rolls of a pair of dice) or real (consumption expenditures of Detroit residents), finite (expenditures for pollution control by U.S. cities) or infinite (the income levels of all past, present, or future visitors to Miami Beach).

See also Sampling.

POPULATION GROWTH, trends of increases and decreases in population and, more broadly, effects of population changes on a nation's economy, ecological equilibrium, and growth trends.

In 1798, Thomas Malthus observed that the population tended to double every 25 years in the American colonies, where resources were abundant, and postulated a universal tendency for population to grow in a geometric progression unless checked by food supply. The means of subsistence, however, increased in an arithmetic progression. Thus, theorized Malthus, growing rates of population result in diminishing return to workers.

According to neo-Malthusian theory,

BUSINESS EXPENDITURES FOR NEW PLANT AND EQUIPMENT
(BILLIONS OF DOLLARS)

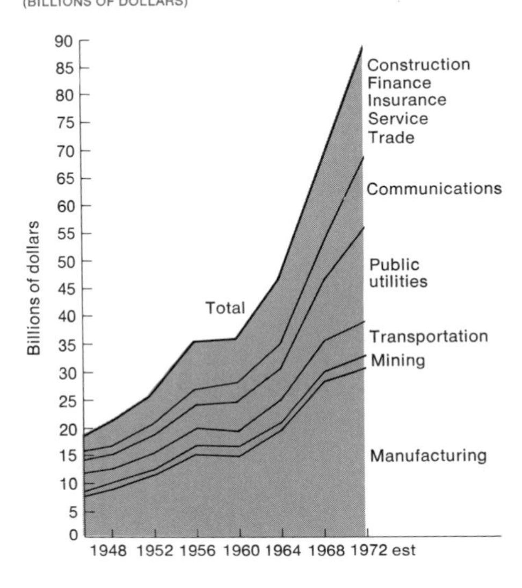

POPULATION GROWTH

Developed Countries	Percentage rate of growth	Number of years for population to double
Australia	2.0	35
Canada	1.6	44
Czechoslovakia	0.5	140
France	0.9	78
Israel	2.9	24
Japan	1.1	64
Union of Soviet Socialist Republics	1.1	64
United Kingdom	0.6	117
United States	1.2	58
West Germany	1.0	70
Less-developed Countries		
Algeria	3.0	23
Brazil	3.0	23
Chad	1.5	47
China (mainland)	1.4	50
India	2.5	28
Kenya	2.0	35
Pakistan	2.1	33
Peru	3.1	23
United Arab Republic	2.5	28
Venezuela	3.5	20

POPULATION GROWTH
POPULATION OF THE UNITED STATES

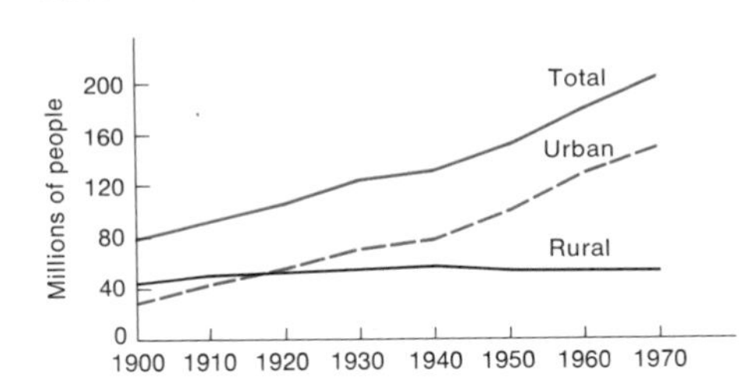

POVERTY

For one way of delineating the poverty sector, see the article on POVERTY LINE. A wide variety of programs, old and new, to alleviate poverty or assist those suffering from it are discussed in the articles on AID TO FAMILIES WITH DEPENDENT CHILDREN, GENRERAL ASSISTANCE, OLD-AGE ASSISTANCE, PUBLIC ASSISTANCE, MINIMUM WAGE, SOCIAL DIVIDEND, INCOME MAINTENANCE, and NEGATIVE INCOME TAX. General approaches are discussed in SUBSIDY and INCOME REDISTRIBUTION.

The Subject Maps accompanying FEDERAL BUDGET and WAGES display the interrelationships of many of these concepts.

POVERTY LINE

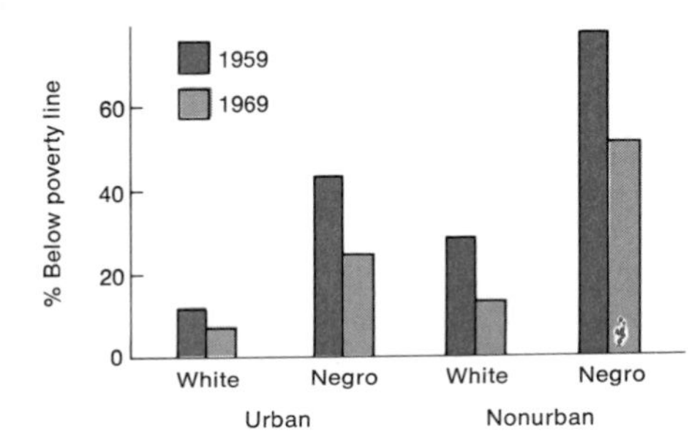

Poverty: simple to recognize; complex to remedy.

the pressures of overpopulation will be lessened through war, pestilence, and famine. In many underdeveloped countries, in which overpopulation is common, a high rate of disease and hunger shorten life expectancy and, therefore, effectively reduce the overburdened means of subsistence. Such countries are working to control their population growth through birth control and family planning programs. These countries are also trying to increase their food supplies with the use of pesticides and fertilizers, as well as modern farming equipment and growing methods, and thus strike a balance between their populations and means of subsistence.

Population Trends. In Western Europe and the United States, the net reproduction rate, a measurement of population growth, appears to be declining, although the birth rate in the United States is higher than in most advanced or wealthy nations. This growth rate, however, affects the nation's ecological equilibrium. Ecologists maintain that a child born in the United States is more a burden on the environment than a child born, for example, in India, because he generates more waste, uses more electrical power, and contaminates the air with more toxic gases. Thus, population growth, as well as technological progress is a major cause of ecological imbalance.

If however, the current trend in population growth continues, the United States will reach zero population growth (ZPG) during the late 1970s. Some people think that ZPG is compatible with environmental equilibrium and that it will eventually aid solution of the problem of poverty.

See also Malthus, Thomas; Net Reproduction Rate.

—Charles Staelin, *University of Michigan*

PORTFOLIO, in financial markets, all the stocks, bonds, or other securities held by an individual or corporation for investment purposes. In banking, the term is sometimes stretched to include cash and loans.

See also Balance Sheet, Bank; Portfolio Balancing.

PORTFOLIO BALANCING, the attempt on the part of investors, particularly, to arrange their holdings of monetary assets—including long-term securities, short-term securities, loans, and cash—to earn the maximum income consistent with maintaining the liquidity needed for day-to-day operations. Holding all cash yields no income, but tying up all assets in long-term commitments may lead to bankruptcy if immediate payments exceed the cash on hand.

PORTFOLIO INVESTMENT. *See* Direct Investment.

POSITIVE THEORY OF CAPITAL (1889). *See* Böhm-Bawerk, Eugen.

POVERTY LINE, the level of income below which people cannot achieve an adequate standard of living. The poverty line changes with changes in the cost of living.

Because of the unequal distribution of income in the United States, many people live far below the average income level. In 1971, the poverty line for a family of four was $4,113. This figure represents only one-third of the average income of all four-person families.

The most depressing aspect of poverty is that unemployment is not necessarily the main cause. In 1971, about 40% of all families headed by men had a source of wage income, but were still unable to raise themselves out of poverty. One reason is that most victims of poverty have a low educational level, also many of the jobs they hold are not covered by minimum-wage laws.

POWER TRANSMISSION INDUSTRY. *See* Regulated Industries.

PPBS. *See* Planning-Programming-Budgeting System.

PRECAUTIONARY DEMAND. *See* Liquidity Preference.

PRECONDITIONS, a transitional stage of growth in which the political and social structure of the traditional society is moving toward a modern industrial society, accompanied by the development of an infrastructure centering on transport, communications, refining raw materials, and the beginnings of modern manufacturing. Such preconditions existed in Western Europe during the late 17th and early 18th centuries.

See also Stages of Growth.

PREDATORY PRACTICES, those actions by a dominant firm in a market having the intent of damaging or eliminating competitors and thereby ensuring monopolistic advantages to the dominant firm. Because of these anti-competitive effects, predatory practices such as local price discrimination, sales below cost, or malicious interference with a competitor's product or business operations, have been regularly condemned by Federal courts under the antitrust laws.

In economic analysis there is often a thin line between price competition and practices deemed predatory, and the evidence of predatory intent is not often easily detected.

See also Antitrust Policy; Monopolizing; Sherman Antitrust Act.

PREFERENCE, CONSUMER'S. *See* Consumer's Preference.

PREFERENCE, TIME. *See* Time Preference.

PREFERENCE ORDERING. *See* Utility Function.

PREFERENCE STOCK. *See* Preferred Stock.

PREFERENCES, PLANNER'S. *See* Planner's (State) Preferences.

PREFERRED STOCK, a type of capital stock, is that stock on which dividends must be paid before they are paid on common, or ordinary, stock. It also has preference in the distribution of net assets as well as of a specified amount of the profits. Preferred stock, also called prior stock or preference stock, is often divided into Class A and Class B, where Class A stock has priority over Class B stock. Unlike common stock, preferred stock is not issued by all corporations.

See also Stock.

PRE-MARXIAN SOCIALISM can be conveniently divided into two basic schools of thought: (1) utopian socialism and (2) analytical, or Ricardian, socialism.

Utopian socialist thought, represented by men such as Saint-Simon, F.M.C. Fourier, and Robert Owen, was aware and critical of the evils of capitalism. However, the Utopians rarely had much beyond a humanitarian basis for their criticism and thus had little influence upon economic thought.

Analytical or Ricardian socialism, however, used existing economic techniques to criticize the classical analysis of capitalism. Writers such as Sismondi, Proudhon and Hodgskin rejected the optimism and harmony of interest which characterized classical economics. Sismondi, for example, felt that competition and the separation of labor and capitalists would lead to over-production and crises. These writers provided Marx with many of the ideas central to his criticism of capitalism.

See also Das Kapital; Owen, Robert; Ricardo, David.

PRESENT COST. *See* Reproduction Cost.

PRESENT VALUE, the capitalized value of a future income stream. It is the future value discounted down to the present at a specific rate. For example, at a 6% rate, $106 due a year from now is worth $100 today. The present value of a series of payments is the sum of the present values for each year the payment is to be received.

See also Discounted Value; Net Productivity of Capital.

Consult (22) Bach, 1971.

PRICE is the pecuniary consideration that induces the exchange of a unit of that commodity or service between two individuals. Assuming that the exchange involved is voluntary, price may be thought of as a manifestation of a "meeting of minds."

Exchange takes place in markets and in the typical market a large number of units change hands at a single market price. By analogy market price can be thought of as representing a meeting of minds for a group of individuals—frequently a large group. An individual purchaser has an implicit schedule of quantities that he would purchase at various prices, and, similarly, sellers have schedules of quantities that they would be willing to sell at various prices.

These individual schedules may then be aggregated to yield market demand and supply schedules which may then be graphed as market demand and supply curves (such as D and S in the figure). Market price is given by the intersection of the demand and supply curves and is that price at which the quantity that demanders wish to buy is just the quantity that suppliers wish to sell.

See also Demand; Supply.

Consult (14) Marshall, 1920.

—Clarence C. Morrison, *Indiana University*

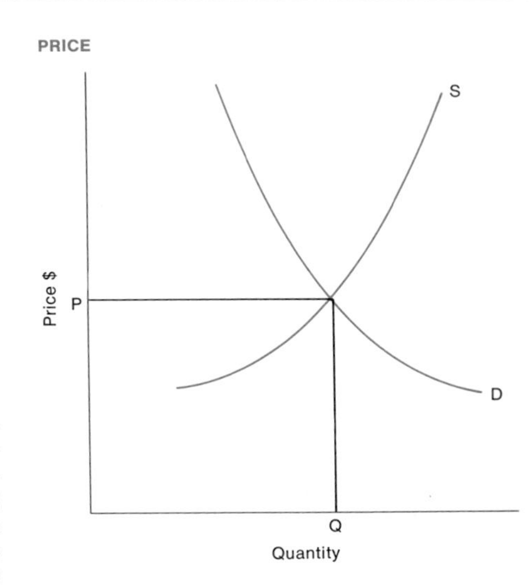

PRICE, SHADOW. *See* Shadow Price.

PRICE COMPETITION, a means of competing for greater shares of the market. Pure price competition occurs in those market structures where products are homogeneous and cannot compete by product differentiation, such as advertising and variations in design of the product.

A homogeneous product is a product (such as nails) that is identical in all firms in the industry that sell it. All products of purely competitive markets are homogeneous. In purely competitive markets price competition is the only means of competition available.

In other market structures, such as monopolistically competitive industries, price competition also occurs, often in the form of price wars. Price wars begin when one firm in the industry lowers its price below the prevailing market price. In order to retain their share of the market, all other firms in the industry must lower their prices. This type of price competition is sometimes found among gasoline companies.

PRICE DETERMINATION. *See* National Income Determination.

PRICE DISCRIMINATION occurs when a firm sells a product to two different buyers at different prices where all other material aspects of the sales are the same. Some forms of price discrimination are routine and legal: different electric power rates to residential and indus-

PRICE LEVEL

Ways of measuring the level of prices are explained in the article on PRICE INDEXES. For a description of one such index, see CONSUMER PRICE INDEX. Theoretical explanations of the determination of the price level are presented in EQUATION OF EXCHANGE and INFLATIONARY GAP. One consequence of a changing price level is explained in INCOME REDISTRIBUTION. And for a fuller discussion of changes in the price level, see the articles on INFLATION and DEFLATION.

The Subject Maps accompanying this article and the article on FEDERAL BUDGET display many of the factors affecting price level.

"GOOD GRACIOUS, YOU MEAN TO SAY SOMETHING'S BEEN GOING ON HERE FOR FIFTY YEARS?"

Electric company executives called on the carpet for price fixing in 1961 tried to shift the blame to subordinates.

trial users; higher adult than children's theater ticket prices. Other forms are illegal where the effect is to lessen competition substantially either at the seller's (Clayton Act, Section 2) or buyer's (Robinson-Patman Act) level of competition. The principal thrust of the prohibition is against the mass distributor who, through his ability to absorb losses in other parts of his market, may price products lower in a locality where competition is especially vigorous, thereby damaging the local (often smaller) competitor.

See also Antitrust Policy; Clayton Act; Robinson-Patman Act; United States v. New York Great A & P Company.

PRICE EFFECT. *See* Consumer Equilibrium.

PRICE ELASTICITY OF DEMAND. According to the law of demand, the quantity of a product demanded is inversely related to its price. This concept of demand defines the nature of the relationship between price and quantity demanded. The responsiveness, or price elasticity of demand, is calculated by dividing the percentage change in quantity demanded by the percentage change in the price of a commodity.

PRICE FIXING is agreement (conspiracy) among several or all firms in an industry to set prices jointly to yield a profit greater than would result if price competition prevailed. Price fixing is challenged in antitrust law because it eliminates business firm efficiencies flowing from the pressure of price competition. Federal courts have consistently ruled that overt price-fixing agreements (cartels, bidding rings), being restraints of trade forbidden under Section 1 of the Sherman Act, are *per se* illegal, as are output-limitation agreements (market sharing, quotas) in support of price fixing.

An alternate method of securing the same end as overt price fixing is conscious parallelism of action, or tacit compliance in the price set by a competitor. This pricing agreement is difficult to prosecute, however, because of the absence of clear intent.

See also Collusion; Conscious Parallelism; Conspiracy Doctrine; Market Sharing; Restraint of Trade; Trade Association.

PRICE INDEXES, indicators of the general level of prices, and attempts to average price changes of individual goods and services into a composite that will reflect the net effect of all the price changes upon the general level of prices.

The Consumer Price Index (CPI) is the index most frequently quoted in reference to the price level. CPI is a statistical measure of changes in the prices of commodities that are deemed essential to maintain a standard of living for an urban working class family unit. Each item is given a weight equal to its importance in the family budget, as determined from consumer spending patterns in the early 1960s. CPI is compiled by the Bureau of Labor Statistics of the Department of Labor and is often referred to as the cost-of-living index. This cost-of-living index is sometimes used to compute pay increases in labor-management contracts.

The Wholesale Price Index (WPI) is a statistical composite of price changes in the primary markets based on large lot sales of selected commodities in primary markets. It is particularly useful in determining long-run trends. Because CPI and WPI do not measure and weigh the same commodities, they do not necessarily move in the same direction.

The Gross National Product Implicit Price Deflator measures changes in the average price of final goods and services by combining several other indexes and applying them to GNP in current dollars to derive GNP in constant dollars relative to a base period.

See also Consumer Price Index; GNP Deflator; Wholesale Price Index.

Consult (7) Ludtke, 1967.

—William D. Wagoner, *Louisiana State University*

PRICE LEADERSHIP refers to the situation in which one or more firms act as a leader in setting a price that other firms in the industry follow. The firm that becomes the leader in price setting is usually the firm with the lowest cost. Due to low cost, a lower price can be charged the consumer. As a result, the other firms in the industry, in order to capture any part of the market, must charge the same price as the price leader.

A second way in which price leadership occurs is in oligopolistic situations, where there are only a few firms in the industry. In this case, the firm that sets the price is very often the largest or dominant firm.

PRICE LEVEL, the average level of money prices, a general indicator of the state of the economy.

Measurement. The price level is usually measured by a price index, which relates current prices to prices of a base period in the past and indicates periods of inflation and deflation. The Consumer Price Index measures changes in the power of the dollar to purchase typical items in a consumer's budget. The Wholesale Price Index measures shifts in the primary markets by examining large commercial transactions. The Gross National Product Implicit Price Deflator measures movements in the average price of final goods and services included in GNP.

PRICE LEVEL

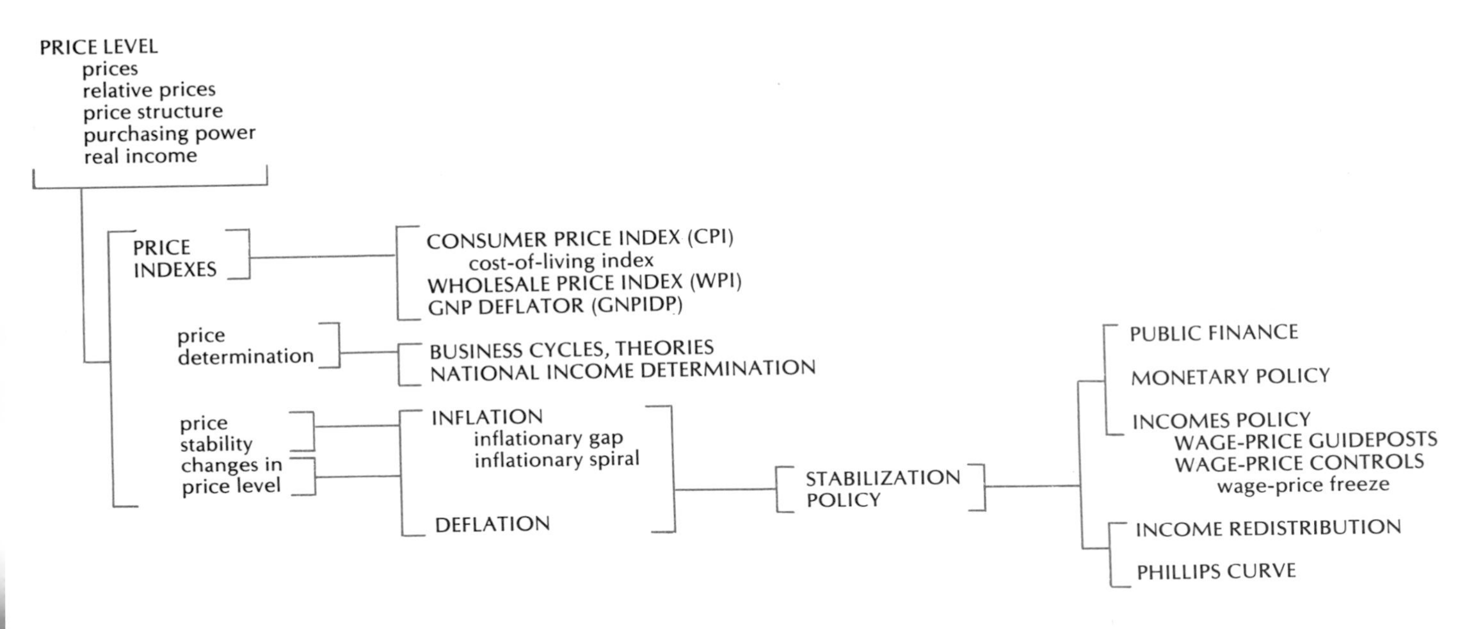

The Subject Maps in the Encyclopedia illustrate the coverage of particular aspects of economics, showing the interrelationships among the articles in twenty-one critical areas of study. Entries in capital letters are subjects for which there are separate articles in the Encyclopedia. Entries in small letters are references to the article immediately above and provide some idea of content.

The Subject Maps are arranged alphabetically in the Encyclopedia under the following titles:

Antitrust Policy
Banking System
Business Cycles
Capital
Circular Flow of Income
Demand Theory
Economic Systems
Factor Markets
Federal Budget
History of Economic Ideas
International Trade Theory
Labor Market
Labor Movement
Market System
Money and Monetary Policy
National Income
Price Level
Regulation
Supply
Theory of the Firm
Wages

Got to Come Down to Earth Sometime

—Seibel, in *The Richmond Times-Dispatch*

Agriculture Secretary Benson's program of flexible price supports was frozen out by the farm bloc in Congress.

Changes. Inflation is a general rise in the prices of goods and services. Unless money incomes rise at the same rate as prices, inflation causes real income of individuals to fall, because the amount of goods and services they can buy with a given money income decreases. When the purchasing power of consumers decreases, their total welfare is decreased. On the other hand, deflation is a fall in the general level of prices. Deflation gives fixed amounts of income more purchasing power. Therefore, deflation improves the welfare of individuals if their money income does not fall with prices.

Theories of Inflation. The demand-pull theory of inflation states that inflation occurs because there is excess demand in the economy; fiscal and monetary policy can often be used to correct this type of inflation. The cost-push theory is that resource prices rise because of such costs as labor unions' wage victories, and that these higher resource prices inflate the prices of finished goods; price guideposts and freezes are sometimes used to correct this type of inflation. The structural imbalance (sectoral) theory states that a large and rapid shift in the makeup of demand can cause a sharp increase in the prices of those sectors where demand has increased; because of factor immobility and price reluctance to fall, price increases in the new higher demand sectors are not offset by decreases in the other sectors.

Remedies. Because major changes in the general level of prices indicate upsets in the economic system, the United States has set the stabilization of prices as one of the national economic objectives. When costs get out of control, the government sometimes takes action to stabilize them. Two methods used are price guideposts and price freezes, essentially war-time controls. Guideposts are essentially voluntary guidelines for management to follow. In 1971, when price guideposts proved ineffective, President Nixon enforced a 90-day freeze on prices.

Significance. Because prices act as allocators of economic goods, they are the mechanism that determines what goods are to be produced in an economy, who is to produce them, and how they are to be distributed. In this sense, therefore, prices act as the basic force in a capitalistic economy.

See also Price Indexes.

Consult (7) Ferguson, 1968; Leftwich, 1970; Liebhafsky, 1968.

—William D. Wagoner, *Louisiana State University*

PRICE MAINTENANCE. *See* Resale Price Maintenance.

PRICES. *See* Price Level.

PRICE SETTING. *See* Public Utilities.

PRICE STRUCTURE. *See* Price Level.

PRICE-SUPPORT PROGRAMS are governmental means of assisting farm income by putting floors under prices received by farmers. A program usually involves both holding a commodity price at or above a certain level and dealing with the resulting imbalance between production and consumption. Virtually all countries have agricultural price- or income-support programs of some kind.

The usual device for supporting prices of crops in the United States is the nonrecourse loan. The means of supporting the price of milk for manufacturing purposes is even simpler: the government merely stands ready to buy cheese, butter, and dry nonfat milk at prices that will return a desired price to farmers for the milk used for such products.

In the absence of support, the price of a farm commodity moves to a point where the amount removed from the market by private buyers equals the amount supplied to the market. When support prices are above market-clearing prices—as they usually are intended to be—the amount demanded falls short of the amount supplied. The unmarketable surplus must somehow be dealt with by the government. The usual first step is for the government to acquire the surplus and store it if the commodity is or can be made storable. In order to avoid endless accumulation of surpluses, however, it may (1) give the commodities to the poor or to a special outlet like the School Lunch Program; (2) give the commodities to poor countries; (3) sell them in commercial markets abroad by means of export subsidies, and (4) control production so that no surpluses are produced.

A sustainable price support program for an exported crop may include government commodity loans to maintain a floor price, storage of any unmarketable surpluses, export subsidies to permit sales abroad, prohibitions on imports of the commodity, and production control to keep farmers from growing more than can be utilized. Such programs can be costly to the government and may conflict with international trade policy.

Origin and Use. Price support programs in the United States have evolved over the years. They began in a tentative way with the Farm Board of 1929 and became firmly established in 1933 after years of extreme depression. Following World War II, the principal source of economic pressure on farmers was rapid technological advance, which increased production, depressed farm prices relative to other prices, and greatly reduced the farm population. Programs have been directed mainly to the principal field crops—feed grains, wheat, cotton, tobacco, rice, peanuts, and sugar beet and cane. Dairy products have been almost continually supported, but meat animals and poultry products have had only occasional and comparatively unimportant support.

Under the Agricultural Acts of 1965 and 1970, market prices of feed grains, wheat, and cotton were supported at comparatively low levels, at or near world trade prices. Production was restricted by acreage controls. Payments offered to farmers to induce them to comply with acreage controls substantially augmented incomes, especially of cotton and wheat growers. Tobacco, rice and peanuts had high-level supports and were under compulsory acreage controls.

See also Commodity Loans; Crop Restrictions; Marketing Orders, Agricultural; Parity Prices.

—George E. Brandow, *Pennsylvania State University*

PRICE TAKER, a firm in a purely competitive market structure that has no individual control over price and "takes" the price that is set by the market in order to gain a share in the market. This is possible because purely competitive markets have homogeneous products. Because these firms have no voice in pricing their products, they must adjust their output in order to cover any expenses that are incurred.

Price takers are not found in the non-competitive market structures because any deviation from pure competition allows a firm to have some control over price because of the ability to differentiate products.

PRICE THEORY, a branch of economics that analyzes how prices for individual goods are determined and how firms in various types of industries will maximize profits under stipulated conditions. It also examines the social consequences of these profit-maximizing decisions. Price theory is, thus, greatly concerned with resource allocation decisions.

Labor Value and Marginal Utility. The ancient and medieval writers attempted to lay down moral rules for the conduct of sellers when they set prices. Aristotle and Thomas Aquinas argued that a just price should be charged by all sellers. Although many scholars in the late Middle Ages and during the Renaissance, endeavoured to determine why goods had value, Adam Smith in his *Inquiry into the Nature and Causes of the Wealth of Nations* (1776) still had no firm answer. He posed the famous paradox of value: why is it that diamonds, which are not extremely useful, have a relatively high market value, whereas water, which is extremely useful, has a comparatively low market value? Although Smith could not solve this conundrum, he hinted that prices of goods will tend to equal their costs of production.

David Ricardo (1772–1823) argued that the relative quantities of labor required to produce commodities determined their relative prices. This became known as the labor theory of value. On closer examination of this theory, however, Ricardo himself recognized that it held only when labor was the only scarce input. Ultimately Ricardo concluded that the prices of reproducible goods will in the long run tend to equal their costs of production. Non-reproducible goods, such as works of art, are not included in the Ricardian analysis. If in the short run the price of a good is greater than its cost of production (including a normal profit to the producer), more of the product will be produced, the supply of the good will increase, and the price will fall until it equals the cost of production. The reverse will occur if the short-run price of a good is less than the cost of production. Ricardo's theory therefore emphasizes supply as the primary determinant of long-run price tendencies. In arriving at these conclusions, Ricardo assumes that pure competition exists. Even Karl Marx's dogmatic labor theory of value has no validity except under conditions where labor is the only factor of production.

Starting in 1862 with a paper by the Englishman Stanley Jevons, a group of economists, including Carl Menger, Friedrich Von Wieser, Eugen Von Böhm-Bawerk, and Leon Walras, uncovered the importance of marginal analysis in analyzing prices. Returning to Smith's paradox of value, they argued that the total utility or total satisfaction received from a good does not determine its market value. Rather, the market value is determined by the marginal utility or additional satisfaction received from a small increment of the good. Because water is plentiful, a very small addition to its total quantity would not add much total satisfaction. In other words, the marginal utility of water is low, so its price is low even though the total utility is high. The reverse is true for diamonds. In this way the marginalists emphasized the marginal utility of the good to the buyer (and the demand side of the market) in the determination of short-run prices.

The Neoclassical School. It remained for the turn-of-the-century English economist Alfred Marshall and his co-workers to synthesize the cost-of-production and marginal-utility analyses. This synthesis constitutes the core of modern price theory. At any given moment a buyer of a particular good will normally receive more marginal utility from the first unit of a good than he will from the second, and he will receive still less marginal utility from the third unit. Thus, additional units must be sold at progressively lower prices. The lower the price for a given good is, the more of it buyers will stand ready to buy. One can, therefore, formulate a demand schedule of various possible prices and the corresponding quantities of the good that buyers will stand ready to purchase.

Similarly, under usual conditions, the price varies directly with the quantity of the good that sellers will stand ready to sell. A supply schedule can then be formulated to show the various price-quantity combinations. In most cases there is one price at which the quantity that buyers wish to buy equals the quantity that sellers stand ready to sell. This price-quantity point will prevail in the market place providing there are many informed potential buyers and sellers, and a uniform good is being offered by all sellers.

The demand and supply schedules demonstrated the determination of the day-to-day market prices of goods under competitive conditions. Marshall, Edgeworth, and the other members of the neoclassical school then went on to show, in a manner similar to Ricardo, that the long-run price would tend to equal costs of production under competitive conditions. Ricardian theories were, thus, synthesized with marginal analysis to form a theory of short- and long-run prices involving demand and supply.

Modern Price Theory. Although Marshallian analysis still constitutes the core of modern price theory, the analysis emphasized conditions of pure competition and touched only lightly on cases when only a few sellers prevailed in the marketplace or when similar products were differentiated in the minds of potential buyers by advertising or other factors. The American economist Edward Chamberlin did much to plug these gaps during the 1930s. His analysis of the spectrum between pure competition and pure monopoly is incorporated, with refinements, into modern price theory. Chamberlin shows that pure competition allocates resources most efficiently, with least cost, and with the lowest price to the consumer in the long run. Monopoly will usually result in relatively high prices, less efficient production, and improper resource allocation. Such an analysis forms the intellectual underpinning for antitrust legislation. The social conclusions, however, have been challenged by Joseph Schumpeter, who argued that large firms are socially desirable, because they hold out the possibility of high profits. The hope of attaining such profits would encourage persons to innovate, yielding long-term economic growth.

Modern price theory includes many additional tools and topics. Indifference curve analysis is used to demonstrate consumer and producer equilibria, various production functions are examined in detail, and numerous concepts of elasticity are utilized for many analytical purposes. The most common of the elasticity concepts, price elasticity of demand, measures the response of potential buyers to a change in the price of a product. Similarly, income elasticity of demand measures the response of potential buyers to a change in their incomes. Recently game theory and linear and non-linear programming have been employed to give fresh insights into many related problems. In addition, price theory has been utilized to cover wider areas of the economy, thereby presaging a possible merger with its sister, macroeconomic analysis, in which broad economic variables, such as the overall price level and employment rates, are analyzed. The tools of price theory have also been utilized widely to analyze the market for labor, land, and capital. Price theory has figured prominently in many of the allied fields of economics, such as agricultural economics.

—Allan B. Mandelstamm, *Michigan State University*

PRIMARY BOYCOTT. *See* Boycott.

PRIME RATE, the interest rate that large commercial banks charge to their very best customers for commercial and industrial loans. Beginning in the thirties this rate was published and changed only infrequently—not more than once or twice a year. In 1972, however, after two years of frequent change, some banks adopted a *floating prime rate,* adjusted weekly to changes in the interest rate on Treasury bills or other sensitive market rates. There is some feeling that a published prime rate is misleading and should be abandoned.

PRINCIPLES OF ECONOMICS (1890). *See* Marshall, Alfred.

PRINCIPLES OF ECONOMICS AND TAXATION (1817). *See* Ricardo, David.

PRINCIPLES OF POLITICAL ECONOMY (1848). *See* Mill, John Stuart.

PRIOR STOCK. *See* Preferred Stock.

PRIVATE COSTS. Normally there exists close correspondence between private and social costs. The latter measure what society must forego for some commodity. Institutionally, market economies require firms to pay resource owners for inputs. The firm produces up to the point where marginal private benefit (price received) equals marginal private cost (marginal cost). However, if a firm avoids private costs by polluting it will impose costs on society. Equilibrium for the firm (equating of price and marginal cost) now implies that marginal social costs are greater than marginal social benefit (price). Market price will be too low and output too large. Since self-interest will not maximize group welfare, external intervention may be required.

See also Social Costs.

PRIVATE INVESTMENT. *See* Gross Investment.

PRIVATE PROPERTY, a legal right of a person, natural or corporate, to own and control an economic good within the limits imposed by law. For example, a person in a Western democracy organized on capitalistic or mixed lines may own and hold legal title to a home, a business, a rental property, and so on, and use such economic goods for personal use.

PROBABILITY, an underlying concept of statistics. There is some disagreement among statisticians as to its meaning. There are two basic approaches to a definition of probability. The *frequency definition* denotes probability as a relative frequency or ratio between the number of times an outcome occurs and the total number of occurrences. The theory rests on the law of large numbers which states that the probability of an event is its relative frequency as the number of observations increases indefinitely.

An alternative is the *Bayesian approach* which defines probability as a subjective, or personal, value. This value is determined by each individual on the basis of his belief in the likelihood of an occurrence, and is modified by experience. The frequency definition is most common, but the Bayesian approach is gaining favor.

See also Frequency Distribution; Probability Distribution; Statistics.

Consult (27) Freund, 1967; Schlaifer, 1959.

PROBABILITY DISTRIBUTION, a function giving the probabilities corresponding to values of a random variable. Commonly used probability distributions include the normal and binomial distributions. The normal distribution is the most widely used because almost any distribution can be closely approximated by a normal curve if the number of observations is large enough.

See also Frequency Distribution.

PRODUCER GOODS, buildings and equipment, excluding raw materials, necessary for production of consumer products.

See also Goods.

PRODUCERS' COOPERATIVES. *See* Cooperativism.

PRODUCT DEMAND. *See* Market Demand.

PRODUCT DIFFERENTIATION, a device used by business firms to distinguish their product from products of other firms in the same industry. Product differentiation is a form of non-price competition found chiefly in oligopolistic and monopolistically competitive markets. Oligopolistic markets usually have such few firms that price competition is very harmful; monopolistically competitive markets have products so similar that price competition is ineffective. Product differentiation usually takes the form of either advertising or variations in the design and quality of the product.

Often, by advertising, even products that are identical in nature can be differentiated by the use of brand names. For example, aspirin tablets must all conform to certain specifications and are all equally effective. However, through successful advertising, some brands are able to outsell others. The second form of product differentiation, variations in quality and design of a product, occurs, for example, in the automotive industry, where companies innovate to achieve a greater share of the market. Chrome, metallic paints, and fast-backs tend to differentiate otherwise identical body frames.

See also Non-price Competition; Promotional Competition.

Even virtually identical products may be differentiated by brand name, packaging, or design.

PRODUCT HOMOGENEITY implies that all products in a particular market are identical in nature. A condition of pure and perfectly competitive markets, it indicates that each seller in the market has the exact same product as every other seller in that market. When products are homogeneous in nature, such as milk, wheat, and other agricultural products, buyers cannot differentiate and, therefore, will buy at the lowest price.

When product homogeneity exists in markets that are not purely competitive, product differentiation can be used to distinguish one product from another. For example, although all aspirins are identical in nature, certain brand names have been able to gain a large share of the market.

PRODUCTION. Utility in economic literature means the capacity to satisfy wants. Production is the creation of utility in material things or the rendering of services for markets. A market is made up of actual or potential buyers and sellers engaged in transactions related in time, location, and types of products. It is the supply side of markets that production theory analyzes. The basic decision-making unit in the productive process is the firm; the basic producing unit is the plant.

Productive activities can be placed in three categories. Production involved with agriculture, raw materials, extractive industries, and other natural resources is primary. Secondary activities are manufacturing and all forms of fabrication involved with changing the form of materials to make them have more utility. Tertiary activities involve production in the service industries. The more highly developed an economy, the greater is its proportion of

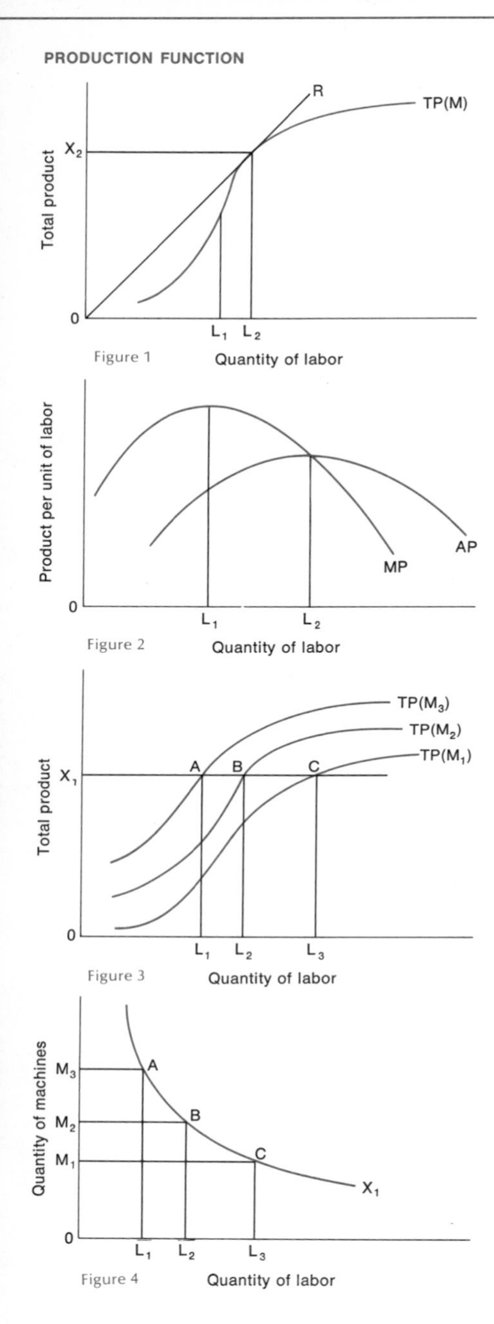

Figure 1

Figure 2

Figure 3

Figure 4

total production involved with tertiary activities.

The production function is a technical relationship concerning inputs and outputs at a given time using existing technology. If it is assumed that an individual firm wishes to maximize its profits, then it wishes to produce a given output at the least cost: in the mix of input factors, cheap factors will be substituted for more expensive ones where possible. As variable factors are added to a given amount of fixed factors, the increase in output attributable to the various factors may rise, then rise at a decreasing rate, and then fall. For example, only a given number of men could farm ten acres of land with a given number of tractors. To keep adding either men or machinery could ultimately lead to the entire acreage becoming a parking lot. Variable inputs are subject to diminishing returns: there is an increased cost per unit of output because if each input is paid the same, but added output (the marginal product) goes down, then the cost of each unit of product goes up.

The firm makes its short-run decisions on the basis of those factor combinations that will give it the same product. Then the firm looks at the costs of the input factors involved to ascertain those combinations with the same costs. There will be no incentive to change the existing productive mix when the equal-product determination (isoquants) is equal to the input costs (isocosts). The firm is in equilibrium where the isoquants are tangent to the isocosts, if the curves were plotted on a graph, and this position shows the exact mix of input factors to use and the cheapest way to produce the output desired. These points of tangency describe the expansion path for the firm or industry in question if increased output is desired. Should relative factor prices change, the methods of production will change.

Opportunity Cost. If all the factors of production in a country are fully employed and used in the most efficient way, the country is said to be operating on its production possibility frontier, or product transformation curve. To move from one point to another on this frontier indicates how much of other goods or services must be given up to get more of a particular good or service: the opportunity cost of more automobiles could be measured by the schools that cannot be built. Opportunity cost permeates the entire productive process at all stages and is implied in the production function faced by firms. If there are hidden costs, or costs to society, not considered in the cost calculations of individual producing firms, these social costs may exceed private costs, and efficient production from the firm or industry viewpoint would not imply a wise allocation of resources for society. These diseconomies are matters of public policy and, if the costs involved become part of the pecuniary calculus of the productive process, would lead to higher costs and less production.

See also Opportunity Cost; Production Possibility Frontier.

Consult (1) Lipsey and Steiner, 1969; Mansfield, 1970; Samuelson, 1973.

—John R. Matthews, Jr., *College of William and Mary*

PRODUCTION, ROUNDABOUT METHODS OF. *See* Roundabout Methods of Production.

PRODUCTION AND DISTRIBUTION THEORIES (1947). *See* Stigler, George J.

PRODUCTION FUNCTION. The act of production may be thought of as a process that transforms inputs, or factors of production, into an output. In general, such a transformation can be described by a mathematical relationship, and this relationship is called a production function. For a production process using two inputs, the production function can be illustrated graphically as in Figure 1, where the output X is measured on the vertical axis, and the input L (say, labor hours) is measured on the horizontal axis. The curve labeled TP(M) is called the *total product curve* of L, and the notation in parentheses indicates that the position of the TP curve depends on the amount of the second input M (say, machine hours).

Marginal Product. The TP curve of L shows the quantities of product X that can be produced with various amounts of input L, and some fixed amount of input M. The TP curve has a positive slope, which indicates that when the amount of one input is increased, the amount of the output increases as well. For a small increment in an input, the resulting increment in output is called the *marginal product* of the input. For a sufficiently small increase in an input, the marginal product is measured by the slope of the TP curve. Thus, the slope of the TP curve in Figure 1 measures the marginal product of L.

Starting from a very small amount of L, and increasing L up to the point L_1, the curvature of the TP curve shows that the amount of X increases at an increasing rate; that is, in that range the marginal product of L increases. Increasing L beyond L_1 causes X to increase at a decreasing rate; that is, beyond L_1 the marginal product of L decreases. Thus, at levels of L beyond L_1 the production function is said to exhibit *diminishing returns* with respect to input L. The curvature of the TP curve implies, therefore, that the marginal product (MP) of L attains its maximum at L_1 (the point of inflection of the TP curve), so that the MP curve has the general shape shown in Figure 2.

Average Product. Another concept of productivity is that of *average product* (AP). It is defined as total product divided by the total amount of one of the inputs used. For example, the AP of labor is defined as X/L, where both X and L are co-ordinates of some point on the TP curve of L. Geometrically, the AP can be represented by the slope of a ray from the origin to the appropriate point on the TP curve. At the L_2 in Figure 1, the AP of L is equal to the slope of the ray OR shown in that diagram. Since the ray OR is tangent to the TP curve at L_2, the AP attains its maximum at that point. Thus, like the MP curve, the AP curve has the shape of an inverted bowl, and it intersects the MP curve at the point at which the latter curve has its maximum, as shown in Figure 2.

Isoquants. If the amount of input M is changed, the TP curve of L shifts. From the assumption that all marginal products are positive, it follows that if the amount of M is increased, the TP curve of L shifts up. Figure 3 illustrates three TP curves for three levels of M, where $M_3 > M_2 > M_1$. Among other things, the diagram shows that any particular level of output can be produced with several different input combinations; for example, the combinations L_1, M_3 (point A); L_2, M_2 (point B); or L_3, M_3 (point C). The points A, B, and C can be mapped into the input plane as shown in Figure 4. The other points on that curve are obtained in a similar fashion. In other words, the curve in Figure 4 is the result of mapping all the points on the horizontal line at X_1 in Figure 3 into the input plane. Any point on the curve in Figure 4 represents an input combination which yields X_1 units of product X. Such a curve is called an *isoquant* (iso-product curve). Since all marginal products are positive, an isoquant has a negative slope. Thus, if output is to be held constant, increasing (decreasing) one input requires a decrease (increase) in another input. The slope of the isoquant measures the rate at which one input must be substituted for another so as to keep the output constant, and is referred to as the *marginal rate of technical substitution*. When an isoquant is convex to the origin, as the one in Figure 4, its slope becomes flatter as the amount of L is increased. This property is known as *diminishing marginal rate of technical substitution.*

One can draw an isoquant for any arbitrary level of output. Several isoquants drawn on one diagram constitute an *isoquant map.* No two isoquants can touch one another. For any two isoquants, the one farther from the origin represents a higher level of output.

Consult (13) Ferguson, 1972; Hadar, 1973; Leftwich, 1970; Stigler, 1966.

—Josef Hadar, *Case Western Reserve University*

PRODUCTION POSSIBILITY FRONTIER, frequently used by economists to explain the costs to the economy of producing more of one good in terms of the resultant lost quantities of other goods. Price theory, growth theory and international trade theory employ the tool. At each moment in the time a nation has given techniques of production and given quantities and types of basic resources (land, labor, capital, and enterprise). It might be possible to produce, say, 30 million units of good A, provided all resources were devoted to its production. The nation, however, may also produce some of good B by transferring some resources out of the production of A into the production of B. In this case, less than 30 million units of A could be produced, because not all of the nation's resources would be left to produce A. Perhaps 5 million units of B could be produced, with 29 million units of A. Further transfers of resources from A to B might yield 10, 15, 20, and 25 million units of B, with 26, 21, 12, and 0 million units of A respectively. The combinations of A and B are summarized in the production possibility table.

The production possibility curve, or production possibility frontier, is a graph of this table, such as curve LM.

The graph depicts the various combinations of A and B that the nation can produce under conditions of full employment. A combination of A and B inside the curve, such as at point X, is produced with less than full employment of available resources and yields less of both A and B. With full employment it is impossible to produce more of B without producing less of A, as shown by the curve's negative slope. A point beyond the curve, such as Z, is unattainable with present techniques and resources, though such a combination of A and B may be attained in the future, as resources grow and techniques improve.

Cost Analysis. The production possibility frontier is bulged outward because of the presence of increasing costs. As the economy produces more and more of B, the cost of B, in terms of A lost, increases. Increasing costs occur because the first resources to be transferred from A to B tend to be those resources most capable of producing B and least capable of producing A. As more of B is produced, however, resources must be transferred that are less and less capable of producing B relative to A. As a result, more and more of A is lost for each increment of B.

—Allan B. Mandelstamm, *Michigan State University*

PRODUCTION QUESTION. *See* Market Mechanism.

PRODUCTIVITY, FACTOR. *See* Factor Productivity.

PRODUCTIVITY, PHYSICAL. *See* Physical Productivity.

PRODUCTION POSSIBILITY TABLE

Units of A (millions)	30	29	26	21	12	0
Units of B (millions)	0	5	10	15	20	25

PRODUCTION POSSIBILITY CURVE

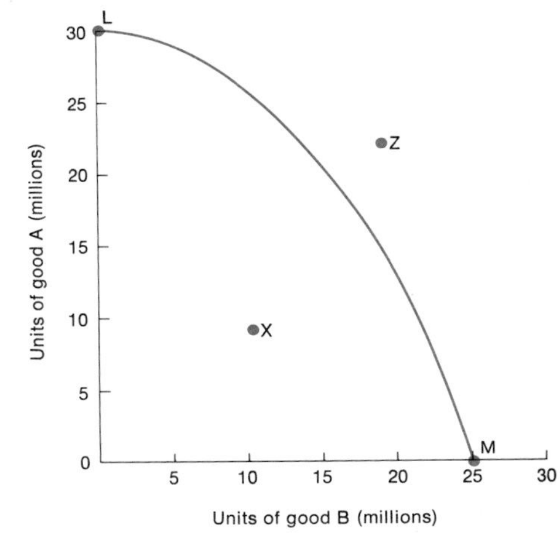

PROFITS

For a full understanding of the role of profits in our economic system, see the articles MARKET SYSTEM, and PROFIT SYSTEM. A bit more specifically, perhaps, the economic function of profits is shown in ALLOCATION.

The significance of profits to the individual firm is described in the articles on EQUILIBRIUM OF THE FIRM, THEORY OF THE FIRM, and PROFIT MAXIMIZATION. Narrower but important aspects of profits can be found in NORMAL PROFITS, MONOPOLISTIC PROFITS, and ACCOUNTING PROFITS.

The Subject Map accompanying THEORY OF THE FIRM displays many of these related concepts.

PROFIT-AND-LOSS STATEMENT. *See* Income Statement.

PROFIT MAXIMIZATION. In economic theory it is assumed that the primary goal of the firm is to make profit and that a firm is in equilibrium when its profits are maximized. Firms secure profits by selling goods and services (output) for more than it costs to employ factors of production input. When the market structure in which the firm operates and the technical relationship between inputs and outputs are specified, maximizing profit implies a particular input pattern. This pattern can be described in two equivalent ways.

The more explicit description of profit maximization is directly in terms of inputs. The technical relation between inputs and outputs is called the production function. If we specify this function we specify how output varies as we vary inputs; with input and output price relationships given we specify how cost and revenue, hence profit, vary with inputs. We assume that the firm opts for whatever input pattern yields the largest profit.

As an alternative we can describe profit maximization in terms of output. If we assume that the firm's goal is to maximize profit it follows that the firm will seek to minimize the cost of whatever output it produces. Minimizing cost for a given output will specify an input pattern for each output. Thus both cost and revenue can be calculated in terms of output. In this approach the firm chooses that output that maximizes profit.

The two approaches are equivalent because the proft maximizing input pattern in the first approach also implies a particular output and the profit maximizing output in the second approach also implies a particular input pattern. Equivalent equilibrium conditions are also implied. The marginal revenue product for each factor must equal the marginal cost of its employment and marginal cost of output must equal marginal revenue.

See also Equilibrium of the Firm; Marginal Cost; Marginal Revenue; Total Cost; Total Revenue.

—Clarence C. Morrison, *Indiana Univ.*

PROFIT MAXIMIZING LEVEL OF OUTPUT. *See* Profit Maximization.

PROFITS, the difference between total income or revenue and total costs of a firm. However, there are several different types of profits. For example, accounting profits represent the difference between the total expenses of a firm and the total revenue of that firm that occurs over a designated period of time, usually a year. Accounting profits are calculated on an income statement of a business and all expenses, including non-cash items such as depreciation, are recorded. Profits can be either positive (gains) or negative (losses).

Profits act as a prime mover of a capitalistic economy and influence both the allocation of resources, by channeling capital funds into alternative uses, and their level of utilization. Because entrepreneurs expect profits, profits can be said to act as a stimulator of output.

In economics there are two major types of profits, normal profits and economic or pure profits.

Normal profits can be defined as the minimum return to the factors of production that a firm uses in order to keep up a certain level of production. In other words, all costs, including a return to entrepreneurship, have to be covered by a firm's revenue in order for normal profits to be earned. A firm must earn normal profits in order to remain competitive, and any firm that fails to earn normal profits is eventually forced to leave the industry because it is operating at an economic loss. Because of the ease of market entry and exit, firms in a purely competitive market structure, in the long run, can earn only normal profits.

Pure, or economic profits, however, represent that amount of revenue a firm earns over and above its normal profits and are not necessary for the maintenance of a given productive activity.

Economists advance two general theories as to why economic profits exist. First, because entrepreneurs take on certain amounts of risk and elements of uncertainty, including unexpected changes in revenue and cost. Economic profits can be said to be the reward for the assumption of these risks. A second explanation is based on the possibility of attaining monopoly power. When a firm is able to attain a certain amount of monopolistic influence, it is able to charge a higher price than in a competitive market and is therefore able to earn economic profits. For example, if one firm can gather exclusive control over a natural resource it then can charge a higher price for its product than if other firms also had access to the resources.

Economic profits are often referred to as monopolistic profits because they are found only in imperfectly competitive market structures.

See also Economic Profits; Normal Profits.

—William D. Wagoner, *Louisiana State University*

PROFITS, ACCOUNTING. *See* Accounting Profits.

PROFITS, ECONOMIC. *See* Economic Profits.

PROFITS, EXCESS. *See* Excess Profits.

PROFITS, MONOPOLISTIC. *See* Monopolistic Profits.

PROFITS, NORMAL. *See* Normal Profits.

PROFITS, UNDISTRIBUTED. *See* Undistributed Profits.

PROFIT SHARING, a means used by employers to give employees a greater incentive to work, calls for distribution to workers of a share in the profits of a company after all ordinary expenses have been met. The usual form of this plan is either the periodic payment of cash to a worker or payments into a trust fund earmarked for employee benefits.

There are several problems with profit sharing as an incentive program. The major one is that profits do not always correlate with production, therefore, if there is an increase in production but profits are reduced for some reason, profit-sharing may very easily become a contra-incentive.

PROFIT SYSTEM, the force that motivates entrepreneurs and allocates resources in the free enterprise, market economy. Business firms are assumed to maximize profits by producing to the point where the revenue derived from the sale of the last marginal unit just equals the cost of producing it. All previously sold units bring in more revenue than they cost.

Profits, to accountants, are the difference between total revenue and total costs; to economists, profits are only that return which exceeds the normal in a particular industry. Even accounting profit at times includes implicit interest, rent, and wages that accrue to the owners for self-use of factors. So profits are returns beyond all explicit and implicit costs.

Competitive Market. In a competitive market in equilibrium, all firms will realize the same return, which is the amount necessary to keep resources committed to that industry. Returns beyond this will cause additional firms to enter to participate in the excess. Any return below this will cause resources to be withdrawn because of economic losses. Economists consider normal returns a cost, and economic profits emerge when returns exceed that amount. In long-run equilibrium under competitive conditions, the entry or withdrawal of firms assures the elimination of economic profits and losses. Their presence in any type of market implies either short-run disequilibrium or monopoly conditions that prevent free entry and exit of firms.

Profit Sources. Karl Marx was virtually the first economist to have an explicit profit theory; his surplus value was profit, and its rate was the rate of exploitation. To economist J. A. Schumpeter, profits came with the emergence of the entrepreneur as a reward to enterprise and innovation including the concomitant financial risks. Professor Frank Knight believed that all true profit is linked with uncertainty and that abnormal returns are necessary to induce entrepreneurs to undertake uncertain venture. Goods involving uncertainty and uninsurable risks must be priced to cover wages, interest, etc., and "profits."

As indicated, profits can arise from monopoly behavior. People with unusual talents, and owners of particularly fertile or strategically located land, get higher than normal returns as a result of natural scarcity; these cannot be competed away. In addition, there are "contrived scarcities" arising from behavior of firms in less than purely competitive markets, and profits derived from them will not be competed away because of market imperfections.

The profit system in socialist and communist countries is either nonexistent or used sparingly as a motivating device to spur output but never to allocate resources.

See also Demand for Capital; Entrepreneur; Excess Profits; Innovator; Risk; Surplus Value; Uncertainty.

Consult (22) Abbott, 1960; Bach, 1971; Fusfeld, 1972; Samuelson, 1973.

—John R. Matthews, Jr., *College of William and Mary*

PROGRESS AND POVERTY. *See* George, Henry.

PROGRESSIVE TAX, a tax whose rate increases as the base of the tax grows larger. Income is generally used as the tax base in the United States. A progressive tax on income would mean that taxes paid *as a percentage of income* would increase as income increases. The marginal rate is greater than the average rate as the tax base increases. The Federal Income Tax is the best example of a progressive tax in the United States.

See also Regressive Tax; Taxation.

PROHIBITIVE TARIFFS. *See* Tariffs.

PROLETARIAT, a large, propertyless, working class dependent on their own labor, or its sale, for their existence. The rise of capitalism created conditions that separated workers from the land and the materials with which they worked. This, according to Marx, created only two mutually hostile classes, and dictatorship of the proletariat would ultimately supplant that of the capitalistic bourgeoisie.

See also Economic Interpretation of History; Marx, Karl; Revolutionary Socialism.

Consult (26) Grossman, 1967.

PROLETARIAT, DICTATORSHIP OF THE. *See* Dictatorship of the Proletariat.

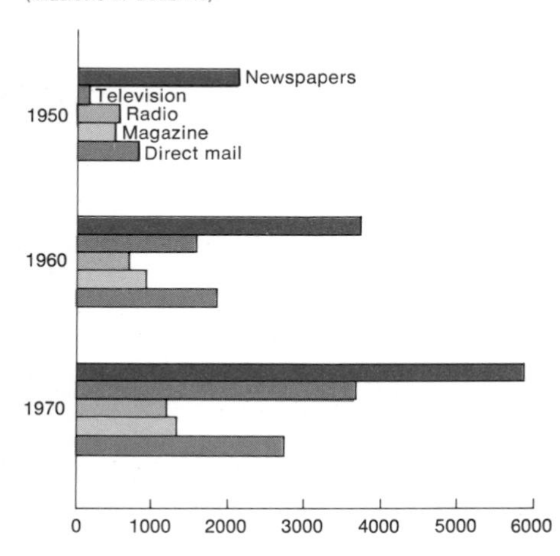

PROMOTIONAL COMPETITION, a form of non-price competition in which firms in an industry compete with each other through advertising and other promotional medias. Promotional competition is very common in monopolistically competitive market structures where all firms in the industry produce essentially the same type of product but try to differentiate by clever advertising campaigns. One form of promotional competition, common in the toothpaste industry, the aspirin industry, and the soap powder industy, is the use of brand names as a means of gathering a greater share of the market. By convincing the public to associate "quality" with its brand, a company can make it difficult for off-brands to enter the market.

See also Product Differentiation.

PROPENSITY TO CONSUME. *See* Consumption Function.

PROPENSITY TO SAVE, the idea that the amount that households save depends on their disposable income and their expectations of future wealth, incomes, and uses for their savings. When the idea is expressed as an exact relationship, it is called a savings function or savings schedule. The propensity to save, the savings function, and the savings schedule are the obverse of the propensity to consume, the consumption function and the consumption schedule, because savings plus consumption always, by definition, uses up all disposable income.

See also Consumption Function.

PROPERTYLESS CLASS. *See* Proletariat.

PROPERTY TAX. *See* Taxation; Taxes.

PROPORTIONAL SUBSTANTIALITY. *See* Quantitative Substantiality.

PROPORTIONAL TAX, a tax whose *rate* remains constant as the tax base grows larger. With income as the tax base, taxes paid as a percentage of income do not change as income increases. The marginal rate is equal to the average rate. A tax on income at a 20% rate, regardless of the amount of income, is an example of a proportional tax.

PROPRIETORSHIP refers to a single private owner of a business enterprise, and represents the most usual type of legal organization in business. However, these businesses usually are small, and the total output of all proprietorships represents only a small portion of the national total output.

See also Corporation; Partnership.

PROSPERITY. *See* Business Cycles, Phases.

PROTESTANT ETHIC. Max Weber observed in *The Protestant Ethic and the Spirit of Capitalism* (1904-5) that, historically, business and economic leaders, skilled labor and trained personnel, and owners of capital in centers of capitalist development were overwhelmingly Protestant. He found the explanation in the Calvinistic doctrine of predestination, in which man is either saved or condemned eternally by God. Hard work could allay anxiety in this regard, and individual economic success could be construed as a sign of election for ultimate redemption. The income from hard work was not to be used for self-indulgence, so the righteous individual lived frugally with savings accumulating as sources of investment funds.

Consult (26) Giddens, 1971; Weber, 1958.

PSYCHOLOGICAL THEORY OF BUSINESS CYCLES states that the reactions of people, waves of optimistic and pessimistic expectations, initiate fluctuations in economic activity. The influence of such external forces as politics and social events, prospects for war or peace, and changing consumer taste, as well as internal economic activity, such as anticipated returns on investment and profit expectations, triggers psychologically based decisions which result in changes in investment and spending. All of these reactions and decisions contribute to the psychological attitude of business, and hence to the level of business activity, a major force contributing to cyclical changes in the economic system.

See also Business Cycles, Theories.

PUBLIC ASSISTANCE, government program created to improve the welfare of poor families by providing them with financial assistance and other services. Sometimes referred to as "welfare" or "relief," the program is administered by local offices operated by state or local governments.

A family or individual in need must apply to the welfare agency for admission to the program. Recipients must pass a "means" test, which restricts eligibility to those with incomes and property below certain levels. Applicants may be required to accept additional conditions in order to qualify for assistance. For example, the family head may be required to accept work or job training if it is available unless this is precluded by poor health or household responsibilities. The family may also be required to subscribe to standards of morality and life style demanded by the agency.

The welfare agency assigns each family to a caseworker who makes periodic visits. In principle, the caseworker is supposed to evaluate the family's needs and make recommendations on the type and amount of help required.

The caseworker is also supposed to provide guidance to the family on matters of employment and job training, consumer education, and family life. The latter functions are designed to rehabilitate the family unit and help it become self-supporting. In addition, the caseworker is expected to screen welfare recipients to make sure that they meet all eligibility requirements. In effect, policing and assistance functions are combined, a practice likely to create suspicion among welfare recipients and undermine efforts at rehabilitation.

Cost and Benefits. Benefits are generally tailored to the needs of the individual family. Each state welfare agency prescribes a budget for families of different size that is supposed to provide for minimum necessities. A family with no other source of income will presumably receive a monthly payment equal to the estimated cost of the minimum budget, although in many states low appropriations force payments to fall below the state's own minimum. If family earnings exceed a minimum (commonly $30 per month), benefits are reduced. Agencies are allowed to make additional payments to families with special needs.

In the United States, the cost of public assistance is split among federal, state, and local governments. The federal government absorbs about half the cost through matching funds. Only the categorical programs for families with dependent children, the elderly, the needy blind, and the totally disabled receive federal funds. General assistance for other needy persons, including many working poor, is financed fully from state and local sources.

Although there is some federal control over the categorical programs, there are great interstate differences in benefits and eligibility requirements. For example, maximum payments to a family of four under the AFDC program (aid to families with dependent children) ranges from $55 in Mississippi to $332 in New Jersey. Even within states nonuniformity is generated by lax administrative control and the social work philosophy, which leaves a great deal to the discretion of the social worker.

See also Aid to Families with Dependent Children; Aid to the Needy Blind; General Assistance; Medicaid; Negative Income Tax; Old-Age Assistance; Social Dividend; Social Insurance.

—Charles W. Meyer, *Iowa State University*

PUBLIC EMPLOYMENT SERVICE. The Wagner Act (1933) provided federal matching funds for states to establish employment services, with the primary goals of 1) administering the work test for unemployment insurance claimants and 2) providing employers with qualified workers. Just recently, a third goal, to give priority to the employment problems of the disadvantaged, was added. In the sixties, the public employment service underwent drastic changes because of the new emphasis on manpower programs, which opened up numerous agencies concerned with the problems of unemployment.

PUBLIC EXPENDITURES. *See* Federal Budget.

PUBLIC FINANCE, the study of the use of the budgetary process for carrying out the allocative, redistributive, and stabilization functions of the modern state. The fiscal instruments available to governments for carrying out these functions are the taxing, spending, and borrowing powers. Each of these instruments may have an impact upon the three functional objectives depending upon their theoretical incidence and economic effects.

The allocative function is concerned with the way a nation's resources are used, whether for the production of "guns or butter;" the redistributive function is concerned with changing the market-determined distribution of income so that it conforms to some predetermined notion of equality; the stabilization function is concerned with assuring a nation's growth with a minimum of unemployment or inflation.

All levels of government carry out public financial activities, though usually the central government has at its command more resources and more powerful control over the tools necessary for carrying out fiscal objectives. In federal countries such as the United States, inter-governmental fiscal relations, particularly subsidies and transfers, are an integral component of the study of public finance.

—Irving J. Goffman, *University of Florida*

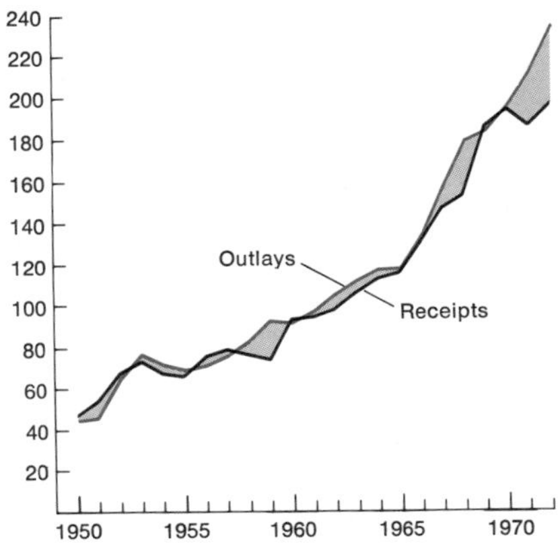

PUBLIC INTEREST DISPUTES, strikes that may jeopardize the national health and safety, such as policemen's and firemen's strikes, sometimes called "emergency-strikes." In order to protect the public in these situations, the emergency strike provisions of Federal and state laws may be invoked. The Taft-Hartley Act provides for public action in these disputes.

See also Emergency Strike; Strike; Taft-Hartley Act (1947).

PUBLIC LAW (P.L.) 480, enacted in 1954 and later called Food for Peace or Food for Freedom, established procedures for sale of surplus farm products by the United States to poor, underdeveloped countries under terms highly favorable to buyers. Sales for local currencies of recipient countries, convertible to dollars only in limited amounts, have accounted for most P. L. 480 shipments, but outright donations in emergencies and for special purposes

FEDERAL BUDGET RECEIPTS AND OUTLAYS (1950-1972)
(BILLIONS OF DOLLARS)

PUBLIC UTILITIES

Further information closely related to the public utility concept can be found in the article on REGULATED INDUSTRIES, and for additional material on a major economic condition underlying the public utility industries see ECONOMIES OF SCALE and NATURAL MONOPOLY. To see what is involved in the regulation of public utilities, consult REGULATION, REGULATORY COMMISSIONS, and PUBLIC UTILITY COMMISSIONS. For some specific aspects and methods of public utility regulation, refer to CERTIFICATE OF PUBLIC CONVENIENCE AND NECESSITY, INTERSTATE COMMERCE COMMISSION, FEDERAL POWER COMMISSION, and FEDERAL COMMUNICATIONS COMMISSION. Two landmark court decisions in the public utility area are discussed in the articles on SMYTH v. AMES and HOPE NATURAL GAS CASE.

The Subject Map accompanying the article on REGULATION displays many of those relationships.

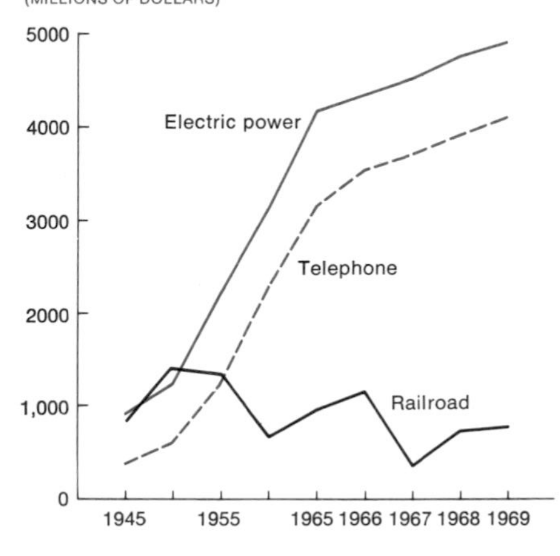

have also been used. Shipment of foods not in surplus was authorized in 1966. Expenditures under the program gradually increased to $1.6 billion in 1965. The amendment in 1966 required a gradual shift from sales for foreign currencies to dollar sales with long-term credit at low interest. These less favorable terms, together with the Green Revolution in some of the underdeveloped world, reduced P. L. 480 shipments after the mid-1960s.

See also Green Revolution.

PUBLIC OWNERSHIP. *See* Nationalization.

PUBLIC REGULATION. See Regulated Industries.

PUBLIC SERVICE COMMISSIONS. *See* Public Utility Commissions.

PUBLIC SERVICES. *See* Infrastructure.

PUBLIC UTILITIES, industries with certain economic characteristics that are subject to public regulation. These industries, which are referred to as "public utilities," are presumed to offer indispensable services to consumers and to be natural monopolies. Because consumers have no good alternatives to these necessary services, the natural monopolists, in effect, perform a public function. In order to prevent these firms from exploiting their monopoly positions, the government substitutes public regulation for competition.

Natural Monopolies. Industries are considered to be natural monopolies when the cost per unit of output (average cost) falls as output increases. Thus, if production efficiency (low average cost) is to be attained, there is only room for one firm or, at most, a few firms to carry on business in a given market. Consequently, competition cannot be depended on to keep prices low.

Another reason given for regulation of such industries is that price competition could become destructive. When a firm has declining average costs, it has an incentive to cut its price so as to increase its sales. If all of the industry's firms end up in a price cutting war, price could fall below per unit costs and drive some firms out of business. This reduction of industry productive capacity may be undesirable to society if the service produced is essential to consumers.

Price Setting. In regulating public utilities, regulatory agencies are primarily concerned with controlling prices. Various methods have been considered for setting utility prices.

First, many economists have maintained that society will benefit most if price is set equal to the incremental cost (that is, marginal cost) of the last unit of the utility service produced. However, if the firm has declining average costs, incremental cost is less than average cost at each possible level of output. Therefore, if price is set equal to incremental cost, price will be below average cost and the firm's total dollar receipts (price times output) will be less than its total dollar costs (average cost times output) and the firm will suffer a loss. If this pricing method is followed, the government must subsidize public utilities by the amount of their losses if the firms are to remain in business. Such subsidies out of general tax revenues have been criticized for various reasons. One criticism is that they represent a redistribution of income away from taxpayers who do not use a utility's services and toward people who do buy the services.

A second pricing method is to set utility price equal to average cost. With this method, total dollar receipts will just cover the utility's total costs. A third possible pricing method is to set prices for utility services so that the average price of the services is equal to the average cost of the services. This method, which may involve some price discrimination—for example, different prices for different units of a service that have the same incremental cost—will also allow total receipts to cover total costs.

Of these three, the second and third pricing methods come closest to describing the actual methods used by regulatory agencies. For the most part, the first method has not been attempted in the United States.

See also Regulated Industries; Regulation.

Consult (17) Coase, 1970; Lerner, 1964; MacAvoy, 1970.

—Joseph Jadlow, *Oklahoma State University*

PUBLIC UTILITY COMMISSIONS, semi-independent regulatory commissions that operate under general legislative powers. These agencies, which exist in every state, are usually known as public utility commissions, public service commissions, railroad commissions, or corporation commissions. Most of these state commissions have jurisdiction over motor carriers, railroads, and gas, water, electric and telephone service. They usually have the authority to regulate rates and the quantity and the quality of services. The members of state commissions are appointed by the governor in many states and are elected by the people in others. Most state commissions suffer from such problems as technically incompetent, low-salaried commissioners, and inadequate budgets and staffs.

See also Regulatory Commissions.

PUBLIC UTILITY CONCEPT. *See* Public Utilities.

PUBLIC UTILITY ENTRY, control by a regulatory commission of entry into a regulated industry. Ordinarily, a firm entering such an industry must first obtain approval from the commission in the form of a certificate of public convenience and necessity. By restricting entry, it is thought that destructive competition may be avoided so that public utilities have financial stability and provide continued service.

See also Certificates of Public Convenience and Necessity; Public Utilities; Regulated Industries.

PUBLIC UTILITY PRICE, the rate charged per unit of use of a public utility's service. Control of such rates is the heart of public utility regulation. A regulatory commission tries to keep a public utility's rates from being unreasonably high but high enough for the utility to attract capital from investors.

See also Public Utilities; Rate Level.

PUBLIC UTILITY SERVICE, the quantity, quality, and conditions of service supplied by a public utility, usually controlled by a regulatory commission. Control of utility prices has little meaning unless the quality of service offered at regulated prices is also controlled.

See also Regulation.

PUBLIC WORKS, capital investment by various governmental bodies for social use. Common examples include roads and highways, multipurpose flood control projects, airports, inland waterways, and harbor facilities. Construction may be performed by public agencies, but in the United States most work is performed by private contractors. The facilities are typically operated and maintained by government. They are often financed in part from user fees and sales of services such as hydroelectric power.

PUMP PRIMING, term widely used in the early 1930s to refer to the policy resulting from the belief that the depression was a reflection of a lack of confidence on the part of the business sector. It was felt that if the government would institute some spending programs, employment would increase, followed by an increase in consumer spending, which would then restore confidence in the economy and hence result in increased private investment. What the economy needed, adherents argued, was a "shot in the arm" to get things moving again. If indeed, a one-time discretionary set of expenditures does build up sufficient confidence, the desired result might very well be generated. For many reasons, economic and political, the "pump priming" activities of the early '30s did not generate sufficient confidence on the part of private investors.

PURCHASES, the value of goods and services acquired by individuals and businesses during a given period. Changes in the rate of purchases are useful indicators of changes of aggregate individual decisions allocating disposable income between consumption and savings.

PURCHASING POWER. *See* Price Level.

PURCHASING POWER OF MONEY (1911). *See* Fisher, Irving.

PURE COMPETITION. *See* Perfect Competition.

PURE PROFITS. *See* Economic Profits.

PURE RENT. *See* Economic Rent.

PYRAMID OF CREDIT, the situation in which a nation expands its money supply on the basis of a relatively small gold stock. If, for instance, the central bank must maintain a 25% gold reserve against its deposit liabilities (which are the reserves of member banks), and the member banks must keep 20% reserves against demand deposits, then $25 of gold will support $100 of reserves, which will support $500 of demand deposits (money). Gold as a monetary base is no longer extensively used, and bank deposits now rest solely on the arbitrarily determined volume of central bank credit.

See also Bank Multiplier; Federal Reserve System; Reserve Requirement.

QUADRATIC FUNCTIONS. *See* Function.

QUALITATIVE CONTROLS are restrictions placed by the federal reserve system on particular types of loans by commercial banks or financial intermediaries in order to implement the goals of monetary policy. While quantitative controls restrict (or encourage) changes in the total money supply, qualitative controls have the effect of channeling a given total of loans away from particular types of financing.

Margin requirements restrict the amount of money that can be borrowed to purchase stock. *Installment credit controls* regulate the amount that can be borrowed for the purchase of consumer goods, while *mortgage lending controls* limit the amount that can be borrowed for the purchase of residential housing. The dangers of diversion of funds into consumer markets are greatest during periods of war when resources generally are scarce, and controls over these purchases have been limited to war periods.

A different form of qualitative control prescribes *interest rate ceilings* that may be paid by *commercial banks.* These controls are intended primarily to prevent banks from entering into competitive races to pay higher rates than they can safely afford in order to attract funds away from other institutions. Al-

Pump priming operated on the principle that input from the top (government) would start a flow of private investment resources.

FEDERAL EXPENDITURES FOR PUBLIC WORKS

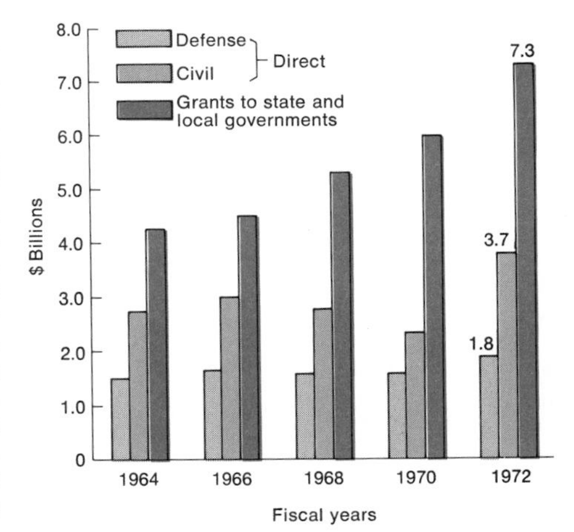

though the federal reserve system normally has control only over member banks, its powers to supervise qualitative controls extend to practically all lenders.

See also Monetary Policy; Quantitative Controls.

—Walter W. Haines, *New York University*

QUALITY COMPETITION, a form of non-price competition in which individual firms in an industry attempt to gather the largest possible share of the market by improving the quality of their products. A form of product differentiation, it is found most often in oligopolistic and monopolistically competitive market structures.

Quality competition has advantages for the consumer, because constant research on the products placed on the market results in a greater variety of styles and types from which he can select. However, these industries, because of the intense non-price competition, tend to be the least efficient.

See also Product Differentiation.

QUANTITATIVE CONTROLS of the federal reserve system, instruments of monetary policy that directly affect the quantity of money in circulation. The three major quantitative controls are changes in reserve requirements, changes in the discount rate, and open-market operations. All such controls influence the multiple expansion of the money supply through their effect on excess reserves. Any action that reduces actual reserves or increases required reserves has the effect of reducing excess reserves, putting downward pressure on the money supply by reducing demand deposits of commercial banks.

The effect of changes in reserve requirements is direct and obvious, immediately affecting excess reserves and the bank multiplier. A 1 percent change in reserve requirements on just demand deposits produces a $2 billion change in excess reserves, which is frequently too large to do what is required. Such changes, therefore, have been infrequent.

A change in discount rates alters the cost of acquiring additional reserves by borrowing from the federal reserve banks and, hence, tends to affect actual reserves. In practice, however, banks have been encouraged to reduce their borrowings to the absolute minimum, and changes in the discount rate have little practical effect. They do, however, signal the thinking of the central bank, thus influencing the banks psychologically or morally.

Open-market operations are by far the most important tool of monetary policy. Aside from affecting the money supply directly, they change the actual reserves of the commercial banks, as well as influencing interest rates on government securities. Open-market dealings can be carried out in any volume over any time period, and they can be reversed instantly if necessary.

See also Discount Rate; Open Market Operations; Qualitative Controls; Reserve Requirement.

Consult (10) Mayer, 1968.

—Walter W. Haines, *New York University*

QUANTITATIVE SUBSTANTIALITY. In interpretation of the Clayton Act, it must be determined if firms engaging in practices prohibited by that act tend to lessen competition substantially. Until recent years, the rule of "proportional substantiality," or percent of the market affected by the practice, was emphasized. Now attention is shifting to the rule of "quantitative substantiality," or the absolute dollar volume of trade affected irrespective of the percent of the market involved.

See also Substantial Lessening of Competition.

QUANTITY DEMANDED, the number of units of a commodity that are or would be purchased per time period at a specific price. Quantities of a commodity purchased change from one time period to another but the change is called a change in quantity demanded only if the different purchase level is caused by a price change. Changes in quantities demanded occur from movements along a given demand curve in response to price changes and not from changes in tastes, prices of related goods, or expectational changes. Parametric changes of the latter sort cause entire demand functions to change, and the result is called a change in demand and not a change in quantity demanded.

QUANTITY SUPPLIED is, technically speaking, merely a point on the supply curve. At any given price, quantity supplied can be found at the perpendicular from the curve to the X-axis. The often-missed, but essential, distinction is that supply and demand are schedules, not points.

Since supply is a schedule of intentions, then a change in supply implies a new functional relationship between price and quantity supplied. At any given price, quantity supplied will be different. Or putting it in a more meaningful context since one of the variables previously held constant has now varied, then before a *given* quantity will be voluntarily supplied by a producer, price must be higher or lower (depending on the circumstances).

Contrasted with this is a change in quantity supplied which can result (holding supply, the schedule, constant) only from a change in price. Given the supply schedule, a change in price can occur only due to a change in the demand schedule. Geometrically, a change in supply is represented by a shift upward or forward from the original schedule; a change in quantity supplied is a movement along the original supply schedule.

—Robert L. Brite, *Louisiana State University*

QUANTITY THEORY OF MONEY. *See* Equation of Exchange.

QUARTILE. *See* Central Tendency.

QUASI RENT, the payment in the short-run period of an amount in excess of the minimum necessary return that a resource owner must receive in order to keep the resource in the current use. Quasi rent differs from economic rent in that the latter is a payment in excess of opportunity cost in the long-run while the former is an excess payment in the short-run and is temporary in nature. One of the most important examples of quasi rent is the difference between a business firm's total revenue and its total variable cost. Since a firm will continue to operate in the short-run so long as it covers all of its variable cost, any return in excess of variable cost is a quasi rent.

See also Economic Rent; Rent.

—John P. Formby, *University of North Carolina at Greensboro*

QUESNAY, FRANÇOIS (1694–1774), the leader and most important thinker among the Physiocrats. The personal physician to Louis XV, Quesnay first wrote on medicine and philosophy, then turned to economics late in his career, making contributions in a number of areas.

The role of a natural order was central to Quesnay's system, with the natural order being determined according to the principle of economic individualism: In working for himself, every individual would be working in the best interest of the society. This concept became the central theme in the works of Adam Smith and other classical economists. However, Quesnay's most significant contribution was the *Tableau èconomique* (1758), the first macroeconomic circular flow model.

See also Invisible Hand; Physiocrats; Tableau Economique.

QUOTAS. Import quotas set limits, in physical or value terms, on the amount of a good that can be received into a country during a given time. The limits may be on a country or global basis. A "tariff quota" does not set a fixed limit on imports but sets the amount beyond which higher duties apply. A licensing system is usually necessary in the administration of quotas and, unless the licenses are auctioned off, windfall profits can accrue to fortunate applicants. From the standpoint of the country using them, quotas have advantages over tariffs: they are a more certain and precise instrument of control and they can be changed by administrative decree.

See also Tariffs; Trade Barriers.

Consult (23) Snider, 1971.

RADNER, ROY (1927-), American educator, economist, and statistician noted for research on the theory of decision under uncertainty and theory of economic growth and planning. He received a Ph.D. in Mathematical Statistics from the University of Chicago (1956). His publications include *Notes on the Theory of Economic Planning* (1963), *Optimal Replacement Policy* (1966, with D.W. Jorgenson and J.J. McCall), and *Economic Theory of Teams* (1970, with J. Marschak). Radner has been an advisor to various firms and government agencies, and also a consultant on higher education. He became professor of economics and statistics at Berkeley in 1961.

RAILROAD ADJUSTMENT BOARD. *See* Railway Labor Act (1926).

RAILWAY LABOR ACT (1926) tried to promote labor and management organization, so that the collective bargaining of new contract interpretation disputes would promote labor-management harmony and, hence, uninterrupted railway service. It was the outgrowth of the government's regulation of railroads and its intention was that free collective bargaining, protected by law, be an essential feature of the rail industry's operation.

Provisions. Among its most significant features was its specification of ways in which peaceful settlements of contract disputes were to be reached when private collective bargaining failed. Alternative methods of dispute resolution were: (1) mediation of disputes in contract interpretation over pay, work rules, and working conditions by the Railroad Adjustment Board, a new agency set up by the act or, if the dispute was over new contract terms, by the National Mediation Board; (2) voluntary arbitration; (3) action by Congress following the report of a presidentially-appointed fact-finding board.

—Leonard G. Schifrin, *College of William and Mary*

François Quesnay

RANDOM NUMBERS. A useful aid in selecting a random sample is a table of random numbers, numbers printed in random fashion. By numbering items in the population and selecting those items whose numbers occur in the random number table, we can be assured of a random sample.

See also Sampling.

RANDOM SAMPLE. *See* Sample.

RANK CORRELATION. *See* Correlation.

Stamps and tokens were used in World War II to ration purchases of scarce food items and gas.

RATE BASE, term referring to fair value for rate evaluation purposes. The figure determined as the rate base is multiplied by the rate of return to establish the rate level. The determination of the rate base varies by jurisdiction but the most popular formulas use original cost, reproduction cost, or a combination of the two.

See also Rate Level.

RATE LEVEL, the general level of rates (prices) of a regulated company. The primary concern of regulatory commissions is to control rate levels so as to prevent regulated firms from exploiting their monopoly position by setting unreasonably high prices, restricting output, or receiving excessive profits.

See also Public Utility Price; Regulation.

RATE OF RETURN, the earnings of a regulated company as a percentage of its rate base (the value of the property it uses to provide its services). Earnings are calculated by deducting current operating costs and depreciation from the firm's revenues for the relevant time period. Usually, regulatory commissions attempt to establish a rate of return that prevents firms from receiving unregulated monopoly profits but still allows them to attract new capital.

See also Rate Base; Regulation.

RATE OF SUBSTITUTION. *See* Marginal Rate of Substitution.

RATE STRUCTURE, the entire set of specific rates (prices) a regulated company charges for particular units of service to different classes of customers. When rate differences are not determined by differences in costs, rate discrimination occurs. Regulatory commissions try to keep discrimination from being unfair and unreasonable.

RATIONAL FUNCTIONS. *See* Function.

RATIONAL WAGE DIFFERENTIALS, often referred to as equalizing wage differentials, are wage differentials given to workers in order to compensate for non-monetary differences in jobs, such as unpleasant tasks, inconvenience, or danger. Differentials are usually paid, for example, to those workers who are employed on graveyard shifts, who work more than six days without an off-day and who work overtime. In addition, jobs involving an element of danger, such as parachutist or skin diver, carry wage differentials of a rational nature.

See also Wage Differentials.

RATIONING in an economic system may be accomplished in two ways. The first, and by far the most important, is the rationing effect of prices in the market. One of the most important functions of prices and price changes is to ration the available goods or services among the various possible uses or users. For example, if a shortage develops in the market for a particular commodity desired by consumers, and they express their willingness to continue to purchase the commodity at the higher price now charged, their constant incomes will necessarily reduce purchases of other items normally purchased. This action frees resources from one industry to move into the industry with higher prices. As a result, productive factors flow into the shortage area, and output is increased. On the other hand, if consumers refuse to pay the higher prices and shift purchases into other products, factors are freed from the industry characterized by the shortage. So, goods are automatically rationed.

However, at times rationing through the price mechanism seems too harsh. For example, the shortage may involve a necessity, and citizens would suffer greatly if unable to purchase it. In this situation, governments often freeze prices and issue ration tickets to consumers. In effect, a two-price system has been established. A consumer now must offer both the money price and the ticket price of the commodity. Money price, because of the freeze, can no longer function to ration the good. The ration tickets or coupons serve this function in this situation, and these coupons are issued independently of income.

—Robert L. Brite, *Louisiana State University*

RATIONING IN WARTIME. During World War II the United States and other countries found it necessary to divide the available output of consumer goods on some basis unrelated to price. The nations generally turned to some double-price system, using money prices and coupon prices. The coupons were issued to the population and were given to the merchant when a purchase was made.

REAL FLOW involves the physical movement of goods, services, or factors of production within or between sectors of the economy. Goods and services generally flow from the producers (business firms and government) to the consumers (households), while factors of production generally move in the opposite direction. Because it would be difficult for a modern, industrial economy to operate with a barter system, money is used to facilitate these real flows. Thus the movements of real goods, services, and factors of production are offset by equal but opposite flows of money. It is the combination of these real and money flows that is one of the most important aspects of the economy and it is up to the economic system to regulate and direct these flows.

See also Circular Flow of Income; Money Flow.

REAL INCOME. *See* Price Level.

REAL INCOME PER CAPITA. *See* Per Capita Real Income.

REALIZED INVESTMENT. *See* Actual Investment.

REAL PROPERTY is land and any asset permanently attached to it, including buildings and trees and any asset that occurs naturally under the surface of it, including petroleum, sand, minerals, and so forth. A house is real property and is distinguished legally from chattels or personal property.

In an economic system in which real property is predominantly privately owned, there are necessarily restrictions on the owners' rights with respect to the property. Property rights are governed by law and are protected by the Constitution.

The supply of land and the resources that occur naturally under the surface of land are fixed in absolute quantity. While it is possible to find substitutes for these real property resources, we cannot generally augment their quantities. As population and income grow, the demand for real property resources tends to rise. Rising prices may lead to economic rents and increasing wealth for the owners.

See also Rent.

—John P. Formby, *University of North Carolina at Greensboro*

REAL WAGES are the purchasing power of money wages: the amount of goods and services that can be purchased with the money wages received for labor rendered. Because real wages are a reflection of the cost of living, they can change without money wages changing.

RECALL, the term used when employees who have previously been laid off by a company are called back to work. In keeping with seniority rights, the last person laid off is usually the first person to be recalled.

RECESSION. *See* Business Cycles, Phases.

RECIPROCAL DEALING. *See* Conglomerate.

RECIPROCAL TRADE AGREEMENTS ACT. The Hawley-Smoot Tariff (1930) raised U.S. tariffs to the highest levels in history. The Reciprocal Trade Agreements Act (1934) gave the president the power to negotiate treaties with foreign countries to reduce tariff barriers on a reciprocal basis by as much as 50%. Later, the base for the 50% limit was tariffs prevailing on January 1, 1945. Before the General Agreement on Tariffs and Trade (1947) the United States had negotiated trade agreements with 29 countries. U.S. tariffs were reduced by more than 75% between 1934 and the final expiration of the Reciprocal Trade Agreements Act in 1962. The act had been renewed 11 times over that span of years and the last renewals had included weakening amendments related to escape clauses, peril-point provisions, and national security clauses.

See also Multinational Trade Agreements.

RECOGNITION, employer acceptance of a union as the bargaining agent for a group of workers. Usually, the union must prove it is the choice of the majority of workers in the bargaining unit by winning an election conducted by the National Labor Relations Board (NLRB). By law, the employer must recognize and bargain with a union certified by the NLRB as the representative of the workers.

See also Bargaining Unit; Representation.

RECONSTRUCTION OF ECONOMICS (1950). *See* Boulding, Kenneth E.

RECOVERY. *See* Business Cycles, Phases.

REDISCOUNT RATE. *See* Discount Rate.

REDISTRIBUTION OF INCOME. *See* Income Redistribution.

REDISTRIBUTION OF LAND. *See* Land Reform.

REDUNDANT CAPACITY. *See* Excess Capacity.

REFORM, LAND. *See* Land Reform.

REFUSAL TO BARGAIN, failure by a negotiating party to bargain in good faith with the other. Either's refusal to bargain is a violation of federal labor law and is thus an unfair labor practice with potentially serious consequences for the offending party.

REGRESSION. *See* Curve Fitting.

REGRESSIVE TAX, a tax whose rate decreases as the tax base increases. With income used as the tax base, taxes paid *as a percentage of income* will decrease as income increases. This means that the marginal rate is less than the average rate as the tax base increases. The sales tax is an example of a regressive tax because the same tax rate causes people with lower incomes to pay a relatively larger percentage of their incomes.

See also Progressive Tax; Taxation.

REGULATED INDUSTRIES, as designated by Congress and state legislatures certain industries, regulated by semi-independent commissions. Among the industries subject to public regulation are the transportation, aviation, power transmission, communications, and atomic energy industries. Because many of these industries are natural monopolies that provide customers with essential services for which no good substitutes exist, the prices and the quantity and quality of their services are regulated so as to ensure that consumers can obtain desired amounts at reasonable prices.

Regulatory Agencies. The interstate transmission and sale for resale of electricity and natural gas is regulated by the Federal Power Commission (FPC). These products, which are sold by natural monopolists, are essential to consumers and there are few good substitutes for them. The FPC also regulates the prices of natural gas producers. This control does not seem justified because there are thousands of competing producers; moreover, ceilings imposed on producers' prices seem to have resulted in a shortage of natural gas.

The railroad, motor carrier, water carrier, and oil pipeline industries are regulated by the Interstate Commerce Commission. Although public regulation may at one time have been necessary in most of these industries, its usefulness has been questioned increasingly in recent years as competition has grown among different transportation modes. For similar reasons, there is now some doubt about the desirability of economic regulation of commercial air transportation by the Civil Aeronautics Board.

The Federal Communications Commission regulates broadcasting (radio and television) and interstate telephone and telegraph services. Telephone and telegraph services are regulated because they are essential to consumers and are produced by natural monopolists. Broadcasting is regulated because of the limited space available on the radio spectrum. Some people argue, however, that there is little economic justification for FCC regulation of broadcasting and that the limited air space could be allocated by allowing broadcast licenses to be bought and sold in the market like other property rights.

See also Atomic Energy Commission; Civil Aeronautics Board; Federal Communications Commission; Federal Power Commission; Interstate Commerce Commission; Public Utilities.

Consult (17) Coase, 1959; Cordtz, 1971 (a); Cordtz, 1971 (b); Friedman, 1969; MacAvoy, 1971.

—Joseph Jadlow, *Oklahoma State University*

REGULATION, the social control of regulated industries. The three basic devices are regulation of entry, regulation of price, and regulation of service. These three are interrelated, and it is necessary to utilize all three in order for regulation to be even minimally effective.

Entry. Entry is controlled by use of certificates of public convenience and necessity, franchises, licenses and permits. One, or a limited number of firms are allowed to operate in a given service territory with the explicit idea that the public will be better served by one large supplier than by many smaller competing firms. Also, since regulated industries use public streets, highways, and thoroughfares, the public will be inconvenienced less by one firm than by many. In return for this monopoly privilege, the firm must serve all comers and assume other "common law" and common carrier obligations.

Price. In order that the supplier does not exploit his monopolistic position, prices must be controlled. Discrimination in price and service must be avoided. Likewise, it has been deemed to be in the public interest that the supplier firm be economically sound and able to serve. Hence the *rate level* must be such that the firm earn a fair return on a fair value.

Service. Finally, the service offered is controlled in some ways because (a) there is a natural tendency of a monopolistic supplier to maximize his return by lowering service levels under regulated prices and (b) there is a need to impose some level of service capability as a substitute for the natural action of the market mechanism under competition. Service competition regulation takes many forms, such as levels of safety, frequency, and routes in transportation and reliability, minimum physical attributes of service, and obligation to serve all customers in utilities.

See also Public Utilities.

Consult (17) Posner, 1970; Stigler and Friedland, 1962.

—Martin T. Farris, *Arizona State University*

REGULATION Q. *See* Interest Rate Ceiling.

REGULATION T. *See* Margin Requirement.

REGULATION U. *See* Margin Requirement.

REGULATION W. *See* Installment Credit Controls.

REGULATION X. *See* Mortgage Lending Controls.

REGULATORY COMMISSIONS, semi-independent agencies that control industries by public regulation. Such a commission usually consists of three to seven members who are appointed or elected for five to seven-year overlapping terms. Ordinarily, the law requires that a political party have no more than a one-man majority of commission members, that a commissioner be discharged only for neglect of duty, and that a commission be independent of the executive branch of government but subject to judicial review.

It was once assumed that independent

REGULATION

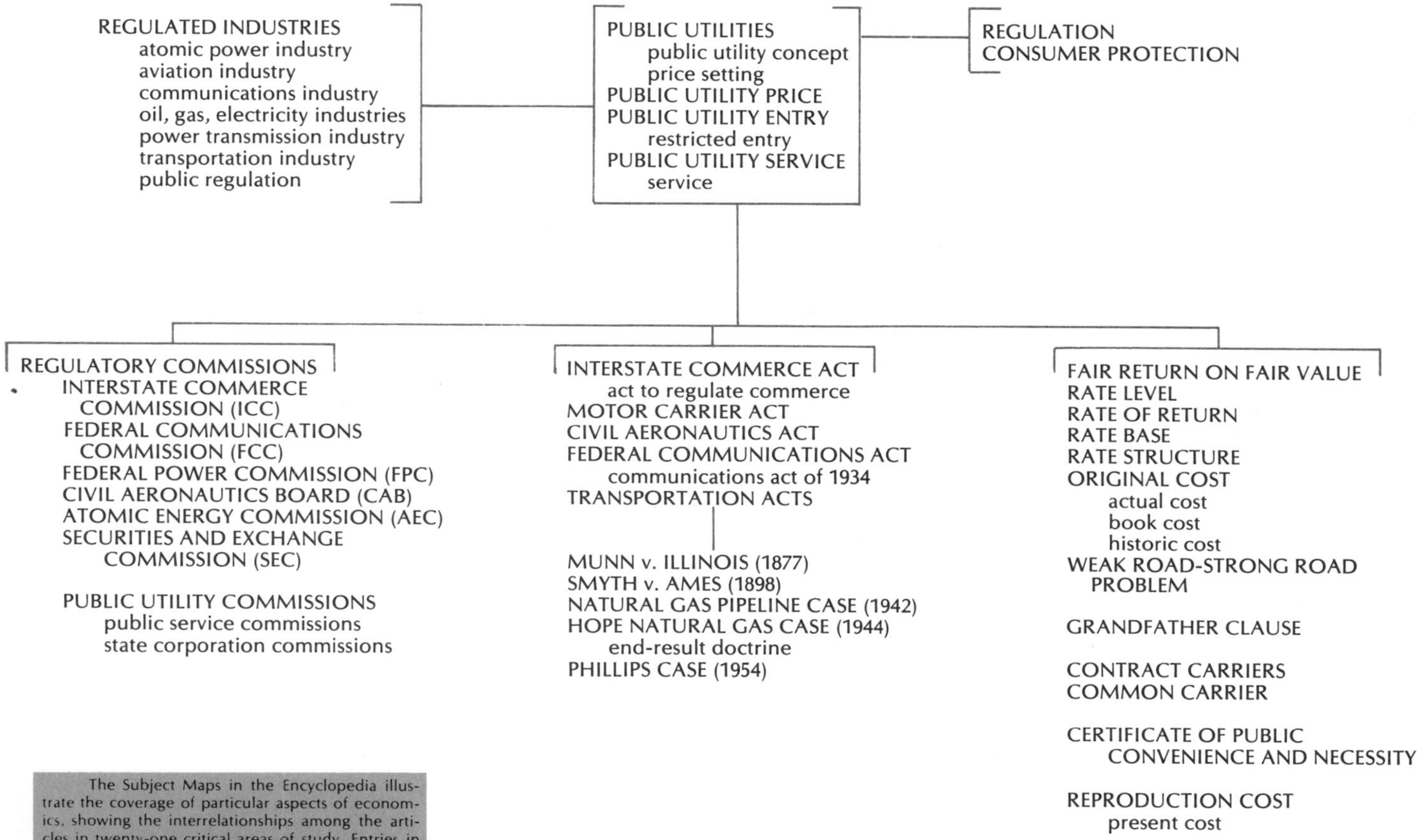
REGULATED INDUSTRIES
atomic power industry
aviation industry
communications industry
oil, gas, electricity industries
power transmission industry
transportation industry
public regulation
PUBLIC UTILITIES
public utility concept
price setting
PUBLIC UTILITY PRICE
PUBLIC UTILITY ENTRY
restricted entry
PUBLIC UTILITY SERVICE
service
REGULATION
CONSUMER PROTECTION
REGULATORY COMMISSIONS
INTERSTATE COMMERCE COMMISSION (ICC)
FEDERAL COMMUNICATIONS COMMISSION (FCC)
FEDERAL POWER COMMISSION (FPC)
CIVIL AERONAUTICS BOARD (CAB)
ATOMIC ENERGY COMMISSION (AEC)
SECURITIES AND EXCHANGE COMMISSION (SEC)
PUBLIC UTILITY COMMISSIONS
public service commissions
state corporation commissions
INTERSTATE COMMERCE ACT
act to regulate commerce
MOTOR CARRIER ACT
CIVIL AERONAUTICS ACT
FEDERAL COMMUNICATIONS ACT
communications act of 1934
TRANSPORTATION ACTS
MUNN v. ILLINOIS (1877)
SMYTH v. AMES (1898)
NATURAL GAS PIPELINE CASE (1942)
HOPE NATURAL GAS CASE (1944)
end-result doctrine
PHILLIPS CASE (1954)
FAIR RETURN ON FAIR VALUE
RATE LEVEL
RATE OF RETURN
RATE BASE
RATE STRUCTURE
ORIGINAL COST
actual cost
book cost
historic cost
WEAK ROAD-STRONG ROAD PROBLEM
GRANDFATHER CLAUSE
CONTRACT CARRIERS
COMMON CARRIER
CERTIFICATE OF PUBLIC CONVENIENCE AND NECESSITY
REPRODUCTION COST
present cost

The Subject Maps in the Encyclopedia illustrate the coverage of particular aspects of economics, showing the interrelationships among the articles in twenty-one critical areas of study. Entries in capital letters are subjects for which there are separate articles in the Encyclopedia. Entries in small letters are references to the article immediately above and provide some idea of content.

The Subject Maps are arranged alphabetically in the Encyclopedia under the following titles:

Antitrust Policy
Banking System
Business Cycles
Capital
Circular Flow of Income
Demand Theory
Economic Systems
Factor Markets
Federal Budget
History of Economic Ideas
International Trade Theory
Labor Market
Labor Movement
Market System
Money and Monetary Policy
National Income
Price Level
Regulation
Supply
Theory of the Firm
Wages

Research and development is essential for success with competitive products such as computers.

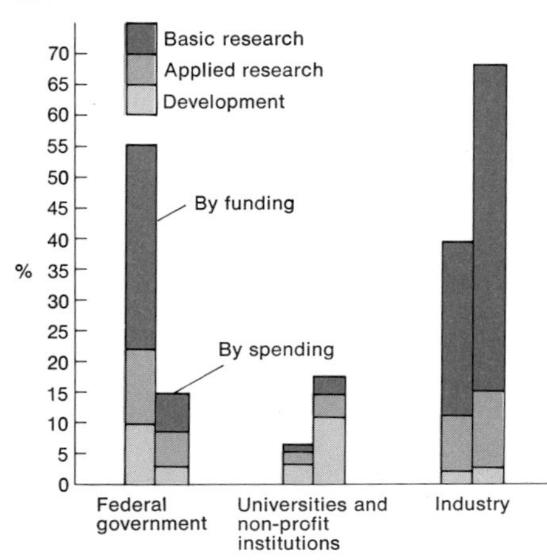

regulatory commissions would be composed of experts, that they would be free from political pressures, that overlapping terms would ensure continuity and consistency of decisions, that their procedures would be flexible, and that they would act quickly. Instead, politicians have tended to be appointed or elected to commissions, commission decisions have often been inconsistent, procedures have become rigidly institutionalized and slow, and pressures from the government and industry have influenced commission decisions. In 1971, the President's Advisory Council on Executive Organization noted these problems and recommended that regulatory efficiency and accountability would be improved if certain commissions were replaced by single administrators.

See also Public Utility Commissions.

Consult (17) Bernstein, 1955.

—Joseph Jadlow, *Oklahoma State University*

RELATIVE FACTOR PRICES, the ratio of input prices, play an important role in profit maximization for the entrepreneur. The firm must choose a combination of inputs, out of the manifold possibilities, that minimizes the cost of producing a given output. To do so, the firm must take into consideration relative factor prices and factor substitutability. Relative factor prices and the respective quantities of the factors in an economy determine the distribution of income. The supply of the respective factors, interacting mutually with the demand for these factors, determines relative factor prices.

RENT has a number of distinct meanings in economics.

Rent is a payment to the owners of real property, such as land, housing, commercial space or some other durable good for use of the real property. Rental payments in this sense are made not only for the use of land but also for physical capital, including interest and depreciation on the capital, and possibly even for janitorial service, protection service, and repair service. It is this concept of rent that is most common in everyday usage. However, from the point of view of economic analysis, this concept of rent is not very useful. The payment of rent for use of land alone—excluding any physical capital on the land—is the return to the resource "land" in the same sense as wages and salaries are the return to the resource "labor."

Rent in the National Income and Product Accounts is denoted as rental income of persons and is one of four major sources of national income. In 1971, the rental income of persons totalled $24 billion. The rental income of persons consists of net rents of non-farm persons, the imputed value of net rental income from owner-occupied housing, and net rents of farm realty. Property taxes, depreciation, interest, and maintenance expenses are deducted from gross rent to arrive at net rent. Rental income of business firms is not included as rent in the National Income and Product Accounts, but rather as profits. It should be clear that the net rental income of persons really represents the profits accruing to individuals from their rental activities.

Economic Rent is any payment in the long-run period to an owner of a resource (factor of production) that is not necessary to keep the resource in its current use. The resource may either be a property resource or a human resource. The payment necessary to keep a resource in its current use is the opportunity cost of the resource, that is, the value of the resource in the best alternative use. The opportunity cost is the real social cost of the resource. Economic rent, or pure rent, as it is occasionally designated, is a payment in excess of the real cost of the resource and constitutes a socially unnecessary payment that could be, if identifiable, taxed away with no change in the allocation of resources. Even if it is not a social cost, rent will be reckoned as a private cost by the person (or firm) paying it. To the recipient rent is a source of income.

Classical Land Rent is the payment to the owner of land which has only one use. The opportunity cost of such land is zero. In classical economics land was defined as "the indestructible powers and qualities of the soil." It was assumed implicitly by David Ricardo, one of the greatest of the classical economists and an important contributor to rent theory, that such land had only one use. Any payment to the owner of land is, thus, an economic rent. Ricardo and other economists failed to realize that the owners of resources other than land may receive economic rents and that land, like other resources, has more than one use.

See also Economic Rent; Implicit Rent; Quasi Rent; Real Property.

—John P. Formby, *University of North Carolina at Greensboro*

RESEARCH AND DEVELOPMENT, usually a branch or part of a firm devoted to improving existing products and developing new ones. Research and development programs are seldom found in purely competitive market structures, but are quite common in imperfectly competitive market structures, such as monopolistically competitive, oligopolistic, and monopolistic industries.

Because imperfectly competitive market structures often use nonprice competition to gather shares of the markets, it is essential that firms constantly make improvements in their products in order to remain competitive with each other. This is especially important in monopolistically competitive markets where product differentiation plays a major role in distinguishing products of one firm from those of others in the industry. Also, in oligopolistic markets where there are only a few firms, a firm that did not improve its product could easily be forced out of the market.

See also Product Differentiation.

RESERVE-ASSET COMPOSITION. *See* Intervention Currency.

RESERVE BANK CREDIT is the amount of money provided by the federal reserve banks to the banking system as a result of their loans and purchases of securities.

See also Discount Rate; Federal Reserve System; Open Market Operations.

RESERVE CITY BANK. *See* Member Bank.

RESERVE CURRENCY. *See* International Monetary System.

RESERVE RATIO. *See* Reserve Requirement.

RESERVE REQUIREMENT, or LEGAL RESERVES, the minimum amount of reserves that a bank must maintain, stated as a percentage of its deposit liabilities. If a bank has $100 million in deposits and a 16% reserve requirement, it must hold $16 million in reserves. Although a few states set requirements for savings banks, reserves are normally applicable only to commercial banks. Reserve requirements for member banks of the federal reserve system are established by its Board of Governors within limits set by Congress. Against time deposits the range is 3% to 10% with recent actual requirements near the minimum (except for banks holding more than $5 million in time deposits, for which the requirement has been 5% or 6%). Against demand deposits the range is 7% to 22%.

Legal reserves for member banks consist only of vault cash and deposits with the federal reserve banks. The legal reserve ratios for nonmember state banks, determined by state law, are frequently similar in amount to requirements of the federal reserve but may include deposits in other commercial banks. In foreign countries various forms of securities may be counted as part of legal reserves.

Changing reserve requirements can be a strong instrument of monetary policy: the multiple expansion of the money supply depends on banks having excess reserves over the legal requirement. Thus, raising reserve requirements reduces excess reserves and the bank multiplier, putting downward pressure on the money supply; lowering requirements has exactly the opposite effect. In practice changes of reserve requirements have been rather rare, because they are considered overly blunt, causing more extensive swings in the money supply than is usually desired.

—Walter W. Haines, *New York University*

RESERVES, currency or certain other liquid assets retained by a bank as a fund that can be used to meet the demands of depositors who wish to withdraw cash from their accounts. Reserves may be stated as a dollar amount or, more commonly, as a percentage of the bank's deposit liabilities, the reserve ratio.

Form of Reserves. The particular form that reserves may take varies according to circumstances and often is defined by law. Vault cash is the only thing that can be paid out on the spot and, thus, is the basic form of reserves, but deposits in other banks are becoming increasingly important as a form of reserve. When a bank maintains a deposit account in another bank (referred to by the depositing bank as "due from banks"), it can speedily withdraw cash from this account to meet the demands of its own customers. In the United States most large banks hold such deposits in the federal reserve bank of which they are members, but they may also maintain deposits in other ordinary banks, and smaller banks invariably hold such accounts. When a bank maintains a deposit account in another bank, both banks are referred to as correspondents of each other. Serving also for clearing checks between banks, correspondent balances are more useful, though a little less readily available, than vault cash.

Other assets that are highly liquid may be readily sold to obtain cash if needed, and these assets are frequently called secondary reserves, because they can be called upon when primary reserves are exhausted. Secondary reserves earn interest for the bank. Secondary reserves may include Treasury bills or other government securities, bank acceptances, or call loans.

Size of Reserves. Because primary reserves do not earn interest, a bank likes to keep them as low as possible, but maintaining too low a level invites bank failures if depositors ask for cash in unexpectedly large amounts. In the absence of legal requirements each bank must decide for itself what level is safe by weighing past experience with the current practices of the business community. The more readily that checks are accepted as money, the lower that the reserve ratio may safely be. In the earliest days of banking, 100% reserves were kept, but as checks became more and more common, the reserve ratio fell, to its present level below 20%.

Today most countries establish reserve requirements by law, specifying how much a bank must keep in reserves. Because these reserves must be on hand at all times, they cannot be used to pay depositors and no longer, therefore, serve as a fund available to meet withdrawals.

See also Reserve Requirement.

—Walter W. Haines, *New York Univ.*

RESOURCE MOBILITY refers to the relative freedom with which resources are able to move among alternative uses. Ideally, when all restraints are removed, resources—chiefly land, labor, capital, and entrepreneurship—should be able to move to the situation that offers the best opportunity or is the most profitable. Workers, for example, should be free to enter and exit jobs as better opportunities arise, and capital should be used in the most profitable ventures.

However, certain economic restraints hinder resource mobility. Among the major restraints is the lack of perfect knowledge of the market. Thus workers and investors may not even know about opportunities that exist. A second restraint results from monopoly and monopsony structures that control such things as employment and natural resources. Other restraints include government intervention, geography and political policies.

See also Labor Mobility.

RESOURCE RIGHTS, the right to own and use certain scarce resources, usually the type that are fixed in terms of known available quantities. Examples are land, certain minerals, and fresh water. Confronted with conditions of unlimited human economic wants and nationally determined goals (a certain economic growth rate, national defense, etc.) and that of the fixed character of certain natural resources, a society must determine the rules dealing with ownership and utilization of scarce resources.

In the free market society, resource rights are based on a variety of rules: (1) the concept of private ownership of property, (2) licensing by a government agency providing rights to a firm to mine or to take a natural resource, (3) setting of quotas on the amount of the resource that may be taken in a given time period. The reasons for restrictions include the public's need for certain resources for present and future use and the need to maintain a livable environment.

Resource rights may also have an international dimension. When scarce resources are owned by foreign capital, a government may decide to confiscate such resources for national purposes.

—Francis W. Rushing, *College of William and Mary*

RESOURCES, the inputs with which products are produced. Economists distinguish four basic resources: land, labor, enterprise, and capital. *Land* refers to all natural resources. *Labor* is usually defined to include the productive contribution of all human beings, with the exception of the entrepreneur. *Enterprise* is the contribution of the entrepreneur, who initiates productive activity, takes risks, and makes important production decisions. *Capital* includes all producers, buildings, machines, and tools, as well as various types of materials.

Resources are usually scarce, not available in unlimited quantities relative to the demand for them. They must, therefore, be paid some return. Specificially, land, labor, enterprise, and capital receive rent, wages, profits, and interest, respectively. All other resources are combinations of the four basic resources. Aluminum, for example, comes from land and is worked on by labor, capital, and enterprise before emerging as a widely used input.

RESTRAINT OF TRADE, collusive action by a business firm or firms to control or eliminate competition or to prevent the emergence of new competitors. The effect sought is the enhancement of price and thereby the profits of the agreeing firms. The specific practices used range from tight-knit combinations such as cartels and bidding rings to basing-point systems, trade associations, and conscious parallelism of action. Enhancement of price is also facilitated by indirect methods such as market sharing, quotas, and other forms of territorial allocation whereby the downward price pressure exerted by direct competition is avoided.

Contracts, combinations, and conspiracies in restraint of trade are prohibited in the Sherman Antitrust Act (along with monopolization). The keys to enforcement of this prohibition are (1) the availability to government prosecutors of evidence of agreement among nominal competitors and (2) the nature of the agreement. Certain practices are considered illegal *per se* where evidence indicates overt agreement to fix prices or share markets. Such violations are not defensible on the grounds that either the action or the result was "reasonable." Where evidence of agreement is less certain, such as in price-reporting plans of trade associations, courts must consider how seriously competition was affected adversely. Similarly, difficult interpretation attends the practice of "conscious parallelism" where the effect of price fixing is achieved oftentimes without any overt agreement among competitors.

The prohibitions on restraint of trade and monopolization state in law the society's conviction (1) that price competition, as the impersonal and automatic regulator of activity in a market economy, is most satisfactory and efficient, and (2) that artificial barriers to the operation of competition should be condemned.

See also Antitrust Policy; Collusion; Conscious Parallelism; Market Sharing; Price Fixing; Rule of Reason; Trade Associations.

—Thomas O. Depperschmidt, *Memphis State University*

RESTRICTED ENTRY. *See* Public Utility Entry.

RESTRICTION OF NUMBERS, a term used to describe the policy of certain labor groups that try to limit the number of workers in that group. Certain trade unions, in order to keep the price of their labor high, restrict the number of workers that can enter the union.

RESTRICTION OF OUTPUT, a method used chiefly in oligopolistic or monopolistic market structures to keep prices high. When an industry has complete control over the production of an item, it may be advantageous for that industry to restrict output in such a way that individuals are willing to pay higher prices to obtain the product.

RETAIL PRICE MAINTENANCE. *See* Price Fixing.

RETAINED EARNINGS or UNDISTRIBUTED PROFITS, a business' income after taxes and dividends have been paid. Retained earnings serve as an internal source of funds for business expansion and allow a company to finance its growth without diluting stockholders' equity or increasing fixed-interest obligations.

RETRAINING. The retraining of labor is a concept that has received major attention in the last decade because of the passage of the Manpower Development and Training Act of 1964. This act provided federal money to be allocated to the retraining of the unemployed who have been displaced due to technological or structural problems in the economic system. Retraining usually involves the training of a worker in a particular skill or trade that he is unfamiliar with because his original training is no longer of any economic value. Large-scale retraining usually becomes necessary when automation displaces workers and when plants shut down or relocate.

REUTHER, WALTER PHILIP (1907-70), American labor leader. Educated at Wayne University, Reuther worked as a tool and die maker for Wheeling Steel until 1927. In 1933, after his discharge from Ford Motor Company for union activism, he went abroad, spending eighteen months traveling in Europe and Russia. While in Russia, he worked at the Ford Plant in Gorki. In 1935 Reuther assisted in the founding of the United Automobile Workers. He became UAW vice president in 1942 and was its president from 1946 until his death.

REVEALED PREFERENCE THEORY OF DEMAND, a relatively new theory in microeconomics, attempts to derive indifference curves based on actual behavior, rather than from a person's stated preferences. The method is behaviorist: observe what a person does rather than what he says he does.

Given a person's preference system (tastes), then money income and prices can be varied experimentally; reaction to these changes can be recorded. Thus, in principle a person chooses one bundle of goods and services over another either because he prefers it or because it is cheaper. If prices are varied so that both bundles cost the same, and the same bundle is chosen, it may be deduced that this bundle is preferred. Advanced texts indicate how, graphically, this procedure can be carried out often enough to eliminate zones of ignorance as to where the indifference curve is located. Though not a practical method, revealed preference is, nevertheless, theoretically important as a possible solution.

REVENUE SHARING. *See* Taxation: *Glossary.*

REVISIONISM, an approach to socialism based on the systematic reexamination and correcting of Marx's doctrines. Led by Edward Bernstein (1850-1932) in Germany, who contended that many accepted Marxian theories had proved incorrect, the revisionists believed that socialism would be reached by evolutionary means, consciously reconstructing the social system, not through the breakdown of capitalism as Marx had predicted.

See also Evolutionary Socialism; Fabian Society.

Consult (26) Halm, 1968.

REVOLUTIONARY SOCIALISM implies the necessity of using force to secure desired social changes and attain a socialist society. The doctrine assumes that (1) capitalism involves a constant class war between capitalists and workers; (2) if capitalists have power bestowed upon them via ownership of capital, they will then exploit the workers; (3) government and laws would assist in this exploitation, primarily by enforcing property rights; and (4) the proletariat, therefore, cannot acquire power over the economic system without gaining possession of the political state. The basic work for revolutionary socialism is the *Communist Manifesto* (1848) of Karl Marx and Friedrich Engels.

See also Evolutionary Socialism; Lenin, Vladimir; Marx, Karl.

Consult (26) Hunt, 1972.

A worker whose skills are no longer in demand can become employable again through retraining.

Walter Philip Reuther

David Ricardo

Lionel Robbins in an academic procession at Berkeley in 1965.

RICARDIAN SOCIALISM. *See* Pre-Marxian Socialism.

RICARDO, DAVID (1772–1823), considered by some to be the greatest classical economist, was the first major economist to develop a rigorous theoretical model based upon abstract thought and building upon the works of his predecessors. However, Ricardo shifted from the Smithian focus upon development to an emphasis upon distribution; he foresaw economic progress leading not toward a bright future but toward a dim future, with subsistence being the lot of most of the people.

Ricardo's contribution in his *Principles of Economics* (1817) fall into several categories:

Value Theory. While Ricardo had a general cost-of-production theory of value, he was interested in changes in the rate at which exchange between goods occurs. He felt this rate was the result of changes in the relative content of labor embodied in the goods. This assumption served as a foundation for Marx's labor theory of value.

Differential Theory of Rent. Combining the concept of diminishing returns with the principle of intensive and extensive margins, Ricardo developed a theory of the return to land which was in essence a marginal productivity theory.

Wage Theory. Ricardo held a subsistence view of wages based upon the wages fund doctrine.

International Trade. Building upon Smith's discussion of absolute advantage as a basis for international trade, Ricardo developed the concept of comparative advantage.

See also Classical Economics.

Consult (25) Rima, 1967; Spiegel, 1971.

—Clyde A. Haulman, *College of William and Mary*

RIGHT-TO-WORK LAWS. *See* Agency Shop; Union Shop.

RISING EXPECTATIONS. *See* Demonstration Effect.

RISK, the possibility of gain or loss in an investment. As Frank Knight pointed out in *Risk, Uncertainty and Profit* (1921), many kinds of risk can be insured against because previous experience provides sufficient samples for actuarial calculations. The best-known example is the risk of loss from theft or fire. Though unpredictable for a given building, the likelihood of fire loss for a group of buildings is reasonably predictable. By pooling the premiums on a large number of buildings, insurance companies can eliminate risk.

See also Profit System; Uncertainty.

RISK AVERSION. *See* Expected Utility.

RISK, UNCERTAINTY AND PROFIT (1921). *See* Knight, Frank H.

ROAD TO SERFDOM (1944). *See* Hayek, Friedrich von.

ROBBINS, LIONEL (1898–   ), English economist and professor at the London School of Economics. His most important work is the influential *Essay on the Nature and Significance of Economic Science* (1932). In this methodological work, Robbins takes the position that the scope and function of economics should be limited to the problem of choice as it appears in the allocation of scarce resources among alternative ends. Thus, the role of economists is to present the alternative means of obtaining a specific goal while being neutral as to the desirability of that goal. Robbins also is a firm supporter of individualism and the use of markets as the means of organizing the economic system.

ROBINSON, JOAN (1903–   ), published her *The Economics of Imperfect Competition* (1933) a few months after Edward Chamberlin's *The Theory of Monopolistic Competition* appeared. Both studies covered the same basic material in developing the concept of monopolistic competition. In addition, Robinson considered the problem of the exploitation of labor in her discussion of distribution.

Since the appearance of this work, Robinson has expanded her studies to include Keynesian theory, international trade, and Marxian economics. Her *Essay on Marxian Economics* (1942) is an excellent critique of Marx's analysis and her *The Accumulation of Capital* (1956) expanded upon her earlier work. Her attention has also turned toward the problems of growth and the development of a long-run version of the Keynesian system.

ROBINSON-PATMAN ACT (1936), amends Section 2 of the Clayton Act, prohibiting price discrimination where the effect may be to lessen competition substantially. Its passage and subsequent interpretation have brought some confusion into antitrust policy since, paradoxically, the law often protects competitors at the expense of price competition.

Interpretation of Section 2 of the Clayton Act confined the prohibition on price discrimination to the impact on the seller's competition, with no concern for the effect on the buyer's plane of competition. That is, competition among buyers could be affected adversely as certain favored buyers (typically the mass-distributing chain stores) received the lower prices.

The Robinson-Patman Act added protection for competition at the buyer's level. An unfavored, local buyer, for example, now has redress against a favored competitor who, because of size, efficiency, or bargaining power, can secure a lower price from the seller and deliver the product to consumers at lower prices.

See also Clayton Antitrust Act; Price Discrimination.

Consult (16) Blummer and Heftner, 1968.

—Thomas O. Depperschmidt, *Memphis State University*

ROSENSTEIN-RODAN, PAUL NARCYZ (1902–), Polish-born educator noted for his contributions to the theory of economic development and development planning. He received his doctoral degree from the University of Vienna. His extensive public service includes a position as head economic adviser to the International Bank for Reconstruction and Development in Washington (1947–53). He also served with the Alliance for Progress 1961–66. Rosenstein-Rodan has been on the faculty at both the University of London and M.I.T.

ROSOVSKY, HENRY (1927–), Polish-born educator and expert on the Japanese economy. A graduate of the College of William and Mary (1949), he received his M.A. (1953) and Ph.D. (1959) from Harvard. His publications include *Capital Formation in Japan, 1868–1940* (1961), *Quantitative Japanese Economic History* (1961), and *Industrialization in Two Systems* (1966). Rosovsky has been chairman of the department of economics at Harvard since 1969 and associate director of the East Asia Research Center at Harvard since 1967.

ROUNDABOUT METHODS OF PRODUCTION, production via capital in which consumer goods are not produced by the direct application of labor to natural products. The roundabout or indirect concept is associated with Eugen von Böhm-Bawerk, an Austrian economist studying the nature of capital. He pointed out one could obtain a drink of water by drinking from a spring with cupped hands, making a bucket and storing the water, or constructing a pipeline to bring the water to his house. The more roundabout the method, the longer the time from expenditure of labor to availability of water but the more rewarding the result.

See also Böhm-Bawerk, Eugen; Demand for Capital; Technological Change.

Consult (22) Spiegel, 1971.

RULE OF REASON, in Sherman Antitrust Act litigation, a legal dictum with which a federal court views restraints of trade and monopolization in terms of "reasonableness" of the methods used and results achieved by the alleged violator, rather than in terms of the literal legal proscription against every violation (holding the actions to be inherently illegal or *per se* violations). A court might find for a firm attempting to monopolize, for example, if the firm's defense shows that its actions did not yield exorbitant profits (the price charged was "reasonable") or that predatory practices did not damage competitors severely.

See also Per Se Illegality; United States v. Standard Oil Co. of New Jersey.

RUNAWAY INFLATION. *See* Hyperinflation.

RUN ON THE DOLLAR, all governments hastening to convert their dollars into gold—comparable to a run on a commercial bank—as they see that the United States has less and less gold relative to its dollar liabilities. Alternatively, they fear that the United States might increase the dollar price of gold (as actually occurred in December 1971), thus reducing the gold value of their dollar holdings; or, finally, they fear that the United States might demonetize gold, that is, abrogate the gold convertibility of official dollars.

SALARIES, one of the costs of production, the payments made to white-collar workers to compensate for services rendered. Salaries include cash payments as well as in-kind income, which refers to such items as room and board. Wages are payments to factory and manual labor workers. Wages and salaries make up nearly two-thirds of national income and are very often one of the largest costs of a firm.

See also Factor Prices.

SALES TAXES, often called commodity or consumption taxes, may be imposed at any of the stages of production and distribution of an economic good—manufacturing, wholesale, or retail. A sales tax may be placed at any one or a combination of these transaction points.

SAMPLE. Since it is usually impractical or impossible to examine every member of a statistical population, it becomes necessary to examine a chosen set of members—the sample—and make inferences concerning the rest. A sample that contains all the members of a population is called a census. The random sample, in which each possible sample has an equal chance of being chosen, is the basis for statistical inference.

See also Inference; Population, Statistical; Sampling.

SAMPLING refers to the process of selecting for study a limited number of items from a population in order to make inferences concerning the entire population. Although inference relies on random sampling, there are many sampling procedures that preserve ran-

Henry Rosovsky

Paul Anthony Samuelson

SAVINGS

For the role of savings in the macroeconomy, see the articles on CIRCULAR FLOW OF INCOME, WITHDRAWALS, and SAVINGS-INVESTMENT EQUALITY. The relationship between income and savings is also discussed in MARGINAL PROPENSITY TO SAVE. Some of the microeconomic aspects of savings are discussed in the articles on FACTOR SUPPLY, LOANABLE FUNDS, INTEREST, and INTEREST RATES.

The Subject Maps accompanying CIRCULAR FLOW OF INCOME and NATIONAL INCOME display additional aspects of savings.

domness: stratified samples, cluster samples, and others.

The target population is the population whose characteristics we wish to infer; the sampled populations should therefore be identical. If the target population is all residents of Chicago, for example, a random sample from the telephone book will result in a sample population of Chicagoans who have telephones, and inferences based on this sample may not apply to the target population.

See also Inference; Population, Statistical; Sample.

Consult (27) Leabo, 1972.

SAMPLING DISTRIBUTION. If we take several random samples and compute the sample mean for each, it is likely that these sample means will not all be equal. The distribution of sample means is called the sampling distribution of means. The mean of the sampling distribution of means is the true population mean.

See also Sample; Sampling.

SAMPLING THEORY. A fundamental concept in statistical inference is the sampling distribution. The central limit theorem states that any sampling distribution of means will approach a normal distribution as the number of sample observations increases. In fact, for samples of 30 observations or more ("large samples") the normal curve is a close approximation of the sampling distribution and can be used for significance tests. For samples less than 30, the normal curve is not as good an approximation and other distributions must be used.

See also Confidence Interval; Hypothesis; Inference; Significance.

SAMUELSON, PAUL ANTHONY (1915-), one of the most important American contributors to economics. His early work concerning the interaction of the multiplier and accelerator helped to develop an important area of the Keynesian system. However, Samuelson's most important work is his *Foundations of Economic Analysis* (1947). In this work he used mathematics to support his position that the similarities among economic theories suggest the existence of a more general concept which binds together the various areas of economics. According to Samuelson, this concept was the equilibrium as a maximizing or minimizing situation, and the analyses of the forces around equilibrium and movements away from equibibrium are the main points of economic theory.

Samuelson applied his views to the theory of cost and production, to the theory of consumer demand, and to welfare economics. Of these, his revealed preference theory of consumer behavior is best known. Yet, Samuelson's most important contribution was his development of the concept of economic dynamics.

In addition to his *Foundations,* Samuelson has written numerous articles and books in many areas of economics including macroeconomic theory and policy and international trade. His widely-used introductory textbook, *Economics,* has taught a new generation of economists. Also, his famous debate with Milton Friedman concerning the role of fiscal versus monetary policy has helped to bring important economic policy questions into focus.

For his many contributions, Samuelson was awarded the Nobel Prize in Economics (1970).

—Clyde A. Haulman, *College of William and Mary*

SATISFACTION. *See* Utility.

SAVING, CAPITAL. *See* Capital Saving.

SAVING, LABOR. *See* Labor Saving.

SAVINGS, withdrawals from the income stream, dollars of income not spent. When households save part of disposable income, they are not demanding the production of goods and services, the employment of labor, and the payment of incomes to the factors of production. When businesses retain earnings, the owners of the businesses do not spend the retained earnings on consumption goods and services. These business savings are considered the equivalent of savings by the owners, who have "left their savings" with the business.

Households frequently save with consumption in mind: old age, vacations, and so on. Households often save by making so-called "investments" (buying stocks or bonds but not capital goods) and may sometimes genuinely invest in capital goods. For instance, a family may save to obtain the purchasing power to start a business.

Firms save, because they spend on investment goods and buy property, other firms, and existing goods, none of which are purchases of currently produced goods. A firm may save now to buy capital goods later or to repay old debts that financed past investment spending. Even when a firm is saving as it invests it is extremely unlikely that the earnings retained will exactly equal the amount spent on new investment goods; and lack of saving by a business does not stop it from investing in new capital goods, because it can borrow to pay for the new capital goods. It is because it is current investment spending, not past or future spending, that national income theory treats both household and business savings separately from investment spending.

See also Consumption.

—Anne Mayhew and Walter C. Neale, *University of Tennessee*

SAVINGS ACCOUNTS. *See* Savings; Time Deposits.

SAVINGS AND LOAN ASSOCIATIONS. *See* Financial Intermediaries.

SAVINGS BONDS. *See* Bonds; Government Securities.

SAVINGS FUNCTION. *See* Propensity to Save.

SAVINGS-INVESTMENT EQUALITY. National income determination is frequently explained by using a simple model of an economy in which there is no foreign trade (or in which exports equal imports) and no government expenditures or taxes (or one in which G = taxes). In this case the equilibrium level of income will be that level at which savings equal investment.

See also National Income Determination: *Changes.*

SAVINGS SCHEDULE. *See* Propensity to Save.

SAY'S LAW, named after one of its early formulators, the French economist J.B. Say, maintains that supply creates its own demand. Thus, there can be no general oversupply or "glut" of goods and services, because the total value of goods and services produced will be available for their purchase. It is implied that resources not consumed (released by saving) would be employed by investment expenditure. This law was important in the pre-Keynesian explanation of why, in the absence of interference with market mechanism, overproduction or underconsumption would not occur.

SCARCITY, a crucial element of economics, the limitation of the means of production (resources and technology). Scarcity limits the total output possible from the economy. The economic problem at any point in time, therefore, becomes one of choosing what goods and services to produce, how they should be produced, and who should get them, given the economy's limited means of production. Scarcity, however, does not imply that the amount of resources or state of technology is fixed over time; as the means of production change, corresponding changes in the economy's output occur.

SCARF, HERBERT ELY (1930-), American educator and mathematical economist noted for his contribution to general equilibrium theory. A graduate of Temple University (1951), he received his Ph.D. in mathematics from Princeton (1954). He is author of *Studies in the Mathematical Theory of Inventory and Production* (1958, with Arrow and Karlin), *Studies in Applied Probability and Management Science* (1962), and *Multistage Inventory Models and Techniques* (1963, with Gilford and Shelly). Scarf has served as a consultant to the General Electric Company (1956), the RAND Corporation (1958), the Planning Research Corporation (1958), and the Defense Department (1963). He became a professor at Yale in 1963 and director of the Cowles Foundation in 1967.

SCATTER DIAGRAM. If we take observations on two variables that we suspect are functionally related and plot each pair of observations as points on graph paper, the result is a group or scatter of points called a scatter diagram. The shape of the scatter may give clues to the actual relationship.

See also Functional Relationship.

SCHECTER BROS. v. U.S. *See* National Industrial Recovery Act (NIRA).

SCHELLING, THOMAS CROMBIE (1921-), American economist. He graduated from the University of California at Berkeley in 1943 and he received his Ph.D. from Harvard in 1951. His publications include *National Income Behavior* (1951), *International Economics* (1958), *The Strategy of Conflict* (1960), and *Arms and Influence* (1966). A professor at Harvard since 1958, Schelling has worked as an economist for the U.S. Government in Copenhagen, Paris, and Washington (1948-53), as a member of the Air Force science advisory board (1960-64), and as a member of the defense science board of the Department of Defense beginning in 1966.

SCHULTZ, THEODORE WILLIAM (1902-), American economist who has achieved recognition for his contributions to agricultural economics and human capital theory. A graduate of South Dakota State College, he received his M.S. (1928) and Ph.D. (1930) from the University of Wisconsin. He became professor of economics at the University of Chicago in 1943. His numerous publications include *The Economic Organization of Agriculture* (1953), *The Economic Value of Education* (1963), *Transforming Traditional Agriculture* (1964), and *Economic Growth and Agriculture* (1968). Schultz has served as a consultant or economic adviser to many organizations and government agencies. He has been director of the National Bureau of Economic Research since 1949, and he was president of the American Economic Association in 1960.

SCARCITY

Scarcity is a pervasive and central economic phenomenon. For other articles that describe the impact of the fact of economic scarcity see CHOICE, ALLOCATION, and OPPORTUNITY COST. Analytical concepts that deal with economic decisions in the context of scarcity are presented in MARGINAL ANALYSIS.

Thomas Crombie Schelling

Charles Schultze

Joseph Alois Schumpeter

SCHULTZE, CHARLES LOUIS (1924-), American educator and principal architect of economic policy during the Kennedy and Johnson administrations. He has made significant contributions to inflation theory and government spending. He received his B.A. (1948) and M.A. (1950) in economics from Georgetown University. He received his Ph.D. from the University of Maryland in 1960. His publications include: *Recent Inflation in the United States* (1959), *The Politics and Economics of Public Spending* (1969), and *Setting National Priorities, the 1973 Budget.* Schultze served as director of the Bureau of the Budget from 1965-67. He is presently senior fellow at the Brookings Institution and professor of economics at the University of Maryland.

SCHUMPETER, JOSEPH ALOIS (1883-1950), outstanding Austrian-American economist who constructed, in his *Theory of Economic Development* (1912) and *Business Cycles* (1939), an economic theory to explain both the development of capitalism and the existence of business cycles in such a system. Schumpeter's system focuses upon the entrepreneur or businessman and his role of introducing innovations. According to Schumpeter, innovation is any change in supply techniques; invention means nothing until it is applied, thus becoming an innovation.

It is the innovating entrepreneur, seeking profit, whom Schumpeter sees as the key to economic development, which comes from within the system. However, innovations occur in clusters rather than continuously because one important innovation creates a situation within which other innovations are favored. This results in an economic boom. But the boom brings conditions which work against further innovation. Thus, the very process which creates economic growth also generates the business cycle—a system of creative destruction.

Schumpeter's *Capitalism, Socialism and Democracy* (1942) suggested that capitalism was beginning to fail because (1) the entrepreneur had become obsolete, (2) the political strata which had protected capitalism had been destroyed, and (3) the institutional framework within which capitalism operated was disappearing.

Finally, Schumpeter's posthumous *History of Economic Analysis* (1954) is an outstanding work which presents one of the most detailed, scholarly histories of economics.

—Clyde A. Haulman, *College of William and Mary*

SCHWEGMANN BROTHERS V. CALVERT CORP. *See* McGuire-Keogh Act.

SCIENCE OF HUMAN HISTORY. *See* Scientific Socialism.

SCIENTIFIC SOCIALISM. To give socialist doctrine and tactics a scientific rather than utopian cast, Marx adapted Hegelian philosophy into a "science of human history." Its basic premise is that changes occur in society only as real conditions change mental states. Therefore, only an oppressed class, never a prosperous one satisfied with its condition, would be receptive to new ideas, hence to socialist reasoning or change.

Historically, change occurs when (1) the oppressed realize their interests and the conditions of their fulfillment while (2) the oppressors have become weak. The proletariat revolution will succeed but, with no class below it to be oppressed in turn, will be the last. The result is a classless society with antagonisms gone.

See also Class Conflict; Economic Interpretation of History; Marx, Karl; Revolutionary Socialism.

SCIENTIFIC TARIFF. *See* Tariffs.

SCITOVSKY, TIBOR (1910-), Hungarian-born economist noted for his contributions to microeconomic theory and international trade. He received a doctoral degree from the University of Budapest in 1933, and an M.A. from the London School of Economics in 1938. His publications include *Welfare and Competition* (1951), *Economic Theory and Western European Integration* (1958), and *Money and the Balance of Payments* (1969). A professor of economics at Yale from 1968, Scitovsky served as an economist with the Department of Commerce in Washington (1946), and as a fellow for the Development Centre at the Organization for European Cooperation and Development (1966-68).

SEASONAL FLUCTUATIONS, regularly recurring, noncyclical variations in economic activity, particularly evidenced in sales and agricultural employment. Typically, retail sales are high around Easter and Christmas, and agricultural employment peaks during the harvest seasons. In measuring business cycles, seasonal fluctuations are not in themselves important because their effect is averaged out over the entire year.

See also Business Cycles, Types; Short-Term Business Cycles.

SEASONAL UNEMPLOYMENT occurs as the result of changes in the demand for labor due to the changing seasons. For example, summer months and holiday seasons such as Christmas and Easter usually bring increased demand for labor because there is an increased demand for products. Similarly, post-summer and post-holiday seasons decrease the demand for products and thus labor, resulting in seasonal unemployment. Another cause is weather conditions; as when winter months decrease the demand for labor in the building trades and the agricultural sector.

See also Unemployment of Labor.

SECONDARY BOYCOTT. *See* Boycott.

SECONDARY RESERVES. *See* Reserves.

SECTION 7. *See* National Industrial Recovery Act (NIRA).

SECTORAL INFLATION, also called demand-shift, structural, or bottleneck inflation, occurs when market imperfections exist in important industries or sectors of the economy, resulting in prices and wages that can easily rise but cannot easily fall. A shift in demand, say, from metal to plastic containers, will cause prices and wages to rise in the chemical industries without an offsetting decline in the metal industry. Moreover, the wage increases in the chemical sector may spill over into other sectors. The result could be inflation even in the face of deficient aggregate demand.

SECULAR STAGNATION. The "stagnationist thesis" was defended strongly during the 1930s as an explanation of the Great Depression. Its leading advocate was Alvin Hansen who argued that the major problem of that period was a lack of investment opportunities for the savings that were accumulating. The stagnationists believed that the inadequacy of investment opportunities resulted from a long-run decline in the rate of population growth and the apparent reduced rate of technological progress. Both these factors, it was argued, had provided the prime stimuli for investment, and in their absence government expenditure action was called for. This thesis was hotly debated in the late '30s but the advent of World War II and the resulting military expenditures rendered it academic.

SECURITIES AND EXCHANGE COMMISSION (SEC), independent federal agency that supervises all aspects of the securities industry—including brokers, investment companies, the stock exchanges, and the actions of corporate officials. The SEC, which consists of five members appointed by the President for five-year terms, was established by the Securities Exchange Act of 1934. The main purpose of the commission is to preserve the integrity of the securities industry. Concentrating on prevention of abuses rather than punishment, the SEC relies primarily on self-regulation within the industry. The SEC has long been considered to be the most successful regulatory agency.

SECURITIES EXCHANGE. *See* Stock Market.

SECURITIES EXCHANGE ACT (1934). *See* Securities and Exchange Commission (SEC).

SECURITIES MARKET. *See* Stock Market.

SELECTIVE CONTROLS. *See* Qualitative Controls.

SELF-SUSTAINED GROWTH, a stage of economic growth at which the very processes of production have reached the point of generating increased production. Self-sustained growth usually occurs when an economy's technological and entrepreneurial skills as well as its foreign trade have developed to the point where almost anything can be produced at will. At that point, the fertile imaginations of the population generate ever new products, the ideas for which create their own demand and, thereby, increase investment to support production of the newly invented items.

Self-sustained growth is used in another sense in the case of Less Developed Countries (LDC's) to refer to that point of economic maturity at which the internal economy has developed to such a point that continued growth can be financed out of internally generated funds, without reliance on external infusions of capital and purchasing power.

See also Stages of Growth.

SELLERS INFLATION. *See* Cost-Push Inflation.

SENIORITY. Prior to the development of a shop constitution through collective bargaining, management had the right to exercise its power of hiring and firing in an entirely arbitrary manner. Considerations such as length of service did not always enter into personnel policies and employment practices. Seniority clauses in collective bargaining contracts generally provide that long-service employees in a plant or subdivision thereof shall receive preference in layoffs and rehiring. The seniority system applies also to the determination of the order of promotion of equally qualified workers.

SERVICE. *See* Public Utility Service; Regulation.

SERVICES. The difference between a good transaction and a service transaction hinges on whether or not a commodity is exchanged. If a commodity—something with physical substance—is exchanged, a commodity or good transaction has taken place; if not, a service transaction has taken place.

Services, considered as final output, are purchased by three sectors of the economy. Services purchased by consumers are broken down by the Department of Commerce into four major categories: household operations, housing, transportation, and other (such items as private higher education, physician services, and lawyer services). Services are also purchased by all levels of government. The major type of service purchased by government is

Tibor Scitovsky

Courtesy of the Minneapolis Journal

"DEAD RETURNED TO LIFE"

Theodore Roosevelt, in 1902, renewed the fight against trusts

Moribund for a decade, the Sherman Act packed new punch under trust-buster Theodore Roosevelt.

Eli Shapiro

labor services (compensation of employees). Services are also exchanged with the rest of the world and are calculated on a net basis from the international balance of payments. From the sum of such inpayments as receipts of income on United States investments abroad and transportation on United States carriers by foreigners are deducted corresponding outpayments to arrive at the net services portion of net exports of goods and services. The fourth sector, business, does not receive or purchase services in terms of final output.

See also Final Outputs; Goods; Real Flow.

—Frank J. Bonello, *University of Notre Dame*

SHADOW PRICE, the value of a factor of the economy that is lost when it is shifted from its current use to the use being analyzed; that is, its value in its best alternative employment. Shadow price is most often associated with the valuation of unskilled labor.

See also Opportunity Cost.

SHAPIRO, ELI (1916-), American educator and economist noted for his work in the fields of monetary economics and finance. He is a graduate of Brooklyn College (1936), and he received a Ph.D. from Columbia (1945). He later earned an A.M. from Harvard (1962). His publications include *Money and Banking* (1953, with Steiner), *Measurement of Corporate Sources and Uses of Funds* (1964, with D. Meiselman), and *Consumer Credit* (1968). A professor of financial management at Harvard Business School since 1968, Shapiro has also served as deputy director of the Research Committee on Money and Credit of the Institute of Defense Analysis (1959-61), and project director of the Committee of Economic Research (1966-69).

SHARES. *See* Stock.

SHAW, EDWARD STONE (1908-), American economist noted for his contribution to monetary theory, particularly the Gurley-Shaw hypothesis. He received his Ph.D. (1936) from Stanford. His publications include *Money, Income, and Monetary Policy* (1950), *Money in the Theory of Finance* (1959, with John G. Gurley), and *Savings and Loan Market Structure and Market Performance* (1963). Shaw has served as a consultant to many government agencies and private organizations, including the board of governors of the Federal Reserve System (1954-57 and 1963-64), the Agency for International Development in Korea (1964-67), and the Ford Foundation in Uruguay (1967). He has been a member of the faculty in the department of economics at Stanford since 1929.

SHERMAN ANTITRUST ACT (1890), the first piece of national antitrust legislation, designed to encourage and maintain a more competitive economy. With the Interstate Commerce Act of 1887, its passage marked the beginning of the era of government's attempt to affect the nature and performance of the American economy.

The principal thrust of the Sherman Act is found in its first two sections. Section 1 makes it a misdemeanor for business rivals to contract, combine, or conspire in restraint of trade. Section 2 makes it a misdemeanor to monopolize, attempt to monopolize, or combine or conspire to monopolize trade. The act applies to interstate commerce as well as to the District of Columbia, American territories, and foreign companies doing business in the United States. It provides that a private party injured by the illegal activities proscribed in Sections 1 and 2 may sue for triple damages. And it defines as a person a corporation or association.

What restraint of trade and monopolization mean in the Sherman Act, as interpreted by the federal courts, is not the same as what they meant in common law. The common law on monopoly was aimed at privilege, especially at monopolistic grants by the Crown in England. Now monopoly means the power to dominate markets, in regard to pricing, market sharing, and exclusion of competitors. The common law on restraint of trade arose out of protection of value in a sales contract, where a seller was allowed by the buyer to set limited conditions on competition. The Sherman Act prohibition focuses on anticompetitive behavior, particularly division of sales territories, joint action on pricing, and exclusion of potential rivals by business competitors.

Principal responsibility for enforcement of the act rests with the Antitrust Division, Department of Justice.

See also Ancillary Agreement; Interstate Commerce Act; Market Sharing; Monopolizing; Predatory Practices; Price Fixing; Restraint of Trade.

Consult (16) Letwin, 1965.

—Thomas O. Depperschmidt, *Memphis State University*

SHIFT IN SUPPLY. *See* Changes in Supply.

SHOP. For articles on various types of shops, *see* Agency Shop; Closed Shop; Open Shop; Union Shop.

SHORTAGE. *See* Excess Demand.

SHORT RUN, a period of time so short that some factors of production cannot be varied. There are two types of factors of production, the fixed and the variable. In the short run the variable factors are labor and raw materials. Capital cannot be varied in the short run and is, therefore, a fixed factor of production. The period defined as the short-run will vary considerably depending on the industry under discussion. Short run analysis of a firm is conducted by holding the amount of capital equipment constant and varying the other factors of production. In this way, it is possible to determine the variable costs of production for a given quantity of capital.

See also Long Run.

SHORT-RUN ELASTICITY OF DEMAND measures the responsiveness of purchasers to price changes during a time period sufficiently small that the determinants of the purchasers' demand cannot change. Assuming incomes, tastes, and prices of other goods to be constant, short-run elasticity measures the responsiveness in quantity demanded that is produced by a change in the price of that commodity. Although short-run elasticities can take either high or low values, the tendency is for the elasticity of demand to be smaller in the short run than in the long run.

SHORT-RUN ELASTICITY OF SUPPLY refers to the ability of a firm or industry to react to price changes in the short run. Since the short run implies a fixed amount of capital, increases or decreases in output will be effected by using existing plant and facilities more or less intensively. Starting from equilibrium, assume an increase in demand, which increases price. The firm can increase output by having labor work overtime, adding another shift, etc. Marginal cost will rise rapidly, and output response will therefore be slight in the short run.

See also Elasticity of Supply.

SHORT-RUN EQUILIBRIUM OF THE FIRM. *See* Equilibrium of the Firm, Short-Run.

SHORT-TERM BUSINESS CYCLES, fluctuations in economic activity, particularly prices, production, and employment, averaging from 2 to 10 years in the opinion of Alvin Hansen, or about 40 months according to Joseph Kitchin, who was the first analyst to study short-term cycles in detail. He contended that such fluctuations were caused by changes in inventory investment and small waves of innovation created by invention of equipment that can be produced quickly.

SHULTZ, GEORGE PRATT (1920-   ), American university dean who has made significant contributions to the study of business. A graduate of Princeton (1942), he received his Ph.D. in industrial economics from M.I.T. (1949). His publications include *Management Organization and the Computer* (1960) and *Strategies for the Displaced Worker* (1966, with Arnold R. Weber). Shultz was senior staff economist of the President's Council of Economic Advisers (1955-56), and later staff director of the national labor policy study for the Committee on Economic Development (1961). He became dean of the Graduate School of Business at the University of Chicago in 1962. After serving as President Nixon's first labor secretary and as chairman of the FTC he was named director of the new Office of Management and Budget in 1970. He became treasury secretary (1972) and, as chairman of the Council on Economic Policy, was one of Nixon's special assistants in the reorganized executive branch.

SHUT-DOWN POINT, the point a firm reaches when it cannot generate enough income from sales to cover its fixed and operating expenses and is operating below the break-even point (where income equals expenses).

Two situations can arise in businesses that indicate the need for a firm to shut down. The first occurs when income covers fixed costs but does not cover marginal costs. However, if a firm has a large fixed cost investment it may be more advantageous to stay in business, because it may be able to minimize its losses. In the second situation, in which income does not meet the fixed costs of a firm, there is a need to shut down, because the firm is maximizing its losses by remaining in operation.

SIGNIFICANCE, the probability that a given result in sampling could occur entirely by chance. In testing an hypothesis significance is the risk we are willing to take of erroneously rejecting a null hypothesis that is actually true. This risk can be made as small as necessary.

See also Hypothesis; Population, Statistical.

SINGLE TAX. *See* George, Henry.

SILVER CERTIFICATES, paper notes of the U.S. Treasury, fully backed by silver in its vaults at the rate of 371.25 grains (about four-fifths of an ounce) per dollar. First issued in 1878, silver certificates constituted the bulk of $1 bills (and some larger denominations) until 1963, when one-dollar federal reserve notes were introduced to replace them. They have now been retired, and the silver that backed them has been disposed of.

See also Money; Money Supply.

SIT-DOWN STRIKE. *See* Strike.

SKEWNESS is the amount by which a distribution departs from symmetry. If the distribution has a longer "tail" to the right it is said to be positively skewed. If the long tail runs to the left it is negatively skewed.

SKEWNESS

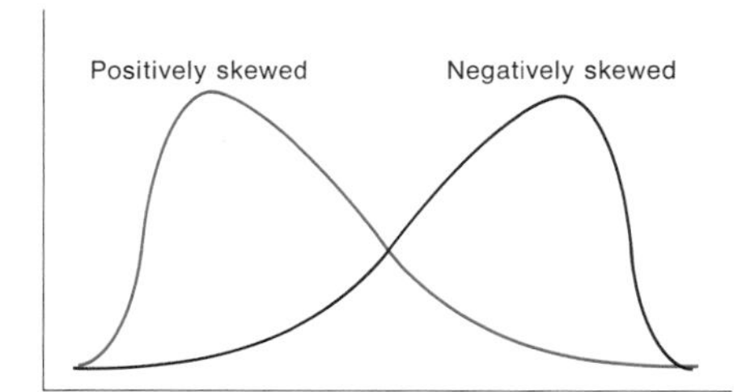

Adam Smith, a copper engraving of 1790.

Deterioration in the quality of our air is a social cost of whatever this plant produces.

SLIDING PEG. *See* Exchange Rate.

SMALL SAMPLES. *See* Sampling Theory.

SMITH, ADAM (1723-90). The founder of the classical school of economic thought and considered by many the father of economics, Adam Smith developed the first systematic analysis of economic phenomena. His first work, *The Theory of Moral Sentiments* (1759), was a philosophical discussion of the ethical forces which are necessary for a society to operate.

Smith's most important work, however, was *The Wealth of Nations* (1776). Having traveled in France and there become familiar with the Physiocrats, Smith combined many of their ideas with his own and those of others to formulate a general theory of economic activity. In Smith's view, the mercantilist policy which had dominated Europe actually worked against economic growth and development. His system, based upon the division of labor, widening markets and the harmony of self-interest, suggested a limited role for the government with dependence placed upon market forces as the means of solving economic problems.

Smith was generally optimistic and did not see the possibility of economic problems such as unemployment and the business cycle in his system. However, as the first to bring together in one volume the consideration of all aspects of economic activity, Smith provided the basis for the development of economics as a discipline.

See also Classical Economics; Invisible Hand; Mercantilism; Physiocrats; Wealth of Nations.

Consult (25) Rima, 1967; Spiegel, 1971.

—Clyde A. Haulman, *College of William and Mary*

SMITHIES, ARTHUR (1907-), Australian-born economist noted for his contributions to the macroeconomic theory of consumption function and fiscal policy. He is a graduate of Magdalen College, Oxford University (1932), and he received his Ph.D. from Harvard (1934). His publications include *The Budgetary Process in the United States* (1954) and *Readings in Fiscal Policy* (1955, ed., with J. Keith Butters). Smithies has been active in government, having served as chief of the economic branch of the U.S. Bureau of the Budget (1943-48), director of the Fiscal and Trade Policy Division of the Economic Cooperation Administration (1948-49), economic adviser to the Office of Defense Mobilization (1951-52), and as a member of the research advisory committee on economic development (from 1956). He has been a professor of economics at Harvard since 1949.

SMYTH v. AMES (1898), in which the Supreme Court set forth criteria by which to judge public utility commission valuations and declared that rates should be set so that the regulated firm receives "a fair return upon. . .the fair value of the property being used by it." Earlier, in an 1877 decision (*Munn v. Illinois*), the court held that public utility rates fixed by the government are not subject to judicial review. However, that position was reversed in 1886 (*Stone v. Farmer's Loan and Trust Co.*), when the court said that rates fixed under legislative authority are subject to judicial review and may be set aside if they are found to deprive investors of their property without due process of law.

Unfortunately, most of the criteria enumerated by the court in *Smyth v. Ames* for determining fair value were either irrelevant, inconsistent, or illogical. Following this decision, the orginal cost and reproduction cost of construction became the main items considered by the courts in determining the fair value of public utility property.

See also Fair Return on Fair Value; Munn v. Illinois; Reproduction Cost.

—Joseph Jadlow, *Oklahoma State University*

SOCIAL ACCOUNTING SYSTEMS are designed to give governments and other institutions concerned with the operation of modern economies a factual record of the economy's performance during a specific time period. The most common system is the National Income Account, which measures the value of the total production or output of the economy during a year (GNP) and indicates the various sources and uses of this production. Such systems, however, generally measure only market-oriented production, thus ignoring some of the economy's output, such as the work of housewives, and overlooking the environmental costs associated with production.

SOCIAL COSTS, those costs society pays when its resources are used to produce a given quantity of some particular commodity, are clearly related to opportunity costs. The benefit given up must be weighed against the advantage gained. The economic problem that society faces is the "proper" composition of total output. Society is optimizing when it produces a given commodity up to the point where the marginal social benefit is equated to the marginal social cost of producing that last unit. Social costs assume significance mainly when contrasted with private costs; the divergence of private and social costs creates social problems for a free enterprise economy.

See also Private Costs.

SOCIAL DIVIDEND, a plan for a per capita

grant to be paid to everyone regardless of financial wellbeing. It would provide a guaranteed income for all individuals. The amount could be the same for everyone or higher for adults than for children. Payment is not reduced directly as income rises (in contrast to the negative income tax), but in order to finance the program it would be necessary to raise the taxes of higher income families by more than they receive in grants. Since everyone receives the grant, the stigma associated with being on welfare is eliminated. A major objection to the program is its very high cost, especially if the dividend is to be large enough to replace existing welfare programs.

See also Negative Income Tax; Public Assistance.

SOCIAL ECONOMICS. *See* Economic Systems.

SOCIAL INSURANCE, a program designed to give insured citizens and their dependents minimal protection against loss of income owing to the retirement, unemployment, disability or death of the insured. In some cases, coverage may include medical care. In the United States, social insurance is provided primarily through the social security system.

Social insurance is generally compulsory for eligible persons. Under social security those eligible include most wage earners (except for employees of the federal government and railroads, who are under similar compulsory federal programs) and most self-employed. The program is funded through a payroll tax levied on employers and employees and on income from self-employment. Because benefits are financed by earmarked payments to a trust fund rather than from general tax revenue, they are regarded as a form of insurance. Benefits are prescribed by law, rather than by contract, as in the case of private insurance, but with the understanding that they are earned through payment of the compulsory tax or "contribution" to the benefit fund. Eligibility is determined by statutory formulas. There is no necessity for recipients to prove that they are in need of help, as in the case of public assistance. Consequently, social insurance is free of the stigma of dependence associated with being on public welfare.

Transferring Income. Although payments are a function of previous contributions, a considerable amount of redistribution does take place among participants who include all insured, only a fraction of whom are receiving benefits at any point in time. For example, most persons now receiving retirement benefits under social security entered the labor force before they entered the program, which dates to 1935. Some, notably farmers, worked in occupations that came under the program years after it started, thus typically receive benefits well in excess of their contributions. The program also favors insureds with large numbers of dependents, since they pay no more tax, but they or their survivors are eligible for higher potential payments. Benefit increases voted periodically by Congress, notably the periodic cost-of-living adjustments, increase the redistribution from contributors to beneficiaries. These forms of redistribution are necessary if the goal of providing a minimum level of protection for all participants is to be realized.

All of the components of the OASDHI (old age, survivors, disability, and health insurance) part of the social security program have counterparts in the field of private insurance. Private insurance, often purchased voluntarily to supplement social insurance, is funded on the actuarial principle, which requires that payments by the typical beneficiary plus accumulated interest on premiums equal the expected cost of serving the beneficiary. Social insurance cannot meet this criterion once the principle of redistribution described above is adopted. The OASDHI program is thus better described as a device for transferring income from current contributors—the working population—to current beneficiaries. It is operated on a pay-as-you-go basis with annual receipts approximating annual benefits.

The unemployment compensation program is administered jointly by the Social Security administration and the states. It is financed by a joint federal-state tax on payrolls under rules set within federal guidelines by the individual states. Taxes are higher on firms with high layoff rates, a feature designed to provide a financial incentive for reducing cyclical hiring practices.

See also Disability Insurance; Medicare; National Health Insurance; Old-Age Insurance; Public Assistance; Social Security; Survivors Insurance; Unemployment Insurance.

Consult (6) Brinker, 1968; Turnbull, 1967.

—Charles W. Meyer, *Iowa State University*

SOCIALISM, a body of thought from which a set of economic and social objectives are derived. The organization and methods of accomplishing these objectives are varied.

Socialist Aims. Adherents to socialism generally hope to achieve: (1) a reduction in the private ownership of the means of production by a transfer of ownership and general control to the state; (2) more equitable distribution of incomes; (3) a smooth growth path facilitated by a steady flow of funds into investment; (4) economic planning of some level and scope; (5) elimination of "capitalist waste" that results from duplications of output, aborted investments, and luxury goods.

To accomplish these objectives, social-

DISTRIBUTIONS OF ALL FEDERAL HEALTH DOLLARS

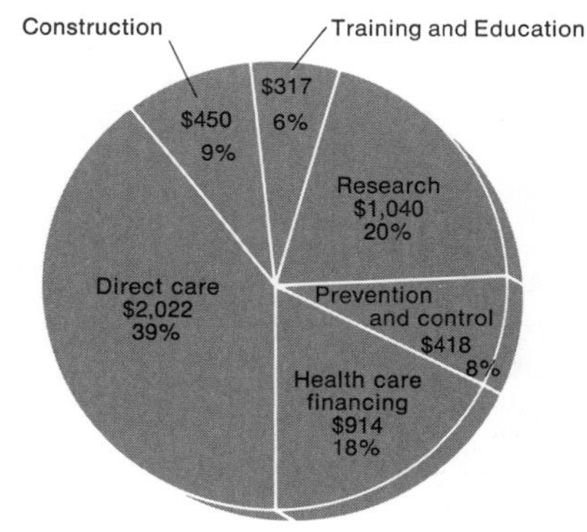

Fiscal year 1965
($5.1 Billion)
(4.4% of total federal outlays)

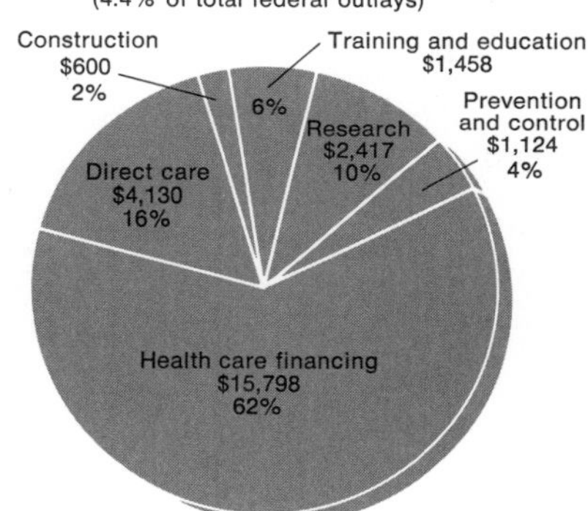

Fiscal year 1973
($25.5 Billion)
(10.3% of total federal outlays)

USSR State Bank. Government control of factors of production is typical of socialism.

Norman Thomas, American Socialist party leader and six times its candidate for the presidency.

A Poor Place to Stand These Days
—Bishop in the St. Louis *Star-Times*

1935 cartoon shows Social Security legislation gaining momentum as it nears passage that year.

ists seek to obtain political power in the state, then to replace the old order with socialist institutions. This can be achieved through an evolutionary process such as success in political elections. The Labour Party in Britain was elected in 1945 with a nationalization program in its platform, as was Salvador Allende in Chile in 1970. By contrast, Fidel Castro came to power in Cuba through the revolutionary process.

Mechanics of Socialism. The present socialist states are of two principal types: the democratic socialist like Britain and India, and the authoritarian socialist like China, Soviet Union, and eastern European states. In any socialist system individual preferences and choices must be restricted to some extent in order for state preferences to be expanded. The socialist state generally attempts to maximize the state welfare.

The democratic socialists hope to remain responsive to the desires of the population, whereas the authoritarian system may require some major economic sacrifices by its population for extended periods of time. The socialist states, in attempting to rectify the inconsistencies of the market place in the free enterprise system, frequently find the ineptness of bureaucracies and the dangers of ineffective planning to be serious obstacles to the attainment of their objectives.

Consult (26) Cole, 1950; Hayek, 1935; Lange and Taylor, 1965; Schumpeter, 1942; Sweezy, 1949.

—Francis W. Rushing, *College of William and Mary*

SOCIALISM, DEMOCRATIC. *See* Democratic (Liberal) Socialism.

SOCIALISM, EVOLUTIONARY. *See* Evolutionary Socialism.

SOCIALISM (PLANNING). *See* Planning (Socialism).

SOCIALISM, REVOLUTIONARY. *See* Revolutionary Socialism.

SOCIALISM, SCIENTIFIC. *See* Scientific Socialism.

SOCIALISTIC DICTATORSHIP. *See* Dictatorship of the Proletariat.

SOCIALIST MARKET SYSTEM. *See* Economic Systems.

SOCIALLY OPTIMAL OUTPUT. *See* Externalities.

SOCIAL SECURITY, a federal program of social insurance that provides payments to eligible participants and their dependents. When introduced in 1935 the program included old-age insurance for persons over 65 and a federally subsidized, state-administered program of unemployment insurance. Coverage has since been extended to include benefits to survivors and the disabled. Health insurance (Medicare) for the elderly was added in 1965.

Originally only wage earners in selected occupations participated in the program. Now nearly all wage earners and self-employed are covered, except for employees of railroads and the federal government who are under separate but similar federal programs.

Benefits are paid out of a special trust fund that is financed by taxes on payrolls and self-employment income. The payroll tax is split equally between employer and employee. Each currently pays 5.2 percent on wage and salary income up to $9000; the self-employment rate is 1½ times the rate paid by an employee. Rapid increases in benefit levels have necessitated frequent increases in rate and base, placing the social security tax second to the personal income tax as a source of federal revenue.

See also Disability Insurance; Medicare; Old-Age Insurance; Social Insurance; Survivors' Insurance; Unemployment Insurance.

—Charles W. Meyer, *Iowa State University*

SOCIAL SECURITY ACT (1935), the basis of extensive U.S. social insurance programs. The current characteristics of the social security program largely reflect the numerous and substantial amendments that have been made to the original act. Spurred by the massive unemployment and poverty of the depression and confronted with the inability of state and local governments to provide assistance on a significant level, the federal government in the early 1930s began to provide several forms of financial assistance to the states to help them aid people.

As the focal point of public policy in this area shifted from the short-run alleviation of poverty to its long-run prevention, the federal government adopted broad-based, compulsory insurance programs against income interruption because of unemployment and old age. The third major element of the law was a public assistance (welfare) program for those remaining in need or not helped by these insurance programs.

Federal Grants. The act provides for a system of federal grants to the states to support their own programs of assistance to the needy, conditional on the programs' compliance with certain federal requirements. Welfare benefits, in the form of income payments and medical care, are provided under programs to benefit the needy aged, dependent children, and the blind and under the maternal and child welfare program.

Pensions and Compensation. The insurance programs set up in the act were those for old-age retirement pensions and unemployment compensation. The old-age retirement pension program, popularly but not quite correctly referred to as "social security"—it is only one part of the social security program—has been expanded to provide income benefits for the retiree's dependents or his surviving dependents, benefits for disabled workers, and medical insurance benefits for the aged.

The unemployment compensation benefits are payable to covered, eligible recipients through individual state programs. If these state programs meet certain federal standards, federal grants pay their administrative expenses. The actual financing of benefits comes through payroll taxes levied by the state, most or all of which can be deducted by the employer from his federal payroll tax liability. Thus, in large part, the state unemployment compensation systems are financed by tax money that otherwise would have gone to the federal government.

—Leonard G. Schifrin, *College of William and Mary*

SOCIAL VALUE. *See* Externalities.

SOIL BANK, an acreage-control program which offered payments to farmers for removing land entirely from crop production. Most prior programs permitted land taken out of controlled crops to be used for growing other crops. Thus surpluses suppressed in one crop showed up in others.

The Acreage Reserve (1956-58) took some land out of selected crops on farms of all levels of productivity, one year at a time. The Conservation Reserve (1956-60) offered payments for removing farms of low productivity entirely from crop production for periods of three to ten years. The chief objection to the Conservation Reserve was that poor land was geographically concentrated and its retirement depressed extensive rural areas. The principle of the Acreage Reserve was used in modified forms in the feed-grain acts of the early 1960s and in the Agricultural Acts of 1965 and 1970.

SOLOW, ROBERT MERTON (1924-   ), American educator, economist, and developer of the Solow growth model, who has achieved recognition for his contributions to macroeconomic theory and the production function. He is a graduate of Harvard (1947), where he also received his M.A. (1949) and Ph.D. (1951). His publications include *Capital Theory and the Rate of Return* (1963), *The Sources of Unemployment in the United States* (1964), and *Growth Theory: An Exposition* (1970). Solow has been senior economist on the Council of Economic Advisers (1961-62), a member of the President's Commission on Income Maintenance (1968-70), and vice president of the American Economic Association (1968). He became a professor of economics at M.I.T. in 1958.

SOMBART, WERNER (1863-1941), German historical economist, whose avid support of Nazism, toward the end of his career, rested in part upon his explanation of the rise and development of the capitalistic system. He felt that the growth pattern contained three distinct stages: early capitalism, high capitalism and late capitalism. In the late capitalistic stage, Sombart felt, the decadent tendencies of capitalism would become so entrenched that a new economic organization must arise. He believed that the stage had been reached following World War I and that the Nazi system was its logical replacement.

See also Historical School.

SOREL, GEORGE. *See* Syndicalism.

SOVEREIGNTY, CONSUMER. *See* Consumer Sovereignty.

SPECIALIZATION. International trade leads to a wider market and more benefits from the division of labor. Each nation should specialize by applying the law of comparative advantage to its resource endowment. If sufficient quantities of goods can be produced to meet their demand without raising costs then specialization will be complete among countries. Country A will specialize in X, if that is where its comparative advantage lies, and produce all X demanded by itself and Country B. It will obtain from B its Y since B produces enough for both. If costs rise as outputs increase, specialization will not be complete; trade will be carried to the point where costs are equalized in the countries.

See also Comparative Advantage; International Trade Theory.

Consult (23) Snider, 1971.

SPECIE, coin, usually gold or silver, whose metallic worth is equal to its face value.

See also Money.

SPECIFIC EXCISE TAX, an excise tax whose tax base is defined in terms of the number of units of the commodity purchased, such as federal and state taxes on gallons of gasoline. Because of the difficulties in applying this type of tax to a large number of economic goods, specific excise taxes are generally applied to one or very few commodities.

SPECIFIC TARIFF. *See* Tariffs.

SPECULATION, the purchase or sale of title to goods or financial obligations in the expectation that the price will rise or fall. When

$20 gold coin, no longer in circulation.

purchasing, possession of title to the good is sometimes taken immediately. When selling, the contract usually calls for future possession, the seller hoping to fulfill the contract at a lower price in the future. Such speculative investments have no role in national income analysis; in monetary analysis, speculation is not another term for investment as defined in economics.

SPECULATIVE DEMAND. *See* Liquidity Preference.

SPENGLER, JOSEPH JOHN (1902–), American educator and expert on the economic aspects of population and the history of economic thought. He received his A.B. (1926), M.A. (1929), and Ph.D. (1930) from Ohio State University. His publications include *Demographic Analysis* (1956), *Population Theory and Policy* (1956), *The Population Crisis and the Use of World Resources* (1964), and *Indian Thought: A Preface to Its History* (1971). A professor of economics at Duke University since 1955, Spengler has served as a consultant to the U.S. government and is a former president of the American Population Association and former vice-president of the Economic History Association.

Joseph John Spengler

SPURT. *See* Take-Off.

STABILIZATION POLICY, a policy that has as its chief goals the control of runaway prices caused by inflationary pressures and the prevention of chronic or excessive unemployment and stagnant growth. There has been no serious American deflation since the late 1930s. There are three major stabilization strategies: fiscal policy, monetary policy, and incomes policy.

THE IMPACT OF PHASE II ON THE CPI (PERCENT OF CONSUMER PRICE INDEX)

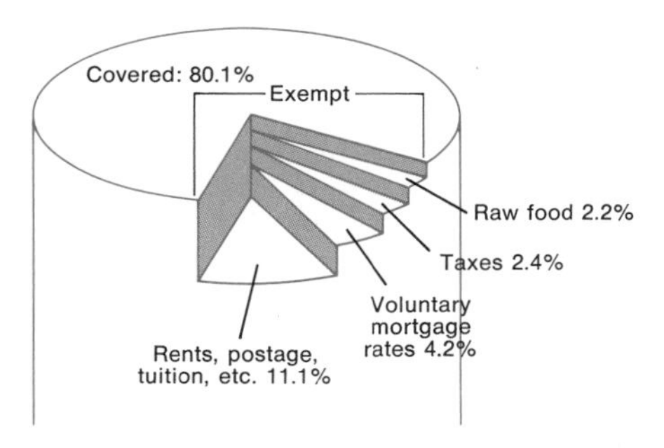

Fiscal policy, as a stabilizer, is a relatively new weapon against unemployment and inflation, having emerged with the economics of John Maynard Keynes in the 1930s. The government uses taxation as a stabilizer in two ways. First, there are built-in stabilizers that react automatically to any changes in the economy. For example, the progressive income tax guarantees that as a person's income decreases, his rate of taxes will also decrease. Another automatic stabilizer is unemployment compensation, which allows laid-off workers to receive an income.

A second form of taxation as a stabilizer is known as discretionary fiscal policy and involves a decision by Congress and the president to change the existing tax structure. For example, in the early 1960s a general decrease in taxes was passed to stimulate spending and ward off a recession. Several years later a 10% surtax was placed on incomes to curb inflationary pressures.

The federal government also uses public expenditures to regulate the economy, which stem from discretionary fiscal policy by the legislature and the president. In depressions government decisions usually involve large-scale spending to stimulate the economy and aid in the reduction of unemployment. In addition, the government may initiate spending in public works, such as the building of roads, and acts directly as an employer, creating jobs for the unemployed. In the same manner, during inflationary periods government policy may involve the reduction of public expenditures. When a substantial decrease in government spending occurs, the result is often a halt in rising prices, due to a decrease in general demand. One of the major problems of the use of public expenditures as a stabilizing policy is that there is often a large gap in the time periods between when the programs are initiated and when the effects of the programs occur. Fiscal policy, to be an effective stabilizer, must work with monetary policy in the fight against inflation and unemployment.

Monetary policy, in some form or another, has been around almost as long as the existence of money. The policy's effectiveness lies in its immediacy of operation. The United States, however, has adopted a monetary policy with its main objective to assist the economy in achieving a full-employment noninflationary level of total output. With this stabilizing objective, the Federal Reserve Act (1913) established a federal reserve system. Among its many objectives is the regulation of the money supply to correspond with the needs of the economy. Because the country's commercial banking system has the ability to effectively create additional money through money lending, the need for a central control over the money supply is essential. The federal reserve system can control the money supply in three main ways: by regulating the reserve ratio, by changing the discount rate, and by buying and selling securities on the open market. The reserve ratio is a specified percentage of a bank's total deposit liabilities that must be kept in the Federal Reserve Bank. By decreasing or increasing the reserve ratio, the Federal Reserve can limit (in inflation) or expand (in deflation) a bank's lending ability and, thus, the money supply.

A second way in which the Federal Reserve can control the money supply is by use of the discount rate. The discount rate is the interest rate at which the Federal Reserve Bank lends money to commercial banks. The higher the discount rate, the less willing these banks are to borrow money. An increased discount rate will contract the money supply, and a decreased discount rate will expand the money supply.

The third and most effective way in which the Federal Reserve controls the money supply is by open-market buying and selling of securities. To contract the money supply, the Federal Reserve sells government bonds to commercial banks and the general public, removing money from the public and the banks, decreasing banks' lending potential, and, therefore, further decreasing the money supply. The Federal Reserve usually sells bonds during inflationary periods and buys during deflationary periods.

Incomes policy is the third type of stabilization strategy. Incomes policies affect the real income of individuals and usually effect changes in wages and prices. There are essentially two types of incomes policy: guideposts and controls. Wage and price guideposts are voluntary guidelines set up for labor and management to follow to curb inflationary pressures. Because these guideposts are voluntary, there is no penalty for violation. In 1962 President Kennedy set forth the first peacetime guideposts to ward off an impending inflation. These guideposts proved to be very effective for several years. In 1969, however, President Nixon issued another set of guideposts, which were virtually ineffective in curbing unemployment and inflation.

A second incomes policy is wage and price controls, employed three times since 1940. These controls have always been a wartime policy, because the diversion of production from consumer to war goods results in more dollars chasing fewer consumption goods. During World War II the National War Labor Board (the Wage Board) and the Office of Price Administration aided in the success of keeping both wages and prices stable (1941–46). During the Korean War these controls were carried out by the Office of Price Stabilization but proved to be relatively ineffective because they were not strictly enforced (1950–53).

In 1971 Nixon instituted a ninety-day wage and price freeze (Phase I), regulated by the Cost of Living Council and the Price Commission, and enforced by IRS. Immediately after Phase I and still operative, Phase II concerned itself with granting price and wage increases sufficiently small to reduce annual inflation to a tolerable level (2–3%) and to decontrol selected segments of the economy. As of August 1972, 1970's 6% annual inflation had been halved.

See also Fiscal Policy; Incomes Policy; Stabilizers.

—William D. Wagoner, *Louisiana State University*

STABILIZERS refers to either qualities inherent in the economic system or policies specifically designed to bring stability in price, income, and employment to the economy. Those qualities inherent or built into the system are generally termed automatic stabilizers whereas those specifically designed to maintain or restore stability are called discretionary stabilizers. All stabilizers operate by affecting the spending-saving streams either in the public or private sectors or both.

Automatic Stabilizers, or Built-in Stabilizers. These refer to automatic forces inherent in the modern fiscal system, or built into that system, which help to keep the economy stable. Automatic changes in tax receipts are the most significant automatic stabilizers. Because of a heavy reliance on progressive income taxes (both personal and corporate) during a recession, as incomes in the economy decline, the government receives proportionately less tax revenues. This leads to increased availability of funds for personal consumption, which leads to larger production, which in turn pushes incomes upward. Therefore, income fluctuations are moderated automatically. The reverse occurs during an inflation. In this case, tax receipts increase as incomes increase. This, too, moderates income fluctuations.

Unemployment compensation and other welfare transfers also serve as automatic stabilizers. During prosperous years, when employment is high, unemployment compensation reserves grow and exert downward pressure on spending. Conversely, during years of higher unemployment, the reserve funds are used to pay out income, which moderates the decline in income by sustaining a higher level of consumption than would otherwise occur.

Government farm aid programs serve to automatically stabilize prices of farm products. When surpluses exist, the government absorbs them, thereby causing the prices on these products to decline. In the opposite case, when prices begin to rise, the government sells its surpluses, thereby holding the prices down.

Another automatic stabilizer is inherent in our private institutions. The custom of corporations maintaining dividends regardless of short-run changes in their incomes results in an automatic stabilizer. Also, families maintaining a certain standard of living rather than making quick adjustments to income fluctuations results in greater stability.

Discretionary Stabilizers. Stabilization policies that deliberately alter taxes or expenditures for the purpose of achieving full-employment and stable price levels are termed discretionary policies. Another primary objective of these policies is to moderate economic fluctuations by stabilizing total spending or demand. This is achieved either by government spending, which compensates for changes in private spending, or by cyclical variations of tax rates.

When unemployment increases and the economy contracts due to a fall in private demand, government spending should rise. When economic expansion and inflation occur, government spending should fall. In other words, the existing economic conditions determine which expenditure policy the government chooses. Expenditure programs such as those initiated during Franklin Roosevelt's New Deal provide employment and increase aggregate demand in the economy. Making transfer payments to individuals is another way government stimulates demand.

Variations in tax rates help governments attain economic stability. A cut in tax rates can help offset an economic recession by encouraging business and consumer expenditures. An increase in the tax rates can have the opposite effect and dampen inflation. A weakness in the case for this policy is that once tax rates are lowered to fight a recession, it may be politically difficult to return them to the higher level after the recession has ended.

—Irving J. Goffman, *University of Florida*

STABLE EQUILIBRIUM, an equilibrium that will be restored if disturbed: the price and quantity of the commodity will tend to return to their equilibrium levels. An unstable equilibrium is one in which the price and quantity will not be restored if disturbed: there will be an explosive divergence of the price away from the equilibrium. In this situation the market price cannot be restored if once disturbed. A stable equilibrium is one from which there is no tendency to move.

STAGES OF A COUNTRY'S BALANCE OF PAYMENTS. The balance of trade is the single most important item in a nation's balance of payments. Merchandise imports and exports represent movements of real consumer goods or real investment goods. When exports exceed imports the trade balance is favorable; the balance is unfavorable when imports exceed exports. These terms pertain only to the technical definition of the trade balance, not to its status in the overall balance of payments. Whether the trade balance is favorable in this greater sense depends on the stage of economic development of the nation.

Young Debtor. Any nation embarking on a program of economic growth must have an unfavorable trade balance. The nation's productive capacities are poorly developed, so that it has little to export, with most goods needed for domestic consumption. Because the lack of capital means high returns, investment is attractive to foreigners. Hence, imports will exceed exports and be financed by capital imports; this is owned by foreigners, and payments of interest and principal will grow.

Mature Debtor. As growth in the economy occurs via domestic savings and continued import of capital, exports can be expected to increase more rapidly than imports, and a favorable balance of trade is achieved. The nation's own foreign investment will begin to grow, but not fast enough to offset interest and principal owed annually to foreigners. The favorable trade balance procures the exchange necessary to pay for this interest and principal.

Young Creditor. As foreign investments continue to grow while foreign debts mature and are paid off, payments of interest and principal by foreigners will exceed amounts paid to them, and the nation becomes a net creditor with a continuing favorable balance of trade.

Mature Creditor. The continued build-up of foreign investments brings in larger amounts of interest and principal payments each year. These funds can finance larger imports, and the nation's citizens will consume increased imports. Therefore, the balance of trade must turn unfavorable.

See also Balance of Payments; Balance of Trade; Capital Account; Capital Movement; Foreign Investment.

—John R. Matthews, Jr., *College of William and Mary*

STAGES OF GROWTH, the levels of technical, industrial, and agricultural achievement that a society experiences as it develops. The first stage of growth begins with the development of some ad hoc technical innovations in a traditional society that is largely based on pre-Newtonian science, technology, and attitudes toward the physical. As the society begins to move out of its agrarian economy and begin the slow process of transition to an industrial economy, it is experiencing the second stage of growth, a period in which the preconditions for a modern state are developed.

Take-Off. The third stage of growth, the take-off or spurt, is the level at which old societal values and resistances are overcome, and a modern industrial economy emerges. Along with a surge of technical development, industries yield profits and begin to reinvest those profits in new plants and equipment.

Drive to Maturity. Following the take-off is a long, sustained period of growth, the drive to maturity, during which the society demonstrates the capacity to move beyond the original industries that powered the take-off, and to develop the technological and entrepreneurial skill to produce almost anything it chooses. At this stage, the society increases its foreign trade so that its dependence is a matter of economic or political choice rather than geographical, technological, or institutional necessity.

High Mass Consumption. The final stage of growth, the age of high mass consumption, stresses durable consumer goods and services, and personal real income rises to a point that transcends basic food, shelter, and clothing.

See also Preconditions; Take-Off; Traditional Economy.

—Charles Staelin, *University of Michigan*

STAGNATION, the failure of real output of the economy to grow sufficiently rapidly over a period (longer than a year or two) to provide for full employment. In the 1930s Alvin Hansen of Harvard (and others) argued that the depression was the result of the disappearance of two of the three main sources of growth during the 19th and early 20th centuries: (1) rapidly increasing population, which meant increased demand for goods and therefore many investment opportunities; and (2) expansion into new territories. The third major source of growth had been, according to Hansen, technological progress (e.g., railroads, automobiles), but Hansen and others doubted that the rate of technological change would be rapid enough in the future to give rise to enough more investment spending to offset household saving at the full employment level of income. Without population growth and territorial expansion to call forth additional investment, technological change would have to be more rapid than it had been in the past to ensure full employment.

In the post-World War II period some have argued that private investment would have been inadequate to ensure full employment, but that high levels of government spending have been responsible for the lack of stagnation since 1945. The argument is essentially the same as Hansen's: in a "mature" economy (such as that of the United States and those of Western Europe) investment opportunities will be insufficient to give rise to the level of private investment necessary to maintain full employment.

—Anne Mayhew, *University of Tennessee*

STALIN, JOSEPH (1879-1953), the chief architect of the economy of the Soviet Union. As a reward for his loyalty and activities on behalf of the Communist Party, before and during the Russian Revolution, Stalin was appointed to the Council of People's Commissars in 1917. In 1922, Lenin named him general secretary of the Communist Party, a position that Stalin then used to eliminate Leon Trotsky as his rival to succeed Lenin. By 1927 he had either removed or neutralized his opposition within the party and established himself as leader of the USSR.

Economic Policies. Stalin helped design and get approved the First Five Year Plan initiated in 1928. With this plan the Soviet system became a command economy, with rapid industrialization as its principal objective. In order to generate sufficient investment funds to support this plan, Stalin dramatically collectivized agriculture. During the 1930s the Soviet industrial output grew rapidly, but so did opposition to Stalin's extreme economic methods. During 1935-37, he purged the party of his opponents and then ruled in a police state environment.

Stalin's war-time leadership and postwar political maneuvering established the USSR as the dominant military, political, and economic power in eastern Europe. His death in 1953 permitted a relaxation of the stringent political controls, but his economic model has remained principally intact.

Consult (26) Deutscher, 1949.

—Francis W. Rushing, *College of William and Mary*

STANDARD DEVIATION. *See* Dispersion.

STANDARD OF LIVING, the scale of consumption, including necessities, comforts, and luxuries, that a nation can achieve with its per capita real income. According to theories of David Ricardo and Thomas Malthus, optimum per capita real income (or an ultimate standard of living) is reached at optimum population, the point past which average output per capita begins to decline.

In the United States, during the period 1890-1970, the standard of living, measured in terms of annual per capita real income, rose steadily, and the average working hours per man declined. Although, on a national average, the standard of living has risen, and the United States is now experiencing the stage of growth known as high-mass consumption, the per capita real income does not reflect the unequal distribution of income among individual households. Thus, to alter income distribution and thereby raise the standard of living among low income groups, governments are being forced to assume the responsibility for the income redistribution.

Redistribution Methods. Redistribution is achieved, in some measure, through a variety of public assistance programs and direct interventions in the market pricing system, through, for example, price supports for farmers, minimum wage legislation, and channeling public expenditures. The primary device used to alter the distribution of income among individual households and to raise their standard of living has universally been the progressive income tax, which takes more from those who earn more and less from low-income households.

See also Income Redistribution; Per Capita Real Income; Stages of Growth.

—Charles Staelin, *University of Michigan*

Joseph Stalin

STANDARD OF VALUE. *See* Money.

STANDARD OIL CASE. *See* United States v. Standard Oil Co. of New Jersey.

STATE BANK, a commercial bank that is chartered by one of the fifty individual states. The bank is subject to the laws of the chartering state and is controlled by the state superintendent of banks or similar official or board. State banks may join the federal reserve system if they wish. Two-thirds of the commercial banks in the United States are state-chartered, but these banks hold only one-third of the total volume of deposits.

See also Commercial Bank.

STATE-CONTROLLED ECONOMY. *See* Government-Controlled Economy.

STATE CORPORATION COMMISSIONS. *See* Public Utility Commissions.

STATE PLANNING COMMITTEE (USSR). *See* Gosplan.

STATE PREFERENCES. *See* Planner's (State) Preferences.

STATIC EQUILIBRIUM. *See* Theory of the Firm.

STATIONARY STATE, stage of economic development at which a full-employment economy can be sustained on the basis of consumer expenditures without investment in new plant and equipment. Such a state exists in the traditional economy, but has not been achieved in other stages of growth. Ricardo, Marshall, and Keynes thought a stationary state would be reached when an economy consumed 100% of full-employment income.

See also Zero Economic Growth.

STATISTICAL POPULATION. *See* Population, Statistical.

STATISTICS, the science concerned primarily with the analysis of empirical data. The word can also refer to the data itself—population counts, tax receipts, import duties—or to the characteristics of a sample, such as the sample mean and standard deviation.

Statistics and the Scientific Method. The primary goal of statistics is to allow the researcher to proceed from knowledge derived from a sample to a statement concerning the entire population from which the sample was taken. This is the process of inference, drawing conclusions concerning the whole on the basis of a careful examination of the parts. It is basically the scientific method.

Statistics in the Social Sciences. Much of social science, including economics, relies heavily on statistical techniques and methods. Because of its ability to separate the effects of systematic variation of a variable from the effects of chance variation, statistics allows the scientific method to be applied to phenomena that cannot be controlled in laboratory conditions. Moreover, statistics allow us to make exact statements of confidence concerning the characteristics of the population on the evidence supplied by the sample.

Hypothesis and Belief. We all formulate beliefs concerning the world on the basis of the evidence supplied by our senses. An important branch of statistics is concerned with the testing of these beliefs, called hypotheses, by confrontation with the facts. Suppose we are interested in reducing the crime rate. If we believe that increased police protection will reduce crime, we can test the hypothesis by hiring more police in some cities while maintaining existing levels in others. Suppose the mean crime rate in those cities with increased police protection drops by 10% in comparison with the other cities. Can this decrease be attributed to the expenditure on police or could it be merely due to chance? Statistics has the power to answer such questions, questions which can have profound implications for society.

Consult (27) Freund, 1967; Mansfield, 1970; Moroney, 1956.

—Carlisle E. Moody, *College of William and Mary*

STEWARD, in labor unionism, the lowest member of the union official structure (not always considered a union officer), typically elected to represent the employees in one shop, or workplace. A large local may have many shop stewards. The steward's most important job is involved with contract administration at the shop or floor level, and he is the one who first takes a worker's case to management. Normally, if the steward and the foreman cannot work out an agreement over a specific management action, the case goes on to the next higher level of both the union and management.

STIGLER, GEORGE JOSEPH (1911-). An outstanding authority in the areas of price theory and the history of economic thought, Stigler has educated many young economists through his textbooks *The Theory of Price* (1952) and *Production and Distribution Theories* (1947). A member of the Chicago school, Stigler has significantly contributed to many aspects of microeconomic theory.

George Joseph Stigler

Stigler's work in the history of economic ideas has been collected in the volume *Essays in the History of Economics* (1965). He assigns "a minor, and even an accidental, role to the economic environment in the development of economic theory since it has become a professional discipline." *(Essays)* While many economists agree with this position, many feel that environmental forces have shaped economic ideas.

STOCK as used in the financial sense, is a certificate showing ownership in a corporation. When a corporation is formed, stock is issued to individual purchasers. In this way, capital is accumulated. When additional capital is needed, the corporation may issue additional stock.

Capital stock is divided into shares with each share representing proportional ownership in the corporation. Shares of stock, in the form of stock certificates, can usually transfer ownership by endorsement of the current owner. Most stock transactions go through what is known as the stock or securities market, with a broker being used as an intermediary.

Classes. Stock is divided by types into various classes. A popular type is called common or ordinary stock. This is stock that has claim to both the net assets and the profits of the corporation. Some corporations also issue preferred or prior stock. When preferred stock is issued, it has priority over common stock in the claiming of assets and profits. Preferred stock can also be divided into classes, such as Class A and Class B, or first and second preferred stock. These subclasses are called classified stock.

Rights and Limitations. Most stocks have certain rights and privileges as well as special limitations. These rights or limitations are often indicated in the name of the stock. For example, a convertible stock grants the owner the right or option to exchange it for some other type of security. A callable preferred stock gives the corporation that issued the stock the option to buy it back from the stockholder at any time after due notice has been given. And, an assessable stock is subject to an assessment if the corporation's financial affairs deem it necessary. Other stocks of this nature include full-paid or paid-up stock, guaranteed stock, participating preferred stock, and redeemable preferred stock.

Other Characteristics. In addition, other stocks are named for a particular characteristic they contain. For example, on the stock market there are so-called active stocks, stocks bought and sold continuously in heavy volume. A listed stock is one traded on a recognized stock exchange. Barometer stocks are indicators of market conditions. Other stocks that are indicators include clearinghouse stock, handled on the New York Stock Exchange, and curb stock, listed by the American Stock exchange.

Some stocks carry with them the privilege of stock dividends. Paid in the form of shares of capital stock, these dividends usually do not change the financial condition of the corporation because they simply transfer funds from the undistributed corporate profits account to the capital stock account. Shares of capital stock may or may not carry a par or face value.

See also Common Stock; Equity; Preferred Stock.

—William D. Wagoner, *Louisiana State University*

STOCK, as a component of bank portfolio. *See* Balance Sheet, Bank.

STOCK, CAPITAL. *See* Capital Stock.

STOCK BROKER. *See* Stock Market.

STOCK MARKET, a group of financial institutions developed in the United States to aid in the distribution of new securities and the buying and selling of existing ones. Also called security exchanges, these institutions are subject to regulation at both the state and federal level.

Because of the major financial disaster that hit the stock market in 1929, Congress, in 1934, passed the Securities Exchange Act. This act required all security exchanges to register with the Securities and Exchange Commission (SEC) and subjected them to SEC regulation.

Organized Security Exchanges. These organized exchanges provide a centralized medium of exchange for the buying and selling of listed securities. Sellers attempt to receive the highest price for their securities while buyers attempt to buy at the lowest possible price. When a price is agreed upon, a securities transaction occurs. This is usually facilitated by the aid of a member of the exchange, often referred to as a broker, who receives a fee (commission) for each transaction he handles. The broker often enlists the aid of a securities specialist if he is unable to carry out orders in many different stocks at the same time. The specialist often accepts buy and sell orders to be executed at specified prices, or he may aid in decreasing the gap between buying price and selling price.

For a security to be listed on an organized stock exchange, the corporation issuing the security must apply to the exchange and prove that the security satisfies all necessary conditions established by that exchange. These may include a written history of the company; descriptions of the firm's properties, securities, dividend record and policies; and financial statements. The exchange reviews the application and decides whether or not to grant listing. If a company fails to observe the necessary conditions and standards of the exchange, it can be delisted from the exchange.

There are two major organized security exchanges in the United States: the New York Stock Exchange and the American Stock Exchange. Located in New York City, these two exchanges account for nearly 90% of all trading on national exchanges. In addition, there are regional exchanges, such as the Pacific Stock Exchange. On the national exchanges, over 2,500 companies are listed. Twice as many stocks as bonds are listed.

Over-the-Counter Markets. Security transactions take place in over-the-counter se-

Typical bustling activity at N.Y. Stock Exchange.

Striking workers wave signs showing provisions they want contract under negotiation to cover.

curity markets as well as in organized security exchanges. In over-the-counter transactions, prices are determined by negotiations between buyers and sellers instead of by centralized bids. In addition, there is considerable diversity in the broker-dealer firms that operate in over-the-counter markets. For example, certain dealer firms tend to specialize in particular types of securities.

Investment Banking. The group of financial institutions known as the investment banking industry is comprised of investment banking firms, commercial banks' underwriting departments, and banker-dealer firms. About fifty investment banking firms handle security offerings in the United States, and together these firms form a highly centralized and efficient mechanism for the distribution of securities.

Government Securities. There are several ways in which US government securities are distributed. Treasury bills are sold to the highest bidder in the competitive market, while intermediate and long-term securities are sold to all those who are willing to buy them. State and local governments usually distribute their securities by the use of competitive bidding.

Regulation. As noted earlier, security markets are subject to both state and federal legislation. The Securities Act of 1933 was the first federal law requiring issuers of securities to make full disclosures at the time new issues are offered to the public. A year later, the Securities Exchange Act made several provisions regarding the buying and selling of securities including the registration and regulation of security exchanges, of brokers and dealers, and of all securities. In addition, the submission of financial reports of issues of registered securities, and the submission of reports on transactions in registered securities of officers, directors, and principle security holders was required. Lastly, the Board of Governors of the Federal Reserve System was given the responsibility to regulate the use of credit in all security transactions.

In 1938, the Maloney Act introduced several amendments to the act of 1934. It provided for the registration of any national securities association with the SEC and established certain standards for these associations. In 1972 the only association registered with the SEC was the National Association of Securities Dealers, Inc. (NASD), established for cooperative regulation of the over-the-counter market. Additional changes in legislation occurred in the mid-1960s. As a result, the SEC imposed comprehensive regulations concerning qualifications, experience, and business practices upon registered broker-dealers who were not members of the registered national association.

In 1966 the New York Stock Exchange adopted rules allowing member firms to execute offboard trading in listed stocks through nonmember firms. And, in 1966 the SEC, in its report on mutual funds, criticized the size of sales commissions and fees paid for management of the funds' portfolios.

—William D. Wagoner, *Louisiana State University*

STOPPAGE, WORK. *See* Work Stoppage.

STRIKE, a collective refusal by employees to work. Although organized workers may act together and refuse to work, perhaps to gain recognition of their union or to obtain some demand from the employer, strikes are mainly associated with unions and take place in the context of collective bargaining.

Role in Bargaining. As a labor-management contract nears expiration, the two parties begin to bargain over the terms of the new contract, employing various strategies as they argue, make concessions, and work toward a compromise of their differences. Among the strongest pressure each side can exert is that of severing the work relationship until a new contract is agreed upon: management's weapon is the lockout, labor's the strike.

The threat or possibility of a strike is a factor influencing management's resistance to union demands, whether or not one actually occurs. The threat exists to the extent that the union has previously demonstrated its willingness to strike.

Strikes thus in a real sense contribute ultimately to settlements. When they occur they impose economic loss on both sides and create an urgency to the bargaining that may hasten a resolution. Also, compromises may appear less unattractive than before, when weighed against losses of profits and wages.

Types of Strikes. Other than contract strikes, there are those called when unions object to management actions during the life of a contract. These are usually in violation of that contract and because of their unauthorized nature are called "wildcat strikes." There are also emergency strikes, public interest disputes, jurisdictional strikes, and the colorful and dramatic "sit-down" strikes of days gone by.

See also Lockout; Picketing, Public Interest Disputes; Wildcat Strikes.

—Leonard G. Schifrin, *College of William and Mary*

STRIKES, EMERGENCY. *See* Emergency Strikes.

STRIKE, WILDCAT. *See* Wildcat Strike.

STRIKE BENEFITS, payments by a union to its striking members in order to help them to stay off the job, thus maintaining pressure on the employer. While workers are on strike and the employer is experiencing partial or total loss of production and sales, each side is suffering economic loss and is under financial pressure to come to terms. The greater this pressure is on either side, the sooner it may capitulate to the other's terms, and the further it may be compelled to go in effecting a compromise. To enhance its staying ability, each side has various methods of reducing or offsetting its losses.

Benefit Characteristics. The main method used by the union is to provide strike benefits. Because striking workers are ineligible for unemployment insurance, their unemployment being presumed voluntary, most unions provide payments sufficient to meet essential minimum living expenses. These may be flat-rate, a fixed percentage of regular or base wages, or a variable amount depending on family dependency status or other differences among workers.

Benefits are paid from a strike fund, which is built up in anticipation of need. If the fund becomes depleted during a strike, it frequently is supplemented through special assessments levied on non-striking members of the union or by contributions or loans from other unions.

—Leonard G. Schifrin, *College of William and Mary*

STRIKE NOTICE, notice served on the employer by a union wishing to impose a deadline on the bargaining over a new labor contract. The notice states that as of some specific date, the workers will no longer work without a contract. The strike notice is both an expression to the employer of the seriousness of the union's position and an announcement to the workers that a work stoppage is impending.

STRUCTURAL INFLATION. *See* Sectoral Inflation.

STRUCTURAL UNEMPLOYMENT occurs because of changes in the basic characteristics of an economic structure, such as shifts in industrial location, variations in the rate of population growth, and changes in the type of labor demanded. For example, if a major firm decided to relocate in a different part of the country, many people who for any reason could not move with the company would be left unemployed. Likewise, the decision to kill the supersonic transport program in 1971 left Seattle a city plagued with unemployment. Other areas of the country hit with structural unemployment include Appalachia and the Ozark Plateau.

See also Unemployment of Labor.

STRUCTURE, INTEREST RATE. *See* Interstate Rate Structure.

STRUCTURE OF AMERICAN ECONOMY (1941). *See* Leontief, Wassily.

SUBSIDIES, AGRICULTURAL. Agricultural subsidies are monies paid out by government for the purpose of assisting farmers rather than for value received in the form of goods and services from agriculture. Payments made to wool growers because wool prices are deemed too low are subsidies; purchases of food for the armed forces are not subsidies.

Most nations have agricultural subsidies of one kind or another. In the United States, the important subsidies wholly chargeable to agriculture include: (1) losses on farm price supports, (2) direct payments to producers of several crops and wool, (3) direct payments for certain practices such as liming pastures or building ponds, and (4) export subsidies on some farm products. Aid to poor countries in the form of farm products (P.L. 480) and food aid to domestic poor families and to school children were originated principally to help farmers, but now the purpose of helping people other than farmers appears to be dominant.

See also Crop Restrictions; Price-Support Programs; Public Law 480.

—George E. Brandow, *Pennsylvania State University*

SUBSIDY, a type of financial assistance or a concession having economic value granted by a government to certain producers. The usual purpose of a subsidy is to encourage a producer to undertake or continue a given type of production that, though unprofitable, is considered essential to public welfare, such as steel mills for domestic self-sufficiency or merchant marine shipbuilding for national defense.

SUBSISTENCE ECONOMY, one in which all economic activity occurs outside the market. With households caring for their own economic needs directly, independent of the rest of the community, money and trade are absent. All goods are homemade, and both productivity and consumption are very low. Hunting, fishing, and foraging supplement the meager subsistence from primitive agriculture, in which, with no surplus production possible, small failure in harvest means famine. The term subsistence economy is associated with peasant economies, and today's closest approximations are in underdeveloped areas.

Consult (26) Griesbrecht, 1972.

SUBSISTENCE THEORY OF WAGES states that wages tend to equal what the worker needs to maintain a bare subsistence level of living. This theory emerged in the early nineteenth century as a result of the writings of two classical economists, David Ricardo and Thomas Malthus.

"SAY, YOU HAVE QUITE A GREEN THUMB."

Biggest benefits of soil bank's acreage-control program were reaped by the largest landowners.

SUPPLY

Major articles fully describing the role of supply in a market economy include MARKET MECHANISM and LAW OF SUPPLY AND DEMAND. Facets of market supply are discussed in the articles on SUPPLY CURVE, SUPPLY SCHEDULE, CHANGES IN SUPPLY, and ELASTICITY OF SUPPLY. And one application of supply analysis is presented in FACTOR SUPPLY. See also the Subject Map accompanying the article on SUPPLY.

Among sufficiently interchangeable goods, only relative price would determine relative demand.

According to the subsistence theory, when a worker receives a higher wage than he needs for mere subsistence, the result will be an increase in the number of children and eventually an increase in the number of workers. As more people become workers, either competition reduces wages paid to workers, or increased demand for food raises the cost of food. In either case, real income is reduced. Therefore, a worker cannot receive a permanent increase in wages. This theory, by the twentieth century, had given way to more progressive theories.

See also Wage Theories.

SUBSTANTIAL LESSENING OF COMPETITION. In determining whether a firm has violated the Clayton Act prohibitions against price discrimination, exclusive dealer-ships and tying contracts, and mergers, the Federal Trade Commission and federal courts must consider whether the effect of the firm's practices "may be to substantially lessen competition."

Apart from the evidence of a violation, at least three areas of interpretation are called for in litigation under the Act. "May be" has come to mean a reasonable probability, not just possibility, of injury to competition. Lessened competition has been found in elimination of rivals or diversion of trade from rivals. (These effects actually show an impact on competitors rather than competition.)

What is "substantial" has not been determined precisely. For some time prior to World War II, courts emphasized the test of "proportional substantiality," an assessment of the percent of the market affected. No "magic number" as to percent necessary to show violation was announced, however. Since that time, more, but not exclusive, emphasis has been placed on "quantitative substantiality," a test based on the absolute dollar volume of trade, rather than the percent of the market affected.

See also Clayton Act; Exclusive Dealership; Merger; Price Discrimination; Quantitative Substantiality; Tying Contract; United States v. New York Great A & P Co.

Consult (16) Bain, 1968.

—Thomas O. Depperschmidt, *Memphis State University*

SUBSTITUTE GOODS, in the consumption process, goods that are to some extent interchangeable with each other. If the price of one good fell, the demand curve for the substitute good would almost certainly fall, because people would opt for the less expensive good, instead. For substitute goods there is a direct relationship between the price of one good and the demand curve of another.

SUBSTITUTION EFFECT, the change in the quantity demanded of a commodity as a result of a compensated price change, where the compensation is designed to keep the consumer's real income constant. The own substitution effect is always negative, and this property is known as the law of demand. Cross-substitution effects may be either positive, negative, or zero.

See also Consumer Equilibrium; Compensated Price Effects.

SUPERIOR GOOD. *See* Income Effect.

SUPPLEMENTAL UNEMPLOYMENT BENEFITS, as sought by the steelworkers and the automobile workers in the 1950s, are benefits which, under certain conditions, an employee receives in addition to unemployment compensation. There are basically two types: the insurance fund and the individual account plan.

Under the insurance fund, a company contributes to a trust fund established for the benefit of the employees a certain amount of money up to a certain maximum level. When a worker becomes unemployed for reasons beyond his control, he receives unemployment compensation from the company plan as well as from the state.

The individual account plans establish an individual account for each employee, to which the employer contributes a designated amount of money. The worker may draw from it when he is laid off, is ill, retires, or leaves the company. This is, therefore, a much broader plan, but is not as popular as the insurance fund.

SUPPLY is a functional relationship between quantity supplied and a host of other variables, the most important of which is usually considered to be price. The supply relationship defines the conditions under which a producer will voluntarily produce and offer for sale differing outputs. It is a flow concept and is therefore defined per unit of time. Variables other than price which are potential determinants of supply are (1) the price of such inputs as labor and raw materials, (2) the current level of technology in the industry in question, (3) future price expectations, and (4) the prices of alternative commodities that the firm potentially can produce in the short run. Moreover, if we are concerned with the short run then certain inputs such as land and capital are considered to be fixed.

It is important to note that, unless specified otherwise, demand considerations are ignored. Thus the supply schedule shows conditions under which outputs will be voluntarily offered; whether they can actually be sold or not is important but not immediately relevant. The fact that supply and demand are considered independent implies that a change in one

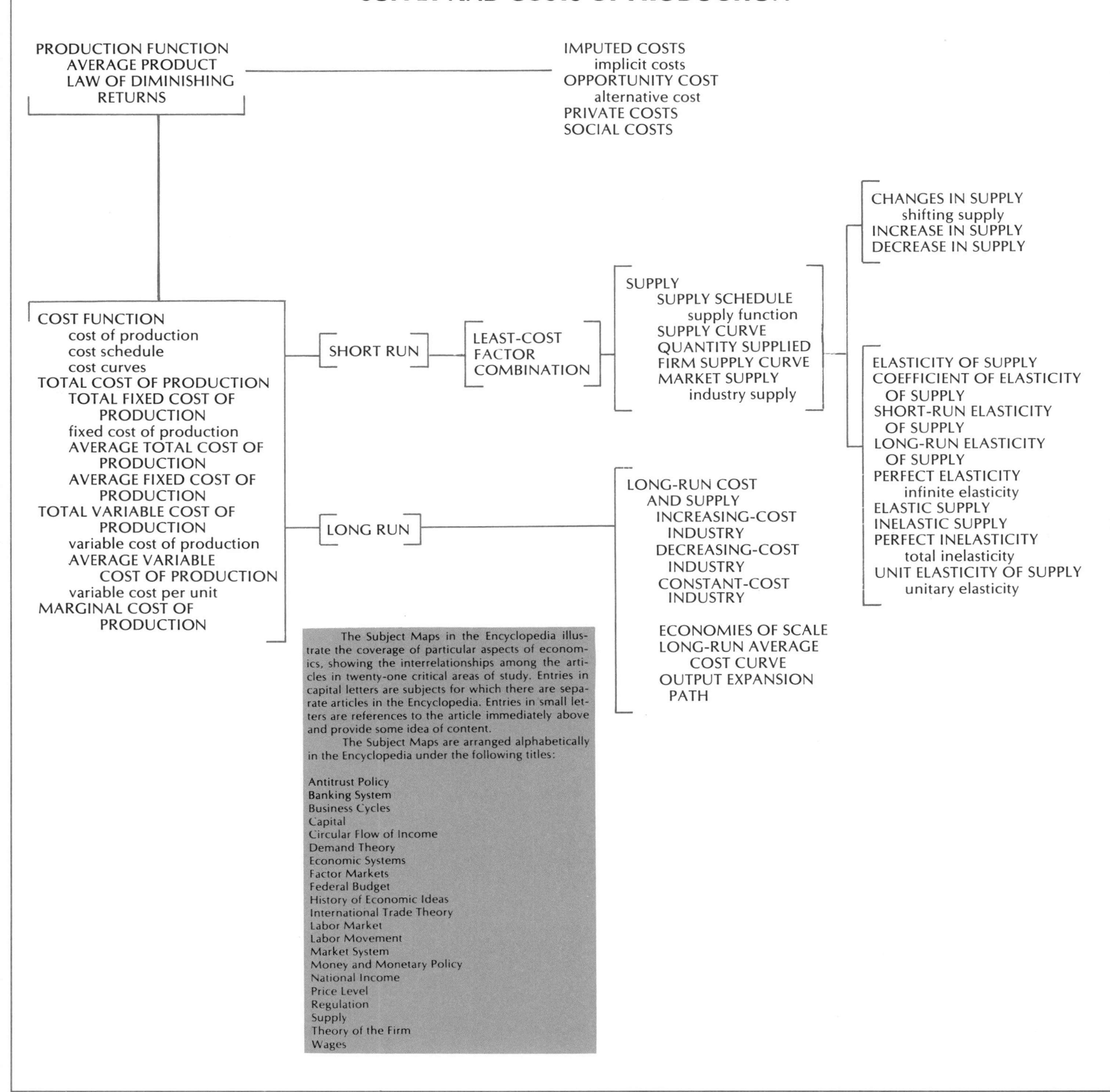
SUPPLY AND COSTS OF PRODUCTION
PRODUCTION FUNCTION
AVERAGE PRODUCT
LAW OF DIMINISHING RETURNS
IMPUTED COSTS
implicit costs
OPPORTUNITY COST
alternative cost
PRIVATE COSTS
SOCIAL COSTS
COST FUNCTION
cost of production
cost schedule
cost curves
TOTAL COST OF PRODUCTION
TOTAL FIXED COST OF PRODUCTION
fixed cost of production
AVERAGE TOTAL COST OF PRODUCTION
AVERAGE FIXED COST OF PRODUCTION
TOTAL VARIABLE COST OF PRODUCTION
variable cost of production
AVERAGE VARIABLE COST OF PRODUCTION
variable cost per unit
MARGINAL COST OF PRODUCTION
SHORT RUN
LEAST-COST FACTOR COMBINATION
SUPPLY
SUPPLY SCHEDULE
supply function
SUPPLY CURVE
QUANTITY SUPPLIED
FIRM SUPPLY CURVE
MARKET SUPPLY
industry supply
CHANGES IN SUPPLY
shifting supply
INCREASE IN SUPPLY
DECREASE IN SUPPLY
ELASTICITY OF SUPPLY
COEFFICIENT OF ELASTICITY OF SUPPLY
SHORT-RUN ELASTICITY OF SUPPLY
LONG-RUN ELASTICITY OF SUPPLY
PERFECT ELASTICITY
infinite elasticity
ELASTIC SUPPLY
INELASTIC SUPPLY
PERFECT INELASTICITY
total inelasticity
UNIT ELASTICITY OF SUPPLY
unitary elasticity
LONG RUN
LONG-RUN COST AND SUPPLY
INCREASING-COST INDUSTRY
DECREASING-COST INDUSTRY
CONSTANT-COST INDUSTRY
ECONOMIES OF SCALE
LONG-RUN AVERAGE COST CURVE
OUTPUT EXPANSION PATH
The Subject Maps in the Encyclopedia illustrate the coverage of particular aspects of economics, showing the interrelationships among the articles in twenty-one critical areas of study. Entries in capital letters are subjects for which there are separate articles in the Encyclopedia. Entries in small letters are references to the article immediately above and provide some idea of content.
The Subject Maps are arranged alphabetically in the Encyclopedia under the following titles:
Antitrust Policy
Banking System
Business Cycles
Capital
Circular Flow of Income
Demand Theory
Economic Systems
Factor Markets
Federal Budget
History of Economic Ideas
International Trade Theory
Labor Market
Labor Movement
Market System
Money and Monetary Policy
National Income
Price Level
Regulation
Supply
Theory of the Firm
Wages

will not directly lead to a change in the other. This theoretical contrivance is called partial equilibrium analysis.

—Robert L. Brite, *Louisiana State University*

SUPPLY, CHANGES IN. *See* Changes in Supply.

SUPPLY AND DEMAND, LAW OF. *See* Law of Supply and Demand.

SUPPLY CURVE

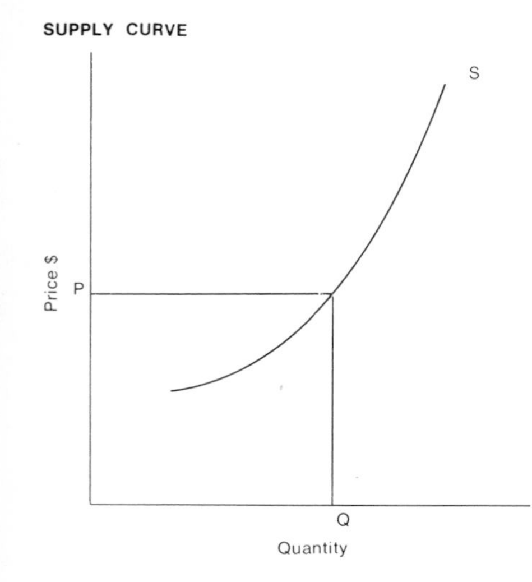

SUPPLY CURVE, the graphical representation of a supply schedule. It is two-dimensional, showing the relationship between prices and quantities supplied, holding other potentially important variables constant. Because it is a flow concept, the axis should be labeled per unit of time.

Mathematically it is the convention to put the dependent variable on the Y axis and the independent variable on the X axis. However, following the convention originating with Alfred Marshall (the famous neo-classical Cambridge economist) economists usually plot price on the Y axis and quantity supplied—the dependent variable—on the X axis. Since the Y intercept and the slope change with the labeling of the axis, this is an important consideration and care must be taken to avoid confusion in the more mathematical treatments of supply schedules.

Since negative prices and outputs are not economically meaningful, the supply schedule will lie entirely in the first quadrant of the coordinate system. To reflect the inverse relationship between price and quantity supplied, the supply schedule should slope upward from left to right. The positive slope reflects the fact that the marginal cost of output rises due to diminishing returns to labor. The firm will voluntarily increase its output per unit of time only if price rises to offset this increased marginal cost of later units of output.

The supply curve can also be viewed as the locus of all points representing potential or possible equilibrium positions for the firm. Since the supply curve defines the outputs voluntarily supplied under differing circumstances (prices) it must simultaneously define the profit maximizing positions for the firm, following the assumption that the producers are rational and attempt to maximize profits.

—Robert L. Brite, *Louisiana State University*

SUPPLY FUNCTION. *See* Supply Schedule.

SUPPLY OF LABOR. *See* Labor Supply.

SUPPLY SCHEDULE, a two-dimensional relationship often depicted in a table showing the various amounts that a firm will voluntarily offer under differing prices, assuming that all other determinants than price (such as wage rates, technology, expectation) remain constant. This is the famous *ceteris paribus* ("other things being the same") assumption, an extremely useful pedagogical device in economics, as well as other scientific disciplines.

Supply schedules show an inverse relationship between price and quantity supplied; this is usually referred to as the law of supply. The fact that low prices are associated with small outputs voluntarily offered and high prices with larger quantities offered is of paramount importance in economics and is accounted for largely by the law of diminishing returns.

The supply schedule we are concerned with is the short-run relationship between price and quantity supplied. Since land and capital (as well as technology) are considered to be constant in the short run the firm can only increase output by taking on more labor. Adding more and more quantities of labor to fixed inputs inevitably causes diminishing returns to occur; the marginal product of labor falls, whereupon, assuming constant wage rates, marginal cost of output rises. If wage rates = $1.00/hr. and the marginal product of the last worker equals 10, then the marginal cost of output equals roughly 10 cents. If marginal product falls to 5 for the next laborer, the last unit now costs roughly 20 cents. Since later units of output cost more than earlier units the firm will voluntarily offer larger amounts only if price rises to offset increased marginal cost.

—Robert L. Brite, *Louisiana State University*

SUPPORT PRICES. *See* Price-Support Programs.

SURPLUS BALANCE OF TRADE. *See* Balance of Trade.

SURPLUS FINANCE. When the government collects more in revenues than it spends, a surplus results. This surplus has contractionary effects on the economy. The way in which this surplus is used can either reinforce or neutralize the contractionary effect. Maximum economic contraction results when the surplus is held idle and not allowed to reenter the private sector. If the surplus is distributed to those who would immediately spend it, the contractionary effect is substantially offset; if it is used to retire government debt that already exists, the contractionary effect is partially offset. The degree to which the contraction is offset depends upon who holds the debt that is to be retired, whether they are spenders or savers.

SURPLUS VALUE, the difference between the value of commodities produced by labor and the wage payment to labor. According to Marx, surplus value, the source of capitalist profits, arose because in the average working day, a laborer produced more than enough to provide for his own subsistence.

See also Economic Interpretation of History; Marx, Karl; Proletariat.

SURVIVORS' INSURANCE. Survivors of workers covered by social security are eligible for children's benefits to age 18 (22 if in school) and a mother's benefit until the youngest child reaches 18. The widow again becomes eligible at age 62 if she is unmarried.

See also Social Insurance; Social Security.

SYNDICALISM, revolutionary movement that originated in France in the late 19th century, with Georges Sorel as one of its intellectual leaders. Deeming class conflict the dominant characteristic in society, syndicalists believed workers must liberate themselves from employers and the state through boycotts, sabotage, mass demonstrations, and strikes. A general strike would overturn the existing system, and industries would be operated by associations of workers to be formed from existing labor unions.

See also Anarchistic Communism; Revolutionary Socialism.

SYSTEMS, ECONOMIC. *See* Economic Systems.

TABLEAU ECONOMIQUE, the first macroeconomic model combined with the first analysis of aggregate economic relationships. François Quesnay's *Tableau èconomique* (1758) attempted to indicate the flows of goods and money between economic sectors in a competitive economy. Of the three sectors considered—landlords, tenant farmers, and manufacturers-merchants—only the tenant farmers were deemed productive, following the Physiocrats' view that only nature can produce a net product. The *Tableau* then indicates how the net product of the agricultural sector circulates and how it is reproduced from one year to the next. Quesnay's work provided the basis for some aspects of macroeconomics, including national income accounting and the circular flow.

See also Physiocrats; Quesnay, François.

TACIT AGREEMENT, an agreement that is only inferred or implied and is never directly stated. Agreement is usually in the form of silent consent.

Tacit agreements are sometimes found in oligopolistic market structures where firms tend to "agree" on a market price or any other policy without formal or written contracts. For example, if one firm establishes a price for its product, by a tacit agreement all other firms may use this same price for their products. Agreements of this type are often used as substitutes for illegal forms of collusion.

TACIT COLLUSION. *See* Collusion.

TAFT, PHILIP (1902-), American educator and expert on labor economics and the labor movement. He received his B.A. (1932) and Ph.D. (1935) from the University of Wisconsin. His publications include *The History of Labor in the United States 1896-1932* (1935), *The A.F.L. from the Death of Gompers to the Merger* (1959), *Organized Labor in American History* (1968), and *Movements for Economic Reform* (1971). Taft has been associate economic analyst for the Social Security Board (1935-36), and a consultant to the Rhode Island Department of Employment Security. He became professor emeritus at Brown University in 1968.

TAFT-HARTLEY ACT (1947), also known as the Labor-Management Relations Act of 1947, amended the Wagner Act of 1935 and also added several new features to federal labor legislation. These changes reflected the one-sidedness of the original Wagner Act in labor's behalf, which in 1935 may well have been justified but by 1947 no longer was. The great growth of unionism between the mid 1930s and the end of World War II had brought labor to its greatest strength, and equality in collective bargaining now made necessary some restraints on this power, of a sort similar to those imposed on management in the earlier law.

Wagner Act Changes. Section 7 of the Wagner Act protected the right of employees to join unions and bargain collectively. Taft-Hartley added the protection of the workers' right not to join unions. Section 8 of the Wagner Act, which specified the "unfair labor practices" prohibited to employers was left almost unchanged. But Taft-Hartley added protections for both employers and workers by designating unfair labor practices prohibited to labor organizations or their representatives. Taft-Hartley also amended the Wagner Act in regard to the structure and operation of the National Labor Relations Board (NLRB).

New Features. The act required unions to file certain information with the government in order to remain under NLRB protection and set forth a detailed procedure for resolving "national emergency strikes."

In strikes that may seriously affect the national safety and well being, the President may ask the Attorney General to seek an 80-day strike injunction. During the first 60 days, mediation is attempted and a fact-finding board studies the situation. The board then reports to the President, and a "last-offer" vote is conducted among the employees. After 80 days, if no resolution has occurred despite these steps, the strike may resume, and any further action is left to labor and management.

Effect. All in all, the Taft-Hartley Act is a complex and detailed law with several aims. It seeks to re-establish a "balance of power" in labor-management relations, to protect the uninvolved third parties from economic harm resulting from labor disputes, and to protect the public from strikes that seriously affect its safety and well-being.

See also Unfair Labor Practices; Wagner Act.

—Leonard G. Schifrin, *College of William and Mary*

TAKE-OFF (Spurt), the stage of growth during which the old societal values and resistances to growth are overcome and a modern industrial society emerges. The state is characterized by a surge in technological development, the reinvestment of business profits in new plant and equipment, and an increase in private savings and investment. Western Europe experienced the take-off phase of its development during the late 18th and early 19th centuries.

See also Preconditions; States of Growth.

TARGET PRICING refers to that policy of a business firm that establishes a designated or target rate of profit to be earned in a certain period of time.

Because of their independent nature, target pricing policies are usually found in noncompetitive market structures where individual firms have some voice in pricing policies. Target pricing is especially popular in monopolistic industries where price can be set by the individual firm. Purely competitive firms cannot successfully use target pricing because price is usually established by the market.

Frank William Taussig

TARIFF HISTORY OF THE UNITED STATES (1888). *See* Taussig, Frank W.

TARIFFS, taxes placed on imports either by value (ad valorem duty) or per unit of quantity (specific duty). A single-columned tariff schedule has the same rate on a particular good irrespective of the country of origin; a multicolumned tariff discriminates according to the country of origin. The chief purpose of tariffs today is protection of import-competing domestic firms, but the original purpose of American tariffs was revenue.

Effects. The imposition of a duty may affect the price and production of the taxed good in the importing country in several ways. There may be no effect when the duty is placed on a commodity also exported by the country, or when the entire duty is borne by the foreign exporter. The price may rise by the amount of the duty when the commodity taxed is produced abroad at constant costs. Finally, the price may rise by less than the duty. Under increasing cost conditions a duty will cause the foreign and domestic price to differ by an amount equal to the duty, unless the duty is so high as to be prohibitive, but the price rise in the importing country is equal to the duty less the fall in price in the exporting country. This effect is the most general. The burden of the duty will always be shifted toward the area of least elasticity: the more elastic the supply is in the exporting country, the higher will be the price increase in the importing country.

Arguments for tariffs come in many forms: improve terms of trade, reduce unemployment, encourage industrialization, further military security, prevent pauperization of labor, keep money at home, effect retaliation, and increase bargaining power. The terms-of-trade argument is valid, if the foreign exporter will bear the burden. The infant-industry argument is rational for any underdeveloped country, which needs a protected market until economies of scale are reached and lower costs allow the country to compete internationally. A problem arises in determining responsive industries and realistic time goals and in avoiding retaliation. Economically, tariffs would equalize costs of production at home and abroad, completely destroying the whole basis for trade. Therefore, most pleas for tariffs reduce to pleas for subsidies.

See also Balance of Trade; Terms of Trade; Trade Barriers.

Consult (23) Ingram, 1970; Wexler, 1972.

—John R. Matthews, Jr., *College of William and Mary*

TAUSSIG, FRANK WILLIAM (1859–1940), presented a body of economic thought very much in the classical tradition and in many respects can be called the American Alfred Marshall. Taussig's most important contributions were in the fields of tariffs and international trade. His *Tariff History of the United States* (1888) was an attempt to integrate theory with empirical data to provide a better understanding of tariff questions. This work provided much of the foundation of his book *International Trade* (1927) in which he combined the theory of international trade and comparative advantage with the effects of monetary and credit systems.

Taussig is also an important figure because of his significant role as teacher of an important generation of American economists.

TAUT PLANNING. *See* Centralization.

TAXATION. Since the beginning of the twentieth century the size and importance of government activities have increased dramatically. As this has occurred, the amount of tax revenues and the complexity of the tax structure have also increased.

Kinds. In 1970 property taxes accounted for approximately 85% of the tax receipts of local governments in the United States. Sales taxes and excise taxes (that is, special levies on individual products, such as gasoline and liquor) constituted somewhat less than 10% of the total tax collections. Most of the remaining revenues of local governments, not counting those received from higher levels of government, came from the sale of various licenses and permits.

State governments, on the other hand, rely primarily on sales and excise taxes (approximately 55% of their tax revenues), with income taxes (15%) becoming more common recently. Other major sources of state tax revenue include licenses and permits (15%) and corporate income taxes (8%). Property, death, and gift taxes provide states with a small proportion of their total tax collections.

The federal government in 1970 received almost $200 billion in tax revenues, 45% from the personal income tax, 20% from corporation income taxes, 22% from social insurance payroll taxes, and the remainder from excise taxes, customs duties, estate and gift taxes, and miscellaneous receipts.

Funding Government. The federal government, if it wished, would not have great difficulty in raising sufficient taxes to meet its payments for government goods and services. In recent years, however, the government frequently has run a deficit to redistribute income or to use fiscal policy as a stimulant for the economy.

On the other hand, even though state and local tax receipts have recently risen relative to federal receipts, the lower governments have lately experienced a difficult time raising sufficient revenues to defray their rapidly increasing expenses for highways, education, pollution control, crime control, and social services. As a result, there has been an increasing tendency for higher levels of government to give grants to lower levels. The states now give substantial aid to local governments, and the federal government has given large grants to lower governments. In the past these grants have been given on condition that they be used for specific purposes and that the state and local governments put up a certain amount of their own funds. Recently several leading economists have proposed that federal subsidies be given to states and localities on a no-strings-attached basis. A federal revenue-sharing proposal of this type has been presented to Congress by President Nixon.

Redistributing Income. Although ostensibly the tax system has attempted to redistribute income from the wealthy to the poor, there is some question as to how effectively this objective has been accomplished. In this connection, taxes may be classified as progressive, proportional, or regressive. A tax is *progressive* if its percentage rate increases as income increases. A *proportional* tax takes the same percentage of each person's income, regardless of how large his income is. A *regressive* tax is one whose percentage rate declines as income increases. Insofar as the tax system is progressive, it places the main burden of tax payment on the higher income groups. The reverse is true if the tax system is regressive. A progressive tax structure, therefore, will generally create a more equal distribution of income after taxes.

Economists have generally agreed that the federal personal income tax is highly progressive, but property, sales, and social security payroll taxes are regressive. The value of taxed property constitutes a larger percentage of a poor person's income than of a wealthy person's income. The poor person spends a larger percentage of his income on consumer goods, which are subject to the sales taxes. The social security taxes apply (as of 1972) only to the first $9,000 of each person's income.

Unfortunately, it is not always a simple matter to determine whether some taxes are progressive, proportional, or regressive. This is because the incidence of a tax may be shifted. An excise tax levied against a liquor company, for example, may be paid finally by the purchaser of the liquor, because the company raises the price to cover the tax. The incidence of the tax is then said to have been shifted forward from the manufacturer to the consumer. The tax may also be shifted backward from the manufacturer to his suppliers; that is, the manufacturer pays the suppliers less than had there been no tax.

Economists have not been able to determine the exact incidence of most levies on firms, so it is impossible to say for certain whether such taxes are progressive, regressive, or proportional. Intensive studies have, nevertheless, come to the tentative conclusion that when all taxes levied in the United States are taken into consideration, the regressive taxes roughly cancel out the progressive taxes, so that the overall tax structure is approximately proportional. If so, taxes in the United States have no important effect on income distribution.

Controlling the Economy. The majority of economists believe that an alteration of taxes may have a powerful effect on the total demand for goods and thereby affect the level of inflation and employment. A decrease in taxes may be expected to raise incomes after taxes and thereby increase the total demand for goods and reduce the level of unemployment. On the other hand, an increase in taxes should decrease incomes after taxes, decreasing the total demand for goods and dampening inflation. In recent years, however, some

TAXATION

Taxes have a bearing on the economic system in many and varied ways. For the role of taxes in regard to the macroeconomy as a whole, see the articles on CIRCULAR FLOW OF INCOME, WITHDRAWALS, and PUBLIC FINANCE. The details of taxes and taxation are presented in numerous articles, particularly FEDERAL BUDGET. Types of taxes are described in EXCISE TAX, SALES TAX, and PERSONAL INCOME TAX. And for details on two types of tax currently receiving much attention, see VALUE ADDED TAX and NEGATIVE INCOME TAX.

The Subject Map accompanying FEDERAL BUDGET displays these and other relationships.

IRS provides citizens with assistance to assure their returns are accurate, payments correct.

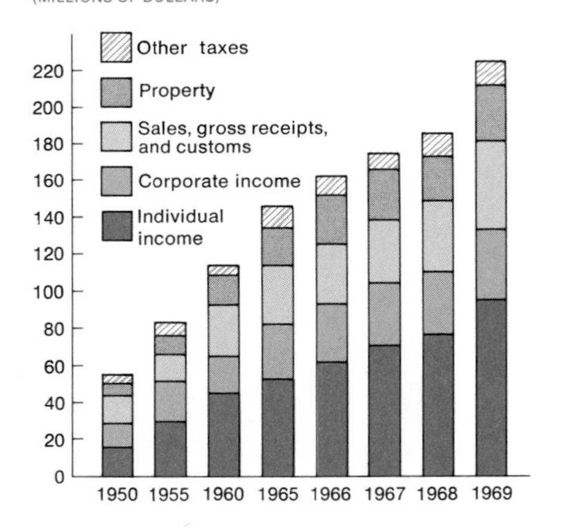

INTERNAL REVENUE SERVICE COLLECTIONS, COST OF COLLECTIONS, TAX PER CAPITA 1870-1970

Fiscal year	Collections ($ millions)	Cost of collecting $100	Tax per capita
1870	184	4.47	4.62
1875	110	4.83	2.44
1880	123	3.63	2.47
1885	112	3.96	1.98
1890	142	2.87	2.26
1895	143	2.88	2.06
1900	295	1.58	3.88
1905	234	2.01	2.79
1910	289	1.74	3.14
1915	415	1.64	4.13
1920	5,407	.50	50.79
1925	2,584	1.44	22.31
1930	3,040	1.13	24.68
1935	3,299	1.29	25.91
1940	5,340	1.12	40.28
1945	43,800	.33	311.82
1950	38,957	.59	255.84
1955	66,288	.42	399.50
1960	91,774	.40	507.98
1965	114,434	.52	589.15
1970	195,722	.45	960.67

economists have expressed strong doubts as to the extent of these effects.

—Allan B. Mandelstamm, *Michigan State University*

Taxation Glossary

Ad Valorem Tax, tax on percentage of an item's value, such as sales taxes or real estate taxes.
Capital Gains Tax, tax on net income from the sale of a capital asset, such as stocks.
Capital Levy, tax that appropriates part of the assets of individuals and businesses, usually assessed to reduce large debts.
Corporation Tax, tax, either federal, state, or local, on the income of corporations.
Custom Duties, taxes collected by a government on items imported into or, occasionally, exported from a country.
Depletion Allowance, tax credit extended in the United States to owners of exhaustible natural resources, such as petroleum, minerals, and timber.
Double Taxation, application of two taxes on the same object of taxation, such as the taxation of corporate income and individuals' corporate dividends, both of which are part of corporate income.
Estate Tax, tax on the entire estate of a deceased person, made before the estate is distributed.
Excess Profits Tax, tax on profits above a predetermined "normal" level, usually applied in war time.
Excise Tax, tax on a specific item, usually made on the manufacturer.
Exemption, the amount and types of income exempt from taxes.
Gift Tax, tax on donated property; designed to prevent avoidance of estate and inheritance taxes.
Income Tax, tax on personal and corporate incomes, used to finance federal, state, and local government.
Inheritance Tax, tax on the portion of an estate received by an individual, usually levied at a progressive rate.
Negative Income Tax, tax plan in which people with incomes below a certain level would receive payments from the government, rather than paying taxes.
Progressive Tax, levy that takes a higher proportion of high incomes in taxes than it takes from low income.
Property Tax, tax on real estate, including the land and the structures on it; exercised by state and local governments in the United States.
Revenue Sharing, practice by which one level of government, such as the federal, shares its income from a tax with another level of government.
Sales Tax, general tax on sale price of goods, usually applied at retail level.
Single Tax, tax plan, popularized by Henry George, that would tax only the income from land.
Tariffs, alternate name for Custom Duties.
Tax Evasion, avoidance of taxes through illegal means.
Tax Loophole, inconsistency in the tax laws, either unintentional or designed to provide benefits for particular activities, that permits the avoidance of taxes.
Tax Reform, revision of the tax laws, generally aimed at closing loopholes and producing a more equitable tax system.
Tax Shelter, financial program to protect income by utilizing opportunities provided by the tax laws.
Turnover Tax, a levy, also called a general sales tax, that taxes items at each step of manufacturing and distribution.
Use Tax, tax on the initial use, rather than the sale of an item; designed to compensate for avoidance of sales taxes and generally limited to expensive items, such as automobiles.
Value-Added Tax, tax on difference between the value of materials and supplies used by the manufacturer and the value of the finished product.
Withholding Tax, tax, usually progressive, by federal, state, or local authorities that is withheld from payments by employers to employees.

TAXES, the income of governments. Originally confined almost exclusively to import duties, the incidence and extent of taxation by the United States government have expanded throughout the country's history as a function both of the increasing demand for governmental services and, more recently, of the post-Keynesian emphasis on regulation of the economy through fiscal policy.

Kinds. Taxes are of many types, the most common of which, in addition to income tax, are tariffs (import duties), sales, excise, estate, gift, value-added, and property taxes. The type of tax imposed and its rate depend on a variety of factors, the most prominent being the political acceptability of the tax, the need for revenue, and the ease with which the tax may be collected.

Tariffs are frequently imposed because of a government's desire to bolster its own economy by restricting outside competition, a goal that is eminently acceptable, because it is usually desired by the people and opposed only by foreigners. *Estate Taxes* are primarily a means of redistribution of wealth. As compared to tariffs, estate taxes are a new development, imposed only since disproportionate wealth has become socially undesirable. *Gift Taxes* are a nuisance to both governments and individuals and are subject to easy evasion. They are used only to support estate taxes; without a gift tax, most individuals could avoid estate taxes by arranging to have no estate.

Property Taxes, long the mainstay of taxation at the local level, recently have been questioned on constitutional grounds in both state and federal courts. From the viewpoint of local governments, this development is likely to prove unfortunate. Property taxes may be the ideal tax for local governments. The tax is difficult to evade or escape: real estate can be neither concealed nor removed. More importantly, local governments, because of the nature of their responsibilities, need the tax's stable source of revenue.

For the federal government, concerned more with fiscal policy than with stable income, and better able than a state or local government to finance deficits through the money markets, income taxes, varying with income levels, which, in turn, vary with economic cycles, are a more satisfactory instrument from which to gain needed revenue than any other tax. The federal income tax began in 1913 with an amendment to the Constitution.

See also Public Finance.

TAX INCIDENCE. When a tax is shifted many times, there may not be any direct connection between the original taxpayer and those who ultimately bear the burden of the tax in the form of lower wages, higher interest rates, higher prices paid, or lower prices received. In this situation, the incidence of the tax has become diffused. The tax incidence is the place where the burden of a tax ultimately rests after all the effects on commodity prices, factor prices, resource-allocation effort, and composition of production and consumption are accounted for—in other words, after the tax can no longer be shifted again.

TAX LOOPHOLE. *See* Taxation: *Glossary.*

TAX RATE, the percentage or absolute amount to be applied to the tax base in order to determine the tax liability. The tax base may be income, sales, gallons of gasoline, or any other specified unit. The tax rate can be a percentage of income or of sales, or a specific nominal amount per unit.

TAX SHELTER. *See* Taxation: *Glossary.*

TAX SHIFTING is the passing on by one taxpayer to another all or part of the tax payment. This is accomplished through the adjustment of prices and incomes. As a consequence of a tax, the prices of goods or services sold may increase or the tax may be said to have been shifted forward. Alternately, prices of factors of production (materials, rent on land and buildings, interest on borrowing, and wages to employees) may fall because of the tax. In this case, the tax is said to have been shifted backward. Shifting may also be a combination of forward and backward. In many cases, the shifting procedure is minimal, as in the case of the personal income tax, and in others, such as the tax on corporate profits, the final resting place (or incidence) is in doubt.

TAX STRUCTURE refers to the *actual* or *effective* rates of taxation paid by individuals or firms, at different levels of income. Specifically, this measures whether the tax system is actually progressive, proportional, or regressive. Though the statutory rates may suggest progression, special treatment (deductions, exemptions, etc.) of certain types of income will reduce considerably the actual progressivity.

TECHNICAL COOPERATION ADMINISTRATION. *See* Point Four Program.

TECHNOLOGICAL CHANGE is brought about within a technology by invention, innovation, imitation, improvement, adaptation to local conditions, and development of full-scale plans. Economic demand, physical resources, costs, and profitability are factors determining the effort devoted to, and the magnitude of, technological change.

As a nation's production-possibility frontier is advanced through such change, the interrelated nature of production tends to cause a clustering of inventions and innovations, with a corresponding increase in capital investment, which leads to economic expansion. Change that increases the productivity of existing resources, and makes new equipment more productive than old, makes economic growth easier.

See also Technology.

Consult (22) Fusfeld, 1972.

Through technological change, the compact computer below exceeds capacity of the full wall array above.

TECHNOLOGICAL QUESTION. *See* Market Mechanism.

TECHNOLOGICAL UNEMPLOYMENT results when a particular type of labor is displaced either by machines or by a different type of labor. When advances in technology make machinery less expensive to use than manpower, jobs become obsolete. Likewise, if newer and cheaper products or methods of production come about, jobs pertaining to the old products or methods of production may be eliminated. Technological unemployment can involve as few as one or two jobs in an industry (the burglar alarm replacing the watchman), or may involve an entire industry or skill (blacksmiths).

See also Unemployment of Labor.

TECHNOLOGY, a body of skills and knowledge that provides techniques for accomplishing desired goals. A particular technology involves inputs and outputs and the quantitative relations between the amounts of each. If a technology can produce several outputs in variable proportions, production functions can be used to derive an output-possibility curve

Henri Theil

or "efficiency frontier," summarizing the production choices open to a nation with given resources and technology.

See also Demand for Capital; Technological Change.

Consult (22) International, 1968.

TENDENCY TOWARD A SUBSTANTIAL LESSENING OF COMPETITION. *See* Substantial Lessening of Competition.

TERMS OF TRADE, the ratio at which goods are exchanged internationally, usually measured in terms of export and import prices. In barter terms it refers to the quantity of exports that must be given up to obtain a given quantity of imports. If more exports have to be sent abroad to get the same amount of imports, the terms of trade have turned against the country in question. They have turned favorable when fewer exports will command the same or more imports.

The terms of trade can better or worsen irrespective of the status of the balance of trade, which is the difference between merchandise exports and imports.

See also Barter; Comparative Advantage.

Consult (23) Ingram, 1970.

THEIL, HENRI (1924-), Dutch-born econometrician, management scientist, and expert on economic forecasting. He received his Ph.D. from the University of Amsterdam in 1951. His publications include *Economic Forecasts and Policy* (1958), *Applied Economic Forecasting* (1966), *Economics and Information Theory* (1967), and *Principles of Econometrics* (1971). Theil was director of the Econometric Institute of the Netherlands School of Economics from 1955-56. A former president of the Econometric Society (1961), he became a professor at the University of Chicago, and also director of its center for Mathematical Studies in Business and Economics, in 1965.

THEORY, ECONOMIC. A theory consists of definitions, assumptions, and hypotheses. The purpose of theory is to develop valid generalizations to predict how people, things, and systems will behave under given conditions. Economic theory attempts to explain how and why certain economic processes, such as production, consumption, allocation of scarce resources, determination of prices, levels of employment, and conditions of competition, behave in a given manner. Economic theory also attempts to enable business and government leaders to predict future behavior of general levels of production, employment, demand, and other significant economic processes. There are a variety of specific economic theories, such as the law of supply and demand, the theory of marginal utility, and the theory of price elasticity.

Schools. There are basic schools of economic thought that represent generally accepted sets of empirical and philosophical tenets, the composite of which is commonly referred to as economic theory. These composite economic theories or schools of economic thought are commonly categorized into three groupings: Classical economic theory prevailed from about 1750 to the early 1900s. Neoclassical economic theory, which developed during the last two decades of the nineteenth century, culminating in Alfred Marshall's *Principles of Economics* (1890), dominated economic theory for the first half of the twentieth century. Many of the school's postulates are still considered valid. Keynesian economic theory (national income theory) was initiated by Lord Keynes in *The General Theory of Employment, Interest, and Money* (1936). National income theory has dominated much of advanced economic theory since 1940.

See also National Income Determination; Neoclassical Economics.

—Algin B. King, *College of William and Mary*

THEORY OF ECONOMIC DEVELOPMENT (1912). *See* Schumpeter, Joseph A.

THEORY OF MONOPOLISTIC COMPETITION (1933), by Edward H. Chamberlin, developed the theory of the firm to include the great area between pure competition and pure monopoly. Chamberlin's work appeared a few months before Joan Robinson's *The Economics of Imperfect Competition* although both books covered much the same ground.

Chamberlin attempted to combine elements of competition and monopoly in developing the theory of monopolistic competition. Like monopolists, many firms face downward sloping demand curves for their products; yet, like the competitive situation, most firms operate in industries with freedom of entry and exit. Under these conditions the equilibrium position of the firm is quite different from the competitive or monopolistic situation.

See also Chamberlin, Edward H.

THEORY OF MORAL SENTIMENTS (1759). *See* Smith, Adam.

THEORY OF PRICE (1952). *See* Stigler, George J.

THEORY OF THE CONSUMPTION FUNCTION (1957). *See* Friedman, Milton.

THEORY OF THE FIRM. In economic theory the word "firm" is used to denote any organizationally independent production unit. At the broadest level of abstraction, the definition of the firm encompasses both corporate giants such as General Motors and economically minuscule individual proprietorships such as the television repairman with a workbench in his basement and the lady who feeds her family and operates a catering service from the same kitchen.

Classification of Firms: *By Product Type.* Although precise classification by product type is not always possible, a collection of firms that produce and sell the same or closely related products or services is referred to as an industry. Thus we speak of the automobile industry, the television repair industry, and the food service industry.

By Ownership. Legally, firms are classified in terms of their form of ownership. A single proprietorship is a firm that is owned by one individual. A partnership is jointly owned by two or more persons who share the profits and losses of the firm and who are individually liable for the full extent of any financial obligations of the firm. A corporation is also jointly owned, but the corporation is itself an individual in the sight of the law, and if it fails the owners (stockholders) stand to lose only what they have previously invested.

By Market Power. On the economic side, a firm is classified by its relation to the various markets in which it operates. Conceptually, this classification is based on a scale of market power with monopoly at one end and competition at the other. The word "monopoly" means literally "single seller" and the term "competition" suggests numerous competitors, but the manifestation of market power that is most widely used in economic theory is the ability of the firm to influence price in any of the markets in which it either purchases factors of production or sells output. (On the purchasing side, the classification scale runs from monopsony to competitive purchasing.) Defining market power in terms of ability to influence market price is so firmly entrenched in formal economics that it has been suggested that the terms "price-taking" and "price-searching" should be substituted respectively for competition and monopoly-monopsony. The terms are descriptive since a firm with no market power simply *takes* that price that is dictated by the market while a firm with any measure of market power *searches* for that price which is most profitable.

The Place of the Firm in Economic Theory. The purpose of economic theory is to explain how various economic systems work. We are primarily interested in understanding our own and similar economies. To this end, we borrow an approach from the more exact engineering and natural sciences and construct models that are intended to analogue the essential functional processes and interrelationships of the system we wish to study. (What makes economics a "soft" science relative to the engineering and natural sciences is that in economics we are not able to test our models under controlled laboratory conditions and must settle for testing by less exact statistical techniques.) In the generalized model employed in economics, production units (firms) and consumption units (consumers) comprise the fundamental "atoms" of the model. Analytically there are many similarities as well as differences between firms and consumers. The similarities stem from the assumption of maximizing behavior on the part of both.

Description of the Model of the Firm. As a theoretical abstraction, the firm consists of a number of market relationships and a process which transforms inputs into outputs. This process includes a decision making unit that coordinates the process.

A firm acquires inputs (factors of production) and sells outputs and thus operates in a variety of markets. Certain factors of production may be owned by the firm and thus incorporated into its productive process without a formal purchase transaction taking place; but it is convenient analytically to pretend that these factors have also been purchased and impute a cost to them equal to their market value. As an example, the single proprietorship owner will usually contribute his own labor to the productive process without entering a cost for this labor on the books. Economists include the market value of this labor as a cost to the firm.

The technical relationships between the inputs and outputs for the firms constitute the production function: the maximum amount of a given output that can be obtained from a given set of input quantities and given levels of any other outputs. The economist does not concern himself with the engineering aspects of these relationships but simply takes them as being given. The inputs of the productive process can be divided into labor services and the services of inanimate objects such as buildings and machines.

One human component of the firm deserves special mention. Production requires organization, and there can be no effective organization without a decision-making process. The technical name for this function within the firm is "entrepreneurship." Entrepreneurship can be exercised individually or collectively and is not necessarily connected with ownership although the great entrepreneurs of economic and business history, such as Henry Ford, Sr., both owned and managed the firms that made them famous. In modern corporate structure, however, the entrepreneurial function is often exercised by hired professional managers whose ownership relation to the firm is minimal and somewhat incidentally related to their wages in the form of stock options.

Operation of the Model. We have now described the general nature of the economic model of the firm except for what makes it

THEORY OF THE FIRM

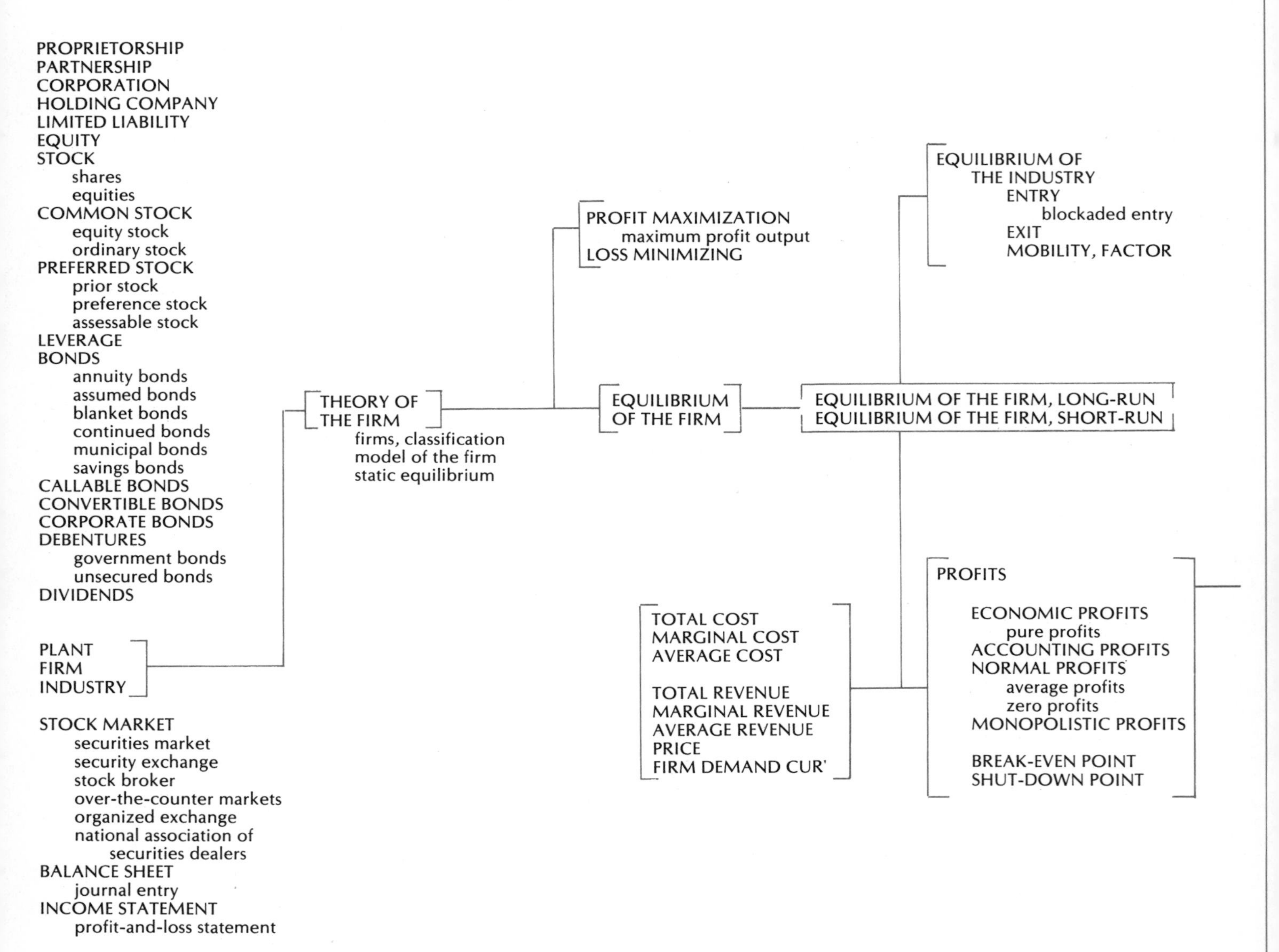

The Subject Maps in the Encyclopedia illustrate the coverage of particular aspects of economics, showing the interrelationships among the articles in twenty-one critical areas of study. Entries in capital letters are subjects for which there are separate articles in the Encyclopedia. Entries in small letters are references to the article immediately above and provide some idea of content.

The Subject Maps are arranged alphabetically in the Encyclopedia under the following titles:

Antitrust Policy
Banking System
Business Cycles
Capital
Circular Flow of Income
Demand Theory
Economic Systems
Factor Markets
Federal Budget
History of Economic Ideas
International Trade Theory
Labor Market
Labor Movement
Market System
Money and Monetary Policy
National Income
Price Level
Regulation
Supply
Theory of the Firm
Wages

MARKET STRUCTURE

- PERFECT COMPETITION
  - pure competition
    - PRICE COMPETITION
    - MARGINAL COST PRICING
    - ECONOMIC EFFICIENCY
      - waste
    - EFFICIENT RESOURCE ALLOCATION
    - RESOURCE MOBILITY
    - RESEARCH AND DEVELOPMENT
- IMPERFECT COMPETITION
  - MONOPOLISTIC COMPETITION
    - PRICE LEADERSHIP
    - FULL-COST PRICING
      - cost-plus pricing
    - TARGET PRICING
    - ADMINISTERED PRICES
    - MARK-UP PRICING
    - INTERDEPENDENCE, OLIGOPOLISTIC
    - TACIT AGREEMENT
    - NON-PRICE COMPETITION
    - QUALITY COMPETITION
    - PROMOTIONAL COMPETITION
      - advertising competition
  - OLIGOPOLY
    - KINKED DEMAND CURVE
    - JOINT PROFIT MAXIMIZATION
      - group profit
    - MONOPOLY PROFITS
    - EXCESS CAPACITY
      - redundant capacity
      - cyclical excess capacity
    - ABSOLUTE COST ADVANTAGE
    - RESTRICTION OF OUTPUT
  - MONOPOLY
    - NATURAL MONOPOLY
- PRODUCT DIFFERENTIATION
- PRODUCT HOMOGENEITY
- BARRIERS TO ENTRY
- PRICE TAKER
- CONCENTRATION RATIO
  - concentration
- MARKET CONCENTRATION
- FREE ENTRY

work. That requires some kind of motive force, which, as a first approximation, we take to be profit seeking. Profit is defined as the difference between revenue (the proceeds from selling outputs) and costs (derived from explicit and implicit purchase of factors of production). Generally it is assumed that the firm maximizes profit, although in some more refined and specialized models this motive force is modified by other considerations such as sales maximization and other managerial motivations.

See also Equilibrium of the Firm, Short-run; Equilibrium of the Firm, Long-run.

Consult (14) Vickrey, 1964.

—Clarence C. Morrison, *Indiana University*

THEORY OF THE LEISURE CLASS (1899). *See* Veblen, Thorstein.

THEORY OF WAGES (1932). *See* Hicks, John R.

THIRD-PARTY INTERVENTION. *See* Conciliation; Fact Finding; Mediation.

THORP, WILLARD LONG (1899-   ), American economist, active in business and government and noted for his work in the fields of international economics and economic growth and development. He is a graduate of Amherst College (1920), and he received his Ph.D. from Columbia (1924). His publications include *Trade, Aid or What?* (1954), *Development Assistance Efforts and Policies* (1963-67, editor), and *The Reality of Foreign Aid* (1971). Thorp has served as assistant secretary of state (1946-52), chairman of the development assistance committee of the Organization for European Cooperation and Development in Paris (1963-67), and director of the National Bureau of Economic Research beginning in 1956. He became professor emeritus of economics at Amherst in 1965.

TIGHT-KNIT COMBINATIONS. *See* Merger.

TIGHT-MONEY POLICY. *See* Monetary Policy.

TIME DEPOSITS, deposits in a commercial bank or savings bank for which the bank may, or must, require advance notice of withdrawal and for which interest is normally paid. The maximum interest that may be paid by member banks on time deposits is set by the federal reserve system. For other banks such limits may be set by state regulation. Time deposits are of three kinds:

Savings Deposits are restricted by law to accounts of individuals or nonprofit organizations. The bank may require up to thirty days notice of withdrawal but in practice never does.

Time Certificates of Deposit may be purchased by anyone, including corporations. The certificates represent a deposit of a specific sum of money for a specified period of time, not less than thirty days, and they cannot be redeemed prior to the date specified. If the certificate is negotiable, it may be sold to someone else. Both savings and commercial banks provide certificates of deposit for small savers, but the great bulk of such deposits are owned by corporations, frequently in denominations of a million dollars or more.

Time Deposits, Open Account, are primarily corporate deposits made without a specified maturity date. By law they cannot be withdrawn without thirty days' advance notice.

See also Interest Rate Ceiling.

—Walter W. Haines, *New York University*

TIME PREFERENCE, a concept that assumes that individuals prefer the present over the future. Although current capital investment will yield more consumer goods at some future time, most people will choose assured present consumption over uncertain future consumption. Therefore, to induce people to abstain from present consumption so that new capital equipment can be manufactured, the increased future consumption (reflected in interest payments) must be enough to overcome their current time preference.

See also Capital Deepening; Demand for Capital; Net Productivity of Capital.

Consult (22) Fusfeld, 1972.

TIME SERIES. Observations of variables taken at various points in time (monthly, quarterly, yearly) generate a time series, which can exhibit trends, cycles, and seasonal and random variation. Analysis of time series is usually concerned with predicting or forecasting future values of the variables in question on the basis of past experience.

TOBIN, JAMES (1918-   ), American economist who, after early work on consumption and saving behavior, has consistently contributed to macroeconomic theory. The unique aspect of Tobin's work is the emphasis upon asset portfolio choice. He feels that the balance sheet as well as the current account must be considered and uses a micro approach in analyzing the balance sheet. For example, Tobin's work with growth models includes the unique feature of capital asset choice.

Tobin also possesses a distinctive ability to summarize and clarify the existing state of a subject. While much of his technical work has been very mathematical, Tobin is also a political economist who served on the Council of Economic Advisors under President Kennedy. He has maintained a keen interest in many public issues such as the negative income tax and poverty.

James Tobin

TOTAL COST is the cost of producing a given output. It is the sum of total fixed cost and total variable cost.

See also Average Cost; Marginal Cost.

TOTAL COST OF PRODUCTION (TC), the cost of all the inputs used to produce some level of output. It is the sum of all the variable and all the fixed costs; that is, TC = TVC (total variable cost) + TFC (total fixed cost). TC is an increasing function of the level of output.

See also Cost Function.

TOTAL FIXED COST OF PRODUCTION (TFC), the cost of all the inputs which are independent of the level of output, that is, costs which a producer has to pay regardless of whether he is producing anything or not. Sometimes these costs are referred to as overhead costs.

See also Cost Function.

TOTAL INELASTICITY. *See* Perfect Inelasticity.

TOTALLY ELASTIC DEMAND. *See* Elastic Demand.

TOTALLY INELASTIC DEMAND. *See* Inelastic Demand.

TOTAL REVENUE is the sum of all the receipts of a firm in a given time interval. For a firm producing a single output, total revenue is simply the number of units sold times the selling price.

See also Average Revenue; Marginal Revenue.

TOTAL-REVENUE TEST. *See* Elasticity of Demand.

TOTAL VARIABLE COST OF PRODUCTION (TVC), the cost of all the variable inputs used to produce some level of output. TVC is an increasing function of the level of output; when the level of output is zero, TVC is zero.

See also Cost Function.

TRADE ASSOCIATION, an organization of firms in an industry (ordinarily less tightly knit than a cartel) to promote the interests of member firms, represent the industry to the public and governmental bodies, and regulate industry standards and practices.

From an economic standpoint, the importance of trade associations relates to possibly anti-competitive practices a trade association may encourage. Especially significant are discussions by members relating to price and output, which may be encouraged by "disorderliness of the market," meaning rapid shifts in price by one or more member firms tending to disrupt the established patterns of distribution. Such concern may foster collusive activities to stabilize the market by price fixing or market sharing. In the latter practices, trade associations run afoul of the Sherman Antitrust Act prohibition on restraint of trade.

See also Collusion; Market Sharing; Price Fixing; Restraint of Trade; Sherman Antitrust Act.

TRADE BARRIERS. International trade theory dictates that trade be free based on the law of comparative advantage, but nations have seen fit to incorporate barriers to trade as elements of commercial policy. The most prominent is the tariff. Quotas are also important when definite restrictions on quantities are sought. A host of non-tariff (or quota) barriers has also arisen. Customs administrations, or red-tape, may provide barriers far more difficult to surmount than formal tariffs. The procedure for setting customs classifications often leads to uncertainty as to the exact amount of duty to be paid. Administration of anti-dumping laws, whereby imports are alleged to have entered a country at unfair low prices, sets obstacles to exporting—it generally takes an inordinate amount of time to get a decision. National patent and trade-mark systems are employed by domestic sellers to curb goods originating in other countries. Health and safety rules either block imports or add appreciably to the cost of importing. The same is true of labeling requirements. Buy-at-home campaigns, subsidies, mixing and milling requirements, taxes, import-export licensing, and currency controls also operate as barriers to trade.

See also Balance of Trade; Quotas; Tariffs.

Consult (23) Massel, 1965.

TRADE EXPANSION ACT. *See* General Agreement on Tariffs and Trade.

TRADE PRACTICE RULES. *See* Federal Trade Commission.

TRADE REGULATION RULES. *See* Federal Trade Commission.

TRADE RESTRICTIONS. *See* Trade Barriers.

TRADITIONAL ECONOMY, the economy of a traditional society. Such a society, and its economy, is usually based on a simple agrarian structure and characterized by limited productivity. Because of the lack of the potentialities created by modern science and technology, the reasonable output per man is quite limited. The traditional society is in the first stage of economic growth, and the populace is subject to the vagaries of external influences that neither the economy nor the political structure of society has learned to control, such as varying output per harvest, war, various plagues, and famine.

See also Stages of Growth.

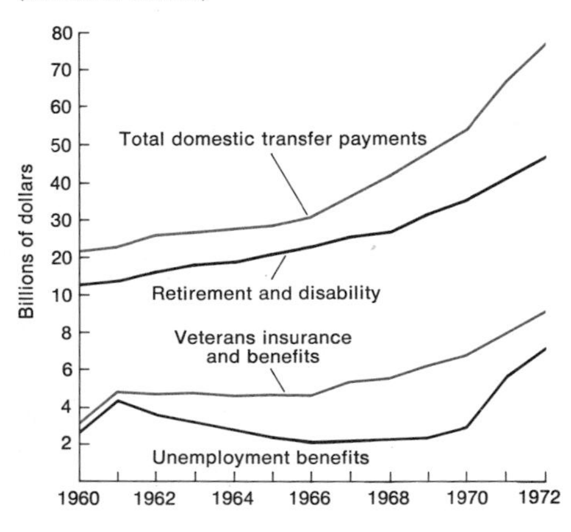

The most widely circulated of U.S. governmental signatures is surely that of the Treasurer.

TRANSACTIONS DEMAND. *See* Liquidity Preference.

TRANSCENDENTAL FUNCTIONS. *See* Function.

TRANSFER PAYMENTS, expenditures for which no goods or services are exchanged. Governments, federal, state, and local, are the largest distributors of transfer payments, which include welfare payments, social security benefits, and unemployment compensation. These payments amount to about 22% of all government expenditures. Some government subsidies, such as farm price supports, are considered transfer payments. Repatriation payments from one country to another are also considered transfer payments, because they involve no output. Business transfer payments, which amount to several billion dollars each year, include payouts under deferred compensation arrangements, gifts, and donations.

Transfer payments, both public and private, essentially redistribute income from the employed to the unemployed, from the urban areas to the farms, and from corporations to individuals. In effect, transfer payments alter private goods production in favor of the recipients of the payments and provide injections into the circular flow of income. Transfer payments by governments also have a stabilizing effect on the economy. During boom years the unemployment reserve funds grow and exert stabilizing pressure to prevent too great spending. Conversely, during slack years reserve funds are used to moderate the decline and sustain consumption. Welfare programs and government subsidies also show an automatic anticyclical type of stabilizing behavior.

TRANSITIONAL GROWTH. *See* Preconditions.

TRANSITIONAL UNEMPLOYMENT describes the loss of work that occurs due to the changing of jobs and the relocation of workers. Often referred to as frictional unemployment, this condition is almost always temporary and poses no real threat to the economy. It occurs even during the most prosperous times, for many reasons such as health, relocation, and family pressures. Transitional unemployment often occurs during the interim between school and the acceptance of a first job as well as between jobs.

See also Unemployment of Labor.

TRANSPORTATION ACTS. In the 20th century, Congress has enacted three transportation acts (1920, 1940, and 1958), each essentially an amendment to an original act of 1887. The Transportation Act of 1920 directed the Interstate Commerce Commission (ICC) to maintain railroad rates which would yield efficient carriers a "fair return." The act of 1940 called for "impartial regulation of all modes of transportation" so as to "preserve the inherent advantages of each" and develop "a national transportation system." The act of 1958 directed the ICC not to hold the rates of one mode up to a level so as to protect another mode unless it was necessary to protect inherent advantages or the national defense.

TRANSPORTATION INDUSTRY. *See* Regulated Industries.

TREASURER OF THE UNITED STATES, a presidential appointee whose functions are to receive, hold, and pay out the public monies of the federal government. Receipts of the government are paid to the Treasury, and all checks written by the government are drawn against the Treasury account, which is kept in the federal reserve banks. The Treasury also supervises the issue and retirement of all United States paper currency. By tradition the Treasurer of the United States is a woman.

TREASURY BILLS. *See* Government Securities.

TREATISE ON MONEY (1930). *See* Keynes, John Maynard.

TREBLE DAMAGES. *See* Triple Damages.

TRENDS IN BUSINESS CYCLES, long-term, noncyclical patterns of economic activity which occur over the course of many business cycles or period fluctuations. A trend or pattern of activity concerning the Gross National Product can be identified readily by examining its movement over a period of time, say 100 years. An example of such a trend is the steady growth of the per capita GNP at an average of 2% per annum since 1870.

See also Business Cycles, Types.

TRIFFIN, ROBERT (1911–), an American economist best known as the author of the Triffin Plan for reforming the system of international payments established after World War II. In his *Gold and the Dollar Crisis* (1960), Triffin correctly analyzed the problem of the gold-exchange standard and its tendency to be extremely vulnerable to crisis. He felt that the system was self-destructive and only a massive reform centering on the role of the International Monetary Fund would correct the situation. Many of Triffin's ideas are elements in the current changes in the system of international payments.

See also Triffin Plan.

TRIFFIN PLAN, reform in the international monetary system calling for the establishment of a world central bank (international bank), or an expanded International Monetary Fund (XIMF), proposed first by Lord Keynes and later elaborated by Robert Triffin. The international bank would operate with countries' central banks exactly as an individual country's central bank operates with the country's commercial banks. All reserves would be held in the form of deposits at the international bank (called *bancor deposits* or bancor balances). International liquidity would be created by the bank making loans to central banks and investing in countries' government securities. The amount and distribution of additional international liquidity would be decided nationally by the international civil servants managing the world bank. The principal problem with this scheme is the requirement that countries give up substantial national sovereignty to the world bank, perhaps a highly desirable but also unlikely prospect.

TRIGONOMETRIC FUNCTIONS. *See* Function.

TRIPLE DAMAGES, also treble damages, are a remedy in antitrust law (Sherman and Clayton acts) whereby a competitor damaged as a result of proved illegal (anticompetitive) behavior of a defendant may recover from the defendant three times the amount of actual monetary damages sustained.

See also Antitrust Policy.

TROUGH. *See* Business Cycles, Phases.

TRUSTEESHIP, in labor unionism, a control technique under which a national union can assume the decision-making functions of a local union by suspending its autonomy. Now limited by the Labor Management Reporting and Disclosure Act of 1959, trusteeships have sometimes been used illegally to assume control of the subordinate organization.

TRUTH IN LENDING. In 1968 the U.S. Senate and the House, riding on a wave of consumerism (an attempt to ban practices that infringe upon individuals' rights as consumers), passed the so-called "Truth-in-Lending Bill". This bill was widely hailed as a significant step forward in consumerism in general and, specifically, in the movement toward full disclosure of the rates on finance charges and other aspects of consumer credit transactions. This law has the dubious merit of merely disclosing credit rates and, therefore, slightly aiding the sophisticated, credit-shopping, middle class; poverty groups still endure outright fraud and higher prices on commodities financed by sellers.

TUCKER, DONALD SKEELE (1884–), American educator noted for contributions to the field of business finance and investment. He is a graduate of Colorado College (1906), receiving an M.A. from Williams College (1912), and a Ph.D. from Columbia (1922). His publications include *Evolution of People's Banks* (1922), *America's Output and Income* (1935), and *Changes in Business Finance* (1949). Tucker, now retired, has been on the faculty at M.I.T., DePauw University, and Northeastern University.

TURNOVER TAX, a tax imposed on the gross monetary value of all business transactions, both productive and distributive, through which a tangible economic good passes. This tax is different from a gross income tax because the latter includes intangible services as well as tangible economic goods.

TWO-TIER GOLD SYSTEM. In addition to the official gold market, meaning the gold-convertibility of official dollars, there is a private gold market, located principally in London. From 1961 to 1968 the private gold price was stabilized at the official gold price of $35 an oz. by means of the *gold pool*. Members of the gold pool were the United States and seven other major countries, and together they bought or sold gold to satisfy any excess demand or excess supply of gold at the pegged price. However, the private demand for gold, especially toward the end of the period, was so great that the gold reserves of these countries were greatly reduced; so in March 1968 the gold pool was disbanded and the private gold price was left free to find its own level. The resulting situation—a free private market for gold coupled with a pegged official price of gold—is called the two-tier gold system.

TYING AGREEMENTS. *See* Tying Contract.

TYING CONTRACT, an agreement between a producer and retailer of a product whereby the retailer, as a condition of acquiring a preferred product for resale, must agree to handle one or more other products of that producer. A variant is "full-line forcing," under which the retailer must handle all products of a producer's line. Tying contracts limit competition by preventing the access of rival producers to a retail market. For example, the retailer may be prevented from carrying a competitor's product available at a lower cost. Or a monopolist may force a tying agreement with several retailers to sustain his position against potential competitors. Tying contracts are prohibited, where their effect is to limit competition substantially, under the Clayton Act, Section 3.

See also Clayton Act; Exclusive Dealership; Full-Line Forcing.

UAW. *See* United Auto Workers.

UNAUTHORIZED WORK STOPPAGES. *See* Wildcat Strikes.

UNBALANCED GROWTH. *See* Balanced Growth.

Robert Triffin

School for weavers in Nigeria exemplifies one way underdeveloped nations try to broaden their economic base by developing new skills, products.

UNCERTAIN PROSPECT. *See* Expected Utility.

UNCERTAINTY, a factor treated some 50 years ago by Frank Knight, University of Chicago economist, in his analysis of profits. He considered profits to be a residual earned by entrepreneurs as a result of correct decisions made in the present that bore fruit at some uncertain future time. Risk did not give rise to profits because risk could be insured against. Under conditions of uncertainty, however, where insufficiency of data makes probability calculation impossible, the decision-maker must rely heavily on intuition and judgment.

See also Entrepreneur; Profit System; Risk.

Consult (22) International, 1968.

UNDERCONSUMPTION THEORY OF BUSINESS CYCLES. This internal theory contends that recessions result from consumption falling behind output as a result of the retention of more income from the amount that might be invested. Underconsumption, therefore, may result from unequal distribution of income, preventing all goods produced from being purchased, or too great a portion of income going into savings, particularly by wealthy or thrifty people. As one major internal force contributing to business cycles, underconsumption acts to lower aggregate demand and causes prices to decline to an unprofitable level.

See also Business Cycles, Theories; Internal Theory.

UNDERDEVELOPED COUNTRIES. *See* Developing Nations; Less Developed Countries.

UNDERDEVELOPMENT, the state of an economy permeated by underemployment of human and material resources. Such economies are typified by low real incomes per capita in comparison with those of the United States, Canada, and Western Europe; illiteracy; poverty; overpopulation; and disease.

About two-thirds of the world's population lives in underdeveloped countries. Income in such countries is usually unequally distributed between a few wealthy land owners and the poor. Often, no middle class of shopkeepers and professional persons exists. A few underdeveloped countries have well-established governments that plan education and highways and offer some degree of social services, but most have limited services and weak government structures. Often, tribal chieftains and religious leaders tend to occupy influential positions.

Development. To raise the general standard of living in underdeveloped countries, many developed nations are providing technical assistance and financial aid, either bilaterally or through international organizations, such as the United Nations and the International Bank for Reconstruction and Development (World Bank). In addition, the private sector is investing in, or constructing plants for, underdeveloped countries, often with the help of credits granted or guaranteed by the developed nations' governmental agencies.

See also Developing Nations; Less Developed Countries; Stages of Growth; Standard of Living.

—Charles Staelin, *University of Michigan*

UNDEREMPLOYMENT refers to a decrease in demand that leads to the withdrawal of labor into occupations with little or no marginal productivity. In other words, employed resources are not being used most efficiently. In industry, for example, when an employer retains a greater number of workers than required during a decrease in demand in order to have sufficient experienced labor available when demand increases, his resources are being underemployed. The result of this underemployment is disguised unemployment. Although the labor is not actually unemployed, it is underemployed.

In rural areas, particularly in underdeveloped countries, there is a high rate of underemployment, stemming from the large percentage of the population engaged in agriculture, which, because it is seasonal, is inherently inefficient. These people cannot be labelled unemployed in the technical sense because they are not seeking work. This underemployment phenomenon also exists in the cities, where people with skills and educations are engaged in low income and underproductive work, when productive, high-income employment is available.

UNDEREMPLOYMENT OF CAPITAL. *See* Underemployment of Productive Capacity.

UNDEREMPLOYMENT OF LABOR. *See* Underemployment of Productive Capacity.

UNDEREMPLOYMENT OF PRODUCTIVE CAPACITY, a level of production making less than optimal use of all of the available factors of production. The productive capacity of an economy is the quantity of goods and services that can be produced using all available factors efficiently. Thus, the productive capacity is determined by the size of the labor force and its skills, the amount of capital equipment and its technology, the quantity and quality of land and other natural resources, and the ability of entrepreneurs to organize these other factors of production. The productive capacity of an economy changes as the quantity or quality of inputs changes.

Underemployment of Labor. In national

income analysis, underemployment of productive capacity is usually defined as a state in which more than 3% to 4% of the labor force is unemployed. Labor is a basic index, because it is the most basic, evident, and easily measured input to use. An unemployed man is a problem to himself, his family, and society. Furthermore, unemployment of labor is often a strong political pressure against congressmen and presidents in office. An owner of a factory may be unhappy about having an idle machine, but it does not threaten the livelihood of other households or the political lives of public officials in the same way that unemployment of labor does.

Underemployment of Capital and Natural Resources. Underemployment of productive capacity is sometimes used to describe a state in which plants and equipment are not being fully utilized. When there is underutilization of capacity in steel and most other major industries, there is, almost certainly, general unemployment; but in small industries, or in industries producing goods for which demand is decreasing, or in industries that have expanded their capacity for their own good, underutilization of capacity need not be accompanied by general unemployment of labor, and such underutilization would not be regarded as a serious general problem.

Underemployment as Inefficent Use. Full employment of productive capacity also means that inputs are being used to produce as much as possible. Some economists speak of underemployment of labor as a problem in achieving full use of productive capacity, meaning that some workers are not being as fully or efficiently employed as they might be. In the study of economic development this interpretation is often used, even though it is impossible to measure or estimate with any confidence.

See also Full Employment.

—Anne Mayhew, *University of Tennessee*

UNDERPRODUCTION occurs when the market price is below the equilibrium price, inducing producers to produce less than consumers are willing to purchase. Overproduction would occur at a price higher than equilibrium, when producers are inclined to produce in excess of demand.

UNDERSUPPLY. *See* Excess Demand.

UNDERVALUATION. A persistent surplus in a nation's balance of payments and a build-up of international reserves reflect an undervalued currency. The rates of exchange prevailing in that country and/or controlled domestic prices make its goods cheaper internationally than they would be if the balance of payments were in equilibrium. Deliberate undervaluation operates to spur exports and dampen imports.

See also Devaluation; Exchange Rates.

Consult (23) Ingram, 1970.

UNDISTRIBUTED PROFITS, post-tax earnings retained after dividend payments. Distributed profits constitute taxable income in the year received; if undistributed, the corporation pays the tax on its taxable earnings but the stockholder gets the advantage of capital appreciation while postponing taxes. Undistributed profits are recorded as part of national income but not in personal income.

See also Corporate Earnings Dividends.

Consult (22) Samuelson, 1973.

UNEMPLOYMENT, DISGUISED. *See* Disguised Unemployment.

UNEMPLOYMENT COMPENSATION. *See* Unemployment Insurance.

UNEMPLOYMENT INSURANCE, temporary income maintenance for workers who become unemployed under the unemployment compensation provisions of the Social Security Act. Recipients receive benefits equal to a fraction of previous wage income (subject to upper and in some states, lower limits). Benefits are financed by federal and state payroll taxes paid by employers.

UNEMPLOYMENT OF LABOR, a term denoting the percentage of people in the labor force who are not working. By definition, those not seeking employment (students, housewives, others) are not in the labor force and thus not considered unemployed. Usually there is said to be excessive unemployment when less than 96% of the labor force is employed. Thus an unemployment rate of about 4% is still considered full employment. The economic cost of unemployment falls both on the society as a result of lost output, and on the individual as a result of lost income.

There are several types of unemployment, including seasonal, frictional, structural, cyclical, and technological.

Seasonal unemployment results from a decrease in the demand for labor due to the changing of the seasons; it is usually found in such fields as agriculture and construction.

Frictional unemployment is the loss of work that occurs when workers change jobs or locations. This is not considered a serious type since it is usually temporary.

Structural unemployment usually results from a major industrial change in a region, causing many people to lose their jobs, as when a major industry either shuts down or relocates.

Cyclical unemployment is the relation-

UNEMPLOYMENT OF LABOR

For the opposite side of the unemployment picture, see the article on FULL EMPLOYMENT. Some of the numerous causes of unemployment are discussed in the articles on CYCLICAL UNEMPLOYMENT, STRUCTURAL UNEMPLOYMENT, and LABOR MOBILITY. For macroeconomic explanations of unemployment see DEFLATIONARY GAP; the unemployment-inflation dual occurrence is explained in PHILLIPS CURVE.

Macroeconomic policy measures designed to reduce unemployment are explained in the article on STABILIZATION POLICY. Specific methods of reducing unemployment or alleviating its impact are described in the articles on MANPOWER POLICY, RETRAINING, MANPOWER DEVELOPMENT AND TRAINING ACT, PUBLIC EMPLOYMENT SERVICE, and UNEMPLOYMENT INSURANCE.

The Subject Maps accompanying LABOR MARKET and WAGES display these and other relationships.

UNEMPLOYMENT RATES, 1971

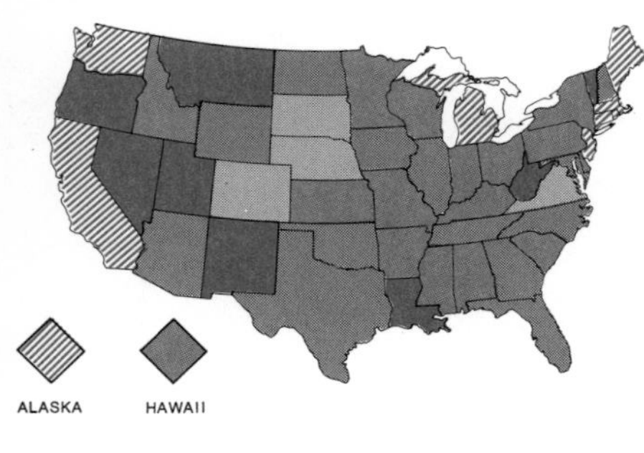

7% or more
6 to 6.9%
5 to 5.9%
4 to 4.9%
Under 4%

SOURCE: *Department of labor.*

UNEMPLOYMENT RATE (PERCENT) 1948-71

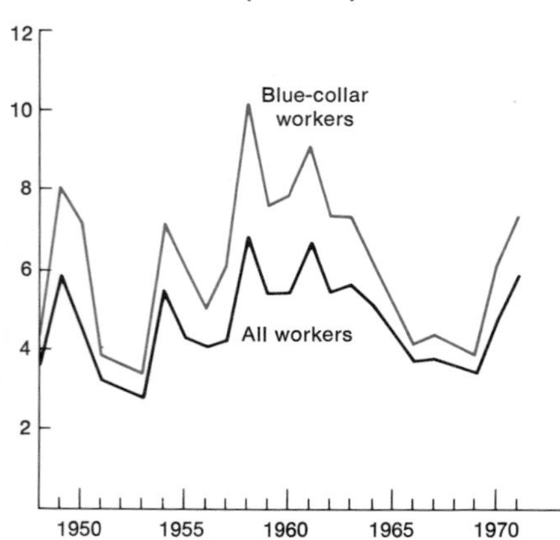

ship between unemployment and the business cycle: the more prosperous the economy, the lower the unemployment rate. This type of unemployment is most severe because it reflects upon the entire nation and not just a subgroup.

Technological unemployment is the displacement of labor that occurs when new techniques, products, or methods of production make jobs obsolete, or too expensive to maintain.

There are also several types of unemployment that are particular to certain groups. For example, there is *hard-core unemployment* which is the unemployment of people with particular problems that keep them from securing employment even in the most prosperous economy. Included in this group are many minority groups, the unskilled and uneducated, as well as the emotionally disturbed.

A second type of discriminatory unemployment is entry unemployment, which is the unemployment that results when workers with no experience find that the competition of the more experienced keeps them from securing employment.

Consult (20) Levitan, 1972.

—William D. Wagoner, *Louisiana State University*

UNFAIR AND DECEPTIVE PRACTICES are those activities of business firms that damage consumers and/or have an adverse effect on competition. Examples are "bait advertising," deceptive pricing, and misbranding and mislabeling. Under Section 5 of the original Federal Trade Commission Act, the FTC was authorized to proceed against business practices doing potential or actual damage to competition (a less rigorous test of damage than restraint of trade found in the Sherman Act). With the Wheeler-Lea Act of 1938, the prohibition was extended to include unfair practices outside the normal antitrust category as well as practices unfair to the general consuming public.

See also Antitrust Policy; Deceptive Advertising; Federal Trade Commission; Unfair Methods of Competition; Wheeler-Lea Act.

UNFAIR LABOR PRACTICES, anti-union actions by employers. The 1930s marked a great turning point for organized labor, and no law aided its cause more than the Wagner Act (1935), which allowed unions to organize and bargain collectively. It also contained unfair labor practices in which employers were forbidden to engage. No comparable restrictions, however, were imposed on unions.

Restrictions on Management. The five unfair labor practices denied to employers were:

(1) to interfere with, restrain, or coerce employees in the exercise of their rights to organize and bargain collectively through representatives of their own choosing;

(2) to dominate or interfere with the formation or administration of any labor organization;

(3) to encourage or discourage membership in unions through discrimination in hiring or in any other phase of employment;

(4) to discharge or otherwise discriminate against an employee because he has filed charges or given testimony under the act;

(5) to refuse to bargain collectively with the representative of his employees.

Restrictions on Labor. The one-sidedness of the Wagner Act was changed by the Taft-Hartley Act (1947), which retained the prohibition of unfair labor practices to the employers but, among other provisions, added a set of seven labor practices denied to labor:

(1) to establish a closed shop;

(2) to cause an employer to discriminate against a worker who has been dismissed from union membership for any reason other than non-payment of dues;

(3) to restrain or coerce workers in exercising their rights to organize;

(4) to refuse to bargain with the employer;

(5) to strike or boycott to force the employer to commit certain acts prohibited in the law;

(6) to charge excessive initiation fees under a union shop;

(7) to cause or attempt to cause an employer to pay for work not performed (the so-called anti-featherbedding provision).

See also Landrum-Griffin Act; Taft-Hartley Act; Wagner Act.

—Leonard G. Schifrin, *College of William and Mary*

UNFAIR METHODS OF COMPETITION are practices designed to damage or eliminate a business firm's competitors illegally. The term is comprehensive, applying to the specific activities prohibited by the Sherman and Clayton Acts as well as the less sharply defined violations of the Federal Trade Commission Act. The prohibition applies to any activity causing a diversion of trade from a competitor other than through normal and legal competition. Though its thrust is on damage to competition or competitors, "unfair and deceptive practices" are also prohibited if the consuming public is damaged. For example, maliciously misrepresenting a competitor's product to weaken its attractiveness to his customers (and divert trade to the violator) would be an unfair method of competition. Deceptive pricing, having the effect of increasing the violator's sales, might damage both competition and the consumer, and would be an "unfair or deceptive practice."

The Federal Trade Commission is given authority to prosecute unfair methods of competition in Section 5 of the Federal Trade Commission Act.

See also Antitrust Policy; Federal Trade Commission; Unfair and Deceptive Practices.

Consult (16) Wilcox, 1971.

—Thomas O. Depperschmidt, *Memphis State University*

UNFAVORABLE BALANCE OF TRADE. *See* Balance of Trade.

UNINCORPORATED BUSINESS INCOME. *See* Income of Unincorporated Business.

UNINTENDED INVESTMENT. *See* Disinvestment.

UNION CONSTITUTION, the document containing the rules and regulations of the organization. Typically the constitution begins with a preamble setting forth the broad goals of the union, and then goes on to outline the internal structure. It will include statements on union government, election of officers, powers of elected officials, membership criteria, and many other subjects of interest, including amendment procedure. The Labor-Management Reporting and Disclosure Act of 1959 specified certain contents of the document.

UNION CONVENTION, the supreme authority in the union structure, holding the legislative, judicial, and executive power of the organization. The unions hold conventions at will (every two years on the average), but under current legislation elections of officers must take place at least every five years. Each local sends delegates to the convention, and each votes based on the number of dues-paying members. The actual conventions range from a managed exercise in union good-will to open fights over issues. Perhaps the greatest effect of the convention results from the informal discussion between leaders of various sections of the country. Thus ideas and methods are spread rapidly throughout the organization.

UNION JURISDICTION. *See* Jurisdiction, Union.

UNION LABEL, a tag or stamp placed on a commodity to show that it has been made by members of a labor union or that it has been made in a union shop. Its purpose is to promote the use of union-made goods.

UNION PAYMENTS. *See* Strike Benefits.

UNION RECOGNITION. *See* Recognition.

UNION SECURITY, the requirements on workers to belong to and support the union that represents them in bargaining. It means, in particular, the type of shop that exists—closed, union, open, agency, or some other type of shop. The union security provisions are stated in the collective bargaining contract and are enforced by the union.

See also Agency Shop; Closed Shop; Open Shop; Union Shop.

UNIONS. *See* Labor Movement.

UNION SHOP, one in which all workers must belong to the union that represents their bargaining unit. The employer may hire whomever he chooses, but new workers who do not belong to the union are required to join, usually within 30 days after they begin work. The union shop arrangement is permissible under federal labor law, although the Taft-Hartley Act modifies it somewhat and, more important, permits its prohibition by individual states in "right-to-work" laws.

UNITARY ELASTICITY. *See* Unit Elasticity.

UNITED AUTOMOBILE WORKERS (UAW), the second largest union in the United States. Organized in the early 1930s by merging a number of AFL locals in the industry, it withdrew in 1936 and joined the CIO. The new organization effectively used the sit-down strike, and in spite of a general protest over the technique, secured union recognition at both General Motors and Chrysler.

Under the expert leadership of Walter Reuther, the UAW continued to grow and to add to its membership workers in areas outside the automotive industry. Its membership currently numbers 1,500,000. In 1967, Reuther withdrew the UAW from the AFL-CIO. In 1970, Reuther died and was succeeded by Leonard Woodcock. Fears that Reuther's death would weaken the union were dispelled when Woodcock successfully led a major strike against General Motors in 1971.

United Auto Workers' president Walter Reuther (right) and vice president Leonard Woodcock at 1967 press conference preceding a major strike.

UNITED STATES NOTES, or greenbacks, were first issued during the Civil War without any backing at all to finance the fighting. After the war they were given a partial gold backing, and in 1878 Congress fixed the total amount in circulation at $347 million (later reduced to $323 million). That quantity still circulates, all of it in $5 bills. In spite of a 50-percent gold backing, the notes are nevertheless not redeemable in gold.

See also Money; Money Supply.

UNITED STATES v. ALUMINUM CO. OF AMERICA, 148 F. 2d 416 (1945). Alcoa had long been the dominant firm in aluminum production, and was the sole domestic manufacturer of virgin ingot in 1937 when the government charged it with monopolizing in violation of the Sherman Act. Judge Learned Hand determined, after considering several alternative definitions, that Alcoa's share of the pertinent market (which excluded secondary aluminum but included Alcoa's primary production for its own use) was 90%.

This market share, said the court, amounted to monopoly. The remaining legal issue was whether the monopoly had been achieved or maintained by means that would indicate illegal monopolization. Judge Hand, in a novel and bold decision, argued that the distinction between the existence and exercise of monopoly power is "purely formal." Alcoa could escape a Sherman Act conviction, he stated, only by showing that monopoly had been thrust upon it, that it was the "passive beneficiary of a monopoly."

Under this extremely stringent standard, Alcoa was found to have monopolized illegally. However innocent its behavior, Judge Hand concluded, it did act purposefully to maintain its market position. This strong presumption against market power which marks the Alcoa decision has not generally been followed in later Sherman Act cases.

See also Abuse Theory; Monopoly Thrust Upon a Firm; United States v. United States Steel Corp.

—Peter Asch, *Rutgers University*

UNITED STATES v. AMERICAN TOBACCO CO., 211 U.S. 106 (1911). In a companion case to *Standard Oil,* the original "tobacco trust" was found by the Supreme Court to violate the Sherman Act. The trust, consisting of five major tobacco manufacturers, controlled about 95 percent of the domestic cigarette industry, and drove numerous competing firms from the market. The Supreme Court held that a dominant market position was not alone sufficient to infer a violation of law. Under the *rule of reason,* the company's intent as evidenced by overt acts was a critical basis for judging legality. The Court found that the record of predatory and ruthless behavior on the part of the tobacco manufacturers supported the claim of Sherman Act violations.

See also United States v. Standard Oil Co. of New Jersey.

UNITED STATES v. E. I. DUPONT AND CO., 353 U.S. 586 (1957). The duPont Company is a major supplier of auto finishes and fabrics to General Motors, the nation's leading automobile manufacturer. The supplier-customer relationship between these two large companies was complicated by the fact that duPont held a 23 percent stock interest in General Motors, an interest acquired several decades earlier. In 1949, the government charged that the original stock acquisition violated Section 7 of the Clayton Act by tending to substantially lessen competition. The government's main argument was that duPont's interest in General Motors had prevented GM from purchasing supplies from duPont's competitors.

The defendant companies argued that their customer-supplier relationship was based solely on objective business considerations. The Supreme Court, however, noting that duPont always supplied the bulk of General Motors' fabric and finish requirements, concluded that the stock acquisition violated original Section 7, and ordered duPont to rid itself of its General Motors holdings.

See also Clayton Antitrust Act.

UNITED STATES v. FIRST NATIONAL CITY BANK. *See* Bank Merger Acts.

UNITED STATES v. NEW YORK GREAT A & P CO., 67 F. Supp. 626 (1946), one of the most controversial cases in antitrust litigation. A & P was charged with price discrimination under Section 2 of the Clayton Act (as amended by Robinson-Patman, 1936) for selling grocery products in certain localities at prices below those of local competitors, to the detriment of those competitors. It was able to do so because of concessions that it, as a major purchaser, was able to extract from manufacturers. A consent decree was negotiated, forbidding A & P to price products so as to eliminate competition, and requiring other minor adjustments in A & P business practices.

The result is controversial because of the intent of antitrust policy being served by the consent decree. A & P clearly was engaging in price competition. It attributed the price concessions on its purchases, which permitted its charging lower prices to customers, to the shrewd bargaining of its buyers. However, local competitors, damaged as a result of the price competition, were provided redress in the decree.

See also Price Discrimination; Robinson-Patman Act.

—Thomas O. Depperschmidt, *Memphis State University*

UNITED STATES v. PHILADELPHIA NATIONAL BANK. *See* Bank Merger Acts.

UNITED STATES v. PROVIDENT NATIONAL BANK. *See* Bank Merger Acts.

UNITED STATES v. STANDARD OIL CO. OF NEW JERSEY, 221 U.S. 1 (1911), is significant in the development of antitrust policy for two reasons. The break-up of Standard Oil into 11 parts was the first major dissolution ordered under the Sherman Act where monopolization was found. And the Supreme Court, despite the judgment against Standard Oil, announced the "rule of reason." Whereas the Sherman Act prohibited every contract, combination, or conspiracy in restraint of trade and every attempt to monopolize, the Standard Oil decision showed that the Court would condemn only "unreasonable" restraints and attempts to monopolize. The rule in effect marked a relaxation of governmental prosecution of antitrust law violations. Standard Oil violated the Sherman Act not by virtue of its position alone, but because its predatory behavior indicated "the intent to drive others from the field and to exclude them from their right to trade."

See also Monopolizing; Predatory Practices; Restraint of Trade.

UNITED STATES v. U. S. STEEL CORPORATION, 251 U.S. 417 (1920). The government charged U.S. Steel with monopolizing and restraining trade in violation of the Sherman Act. The company, which had been formed by consolidation of about 180 separate concerns at the turn of the century, had accounted for about 50 percent of national iron and steel capacity, although its share had since fallen to about 41 percent.

The Supreme Court, upholding a District Court decision, concluded that U. S. Steel had not monopolized in violation of the Sherman Act. In one of the most famous phrases in modern antitrust, the Court stated: ". . . the law does not make mere size an offense, or the existence of unexerted power an offense . . ." U. S. Steel thus could not be found to have monopolized by virtue of its market position alone. In addition, the Court could find no "overt acts" in the company's history that would indicate intent to monopolize. The company was therefore acquitted despite a position indicating significant market power. This case provided a clear antitrust precedent for many years: a company does not violate the law simply by growing large; it must also engage in somehow wrongful conduct in the process of achieving its growth.

See also Monopolizing; Sherman Antitrust Act; United States v. Aluminum Co. of America.

—Peter Asch, *Rutgers University*

UNIT ELASTICITY, or UNITARY ELASTICITY, of supply. The supply of a product is said to be of unitary elasticity, over some small price range, when the computed coefficient of elasticity is equal to 1. Assume that the price of commodity "Z" changes by some small percentage. If the response on the part of the producers of that commodity is such as to increase output by an identical percentage, then the computed coefficient of elasticity will exactly equal one and this would be called unitary elasticity. The importance of this concept is that it is a watershed; coefficients greater than 1 are called elastic, coefficients less than one are considered inelastic.

UNIT ELASTICITY OF DEMAND. A demand curve is said to possess unitary elasticity of demand if a given percentage change in the price of the commodity in question results in the same percentage change in quantity demanded. The coefficient of elasticity in such a case will be minus one. Every downward sloping demand curve will have at least one point on it with unitary elasticity. For the typical downward sloping linear demand curve, this point of unitary elasticity will occur at the point on the quantity-demanded axis where the marginal revenue of additional price change equals zero. A special class of demand curves possess unitary elasticity throughout. When these curves are graphed, they always assume the shape of a rectangular hyperbola asymptotic to both axes of the graph.

UNIT OF ACCOUNT. *See* Money.

UNSECURED BONDS. *See* Debentures.

UNSTABLE EQUILIBRIUM. *See* Stable Equilibrium.

USE TAX. *See* Taxation: *Glossary.*

UTILITIES, PUBLIC *See* Public Utilities.

UTILITY. Underlying the basic theory of consumer behavior are two fundamental assumptions: (1) when considering any set of commodity bundles, the consumer is always able to rank these bundles in the order of his preferences; (2) when making a choice among the bundles that are within his budget, the consumer always chooses the most preferred bundle. More formally, the first assumption postulates the existence, for each consumer, of a complete *preference ordering,* while the second assumption says in effect that the consumer is a hedonist.

Utility Index. Given the preference ordering of a consumer, it is possible (with an additional assumption of a technical nature) to assign numbers to all commodity bundles in such a way that they reflect the order of the consumer's preferences. The number assigned to a particular bundle is called a *utility index.* It has no intrinsic meaning, and should *not* be interpreted as a measure of the satisfaction which the consumer derives from the respective commodity bundle. The utility index of a commodity bundle assumes a meaning only when compared with that of another bundle, and all that can be inferred from such a comparison is that, for any two bundles, the bundle with the higher utility index is preferred by the consumer to the other bundle.

Utility Function. It may be possible to describe the relationship between the quantities of the various commodities in a particular bundle and the utility index of the bundle by

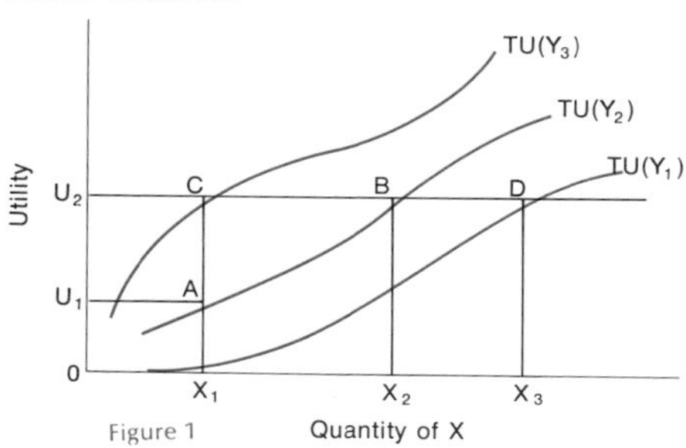

Figure 1

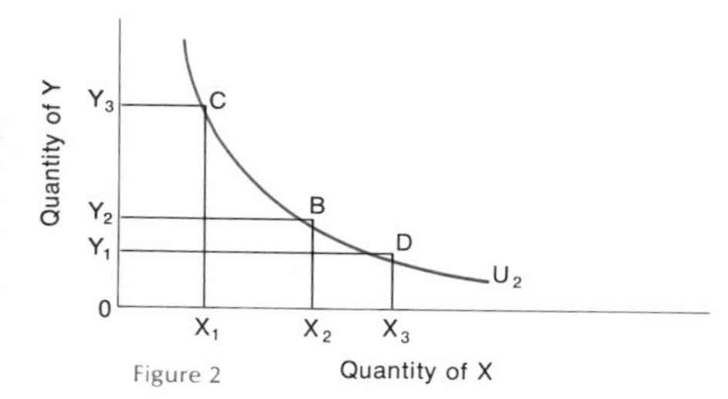

Figure 2

means of a mathematical formula, or function; such a function is called a utility function. Consequently, when a consumer chooses the most preferred bundle, he is in fact choosing a bundle for which the utility function attains its maximum value. It is for this reason that theories of consumer behavior are often formulated as a utility maximization problem.

—Josef Hadar, *Case Western Reserve University*

UTILITY COMMISSIONS. *See* Public Utility Commissions.

UTILITY ENTRY. *See* Public Utility Entry.

UTILITY FUNCTION. The modern theory of consumer behavior is based on the notion of a preference ordering, a ranking of all commodity bundles in accordance with the preferences of a consumer. It is also assumed that it is possible to assign numbers (utility indexes) to all commodity bundles to reflect the consumer's preference ordering; that is, for any two different bundles, the preferred bundle is assigned a higher number, and if the consumer considers the two bundles as being equally desirable, they are assigned the same number. The functional relationship between commodity bundles and the utility index is referred to as the utility function.

Utility Curves. Figure 1 illustrates a utility function for the case of bundles with two commodities, X and Y. Commodity X is measured on the horizontal axis, and the utility index U on the vertical axis. The curves shown are total utility curves: each curve shows the utility associated with various bundles containing some fixed amounts of commodity Y, and $Y_3 > Y_2 > Y_1$. For example, the curve TU (Y_2) shows the utility of bundles containing Y_2 units of Y and various amounts of X. The fact that each TU curve has a positive slope reflects the assumption of greediness; that is, a consumer always prefers a larger bundle to a smaller one, where a larger bundle is one with more of at least one commodity and no less of any other commodity, compared to the other bundle. Thus, the bundle denoted by B is larger than bundle A, and, therefore, the utility of bundle B is higher than the utility of bundle A. Similarly, bundle C is preferred to bundle A.

The change in the utility index resulting from a small increase in one commodity is called the marginal utility of that commodity. For example, moving along the curve TU (Y_2) in Figure 1 from bundle A toward bundle B causes the utility index to increase. These increases in utility are the marginal utilities of successive increments in X. Geometrically speaking, the marginal utility of X is measured by the slope of the respective TU curve. The greediness assumption says, in effect, that the marginal utility of every good is positive.

Indifference Curves. A utility function may also be represented by certain curves in the commodity space, the XY-plane. For example, mapping the points C, B, and D from Figure 1 into the XY-plane yields the three points shown in Figure 2. Because these three bundles have the same level of utility, they are considered to be equally desirable by the consumer. He is indifferent between them. If all the points on the horizontal line going through points C, B, and D in Figure 1 are mapped into Figure 2, one obtains a curve such as that labeled U_2. All commodity bundles represented by points on that curve have the same level of utility: the consumer is indifferent between them. For this reason such a curve is called an indifference curve, or isoutility curve.

For any two bundles on an indifference curve, one bundle has more of X and less of Y than the other bundle; in other words, an indifference curve has a negative slope. A movement along the indifference curve in Figure 2 from bundle C to bundle B shows how commodity X is substituted for commodity Y to keep the level of utility constant. The curvature of the indifference curve, that is, the fact that it is convex to the origin, implies that the indifference curve becomes flatter as the amount of X is increased. But the slope of the indifference curve indicates the rate at which commodity Y is reduced for each additional unit of X added. For this reason the slope of an indifference curve measures the marginal rate of substitution (rate of substitution in consumption) between the commodities in question. If the indifference curve is convex to the origin, as in Figure 2, the marginal rate of substitution decreases as X is increased. This property is known as diminishing marginal rate of substitution. One can draw an indifference curve for any level of utility. A diagram of several indifference curves is referred to as an indifference map.

Consult (12) Ferguson, 1972; Hadar, 1973; Stigler, 1966.

—Josef Hadar, *Case Western Reserve University*

UTILITY INDEX. *See* Utility Function.

UTILITY PRICE, PUBLIC. *See* Public Utility Price.

UTOPIAN SOCIALISM. *See* Owen, Robert; Pre-Marxian Socialism.

UZAWA, HIROFUMI (1928–), Japanese-born mathematical economist and contributor to the development of economic growth theory. He received a B.S. from the University of Tokyo in 1951, and a Doctor of Science degree from Tohoku University in 1962. He is author of *Studies in Linear and Nonlinear Programming*

(1958, with Arrow and Hurwicz), *Readings in the Modern Theory of Economic Growth* (1969, with Stiglitz), and various journal articles in the field. Uzawa became professor of economics at the University of Chicago in 1964.

VACATIONS, often termed annual leaves, are paid time off earned by employees for services rendered to their employers. The duration of earned vacations varies with individual companies and usually increases with the length of employment. Average vacations range from two weeks to a month in most companies and can be taken all at once or a day at a time. In many companies, the employee has the option to elect to be paid in cash for annual leave not taken.

VALUE, DISCOUNTED. *See* Discounted Value.

VALUE, PRESENT. *See* Present Value.

VALUE, SURPLUS. *See* Surplus Value.

VALUE ADDED by a firm, approximately equivalent to the difference between its sales and its purchases of intermediate output—ingredients that enter into the fabrication of sold output. The value added by a firm is equivalent to the factor incomes that the firm must pay out. What a firm receives through its sales must be distributed to the firms from which it buys or to the factors it employs. Recognizing this feature yields the conclusion that summing up either the value added or the factor income generated by each firm will yield equivalent dollar magnitudes, equivalent estimates of GNP.

The summation of the value added by each firm is also equivalent to the sum of final output. To make this fact clear, take the cost of a commodity purchased by a consumer. The cost of this item to the consumer will equal the sum of the value added by each firm that participates in the production and distribution of the commodity. Thus, the price of a loaf of bread received by a retailer is partly paid out to factors and to bakers, bakers in turn will distribute its revenues to factors and suppliers, and these suppliers will distribute their proceeds to factors and still other suppliers. Thus, in the calculation of GNP the sales of all firms are not added together, only the value added by each firm. If all sales were added together—taken as final output—many transactions would be counted more than once; total sales far exceeds the sum of factor incomes, the value of final output, or, identically, the sum of the value added by each firm.

—Frank J. Bonello, *University of Notre Dame*

VALUE-ADDED TAX, tax with a base defined as the net "value-added" at each stage of the production process. Value-added is the payment for wages and other factors of production that increase the value of materials and other inputs that a business purchases. It is determined by subtracting the purchase cost of a good from its selling price. Such a tax can be based on sales, with allowances for taxes incorporated in the prices of purchased goods, or it can be based directly on each company's value-added.

This type of tax is in use in several European nations and in at least one state (Michigan) and has recently been the subject of discussion for use in the United States. In other nations, it has usually acted as a substitute for some sales taxes.

VALUE AND CAPITAL (1939). *See* Hicks, John R.

VALUE PRODUCTIVITY. *See* Factor Productivity.

VARIABLE, a symbol, denoted by a letter whose numerical magnitude can change. Some common variables in economics are quantity demanded, consumption, price, and profits. Any variable is allowed to assume different values from a given set of numbers, usually positive real numbers in economics. If these values can be arranged so that there are no gaps or holes in the set, however small, then the variable is said to be continuous. Discontinuous or discrete variables take only certain values from the appropriate number set, such as integer (whole number) values. Whether a variable is considered continuous or discrete often depends on the units in which it is measured and the convenience of the researcher.

If one variable (y) is related to another variable (x) in such a way that the value of x determines the value of y, then y is called the dependent variable and x the independent variable. The set of numbers from which the independent variable can assume its values is called the domain of x. The corresponding set of values for the dependent variable is called the range of y.

—Carlisle E. Moody, Jr., *College of William and Mary*

VARIABLE COST OF PRODUCTION. *See* Average Fixed Cost of Production.

VARIABLE COST PER UNIT. *See* Average Variable Cost of Production.

VARIANCE. *See* Dispersion.

VARIANCE, ANALYSIS OF. *See* Analysis of Variance.

VARIATION. *See* Dispersion.

VAULT CASH, coin and paper currency held on

bank premises to meet the immediate demands of depositors wishing to withdraw cash from their accounts. United States banks keep 2% to 3% of their deposits in vault cash.

Thorstein Veblen

VEBLEN, THORSTEIN (1857-1929), founder of the institutionalist school, a pessimistic American critic of society and the economic system. His most important book, *The Theory of the Leisure Class* (1899), approached economics from a broad evolutionary perspective and introduced such terms as leisure class and conspicuous consumption. Veblen felt that the structure of society and the economy could be best viewed as the outcome of a process of natural selection of institutions. However, institutions do not change as rapidly as society, thus creating a continual state of conflict.

In the *Leisure Class* and other works, Veblen attacked marginalist and conventional economics on a number of grounds. He felt that the view of the entrepreneur as a risk bearer was basically incorrect and that marginalist theory supported the present income and wealth distribution. Veblen wished to replace conventional theory with an exposure of the business system and its effect upon man.

While much was wrong with Veblen's work, it did confront economics with questions and problems which conventional theory had generally ignored until that time.

See also Conspicuous Consumption; Institutionalism.

—Clyde A. Haulman, *College of William and Mary*

VELOCITY OF CIRCULATION, the speed with which money changes hands. Transactions velocity is the number of times on the average that each dollar is spent during a given year. Income velocity is the number of times that each dollar becomes income during the year. Income velocity for a nation can be measured by dividing national income by the money supply.

See also Equation Exchange.

Raymond Vernon

VERNON, RAYMOND (1913-), American economist noted for his work in the areas of international business and economic development. He is a graduate of the City College of New York (1933), and he received a Ph.D. from Columbia (1941), and an M.A. from Harvard (1959). His publications include *Metropolis 1985* (1962), *Dilemma of Mexico's Development* (1965), *The Manager in the International Economy* (1968), and *Sovereignty at Bay* (1971). Vernon has been active in public service, and has served as acting director of the office of economic defense of the Department of State (1949-54) and director of the New York metropolitan region study (1956-59). He became professor at the Harvard Graduate School of Business in 1959.

VERTICAL DEMAND CURVE, a demand curve that intersects the quantity axis of a rectilinear coordinate system and rises from that intersection point with an infinite slope. The economic implication of a vertical demand curve is that a given quantity of the product in question will be demanded regardless of whatever level the price of that commodity might reach. This type of demand curve displays perfectly inelastic demand: the total expenditure on a commodity and its price will always change in the same direction.

VERTICAL MERGER, a combination of firms at different stages of the production process into one business unit. The result of such a merger is also called "vertical integration." A firm is said to integrate "backward" when, for example, it absorbs a firm supplying to it, "forward" when it acquires another firm to which it supplies, such as a wholesale or retail outlet. The legality of vertical mergers is subject to the same test as other mergers: does its effect tend to lessen competition or create a monopoly?

See also Celler-Kefauver Act; Clayton Act; Merger; Monopoly.

VERY LONG RUN, a period in which all variables are subject to change. Under the assumptions of the short run and the long run, technological change was not possible. In the very long run any technological possibility is open to the firm. The technological improvements implemented within the firm may be either internal or external. Decisions in the very long run must take cognizance of technological change.

See also Long Run.

VISIBLE GOODS AND SERVICES. The current account of a balance of payments is made up of *visible* and *invisible* items. Visible items are physical, tangible goods which can pass through customs and be quantitatively identified and on which a value can be placed. These characteristics make visible items subject to the levying of tariffs or imposition of quotas. Merchandise exports and imports are the visible items in the current account and it is with respect to these that the most reliable quantitative data is obtained. An automobile imported from Germany into the United States is an obvious example of a visible item in the current account. Just as visible would be Germans traveling in the United States, but tourist expenditures are classified as invisible items by balance of payments criteria.

See also Invisible Goods and Services.

VOLUNTARY ASSOCIATION. *See* Associationism.

WAGE AND HOUR LAW. *See* Fair Labor Standards Act (1938).

WAGE CRITERIA are devices used by both labor and management to aid in the determination of wage rates. Of the several wage criteria used in collective bargaining, cost-of-living and ability-to-pay are the most frequently used today.

The ability-to-pay criterion states that justified cost of living wage increases can only be granted if management is in a position to be able to pay the higher wage rate.

The cost-of-living wage criterion bases its justification for higher wages on the rise in the cost of living as reflected in higher prices. To adjust for the loss of real income that may occur with inflation, a bargaining contract may include an escalator clause, specifying a precise relationship between changes in the cost of living and changes in the wage rate. These clauses therefore provide for an "open end" increase in wage rates.

Other wage criteria sometimes used are maintenance of take-home pay despite the reduction of hours worked, and improvement in productivity.

Consult (20) Baerwald, 1967; Bloom, 1965; Cohan, 1966.

—William D. Wagoner, *Louisiana State University*

WAGE DIFFERENTIALS, differences in wage rates that occur either for rational or nonrational reasons.

Rational wage differentials, or equalizing wage differentials, are paid to compensate for the non-money differences among jobs. A major job difference is risk or danger, as in steeplejacking, skin diving or combat service. Another rational wage differential is extra pay for unpleasant or inconvenient jobs—workers on a graveyard shift usually receive a night differential, generally a certain percentage of their wage rate.

The nonrational or nonequalizing wage differential is based on such illogical reasons as peculiarities of places and practices, historical accidents, and the relative skill of different groups in gaining wage increases. For example, certain union workers earn more than nonunion workers of the same trade, and many minority group workers are paid less than whites.

WAGE DISPERSION. *See* Wage Structure.

WAGE FLEXIBILITY means that wages change with changing conditions in the labor market. The degree of flexibility determines the impact on employment of a change in the demand for labor. Assuming flexible wages, and a decrease in demand, a reduction in the wages workers are willing to accept permits employment to hold up rather than decrease. Flexible wages, as do flexible prices, permit the market system to operate.

WAGE GUIDEPOSTS. Although wage and price control by government is somewhat acceptable during times of war, in peacetime it is looked upon with disfavor. For this reason, government has experimented with a system of controls known as wage and price guideposts, which indicate to both management and labor the limits of wage and price changes that are compatible with economic stability. Adherence to these guideposts is usually voluntary, with no penalty for violation.

In 1962, when high levels of unemployment existed along with inflation, President Kennedy, through his Council of Economic Advisers, announced a set of voluntary guidelines for wage and price changes. The general guide for noninflationary wage behavior was that the rate of increase in wage rates in each industry be equal to the trend rate of over-all productivity increase. In addition, the guide for noninflationary price behavior called for price reduction if the industry's rate of productivity increase exceeded the overall rate, and it called for price increases if the industry's rate of production increase was below the overall rate. For the case where the two rates were equal, stable prices should exist.

These guidelines seemed to have been fairly successful from 1962 to 1964. In 1965 and 1966, government used its position as a purchaser, subsidizer, and regulator to influence the use of guideposts in such industries as copper, steel, and aluminum. In 1969 and 1970, with inflationary pressures beginning to mount, interest in wage and price regulations was again revived. New wage and price guideposts were administered under President Nixon. However, guideposts did not seem to be as helpful this time in relieving inflationary pressures, and in 1971 a ninety-day wage and price freeze was put into effect.

—William D. Wagoner, *Louisiana State University*

Cartoon reflecting AFL-CIO president George Meany's discontent with Nixon wage-price policies.

WAGE LEVEL of a country is a composite of a wide range of different specific wage rates. Usually the higher the demand for labor in relation to the supply of labor, the higher the wage rates.

The wage level depends upon several factors, including (1) the amount of capital a country has available, (2) natural resources, (3) the level of technology and (4) the extent and nature of education and training of labor. The higher the productivity of labor, the higher the wage level. For this reason, the United States ranks highest in wage levels of all countries.

A problem arising from a rising wage level is that, as money wages begin to increase, the supply of labor available also begins to increase and the price level to rise, often causing a decrease in real wages.

WAGE PATTERNS is a term often used in labor

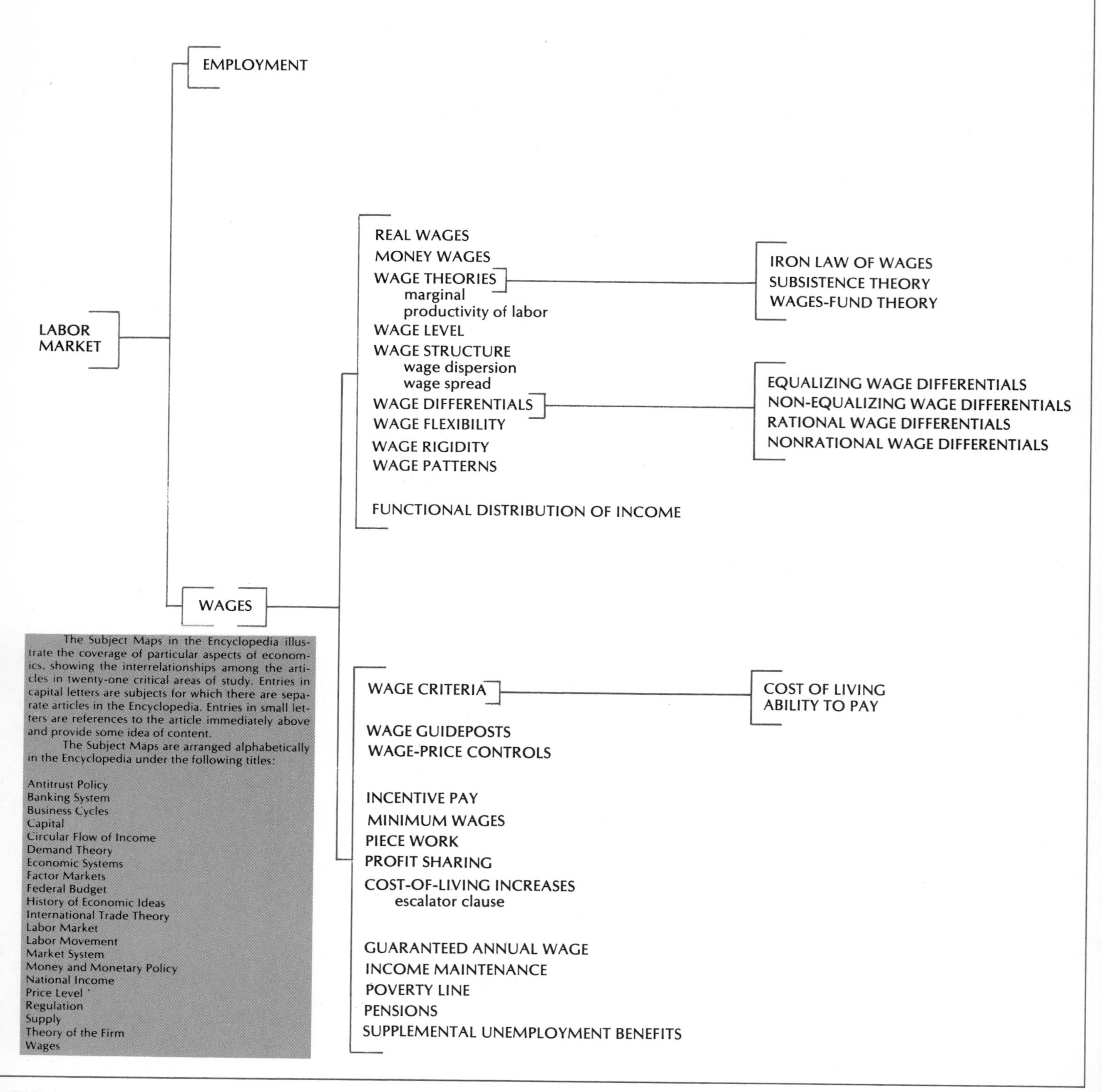
WAGES
EMPLOYMENT
LABOR MARKET
WAGES
REAL WAGES
MONEY WAGES
WAGE THEORIES
marginal productivity of labor
WAGE LEVEL
WAGE STRUCTURE
wage dispersion
wage spread
WAGE DIFFERENTIALS
WAGE FLEXIBILITY
WAGE RIGIDITY
WAGE PATTERNS
FUNCTIONAL DISTRIBUTION OF INCOME
IRON LAW OF WAGES
SUBSISTENCE THEORY
WAGES-FUND THEORY
EQUALIZING WAGE DIFFERENTIALS
NON-EQUALIZING WAGE DIFFERENTIALS
RATIONAL WAGE DIFFERENTIALS
NONRATIONAL WAGE DIFFERENTIALS
WAGE CRITERIA
COST OF LIVING
ABILITY TO PAY
WAGE GUIDEPOSTS
WAGE-PRICE CONTROLS
INCENTIVE PAY
MINIMUM WAGES
PIECE WORK
PROFIT SHARING
COST-OF-LIVING INCREASES
escalator clause
GUARANTEED ANNUAL WAGE
INCOME MAINTENANCE
POVERTY LINE
PENSIONS
SUPPLEMENTAL UNEMPLOYMENT BENEFITS
The Subject Maps in the Encyclopedia illustrate the coverage of particular aspects of economics, showing the interrelationships among the articles in twenty-one critical areas of study. Entries in capital letters are subjects for which there are separate articles in the Encyclopedia. Entries in small letters are references to the article immediately above and provide some idea of content.
The Subject Maps are arranged alphabetically in the Encyclopedia under the following titles:
Antitrust Policy
Banking System
Business Cycles
Capital
Circular Flow of Income
Demand Theory
Economic Systems
Factor Markets
Federal Budget
History of Economic Ideas
International Trade Theory
Labor Market
Labor Movement
Market System
Money and Monetary Policy
National Income
Price Level
Regulation
Supply
Theory of the Firm
Wages

economics to show the spread of an idea in collective bargaining across an industry or the economy. Thus, one firm will be the "pattern setter" in an industry, and the other firms may be expected to follow the pattern set. The wage package—that is, the total of the payments made to an employee—can often be traced from firm to firm and from industry to industry, and the pattern can be easily observed.

WAGE-PRICE CONTROL, an incomes policy to curb inflation through mandatory limits on wage-price changes. Wage-price controls have been wartime policies only. For example, during World War II (1941–46) the National War Labor Board and the Office of Price Administration were set up to stabilize wages and prices. The Office of Price Stabilization effected similar controls during the Korean War (1950–53). However, because these controls were not strictly enforced, they had relatively little effect.

For nearly two decades after the Korean War, the only incomes policy used was the wage-price guideposts, voluntary guidelines for labor and management. The guideposts proved successful under President Kennedy, but in 1971 President Nixon, having been unable to relieve inflationary pressures through guidelines, resorted to a wage-price freeze for ninety days. The first freeze ever placed on wages and prices during ostensible peacetime, the policy met with great controversy but was moderately successful in curbing excessive inflationary pressures.

See also Incomes Policy.

Consult (7) Levitan, 1972.

—William D. Wagoner, *Louisiana State University*

WAGE-PRICE FREEZE. *See* Wage-Price Control.

WAGE-PRICE GUIDEPOSTS, incomes policies used mainly during inflationary periods to stabilize wages and prices through voluntary guidelines for labor and management to follow, preventing real income from decreasing. Unlike wage-price controls, these guideposts carry no penalty for violation.

In 1962 President Kennedy and his Council of Economic Advisors set up some guideposts, which proved to be very successful and lasted through 1964. In other instances, the government has been able to use its influence as a purchaser, regulator, and subsidizer to enforce guidelines. In 1969, with unemployment beginning to rise along with inflationary pressure, new interest in a wage-price policy arose. President Nixon announced a set of guidelines that same year. However, they were unsuccessful and in August 1971 were replaced by a wage-price freeze.

See also Incomes Policy.

WAGE-PUSH INFLATION, essentially cost-push inflation where the prime mover has been identified as union wage demands in excess of productivity gains. The increased costs to the firm are passed to the consumer as higher prices.

WAGE RIGIDITY refers to a situation in which, for whatever reason, wages do not respond to the changing conditions in the labor market. Wage rates are difficult to change, particularly in a downward direction, but to the degree that wages are sticky, the market cannot work as it should. For example, a wage level that does not change in the face of a decreased demand for labor can only result in a decrease in the number of people employers can hire. On the other hand, wages that are variable permit the labor market to work efficiently.

WAGES, the price paid for labor, represent a cost to the employer, income for the worker. As income (constituting about 70% of national income) wages include "in-kind" income, such as room and board furnished to the worker by the employer, as well as cash payments. These represent a worker's money wages, as distinguished from his real wages or purchasing power. If prices increase at a faster rate than an individual's money wages, his real wages are decreasing.

Wages are usually stated as a rate on an hourly basis. For example, the minimum wage in the United States in 1971 was $1.60 per hour. Conflict over what the wage rate of workers should be often arises, wherefore wages often have to be decided upon by the collective bargaining process.

In many industries a wage structure is used. A wage structure is a hierarchy of jobs to which wage rates are attached. This is often done by the use of a labor grade, a ranked classification, with each grade having specifications as to the amount of skill, experience, and seniority a worker needs to qualify for that grade. Within each grade there is often a wage spread with a maximum and a minimum rate.

A second way in which wages are paid is by the incentive system. This system may pay workers according to the amount of work actually done, so much per piece produced or a commission on goods sold. Two other forms of incentive pay are bonuses and profit sharing.

Wages can help allocate labor to its best alternative use. As wage rates in an industry increase, for example, more and more labor becomes available to that industry. Wages also function in determining the overall volume of employment. Up to a certain level, higher wage rates induce more and more people to enter the labor force.

—William D. Wagoner, *Louisiana State University*

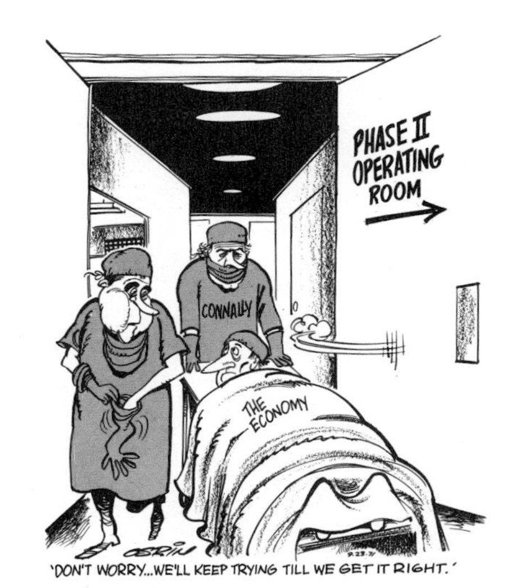

Ailing economy may require such heroic measures as wage-price control, though treatment may induce side effects which need further attention.

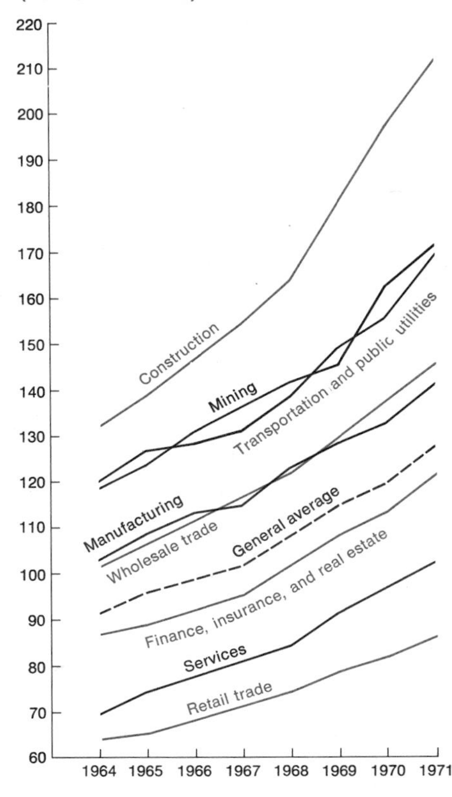

Leon Walras

WAGES-FUND THEORY, evolved in the latter part of the eighteenth century, stated that the rate of wages was a function of the ratio between the amount of funds available for paying wages and the amount of workers. Under this theory, wages could only rise if there was an increase in the fund or "capital," or a decrease in the number of workers. This theory was often used to prove that an attempt by workers to raise real wages was futile.

WAGE SPREAD. *See* Wage Structure.

WAGE STRUCTURE, a hierarchy of jobs, ranked in ascending or descending order according to their importance, with wage rates allotted to each job.

For simplicity, jobs are often classified into labor grades with each grade having a wage spread with a minimum and a maximum rate and usually progressive steps within the grade. The use of this rate range allows management to recognize both seniority and individual merit. Most government jobs use this type of wage structure. A second wage structure method is the concept, pushed by unions, of equal pay for equal work. However, problems often arise in dealing with this type of wage determination because it is often difficult to translate a ranking of jobs into a system of money wages satisfactorily.

Wage structures are set up by management or through the collective bargaining process, and changes in the wage rates within the structure are usually adjusted periodically for increases in the cost of living.

WAGE THEORIES have been in existence almost as long as the science of economics. Although Adam Smith formulated no actual theory of wages, he did set a pattern of thought in regard to minimum levels of pay.

The Iron Law of Wages was one of the first theories of wages. A concept of the classical economists, namely David Ricardo and Thomas Malthus, it stated that wages tend to equal what the worker needs to maintain a bare subsistence level of living. It further stated that higher wages result in increased population, thus increased demand for food, thus rising food prices, thus a drop in real income.

The Iron Law gave way to a more sophisticated wage fund theory presented by John Stuart Mill in 1848. Mill stated that there is a set wage fund at any given time, and that the only way a worker's wages could increase would be by a decrease in the number of workers.

The third major wage theory was the marginal productivity theory, under which the worker is paid a wage rate equal to the marginal output.

Consult (20) Baerwald, 1967.

COMING UP!
—Herblock in Winston-Salem (N. C.) Journal

Cartoon shows Wagner Act bound for 1937 Supreme Court test of constitutionality. It passed.

WAGNER ACT (1935), organized labor's greatest single legislative victory, granting workers the explicit right to organize and bargain collectively and requiring management to recognize these unions and to bargain with them. To promote these ends, the law, also known as the National Labor Relations Act, denied to management certain "unfair labor practices." The National Labor Relations Board was set up to administer the act.

Explicit, bold, and comprehensive in its support of organized labor, much of its content derived from earlier legislation, particularly the Railway Labor Act of 1926 and the short-lived National Industrial Recovery Act (NIRA) of 1933. Passed by Congress within a few weeks of the Supreme Court's decision declaring the NIRA unconstitutional, the Wagner Act resurrected and greatly expanded the protections to labor contained in Section 7 (a) of the defunct law.

Bolstering Labor's Power. The act states that "employees shall have the right to self-organization, to form, join, or assist labor organizations, to bargain collectively through representatives of their own choosing, and to engage in concerted activities for the purpose of collective bargaining or other mutual aid or protection." The law protected these rights by prohibiting management from engaging in certain acts, designated as "unfair labor practices," such as refusal to bargain collectively, or interference with or discrimination against workers or unions in their organization, administration, or bargaining.

The constitutionality of the act could not be taken for granted; however, the Supreme Court, in the landmark case *National Labor Relations Board v. Jones and Laughlin Steel Corporation,* upheld the validity of the law. With this decision, the rapid growth of the labor movement, which would bring it quickly to large size and substantial power, was assured.

Counterbalance Needed. But the growth of the labor movement itself made the Wagner Act too limited to serve as the key labor law. It was recognized as totally one-sided, designed to aid unionism and restrict management in labor relations. Certain restrictions on labor were deemed necessary, lest its newly developed power be used without restraint. Limitations on unions in regard to their actions against employers and non-union employees were therefore added in the Taft-Hartley Act of 1947, and the balance of power between labor and employers, as in 1935, would again move toward equalization.

See also National Industrial Recovery Act; Railway Labor Act; Taft-Hartley Act.

—Leonard G. Schifrin, *College of William and Mary*

WAGNER-PEYSER ACT. *See* Public Employment Service.

WALRAS, LEON (1834–1910), French economist, principally known for his authorship of *Elements of Pure Economics* (1874–77), a classical work in the area of pure economic theory. In addition to including an analysis of value and marginal utility similar to that of Jevons and Menger, this outstanding work was a pioneering effort in applying the tool of mathematical analysis to general economic equilibrium under, in Walras's words, "a regime of perfectly free competition." In other words, it provides a conceptual solution to the problems of price equilibrium, quantities of products, and the productive factors.

In his major attempt to solve the problem of linking the various markets which constitute the economy, Walras developed a system requiring perfect competition, freedom of entry, mobility, and price flexibility. The system's most notable characteristic was Walras's effort to demonstrate, through mathematical analysis, that a perfectly competitive economy would tend to approximate equilibrium positions.

The Walrasian system, being presumed the supreme representation of classical and neoclassical economics, was a prime focus of those who attacked what they saw as a dichotomy between the theories of relative prices and money and the theory of the price level. They argued that in the Walrasian system the price level is indeterminate. With such arguments, the Walrasian system thus provided at least the point of departure for further contributions in the field of economic analysis.

—Clyde A. Haulman, *College of William and Mary*

WASTE. *See* Economic Efficiency.

WEAK ROAD-STRONG ROAD PROBLEM arises because the Interstate Commerce Commission, as a practical necessity, sets uniform rates for whole groups of competing railroads. Under these uniform rates some railroads (strong roads) have more than adequate earnings while other (weak roads) receive insufficient earnings.

Suggested possible solutions to the problem include consolidation of railroads into a few large systems and government ownership and operation of railroads. To the extent that the problem is not dealt with adequately, it is likely that some useful lines will be abandoned.

WEALTH OF NATIONS, THE. Adam Smith's *An Inquiry into the Nature and Causes of the Wealth of Nations* (1776) was the first volume to develop a general theory of economics and apply that theory to the explanation of various aspects of economic life. Two general themes dominate: (1) that the division of labor is the root of much of the economic progress of man; (2) that harmony of interest guides society, wherein each individual seeking to improve his own condition contributes to the betterment of society through his actions. Based upon these concepts, Smith analyzes the workings of the economic system and suggests the policies which he feels are necessary to promote economic growth and development. In addition, the *Wealth of Nations* is centered on the concept that the wealth of a nation stems from its treasury, as the mercantilists felt, or from its agricultural sector, as the Physiocrats believed.

Smith's work is divided into five books or sections dealing with (1) production, (2) distribution, (3) economic development, (4) economic history, and (5) public finance. The first two are the most important since they consider the theory of value, market price, wage theory, the theory of profit, rent theory, and capital. Smith's statement of several value theories and his inability to deal with rent theory create problems. However, his treatment of important aspects of price theory and his consideration of factors creating different wage rates, in addition to his concept of declining profits, laid the foundation for classical economics. This, combined with his treatment of other economic phenomena, marks the emergence of economics as a discipline and set the stage for later advances in theory.

See also Classical Economics; Smith, Adam.

—Clyde A. Haulman, *College of William and Mary*

WEBB, SIDNEY JAMES (1859–1947), and **BEATRICE POTTER** (1858–1943), Lord and Lady Passfield, founders of the London School of Economics (1895) and, with George Bernard Shaw, guiding spirits of the socialist Fabian Society, the Webbs made important contributions to political and social thought in England during the early part of the twentieth century. Central to Fabian thought was the concept of the inevitability of gradualness in the development of socialism, with a democratic government planning and controlling this development. Their approach to economics emphasized the realities of the situation rather than theoretical, abstract concepts.

See also Fabian Society.

WEBB-POMERENE ACT (1918) exempts joint marketing associations of American firms selling in foreign countries from prosecution under the Sherman Act for activities such as market sharing and joint price setting, so long as these association activities are not conducted domestically. About 30 such associations exist.

See also Cartels; Market Sharing; Sherman Antitrust Act.

AN

INQUIRY

INTO THE

Nature and Caufes

OF THE

WEALTH OF NATIONS.

By ADAM SMITH, LL.D. and F.R.S.
Formerly Profeffor of Moral Philofophy in the Univerfity of GLASGOW.

IN TWO VOLUMES.

VOL. I.

LONDON:
PRINTED FOR W. STRAHAN; AND T. CADELL, IN THE STRAND.
MDCCLXXVI.

In this volume, Adam Smith developed the first general theory of economics as a discrete discipline.

Beatrice and Sidney Webb

Max Weber, in a 1920 oil painting.

Murray Weidenbaum

WELFARE ECONOMICS

For one article closely related to welfare economics, consult PARETO OPTIMUM. Additional concepts of relevance are described in the articles on EFFICIENCY, REDISTRIBUTION OF INCOME, PERFECT COMPETITION, and MAXIMIZING BEHAVIOR.

WEBER, MAX (1864-1920), noted German sociologist and political economist who found his main challenge in the Marxist idea of economic determinism. Weber's *The Protestant Ethic and the Spirit of Capitalism* (1904-05), a painstakingly complete historical study, was an attempt to demonstrate that, at least in the specific case under examination, religious and ethical ideas held great sway. Weber then developed the question of historical causation into the even broader issue of discovering what element in the spiritual history of Western civilization was responsible for the development of capitalism, particularly as other cultures failed to produce such an economic system.

Weber's most significant contribution is to economic sociology. Stubbornly adhering to Hume's distinction between what is and what ought to be, and maintaining that there must be no value judgments in social science, Weber laid the groundwork for modern social science's characteristic distinction between personal and professional attitude.

WEIDENBAUM, MURRAY L. (1927-), American economist who has been active in industry and government for many years. A graduate of the City College of New York (1948), he received an M.A. from Columbia University in 1949 and his Ph.D. in economics from Princeton University in 1958. He published *The Modern Public Sector* in 1969, and has written widely in such journals and periodicals as *Dun's Review, Financial Analysts Journal, Journal of Marketing, Public Finance,* and *Saturday Review.* He became a member of the Washington University faculty in 1964 and served as Chairman of the Economics Department from 1966-1969. In the Nixon Administration, Weidenbaum was Assistant Secretary of the Treasury until August 1971, and was appointed by President Nixon in November, 1971, to the Rent Advisory Board.

WEIGHTED AVERAGE. *See* Central Tendency.

WELFARE. *See* Public Assistance.

WELFARE ECONOMICS, a branch of economic study concerned with how an economic system attempts to maximize the welfare of its people. In addition, welfare economics studies the principles by which alternative economic objectives can be ranked in terms of social welfare. The study emerged as a separate discipline with the publication of A.C. Pigou's *The Economics of Welfare* (1920).

Included in the theoretical approaches of welfare economics is the goal of optimizing both resources allocation and product distribution. An economic system maximizes welfare when the marginal productivity of social benefits, the marginal utility of private benefits, and the marginal utility of consumers are equal. For example, if products currently being produced for private consumption could be transferred to social consumption to add a greater amount to total welfare, then the existing system would not be maximizing welfare. The optimal position in maximizing welfare is to reach a point where the marginal rate of substitution between any two goods equals the marginal rate of transformation of the two goods in production.

Usually, in the study of welfare economics the socioeconomic goals of the economy are predetermined by factors other than economic analysis, such as legislation or consumer preference. The optimum is achieved when the welfare of the greatest possible number of people is maximized without regard to the profit of an individual or a firm.

See also Consumer Surplus; Marginal Utility.

—Robert L. Brite, *Louisiana State University*

WELFARE STATE, an economic system committed to providing security to its population in the areas of minimal incomes, health care, job security, and provisions for old age.

An economic system may be described as a welfare state regardless of its degree of public ownership of the means of production. Sweden has a low percentage of public ownership but a highly developed welfare system. To meet its aims of social welfare, the state may tax private property owners or direct incomes from state properties.

WHEELER-LEA ACT (1938) amended the Federal Trade Commission Act, Section 5, to prohibit "unfair or deceptive acts or practices" (including misleading and false advertising). It made more explicit the types of "unfair practices" prohibited in the FTC Act and made the test of legality of such practices not the effect on an offender's competitors (or competition generally) but the effect on the general public. The Wheeler-Lea Act is unique in antitrust legislation in providing such direct protection to consumers.

See also Deceptive Advertising; Federal Trade Commission; Unfair and Deceptive Practices.

WHIPSAW TACTICS. *See* Multi-Employer Bargaining.

WHITE-COLLAR WORKER. Though not a distinct Bureau of the Census classification, white-collar jobs usually fall under the categories of "sales workers," "clerical and kindred workers," and "professional, technical and kindred workers." Since World War II, the number of white-collar jobs has grown very rapidly. By 1956 it had surpassed the number of blue-collar jobs and, since that time, white-collar jobs have been increasing at a faster rate than blue-collar jobs.

WHOLESALE PRICE INDEX (WPI), one of the best known of the price indexes, a statistical composite measure of price movements in wholesale, or primary, markets. Using a sample of over 2,200 commodities, WPI bases its price quotations on the level of the first significant commercial transaction of these commodities. These price quotations are usually those of the producers and reflect their large lot sales and not necessarily sales to wholesale dealers or distributors. The commodities and the weights used for WPI are not the same as the Consumer Price Index and, therefore, both indexes need not move in the same direction in the short run. WPI is very helpful in indicating and tracing long-run price trends and conditions in the economy.

See also Price Indexes.

WICKSELL, KNUT (1851-1926), Swedish monetary economist who made numerous important contributions to monetary theory and developed some of the concepts which became central elements of the Keynesian system.

Wicksell's monetary theory was directed toward an analysis of aggregate price changes and the role of the interest rate in such changes. Because he felt that prices could not be stable until the bank interest rate equaled the natural rate, governmental and central bank monetary controls over interest rates were considered to be crucial in promoting stability.

While Wicksell felt that the normal state of the economy was one of full employment, he did address the question of the relationship between saving and investment and developed the concept of ex-post and ex-ante saving. However, it was left for Keynes to apply these concepts to the situation in which the economy reached an equilibrium at less than full employment.

—Clyde A. Haulman, *College of William and Mary*

WICKSTEED, PHILLIP H. (1884-1927). A theologian and Dante scholar, Wicksteed contributed to economics as one aspect of his broad intellectual interest. A follower of William Jevons, he made independent contributions to distribution theory and to the study of the relationship between supply and demand.

Wicksteed's *Essay on the Co-ordination of the Laws of Distribution* (1894) considered the distribution of output among the various factors of production based upon the marginal productivity principle. He concluded that output would be totally exhausted if each factor received its marginal production. However, *Common Sense of Political Economy* (1910) was Wicksteed's most important work. In it, he considers all the technical implications of pure marginalism in economic theory.

See also Marginalism.

WIESER, FRIEDRICH VON (1851-1926), Austrian follower of Carl Menger and classmate of Eugen Böhm-Bawerk, noted for his introduction of the term marginal utility to describe the concept developed by his mentor and others. Using this concept, Wieser rejected the labor theory of value and, in *Karl Marx and the Close of His System* (1896), presented one of the leading criticisms of Marxian economics. Wieser also developed the doctrine of opportunity cost. The concept that cost can be viewed in terms of opportunities or alternatives foregone has become an essential element of economic analysis.

See also Marginalism; Opportunity Cost.

WILDCAT STRIKES, unofficial or unauthorized work stoppages by employees, usually over a dispute arising during the life of a contract and involving its interpretation of perhaps an issue not covered by the contract. With the maturing of collective bargaining relationships, increased mutual respect of labor and management, and greater reliance on the grievance procedure as a method of resolving disputes under a contract, the frequency and impact of wildcat strikes have diminished.

They are most likely to arise where lingering hostility or militancy between the parties exists, or where the grievance process does not afford an effective means of conflict resolution. This occurs in the construction and long-shoring industries and others where jobs are of short duration, and, therefore, the workers believe immediate confrontation is necessary.

See also Strike.

WILLIAMSON, OLIVER E. (1932-), American educator, noted for his economic theories of organization and management. He graduated from M.I.T. in 1955 and later received his M.B.A. from Stanford University (1960), and his Ph.D. in Economics from Carnegie-Mellon University (1963). His books include *The Economics of Discretionary Behavior: Managerial Objectives in a Theory of the Firm* (1971), and *Corporate Control and Business Behavior: An Inquiry into the Effects of Organization Form on Enterprise Behavior* (1970). In 1966-67 he was special economic assistant to the Antitrust Division of the Department of Justice. He is presently professor of economics, and chairman of the Department of Economics, at the University of Pennsylvania.

WILLITS, JOSEPH HENRY (1889-), American educator and economist noted for his contributions to the area of labor relations. He

WHOLESALE PRICE INDEXES, BY MAJOR COMMODITY GROUPS, (1967=100)

Year	All commodities	Farm products	Industrial commodities
1926	51.6	61.3	53.2
1927	49.3	60.8	50.0
1928	50.0	64.8	49.3
1929	49.1	64.1	48.6
1930	44.6	54.2	45.2
1931	37.6	39.7	39.9
1932	33.6	29.5	37.3
1933	34.0	31.4	37.8
1934	38.6	40.0	41.6
1935	41.3	48.1	41.4
1936	41.7	49.5	42.2
1937	44.5	52.9	45.2
1938	40.5	42.0	43.4
1939	39.8	40.0	43.3
1940	40.5	41.4	44.0
1941	45.1	50.3	47.3
1942	50.9	64.8	50.7
1943	53.3	75.0	51.5
1944	53.6	75.5	52.3
1945	54.6	78.5	53.0
1946	62.3	90.9	58.0
1947	76.5	109.4	70.8
1948	82.8	117.5	76.9
1949	78.7	101.6	76.3
1950	81.8	106.7	78.0
1951	91.1	124.2	86.1
1952	88.6	117.2	84.1
1953	87.4	106.2	84.8
1954	87.6	104.7	85.0
1955	87.8	98.2	86.9
1956	90.7	96.9	90.8
1957	93.3	99.5	93.3
1958	94.6	103.9	93.6
1959	94.8	97.5	95.3
1960	94.9	97.2	95.3
1961	94.5	96.3	94.8
1962	94.8	98.0	94.8
1963	94.5	96.0	94.7
1964	94.7	94.6	95.2
1965	96.6	98.7	96.4
1966	99.8	105.9	98.5
1967	100.0	100.0	100.0
1968	102.5	102.5	102.5
1969	106.5	108.8	106.0
1970	110.4	111.0	110.0
1971	115.9	112.9	114.0

Oliver E. Williamson

Leonard Freel Woodcock

received his A.B. (1911) and A.M. (1912) from Swarthmore, and his Ph.D. from the University of Pennsylvania (1916). His publications include *Labor Relations in Bituminous Coal Mining* (1925), and *Labor Relations in Anthracite Coal Mining* (1925). Willits, now retired, has done a number of studies and surveys on education. In 1962 he became director of a study of excellence and mediocrity in colleges and universities.

WITHDRAWAL OF LABOR. *See* Disguised Unemployment; Underemployment.

WITHDRAWALS. When money flows are received by various sectors of the economy, all of the income may not be passed on directly to other sectors. That part of income not passed on is a withdrawal from the income stream. One of the most important withdrawals in the economy is saving by the household sector. Any income received by households but not spent for goods and services is considered saving. While household saving is generally the most important withdrawal, a number of others exist. Quite similar to household saving is business saving, or what is generally called retained earnings.

An additional withdrawal from the domestic circular flow of income is expenditures for imports. When households purchase goods and services produced in other countries it means that the households' income flow has been diverted from domestic businesses to foreign businesses. In a two-sector (household and business) circular-flow model, another withdrawal to consider is tax payments to the government. This withdrawal may be injected back into the circular flow through government spending or, if the government merely accumulates the funds, may remain outside the circular flow.

Withdrawals are an important consideration in macroeconomic theory because they reduce the spending stream. This is especially important in the analysis of the multiplier and the macroeconomic adjustment process.

See also Circular Flow of Income; Savings.

—Clyde A. Haulman, *College of William and Mary*

WITHHOLDING TAX. *See* Taxation: *Glossary.*

WOODCOCK, LEONARD FREEL (1911–), American labor union leader. Born in Rhode Island, Woodcock spent WWI in England. He returned to the United States with his parents, attended Wayne State University in Detroit, and joined the United Automobile Workers (UAW) in the 1930s. He held many positions in the union, and was an International Vice President in 1970 when, on the death of Walter Reuther, he became the union's fourth president.

WORKABLE COMPETITION, a term developed by J.M. Clark of Columbia University to describe the efficiency with which market prices can reflect the needs of the economy. In order for competition to remain workable, both public and private policies must cooperate in efforts to restrict monopolistic practices that tend to weaken competition. Because it is virtually impossible for all markets to be perfectly competitive, the economic models tend to indicate that there will always be imperfections in the market. However, a certain amount of imperfection still allows competition to be workable.

WORKER-UNION RELATIONS. *See* Union Security.

WORKING CONDITIONS. Under the Taft-Hartley Act of 1947, labor and management were expected to bargain over wages, hours, and working conditions—which encompass every aspect of an employee's situation on the job. Working conditions, first, relate to the work rules of the individual company, regarding such matters as lunch hours, coffee breaks, relief time, smoking and drinking rules, and dress codes. These working conditions may be negotiated through the collective bargaining process if either labor or management is dissatisfied.

Another working condition stressed in collective bargaining is the safety conditions under which an employee must work. Many jobs are dangerous and many safety rules must be obeyed under penalty of law. Other conditions, not covered by law, have to be bargained for to assure a worker maximum safety.

WORK RULES are a code of conduct, included in a collective bargaining contract, that employees are expected to follow in order to carry out their duties effectively and safely. Work rules have been the bases of some bitter battles between labor and management. In 1959, for example, the steelworkers, in an effort to maintain their jurisdiction over work rules which could help protect their jobs, went on strike. Their employers wanted a free hand in introducing and controlling new methods of production. In 1964, General Motors barely escaped a major strike by agreeing to bargain over such things as lunch hours, coffee breaks, and relief time.

WORK STOPPAGE, an interruption in the regular employer-employee work relationship, usually resulting from an impasse in bargaining over a new contract. It may be caused by the union's decision to strike or by management's decision to halt production until an agreement occurs. Thus, the work stoppage is a tactic used by either party to bring pressure on the other. It occasionally occurs while a contract is in force.

See also Strike.

WORLD BANK. *See* International Bank for Reconstruction and Development.

WPI. *See* Wholesale Price Index.

YELLOW-DOG CONTRACT, an agreement between an employer and a worker, whereby, as a condition of employment, the worker agrees not to join a labor union during the time in which he is employed. The condition implies that the worker is subject to automatic discharge if the agreement is violated. This practice of discrimination because of union membership is now illegal, having been outlawed by Congress in 1932.

YOUNG/GROWING DEBTOR. *See* Stages of a Country's Balance of Payments.

Z CURVE. *See* 45° Line.

ZERO PROFITS. *See* Normal Profits.

Selected Readings in Economics

This comprehensive Bibliography is divided into 27 sections, representing the major study areas of economics. The articles in the encyclopedia that have bibliographic references direct the student to the appropriate section of the Bibliography. For example, a citation of "*Consult* (26) Spiegel, 1971" directs the reader to the 1971 book by Henry W. Spiegel listed in Section 26 of the Bibliography.

The 27 sections of the Bibliography are:

1. Concepts and Methodology
2. Models of the Economic System
3. National Income Measurement
4. National Income Determination
5. Business Cycles
6. Fiscal Policy
7. Price Level
8. Money
9. The Banking System
10. Monetary Policy
11. The Market System
12. Demand Theory
13. Supply and Costs of Production
14. Theory of the Firm
15. Agriculture
16. Antimonopoly and Antitrust
17. Government Regulation
18. Theory of Production
19. Rent
20. Wages
21. Unions
22. Capital, Profits, and Interest
23. International Trade
24. Growth and Development
25. History of Economic Thought
26. Economic Systems
27. Statistics

In addition to the specific works cited in the main body of the Bibliography, the student of economics will be interested in a wide variety of publications issued by the federal government. Statistical studies include the *Statistical Abstract of the United States* and *Historical Statistics of the United States: A Statistical Abstract Supplement.* The *Economic Report of the President* and *Special Analyses of the United States Government* are detailed examinations of the U.S. economy. The status of labor is reported in the *Handbook of Labor Statistics* and *Manpower Report of the President.* All of the above may be ordered from the Superintendent of Documents, Government Printing Office, Washington, D.C. 20402. They are also stocked in the Government Printing Office bookstores in Atlanta, Birmingham, Boston, Canton (Ohio), Chicago, Dallas, Denver, Detroit, Kansas City (Missouri), Los Angeles, New York, Philadelphia, and San Francisco.

The Superintendent of Documents also issues free price lists of publications available in several areas of economics. Among these lists are *Census Publications, Commerce, Finance, Labor,* and *Tariff and Taxation.*

1. CONCEPTS AND METHODOLOGY

Boulding, Kenneth E., *Economic Analysis: Microeconomics,* 4th ed. (New York: Harper & Row, 1966).

Boulding, Kenneth E., *Economics as a Science* (New York: McGraw-Hill, 1970).

Bowen, Howard R., *Toward Social Economy* (New York: Holt, Rinehart & Winston, 1948).

Clay, Henry, *Economics for the General Reader* (New York: Macmillan, 1925).

Dernburg, Thomas F., and McDougall, Duncan M., *Macroeconomics,* 3d ed. (New York: McGraw-Hill, 1968).

Ferman, Louis A., and others (eds.), *Poverty in America,* rev. ed. (Ann Arbor: University of Michigan, 1968).

Fusfeld, Daniel L., *The Age of the Economist* (Chicago: Scott, Foresman, 1966).

Galbraith, John K., *American Capitalism,* rev. ed. (Boston: Houghton Mifflin, 1956).

Heller, Walter W., *New Dimensions of Political Economy* (New York: W.W. Norton, 1967).

Knight, Frank H.,. *The Economic Organization* (New York: Harper & Row, 1965).

Krupp, Sherman R. (ed.), *The Structure of Economic Science* (Englewood Cliffs, NJ: Prentice-Hall, 1966).

Leftwich, Richard H., *The Price System & Resource Allocation,* 4th ed. (Hinsdale, IL: Dryden Press, 1970).

Lindauer, John, *Macroeconomics,* 2d ed. (New York: John Wiley, 1971).

Lipsey, Richard G., and Steiner, Peter O., *Economics,* 2d ed. (New York: Harper & Row, 1969).

Mansfield, Edwin L., *Microeconomics* (New York: W.W. Norton, 1970).

Mundell, Robert A., *Man and Economics* (New York: McGraw-Hill, 1968).

Newman, Phillip C., "Development of Economic Thought," *Source Reading in Economic Thought* (New York: W.W. Norton, 1954).

Rogers, Augustus J., III, *Choice: An Introduction to Economics* (Englewood Cliffs, NJ: Prentice-Hall, 1970).

Rostow, Walt W., *The Stages of Economic Growth,* 2d ed. (Cambridge: Cambridge University Press, 1971).

Samuelson, Paul A., *Economics,* 9th ed. (New York: McGraw-Hill, 1973).

Shapiro, Edward, *Macroeconomic Analysis,* 2d ed. (New York: Harcourt, Brace & World, 1970).

Smith, Adam, *Wealth of Nations* (Westminister, MD: Modern Library, 1963).

Will, Robert E., and Vatter, Harold G. (eds.), *Poverty in Affluence,* 2d ed. (New York: Harcourt, Brace & World, 1970).

2. MODELS OF THE ECONOMIC SYSTEM

Bowen, Howard R., *Toward Social Economy* (New York: Holt, Rinehart & Winston, 1948).

Heilbroner, Robert L. *The Making of Economic Society* (Englewood Cliffs, NJ: Prentice-Hall, 1962).

Miernyk, William H., *The Elements of Input-Output Analysis* (New York: Random House, 1965).

Monsen, R. Joseph, Jr., *Modern American Capitalism: Ideologies and Issues* (Boston: Houghton Mifflin, 1963).

3. NATIONAL INCOME MEASUREMENT

Abraham, William I., *National-Income & Economic Accounting* (Englewood Cliffs, NJ: Prentice-Hall, 1969).

Dernburg, Thomas F., and McDougall, Duncan M., *Macroeconomics,* 3d ed. (New York: McGraw-Hill, 1968).

Edey, Harold C., and Peacock, Alan T., *National Income & Social Accounting* (London: Hutchinson & Co., 1966).

Gilbey, Elizabeth W., *A Primer on Economics of Consumption* (New York: Random House, 1968).

Katona, George, *The Mass Consumption Society* (New York: McGraw-Hill, 1964).

Linder, Staffan B., *The Harried Leisure Class* (New York: Columbia Univ. Press, 1970).

Preston, Lee E. (ed.), *Social Issues in Marketing* (Glenview, IL: Scott, Foresman, 1968).

Shapiro, Edward, *Macroeconomic Analysis,* 2d ed. (New York: Harcourt, Brace & World, 1970).

U.S. Department of Commerce, *The National Income and Product Accounts of the United States, 1929–1965* (Washington: 1966).

4. NATIONAL INCOME DETERMINATION

Dillard, Dudley D., *The Economics of John Maynard Keynes: The Theory of a Monetary Economy* (New York: Prentice-Hall, 1948).

Hansen, Alvin H., *A Guide to Keynes* (New York: McGraw Hill, 1953).

Keynes, John Maynard, *The General Theory of Employment, Interest, and Money* (New York: Harcourt, Brace, 1936).

Klein, Lawrence R., *The Keynesian Revolution,* 2d ed. (New York: Macmillan, 1966).

5. BUSINESS CYCLES

Chandler, Lester U., *America's Greatest Depression 1929–1941* (New York: Harper & Row, 1970).

Fishman, Betty G., and Fishman, Leo, *Employment, Unemployment and Economic Growth* (New York: Thomas Y. Crowell, 1969).

Gordon, Robert A., *Business Fluctuations,* 2d ed. (New York: Harper & Row, 1961).

Hansen, Alvin H., *Fiscal Policy and Business Cycles* (New York: W.W. Norton, 1941).

Lee, Maurice W., *Macroeconomics: Fluctuations, Growth and Stability,* 4th ed. (Homewood, IL: Irwin, 1967).

Lindauer, John, *Macroeconomics* (New York: John Wiley, 1968).

Mitchell, Wesley C., "Business Cycles," *Readings in Business Cycle Theory* (Philadelphia: Blakiston, 1944).

Moore, Geoffrey H., "Tested Knowledge of Business Cycles," *Readings in Business Cycles* (Homewood, IL: Irwin, 1965).

Okun, Arthur M. (ed.), *The Battle Against Unemployment* (New York: W.W. Norton, 1972).

Peterson, Wallace C., *Income, Employment and Economic Growth* (New York: W.W. Norton, 1962).

Silk, Leonard S., and Curley, M. Louise, *A Primer on Business Forecasting* (New York: Random House, 1970).

6. FISCAL POLICY

Bator, Francis M., *The Question of Government Spending* (New York: Harper & Row, 1960).

Benoit, Emile, and Boulding, Kenneth E. (eds.), *Disarmament and the Economy* (New York: Harper & Row, 1963).

Brinker, Paul A., *Economic Insecurity and Social Security* (New York: Appleton-Century-Crofts, 1968).

Buchanan, James M., *The Public Finances,* rev. ed. (Homewood IL: Irwin, 1965).

Clayton, James L. (ed.), *The Economic Impact of the Cold War* (New York: Harcourt, Brace & World, 1970).

Eckstein, Otto, *Public Finance,* 2d ed. (Englewood Cliffs, NJ: Prentice-Hall, 1967).

Freidman, Milton, *Capitalism and Freedom* (Chicago: Univ. of Chicago Press, 1962).

Hamovitch, William (ed.), *The Federal Deficit* (Boston: D.C. Heath & Co., 1965).

Haveman, Robert H., *The Economics of the Public Sector* (New York: John Wiley, 1970).

Heilbroner, Robert L., and Bernstein, Peter L., *A Primer on Government Spending,* 2d ed. (New York: Random House, 1970).

Heller, Walter W., *New Dimensions of Political Economy* (New York: W.W. Norton, 1967).

Henderson, William L., and Cameron, Helen A., *The Public Economy* (New York: Random House, 1969).

Herber, Bernard P., *Modern Public Finance,* rev. ed. (Homewood, IL: Irwin, 1971).

Mansfield, Edwin (ed.), *Defense, Science and Public Policy* (New York: W.W. Norton, 1968).

McKean, Roland N., *Public Spending* (New York: McGraw-Hill, 1968).

Newman, Herbert E., *An Introduction to Public Finance* (New York: John Wiley, 1968).

Phelps, Edmund S. (ed.), *Private Wants and Public Needs* (New York: W.W. Norton, 1965).

Sharp, Ansel M., and Sliger, Bernard F., *Public Finance,* rev. ed. (Austin, TX: Business Publications, 1970).

Slesinger, Reuben E. (ed.), *National Economic Policy: The Presidential Reports* (Princeton, NJ: D. Van Nostrand, 1968).

Stein, Bruno, *On Relief* (New York: Basic Books, 1971).

Thurow, Lester C. (ed.), *American Fiscal Policy* (Englewood Cliffs, NJ: Prentice-Hall, 1967).

Turnbull, John G., and others, *Economic and Social Security,* 3d ed. (New York: Ronald Press, 1967).

Ulmer, Melville J., *The Welfare State: U.S.A.* (Boston: Houghton Mifflin, 1969).

7. PRICE LEVEL

Ferguson, Charles E., *Microeconomic Theory* (Homewood, IL: Irwin, 1972).

Friedman, Milton, and Heller, Walter W., *Monetary vs. Fiscal Policy* (New York: Harper & Row, 1972).

Leftwich, Richard H., *The Price System and Resource Allocation,* 4th ed. (Hinsdale, IL: Dryden, 1970).

Levitan, Sar A., and others, *Human Resources and Labor Markets* (New York: Harper & Row, 1972).

Liebhafsky, H.H., *Nature of Price Theory* (New York: Business Press, 1968).

Ludtke, James B., *The American Financial System,* 2d ed. (Boston: Allyn & Bacon, 1967).

Okun, Arthur M., *The Political Economy of Prosperity* (New York: W.W. Norton, 1970).

Sheehan, John, *The Wage-Price Guideposts* (Washington: The Brookings Institution, 1967).

8. MONEY

Angell, Norman, *The Story of Money* (Philadelphia: Lippincott, 1929).

Federal Reserve Bank of Atlanta, *Fundamental Facts About United States Money* (Atlanta, 1967).

Fisher, Irving, *The Purchasing Power of Money* (New York: Macmillan, 1911).

Friedman, Milton, *Studies in the Quantity Theory of Money* (Chicago: Univ. of Chicago, 1956).

Jevons, William S., *Money and the Mechanism of Exchange* (New York: D. Appleton, 1896).

Ritter, Lawrence S., and Silber, William L., *Money* (New York: Basic Books, 1970).

Robertson, Dennis H., *Money* (New York: Pitman, 1948).

9. THE BANKING SYSTEM

Abbott, Charles C., *The Federal Debt: Structure and Impact* (New York: Twentieth Century Fund, 1953).

Bernstein, Peter L., *A Primer on Money, Banking, and Gold* (New York: Random House, 1965).

Board of Governors of the Federal Reserve System, *The Federal Reserve System: Purposes and Functions,* 5th ed. (Washington: 1963).

Chandler, Lester V., *The Economics of Money and Banking,* 5th ed. (New York: Harper & Row, 1969).

Cochran, John A., *Money, Banking and the Economy,* 2d ed. (New York: Macmillan, 1971).

Duesenberry, James S., *Money and Credit: Impact and Control,* 2d ed. (Englewood Cliffs, NJ: Prentice-Hall, 1967).

Federal Reserve Bank of Cleveland, *Money Market Instrument* (Cleveland: 1970).

Federal Reserve Bank of Philadelphia, *Fifty Years of the Federal Reserve Act* (Philadelphia: 1964).

Goldsmith, Raymond W., *Financial Intermediaries in the American Economy Since 1900* (Princeton, NJ: Princeton Univ., 1958).

Haines, Walter W., *Money, Prices, and Policy,* 2d ed. (New York: Harper & Row, 1960).

Klein, John J., *Money and the Economy,* 2d ed. (New York: Harcourt, Brace & World, Inc., 1970).

Procknow, Herbert V. (ed.), *The Federal Reserve System* (New York: Harper & Row, 1960).

Ritter, Lawrence S., and Silber, William L., *Money* (New York: Basic Books, 1970).

Robinson, Roland I., *Financial Institutions,* 3d ed. (Homewood, IL: Irwin, 1969).

Shapiro, Eli, and others, *Money and Banking,* 5th ed. (New York: Harcourt, Brace & World, Inc., 1970).

Smith, Harlan M., *Elementary Monetary Theory* (New York: Random House, 1968).

Wrightsman, Dwayne, *An Introduction to Monetary Theory and Policy* (New York: Free Press, 1971).

10. MONETARY POLICY

Anderson, Clay J., *Evolution of the Role and Functioning of the Discount Mechanism* (Washington: Board of Governors of the Federal Reserve System, 1966).

Carson, Deane (ed.), *Money and Finance* (New York: John Wiley, 1972).

Conrad, Joseph W., *An Introduction to the Theory of Interest* (Berkeley: Univ. of California, 1959).

Federal Reserve Bank of Chicago, *Modern Money Mechanics* (Chicago: 1961).

Federal Reserve Bank of New York, *Open Market Operations* (New York: 1963).

Haines, Walter W., *Money, Prices, and Policy* (New York: McGraw-Hill, 1966).

Homer, Sidney, *A History of Interest Rates* (New Brunswick, NJ: Rutgers, 1963).

Jacoby, Neil H. (ed.), *United States Monetary Policy* (New York: Praeger, 1964).

Lee, Maurice W., *Toward Economic Stability* (New York: John Wiley, 1966).

Mayer, Thomas, *Elements of Monetary Policy* (New York: Random House, 1968).

Mayer, Thomas, *Monetary Policy in the United States* (New York: Random House, 1968).

11. THE MARKET SYSTEM

Allen, Clark Lee, *The Framework of Price Theory* (Belmont, CA: Wadsworth, 1967).

Boulding, Kenneth E., *Economic Analysis: Microeconomics,* 4th ed. (New York: Harper & Row, 1966).

Cohen, Kalman J., and Cyert, R. M., *Theory of the Firm: Resource Allocation in a Market Economy* (Englewood Cliffs, NJ: Prentice-Hall, 1965).

Ferguson, Charles E., *Microeconomic Theory* (Homewood, IL: Irwin, 1968).

Hibdon, James E., *Price and Welfare Theory* (New York: McGraw-Hill, 1969).

Kershaw, Joseph A., *Government Against Poverty* (Chicago: Markham, 1970).

Kohler, Heinz, *Welfare and Planning* (New York: John Wiley, 1966).

Leftwich, Richard H., *The Price System and Resource Allocation,* 4th ed. (Hinsdale, IL: Dryden, 1970).

Liebhafsky, H. H., *Nature of Price Theory* (New York: Business Press, 1968).

Mansfield, Edwin, *Microeconomics: Theory and Applications* (New York: Norton, 1970).

Phelps-Brown, E. H., *The Framework of the Pricing System* (London: Chapman and Hall, 1936).

Ryan, W.J.L., *Price Theory* (New York: St. Martin's Press, 1958).

Stigler, George J., *The Theory of Price,* 3d ed. (New York: Macmillan, 1966).

Stonier, Alfred W., and Hague, Douglas C., *A Textbook of Economic Theory,* 3d ed. (New York: Longmans, Green & Co., 1964).

Watson, Donald S., *Price Theory and Its Uses,* 2d ed. (Boston: Houghton Mifflin, 1968).

Watson, Donald S., *Price Theory in Action,* 2d ed. (Boston: Houghton Mifflin, 1969).

Wilcox, Clair, *Toward Social Welfare* (Homewood, IL: Irwin, 1969).

12. DEMAND THEORY

Bloom, Gordon F., and Northrup, Herbert R., *Economics of Labor Relations,* 6th ed. (Homewood, IL: Irwin, 1969).

Boulding, Kenneth E., *Economic Analysis: Microeconomics,* 4th ed. (New York: Harper & Row, 1966).

Cohen, Sanford, *Labor in the United States,* 3d ed. (Columbus, Ohio: Charles E. Merrill, 1970).

Ferguson, Charles E., *Microeconomic Theory,* 3d ed. (Homewood, IL: Irwin, 1972).

Hadar, Josef, *Elementary Theory of Micro-Economic Behavior,* 2d ed. (Reading, PA: Addison-Wesley, 1973).

Henderson, Hubert, *Supply and Demand* (Chicago: Univ. of Chicago Press, 1958).

Leftwich, Richard H., *The Price System and Resource Allocation,* 4th ed. (Hinsdale, IL: Dryden, 1970).

Mansfield, Edwin, *Microeconomics: Theory and Applications* (New York: W. W. Norton, 1970).

Morgan, Chester A., *Labor Economics,* 3d ed. (Austin, TX: Business Publication, 1970).

Stigler, George J., *The Theory of Price,* 3d ed. (New York: Macmillan, 1966).

Williams, C. Glyn, *Labor Economics* (New York: John Wiley, 1970).

13. SUPPLY AND COSTS OF PRODUCTION

Bain, Joe S., *Industrial Organization,* 2d ed. (New York: John Wiley, 1968).

Bilas, Richard A., *Microeconomic Theory,* 2d ed. (New York: McGraw-Hill, 1971).

Boulding, Kenneth E., *Economic Analysis: Microeconomics,* 4th ed. (New York: Harper & Row, 1966).

Ferguson, Charles E., *Microeconomic Theory,* 3d ed. (Homewood, IL: Irwin, 1972).

Hadar, Josef, *Elementary Theory of Micro-Economic Behavior,* 2d ed. (Reading, PA: Addison-Wesley, 1973).

Henderson, Hubert, *Supply and Demand* (Chicago: Univ. of Chicago Press, 1958).

Leftwich, Richard H., *The Price System and Resource Allocation,* 4th ed. (Hinsdale, IL: Dryden, 1970).

Stigler, George J., *The Theory of Price,* 3d ed. (New York: Macmillan, 1966).

Watson, Donald S. (ed.), *Price Theory in Action,* 2d ed. (Boston: Houghton Mifflin, 1969).

14. THEORY OF THE FIRM

Adams, Walter (ed.), *The Structure of American Industry,* 4th ed. (New York: Macmillan, 1971).

Adams, Walter, and Gray, Horace M., *Monopoly in America* (New York: Macmillan, 1971).

Allen, Roy G.D., *Macro-Economic Theory* (New York: Macmillan, 1967).

Backman, Jules, *Advertising and Competition* (New York: New York Univ. Press, 1967).

Bain, Joe S., *Industrial Organization,* 2d ed. (New York: John Wiley, 1968).

Baratz, Morton S., *The American Business System in Transition* (New York: Thomas Y. Crowell, 1970).

Boulding, Kenneth E., "Welfare Economics," *A Survey of Contemporary Economics,* ed. by B.F. Haley (Homewood, IL: Irwin, 1952).

Cheit, Earl F. (ed.), *The Business Establishment* (New York: John Wiley, 1964).

Colberg, Marshall R., and others, *Business Economics: Principles and Cases,* 4th ed. (Homewood, IL: Irwin, 1970).

Ferguson, Charles E., and Maurice, S. Charles, *Economic Analysis* (Homewood, IL: Irwin, 1970).

Galbraith, John Kenneth, *The New Industrial State* (Boston: Houghton Mifflin, 1967).

Hacker, Andrew (ed.), *The Corporation Take-over* (Garden City, NY: Doubleday, 1965).

Heyne, Paul T., *Private Keepers of the Public Interest* (New York: McGraw-Hill, 1968).

Leftwich, Richard H., *The Price System and Resource Allocation,* 4th ed. (Hinsdale, IL: Dryden, 1970).

Leonard, William N., *Business Size, Market Power, and Public Policy* (New York: Thomas Y. Crowell, 1969).

Lerner, Abba P., *The Economics of Control* (New York: Macmillan, 1947).

Liebhafsky, H. H., *Nature of Price Theory* (New York: Business Press, 1968).

Ludtke, James B., *The American Financial System,* 2d ed. (Boston: Allyn & Bacon, 1967).

Mansfield, Edwin (ed.), *Monopoly Power and Economic Performance,* 2d ed. (New York: W.W. Norton, 1968).

Marshall, Alfred, *Principles of Economics,* 8th ed. (New York: Macmillan, 1920).

McGuire, Joseph W., *Business and Society* (New York: McGraw-Hill, 1963).

Mueller, Willard F., *A Primer on Monopoly and Competition* (New York: Random House, 1970).

Papandreou, Andreas G., and Wheeler, John T., *Competition and Its Regulation* (Englewood Cliffs, NJ: Prentice-Hall, 1954).

Samuelson, Paul A., "Dynamics, Statics, and the Stationary State," *Review of Economics and Statistics* 25 (Feb., 1943).

Scherer, Frederic M., *Industrial Market Structure and Economic Performance* (Chicago: Rand McNally, 1970).

Schumpeter, Joseph A., *Capitalism, Socialism and Democracy,* 3d ed. (New York: Harper & Row, 1950).

Shepherd, William G., *Market Power & Economic Welfare* (New York: Random House, 1970).

Stigler, George J., *The Theory of Price,* 3d ed. (New York: Macmillan, 1966).

Vickrey, William S., *Microstatics* (New York: Harcourt, Brace & World, 1964).

Watson, Donald S. (ed.), *Price Theory in Action,* 2d ed. (Boston: Houghton Mifflin, 1969).

Weiss, Leonard W., *Economics and American Industry* (New York: John Wiley, 1961).

15. AGRICULTURE

Cochrane, Willard W., *The City Man's Guide to the Farm Problem* (New York: McGraw-Hill, 1966).

Hathaway, Dale E., *Problems of Progress in the Agricultural Economy* (Chicago: Scott, Foresman, 1964).

Owen, Wyn F. (ed.), *American Agriculture: The Changing Structure* (Lexington, MA: D.C. Heath, 1969).

Ruttan, Vernon W., and others (eds.), *Agricultural Policy in an Affluent Society* (New York: W. W. Norton, 1969).

Tweeten, Luther, *Foundations of Farm Policy* (Lincoln, NEB: Univ. of Nebraska, 1970).

USDA, "Agricultural Prices and Parity," *Major Statistical Series of the USDA,* Vol. 1, Hbk. No. 365 (1970).

16. ANTIMONOPOLY AND ANTITRUST

Bain, Joe S., *Industrial Organization* (New York: John Wiley, 1968).

Blummer, Disney M., and Hefner, Dennis L. (eds.), *Readings in the Regulation of Business* (Scranton, PA: International, 1968).

Bock, Betty, *Mergers and Markets,* 4th ed. (New York: National Industrial Conference Board, 1965).

Corwin, Edward S., "The Schechter Case—Landmark or What?" *New York University Quarterly Law Review,* Jan. 1936.

Heflebower, Richard B., and Stocking, George W. (eds.), *Readings in Industrial Organization and Public Policy* (Homewood, IL: Irwin, 1958).

Kaysen, Carl, and Turner, Donald F., *Antitrust Policy: An Economic and Legal Analysis* (Cambridge, Mass: 1959).

Letwin, William, *Law and Economic Policy in America: The Evolution of the Sherman Antitrust Act* (New York: Random House, 1965).

Millis, Harry A., and Montgomery, Royal E., *Organized Labor: Economics of Labor,* Vol. 3 (New York: McGraw-Hill, 1945).

Narver, John C., *Conglomerate Mergers and Market Competition* (Berkeley: Univ. of Calif., 1967).

Select Committee on Small Business, 81st Congress, 2d Session, *Congress and the Monopoly Problem—Fifty Years of Antitrust Development, 1900-1950* (House Document 599: 1950).

Sichel, Werner (ed.), *Industrial Organization and Policy: Selected Readings* (Boston: Houghton Mifflin, 1967).

Wilcox, Clair, *Public Policies Toward Business,* 4th ed. (Homewood, IL: Irwin, 1971).

17. GOVERNMENT REGULATION

Bernstein, Marver H., *Regulating Business By Independent Commission* (Princeton: Princeton, 1955).

Coase, Ronald H., "The Federal Communications Commissions," *Journal of Law and Economics,* Vol. 2, pp. 1-40 (October, 1959).

Coase, Ronald H., "The Theory of Public Utility Pricing and Its Application," *Bell Journal of Economics and Science,* Vol. 1, Spring 1970.

Cordtz, Dan, "It's Time to Unload the Regulators," *Fortune,* Vol. 84, July 1971.

Cordtz, Dan, "A Case For Grounding the CAB," *Fortune,* Vol. 84, July, 1971.

Kitch, Edmund W., "Regulation of the Field Market for Natural Gas by the Federal Power Commission," *Journal of Law and Economics,* Vol. 11, Oct. 1968.

Lerner, Abba P., "Conflicting Principles of Public Utility Rate Regulation," *Journal of Law and Economics,* Vol. 7, Oct. 1964, pp. 61–70.

MacAvoy, Paul W. (ed.), *The Crisis of the Regulatory Commissions* (New York: W. W. Norton, 1970).

MacAvoy, Paul W., "The Regulation-Induced Shortage of Natural Gas," *Journal of Law and Economics,* Vol. 14, April 1971, pp. 167–199.

Posner, Richard A., "Natural Monopoly and Its Regulation," *Stanford Law Review* (Feb. 1969).

Stigler, George J., and Friedland, Claire, "What can Regulators Regulate? The Case of Electricity," *Journal of Law and Economics,* Vol. 5, Oct. 1962.

Wilcox, Clair, *Public Policies Toward Business,* 4th ed. (Homewood, IL: Irwin, 1971).

18. THEORY OF PRODUCTION

Chamberlain, Neil W., and Cullen, Donald E., *The Labor Sector,* 2d ed. (New York: McGraw-Hill, 1971).

Heneman, Herbert G., Jr., and Yoder, Dale, *Labor Economics,* 2d ed. (Cincinnati: South-Western Publishing, 1965).

Leftwich, Richard H., *The Price System and Resource Allocation,* 4th ed. (Hinsdale, IL: Dryden, 1970).

Mansfield, Edwin, *Microeconomics: Theory and Application* (New York: W.W. Norton, 1970).

Peterson, Wallace C., *Income, Employment, and Economic Growth,* rev. ed. (New York: W. W. Norton, 1967).

Sirkin, Gerald, *Introduction to Macroeconomic Theory,* 3d ed. (Homewood, IL: Irwin, 1970).

19. RENT

Due, John F., and Clower, Robert W., *Intermediate Economic Analysis,* 5th ed. (Homewood, IL: Irwin, 1966).

Meyers, Albert L., *Elements of Modern Economics,* 4th ed. (Englewood Cliffs, NJ: Prentice-Hall, 1956).

Stonir, Alfred W., and Hague, Douglas C., *A Textbook of Economic Theory,* 3d ed. (New York: Longmans, Green & Co., 1964).

20. WAGES

Baerwald, Friedrich, *Economic Progress and Problems of Labor* (Scranton, PA: International Textbook, 1967).

Bloom, Gordon F., and Northrup, Herbert R., *Economics of Labor Relations,* 6th ed. (Homewood, IL: Irwin, 1969).

Bowen, William G., and Finegan, T. Aldrich, *The Economics of Labor Force Participation* (Princeton: Princeton University, 1969).

Cohen, Sanford, *Labor in the United States,* 2d ed. (Columbus: Charles E. Merrill, 1966).

Galenson, Walter, *A Primer on Employment and Wages,* 2d ed. (New York: Random House, 1970).

Levitan, Sar A., and others, *Human Resources and Labor Markets* (New York: Harper & Row, 1972).

Mangum, Garth L., *The Emergence of Manpower Policy* (New York: Holt, 1969).

McConnell, Campbell R. (ed.), *Perspectives on Wage Determination* (New York: McGraw-Hill, 1970).

Mincer, Jacob, "Labor Force Participation," *International Encyclopedia of the Social Sciences* (New York: Macmillan & Free Press, 1968).

Reynolds, Lloyd G., *Labor Economics and Labor Relations,* 5th ed. (Englewood Cliffs, NJ: Prentice-Hall, 1970).

Terborgh, George, *The Automation Hysteria* (New York: W. W. Norton, 1966).

Thurow, Lester, *Investment in Human Capital* (Belmont, CA: Wadsworth Publishing Co., 1970).

21. UNIONS

Baitsell, John M., and others, *Problems in Labor Relations,* 3d ed. (New York: McGraw-Hill, 1964).

Bloom, Gordon F., and Northrup, Herbert R., *Economics of Labor Relations,* 6th ed. (Homewood, IL: Irwin, 1969).

Cohen, Sanford, *Labor in the United States,* 2d ed. (Columbus: Charles E. Merrill, 1966).

Dulles, Foster R., *Labor in America* (New York: Thomas Y. Crowell, 1966).

22. CAPITAL, PROFITS, AND INTEREST

Abbott, Lawrence, *Economics and the Modern World* (New York: Harcourt Brace, 1960).

Bach, George L., *Economics,* 7th ed. (Englewood Cliffs, NJ: Prentice-Hall, 1971).

Coleman, John R. (ed.), *The Changing American Economy* (New York: Basic Books, 1967).

Eckaus, Richard S., *Basic Economics* (Boston: Little, Brown, 1972).

Fusfeld, Daniel R., *Economics* (Lexington: D.C. Heath, 1972).

Guttman, Peter M. (ed.), *Economic Growth: An American Problem* (Englewood Cliffs, NJ: Prentice-Hall, 1964).

International Encyclopedia of the Social Sciences (New York: Macmillan, 1968).

Landsberg, Hans H., *Natural Resources for U.S. Growth* (Baltimore: Johns Hopkins Press, 1964).

Lipsey, Richard, and Steiner, Peter, *Economics,* 2d ed. (New York: Harper & Row, 1969).

Mansfield, Edwin, *Technological Change* (New York: W.W. Norton, 1971).

Mishan, Ezra J., *Technology and Growth* (New York: Praeger, 1970).

Peterson, Willis L., *Principles of Economics,* Vol. 2 (Homewood, IL: Irwin, 1971).

Samuelson, Paul A., *Economics,* 9th ed. (New York: McGraw-Hill, 1973).

Schumpeter, Joseph A., *Capitalism, Socialism and Democracy,* 3d ed. (New York: Harper & Row, 1962).

Spiegel, Henry W., *The Growth of Economic Thought* (Englewood Cliffs, NJ: Prentice-Hall, 1971).

23. INTERNATIONAL TRADE

Bach, George L., *Economics,* 7th ed. (Englewood Cliffs, NJ: Prentice-Hall, 1971).

Board of Governors, *Federal Reserve Bulletin* (monthly).

Department of Commerce, *Survey of Current Business* (monthly).

Ellsworth, Paul T., *The International Economy,* 4th ed. (New York: Macmillan, 1969).

Ingram, James C., *International Economic Problems,* 2d ed. (New York: John Wiley, 1970).

Kindleberger, Charles P., *International Economics,* 4th ed. (Homewood, IL: Irwin, 1968).

Krause, L.B., *Fixed, Flexible, and Gliding Exchange Rates* (Brookings Institution, Reprint 205, 1971).

Kreinin, Mordechai E., *International Economics, A Policy Approach* (New York: Harcourt, Brace, 1971).

Massel, Mark S., *Non-Tariff Barriers as an Obstacle to World Trade* (Brookings Institution, 1964).

Mikesell, Raymond F., *Financing World Trade* (New York: Thomas Y. Crowell, 1969).

Snider, Delbert A., *International Monetary Relations* (New York: Random House, 1966).

Snider, Delbert A., *Introduction to International Economics,* 5th ed. (Homewood, IL: Irwin, 1971).

Wexler, Imanuel I., *Fundamentals of International Economics,* 2d ed. (New York: Random House, 1972).

24. GROWTH AND DEVELOPMENT

Bhagwati, Jagdish, and Eckaus, Richard S. (eds.), *Foreign Aid* (Baltimore: Penguin, 1970).

Carroll, T.F., "The Land Reform Issue in Latin America," in *Latin American Issues: Essays and Comments* (New York: Twentieth Century Fund, 1961).

Cochran, Thomas C., and Brewer, Thomas B. (eds.), *Views of American Economic Growth,* Vol. II (New York: McGraw-Hill, 1966).

Fabricant, Solomon, *A Primer on Productivity* (New York: Random House, 1969).

Gill, Richard T., *Economic Development Past & Present,* 2d ed. (Englewood Cliffs, NJ: Prentice-Hall, 1967).

Helleiner, G.K., "The Fiscal Role of Marketing Boards in Nigerian Economic Development, 1947-61," in *Economic Journal* (Sept. 1964).

Hirschman, Albert O., *The Strategy of Economic Development* (New Haven: Yale, 1958).

Johnson, H.C., "Planning and the Market in Economic Development," in *Money, Trade and Economic Growth* (Cambridge: Harvard, 1962).

Maddison, Angus, *Economic Progress and Policy in Developing Countries* (London: George Allen & Unwin, 1970).

Meier, Gerald M., *Leading Issues in Economic Development,* 2d ed. (New York: Oxford University Press, 1970).

Morris, Bruce R., *Economic Growth and Development* (New York: Pitman, 1967).

Nurkse, Ragnar, *Equilibrium and Growth in the World Economy* (Cambridge: Harvard, 1961).

Raup, P.M., "Land Reform and Agricultural Development," in *Agricultural Development and Economic Growth,* ed. by H.M. Southworth and B.F. Johnston (Ithaca: Cornell, 1967).

Rosenstein-Rodan, P.N., "Notes on the Theory of the Big Push," in *Economic Development for Latin America,* ed. by Ellis and Wallich (New York: St. Martin's, 1961).

Rostow, Walt W., *The Stages of Economic Growth* (New York: Cambridge Univ. Press, 1960).

Scitovsky, Tibor, "Two Concepts for External Economics," in *The Journal for Political Economy* (April 1954).

Spiegelglas, Stephen, and Welsh, Charles J. (eds.), *Economic Development: Challenge and Promise* (Englewood Cliffs, NJ: Prentice-Hall, 1970).

Streeton, P., "Balanced vs. Unbalanced Growth," *Economic Weekly,* (April 20, 1963).

Waterson, Albert, *Development Planning: The Lessons of Experience* (Baltimore: Johns Hopkins, 1965).

Watson, A., and Dirlan J., "The Impact of Underdevelopment on Economic Planning," in *Quarterly Journal of Economics* (May 1965).

25. HISTORY OF ECONOMIC THOUGHT

Heilbroner, Robert L., *The Worldly Philosophers,* 3d ed. (New York: Simon & Schuster, 1967).

Rima, Ingrid H., *Development of Economic Analysis* (Homewood, IL: Irwin, 1967).

Spiegel, Henry W., *The Growth of Economic Thought* (Englewood Cliffs, NJ: Prentice-Hall, 1971).

Stewart, Michael, *Keynes and After* (Baltimore: Penguin Books, 1967).

26. ECONOMIC SYSTEMS

Balinky, Alexander, *Marx's Economics: Origin and Development* (Lexington: D.C. Heath, 1970).

Bornstein, Morris I., *Comparative Economic Systems: Models and Cases,* rev. ed. (Homewood, IL: Irwin, 1969).

Campbell, Robert W., *Soviet Economic Power* (Boston: Houghton Mifflin, 1960).

Cole, Charles L., *The Economic Fabric of Society* (New York: Harcourt, Brace, 1969).

Cole, G. D. H., *Socialist Economics* (London: Gollancz, 1950).

Davies, R.W., "Economic Planning in the USSR," in *Comparative Economic Systems—Models and Cases,* ed. by Morris Bornstein (Homewood, IL: Irwin, 1969).

Deutscher, Isaac, *Stalin: A Political Biography* (New York: Oxford, 1949).

Dillard, Dudley, *Economic Development of the North Atlantic Community* (Englewood Cliffs, NJ: Prentice-Hall, 1967).

Drewonowski, Jan, "The Economic Theory of Socialism: A Suggestion for Reconsideration," in *Comparative Economic Systems—Models and Cases,* ed. by Morris Bornstein (Homewood, IL: Irwin, 1969).

Ebenstein, William, *Today's Isms,* 6th ed. (Englewood Cliffs, NJ: Prentice-Hall, 1970).

Freedman, Robert (ed.), *Marx on Economics* (New York: Harcourt, Brace, 1961).

Fusfeld, Daniel R., *Economics* (Lexington: D.C. Heath, 1972).

Galbraith, John K., *American Capitalism,* rev. ed. (Boston: Houghton Mifflin, 1956).

Giddens, Anthony, *Capitalism and Modern Social Theory* (New York: Cambridge, 1971).

Griesbrecht, M.G., *The Evolution of Economic Society* (San Francisco: Freeman, 1972).

Grossman, Gregory, *Economic Systems* (Englewood Cliffs, NJ: Prentice-Hall, 1967).

Gruchy, Allan G., *Comparative Economic Systems* (Boston: Houghton Mifflin, 1966).

Halm, George N., *Economic Systems—A Comparative Analysis,* 3d ed. (New York: Holt, Rinehart, 1968).

Hayek, Friedrich A., von (ed.), *Collectivist Economic Planning* (London: Routledge, 1935).

Heilbroner, Robert L., *The Worldly Philosophers,* 3d. ed. (New York: Simon & Schuster, 1967).

Hunt, E.K., *Property and Prophets* (New York: Harper & Row, 1972).

International Encyclopedia of Social Sciences (New York: Macmillan, 1968).

Klaasen, Adrian (ed.), *The Invisible Hand* (Chicago: Henry Regnery Co., 1965).

Lange, Oskar, and Taylor, Fred M., *On the Economic Theory of Socialism* (New York: McGraw-Hill, 1965).

Leeman, Wayne A. (ed.), *Capitalism, Market Socialism, and Central Planning* (Boston: Houghton Mifflin, 1963).

Lenin, Vladimir I., *Collected Works* (Moscow: Foreign Languages, 1960).

Loucks, William N., and Whitman, William G., *Comparative Economic Systems,* 8th ed. (New York: Harper & Row, 1969).

Marshall, Howard D., *The Great Economists* (New York: Pitman, 1967).

Montias, John M., *Central Planning in Poland* (New Haven, CT: Yale, 1962).

Oser, Jacob, *The Evolution of Economic Thought,* 2d ed. (New York: Harcourt, Brace, 1970).

Schumpeter, Joseph A., *Capitalism, Socialism, and Democracy* (New York: Harper & Row, 1942).

Sherman, Howard J., *The Soviet Economy* (Boston: Little, Brown, 1969).

Snavely, William P., *The Theory of Economic Systems: Capitalism, Socialism, and Corporatism* (Columbus: Merrill, 1969).

Spiegel, Henry W., *The Growth of Economic Thought* (Englewood Cliffs, NJ: Prentice-Hall, 1971).

Spulber, Nicolas, *The Soviet Economy: Structure, Principles, Problems* (New York: Norton, 1969).

Sweezy, Paul M., *Socialism* (New York: McGraw-Hill, 1949).

Sweezy, Paul M., *The Theory of Capitalist Development* (New York: Monthly Review, 1956).

Wallich, Henry C., *The Cost of Freedom* (New York: Harper & Row, 1960).

Weber, Max, *The Protestant Ethic and the Spirit of Capitalism* (New York: Scribner's, 1958).

27. STATISTICS

Baumol, William J., *Economic Theory and Operations Analysis,* 2d ed. (Englewood Cliffs, NJ: Prentice-Hall, 1965).

Ellsberg, Daniel, "Theory of the Reluctant Duelist," *American Economic Review,* Vol. 46 (Dec., 1956).

Freund, John E., *Modern Elementary Statistics,* 3d ed. (Englewood Cliffs, NJ: Prentice-Hall, 1967).

Huff, Darrell, *How to Lie with Statistics* (New York: W.W. Norton, 1954).

Kane, Edward J., *Economic Statistics and Econometrics: An Introduction to Quantitative Economics* (New York: Harper & Row, 1968).

Leabo, Dick A., *Basic Statistics,* 4th ed. (Homewood, IL: Irwin, 1972).

L'Esperance, Wilfred L., *Modern Statistics for Business and Economics* (New York: Macmillan, 1971).

Mansfield, John E., *Modern Elementary Statistics,* 3d ed. (Englewood Cliffs, NJ: Prentice-Hall, 1967).

Moroney, M. J., *Facts From Figures,* 3d ed. (Baltimore: Penguin Books, 1956).

Schlaifer, Robert, *Probability and Statistics for Business Decisions* (New York: McGraw-Hill, 1959).

Spiegel, Murray R., *Theory and Problems of Statistics,* Schaum's Outline Series (New York: McGraw-Hill, 1961).

Wonnacott, Thomas H., and Ronald J., *Introductory Statistics,* 2d ed. (New York: John Wiley, 1972).

CREDITS

1. The Bettmann Archive
2. Wide World Photos
5. The Bettmann Archive; Wide World Photos
8. Harvard University News Office
15. Doyle
16. Talbot Lovering
17. HERBLOCK from *Herblock's Here and Now* (Simon and Schuster, 1955)
19. Brown Brothers
25. Bruce Davidson—1970 Magnum Photos; Magnum Photos
28. Harvard University News Office
30. Wide World Photos
31. Culver Pictures
34. Brown Brothers
35. Department of Public Information, Princeton University
38. Playboy Enterprises, Inc.
39. Culver Pictures
40. Wide World Photos
42. Ford Division Public Relations, Ford Motor Company
46. Culver Pictures
50. Brown Brothers
52. Brown Brothers
62. Harvard University News Office
63. Harvard University News Office
75. Wide World Photos
78. 1969 Magnum Photos
80. The Bettmann Archive
81. Jerry Schrader—Stock, Boston
84. The Bettmann Archive
87. Talbot Lovering; U.S. Bureau of Budget and Management, photo by Clif Garboden
88. Talbot Lovering
91. Yale University
95. The Bettmann Archive
98. The Bettmann Archive; Harvard University News Office
99. Harvard University News Office; Brown Brothers
100. The Chase Manhattan Money Museum, photo by Larry Fink
101. The Bettmann Archive; Hugh Rogers—Monkmeyer Press Photo Service
102. Fabian Bachrach
103. Talbot Lovering
105. MIT Office of Public Relations; Harvard University News Office
106. Monkmeyer Photo Service
107. University Relations, University of California
109. Harvard University News Office
110. Talbot Lovering
122. Edwin G. Huffman for World Bank Group
123. The Bettmann Archive
127. Radio Times Hulton Picture Library
128. Charles R. Walgren Foundation for the Study of American Institutions, University of Chicago; Yale University
134. AFL-CIO News
137. The Bettmann Archive; Wide World Photos
138. United Press International Photo
141. Department of Public Information, Princeton University
143. Brown Brothers; Paul Conklin—Monkmeyer Press Photo Service
152. The Bettmann Archive; Historical Pictures Service
153. Harvard University
154. United Press International Photo; United Press International Photo
155. Yale University
156. The Bettmann Archive
157. United Press International Photo
162. Drawing by Ed Fisher; © 1971 The New Yorker Magazine, Inc.
164. AT&T Photo Center
165. HERBLOCK from *Herblock's Special for Today* (Simon and Schuster, 1958)
166. Coca-Cola
168. Wide World Photos
175. Brown Brothers
182. The Bettmann Archive
184. United States Patent Office
185. Chicago Board of Trade
186. Internal Revenue Service
190. Mark L. Rosenberg—Stock, Boston
192. HERBLOCK from *Straight Herblock* (Simon and Schuster, 1964)
194. The New York Public Library
197. J. Steve Murillo
205. Brown Brothers
207. Culver Pictures
208. The Bettmann Archive
212. IBM Corp.
215. Sybil Shelton—Monkmeyer Press Photo Service; UPI Photo; Albertus-Yale News Bureau
216. The Bettmann Archive; Wide World Photos
217. Harvard University News Office
218. United Press International Photo
219. Harvard University News Office
220. The Bettmann Archive
221. Yale University
222. Brown Brothers; Harvard University
224. The Bettmann Archive; Burk Uzzle—Magnum Photos
225. Sovfoto
226. Brown Brothers; Brown Brothers
227. The Chase Manhattan Money Museum, photo by Larry Fink
228. Duke University News Service
231. The Bettmann Archive
232. The University of Chicago
233. New York Stock Exchange
234. Wide World Photos
235. HERBLOCK from *Straight Herblock* (Simon and Schuster, 1964)
236. J. Steve Murillo
240. Brown Brothers
241. Patricia Hollander Gross—Stock, Boston
243. IBM Corp.; IBM Corp.
244. University of Chicago
248. Albertus-Yale News Bureau
250. Talbot Lovering
251. Albertus-Yale News Bureau
252. 1962 Magnum Photos
255. United Press International Photo
260. The Bettmann Archive; Harvard University News Office
261. Editorial cartoon by Pat Oliphant, copyright The Denver Post, Reprinted with permission of Los Angeles Times Syndicate
263. Roy Osrin—The Plain Dealer
264. New York Public Library; Herblock
265. The Bettmann Archive; The Bettmann Archive
266. The Bettmann Archive
268. United Press International Photo

Contributing Artists: Craven and Evans, Natalie Rose, Louise Emmons Merriman

Economics '73–'74 Encyclopedia Staff

Editor	**Peter O'Connell**
Designer	**Louise Merriman**
Photo Researcher	**Tina Schwinder**
Production Supervisor	**Carol Dudley**

This book was set in Optima on the Fototronic CRT by Rocappi/Lehigh, Pennsauken, New Jersey.

The text was printed in web offset lithography and bound by Kingsport Press, Inc., Kingsport, Tennessee.

Text paper is Finch Title '94,' furnished by Pratt Paper Company, Boston, Massachusetts.

The cover material is Lexotone, furnished by The Holliston Mills, Inc., Norwood, Massachusetts.

Covers were printed in offset lithography by The Lehigh Press/Lithographers, Pennsauken, New Jersey.